THE ROUGH GUIDE TO

London

written and researched by

Rob Humphreys and Samantha Cook

with additional contributions by

Andrew Mickel

ROUGH GUIDES

roughguides.com

Contents

Introduction to
London

For the visitor, London is a thrilling place. Monuments from the capital's glorious past are everywhere, from medieval banqueting halls and the great churches of Christopher Wren to eclectic Victorian architecture. You can relax in the city's quiet Georgian squares, explore the narrow alleyways of the City of London, wander along the riverside walkways and uncover the quirks of what is still identifiably a collection of villages. London is also incredibly diverse, ethnically and linguistically, offering cultural and culinary delights from right across the globe. And, of course, it's also very big. In fact, it's the largest capital in the European Union, stretching for more than thirty miles from east to west, and with a population of over eight million. In other words, it really is the archetypal buzzing metropolis.

The capital's traditional landmarks – Big Ben, Westminster Abbey, Buckingham Palace, St Paul's Cathedral, the Tower of London and so on – continue to draw in millions of tourists every year. Things change fast, though, and the regular emergence of new attractions ensures that there's plenty to do even for those who've visited before. London's world-class **museums**, **galleries** and institutions are constantly reinventing themselves, from the V&A to the British Museum. With Tate Modern and the Shard, the city boasts the world's largest modern art museum and Europe's highest building. And thanks to the 2012 Olympics, the East End has had a boost, an entirely new park has been created, and the tourist and transport infrastructure has had a major overhaul.

The biggest problem for newcomers is that the city is bewilderingly amorphous. Londoners cope with this by compartmentalizing their city, identifying strongly with the neighbourhoods in which they work or live, just making occasional forays into the West End, London's busy shopping and entertainment heartland. As a visitor, the key to enjoying London, then, is not to try and do everything in a single trip – concentrate on one or two areas and you'll get a lot more out of the place. And remember to take some

ABOVE THE RIVER THAMES AND SOUTH BANK

time out in the city's surprisingly large expanses of greenery: Hyde Park, Green Park and St James's Park are all within a few minutes' walk of the West End, while, further afield, you can enjoy the more expansive parklands of Hampstead Heath and Richmond Park.

You could spend days just **shopping** in London, too, mixing with the upper classes in the "tiara triangle" around Harrods, or sampling the offbeat weekend markets of Portobello Road, Brick Lane and Camden. The **music**, **clubbing** and **gay and lesbian** scenes are second to none, with an ever-growing selection of clubs and bars around Shoreditch and Dalston and new music festivals cropping up every summer. Mainstream **arts** are no less exciting, with regular opportunities to catch outstanding theatre companies, dance troupes, exhibitions and opera. The city's pubs have always had heaps of atmosphere, but food is a major attraction too, with over sixty Michelin-starred **restaurants** and the widest choice of cuisines on the planet.

What to see

Although most of the city's sights are north of the **River Thames**, which loops through the centre from west to east, there is no single focus of interest. That's because London hasn't grown through centralized planning but by a process of agglomeration. Villages and urban developments that once surrounded the core are now lost within the vast mass of Greater London, leaving London's highlights widely spread, and meaning that visitors should make mastering the public transport system, particularly the Underground (tube), a top priority.

If London has a centre, it's **Trafalgar Square**, home to Nelson's Column and the National Gallery. It's also as good a place as any to start exploring the city, especially as the area to the

MULTIETHNIC LONDON

With around three hundred languages spoken and all the major religions represented, London is Europe's most ethnically **diverse** city. First-, second- and third-generation immigrants make up over thirty percent of the population, with many more descended from French Huguenot refugees. The first immigrants were invaders like the Romans, Anglo-Saxons, Vikings and Normans, while over the last four centuries, the city has absorbed wave after wave of foreigners fleeing persecution or simply looking for a better life. In the postwar period thousands came here from the Caribbean and the Indian subcontinent; today's arrivals are more likely to come from the world's trouble spots (Somalia, Afghanistan, Iraq) or from new EU member states like Poland.

London doesn't have the sort of ghettoization that's widespread in the US, but certain areas have become **home from home** for the more established communities. Brixton and Hackney are the most prominent African-Caribbean and African districts; Dalston, along with Haringey, is also home to the largest Turkish and Kurdish communities; Southall is predominantly Punjabi; Wembley is a Gujarati stronghold; Acton has a sizeable Polish community; Hoxton is a Vietnamese neighbourhood. The East End, London's top immigrant ghetto, has absorbed several communities over the centuries, and is currently the heart of Bengali London, while the Jewish community has more or less abandoned the East End, and now has its largest Orthodox communities in Stamford Hill and Golders Green.

south of here, **Whitehall and Westminster**, is one of the easiest bits to discover on foot. This was the city's royal, political and ecclesiastical power-base for centuries, and you'll find some of London's most famous landmarks here: Downing Street, Big Ben, the Houses of Parliament and **Westminster Abbey**. The grand streets and squares of **St James's**, **Mayfair** and **Marylebone**, to the north of Westminster, have been the playground of the rich since the Restoration, and now contain some of the city's busiest shopping zones: Piccadilly, **Bond Street**, **Regent Street** and, most frenetic of the lot, **Oxford Street**.

East of Piccadilly Circus, **Soho**, **Chinatown** and **Covent Garden** are also easy to walk around and form the heart of the West End entertainment district, where you'll find the largest concentration of theatres, cinemas, shops, cafés and restaurants. Adjoining Covent Garden to the north, the university quarter of **Bloomsbury** is the location of the ever-popular **British Museum**, a stupendous treasure house that boasts a wonderful central, covered courtyard. To the north of Bloomsbury lie King's Cross and St Pancras stations, home to the **British Library** and the city's Eurostar terminal, and now at the centre of a massive redevelopment project.

Welding the West End to the financial district, **Holborn** is a little-visited area, but offers some of central London's most surprising treats, among them the eccentric Sir John Soane's Museum and the secluded quadrangles of the Inns of Court, where the country's lawyers learn and ply their trade. Fashionable **Clerkenwell**, to the east of Holborn on the northern edge of the City, is visited mostly for its many popular bars and restaurants, but also has vestiges of London's monastic past and a radical history to be proud of.

A couple of miles downstream from Westminster, **The City** – or the City of London, to give it its full title – is the original heart of London, simultaneously the most ancient and the most modern part of the metropolis. Settled since Roman times, the area became the commercial and residential heart of medieval London, with its own Lord Mayor and its own peculiar form of local government, both of which survive (with considerable pageantry) to this day. The Great Fire of 1666 obliterated most of the City, and although it was rebuilt, the resident population has dwindled to insignificance. Yet this remains one of the great financial centres of the world, with the most prominent landmarks these days being the hi-tech **skyscrapers** of banks and insurance companies. However, the Square Mile, as it's known, boasts its fair share of historic sights too, notably the **Tower of London** and a fine cache of Wren churches that includes the mighty St Paul's Cathedral.

East of the City, the **East End** and **Docklands** are equally notorious, but in entirely different ways. Traditionally working-class, the East End is not conventional tourist territory, but its long history of immigration is as fascinating as is its more recent emergence as a bolthole for artists. With its converted warehouse apartments and hubristic tower blocks, Docklands is the converse of the edgy East End, with the **Canary Wharf** tower – for three decades the country's tallest building – epitomizing the pretensions of the 1980s' Thatcherite dream.

The **South Bank**, **Bankside** and **Southwark** together make up the small slice of central London that lies south of the Thames. The Southbank Centre itself, London's concrete culture bunker, is enjoying something of a renaissance – thanks, in part, to the nearby London Eye, which spins gracefully over the Thames. Bankside is also going from strength to strength, with the Millennium Bridge linking St Paul's Cathedral with the former power station that's home to **Tate Modern**, London's museum of modern art.

In **Hyde Park** and **Kensington Gardens** you'll find a large segment of greenery that separates wealthy west London from the city centre. The museums of **South Kensington** – the Victoria and Albert Museum, the Science Museum and the Natural History Museum – are a must, and if you have shopping on your agenda you may well want to investigate the hive of plush stores in the vicinity of Harrods, superstore to the upper echelons.

Some of the most appealing parts of north London are clustered around the Regent's Canal, which skirts the northern edge of **Regent's Park** and serves as the focus for the capital's busiest weekend market, held around **Camden Lock**. Further out, in the chic literary suburbs of Hampstead and Highgate, there are unbeatable views across the city from half-wild **Hampstead Heath**, the favourite parkland of thousands of Londoners.

The glory of south London is **Greenwich**, with its nautical associations, royal park and observatory (not to mention its Dome). Finally, there are plenty of rewarding day-trips up the Thames, southwest of the city centre from **Chiswick** to **Hampton Court**, an area that is liberally peppered with the stately homes and grounds of the country's royalty and former aristocracy, from Syon and **Kew**, to **Richmond** and Ham.

When to go

Considering how temperate the London **climate** is (see p.27), it's amazing how much mileage the locals get out of the subject. The truth is that summers rarely get really hot and the winters aren't very cold. In fact, it's impossible to say with any certainty what the weather will be like in any given month. May might be wet and grey one year and gloriously sunny the next; November stands an equal chance of being crisp and clear or foggy and grim. So, whatever time of year you come, be prepared for all eventualities, and bring a pair of comfortable shoes, as, inevitably, you'll be doing a lot of walking.

FROM TOP LITTLE VENICE; GUARDS OUTSIDE BUCKINGHAM PALACE; COVENT GARDEN PIAZZA

17

things not to miss

It's not possible to see everything that London has to offer in one visit
– and we don't suggest you try. What follows, in no particular order, is a
selective taste of the city's highlights, from outstanding art collections and
historic architecture to vibrant markets and picturesque parks. Each
highlight has a page reference to take you straight into the Guide, where
you can find out more.

1 BRITISH MUSEUM
Page 106

The spectacular Great Court and the renovated Round Reading Room have brought new life to the world's oldest and greatest public museum.

2 TOWER OF LONDON
Page 180

Bloody royal history, Beefeaters, lots of armour, the Crown Jewels and ravens – and a great medieval castle.

3 HIGHGATE CEMETERY
Page 305

The city's most atmospheric Victorian necropolis, thick with trees and crowded with famous corpses, with Karl Marx topping the bill.

4 SHOPPING AT LIBERTY
Page 426

Just down the road from the scrum of Oxford Circus, this beautiful department store, housed in a grand, mock-Tudor building, is heaven for label aficionados and window-shoppers alike.

5 HAMPSTEAD HEATH
Page 302

Fly kites, look across London and walk over to Kenwood, for fine art, tea and cakes.

LONDON PUBS
Page 386
Have a pint of traditional real ale in one of the many old and historic pubs found all over the capital.

 TATE MODERN
Page 225
One of the world's greatest modern art collections housed in a spectacularly converted, riverside power station.

 HOUSES OF PARLIAMENT
Page 49
See the "mother of all parliaments" at work from the public gallery, book in advance to attend Question Time or take a summertime guided tour.

 GREENWICH
Page 314
Soak up the naval history at the National Maritime Museum, and climb up to the Royal Observatory in Greenwich Park to enjoy the view over the river.

 NATIONAL GALLERY
Page 38
From the Renaissance to Picasso: the National Gallery is undoubtedly one of the world's great art galleries.

7

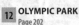

11 BOROUGH MARKET
Pages 230
Feast on all the scrumptious free titbits at London's leading foodie market.

12 OLYMPIC PARK
Page 202
You can still see some of the iconic venues and Orbit Tower, set amid the beautifully landscaped Olympic Park.

13 KEW GARDENS
Page 336
Three hundred acres of beautiful botanic gardens, with the curvaceous Palm House as the centrepiece.

14 SPITALFIELDS AND BRICK LANE
Page 189
Visit the offbeat market stalls, shops, cafés and bars on the edge of the East End.

15 V&A MUSEUM
Page 249
For variety and scale, the V&A is the greatest applied arts museum in the world.

16 THE SHARD
Page 232
Simply the most impressive view in London.

17 HAMPTON COURT PALACE
Page 348
Take a boat to this sprawling red-brick affair, the finest of London's royal palaces.

Itineraries

London's a city of neighbourhoods, and each of these day-long itineraries covers one of the city's most distinctive areas. They can all be covered on foot, or with just a few short hops by bus or tube.

FREE WEST END

London can be an expensive place, but there are lots of things to enjoy that are free. We've picked a few lesser-known sights, in some of the city's poshest parts, none of which will break the bank.

Wallace Collection Escape from nearby Oxford Street and pop into this miniature eighteenth-century French chateau and wallow in the luxury and excess of the Ancien Régime. **See p.90**

Mayfair auction houses Of the area's three major auction houses, Sotheby's is the most approachable. Sift through the lots, imagine what you'd buy if you had the money and then have a coffee at the café. **See p.82**

Royal Institution Not only is the RI one of the country's most venerable scientific institutions, it also has a great building to explore, from the museum to the famous lecture hall. **See p.82**

Lunch In summer, St James's Park (see p.67) is a particularly nice spot for a picnic; in winter treat yourself at *The Wolseley* (see p.367).

Covent Garden buskers Performers in the Piazza have to audition, so a certain quality is guaranteed – expect everything from opera to slapstick. **See p.131**

Horse Guards Don't fret that you missed Changing the Guard at 11am. The 4pm daily inspection by an Officer of the Guard involves lots of cavalry and is just as much fun. **See p.48**

Evensong at Westminster Abbey You can save yourself the hefty entrance fee by turning up for choral evensong at 5pm. **See p.53**

A SOUTH BANK STROLL

You can stroll the wonderful traffic-free footpath for three miles along the South Bank from the London Eye to Rotherhithe.

Southbank Centre London's concrete culture bunker is a vibrant venue for pop-up festivals and outdoor stalls, as well as a great place for theatre, music and art. **See p.215**

Tate Modern Already the largest modern art museum in the world, this awesome edifice is expanding below and behind the original power station. **See p.225**

Shakespeare's Globe Groundling tickets are only just over a fiver, so there's no excuse not to catch a play or visit the museum. **See p.228**

Borough Market This wholesale fruit and veg market becomes a foodie scrimmage from Thursday to Saturday. **See p.230**

Tower Bridge Climb to the top of one of the city's most famous sights, or phone ahead to check the bridge opening times. **See p.187**

Butler's Wharf A lesson in how to preserve and enhance an old warehouse, marking the start of the South Bank's Docklands. **See p.235**

Brunel Museum Rotherhithe is cut off from the rest of London, and all the better for it. This museum tells the remarkable story of the world's first underwater tunnel, and has a pop-up cocktail garden to boot. **See p.236**

Mayflower pub Sink a pint of real ale and survey the river at this historic pub from which the Pilgrim Fathers set out in 1620. **See p.394**

ABOVE COLUMBIA ROAD FLOWER MARKET **OPPOSITE** SUMMER FOUNTAIN OUTSIDE THE SOUTHBANK CENTRE

OFFBEAT CITY

The City of London is one of the world's major financial centres, but dig deeper and you'll find centuries of history just below the surface.

Bank of England Museum Catch a glimpse of John Soane's genius, and get your hands on a real gold bar at the Bank's museum. **See p.172**

Clockmaker's Museum Quality not quantity is the virtue of this museum, which owns the clock with which John Harrison won the Longitude Prize. **See p.171**

Postman's Park Tiny park with a curious, slightly mawkish memorial to have-a-go heroes of the Victorian era (and today). **See p.168**

The Black Friar Settle into an alcove, nurse a pint and soak in this pub's fantastically over-the-top 1905 Art Nouveau interior. **See p.390**

Temple Cut off from the hustle and bustle of the City, the Inns of Court harbour gas-lit courtyards, gardens and medieval masterpieces. **See p.143**

Royal Courts of Justice Security is tight, but you can wander through the Gothic corridors of this vast legal complex on the Strand. **See p.145**

Hunterian Museum Forget the London Dungeon, the pickled bits and bobs here are much more terrifying. **See p.145**

Sir John Soane's Museum The architect's former home is a labyrinth of hidden treasures, including an Egyptian sarcophagus. **See p.145**

HEADING EAST

London's East End is one of the capital's most historic and distinctive quarters, perfect for a Sunday of browsing and grazing.

Columbia Road flower market Start with an early breakfast at the cute old *Jones Dairy* (see p.379) before checking out the fragrant blooms and browsing the lively indie shops. **See p.434**

Geffrye Museum This endearing museum re-creates period living spaces in a set of eighteenth-century almshouses. **See p.197**

Vintage shops You could spend days exploring the markets and artist's spaces near Brick Lane, but vintage is where the area excels. Start with the classy Vintage Emporium, then the copious offerings of Beyond Retro and finally a rummage in Blitz (see p.428), before stopping for a bagel at the venerable *Brick Lane Beigel Bake* (see p.378).

Whitechapel Gallery Check out the cutting-edge art at this fine old establishment, which has brought to public prominence everyone from Frida Kahlo to Gilbert and George. **See p.198**

Tayyabs While the East End has some seriously cool and experimental restaurants, our bet's on old favourite *Tayyabs* for fresh, flavour-filled Pakistani food at low prices. **See p.378**

The George Tavern If you're up for a seriously artsy East End experience, finish your night at this dilapidated but beautiful boozer, where the hip events are nothing if not eclectic. **See p.391**

BUS OUTSIDE ST PAUL'S

Basics

Getting there

Unless you're coming from elsewhere in Britain, or from northwest Europe, the quickest and easiest way to get to London is by plane. The city has five airports (see p.20) and is a major destination for most international airlines, so airfares tend to be keenly competitive. How much you pay to fly to London depends on how far in advance you book, and how flexible you need your ticket to be.

Flights from the US and Canada

All major US and Canadian airlines run direct services from North America to London, Europe's busiest gateway. Two of London's airports – **Heathrow** and **Gatwick** – handle transatlantic flights, and in terms of convenience they're about equal.

Figure on around six hours' flying time from New York; it's an hour extra going the other way, due to headwinds. Add three or four hours more for travel from the West Coast. Most eastbound flights cross the Atlantic overnight, arriving the next morning; flying back, departure times tend to be morning or afternoon, arriving in the afternoon or evening of the same day.

The cheapest return **fares** (including taxes) from New York or Chicago (and even LA) start from around US$600; or from around Can$800 from Toronto; and from around Can$1000 from Vancouver.

Flights from Australia and New Zealand

Flight time from Australia and New Zealand to London is at least 22 hours, and can be more depending on routes and transfer times. There are a wide variety of routes, with those touching down in Southeast Asia the quickest and cheapest on average. Given the length of the journey involved, you might be better off including a night's stopover in your itinerary; some airlines include one in the price of the flight.

The cheapest direct scheduled flights to London are usually to be found on one of the Asian airlines. Average return **fares** (including taxes) from eastern gateways to London are Aus$1500–2500 depending on the season. Fares from Perth or Darwin cost around Aus$200 less. Return fares from Auckland to London range between NZ$2000 and NZ$3000 depending on the season, route and carrier.

By plane or train from Ireland

Travel from Ireland is quickest by **plane**, with the likes of Aer Lingus and Ryanair offering return tickets from Dublin, Derry, Cork or Shannon to London Stansted or Gatwick for as little as €50. From Belfast International, easyJet has return fares to London Luton, Gatwick or Stansted from around £60, if you book far enough in advance; flybe has similar fares from Belfast City to London Gatwick. A fully flexible fare can cost three or four times that amount, but will allow you to change your plans after purchasing the ticket.

Flying may be quick, but the **ferry** and **train** fares are pretty competitive and much more flexible, with Irish Ferries (ⓦ irishferries.com) offering SailRail return fares of around €80 to London (via Holyhead) from anywhere in the Republic; from Belfast (via Stranraer or Holyhead) returns start from £90. Journey time is eight hours from Dublin, ten from Belfast.

AGENTS AND OPERATORS

North South Travel UK ☎ 01245 608291, ⓦ northsouthtravel .co.uk. Friendly, competitive travel agency, offering discounted fares worldwide. Profits are used to support projects in the developing world, especially the promotion of sustainable tourism.

STA Travel UK ☎ 0871 2300 040, US ☎ 1800 781 4040, Australia ☎ 134 782, New Zealand ☎ 0800 474 400, South Africa ☎ 0861 781 781, ⓦ statravel.com. Worldwide specialists in independent travel; also student IDs, travel insurance, car rental, rail passes and more. Good discounts for students and under-26s.

Trailfinders UK ☎ 020 7408 9006, Ireland ☎ 01 677 7888, ⓦ trailfinders.com. One of the best-informed and most efficient agents for independent travellers.

A BETTER KIND OF TRAVEL

At Rough Guides we are passionately committed to travel. We feel that travelling is the best way to understand the world we live in and the people we share it with – plus tourism has brought a great deal of benefit to developing economies around the world over the last few decades. But the growth in tourism has also damaged some places irreparably, and climate change is exacerbated by most forms of transport, especially flying. All Rough Guides' trips are carbon-offset, and every year we donate money to a variety of charities devoted to combating the effects of climate change.

Arrival

The majority of visitors arrive in London at one of its five airports, all but one of which can involve an expensive trip to the centre. Those arriving by train or bus are dropped right in the middle of the city, with easy access to public transport.

By plane

Flying into London, you'll arrive at Heathrow, Gatwick, Stansted, Luton or City airport, each of which is less than an hour from the city centre.

Heathrow

Heathrow (ⓦheathrowairport.com) lies around fifteen miles west of central London, and is the city's busiest airport, with five terminals and three train/tube stations: one for terminals 1, 2 and 3, and separate ones for terminals 4 and 5. The fastest (and most expensive) trains into London are the nonstop **Heathrow Express** (ⓦheathrowexpress .com) services to Paddington station (daily 5am–midnight; journey 15min); tickets cost £20 one way or £34 return (more if you purchase your ticket on board the train). **Heathrow Connect** (ⓦheathrow connect.com) trains stop at some intermediate stations (Mon–Sat 5am–midnight, Sun 6am–11pm; every 30min; journey 30–40min) but tickets cost just £9.50 single and £19 return. An even cheaper alternative is to take the **Piccadilly Underground line** (ⓦtfl.gov.uk), which connects the airport to numerous tube stations across central London (Mon–Sat 5am–11.45pm, Sun 6am–11.30pm; every 5min; journey 50min–1hr); tickets cost just £5.50 single – £5 if you have an Oyster card – or you can buy a Day Off-Peak Travelcard (Zones 1–6) for £8.90 (see p.22).

National Express bus services (ⓦnational express.com) run from Heathrow direct to Victoria Coach Station (5am–9.30pm every 15–30min; journey 40–55min); tickets cost £6 single, £11 return. From 11.30pm, you can take night bus #N9 to Trafalgar Square for a bargain fare of £2.40 (every 20min; journey 1hr 10min). **Taxis** are plentiful, but will set you back between £50 and £80 to central London, and take around an hour (much longer in the rush hour).

Gatwick

Gatwick (ⓦgatwickairport.com) is around thirty miles south of London, and has a train station at the South Terminal. Nonstop **Gatwick Express** trains (ⓦgatwickexpress.com) run between the airport and London Victoria (daily 4.30am–1.30am; every 15min; journey 30–35min); tickets cost around £20 single, £35 return (less online). A cheaper option is to take a **Southern** train service (ⓦsouthernrailway .com) to Victoria (every 15min; journey 35min), which stops at a couple of intermediate stations, or a **First Capital Connect** train (ⓦfirstcapitalconnect .co.uk) to various stations within London (every 15–30min; journey 30–45min), including London Bridge and St Pancras; advance online tickets for either cost from £10 single.

From the North and South terminals **easyBus** (ⓦeasybus.co.uk) runs buses to West Brompton tube near Earl's Court (daily 4.30am–midnight every 20min; 1hr 10min), with online tickets going for as little as £2 single (£10 if you buy on board). **National Express** buses run from Gatwick direct to central London (daily 5am–9.30pm hourly; 1hr 30min); tickets cost around £7 single, £13.50 return. A **taxi** will set you back £100 or more, and take over an hour.

Stansted

Designed by Norman Foster, Stansted (ⓦstansted airport.com) is London's best-looking international airport, and lies roughly 35 miles northeast of the capital. The fastest trains are run by **Stansted Express** (ⓦstanstedexpress.com) to Liverpool Street (daily 5.30am–12.30am; every 15–30min; journey 45min), and cost £20 single, £33 return if you book online. All year round, 24 hours a day, **easyBus** runs buses to Baker Street tube (every 20–30min; 1hr 15min), with online tickets going for as little as £2 single (£10 if you buy on board). **National Express** runs buses 24 hours a day calling at various places in London en route to Victoria Coach Station (every 30min; journey 1hr 30min–1hr 45min), with tickets £9 single. **Terravision** (ⓦterravision.eu) also run coaches to Liverpool Street and Victoria (daily 7.15am–1am; every 30min; journey time 1hr 15min), with tickets £8 single, £15 return. A **taxi** will set you back £100, and take at least an hour.

City Airport

City Airport (ⓦlondoncityairport.com), London's smallest, used primarily by business folk, is situated in the Royal Albert Docks, ten miles east of central London, and handles European flights only. The **Docklands Light Railway** (DLR) takes you straight to Bank in the City (Mon–Sat 5.30am–12.15am, Sun 7am–11.15pm; every 8–15min; journey 20min), where you can change to the tube; single tickets cost around £4.50 (less if you have an Oyster card).

A **taxi** from the airport to the City's financial sector will cost around £20, and take half an hour or so.

Luton

Luton Airport (**W** london-luton.co.uk) is roughly thirty miles north of London and mainly handles charter flights. A free shuttle bus (every 10min) takes five minutes to transport passengers to **Luton Airport Parkway station**, which is connected by train to St Pancras (every 15–30min; journey 25–35min) and other stations in central London; single tickets cost around £13.50. All year round, 24 hours a day, **Green Line** and **easyBus** run the #757 coach from Luton Airport to Victoria Coach Station (every 20–30min; journey 1hr 20min), stopping at several locations en route, including Baker Street. Tickets cost as little as £2 (or as much as £10) if you book with easyBus online. A **taxi** will cost in the region of £70–80 and take at least an hour to central London.

Arriving by train or bus

Eurostar (**W** eurostar.com) trains arrive at St Pancras International next door to King's Cross. Trains from the **Channel ports** arrive at Charing Cross or Victoria, while **boat trains** from Harwich arrive at Liverpool Street. Arriving by train from elsewhere in Britain, you'll come into one of London's numerous mainline stations, all of which have adjacent Underground stations linking into the city centre's tube network. Coming into London by coach, you're most likely to arrive at Victoria Coach Station, a couple of hundred yards south down Buckingham Palace Road from Victoria train station and tube.

City transport

The city's highly complex transport system has improved enormously over the last decade or so. The congestion charge has reduced traffic within central London, and much of the money has been ploughed into improving the bus and tube network. That said, London still has one of the most expensive transport systems in the world.

Transport for London (TfL) provides excellent free maps and details of bus and tube services from its six **Travel Information Centres**: the most central one is at Piccadilly Circus tube station (Mon–Fri 7.45am–7pm, Sat 9.15am–7pm, Sun 9.15am–6pm); there are other desks at the arrivals at Heathrow (terminals 1, 2 & 3), Victoria, Euston, King's Cross and

> ### TRAIN INFORMATION
> For up-to-date information on all train services and ticket prices, contact National Rail Enquiries (**T** 0845 748 4950, **W** nationalrail.co.uk).

Liverpool Street train stations. There's also a 24-hour helpline and website for information on all bus and tube services (**T** 0343 222 1234, **W** tfl.gov.uk).

For transport purposes, London is divided into six concentric zones (plus a few extra in the northwest), with fares calculated depending on which zones you travel through: the majority of the city's accommodation, pubs, restaurants and sights lie in zones 1 and 2. If you cannot produce a valid ticket for your journey, or travel further than your ticket allows, you will be liable to a Penalty Fare of £80, reduced to £40 if you pay within 21 days. Try and avoid travelling during the rush hour (Mon–Fri 8–9.30am & 5–7pm), if possible, when tubes become unbearably crowded and hot, and some buses get so full they won't let you on.

The tube

Except for very short journeys, the **Underground** – or tube, as it's known to Londoners – is by far the quickest way to get about. Eleven different lines cross much of the metropolis, although London south of the river is not very well covered. Each line has its own colour and name – all you need to know is which direction you're travelling in: northbound, eastbound, southbound or westbound (this gets tricky when taking the Circle Line). As a precaution, it's also worth checking the final destination displayed on the front of the train, as some lines, such as the District and Northern lines, have several different branches.

Services are frequent (Mon–Sat 5.30am–12.30am, Sun 7.30am–11.30pm), and you rarely have to wait more than five minutes for a train between central stations. Tickets must be bought in advance from automatic machines or from a ticket booth in the station entrance hall. Single **fares** are expensive – a journey in the central zone costs £4.50 – so if you're intending to make more than one journey, an **Oyster card** or a Travelcard is by far your best option (see p.22).

Buses

London's famous red double-decker buses are fun to ride on, with most running a frequency of five to ten minutes during the day. Some stops have live departure information, or if you've got a smart-phone, there are several apps (and the TfL website) that will do the same for you. The standard walk-on **fare** is £2.40 without an Oyster card, £1.40 with one, (see box below), but you'll need to have the right change or the bus driver may refuse to let you on, and the machines at the bus stops also only take exact change.

A lot of bus stops are request stops (easily recog-nizable by their red sign), so if you don't stick your arm out to hail the bus you want, it will pass you by, and if you don't ring the bell for the bus to stop, it will just keep on going.

Some buses run a **24-hour service**, but most run between 5am and midnight, with a network of night buses (prefixed with the letter "N") operating outside this period. Night-bus routes depart every twenty to thirty minutes, more frequently on Friday and Saturday nights. Tickets are £2.40 from central London, and Travelcards (see below) are valid until 4.30am. All stops are treated as request stops, so you must signal to get the bus to stop, and press the bell in order to get off.

Suburban trains

Large areas of London's suburbs are only served by the suburban train network. Wherever a sight can only be reached by train, we've indicated the nearest train station (and, if relevant, the central terminus from which trains depart). Oyster cards and Travelcards are valid on all suburban train services within Greater London. For information on services, phone National Rail Enquiries on ☎0845 748 4950, or visit ⓦnationalrail.co.uk.

The most useful train line to cross the capital is the **First Capital Connect** service (ⓦfirstcapital connect.co.uk), which runs north–south via St Pancras and Blackfriars (Mon–Sat every 15min, Sun every 30min). Another useful line is the **Overground**, which has transformed itself into a large network stretching out to Richmond in the west and Stratford in the east, and including an orbital railway, a sort of outer Circle Line.

Docklands Light Railway

The Docklands Light Railway, or DLR (☎020 7363 9700), runs driverless trains from Bank in the City,

---

OYSTER CARDS AND TICKETS

The cheapest, easiest way to get about London is to use an **Oyster card**, London's transport smartcard, available from all tube stations and Travel Information Centres, and valid on the bus, tube, Docklands Light Railway (DLR), Tramlink, Overground and all suburban rail services. You can use an Oyster card in one of two ways: you can use it simply to store a weekly/monthly/ yearly **season ticket**, or you can use it as a **pay-as-you-go** card – you can top-up your card at all tube stations and at most newsagents. As you enter the tube or bus, simply touch in your card at the card reader – if you're using pay-as-you-go, the fare will be taken off your card. If you're using the tube or train, you need to touch out again or a maximum cash fare of up to £7.40 will be deducted. A pay-as-you-go Oyster operates daily price-capping so that when you've paid the equivalent of a Day Travelcard, it will stop taking money off your card, though you still need to touch in (and out). Oyster cards are free for those purchasing monthly or yearly tickets; everyone else needs to hand over a £5 refundable deposit; visitors can buy a pay-as-you-go Oyster card for just £3.

If you don't have an Oyster card, you can buy a paper **Travelcard** from machines and booths at all tube and train stations (and at many newsagents too – look for the sign). Anytime Day Travelcards start from £8.80 (zones 1 & 2); Off-Peak Day Travelcards are valid after 9.30am on weekdays and all day at the weekend, and cost £7.30 (zones 1 & 2), rising to £8.90 (zones 1–6). If you need to travel before 9.30am, it's worth considering a 7 Day Travelcard for £30.40 (zones 1 & 2).

Children under 11 travel for free; children aged 11–15 travel free on all buses and trams and at child-rate on the tube; children aged 16 or 17 can travel at half the adult rate on all forms of transport. However, all children over 10 must have an Oyster photocard to be eligible for the discounts – these should be applied for in advance online and will cost £10. Railcard holders can buy a Day Off-Peak Travelcard (zones 1–9) for children aged 11–15 for just £2, providing they're travelling with an adult. All Londoners over 60, and in possession of a **Freedom Pass**, can travel for free on all types of transport – over 60s from elsewhere in the UK can still use their Freedom Pass to travel free on London buses.

and from Tower Gateway (close to Tower Hill tube and the Tower of London) above ground to the financial centre of Docklands, plus other areas in the East End and also below ground to Greenwich and Woolwich. Oyster cards and Travelcards (see opposite) are valid on the network.

Boats

Unfortunately, boat services on the Thames are not fully integrated into the public transport system. If you have a valid Travelcard (either in paper or Oyster form), you're entitled to a third off, but if you have a pay-as-you-go Oyster card, you get just ten percent off. Timetables and services are complex, and there are numerous companies and small charter operators – for a full list pick up a booklet from a TfL information centre (see p.21) or visit Ⓦ tfl.gov.uk.

One of the largest companies is **Thames Clippers** (Ⓦ thamesclippers.com), who run a regular commuter service (Mon–Fri 6am–11pm, Sat & Sun 9am–10.30pm; every 20–30min) between Waterloo and Greenwich (including the Dome), with some boats going as far as Woolwich. Typical fares are £6.50 single, with an unlimited hop-on, hop-off River Roamer costing £13.60, and a weekly ticket costing £41.

Other companies run boats upstream to Kew, Richmond and Hampton Court (see p.329). Look out, too, for the MV *Balmoral* and paddle steamer *Waverley*, which make regular visits to Tower Pier in the summer and autumn (Ⓣ 0845 130 4647, Ⓦ waverleyexcursions.co.uk).

Taxis

Compared to most capital cities, London's metered **black cabs** are an expensive option unless there are three or more of you. The minimum fare is £2.40, and a ride from Euston to Victoria, for example, costs around £12–15 (Mon–Fri 6am–8pm). After 8pm on weekdays and all day during the weekend, a higher tariff applies, and after 10pm, it's higher still. Tipping is customary. An illuminated yellow light over the windscreen tells you if the cab is available – just stick your arm out to hail it. London's cabbies are the best-trained in Europe; every one of them knows the shortest route between any two points in the capital, and they won't rip you off by taking another route. They are, however, a blunt and forthright breed, renowned for their generally reactionary opinions. To order a black cab in advance, phone Ⓣ 0871 871 8710, and be prepared to pay an extra £2.

Minicabs

Minicabs look just like regular cars and are considerably cheaper than black cabs, but they cannot be hailed from the street. All minicabs should be **licensed** and able to produce a TfL ID on demand. There are hundreds of minicab firms in the phone book, but the best way to pick is to take the advice of the place you're at, unless you want to be certain of a woman driver, in which case book a cab from Lady Mini Cabs (Ⓣ 020 7272 3300), or a gay/lesbian-friendly driver, in which case call **London Cabs** (Ⓣ 020 7205 2677). Avoid illegal taxi touts, who hang around outside venues alongside licensed cabs, and always establish the fare beforehand, as minicabs are not metered.

Pedicabs

Last, and definitely least, there's currently a plague of pedicabs or **bicycle taxis** in the West End. The oldest and biggest of the bunch are Bugbugs (Ⓣ 020 7353 4028, Ⓦ bugbugs.com), who have rickshaws operating Monday to Saturday from 7pm until the early hours of the morning. The rickshaws take up to three passengers and **fares** are negotiable, so you should always agree a price beforehand based on a fare of around £3–5 per person.

Driving

Given the traffic jams, parking hassle and pollution caused, driving in London – especially central London – is by far the worst transport option available. However, if you must drive, bear in mind the rules of the road (even if no one else does). Seatbelts are compulsory front and back and the speed limit is 30mph, unless it says otherwise.

CONGESTION CHARGE

All vehicles entering central London on weekdays between 7am and 6pm are liable to a **congestion charge** of £10 per vehicle. Drivers can pay the charge online, over the phone and at garages and shops, and must do so before midnight the same day or incur a £2 surcharge – 24 hours later, you'll be liable for a £130 Penalty Charge Notice (reduced to £65 if you pay within 14 days). Disabled travellers, motorcycles, minibuses and some alternative-fuel vehicles are exempt from the charge, and local residents get a ninety percent discount, but you must register in order to qualify. For more details, visit Ⓦ tfl.gov.uk.

Your biggest nightmare as a driver is undoubtedly **parking**. The basic rules are that double **red and double yellow lines** mean no waiting or stopping, as do the zigzag lines that you'll see near a pedestrian crossing. **Single yellow** and single red lines mean that you can park on them after 6pm or 7pm, and at the weekends, but times vary from borough to borough, so read the signs before leaving your vehicle. Parking at a meter or pay-and-display will cost you up to around £4 an hour, though again meters are often free in the evenings and at weekends. In some boroughs, you'll need a mobile phone and credit card with you to pay for your parking. Finally, you can go to a car park – NCP are the largest operators @ncp.co.uk – which costs up to £10 for two hours during the day. If you park your car illegally, you will get a Penalty Charge Notice (usually £80), possibly get clamped (another £80) or get towed away (£125 and upwards). If you suspect your vehicle has been towed away, phone the police on ☎020 7747 4747.

Cycling

Cycling is more popular than ever in London, not least because it's the cheapest and – in the centre, at least – fastest way to get around. The easiest way to get cycling is to use the city's Barclays Cycle Hire scheme or **Boris Bikes**, as they're universally known, after Boris Johnson, Mayor of London at the time they were introduced. There are over six hundred docking stations across central London. With a credit or debit card, you can buy 24 hours' access to the bikes for just £2, after which you get the first half hour free, so if you hop from docking station to docking station, you don't pay another penny. Otherwise, it's £1 for the first hour, increasing rapidly after that to £15 for three hours. If you're going to use the Boris Bikes a lot, you're best off becoming a member and getting a key – for more details see @tfl.gov.uk.

If you want to rent a better bike for longer than an hour or so, try **London Bicycle Tour Company,** on the South Bank at 1a Gabriel's Wharf, SE1 (☎020 7928 6838, @londonbicycle.com), which has hybrid and mountain bikes for rent at £3–4 an hour or £20 for the first day, £10 per day thereafter, £50 for the week; or On Your Bike, The Vaults, Montague Close, SE1 (☎020 7378 6669, @onyourbike.com), which has a whole range of bikes for rent at £18 a day, £10 per day thereafter.

There are restrictions on taking **bikes on public transport**: no bikes other than folding bikes are allowed on any part of the system (with a few minor exceptions) from Monday to Friday between 7.30am

and 9.30am, and from 4pm to 7pm. Bikes are also restricted on the tube, but allowed on the District, Circle, East London, Hammersmith & City and Metropolitan lines, plus certain sections of other tube lines. Restrictions on the suburban trains vary from company to company, so check before you set out.

Festivals

London hosts an enormous number of festivals throughout the year, several of which are worth planning a trip around. The biggest street festival is still the Notting Hill Carnival, which takes place at the end of August, and the longest-running event is still the Proms, whose series of classical music concerts takes place for around eight weeks over the summer. There are also regular free events held throughout the year on Trafalgar Square, funded by the Mayor of London. The list of events below really just skims the surface – there is also an excellent range of sporting events (see p.435) and music festivals (see p.401).

JANUARY

London Parade Jan 1 @ londonparade.co.uk; admission charge for grandstand seats in Piccadilly, otherwise free. A procession of floats, marching bands, cheerleaders and clowns wends its way from Parliament Square, at noon, to Green Park.

London International Mime Festival Late Jan @ mimelondon .com. Annual mime festival that takes place over much of January at the Southbank Centre, the ICA and other funky venues. It pulls in some very big names in mime, animation and puppetry.

Chinese New Year Late Jan/early Feb @ chinatownlondon.org; free. Celebrations in Soho's Chinatown, Leicester Square and even Trafalgar Square erupt in a riot of dancing dragons and firecrackers – expect serious human congestion.

FEBRUARY

Clowns Service First Sun of month 3pm. Holy Trinity Church, Beechwood Rd, E8 @ clowns-international.com; Dalston Kingsland or Junction Overground; free. The Joseph Grimaldi Memorial Service for clowns, commemorating the great clown, with a clown show afterwards in the church hall.

Pancake Day Shrove Tuesday. Free. There are several places to enjoy a public pancake race: go to Brick Lane for frivolity, and the Guildhall for seriously silly costumes courtesy of the Poulterers' Guild.

MARCH

St Patrick's Day March 15 @ london.gov.uk; free. Events all over London and a parade that sets off at noon and ends up at Trafalgar

Square, where there's a festival of Irish culture; also plenty of events in the week building up to the day.

Head of the River Race Sat in late March or early April Ⓦ horr.co.uk; free. Less well known than the Oxford and Cambridge race, but much more fun, since there are over four hundred crews setting off on the ebb tide at ten-second intervals and chasing each other from Mortlake to Putney.

The Boat Race Last Sat in March or first Sat in April Ⓦ theboatrace.org; free. Since 1829 rowers from Oxford and Cambridge universities have battled it out over four miles from Putney to Mortlake, setting off on the flood tide. The pubs at prime vantage points pack out early.

APRIL

Alternative Fashion Week Late April Ⓦ alternativefashionweek .co.uk. Lots of new designers and no exclusive guest lists at this week-long fashion show, with fifteen shows a day held in Spitalfields.

London Marathon Third or fourth Sun in month Ⓦ london -marathon.co.uk; free. The world's most popular marathon, with around forty thousand masochists sweating the 26.2 miles from Greenwich to The Mall. A handful of world-class athletes enter each year, but most of the competitors are running for charity, often in ludicrous costumes.

MAY

IWA Canalway Cavalcade May Bank Holiday weekend. Little Venice Ⓦ waterways.org.uk; ⊖ Warwick Avenue; free. Lively three-day celebration of the city's inland waterways, with scores of decorated narrow boats, and lots of stalls and children's activities.

May Fayre and Puppet Festival Sun nearest May 9. St Paul's Churchyard Ⓦ punchandjudy.com; ⊖ Covent Garden; free. The gardens of Covent Garden's St Paul's Church play host to puppet booths to commemorate the first recorded Punch and Judy show in England, seen by diarist Samuel Pepys in 1662.

State Opening of Parliament Early May Ⓦ parliament.uk; free. The Queen arrives by coach at the Houses of Parliament at 11am accompanied by the Household Cavalry and gun salutes. The ceremony itself takes place inside the House of Lords and is televised; it also takes place whenever a new government is sworn in.

Chestnut Sunday Sun nearest May 11. Bushy Park Ⓦ royalparks .gov.uk; Hampton Court train station; free. Parade of antique bicycles, classic cars, motorcycles and carriages along Chestnut Ave, with the trees in full blossom.

Boishakhi Mela Second Sun in May. Weavers Fields, Allen Gardens and Brick Lane Ⓦ boishakhimela.org; ⊖ Bethnal Green, Whitechapel or Aldgate East; free. A colourful Bengali New Year open-air festival with vast crowds (120,000 and up), street entertainment, fun fairs and lots of food in Victoria Park.

Chelsea Flower Show Late May. Royal Hospital, Chelsea Ⓦ rhs.org.uk/Chelsea; ⊖ Sloane Square. The world's finest horticultural event with over 150,000 visitors over five days, is a solidly bourgeois affair. RHS members only on the first two days.

London Literature Festival Late May Ⓦ southbankcentre .co.uk. The capital's chief wordfest is held over a fortnight at the Southbank Centre, with music, poetry and debate.

JUNE

Beating Retreat Two consecutive eves in early June 9pm. Horse Guards Parade Ⓦ army.mod.uk; ⊖ Charing Cross, Embankment or Westminster. Annual military display on Horse Guards' Parade over three evenings, marking the old custom of drumming and piping the troops back to base at dusk. Soldiers on foot and horseback provide a colourful ceremony which precedes a floodlit performance by the Massed Bands of the Foot Guards and the Mounted Bands of the Household Cavalry.

Spitalfields Summer Music Festival Mid-June Ⓦ spitalfieldsmusic.org.uk. The festival is held over two weeks in various venues across the East End, focusing on early classical music, with the odd nod to world music.

Trooping the Colour Second Sat in month Ⓦ army.mod.uk; ⊖ Charing Cross, Embankment or Westminster. Celebration of the Queen's official birthday (her real one is on April 21) featuring massed bands, gun salutes, fly-pasts and crowds of tourists and patriotic Britons. The royal procession along the Mall allows you a glimpse for free, and there are rehearsals (minus Her Majesty) on the two preceding Saturdays.

Meltdown Mid-June. Southbank Centre Ⓦ southbankcentre.co.uk; ⊖ Waterloo. Week of groovy gigs, films and other events on the South Bank, chosen and presided over by a different seminal musician each year.

City of London Festival Late June to late July Ⓦ colf.org. For one month, churches (including St Paul's Cathedral), livery halls, corporate buildings and even the streets around the City play host to classical and jazz musicians, theatre companies and other guest performers.

Gay Pride Late June Ⓦ londoncommunitypride.org. Traditional Gay Pride march through the West End, finishing up in Trafalgar Square for speeches, music and dancing. The celebrations continue in Soho until the early hours.

JULY

Hampton Court Palace Flower Show Early July. Hampton Court Palace Ⓦ rhs.org.uk; Hampton Court train station. Six-day international flower extravaganza that rivals its sister show in Chelsea. RHS members only on the first two days.

Doggett's Coat & Badge Race Mid-July Ⓦ doggettsrace.org.uk; free. World's oldest rowing race from London Bridge to Chelsea, established by Thomas Doggett, an eighteenth-century Irish comedian, to commemorate George I's accession to the throne. Six young watermen battle it out in modern sculling boats.

Lambeth Country Show Weekend in mid-July. Brockwell Park Ⓦ lambeth.gov.uk; Herne Hill train station; free. A traditional country show comes to Brixton's Brockwell Park, with best-jam competitions, sheep shearing, a scarecrow competition and a cider stall, as well as a couple of stages of live music.

The Proms or Henry Wood Promenade Concerts Mid-July to early Sept Ⓦ bbc.co.uk/proms. This series of nightly classical concerts, over the course of two months at the Royal Albert Hall (and elsewhere), is a well-loved British institution. See p.413.

Italian Procession Sun nearest July 16. St Peter's Italian Church Ⓦ italianchurch.org.uk; ⊖ Farringdon; free. Big, boisterous Italian Catholic parade, party and stalls, which starts on Clerkenwell Rd and roams the streets of what used to be London's very own Little Italy (see p.151).

Cart Marking Wed 11am in mid-July. Guildhall Ⓦ thecarmen
.co.uk; ⊖ Bank; free. Recalling a 1681 Act which restricted to 421 the
number of horse-drawn carts allowed in the City, this arcane ceremony
involves vintage vehicles congregating in Guildhall Yard in a branding
ceremony organized by the Worshipful Company of Carmen.

AUGUST

Ride London Early Aug Ⓦ prudentialridelondon.co.uk; free. Weekend
festival of cycling, including an eight-mile traffic-free loop around the
capital – more than eighty thousand people take part every year.

Great British Beer Festival Mid-Aug. London Olympia Ⓦ gbbf
.org.uk; ⊖ Kensington Olympia. A five-day binge organized by the
Campaign for Real Ale (CAMRA). With up to eight hundred brews to
sample, the entrance fee is a small price to pay to drink yourself silly.

London Mela Sun in Aug or early Sept. Gunnersbury Park
Ⓦ londonmela.org; ⊖ Gunnersbury; free. Nearly one hundred
thousand revellers come to this big open-air Asian festival of live music,
dance and the arts, washed down with the best festival food in the capital.

Notting Hill Carnival Sun & Mon of Aug Bank Holiday weekend
Ⓦ thenottinghillcarnival.com; free. World-famous two-day street
festival. Carnival is a tumult of imaginatively decorated floats,
eye-catching costumes, thumping soundsystems, live bands, irresistible
food and huge crowds (see p.278).

SEPTEMBER

Great River Race Sat in mid-Sept Ⓦ greatriverrace.co.uk; free.
Hundreds of boats are rowed or paddled for 21 miles from Island Gardens
on the Isle of Dogs to Ham House, Richmond. Starts are staggered and
any number of weird and wonderful vessels take part.

Thames Festival Early Sept Ⓦ thamesfestival.org; ⊖ Southwark;
free. The Mayor of London's very own family-orientated community
festival takes place over the course of a week on both banks of the river,
with river races, a Thames beach, dancing, music, fireworks and a
night-time parade.

Open House Third weekend in month Ⓦ londonopenhouse
.org; free. A once-a-year opportunity to peek inside over seven hundred
buildings around London, many of which don't normally open their
doors to the public. You'll need to book in advance for some of the more
popular places.

Great Gorilla Run Last Sat in month Ⓦ greatgorillarun.org; free
(to watch). Don a gorilla suit and join (or simply watch) 750 gorillas
running 7km through the City for mountain gorilla conservation.

Costermongers Harvest Festival Parade Service Last Sun in
month 1pm. Guildhall to St Mary-le-Bow Ⓦ pearlysociety.co.uk;
⊖ Bank or St Paul's; free. Cockney festival in the City, with donkeys
and carts, marching bands and Pearly Kings and Queens in their
traditional pearl-button-studded outfits.

OCTOBER

Judges' Service First Mon in month Ⓦ westminster-abbey.org.
Westminster Abbey; free. To mark the opening of the legal year
the judiciary, in full regalia, attends a service at 11.30am in the
abbey. Afterwards they process to the House of Lords for their
"Annual Breakfast".

London Film Festival Mid to late Oct Ⓦ bfi.org.uk/lff. A two-week
cinematic season with scores of new international films screened at the
BFI Southbank and some West End venues.

Return to Camden Town Late Oct & early Nov. London Irish Centre,
50–52 Camden Square Ⓦ returntocamden.org; Camden Road
Overground. Two long weekends of traditional Irish music, song and dance
featuring a great line-up of performers as well as talks and workshops.

NOVEMBER

London to Brighton Veteran Car Run First Sun in month. Hyde
Park Ⓦ veterancarrun.com; free. In 1896 Parliament abolished the Act
that required all cars to crawl along at 2mph behind someone waving a
red flag. A rally was set up to mark the occasion, and more than a century
later five hundred or so pre-1905 vehicles still set off from Hyde Park at
sunrise and travel the 58 miles to Brighton along the A23 at the heady
average speed of 20mph.

Bonfire Night Nov 5 or nearest weekend; free. In memory of Guy
Fawkes – executed for his role in the 1605 Gunpowder Plot to blow up
King James I and the Houses of Parliament – effigies of the hapless
Fawkes are burned on bonfires all over the capital. See local listings or
head for Alexandra Palace, which provides a good vantage point from
which to take in several displays at once.

London Jazz Festival Mid-Nov Ⓦ londonjazzfestival.org.uk.
Big ten-day international jazz fest held in all London's jazz venues, large
and small.

Lord Mayor's Show Second Sat in month Ⓦ lordmayorsshow.org;
free. The Lord Mayor begins his or her day of investiture at Westminster,
leaving there at around 9am for Guildhall. At 11.10am, the vast
ceremonial procession, headed by a gilded coach, begins its journey from
Guildhall to the Law Courts in the Strand, where the oath of office is taken
at 11.50am. From there the coach and its train of 140-odd floats make
their way back towards Guildhall, arriving at 2.20pm. After dark, there's a
fireworks display on the Thames.

Remembrance Sunday Sun nearest Nov 11; free. A day of
commemorative ceremonies for the dead and wounded of the two world
wars and other conflicts. The principal ceremony, attended by the Queen
and the prime minister, takes place at the Cenotaph in Whitehall,
beginning with a march-past of veterans and building to a one-minute
silence at the stroke of 11am.

Christmas Lights Late Nov to Jan 5; free. Assorted celebrities flick
the switches, and Bond, Oxford and Regent streets are bathed in festive
illumination from dusk to midnight until January 6. Also, each year since
the end of World War II, Norway has acknowledged its gratitude to the
country that helped liberate it from the Nazis with the gift of a mighty
spruce tree that appears in Trafalgar Square in early December. Decorated
with lights, it becomes the focus for carol singing versus traffic noise each
evening until Christmas Eve.

DECEMBER

Ice rinks Dec–Jan. Ice rinks have become all the rage. You can skate
outside the Natural History Museum, at Somerset House, Marble Arch,
Kew Gardens and elsewhere.

Christmas Day Race Christmas Day. Serpentine Lido
Ⓦ serpentineswimmingclub.com; ⊖ Knightsbrdge; free. Brave

(or foolhardy) members of the Serpentine Swimming Club have taken an icy 100yd plunge and competed for the Peter Pan Cup in the Lido every year since 1864.

New Year's Eve Ⓦ london.gov.uk; free. New Year is welcomed by thousands of revellers who get to enjoy a spectacular firework display centred on the London Eye. Transport for London runs free public transport all night, sponsored by various public-spirited breweries.

Travel essentials

Addresses

London addresses come with postcodes at the end. Each street name is followed by a letter or letters giving the geographical location of the street in relation to the City (E for "east", WC for "west central" and so on) and a number that specifies its location more precisely. Unfortunately, this number doesn't correspond to the district's distance from the centre (as in most cities). So W11 (Notting Hill) for example, is closer to the centre of town than W4 (Chiswick), and SE3 (Blackheath) lies beyond the remote-sounding SE10 (Greenwich). Full postal addresses end with a digit and two letters, which specify the individual block, and will locate a building on Google Maps or a Sat Nav.

Climate

Despite the temperateness of the English climate, it's impossible to say with any degree of certainty that the weather will be pleasant in any given month. English summers rarely get unbearably hot, while the winters don't get very cold – though they're often wet. However, whenever you come, be prepared for all eventualities: it has been known to snow at Easter and rain all day on August Bank Holiday weekend.

Costs

The high cost of accommodation (see p.355), and food (see p.367) and drink, makes London a **very expensive** place to visit. The minimum expenditure for a couple staying in a budget hotel and eating

> ### TIPPING
> There are no fixed rules for **tipping** in London. However, there's a certain expectation in restaurants or cafés that you should leave a tip of about ten percent of the total bill – check first, though, that "optional" service has not already been included. Taxi drivers also expect tips – add about ten percent to the fare – as do traditional barbers. The other occasion when you'll be expected to tip is in upmarket hotels where porters, bellboys and table waiters rely on being tipped to bump up their often dismal wages.

takeaway meals, pizzas or other such basic fare would be in the region of at least £50 per person per day. You only have to add in the odd better-quality meal, plus some major tourist attractions, a few films or other shows, and you're looking at around £75–100 as a daily budget, even in decidedly average accommodation.

Most attractions and many cinemas and theatres offer **concessions** for senior citizens, the unemployed, full-time students and under-16s, with under-5s being admitted free almost every-where – although proof of eligibility will be required in most cases.

Once obtained, **youth/student ID cards** soon pay for themselves in savings. Full-time students are eligible for the International Student Identity Card or **ISIC**, which costs around £10 and entitles the bearer to reduced air, rail and bus fares, and discounts at museums, theatres and other attractions. If you're not a student, but you're 25 or younger, you can get an International Youth Travel Card or **IYTC**, which costs the same as the ISIC and carries the same benefits. Visit Ⓦ isic.org for more details.

Crime and personal safety

The traditional image of the friendly British "bobby" is a bit of a tired old cliché, but in the

AVERAGE MONTHLY TEMPERATURES AND RAINFALL

	Jan	Feb	Mar	Apr	May	Jun	Jul	Aug	Sep	Oct	Nov	Dec
LONDON												
Max/min (°C)	6/2	7/2	10/3	13/6	17/8	20/12	22/14	21/13	19/11	14/8	10/5	7/4
Max/min (°F)	43/36	44/36	50/37	56/43	62/46	69/53	71/57	71/56	65/52	57/45	50/41	44/39
Rainfall (mm)	54	40	37	37	46	45	57	59	49	57	64	48

ENGLISH HERITAGE AND NATIONAL TRUST

A few of London's historic properties come under the control of the private **National Trust** (☎0844 800 1895, ⓦnationaltrust.org.uk), or the state-run **English Heritage** (☎0870 333 1181, ⓦenglish-heritage.org.uk). These properties are denoted in the guide by "NT" or "EH" after the opening times. Annual membership for each organization is around £50 and allows free entry to their respective properties, though if you're only visiting London for a short time, it may not be worth it.

normal run of events the police continue to be approachable, helpful and, for the most part, unarmed. If you're lost in London, asking a police officer is generally the quickest way to pinpoint your destination – police officers on street duty wear a distinctive domed hat with a silver tip. Like any other capital, London has its dangerous spots, but these tend to be obscure parts of the city where no tourist has any reason to be. The chief risk on London's streets is pickpocketing, and there are some virtuosos at work on the big shopping streets and the Underground (tube). Carry only as much money as you need for the day, and keep all bags and pockets fastened.

Should you have anything stolen or be involved in an incident that requires reporting, go to the local police station or phone ☎101 – the ☎999 number should only be used in emergencies. Central 24hr Metropolitan police stations include: Charing Cross, Agar St, WC2 (⊖ Charing Cross); Holborn, 10 Lambs Conduit St, WC1 (⊖ Holborn); Marylebone, 1–9 Seymour St, W1 (⊖ Marble Arch); West End Central, 27 Savile Row, W1 (⊖ Oxford Circus); ⓦmet.police.uk. The City of London Police are separate from the Metropolitan Police and have a police station at 182 Bishopsgate, EC2 (☎020 7601 2222, ⓦcityoflondon.police.uk; ⊖ Liverpool Street). If there's an incident on public transport, you should call the British Transport Police, 55 Broadway SW1 (☎0800 405 040, ⓦbtp.police.uk). If

you have a complaint against the police, take the officer's number and report it to the Independent Police Complaints Commission (☎0845 300 2002, ⓦipcc.gov.uk).

Electricity

Electricity supply in London conforms to the EU standard of approximately 230V. Sockets are designed for British three-pin plugs, which are totally different from those in the rest of the EU and North America.

Entry requirements

Citizens of all European countries – except Albania, Bosnia, Macedonia, Montenegro, Serbia and the former Soviet republics (other than the Baltic states) – can enter Britain with just a passport, for up to three months (indefinitely if you're from the EU). US, Canadian, Australian and New Zealand citizens can stay for up to six months, providing they have a return ticket and adequate funds to cover their stay. Citizens of most other countries require a **visa**, obtainable from the British consular or mission office in the country of application. To check if you need a visa, visit ⓦukba.homeoffice.gov.uk.

Note that visa regulations are subject to frequent changes, so it's always wise to contact the nearest British embassy or High Commission before you travel. If you visit ⓦukvisas.gov.uk, you can download the full range of application forms and information leaflets and find out the contact details of your nearest embassy or consulate.

EMERGENCIES

Alcoholics Anonymous ☎0845 769 7555, ⓦalcoholics-anonymous.org.uk
Police, fire and ambulance ☎999
Rape Crisis ☎0808 802 9999 (daily noon–2.30pm & 7–9.30pm), ⓦrapecrisis.org.uk
Samaritans 24hr counselling helpline ☎0845 790 9090, ⓦsamaritans.org; or drop-in (daily 9am–9pm) at 46 Marshall St, W1 ☎020 7734 2800; ⊖ Piccadilly Circus or Oxford Circus
Sexual Healthline ☎0800 567123, ⓦfpa.org.uk

EMBASSIES AND HIGH COMMISSIONS

Australian High Commission Australia House, Strand, WC2 ☎020 7379 4334, ⓦuk.embassy.gov.au; ⊖ Charing Cross
Canadian High Commission 1 Grosvenor Square, W1 ☎020 7258 6600, ⓦunitedkingdom.gc.ca; ⊖ Bond Street
Irish Embassy 17 Grosvenor Place, SW1 ☎020 7235 2171, ⓦembassyofireland.co.uk; ⊖ Hyde Park Corner
New Zealand High Commission New Zealand House, 80 Haymarket, SW1 ☎020 7930 8422, ⓦnzembassy.com; ⊖ Piccadilly Circus

24 HOUR ACCIDENT AND EMERGENCY

Chelsea & Westminster Hospital 369 Fulham Rd, SW10 ☎020 8746 8080; bus #14 or #414 from ⊖South Kensington.
Royal Free Hospital Pond St, NW3 ☎020 7794 0500; ⊖ Hampstead.
Royal London Hospital Whitechapel Rd, E1 ☎020 3416 5000; ⊖ Whitechapel.
St Mary's Hospital Praed St, W2 ☎020 3312 6330; ⊖ Paddington.
St Thomas's Hospital Westminster Bridge Rd, SE1 ☎020 7188 7188; ⊖ London Bridge.
University College London Hospital 235 Euston Rd, NW1 ☎020 3456 7890; ⊖ Euston Square or Warren Square.
Whittington Hospital Magdala Ave, N19 ☎020 7272 3070; ⊖ Archway.

South African High Commission South Africa House, Trafalgar Square, WC2 ☎020 7451 7299, ⓦ southafricahouseuk .com; ⊖ Charing Cross
US Embassy 24 Grosvenor Square, W1 ☎020 7499 9000, ⓦ london.usembassy.gov; ⊖ Bond Street

Health

For minor complaints, pharmacists (known as chemists in England) can dispense a limited range of drugs without a doctor's prescription. Most pharmacies are open standard shop hours, though some stay open later: Zafash, 233–235 Old Brompton Rd, SW5 ☎020 7373 2798, ⓦ zafash.com (⊖ Earl's Court), is open 24 hours; while Bliss, at 5–6 Marble Arch, W1 ☎020 7723 6116, ⓦ blisslife.co.uk (⊖ Marble Arch), is open daily 9am till midnight.

EU and EEA citizens are entitled to free medical treatment within the National Health Service, on production of an EHIC (European Health Insurance Card). Australia, New Zealand, Russia and several other non-EU countries also have reciprocal healthcare arrangements with the UK. If it's an emergency, go to the Accident and Emergency (A&E) department of your local hospital, or phone for an ambulance (☎999). A&E services are free to all. You can also go to a Minor Injuries Clinic such as the one at St Bartholomew's Hospital, West Smithfield, EC1 ☎020 3465 5869 (Mon–Fri 8am–4pm; ⊖ Farringdon), or get free medical advice from NHS

Direct, the health service's 24-hour helpline ☎111, ⓦ nhsdirect.nhs.uk.

For an emergency dentist turn up as early as possible at the Dental Emergency Care Service at Guy's Hospital, St Thomas St (☎020 7188 1234; Mon–Fri 8am–3.45pm).

Insurance

Even though EU healthcare privileges apply in the UK, it's as well to take out an insurance policy before travelling to cover against theft, loss and illness or injury. Non-EU citizens should check whether they are already covered before buying a new policy.

Internet access

Most hotels and hostels in London have internet access. Otherwise, your best bet is to find a café with wi-fi like the café in Foyles bookshop at 113–119 Charing Cross Rd (⊖ Tottenham Court Road). The Southbank Centre has free wi-fi and the British Library and St Pancras Station both have free wi-fi, too. Some public libraries also offer free access.

Laundry

Most hotels offer a laundry service and most hostels have washing machines. Self-service

ROUGH GUIDES TRAVEL INSURANCE

Rough Guides has teamed up with **WorldNomads.com** to offer great travel insurance deals. Policies are available to residents of over 150 countries, with cover for a wide range of adventure sports, 24hr emergency assistance, high levels of medical and evacuation cover and a stream of travel safety information. Roughguides.com users can take advantage of their policies online 24/7, from anywhere in the world – even if you're already travelling. And since plans often change when you're on the road, you can extend your policy and even claim online. Roughguides.com users who buy travel insurance with WorldNomads.com can also leave a positive footprint and donate to a community development project. For more information go to ⓦ roughguides.com/shop.

laundrettes exist all over London, although they are harder to find in the centre – there's Red & White laundrette at 78 Marchmont St, WC1 ☎020 7387 3667 (daily 6.30am–10.30pm; ⊖ King's Cross). For a central dry cleaners, try Valentino Dry Cleaners, 56b New Oxford St, WC1 ☎020 7436 1660 (Mon–Fri 8.30am–6pm, Sat 9am–1pm; ⊖ Tottenham Court Road).

Left luggage

Airports Gatwick: North Terminal ☎01293 734888 (daily 5am–9pm); South Terminal ☎01293 734887 (24hr). Heathrow ☎020 8759 3344: Terminal 1 (daily 6am–11pm); Terminal 3 (daily 5.30am–11pm); Terminal 4 (daily 5.30am–11pm); Terminal 5 (daily 5.30am–11pm). London City ☎020 7646 0000 (Mon–Fri 5am–10pm, Sat 5am–11pm, Sun 11am–10.20pm). Luton ☎01582 405100 (24hr). Stansted ☎0844 824 3109 (24hr).

Train stations Excess Baggage Company (☎020 7262 0344, ⓦleft-baggage.co.uk): Charing Cross ☎020 7930 5444 (daily 7am–11pm); Euston ☎020 7387 1499 (daily 7am–11pm); King's Cross ☎020 7837 4334 (daily 7am–11pm); Liverpool Street ☎020 7247 4297 (daily 7am–11pm); Paddington ☎020 7262 0344 (daily 7am–11pm); St Pancras ☎020 7837 4334 (Mon–Sat 6am–10pm, Sun 7am–10pm); Victoria ☎020 7963 0957 (daily 7am–midnight); Waterloo ☎020 7401 8444 (daily 7am–11pm).

Lost property

Airports Gatwick (South Terminal) ☎01293 503162 (daily 10am–4pm); Heathrow (Terminals 3 & 5) ☎0844 824 3115 (daily 9.30am–4.30pm); London City ☎020 7646 0000; Luton ☎01582 395219; Stansted ☎0844 824 3109 (daily 1–5pm). **Eurostar** ☎0844 822 4411 (Mon–Fri 10am–5pm). **Train stations** Euston ☎020 7387 8699 (Mon–Fri 9am–5pm); King's Cross ☎020 7278 3310 (Mon–Fri 9am–5pm); Liverpool Street ☎020 7247 4297 (Mon–Fri 9am–5pm); Paddington ☎020 7262 0344 (Mon–Fri 9am–5pm); St Pancras ☎020 7837 4334 (Mon–Fri 9am–5pm); Victoria ☎020 7963 0957 (Mon–Fri 9am–5pm); Waterloo ☎020 7401 7861 (Mon–Fri 7.30am–7pm).

Transport for London Lost Property Office, 200 Baker St, NW1 (Mon–Fri 8.30am–4pm) ☎0343 222 1234, ⓦtfl.gov.uk; ⊖ Baker Street; map p.89. Contact TfL about property lost on buses, tubes or in black cabs.

Mail

The postal service is pretty efficient. First-class **stamps** to anywhere in the UK currently cost 60p and should arrive the next day; if the item is anything approaching A4 size, it will be classed as a "Large Letter" and will cost 90p; if you want to guarantee next day delivery, ask for Special Delivery (from around £6). Second-class stamps cost 50p, taking up to three days; airmail to the rest of Europe costs 88p and should take three days; to the rest of the world stamps cost from 76p and should take five days. Stamps can be bought at post offices, and from newsagents and supermarkets, although they usually only sell books of four or ten first-class UK stamps.

For general postal enquiries phone ☎0845 774 0740 (Mon–Fri 8am–6pm, Sat 8am–1pm), or visit the website ⓦroyalmail.com. Almost all London's **post offices** are open Monday to Friday 9am–5.30pm, Saturday 9am–noon. The exception is the Trafalgar Square Post Office (24–28 William IV St, WC2N 4DL; Mon–Fri 8.30am–6.30pm, Tues opens 9.15am, Sat 9am–5.30pm), to which **poste restante** mail should be sent. In the suburbs you'll find sub-post offices operating out of shops, but these are open the same hours as regular post offices, even if the shop itself is open for longer. To find out your nearest post office, contact ☎0845 611 2970, ⓦpostoffice.co.uk (Mon–Fri 8.15am–6pm, Sat 8.30am–2pm).

Maps

The maps in this book should be adequate for sightseeing purposes. Alternatively, the Geographers' A–Z map series produces a whole range of street-by-street maps of London, from pocket-sized foldouts to giant atlases. Virtually every newsagent in London stocks them, but the best map shop in London is Stanfords, 12–14 Long Acre, WC2 (☎020 7836 1321, ⓦstanfords.co.uk; ⊖ Leicester Square). Free maps of the Underground and bus networks can be picked up at tourist offices and TfL information offices (see p.21).

Media

The free **listings magazine**, *Time Out*, comes out every Tuesday and carries critical appraisals of a selection of the week's theatre, film, music, exhibitions and children's events, though for comprehensive coverage, you need to visit their website ⓦtimeout.com/london. London's only daily **newspapers** are both tabloids: the *Metro* is available on the public transport system in the morning, and the *Evening Standard* all over town from mid-afternoon onwards – both are free. Each of the London boroughs has a local paper, usually printed twice weekly and filled mostly with news of local crimes and cheap adverts.

Money

The currency in the UK is the pound sterling (£), divided into 100 pence (p). Coins come in denominations of 1p, 2p, 5p, 10p, 20p, 50p, £1 and £2. Notes come in denominations of £5, £10, £20 and £50. Many shopkeepers may not accept £50 notes – the best advice is to avoid having to use them. At the time of writing, £1 was worth $1.50, €1.15, Can$1.60, Aus$1.60 and NZ$2. For the most up-to-date exchange rates, visit ⓦ xe.com.

The easiest way to get hold of your cash is to use your **credit/debit card** in a "cash machine" (ATM); check in advance whether you will be subject to a daily withdrawal limit. There are ATMs all over the city, outside banks, supermarkets and post offices – beware of stand-alone ATMs in small shops, which charge up to £2 for each withdrawal. The opening hours for most **banks** are Monday to Friday 9.30am–4.30pm, with some branches opening on Saturday mornings. Post offices charge no commission, and are therefore a good place to change money and cheques. Lost or stolen credit/debit cards should be reported to the police and the following numbers: MasterCard ☎ 0800 964767, Visa ☎ 0800 891725.

PUBLIC HOLIDAYS

You'll find all banks and offices closed on the following Bank Holidays, while everything else pretty much runs to a Sunday schedule (except on Christmas Day when most places shut down): **New Year's Day** (January 1); **Good Friday** (late March/early April); **Easter Monday** (late March/early April); **Spring Bank Holiday** (first Monday in May); **May Bank Holiday** (last Monday in May); **August Bank Holiday** (last Monday in August); **Christmas Day** (December 25); **Boxing Day** (December 26). Note that if January 1, December 25 or December 26 falls on a Saturday or Sunday, the holiday falls on the following weekday.

UK OPERATOR SERVICES

Domestic operator ☎ 100
International operator ☎ 155

Opening hours and public holidays

Generally speaking, **shop opening hours** are Monday to Saturday 9am or 10am to 5.30pm or 6pm – with some places in central London staying open till 8pm, and later on Thursdays and Fridays (around 9pm) – and Sundays and Bank Holidays noon to 6pm. There are still plenty of stores that close completely on Sundays and Bank Holidays. That said, numerous family-run corner shops stay open late every day of the year. The big supermarket chains tend to open Monday to Saturday from 8am to 10pm, Sunday 10am or 11am to 4pm or 5pm. Note that many petrol (gas) service stations in London are open 24 hours and have small shops.

Tourist attractions and **museums** are typically open daily 10am to 6pm, occasionally with shorter hours on Sundays and public holidays (see box below). Most places are closed on December 25 and 26. Several museums now have late-night openings until 9pm or 10pm, once or twice a week. Individual opening hours are given in the main text of this guide.

Phones

Public **payphones** on the streets of London are iconic, ubiquitous and little-used. Most take coins from 10p upwards – the minimum charge of 60p will get you thirty minutes. Paying using a credit card is expensive (20p per minute). Discount phonecards with a PIN number, available from newsagents, are the cheapest way to make international calls.

If you're taking your **mobile/cellphone** with you, check with your provider that roaming is activated (if you're coming from America, you will need a multi-band phone, unless you have a smart phone). Mobiles in Australia and New Zealand generally use the same system as the UK so should work fine. If you're staying for a while, it's easier to buy a handset and SIM card when you arrive – a basic pay-as-you-go phone can cost as little as £20.

London phone numbers are prefixed by the area code ☎ 020. Mobile numbers are prefixed with ☎ 07; numbers with ☎ 0800, 0808 and 0500 prefixes are free of charge (unless calling from a mobile);

PHONING HOME

To Australia ☎0061 + area code without the zero + number
To Ireland ☎00353 + area code without the zero + number
To New Zealand ☎0064 + area code without the zero + number
To South Africa ☎0027 + area code without the zero + number
To US and Canada ☎001 + area code + number

☎03 numbers are charged at local rates; ☎0845 and ☎0870 numbers are charged at special higher rates. Beware of premium-rate numbers which usually have the prefix ☎09, as these are charged at anything up to £1.50 a minute.

For directory enquiries, there are numerous companies offering the service, all with six-figure numbers beginning with ☎118. Whichever one you choose, the minimum charge you'll get away with is 40p. The best known is ☎118 118; for an online UK phone directory, visit ⓦukphonebook.com.

Smoking

Smoking is banned in all indoor public spaces including all cafés, pubs, restaurants, clubs and public transport.

Tax

Most goods in Britain are subject to **Value Added Tax** (VAT), which increases the cost of an item by 20 percent, although the prices displayed nearly always include VAT. Visitors from non-EU countries can save money through the **Retail Export Scheme** (tax-free shopping), which allows a VAT refund on goods taken out of the country. Note that not all shops participate in this scheme (those doing so will display a sign to this effect) and that you cannot reclaim VAT charged on hotel bills or other services. See ⓦhmrc.gov.uk for more details.

Time

Greenwich Mean Time (GMT) is used from the end of October to the end of March; for the rest of the year the country switches to British Summer Time (BST), one hour ahead of GMT. GMT is five hours ahead of the US East Coast; eight ahead of the US West Coast; and nine behind Australia's East Coast.

Toilets

There are surprisingly few public toilets in London. All mainline train and major tube stations have toilets. Department stores and free museums and galleries are another good option.

Tourist information

There is no proper, central tourist office in London, as there is in just about every other major city in Europe. Instead, there's just a tiny window in the **tkts kiosk** on Leicester Square, WC2 (daily 8am–midnight; ☎020 7292 2333, ⓦlondoninformationcentre.com; ⊖ Leicester Square), and a kiosk outside Holborn tube station (Mon–Fri 8am–6pm).

Many of the 32 London boroughs have tourist information offices, with the most central one in the City of London on the south side of St Paul's Cathedral (Mon–Sat 9.30am–5.30pm, Sun 10am–4pm; ☎020 7332 1456, ⓦvisitthecity.co.uk; ⊖ St Paul's). Another useful borough tourist office is Greenwich in the old Royal Naval College (daily 10am–5pm; ☎0870 608 2000; Cutty Sark DLR).

Tours and walks

Standard sightseeing tours are run by several rival bus companies, their open-top double-deckers setting off every thirty minutes from Victoria station, Trafalgar Square, Piccadilly and other conspicuous tourist spots. You can hop on and off several different routes as often as you like with **The Original Tour** for around £25 (daily 8.30am–6pm; every 15–20min; ☎020 8877 1722, ⓦtheoriginaltour.com).

The cheapest option is to hop on a real **London double-decker**. For example, the #11 bus (with its fleet of Boris Buses with open rear platforms and roving conductors) from Victoria station, will take you past Westminster Abbey, the Houses of Parliament, up Whitehall, round Trafalgar Square, along the Strand and on to St Paul's Cathedral. You can also take an old double-decker Routemaster, on two "heritage" routes (daily every 20min 9.30am–7pm): #9 from the Kensington High Street to Trafalgar Square and #15 from Trafalgar Square to Tower Hill.

Walking tours are infinitely more appealing and informative, mixing solid historical facts with juicy anecdotes in the company of a local specialist. Walks on offer range from a literary pub crawl round Bloomsbury to a roam around the East End. Tours cost around £7–10 and take around two hours; normally you can simply show up at the starting

THE LONDON PASS

If you're thinking of visiting a lot of fee-paying attractions in a short space of time, it's worth considering buying a **London Pass** (W londonpass.com), which gives you free entry to some of London's top attractions including Hampton Court Palace, Kensington Palace, Kew Gardens, London Zoo, St Paul's Cathedral, the Tower of London, Westminster Abbey and Windsor Castle. You can choose to buy the card with an **All-Zone Travelcard** thrown in; the extra outlay is relatively small, but does not include travel out to Windsor. The pass costs around £47 for one day (£30 for kids), rising to around £100 for six days (£70 for kids), or £56 with a Travelcard (£34 for kids) rising to around £150 (£100 for kids). The London Pass can be bought online or in person from tourist offices and London's mainline train or chief underground stations.

point and join. **Original London Walks** (T 020 7624 3978, W walks.com) are a well-established and reliably good company, but you'll find many more detailed at W timeout.com/london/walks. If you want to plan – or book – walks in advance, contact W guidelondon.org.uk or W britainsbestguides.org.

Travellers with disabilities

London is an old city, not well equipped for disabled travellers. That said, all public venues are obliged to make some effort towards accessibility and even public transport is slowly improving, with most buses now wheelchair-accessible. The ancient tube and rail systems, designed, for the most part, in the nineteenth century, are still a trial for those with mobility problems. Around 25 percent of all tube stations are step-free – the majority on the Docklands Light Railway – and are indicated by a blue symbol on the tube map. For a more detailed rundown, get hold of the free *Tube Access Guide* or use the TfL website to plan a step-free journey (W tfl.gov.uk).

Tourism For All has lots of useful information on accessibility for visitors to London (T 0845 124 9971, W tourismforall.org.uk). Another valuable service is provided by Artsline (T 020 7388 2227, W artsline .org.uk), who can give up-to-date information and advice by phone on access to arts venues and events in London: theatres, cinemas, galleries and concert halls.

Websites

Aside from the aforementioned tourist authority and local borough websites, there's a vast quantity of useful London-related information online. Below are a handful of good general sites:

W **culture24.org.uk** Useful national website, with up-to-date information on virtually every single museum, large or small, in London (and the UK).

W **derelictlondon.co.uk** Pictorial catalogue of the city's abandoned cinemas, pubs, theatres and even toilets, plus other forgotten derelict gems.

W **londonist.com** London webmag with listings, but also lots of interesting articles on the many faces of London.

W **londonnet.co.uk** Web guide to London with useful up-to-date listings on eating, drinking and nightlife.

W **gumtree.com** Very useful website for anyone living in London, looking for a job, a flat, or to buy or sell anything.

W **smokealondonpeculiar.co.uk** Witty, tongue-in-cheek look at London's more obscure tics and quirks.

W **thisislocallondon.co.uk** Forty of the capital's local newspapers on one local news website.

Working in London

All Swiss nationals and EEA citizens can work in London without a permit, although citizens of Bulgaria, Czech Republic, Estonia, Hungary, Latvia, Lithuania, Poland, Romania, Slovakia or Slovenia must register under the Worker Registration Scheme. Other nationals need a work permit in order to work legally in the UK, with eligibility worked out on a points-based system. There are exceptions to the above rules, although these are constantly changing, so for the latest regulations visit W ukvisas.gov.uk.

Whitehall and Westminster

The monuments and buildings in Westminster include some of London's most famous landmarks – Nelson's Column, Big Ben, the Houses of Parliament and Westminster Abbey, plus two of the city's top permanent art collections, the National Gallery and Tate Britain and its finest architectural set piece, Trafalgar Square. This is one of the easiest parts of London to walk round, with all the major sights within a mere half-mile of each other, and linked by one of London's most triumphant – and atypical – avenues, Whitehall. However, despite the fact the area is a well-trodden tourist circuit, for the most part there are only a few shops or cafés and little commercial life (nearby Soho and Covent Garden are far better for this).

Political, religious and regal power has emanated from **Whitehall** and **Westminster** for almost a millennium. It was King Edward the Confessor (1042–66) who first established Westminster as a royal and ecclesiastical power base, some three miles west of the City of London. The embryonic English parliament used to meet in the abbey and eventually took over the old royal palace of Westminster when Henry VIII moved out to Whitehall. Henry's sprawling Whitehall Palace burnt down in 1698 and was slowly replaced by government offices, so that by the nineteenth century Whitehall had become the "heart of the Empire", its ministries ruling over a quarter of the world's population. Even now, though the UK's world status has diminished and its royalty and clergy no longer wield much real power or receive the same respect, the institutions that run the country inhabit roughly the same geographical area: Westminster for the politicians, Whitehall for the ministers and civil servants.

Trafalgar Square

⊖ Charing Cross

As one of the few large public squares in London, **Trafalgar Square** has been both a tourist attraction and the main focus for political demonstrations for over a century and a half (see box below). Nowadays, most folk come here to see **Nelson's Column**, or to visit the **National Gallery**, though a huge range of events, commemorations and celebrations are staged here throughout the year, from St Patrick's Day shenanigans to Diwali, the Hindu festival of lights. Each December, the square is graced with a giant Christmas tree covered in fairy lights, donated by Norway in thanks for Britain's support during World War II, and carol singers battle nightly with the traffic.

For centuries, Trafalgar Square was the site of the **King's Mews**, established in the thirteenth century by Edward I, who kept the royal hawks and the falconers here (the term "mews" comes from falconry: the birds were caged or "mewed up" there whilst changing their plumage). Chaucer was Clerk of the Mews for a time, and by Tudor times there were stables here, too. During the Civil War they were turned into barracks and later used as a prison for Cavaliers. In the 1760s, George III began to move the mews to Buckingham Palace, and by the late 1820s, **John Nash** had designed the new square (though he didn't live to see his plan executed). The Neoclassical National Gallery filled up the northern side in 1838, followed shortly afterwards by the central focal point, Nelson's Column, though the famous bronze lions didn't arrive until 1868. The development of the rest of the square was equally haphazard, though the overall effect is unified by the safe Neoclassical style of the buildings, and the square remains one of London's grandest architectural highlights.

A HISTORY OF PROTEST

Installed in 1845 in an attempt to deter the gathering of urban mobs, the Trafalgar Square fountains have failed supremely to prevent the square from becoming a focus of **political protest**. The first major demo was held in 1848 when the Chartists assembled to demand universal suffrage before marching to Kennington Common. Protests were banned until the 1880s, when the emerging Labour movement began to gather here, culminating in **Bloody Sunday**, 1887, when hundreds of demonstrators were injured, and three killed, by the police. To allow the police to call quickly for reinforcements, a police phone box was built into one of the stone bollards in the southeast corner of the square, with a direct link to Scotland Yard.

Throughout the 1980s, there was a continuous **anti-apartheid demonstration** outside South Africa House, and in 1990, the square was the scene of the **Poll Tax Riot**, which precipitated the downfall of Margaret Thatcher. Smaller demos still take place here, but London's largest demonstrations – like the ones against military intervention in Iraq and Afghanistan – simply pass through, en route to the more spacious environs of Hyde Park.

WHITEHALL & WESTMINSTER

SEE 'TRAFALGAR SQUARE & WHITEHALL' MAP FOR DETAIL

National Portrait Gallery

Piccadilly Circus

National Gallery

St Martin-in-the-Fields

Charing Cross

Nelson's Column

Trafalgar Square

Canada House

Admiralty Arch

Banqueting House

Green Park

St James's Square

Horse Guards

10 Downing St

MoD

St James's Palace

Clarence House

THE MALL

Duck Island

Lancaster House

Cenotaph

Green Park

St James's Park

Westminster

Victoria Memorial

Churchill War Rooms

Constitution Hill

Buckingham Palace

Big Ben

Buckingham Palace Gardens

Queen's Gallery

St Margaret's

Houses of Parliament

Wellington Barracks

Central Hall

Westminster Abbey

Royal Mews

St James's Park

New Scotland Yard

Jewel Tower

Blewcoat School

Victoria Tower Gardens

Cardinal Place

St John

Victoria

Westminster Cathedral

Royal Horticultural Halls

MI5

Victoria Station

Millbank Tower

Tate Britain

Victoria Coach Station

St James the-Less

Millbank Pier

Pimlico

PIMLICO

River Thames

St George's Tower

VAUXHALL BRIDGE

N

0   200
         yards

THE FOURTH PLINTH

The **fourth plinth**, in the northwest corner Trafalgar Square, was originally earmarked for an equestrian statue of William IV. In the end, it remained empty until 1999, since when it has been used to display works of modern sculpture, which are changed annually (Ⓦlondon.gov.uk/fourthplinth). Highlights have included: Rachel Whiteread's inverted plinth; Marc Quinn's *Alison Lapper Pregnant*, a nude statue of a woman without arms – a larger, inflatable version of which appeared in the 2012 Paralympics opening ceremony; Antony Gormley's *One & Other*, where several thousand individuals each had an hour to occupy the plinth; and Yinka Shonibare's *Ship in a Bottle*.

Nelson's Column

Raised in 1843, and now one of London's best-loved monuments, **Nelson's Column** commemorates the one-armed, one-eyed admiral who defeated the French at the Battle of Trafalgar in 1805, but paid for it with his life. The sandstone statue which surmounts a 151-foot granite column is more than triple life-size but still manages to appear minuscule. The acanthus leaves of the capital are cast from British cannons, while bas-reliefs around the base – depicting three of Nelson's earlier victories as well as his death aboard HMS *Victory* – are from captured French armaments. Edwin Landseer's four gargantuan **bronze lions** guard the column and provide a climbing frame for kids (and demonstrators).

Keeping Nelson company at ground level, on either side of the column, are bronze **statues** of Napier and Havelock, Victorian major-generals who helped keep India British; against the north wall are busts of Beatty, Jellicoe and Cunningham, admirals from the last century. To the right of them are the imperial standards of length – inch, foot and yard – "accurate at 62 degrees Fahrenheit", as the plaque says, and still used by millions of Brits despite the best efforts of the European Union. Above this is an equestrian statue of George IV (bareback, stirrup-less and in Roman garb), which he himself commissioned for the top of Marble Arch, but which was later erected here "temporarily".

South Africa House and Canada House

There's an unmistakable whiff of empire about Trafalgar Square, with **South Africa House** erected in 1935 on the east side, complete with keystones featuring African animals, and a gilded springbok. **Canada House**, constructed in warm Bath stone on the opposite side of the square, was built by Robert Smirke in the 1820s as a gentlemen's club and home for the Royal College of Physicians. It retains much of its original Neoclassical interior, and is now in the hands of the Canadian High Commission.

St Martin-in-the-Fields

Trafalgar Square • Mon, Tues & Fri 8.30am–1pm & 2–6pm, Wed 8.30am–1.15pm & 2–5pm, Thurs 8.30am–1.15pm & 2–6pm, Sat 9.30am–6pm, Sun 3.30–5pm • Free • ☏ 020 7766 1100, Ⓦ stmartin-in-the-fields.org • ⊖ Charing Cross

At the northeastern corner of Trafalgar Square stands the church of **St Martin-in-the-Fields**, fronted by a magnificent Corinthian portico and topped by an elaborate tower and steeple, designed in 1721 by James Gibbs – it was subsequently copied widely in the American colonies. The barrel-vaulted interior features ornate, sparkling white Italian plasterwork and is best appreciated while listening to one of the church's **free lunchtime concerts** (Mon, Tues & Fri) or ticketed, candle-lit evening performances. As the official parish church for Buckingham Palace, St Martin's maintains strong royal and naval connections – there's a royal box on the left of the high altar, and one for the admiralty on the right. Down in the newly expanded **crypt** – accessible via an entrance north of the church – there's a licensed **café** (see p.367), shop, gallery and **brass-rubbing centre**.

1

National Gallery

Trafalgar Square • Daily 10am–6pm, Fri till 9pm • Free • ☎ 020 7747 2885, ⓦ nationalgallery.org.uk • ⊖ Charing Cross

Taking up the entire north side of Trafalgar Square, the sprawling Neoclassical hulk of the **National Gallery** houses one of the world's greatest art collections. Unlike the Louvre or the Hermitage, the National Gallery is not based on a former royal collection, but was begun as late as 1824 when the government reluctantly agreed to purchase 38 paintings belonging to a Russian émigré banker, John Julius Angerstein. The collection was originally put on public display at Angerstein's old residence, on Pall Mall, until today's purpose-built edifice was completed in 1838. A hostile press dubbed the gallery's diminutive dome and cupolas "pepperpots", and poured abuse on the Greek Revival architect, William Wilkins, who retreated into early retirement and died a year later.

The gallery now boasts a collection of more than 2300 paintings, whose virtue is not so much its size as its range, depth and quality. Among the thousand paintings on permanent display are **Italian masterpieces** by the likes of Botticelli, Leonardo and Michelangelo, dazzling pieces by Velázquez and Goya and an array of **Rembrandt** paintings that features some of his most searching portraits. In addition, the gallery has a particularly strong showing of **Impressionists**, with paintings by Monet, Degas, Van Gogh and Cézanne, plus several early Picassos. There are also showpieces by Turner, Reynolds and Gainsborough, but for a wider range of British art, head for Tate Britain (see p.60). **Special exhibitions** are held in the basement of the Sainsbury Wing and usually charge admission.

INFORMATION AND TOURS

Arrival There are four entrances to the National Gallery: Wilkins' original Portico Entrance up the steps from Trafalgar Square, the Getty Entrance on the ground floor to the east, the Sainsbury Wing to the west and the back entrance on Orange St. The Getty Entrance and the Sainsbury Wing both have an information desk, where you can buy a floorplan, and disabled access, with lifts to all floors.

Tours Audioguides (£3.50) are available – much better, though, are the gallery's free guided tours, which set off from the Sainsbury Wing foyer (daily 11.30am & 2.30pm, plus Fri 7pm; 1hr).

Eating By the Getty Entrance is the *National Café* (Mon–Fri 8am–11pm, Sat 10am–11pm, Sun 10am–6pm), which has a self-service area, and a large brasserie, with an entrance on St Martin's Place. More formal dining is available at the *National Dining Rooms*, serving excellent British cuisine, in the Sainsbury Wing (☎020 7747 2525), with views over Trafalgar Square.

The Sainsbury Wing

The original design for the gallery's modern **Sainsbury Wing** was dubbed by Prince Charles "a monstrous carbuncle on the face of a much-loved and elegant friend". So instead, the American husband-and-wife team of Venturi and Scott-Brown were commissioned to produce a softly-softly, postmodern adjunct, which playfully imitates elements of William Wilkins' Neoclassicism and even Nelson's Column and, most importantly, got the approval of Prince Charles, who laid the foundation stone in 1988.

Chronologically the gallery's collection begins in this wing, which houses the National's oldest paintings from the thirteenth to the fifteenth centuries, mostly early Italian Renaissance masterpieces, with a smattering of early Dutch, Flemish and German works.

Giotto to Van Eyck

The gallery's earliest works by **Giotto**, "the father of modern painting", and **Duccio**, a Sienese contemporary, are displayed in room 52. So too, in a "side chapel" is the "Leonardo Cartoon" – a preparatory drawing for a painting which, like so many of Leonardo's projects, was never completed. The cartoon was known only to scholars until the gallery bought it for £800,000 in the mid-1960s. In 1987, it gained further notoriety when an ex-soldier blasted the work with a sawn-off shotgun in protest at the political status quo.

TEN PAINTINGS NOT TO MISS

Battle of San Romano Uccello. Room 54

Arnolfini Portrait Van Eyck. Room 56

Virgin of the Rocks Da Vinci. Room 57

Venus and Mars Botticelli. Room 58

The Ambassadors Holbein. Room 4

Self-Portrait at the Age of 63 Rembrandt van Rijn. Room 23

The Cornfield Constable. Room 34

Rain, Steam & Speed Turner. Room 34

Gare St Lazare Monet. Room 43

Van Gogh's Chair Van Gogh. Room 45

Next door, you can admire the extraordinarily vivid **Wilton Diptych**, one of the few medieval altarpieces to survive the Puritan iconoclasm of the Commonwealth. It was painted by an unknown fourteenth-century artist for King Richard II, who is depicted kneeling, presented by his three patron saints to the Virgin, Child and assorted angels.

Whatever you do, don't miss **Paolo Uccello**'s brilliant, blood-free *Battle of San Romano*, which dominates room 54. The painting commemorates a recent Florentine victory over her bitter Sienese rivals and was commissioned as part of a three-panel frieze for a Florentine palazzo. Another Florentine commission – this time from the Medicis – is *The Annunciation* by **Fra Filippo Lippi**, a beautifully balanced painting in which the poses of Gabriel and Mary carefully mirror one another, while the hand of God releasing the dove of the Holy Spirit provides the vanishing point.

Room 56 explores the beginnings of oil painting, and one of its early masters, **Jan van Eyck**, whose intriguing *Arnolfini Portrait* is celebrated for its complex symbolism. No longer thought to depict a marriage ceremony, the "bride" is not pregnant but simply wearing a fashionable dress that showed off just how much excess cloth a rich Italian cloth merchant like Arnolfini could afford.

Botticelli to Piero della Francesca

You return to the Italians in room 57, which boasts **Leonardo da Vinci**'s melancholic *Virgin of the Rocks* (the more famous *Da Vinci Code* version hangs in the Louvre) and two contrasting Nativity paintings by **Botticelli**: the *Mystic Nativity* is unusual in that it features seven devils fleeing back into the Underworld, while in his *Adoration of the Kings*, Botticelli himself takes centre stage, as the best-dressed man at the gathering, resplendent in bright-red stockings and giving the audience a knowing look. In room 58 is his *Venus and Mars*, depicting a naked and replete Mars in deep postcoital sleep, watched over by a beautifully calm Venus, fully clothed and somewhat less overcome.

Further on, in room 62, hangs one of **Mantegna**'s best early works, *The Agony in the Garden*, which demonstrates a convincing use of perspective. Close by, the dazzling dawn sky in the painting on the same theme by his brother-in-law, **Giovanni Bellini**, shows the artist's celebrated mastery of natural light. Also in this room is one of Bellini's greatest portraits of the Venetian Doge *Leonardo Loredan*. Elsewhere, there are paintings from Netherlands and Germany, among them **Dürer**'s sympathetic portrait of his father (a goldsmith in Nuremberg), in room 65, which was presented to Charles I in 1636 by the artist's home town.

Finally, at the far end of the wing, in room 66, your eye will probably be drawn to **Piero della Francesca**'s monumental *Baptism of Christ*, one of his earliest surviving pictures, dating from the 1450s and a brilliant example of his immaculate compositional technique. Blindness forced Piero to stop painting some twenty years before his death, and to concentrate instead on his equally innovative work as a mathematician.

The main building

The collection continues in the gallery's **main building** with paintings from the sixteenth century to the early twentieth century. This account follows the collection more or less chronologically.

1

Veronese, Giorgione and Titian

The first room you come to from the Sainsbury Wing is the vast Wohl Room (room 9), containing mainly large-scale sixteenth-century Venetian works. The largest of the lot is **Paolo Veronese**'s lustrous *Family of Darius before Alexander*, its array of colourfully clad figures revealing the painter's remarkable skill in juxtaposing virtually the entire colour spectrum in a single canvas. Less prominent in this room are two perplexing paintings attributed to the elusive **Giorgione**, a highly original Venetian painter, only twenty of whose paintings survive. Here, too, at opposite ends of the room, are all four of Veronese's erotic *Allegories of Love* canvases, designed as ceiling paintings, perhaps for a bedchamber.

More Venetian works hang in room 10, including **Titian**'s consummate *La Schiavona*, a precisely executed portrait within a portrait. His colourful early masterpiece *Bacchus and Ariadne*, and his much gloomier *Death of Actaeon*, painted some fifty years later, amply demonstrate the painter's artistic development and longevity. *The Virgin and Child* is another typical late Titian, with the paint jabbed on and rubbed in.

Bronzino, Michelangelo and Raphael

In room 8, **Bronzino**'s strangely disturbing *Venus, Cupid, Folly and Time* is a classic piece of Mannerist eroticism, once owned by François I, the decadent, womanizing, sixteenth-century French king. (Incidentally, Cupid's foot features in the opening animated titles of *Monty Python's Flying Circus*.) Here too is **Michelangelo**'s early, unfinished *Entombment*, which depicts Christ's body being carried to the tomb, and the National's major paintings by **Raphael**. These range from early works such as *St Catherine of Alexandria*, whose sensuous serpentine pose is accentuated by the folds of her clothes, and the richly coloured *Mond Crucifixion*, both painted when the artist was in his 20s, to later works like *Pope Julius II* – his (and Michelangelo's) patron – a masterfully percipient portrait of old age.

Holbein, Cranach, Bosch and Bruegel

Room 4 contains several masterpieces by **Hans Holbein**, most notably his extraordinarily detailed double portrait from the Tudor court, *The Ambassadors* – note the anamorphic skull in the foreground. Among the other works by Holbein is his intriguing *A Lady with a Squirrel and a Starling*, and his striking portrait of the 16-year-old Christina of Denmark, part of a series commissioned by Henry VIII when he was looking for a potential fourth wife. Look out, too, for Holbein's contemporary, **Lucas Cranach the Elder**, whose *Cupid Complaining to Venus* is a none-too-subtle message about dangerous romantic liaisons – Venus's wonderfully fashionable headgear only emphasizes her nakedness.

Next door, in room 5, hangs the National's one and only work by **Hieronymus Bosch**, *Christ Mocked*, in which four manic tormentors (one wearing an Islamic crescent moon

---

BORIS ANREP'S FLOOR MOSAICS

One of the most overlooked features of the National Gallery is the mind-boggling **floor mosaics** executed by Russian-born Boris Anrep between 1927 and 1952 on the landings of the main staircase leading to the Central Hall. The *Awakening of the Muses*, on the halfway landing, features a bizarre collection of famous figures from the 1930s – Virginia Woolf appears as Clio (Muse of History) and Greta Garbo plays Melpomene (Muse of Tragedy). The mosaic on the landing closest to the Central Hall is made up of fifteen small scenes illustrating the *Modern Virtues*: Anna Akhmatova is saved by an angel from the Leningrad Blockade in *Compassion*; T.S. Eliot contemplates the Loch Ness Monster and Einstein's Theory of Relativity in *Leisure*; Bertrand Russell gazes on a naked woman in *Lucidity*; Edith Sitwell, book in hand, glides across a monster-infested chasm on a twig in *Sixth Sense*; and in the largest composition, *Defiance*, Churchill appears in combat gear on the white cliffs of Dover, raising two fingers to a monster in the shape of a swastika.

1

HIDDEN GEMS OF THE NATIONAL GALLERY

Wilton Diptych Room 53
An Allegory with Venus and Cupid
Bronzino. Room 8
Supper at Emmaus Caravaggio. Room 32
A Young Woman standing at a Virginal
Vermeer. Room 25
The Avenue at Middleharnis Hobbema
Room 21

Self-Portrait in a Straw Hat Elisabeth Louise
Vigée le Brun. Room 33
Marriage à la Mode Hogarth. Room 35
Portrait of Hermine Gallia Klimt.
Room 44
After the Bath Degas. Room 46
Boris Anrep's mosaics See box opposite

and a Jewish star) bear down on Jesus. The painting that grabs most folks' attention, however, is **Massys**'s caricatured portrait of an old woman looking like a pantomime dame. Nearby, in room 14, you'll find the gallery's only work by **Jan Bruegel the Elder**, the tiny *Adoration of the Kings*, with some very motley-looking folk crowding in on the infant; only Balthasar looks at all regal.

Claude, Poussin and Dutch landscapes

The English painter **J.M.W. Turner** left specific instructions in his will for two of his Claude-influenced paintings to be hung alongside a couple of the French painter's landscapes. All four now hang in the octagonal room 15, and were slashed by a homeless teenager in 1982 in an attempt to draw attention to his plight. **Claude**'s dreamy classical landscapes and seascapes, and the mythological (often erotic) scenes of **Poussin**, were favourites of aristocrats on the Grand Tour, and made both artists very famous in their time. Claude's *Enchanted Castle*, in particular, caught the imagination of the Romantics, allegedly inspiring Keats' *Ode to a Nightingale*. Nowadays, rooms 19 and 20, which are given over entirely to these two French artists, are among the quietest in the gallery.

Of the Dutch landscapes in rooms 21 and 22, those by **Aelbert Cuyp** stand out due to the warm Italianate light which suffuses his works, but the finest of all is, without a doubt, **Hobbema**'s tree-lined *Avenue at Middelharnis*. The market for such landscapes at the time was limited, however, and Hobbema quit painting at the age of just 30. **Jacob van Ruisdael**, Hobbema's teacher, whose works are on display nearby, also went hungry for most of his life.

Rembrandt and Vermeer

Rooms 23 and 24 feature mostly works by **Rembrandt**, including the highly theatrical *Belshazzar's Feast*, painted for a rich Jewish patron. Look out also for two of Rembrandt's searching self-portraits, painted thirty years apart, with the melancholic *Self Portrait Aged 63*, from the last year of his life, making a strong contrast to the sprightly early work. Similarly, the joyful portrait of Saskia, Rembrandt's wife, from the most successful period of his life, contrasts with his more contemplative depiction of his mistress, Hendrickje, who was hauled up in front of the city authorities for living "like a whore" with Rembrandt. The portraits of Jacob Trip and his wife, Margaretha de Geer, are among the most honestly realistic depictions of old age in the entire gallery.

Room 25 harbours **de Hooch**'s classic *Courtyard of a House in Delft*, and a (probable) self-portrait by Carel Fabritius, one of Rembrandt's pupils. Fabritius died in the explosion of the Delft gunpowder store, the subject of another painting in the room. Also here is the seventeenth-century **van Hoogstraten Peepshow**, a box of tricks that reflects the Dutch obsession of the time with perspective and optical devices. Two typically serene works by **Vermeer** hang here (or in a nearby room) and provide a counterpoint to one another: each features a "young woman at a virginal", but where she stands in one, she sits in the other; she's viewed from the right and then the left, in shadow and then in light and so on.

1

Rubens

Three adjoining rooms, known collectively as room 29, are dominated by the expansive, fleshy canvases of **Peter Paul Rubens**, the Flemish painter whom Charles I summoned to the English court. The one woman with her clothes on is the artist's future sister-in-law, Susanna Fourment, whose delightful portrait became known as *Le Chapeau de Paille* (*The Straw Hat*) – though the hat is actually made of black felt and decorated with white feathers. At the age of 54, Rubens married Susanna's younger sister, Helena (she was just 16), the model for all three goddesses posing in the later 1630s version of *The Judgement of Paris*. Also displayed here are Rubens' rather more subdued landscapes, one of which, the *View of Het Steen*, shows off the very fine prospect from the Flemish country mansion Rubens bought in 1635.

Velázquez, El Greco, Van Dyck and Caravaggio

The cream of the National Gallery's Spanish works are displayed in room 30, among them **Velázquez**'s *Rokeby Venus*, one of the gallery's most famous pictures. Velázquez is thought to have painted just four nudes in his lifetime, of which only the *Rokeby Venus* survives, an ambiguously narcissistic image that was slashed in 1914 by suffragette Mary Richardson, in protest at the arrest of Emmeline Pankhurst.

Another Flemish painter summoned by Charles I was **Anthony van Dyck**, whose *Equestrian Portrait of Charles I*, in room 31, is a fine example of the work that made him a favourite of the Stuart court, romanticizing the monarch as a dashing horseman. Nearby is the artist's double portrait of *Lord John and Lord Bernard Stuart*, two dapper young cavaliers about to set out on their Grand Tour in 1639, and destined to die fighting for the royalist cause shortly afterwards in the Civil War.

Caravaggio's art is represented in the vast room 32 by the typically salacious *Boy Bitten by Lizard*, and the melodramatic *Supper at Emmaus*. The latter was a highly influential painting: never before had biblical scenes been depicted with such naturalism – a beardless and haloless Christ surrounded by scruffy disciples. At the time it was deemed to be blasphemous, and, like many of Caravaggio's religious commissions, was eventually rejected by the customers. One of the most striking paintings in this room is Giordano's *Perseus turning Phineas and his Followers to Stone*, in which the hero is dramatically depicted in sapphire blue, with half the throng already petrified.

British art 1750–1850

When the Tate Gallery opened in 1897, the vast bulk of the National's British art was transferred there, leaving just a few highly prized works behind. Among these are several superb late masterpieces by **Turner**, two of which herald the new age of steam: *Rain, Steam and Speed* and *The Fighting Temeraire*, in which a ghostly apparition of the veteran battleship from Trafalgar is pulled into harbour by a youthful, fire-snorting tug, a scene witnessed first-hand by the artist in Rotherhithe. Here, too, is **Constable**'s *Hay Wain*, painted in and around his father's mill in Suffolk, as is the irrepressibly popular *Cornfield*. There are landscapes, as well as the portraits, by **Thomas Gainsborough** – his feathery, light technique is seen to superb effect in *Morning Walk*, a double portrait of a pair of newlyweds. **Joshua Reynolds**' contribution is a portrait, *Lady Cockburn and her Three Sons*, in which the three boys clamber endearingly over their mother. And finally, the most striking portrait in the whole room is George Stubbs' pin-sharp depiction of the racehorse Whistlejacket rearing up on its hindlegs.

More works by Gainsborough and Reynolds hang in room 35, including the only known self-portrait of the former with his family, painted in 1747 when he was just 20 years old. On the opposite wall are the six paintings from **Hogarth**'s *Marriage à la Mode*, a witty, moral tale that allowed the artist to give vent to his pet hates: bourgeois hypocrisy, snobbery and bad (ie Continental) taste. In the ornate, domed

FROM TOP HOUSES OF PARLIAMENT (P.49); TRAFALGAR SQUARE (P.35); THE NATIONAL GALLERY (P.38) >

1

Central Hall (room 36) hangs Reynolds' dramatic portrait of the extraordinarily effeminate Colonel Tarleton.

French art 1700–1860

The large room of British art (room 34) is bookended with two small rooms of French art. In room 33, among works by the likes of Fragonard, Boucher and Watteau, there's a portrait of Louis XV's mistress in the year of her death and a spirited self-portrait by the equally well-turned-out **Elisabeth Louise Vigée-Lebrun**, one of only three women artists in the National Gallery.

In room 41, the most popular painting is **Paul Delaroche**'s slick and pretentious *Execution of Lady Jane Grey*, in which the blindfolded, white-robed, 17-year-old queen stoically awaits her fate. Look out, too, for **Gustave Courbet**'s languorous *Young Ladies on the Bank of the Seine*, innocent enough to the modern eye, scandalous when it was first shown in 1857 due to the ladies' "state of undress".

Impressionism and beyond

Among the gallery's busiest section are the four magnificent rooms (43–46) of Impressionist and post-Impressionist paintings, where rehangings are frequent. The National boasts several key works by **Manet**, including his famous *Music in the Tuileries Gardens*, and the unfinished *Execution of Maximilian*, one of three versions he painted. There are also canvases from every period of **Monet**'s long life: from early works like *The Thames below Westminster* and *Gare St Lazare* to the late, almost abstract paintings executed in his beloved garden at Giverny.

Other major Impressionist works include **Renoir**'s *Umbrellas*, **Seurat**'s classic pointillist canvas, *Bathers at Asnières* – one of the National's most reproduced paintings – and **Pissarro**'s *Boulevard Montmartre at Night*. There are also several townscapes from Pissarro's period of exile, when he lived in south London, during the Franco-Prussian War. There's a comprehensive showing of **Cézanne** with works spanning the great artist's long life. *The Painter's Father*, one of his earliest extant works, was originally painted onto the walls of his father's house outside Aix. *The Bathers*, by contrast, is a late work, whose angular geometry exercised an enormous influence on the Cubism of Picasso and Braque.

Van Gogh's famous, dazzling *Sunflowers* hangs here, the beguiling *Van Gogh's Chair*, dating from his stay in Arles with Gauguin, and *Wheatfield with Cypresses*, which typifies the intense work he produced shortly before his suicide. Finally, look out for **Picasso**'s sentimental Blue Period *Child with a Dove*; **Rousseau**'s imagined junglescape, *Surprised!*; Klimt's *Hermine Gallia*, in which the sitter wears a dress designed by the artist; and a trio of superb **Degas** canvases: *Miss La-La at the Cirque Fernando*, the languorous pastel drawing *After the Bath* and the luxuriant *La Coiffure*.

National Portrait Gallery

St Martin's Place · Daily 10am–6pm, Thurs & Fri till 9pm · Free · ☎ 020 7306 0055, Ⓦ npg.org.uk · ⊖ Charing Cross

Around the east side of the National Gallery lurks the **National Portrait Gallery** founded in 1856 to house uplifting depictions of the good and the great. Though it undoubtedly has some fine works among its collection of over ten thousand portraits, many of the studies are of less interest than their subjects. Nevertheless, it's interesting to trace who has been deemed worthy of admiration at any one time: aristocrats and artists in previous centuries, warmongers and imperialists in the early decades of the twentieth century, writers and poets in the 1930s and 1940s. The most popular part of the museum by far is the contemporary section, where the whole thing degenerates into a sort of thinking person's Madame Tussauds, with photos and portraits of today's celebrities. However, the special exhibitions (for which there is often a charge) are well worth seeing – the photography shows, in particular, are often excellent.

INFORMATION

Arrival There are two entrances to the NPG: disabled access is from Orange St, while the main entrance is on St Martin's Place. Once inside, head straight for the Ondaatje Wing, where there's an information desk – you can pick up an audioguide (£3.50) which gives useful biographical background on many of the pictures.

Eating There's a little café in the basement, and the excellent but pricey rooftop *Portrait* restaurant on Floor 3, with incredible views over Trafalgar Square (☎ 020 7312 2490).

The Tudors and Stuarts

To follow the collection chronologically, take the escalator to the trio of **Tudor Galleries**, on Floor 2. Here, you'll find Tudor portraits of pre-Tudor kings as well as Tudor personalities: a stout **Cardinal Wolsey** looking like the butcher's son he was and the future **Bloody Mary** looking positively benign in a portrait celebrating her reinstatement to the line of succession in 1544. Pride of place goes to Holbein's larger-than-life cartoon of **Henry VIII**, showing the king as a macho buck against a modish Renaissance background, with his sickly son and heir, **Edward VI**, striking a deliberately similar pose close by. The most eye-catching canvas is the anamorphic portrait of Edward, an illusionistic painting that must be viewed from the side.

Also displayed here are several classic propaganda portraits of the formidable Elizabeth I and her dandyish favourites. Further on hangs the only known painting of **Shakespeare** from life, a subdued image in which the Bard sports a gold-hoop earring; appropriately enough, it was the first picture acquired by the gallery. To keep to the chronology, you must turn left here into room 5, where the quality of portraiture goes up a notch thanks to the appointment of Van Dyck as court painter. Among all the dressed-to-kill Royalists in room 5, **Oliver Cromwell** looks dishevelled but masterful, while an overdressed, haggard **Charles II** hangs in room 7 alongside his long-suffering Portuguese wife and several of his mistresses, including the orange-seller-turned-actress **Nell Gwynne**.

The eighteenth century

The **eighteenth century** begins in room 9, with members of the **Kit-Kat Club**, a group of Whig patriots, painted by one of its members, Godfrey Kneller, a naturalized German artist, whose self-portrait can be found in room 10. Next door, room 11 contains a hotchpotch of visionaries including a tartan-free **Bonnie Prince Charlie** and his saviour, the petite Flora MacDonald. In room 12 there are several fine self-portraits, including a dashing one of the Scot Allan Ramsay. Room 14 is dominated by *The Death of Pitt the Elder*, who collapsed in the House of Lords having risen from his sickbed to try and save the rebellious American colonies for Britain – despite the painting's title, he didn't die for another month.

In room 17, you'll find a bold likeness of **Lord Nelson**, unusually out of uniform, along with an idealized portrait of Nelson's mistress, **Lady Emma Hamilton**, painted by the smitten George Romney. Also here is a portrait of **George IV** and the twice-widowed Catholic woman, Maria Fitzherbert, whom he married without his father's consent. His official wife, **Queen Caroline**, is depicted at the adultery trial at which she was acquitted, and again, with sleeves rolled up, ready for her sculpture lessons, in an audacious portrait by Thomas Lawrence, who was called to testify on his conduct with the queen during the painting of the portrait.

The Romantics dominate room 18, with the ailing **John Keats** painted posthumously by Joseph Severn, in whose arms he died in Rome. Elsewhere, there's **Lord Byron** in Albanian garb, an open-collared **Percy Bysshe Shelley**, with his wife, Mary, nearby, and her mother, **Mary Wollstonecraft**, opposite.

The Victorians

Down on the first floor, the **Victorians** feature rather too many stuffy royals, dour men of science and engineering, and stern statesmen such as those lining the corridor of

1

room 22. Centre stage, in room 21, is a comical statue of **Victoria and Albert** in Anglo-Saxon garb. The best place to head for is room 24, which contains a deteriorated portrait of the **Brontë sisters** as seen by their disturbed brother Branwell; you can still see where he painted himself out, leaving a ghostly blur between Charlotte and Emily. Nearby are the poetic duo, **Robert** and **Elizabeth Barrett Browning**, looking totally Gothic in their grim Victorian dress.

In room 28, it's impossible to miss the striking Edwardian portrait of **Lady Colin Campbell**, posing in a luxuriant black silk dress. Finally, in room 29, there are some excellent **John Singer Sargent** portraits, and several works by students of the Slade: **Augustus John**, looking very confident and dapper at the age of just 22, his sister, Gwen John, **Walter Sickert** (by Philip Wilson Steer) and Steer (by Sickert). Steer founded the New English Arts Club, at which the last two portraits were originally exhibited.

The twentieth century and beyond

The **twentieth-century** collection begins in room 30, with Sargent's group portrait of the upper-crust generals responsible for the slaughter of World War I. The interwar years are then generously covered in room 31. The faces on display here are frequently rotated, but look out for Sickert's excellent small, smouldering portrait of **Churchill**, Augustus John's portrayal of a ruby-lipped Dylan Thomas, Ben Nicolson's double portrait of himself and Barbara Hepworth and a whole host of works by, or depicting, the **Bloomsbury Group**.

Out on the Balcony Gallery, there's a who's who (or was who) of **Britain 1960–90**. Even here, amid the photos of the Swinging Sixties, there are quite a few genuine works of art by the likes of Leon Kossoff, R.B. Kitaj, Lucien Freud and Francis Bacon. The **Contemporary Galleries** occupy the ground floor, and are a constantly changing, unashamedly populist trot through the media personalities of the last decade or so. As well as a host of photo portraits, you can sample such delights as Michael Craig Martin's LCD portrait of architect Zaha Hadid, or the cartoon-like quadruple portrait of pop band Blur by Julian Opie.

Whitehall

Whitehall, the unusually broad avenue connecting Trafalgar Square to Parliament Square, is synonymous with the faceless, pinstriped bureaucracy charged with the day-to-day running of the country. Yet during the sixteenth and seventeenth centuries, it was, in fact, the site of the chief royal residence in London. **Whitehall Palace** started out as the London seat of the Archbishop of York, but was confiscated and enlarged by Henry VIII after a fire at

CHARLES I

Stranded on a traffic island to the south of Nelson's Column, on the site of the medieval **Charing Cross** (see p.136), an equestrian statue of **Charles I** gazes down Whitehall to the place of his execution in 1649, outside the Banqueting House. The king wore two shirts in case he shivered in the cold, which the crowd would take to be fear, and once his head was chopped off, it was then sewn back on again for burial in Windsor – a very British touch. The statue itself was sculpted in 1633 and was originally intended for a site in Roehampton, but was sold off during the Commonwealth to a local brazier, John Rivett, with strict instructions to melt it down. Rivett made a small fortune selling bronze mementoes, allegedly from the metal, while all the time concealing the statue in the vaults of St Paul's, Covent Garden. After the Restoration, in 1675, the statue was erected on the very spot where eight of those implicated in the king's death were disembowelled in 1660. Until 1859, "King Charles the Martyr" Holy Day (Jan 30) was a day of fasting, and his execution is still commemorated here on the last Sunday in January with a parade by the royalist wing of the Civil War Society.

Westminster Palace forced the king to find alternative accommodation; it was here that he celebrated his marriage to Anne Boleyn in 1533, and here that he died fourteen years later. Described by one contemporary chronicler as nothing but "a heap of houses erected at diverse times and of different models, made continuous", it boasted some two thousand rooms and stretched for half a mile along the Thames. Very little survived the fire of 1698 and, subsequently, the royal residence shifted to St James's and Kensington.

Since then, all the key governmental ministries and offices have migrated here, rehousing themselves on an ever-increasing scale. The **Foreign & Commonwealth Office**, for example, occupies a palatial Italianate building, built by George Gilbert Scott in 1868, and well worth a visit on Open House weekend (see p.26). The process reached its apogee with the grimly bland **Ministry of Defence (MoD)** building, completed in 1957, underneath which is Britain's most expensive military bunker, the £125 million Pindar.

Banqueting House

Whitehall • Mon–Sat 10am–5pm • £5 • ☎ 020 3166 6000, ⓦ hrp.org.uk • ⊖ Charing Cross

The only sections of Whitehall Palace to survive the 1698 fire were Cardinal Wolsey's wine cellars (now beneath the Ministry of Defence) and Inigo Jones's **Banqueting House**, the first Palladian (or Neoclassical) building to be built in central London. Opened in 1622 with a performance of Ben Jonson's *Masque of Angers*, the Banqueting House is still used for state occasions (and, therefore, may be closed at short notice). The one room open to the public – the main hall upstairs – is well worth seeing for the superlative ceiling paintings, commissioned by Charles I from **Rubens** and installed in 1635. A glorification of the divine right of kings, the panels depict the union of England and Scotland, the peaceful reign of Charles's father, James I and, finally, his apotheosis.

Given the subject of the paintings, it's ironic that it was through the Banqueting House that **Charles I** walked in 1649 before stepping onto the executioner's scaffold from one of its windows. **Oliver Cromwell** moved into Whitehall Palace in 1654, having declared himself Lord Protector, and kept open table in the Banqueting House for the officers of his New Model Army; he died here in 1658. Two years later **Charles II** celebrated the Restoration here, and kept open house for his adoring public – Samuel Pepys recalls seeing the underwear of one of his mistresses, Lady Castlemaine, hanging out to dry in the palace's Privy Garden. (Charles housed two mistresses and his wife here, with a back entrance onto the river for courtesans.) To appreciate the place fully, it's worth getting hold of one of the free audioguides.

1

Horse Guards: Household Cavalry Museum

Whitehall • Daily: April–Oct 10am–6pm; Nov–March 10am–5pm • £6 • ☎ 020 7930 3070, ⓦ householdcavalrymuseum.co.uk • ⊖ Charing Cross or Westminster

During the day, two mounted sentries and two horseless colleagues are posted to protect **Horse Guards**, a modest building begun in 1745 by William Kent, and originally the formal gateway to St James's Palace. The black dot over the number two on the building's clock face denotes the hour at which Charles I was executed close by in 1649. Round the back of the building, you'll find the **Household Cavalry Museum** where you can try on a trooper's elaborate uniform, complete a horse quiz and learn about the regiments' history. With the stables immediately adjacent, it's a sweet-smelling place, and – horse-lovers will be pleased to know – you can see the beasts in their stalls through a glass screen. Don't miss the pocket riot act on display, which ends with the wise warning: "must read correctly: variance fatal".

Downing Street

ⓦ number10.gov.uk • ⊖ Westminster

London's most famous address, **10 Downing Street**, is the terraced house that was presented to the First Lord of the Treasury, Robert Walpole, Britain's first prime minister or PM, by George II in the 1730s. It has been the PM's official residence ever since, with no. 11 the official home of the Chancellor of the Exchequer (in charge of the country's finances) since 1806, and no. 12 official headquarters of the government's Chief Whip (in charge of party discipline). These three are the only remaining bit of the original seventeenth-century cul-de-sac, though all are now interconnected and house much larger complexes than might appear from the outside. The public have been kept at bay since 1990, when Margaret Thatcher ordered a pair of iron gates to be installed at the junction with Whitehall, an act more symbolic than effective – a year later the IRA lobbed a mortar into the street from Horse Guards Parade, coming within a whisker of wiping out the entire Tory cabinet.

Churchill War Rooms

King Charles St • Daily 9.30am–6pm • £17 • ☎ 020 7930 6961, ⓦ iwm.org.uk • ⊖ Westminster

In 1938, in anticipation of Nazi air raids, the basement of the Treasury building on King Charles Street was converted into the **Churchill War Rooms**, protected by a three-foot-thick concrete slab, reinforced with steel rails and tramlines. It was here that

---

CHANGING THE GUARD

Changing the Guard takes place at two London locations: the Foot Guards hold theirs outside Buckingham Palace (May–July daily 11.30am; Aug–April alternate days; no ceremony if it rains; ⓦroyal.gov.uk), but the more impressive one is held on Horse Guards Parade, behind Horse Guards, where a squad of mounted Household Cavalry arrives from Hyde Park to relieve the guards at the Horse Guards building on Whitehall (Mon–Sat 11am, Sun 10am) – alternatively, if you miss the whole thing, turn up at 4pm for the daily inspection by the Officer of the Guard, who checks the soldiers haven't knocked off early.

If you want to see something grander, check out **Trooping the Colour**, and the **Beating Retreat**, which both take place in June (see p.25).

The Queen is colonel-in-chief of the seven **Household Regiments**: the Life Guards (who dress in red and white) and the Blues and Royals (who dress in blue and red) – princes William and Harry were both in the Blues and Royals – are the two Household Cavalry Regiments; while the Grenadier, Coldstream, Scots, Irish and Welsh guards make up the Foot Guards. The Foot Guards can only be told apart by the plumes (or lack of them) in their busbies (fur helmets), and by the arrangement of their tunic buttons. The three senior regiments (Grenadier, Coldstream and Scots) date back to the seventeenth century, as do the Life Guards and the Blues and Royals. All seven regiments still form part of the modern army as well as performing ceremonial functions such as Changing the Guard.

WHITEHALL STATUES AND THE CENOTAPH

The **statues** dotted along Whitehall recall the days of the empire. Kings and military leaders predominate, starting outside Horse Guards with the **2nd Duke of Cambridge** (1819–1904), whose horse was shot from under him in the Crimean War. As commander-in-chief of the British Army, he was so resistant to military reform that he had to be forcibly retired. Next stands the **8th Duke of Devonshire** (1833–1908), who failed to rescue General Gordon from the Siege of Khartoum in 1884–85. Appropriately enough, **Lord Haig** (1861–1928), who was responsible for sending thousands to their deaths in World War I, faces the Cenotaph, his horse famously poised ready for urination. Before you get to the Cenotaph, there's a striking memorial to the **Women of World War II**, featuring seventeen uniforms hanging on a large bronze plinth.

At the end of Whitehall, in the middle of the road, stands Edwin Lutyens' **Cenotaph**, built in 1919 in wood and plaster to commemorate the Armistice, and rebuilt in Portland stone the following year. The stark monument, which eschews Christian imagery, is inscribed simply with the words "The Glorious Dead" – the lost of World War I, who, it was once calculated, would take three and a half days to pass by the Cenotaph marching four abreast. The memorial remains the focus of the **Remembrance Sunday** ceremony held on the Sunday nearest November 11. Between the wars, however, a much more powerful, two-minute silence was observed throughout the entire British Empire every year on November 11 at 11am, the exact time of the armistice at the end of World War I.

Winston Churchill directed operations and held cabinet meetings for the duration of World War II. By the end of the war, the six-acre site included a hospital, canteen and shooting range, as well as sleeping quarters; tunnels fan out from the complex to outlying government ministries, and also, it is rumoured, to Buckingham Palace itself, allowing the Royal Family a quick getaway to exile in Canada (via Charing Cross station) in the event of a Nazi invasion.

The rooms remain much as they were when they were abandoned on VJ Day, August 15, 1945, and make for an atmospheric underground trot through wartime London. To bring the place to life, pick up an audioguide, which includes various eyewitness accounts by folks who worked here. The best rooms are Winnie's very modest emergency bedroom (though he himself rarely stayed here, preferring to watch the air raids from the roof of the building, or rest his head at the *Savoy Hotel*), and the Map Room, left exactly as it was on VJ Day, with its rank of multicoloured telephones, copious ashtrays and floor-to-ceiling maps covering every theatre of war.

Churchill Museum

When you get to Churchill's secret telephone hotline direct to the American president, signs direct you to the self-contained Churchill Museum, which begins with his finest moment, when he took over as PM and Britain stood alone against the Nazis. You can hear snippets of Churchill's speeches and check out his trademark bowler, spotted bow tie and half-chewed Havana, not to mention his wonderful burgundy zip-up "romper suit". Fortunately for the curators, Churchill had an extremely eventful life and was great for a soundbite, so there are plenty of interesting anecdotes to keep you engaged.

Houses of Parliament

Parliament Square • ☎ 020 7219 4272, ⓦ parliament.uk • ⊖ Westminster

The Palace of Westminster, better known as the **Houses of Parliament**, is among London's best-known icons. The city's finest Victorian edifice and a symbol of a nation once confident of its place at the centre of the world, it's best viewed from the south side of the river, where the likes of Monet and Turner once set up their easels. The building's most famous feature is its ornate, gilded clock tower popularly known as **Big Ben**, at its most impressive when lit up at night. Strictly speaking, it's the

1

Elizabeth Tower – "Big Ben" is just the nickname for the thirteen-ton bell that strikes the hour (and is broadcast across the world by the BBC), after either the former Commissioner of Works, Benjamin Hall, or a popular heavyweight boxer of the time, Benjamin Caunt.

The original Palace of Westminster was built by **Edward the Confessor** in the eleventh century to allow him to watch over the building of his abbey. Westminster then served as the seat of all the English monarchs until a fire forced Henry VIII out, and he eventually decamped to Whitehall. The Lords have always convened at the palace, but it was only following Henry's death that the House of Commons moved from the abbey's Chapter House into the palace's St Stephen's Chapel.

In 1834, a fire reduced the old palace to rubble. Today, save for Westminster Hall, and a few pieces of the old structure buried deep within the interior, everything you see today is the work of **Charles Barry**, who wanted to create something that expressed national greatness through the use of Gothic and Elizabethan styles. The resulting orgy of honey-coloured pinnacles, turrets and tracery is the greatest achievement of the Gothic Revival. Inside, the Victorian love of mock-Gothic detail is evident in the maze of over one thousand committee rooms and offices, the fittings of which were largely the responsibility of Barry's assistant, **Augustus Pugin**.

INFORMATION AND TOURS

Sitting times To find out exact "sitting times" and dates of "recesses" (holiday closures), phone ☎ 020 7219 4272, or visit ⓦ parliament.uk. If Parliament is in session a Union flag flies from the southernmost tower, the Victoria Tower; at night there's a light above the clock face on Big Ben.

Public galleries To watch proceedings in either the House of Commons – the livelier of the two – or the House of Lords, simply join the queue for the public galleries on Cromwell Green, near St Stephen's Gate. The public are let in slowly from about 2.30pm on Mondays, 11.30am on Tuesdays, around 1pm Wednesdays, and 9.30am on Thursdays and Sitting Fridays. Security is tight and the whole procedure can take over an hour, so to avoid the

queues, turn up an hour or so later or on a Sitting Friday.

Question Time UK citizens can attend Question Time – when the House of Commons is at its liveliest – which takes place in the first hour (Mon–Thurs) and Prime Minister's Question Time (Wed only), but they must book in advance with their local MP (☎ 020 7219 3000).

Guided tours Throughout the year there are Saturday tours (9.15am–4.30pm; £16.50) and occasional more specialist tours (£30); during the summer there are more frequent tours (Tues–Sat 9.15am–4.30pm) – in all cases tours take just over an hour and it's a good idea to book in advance (☎ 0844 847 1672), though you can buy tickets on the day from the ticket office by the Jewel Tower. All year round, UK

HOUSES OF PARLIAMENT

residents are entitled to a free guided tour of the palace, as well as a guided tour up Big Ben (Mon–Fri 9.15am, 11.15am & 2.15pm; no under-11s); both need to be organized well in advance through your local MP or a member of the House of Lords. Visitors for Big Ben must enter via Portcullis House, the modern building on Victoria Embankment.

Westminster Hall

Virtually the only relic of the medieval palace is the bare expanse of **Westminster Hall**, which you enter after passing through security. Built by William II in 1099, it was saved from the 1834 fire by the timely intervention of the PM, Lord Melbourne, who took charge of the firefighting himself. The sheer scale of the hall – 240ft by 60ft – and its huge oak hammerbeam roof, added by Richard II in the late fourteenth century, make it one of the most magnificent secular medieval halls in Europe. It has also witnessed some nine hundred years of English history and been used for the lying-in-state of members of the Royal Family and a select few non-royals. Until 1821 every royal coronation banquet was held here and during the ceremony, the Royal Champion would ride into the hall in full armour to challenge any who dared dispute the sovereign's right to the throne.

Until the nineteenth century the hall was also used as the country's highest court of law: **William Wallace** had to wear a laurel crown during his treason trial here; **Thomas More** was sentenced to be hung, drawn and quartered (though in the end was simply beheaded); **Guy Fawkes**, the Catholic caught trying to blow up Parliament on November 5, 1605, was also tried here and actually hanged, drawn and quartered in Old Palace Yard. The trial of **Charles I** took place here, but the king refused to take his hat off, since he did not accept the court's legitimacy. **Oliver Cromwell**, whose statue now stands outside the hall, was sworn in here as Lord Protector in 1653, only to be disinterred after the Restoration and tried here (whilst dead). His head was displayed on a spike above the hall for several decades until a storm dislodged it. It's now buried in a secret location at Cromwell's old college in Cambridge University.

St Stephen's Hall

From Westminster Hall, visitors pass through the tiny **St Stephen's Hall**, designed by Barry as a replica of the palace's Gothic chapel (built by Edward I), where the Commons met from 1550 until the 1834 fire. It was into that chapel that Charles I entered with an armed guard in 1642 in a vain attempt to arrest five MPs who had made a speedy escape down the river – "I see my birds have flown", he is supposed to have said. Shortly afterwards, the Civil War began, and no monarch has entered the Commons since. It was on the steps of the hall, in 1812, that Spencer Perceval – the only British prime minister to be assassinated – was shot by a merchant whose business had been ruined by the Napoleonic Wars.

Central Lobby

Next you come to the bustling, octagonal **Central Lobby**, where constituents can "lobby" their MPs. In the tiling of the lobby Pugin inscribed the Biblical quote in Latin: "Except the Lord keep the house, they labour in vain that build it". In view of what happened to the architects, the sentiment seems like an indictment of parliamentary morality – Pugin ended up in Bedlam mental hospital and Barry died from overwork within months of completing the job.

The House of Commons

If you're going to listen to proceedings in the **House of Commons**, you'll be asked to sign a form vowing not to cause a disturbance and then led up to the Public Gallery. Protests from the gallery used to be a fairly regular occurrence: suffragettes have poured flour, farmers have dumped dung, Irish Nationalists have lobbed tear gas and lesbians have abseiled down into the chamber, but a screen now protects the MPs. An incendiary bomb in May 1941 destroyed Barry's original chamber, so what you see

1

now is a rather lifeless postwar reconstruction. Barry's design was modelled on the palace's original St Stephen's Hall, hence the choir-stall arrangement of the MPs' benches. Members of the cabinet (and the opposition's shadow cabinet) occupy the two "front benches"; the rest are "backbenchers". The chamber is at its busiest during Question Time, though if more than 427 of the 650 MPs turn up, a large number have to remain standing. For much of the time, however, the chamber is almost empty, with just a handful of MPs present from each party.

The House of Lords

On the other side of the Central Lobby, a corridor leads to the **House of Lords** (or Upper House), a far dozier establishment peopled by unelected Lords and Ladies, plus a smattering of bishops. Their home boasts much grander decor than the Commons, full of regal gold and scarlet, and dominated by Pugin's great canopied gilded throne where the Queen sits for the state opening of Parliament in May. Directly in front of the throne, the Lord Chancellor runs the proceedings from the scarlet Woolsack, an enormous cushion stuffed with wool, which harks back to the time when it was England's principal export. Until 1999, there were one thousand plus hereditary Lords (over a quarter of whom had been to Eton) in the House. Most rarely bothered to turn up, but at critical votes, they could be (and were) called upon by the Conservatives, to ensure a right-wing victory. Today, just 92 hereditary peers sit in the House, along with 26 senior bishops, while the rest are made up of life peers, appointed by the Queen on the advice of the Prime Minister. However, for the most part, the Lords have very little real power, as they can only advise, amend and review parliamentary bills.

The royal apartments

To see any more of parliament's pomp and glitter you'll need to go on a **guided tour** (see p.50). Beyond the House of Lords is the **Princes' Chamber**, known as the Tudor Room after the portraits that line the walls, including Henry VIII and all six of his wives. Beyond here you enter the **Royal Gallery**, a cavernous writing room for the House of Lords, hung with portraits of royals past and present, and two 45-foot-long frescoes of Trafalgar and Waterloo. Next door is the **Queen's Robing Chamber**, which boasts a superb coffered ceiling and lacklustre Arthurian frescoes. As the name suggests, this is the room where the monarch dons the crown jewels before entering the Lords. Lastly, you get to see the Norman Porch, every nook of which is stuffed with busts of eminent statesmen, and the **Royal Staircase**, which is lined with guards from the Household Cavalry when the Queen arrives for the annual state opening of Parliament in May.

Jewel Tower

Daily 10am–5pm • EH • £3.90 • ☎ 020 7222 2219 • ⊖ Westminster

The **Jewel Tower** across the road from the Sovereign's Entrance, is the only other major remnant of the medieval palace apart from Westminster Hall. Constructed in 1365 by Edward III as a giant strongbox for his most valuable possessions, the tower formed the southwestern corner of the original exterior fortifications (there's a bit of moat left, too), and was called the King's Privy Wardrobe. Later, it was used to store the records of the House of Lords, and then as a testing centre by the Board of Trade's Standards Department. Nowadays, the tower houses a small exhibition on the history of the Palace of Westminster and on the tower itself.

Victoria Tower Gardens

To the south of Parliament's Victoria Tower are the leafy **Victoria Tower Gardens**, which look out onto the Thames. Visitors are greeted by a statue of Emmeline Pankhurst, leader of the suffragette movement, who died in 1928, the same year women finally got the vote on equal terms with men; medallions commemorating her daughter

Christabel, and a WPSU Prisoners' Badge, flank the statue. Round the corner, a replica of Rodin's famous sculpture, *The Burghers of Calais*, makes a surprising appearance here, while at the far end of the gardens stands the **Buxton Memorial**, a neo-Gothic fountain, made from a real potpourri of exotic materials, erected in 1865 to commemorate the 1834 abolition of slavery in the British Empire.

Westminster Abbey

Parliament Square • Hours can vary: Mon–Fri 9.30am–4.30pm, Wed until 6pm, Sat 9.30am–2.30pm • £18 • ☎ 020 7654 4900, ⓦ westminster-abbey.org • ⊖ Westminster

The Houses of Parliament dwarf their much older neighbour, **Westminster Abbey**, which squats awkwardly on the western edge of Parliament Square. Yet this single building embodies much of the history of England: it has been the venue for every coronation since the time of William the Conqueror, and the site of just about every royal burial for some five hundred years between the reigns of Henry III and George II. Scores of the nation's most famous citizens are honoured here, too – though many of the stones commemorate people buried elsewhere – and the interior is cluttered with literally hundreds of monuments, reliefs and statues.

With over 3300 people buried beneath its flagstones and countless others commemorated here, the abbey is, in essence, a giant mausoleum. It has long ceased to be simply a working church, and hefty admission charges are nothing new: Oliver Goldsmith complained about being charged three pence in 1765. A century or so later, so few people used the abbey as a church that, according to George Bernard Shaw, one foreign visitor kneeling in prayer was promptly arrested because the verger thought he was acting suspiciously. Despite protestations to the contrary, the abbey is now more mass tourist attraction than House of God.

1

INFORMATION AND TOURS

Information If you have any questions, ask the vergers in the black gowns, the marshals in red or the abbey volunteers in green. Note that you can visit the Chapter House, the Cloisters and the College Garden (free admission), without buying an abbey ticket, by entering via Dean's Yard.

Tours There are guided tours by the vergers, which allow access to the Confessor's Tomb (Mon–Sat, times vary; ring for details; 1hr 30min; £3). A free audioguide is available.
Services Admission to the daily services at the abbey (check website for details) is, of course, free. Evensong is at 5pm on weekdays.

Brief history

Legend has it that the first church on the site was consecrated by St Peter himself, who was rowed across the Thames by a fisherman named Edric, to whom he granted a giant salmon as a reward. More verifiable is that there was a small Benedictine monastery here by the tenth century, for which **Edward the Confessor** built an enormous church. Nothing much remains of Edward's church, which was consecrated on December 28, 1065, just eight days before his death. The following January his successor, Harold, was crowned, and, on Christmas Day, William the Conqueror rode up the aisle on horseback, thus firmly establishing the tradition of royal coronation within the Confessor's church.

It was in honour of Edward (who had by now been canonized) that **Henry III** began to rebuild the abbey in 1245, in the French Gothic style of the recently completed Rheims Cathedral. The monks were kicked out during the Reformation, but the church's status as the nation's royal mausoleum saved it from any physical damage. In the early eighteenth century, Nicholas Hawksmoor designed the quasi-Gothic west front, while the most recent additions can be seen above the west door: a series of statues representing twentieth-century martyrs, from Dietrich Bonhöffer to Martin Luther King.

Statesmen's Aisle and the Sanctuary

The north transept, where you enter, is littered with overblown monuments to long-forgotten empire-builders and nineteenth-century politicians, and traditionally known as **Statesmen's Aisle**. From here, you can go straight to the central **Sanctuary**, site of the royal coronations. The most precious work of art here is the thirteenth-century Italian floor mosaic known as the **Cosmati pavement**. It depicts the universe with interwoven circles and squares of Purbeck marble, glass, and red and green porphyry, though it's sometimes covered by a carpet to protect it. The richly gilded high altar, like the ornately carved **choir stalls**, is, in fact, a neo-Gothic construction from the nineteenth century.

The side chapels

Some of the best funereal art is tucked away in **St Michael's Chapel**, east of the Statesmen's Aisle, where you can admire the remarkable monument to **Francis Vere** (1560–1609), one of the greatest soldiers of the Elizabethan period, made out of two slabs of black marble, between which lies Sir Francis; on the upper slab, supported by four knights, his armour is laid out, to show that he died away from the field of battle. The most striking grave, by Roubiliac, is that in which **Elizabeth Nightingale**, who died from a miscarriage, collapses in her husband's arms while he tries to fight off the skeletal figure of Death, who is climbing out of the tomb.

In the **north ambulatory**, two more chapels contain ostentatious Tudor and Stuart tombs that replaced the altarpieces that had graced them before the Reformation. One of the most extravagant tombs is that of Lord Hunsdon, Lord Chancellor to Elizabeth I, which dominates the **Chapel of St John the Baptist**, and, at 36ft in height, is the tallest in the entire abbey. More intriguing, though, are the sarcophagi in the neighbouring **Chapel of St Paul**: one depicts eight "weepers", kneeling children along the base of the tomb – the two holding skulls predeceased their parents – while the red-robed Countess of Sussex has a beautiful turquoise and gold porcupine (the family emblem) as her prickly footrest.

Henry VII's Chapel

From the Chapel of St Paul you can climb the stairs and enter the Lady Chapel, better known as **Henry VII's Chapel**, the most dazzling architectural set piece in the abbey. Begun by Henry VII in 1503 and dedicated to the Virgin Mary, it represents the final gasp of the English Perpendicular style, with its beautiful, light, intricately carved vaulting, fan-shaped gilded pendants and statues of nearly one hundred saints, high above the choir stalls. The stalls themselves are decorated with the banners and emblems of the Knights of the Order of the Bath, established by George I. **George II**, the last king to be buried in the abbey, lies in the burial vault under your feet, along with Queen Caroline – their coffins were fitted with removable sides so that their remains could mingle.

Beneath the altar is the grave of Edward VI, the single, sickly son of Henry VIII, while behind lies the chapel's centrepiece, the black marble **sarcophagus of Henry VII** and his spouse – their lifelike gilded effigies, modelled from death masks, are obscured by an ornate Renaissance grille by Pietro Torrigiano, who fled from Italy after breaking Michelangelo's nose in a fight. James I is also interred within Henry's tomb, while the first of the apse chapels, to the north, hosts a grand monument by Hubert le Sueur to James's lover, George Villiers, Duke of Buckingham, the first non-royal to be buried in this part of the abbey, who was killed by one of his own disgruntled soldiers.

The side chapels

The easternmost **RAF Chapel** sports a stained-glass window depicting airmen and angels in the Battle of Britain and a small piece of bomb damage from World War II. In the floor, a plaque marks the spot where Oliver Cromwell rested, briefly, until the Restoration, whereupon his mummified body was disinterred, dragged through the streets, hanged at Tyburn and beheaded. And the last of the apse chapels contains another overblown Le Sueur monument, in which four caryatids, holding up a vast bronze canopy, weep for Ludovic Stuart, another of James I's "favourites".

North aisle: Elizabeth I and the Innocents

Before descending the steps back into the ambulatory, pop into the chapel's north aisle, which is virtually cut off from the chancel. Here James I erected a huge ten-poster tomb to his predecessor, **Elizabeth I**. Unless you read the plaque on the floor, you'd never know that Elizabeth's Catholic half-sister, "Bloody Mary", is also buried here, in an unusual act of posthumous reconciliation. The far end of the north aisle, where James I's two infant daughters lie, is known as **Innocents' Corner**: Princess Sophia, who died aged three days, lies in an alabaster cradle, her face peeping over the covers, just about visible in the mirror on the wall; Princess Mary, who died the following year aged 2, is clearly visible, casually leaning on a cushion. Set into the wall between the two is the Wren-designed urn containing (what are thought to be) the bones of the **Princes in the Tower**, Edward V and his younger brother, Richard (see p.183).

South aisle: Mary Queen of Scots

The south aisle of Henry VII's Chapel contains a trio of stellar tombs, including James I's mother, **Mary, Queen of Scots**, whom Elizabeth I had beheaded. James had Mary's remains brought from Peterborough Cathedral in 1612, and paid significantly more for her extravagant eight-postered tomb, bristling with Scottish thistles and complete with a terrifyingly aggressive Scottish lion, than he had done for Elizabeth's; the 27 hangers-on (including the Cavalier Prince Rupert and the "Winter Queen", Elizabeth of Bohemia) who are buried with her are listed on the nearby wooden screen. The last of the tombs here is that of **Lady Margaret Beaufort**, Henry VII's mother, her face and hands depicted wrinkles and all by Torrigiano. Below the altar, commemorated by simple modern plaques, lie yet more royals: **William and Mary**, **Queen Anne** and **Charles II**.

1

The Coronation Chair

As you leave Henry VII's Chapel, look out for Edward I's **Coronation Chair**, a decrepit oak throne dating from around 1300. The graffiti-covered chair, used in every coronation since 1308, was custom-built to incorporate the **Stone of Scone**, a great slab of red sandstone which acted as the Scottish coronation stone for centuries before Edward pilfered it in 1296. The stone remained in the abbey for the next seven hundred years, apart from a brief interlude in 1950, when some Scottish nationalists managed to steal it back and hide it in Arbroath. In a futile attempt to curry favour with the Scots before the 1997 election, the Conservatives returned the stone to Edinburgh Castle, where it now resides until the next coronation.

The Shrine of Edward the Confessor

Behind the chair lies the tomb of **Henry V**, who died of dysentery in France in 1422 at the age of just 35, and was regarded as a saint in his day. Above him rises the highly decorative, H-shaped Chantry Chapel, where the body of Henry's wife, Catherine of Valois, was openly displayed for several centuries – Pepys records kissing her corpse on his 36th-birthday visit to the abbey. The chapel acts as a sort of gatehouse for the **Shrine of Edward the Confessor**, the sacred heart of the building, and site of some of the abbey's finest tombs, now only accessible on a guided tour (see p.54). With some difficulty, you can just about make out the battered marble casket of the Confessor's tomb and the niches in which pilgrims would kneel.

Poets' Corner

In the south transept, you'll find the increasingly popular **Poets' Corner**. The first occupant, **Geoffrey Chaucer**, was buried here in 1400, not because he was a poet, but because he lived nearby, and his battered tomb, on the east wall, wasn't built for another 150-odd years. When **Edmund Spenser** chose to be buried close to Chaucer in 1599, his fellow poets – Shakespeare among them (possibly) – threw their own works and quills into the grave. Nevertheless, it wasn't until the eighteenth century that this zone became an artistic pantheon, since when the transept has been filled with tributes to all shades of talent.

Among those who are actually buried here, you'll find – after much searching – grave slabs or memorials for everyone from John Dryden and Samuel Johnson to **Charles Dickens** and Thomas Hardy (though his heart was buried in Dorset). Among the merely commemorated is **William Shakespeare**, whose dandyish statue is on the east wall. Even mavericks like Oscar Wilde, commemorated in the Hubbard window, are acknowledged here, though William Blake was honoured by a Jacob Epstein sculpture only in 1957, and Byron was refused burial for his "open profligacy", and had to wait until 1969.

Among the non-poets buried here are the great eighteenth-century actor **David Garrick**, depicted parting the curtains for a final bow, and the German composer **Georg Friedrich Handel**, who spent most of his life at the English court, and wrote the coronation anthem *Zadok the Priest*, first performed at George II's coronation, and performed at every subsequent one. There's even one illiterate, Thomas Parr, a Shropshire man who arrived in London as a celebrity in 1635 at the alleged age of 152, but died shortly afterwards, and whose remains were brought here by Charles II.

South choir aisle

Before you enter the cloisters, it's worth seeking out several wonderful memorials to undeserving types in the **south choir aisle**, though you may have to ask a verger to allow you to see them properly. The first is to **Thomas Thynne**, a Restoration rake, whose tomb incorporates a relief showing his assassination in his coach on Pall Mall by three thugs, hired to kill him by his Swedish rival in love. Further along lies

WESTMINSTER ABBEY >

1

Admiral Clowdisley Shovell, lounging in toga and wig. One of only two survivors of a shipwreck in 1707, he was washed up alive on a beach in the Scilly Isles, off southwest England, only to be killed by a fisherwoman for his emerald ring. Above Shovell is a memorial to the court portrait painter **Godfrey Kneller**, who declared, "By God, I will not be buried in Westminster – they do bury fools there". In the event, he has the honour of being the only artist commemorated in the abbey (most are in St Paul's); the tomb is to his own design, but the epitaph is by Pope, who admitted it was the worst thing he ever wrote – which is just as well, as it's so high up you can't read it.

The cloisters

Cloisters daily 10am–6pm; Chapter House daily 10.30am–4pm • Free via Dean's Yard entrance

Doors in the south choir aisle lead to the **Great Cloister**, rebuilt after a fire in 1298 and paved with yet more funerary slabs, including, at the bottom of the ramp, that of the proto-feminist writer **Aphra Behn**, upon whose tomb "all women together ought to let flowers fall", according to Virginia Woolf, "for it was she who earned them the right to speak their minds".

At the eastern end lies the octagonal **Chapter House**, built in the 1250s and used by Henry III's Great Council, England's putative parliament. The House of Commons continued to meet here until 1395, though the monks were none too happy about it, complaining that the shuffling and stamping wore out the expensive tiled floor. Despite their whingeing, the paving tiles have survived well, as have sections of the remarkable apocalyptic wall-paintings, which were executed in celebration of the eviction of the Commons. Be sure to check out the southern wall, where the Whore of Babylon rides the scarlet seven-headed beast from The Book of Revelation.

Pyx Chamber and Museum

Daily: Pyx Chamber 10.30am–3.30pm; museum 10.30am–4pm • Free

The nearby **Pyx Chamber** was a medieval high-security safe-deposit box and is one of the few surviving Norman sections of the abbey, along with the neighbouring **Museum**. The latter contains a real mixed bag of exhibits, from replica coronation regalia used during rehearsals to the ring given by Elizabeth I to her lover, the Earl of Essex. The most bizarre items, though, are the lifelike wood and wax royal funereal effigies (several of which are wigless), used in royal burials (1307–1660) instead of an open coffin, including that of Lady Frances Stuart, the Duchess of Richmond and Lennox and model for Britannia on the old penny coin, complete with her pet parrot, which died a few days after she did.

College Garden

Tues–Thurs: April–Sept 10am–6pm; Oct–March 10am–4.30pm • Free

From the Great Cloister you can make your way to the **Little Cloister**, where sick or elderly monks used to live, and where, on the east side, you can look into **St Catherine's Chapel Garden**, a tiny plot dotted medieval ruins. From here a passage leads to the little-known **College Garden**, with a nine hundred-year-old stretch of green, originally used as a herb garden by the monastery's doctor. The garden now provides a quiet retreat and a croquet lawn for pupils of Westminster School; brass-band concerts take place in the summer (July & Aug Wed 12.30–2pm).

The nave

It's only when you finally leave the cloisters that you get to enter the **nave** itself. Narrow, light and, at over a hundred feet in height, by far the tallest in the country, the nave is an impressive space. The first monument to head for is the **Tomb of the Unknown Soldier**, by the west door, with its garland of red poppies commemorating the million British soldiers who died in World War I. Close by is a large floor slab dedicated to **Winston Churchill**, though he chose to be buried in his family plot in Bladon, Oxfordshire.

A tablet in the floor near the Unknown Soldier marks the spot where **George Peabody**, the nineteenth-century philanthropist whose housing estates in London still provide homes for those in need, was buried for a month before being exhumed and removed to Massachusetts; he remains the only American to have been buried in the abbey. On the pillar by St George's Chapel, right by the west door, is a doleful fourteenth-century portrait of **Richard II**, painted at his coronation at the age of 10, and the oldest known image of an English monarch painted from life. Above the west door, **William Pitt the Younger**, prime minister at just 23, teaches Anarchy a thing or two, while History takes notes.

The choir screen and the side aisles

The dried and salted body of the explorer and missionary **David Livingstone** is buried in the centre of the nave – except for his internal organs, which, following the tradition of the African people in whose village he died, were buried in a box under a tree. To the left of the gilded neo-Gothic choir screen is a statue of **Isaac Newton**, who, although a Unitarian by faith, would no doubt have been happy enough to be buried in such a prominent position. Other scientists' graves cluster nearby, including non-believer **Charles Darwin**, who, despite being at loggerheads with the Church for most of his life over *On the Origin of Species*, was given a religious burial in the abbey.

In the far corner of the south aisle, the eighteenth-century marble memorial to **General Hargrave** by Roubiliac, has the deceased rising from the grave in response to the Last Trumpet; at the time there was a public outcry that such an undistinguished man – he was Governor of Gibraltar – should receive such a vast memorial. Another controversial grave is that of poet and playwright **Ben Jonson**, who, despite being a double murderer, was granted permission to be buried here, upright so as not to exceed the eighteen square inches he'd been allowed; his epitaph reads simply, "O Rare Ben Jonson". The so-called **Musicians' Aisle** lies to the east, beyond a barrier, so you'll need to ask a verger for access. In fact, just two musicians of great note are buried here: Ralph Vaughan Williams and Henry Purcell, who served as the abbey's organist. Of the statues lining the aisle, only the tireless anti-slavery campaigner **William Wilberforce**, slouching in his chair, is actually buried in the abbey.

Parliament Square

Parliament Square was laid out in the mid-nineteenth century to give the new Houses of Parliament and the adjacent Westminster Abbey a grander setting, though nowadays it functions primarily as a traffic roundabout and as a favoured protest spot. Statues of notables – Abraham Lincoln, Benjamin Disraeli and Nelson Mandela, to name but a few – are scattered amid the swirling cars and buses, with Winston Churchill stooping determinedly in the northeast corner of the central green. At the beginning of **Westminster Bridge**, you can also spot **Boudicca**, depicted keeping her horses and daughters under control without the use of reins – the imperialist boast "regions Caesar never knew, thy posterity shall sway" adorns the plinth.

St Margaret's Church

St Margaret St • Mon–Fri 9.30am–3.30pm, Sat 9.30am–1.30pm, Sun noon–4.45pm • Free • ⊖ Westminster

Sitting in the shadow of Westminster Abbey, **St Margaret's Church** has been the unofficial parliamentary church since 1614, when Puritan MPs decided to shun the elaborate liturgy of the neighbouring abbey. St Margaret's has also long been a fashionable church to get married in – Pepys and Milton were followed in the twentieth century by Churchill and Mountbatten – and it gets a steady stream of visitors simply by dint of being so close to the abbey (and because it's free, unlike the abbey). The present building dates back to 1523, and features some colourful Flemish stained glass above the altar, commemorating the marriage of Henry VIII and

1

Catherine of Aragon (depicted in the bottom left- and right-hand corners). Constructed in 1526, the window was never intended for St Margaret's, and was only bought by the church in 1758 to replace those smashed by the Puritans. The west window commemorates Walter Raleigh, who was beheaded in Old Palace Yard and buried in the old churchyard. Also interred here is William Caxton, who audited the parish accounts and set up the country's first printing press in the abbey close in 1476.

Supreme Court

Parliament Square • Mon–Fri 9.30am–4.30pm • Free • ☎ 020 7960 1500, Ⓦ supremecourt.gov.uk • ⊖ Westminster

The House of Lords was the country's final court of appeal from medieval times until 2009, when the **Supreme Court** took over and housed itself in the former Middlesex Guildhall, a quasi-medieval Edwardian town hall that sits on the west side of Parliament Square, replete with lugubrious gargoyles and sculptures. The public are welcome to explore the building, view an exhibition on the Supreme Court and sit in on any sessions going on (Mon–Thurs only) – plus there's a very nice **café** with free wi-fi in the tiled and roofed inner light well. A self-guided tour guide is available for £1 from the reception desk.

Central Hall Westminster

Storey's Gate • ☎ 020 7222 8010, Ⓦ c-h-w.com • ⊖ Westminster

Set back from Parliament Square, on Storey's Gate, stands the Methodists' national headquarters, **Central Hall**, established here in 1912. In order to avoid the Gothic of the abbey, and the Byzantine of the nearby Catholic cathedral (see p.63), the Methodists opted for Edwardian Beaux-Arts – as a result, it looks rather like a giant continental casino, which is hardly appropriate given the Methodists' views on gambling and alcohol. Central Hall has been used over the years as much for political meetings as religious gatherings, and was the unlikely venue for the inaugural meeting of the **United Nations** in 1946. If there's no event on, you're free to wander round the building and – after donning black gloves – to look at the Historic Roll, a fifty-volume list of the folk who donated a guinea towards the cost of the building. Free **guided tours** are also available, and allow you to climb the stone balustrade atop the reinforced concrete dome.

Tate Britain

Millbank • Daily 10am–6pm; first Fri of month until 10pm • Free • ☎ 020 7887 8888, Ⓦ tate.org.uk • ⊖ Pimlico or Vauxhall

Founded in 1897 with money from Henry Tate, inventor of the sugar cube, **Tate Britain** showcases British art from 1500 to the present day. In addition, the gallery has a whole wing devoted to Turner, as well as putting on large-scale temporary exhibitions (for which there is a charge) and sponsoring the **Turner Prize**, the country's most infamous modern-art award. Works by a shortlist of four British artists under 50 are displayed in the gallery a month or two prior to the December prize-giving.

Following a major refurbishment, the gallery has returned to a traditional, chronological approach in its permanent displays. There is more space than ever, but what you see is still only a fraction of the collection, and rooms are periodically re-hung. What follows, therefore, is a rundown of the artists usually featured, plus some of the best works Tate owns, many of which are on show more or less permanently.

INFORMATION AND TOURS

Arrival The traditional entrance on Millbank leads up the steps to a small information desk. A larger entrance with disabled access is on Atterbury St, and leads down to information desks and the cloakroom. The Clore Gallery, which houses the Turner Bequest, can be reached via the modern-art galleries, but it also has its own entrance and

information desk to the right of the original gallery entrance.
Tate boat If you're coming from, or going to, Tate Modern, there's a Tate Boat that plies between the two galleries (every 40min; 15min; £5.50); Ⓦ thamesclippers.com.
Tours There are free guided tours (daily 11am, noon, 2 & 3pm; 45min) and you can rent multimedia guides for £3.50.

British art from 1540 to 1810

The collection's earliest works are richly bejewelled portraits of the Elizabethan and Jacobean nobility, the most striking being the richly symbolic Portrait of Captain Thomas Lee, a bare-legged swashbuckling English soldier. Another eye-catching work is the *Cholmondeley Ladies*, who were born on the same day, married on the same day and "brought to bed" on the same day, but are not now thought to be twins. Despite a smattering of English talent – **William Dobson**'s portrait of courtier *Endymion Porter* is a perennial favourite – the Stuarts relied heavily on imported Dutch talent such as Van Dyck and Peter Lely (several of whose "lovelies" are usually on display) and the German Godfrey Kneller, who used to sign himself "Pictor Regis" such was the longevity of his royal patronage.

Hogarth and Constable

You can be guaranteed a good selection of works by the first great British artist, **William Hogarth**, including *O the Roast Beef of Old England*, a particularly vicious visual dig at the French, whom Hogarth loathed. **John Constable**'s most famous work, *Hay Wain*, hangs in the National Gallery, but the same location – Flatford Mill in his native Stour valley in Suffolk – features in many of the paintings owned by the Tate. Another painter to look out for is **George Stubbs**, for whom "nature was and always is superior to art", and who portrayed animals – horses in particular – with a hitherto unknown anatomical precision.

Gainsborough and Reynolds

Works by **Thomas Gainsborough** and **Joshua Reynolds** are sprinkled across several rooms. Of the two, Reynolds, first president of the Royal Academy, was by far the more successful, elevating portraiture to pole position among the genres and flattering his sitters by surrounding them with classical trappings as in *Three Ladies adorning a Term of Hymen*. Gainsborough was equally adept at flattery, but preferred instead more informal settings, concentrating on colour and light, as in *Giovanna Baccelli*. At the outset of his career, Gainsborough was also a landscape artist, often painting the Stour valley in Suffolk, where he – like Constable – was born.

The Pre-Raphaelites

Tate is justifiably renowned for its vast collection of paintings by the **Pre-Raphaelites**, seven of whom formed their Brotherhood, the PRB, in 1848 in an attempt to re-create the humble, pre-humanist, pre-Renaissance world. One of the first PRB paintings to be exhibited was **Rossetti**'s *Girlhood of Mary Virgin*, which was well received by the critics, but his *Annunciation*, with its emaciated heroin-chic Virgin, the model for which was his sister, caused outrage. So too did **Millais**' *Christ in the House of His Parents*; Dickens described the figure of Jesus as "a hideous, wry-necked, blubbering, red-headed boy in a bed-gown". Millais also got into trouble for *Ophelia*, after his model, Elizabeth Siddal, caught a chill from lying in the bath to pose for the picture, prompting threats of a lawsuit from her father. Siddal later married Rossetti, and is also the model in his *Beata Beatrix*, painted posthumously, after she died of an opium overdose in 1862. Other classic PRB paintings in the collection are Arthur Hughes' *April Love*, Henry Wallis's Romantic hero *Chatterton*, John William Waterhouse's *The Lady of Shalott* and Burne-Jones' *King Cophetua and the Beggar Maid*, all inspired by poems by Lord Tennyson.

The Academy and the Impressionists

Throughout Tate Britain, the term "British" is very loosely applied, so you'll find several works by the French artist, **James Tissot**, whose Impressionist take on English life (and, in particular, English ladies in frilly frocks) was very popular. **Lord Leighton**'s *Bath of Psyche* is a typical piece of Victorian soft porn, the likes of which made him by far the most successful Royal Academician of his generation. Moralizing paintings such as

1

A. L. Egg's *Past and Present* abound, as do heavily symbolist efforts like G. F. Watts' *Hope* (once one of the most popular paintings in the Tate). More universally appealing Victorian paintings to look out for include **John Singer Sargent**'s well-known and much-loved *Carnation, Lily, Lily-Rose* and the American-born **Whistler**'s portrait of the precocious *Miss Cecily*, who looks as pissed off as she clearly felt after interminable sittings.

Twentieth-century British art

You'll find works by the same twentieth-century and contemporary British artists displayed in both Tate Modern and Tate Britain, so it's very hard to predict what will be on show here. Works by sculptors **Barbara Hepworth**, Jacob Epstein, Eric Gill, Giacometti and **Henry Moore** usually feature prominently, while paintings by Walter Sickert, Paul Nash, Ben Nicholson and Francis Bacon crop up regularly. Vanessa Bell and Duncan Grant, from the Bloomsbury Group, are represented more often than not, and there are nearly always several paintings by **Stanley Spencer**, who saw his home village of Cookham, on the Thames, as paradise and used it as a background for all his Biblical paintings.

Some less well-known artists to look out for include the Vorticist **David Bomberg**, who forged his own brand of Cubo-Futurism before World War I; **Ivon Hitchens**, whose distinctive use of blocks of colour harks back to the late works of Cézanne; and the self-taught St Ives painter **Alfred Wallis**. There's usually a fairly good selection of work, too, by modern painters such as **Lucian Freud** and R.B. Kitaj, as well as established living artists such as **David Hockney**, Frank Auerbach and op-art specialist Bridget Riley, and contemporary artists such as Rachel Whiteread, Damien Hirst, Chris Ofili and the ever-popular Antony Gormley.

The Turner Collection

J.M.W. Turner, possibly the greatest artist Britain has ever produced, bequeathed over one hundred oil paintings to the nation, and the gallery now has three hundred, plus a staggering 19,000 watercolours and drawings. Turner's one condition was that the paintings should be housed and exhibited together – the original idea behind the Clore Gallery, the strangely childish building by James Stirling from 1987. The Turner Galleries still exhibit probably the world's largest collection of works by Turner, but you'll also find other artists' works here, and several of Turner's major works hang in the National Gallery. Turner was superb at depicting awe-inspiring scenes – what the Romantics liked to call "the sublime" – particularly marine scenes, and one of the finest examples is *The Shipwreck*. Other natural cataclysms include the *Deluge*, and, in this case as part of a grand historical painting, *Snow Storm: Hannibal and His Army Crossing the Alps*. His financial independence allowed him to develop his own style freely and it's worth seeking out Turner's late works, great smudges of colour that seem to anticipate Monet in their almost total abandonment of linear representation. *Snow Storm – Steam Boat off a Harbour's Mouth* is a classic late Turner, a symbolic battle between the steam

---

J.M.W. TURNER (1775–1851)

Born in **Covent Garden**, Turner's childhood was blighted by the death of his younger sister, and the mental illness of his mother, who died in Bedlam in 1804. Nevertheless, he became an extremely successful artist, exhibiting his first watercolours in the window of his father's barbershop in Maiden Lane, while still a boy, and at the **Royal Academy** when he was just 14. He travelled widely in Europe, but when returning to England, lived increasingly as a recluse. He never married, but had two children with an older widow, and lived for thirty years with his father who worked as his studio assistant. Turner's only known **self-portrait** (he had no pretensions as a portraitist and was rather ashamed of his ruddy complexion) is usually on display, as are his personal belongings, such as his pocket watercolour kit and sketchbooks, his fishing rod, and his toothless death mask.

age and nature's primeval force. It was criticized at the time as "soapsuds and whitewash", though Turner himself claimed he merely painted what he saw, having been "lashed to a mast" for four hours.

William Blake

Two rooms on the upper floor of the Turner Wing are devoted to the visionary works of the poet **William Blake**, who was considered something of a freak by his contemporaries. He rejected oil painting in favour of watercolours, and often chose unusual subject matter which matched his highly personal form of Christianity. He earned a pittance producing illuminated books written and printed entirely by himself, and painted purely from his own visions: "Imagination is My World; this world of Dross is beneath my notice", he wrote. He also executed a series of twelve large colour prints on the myth of the Creation, now considered among his finest works, several examples of which are normally on display here. Blake's works were originally intended for a room back in the southern corner of the main building, which is decorated by Boris Anrep's floor mosaics, accompanied by quotes from Blake's poem *The Marriage of Heaven and Hell*.

From Millbank to Victoria Street

The area between **Millbank** – the busy riverside road that runs past Tate Britain – and **Victoria Street** – the link forged in the 1860s between Parliament and the newly built Victoria train station – is home to various governmental ministries that can't quite fit into Whitehall. It's also a favourite place for MPs to have their London bases, and many of the restaurants and pubs in the area have "division bells", which ring eight minutes before any vote in the House of Commons. As for sights, the area boasts one of the city's most exotic and unusual churches, the Catholic Westminster Cathedral.

St John's, Smith Square

Smith Square • ☎ 020 7222 1061, ⓦ sjss.org.uk • ⊖ Westminster

Hidden away in the backstreets west of Millbank is the beautiful early Georgian architectural ensemble of **Smith Square**, home to the church of **St John**, a rare and totally surprising slice of full-blown Baroque, completed in 1728. With its four distinctive towers topped by pineapples, it was dubbed the "footstool church" – the story being that Queen Anne, when asked how she would like the church to look, kicked over her footstool. Bombed in 1941, the interior was totally gutted and has since been restored as a classical music venue, so to visit you'll have to go to a concert. The church's atmospheric restaurant is in the brick-vaulted crypt beyond the box office (access from Dean Stanley St).

St James-the-Less

Vauxhall Bridge Rd • Mon–Fri 9.30am–1pm • Free • ☎ 020 7630 6282, ⓦ sjtl.org • ⊖ Pimlico

Another sight worth seeking out is the remarkable High Victorian church of **St James-the-Less**, designed by George Edmund Street in the 1860s, which lies on the south side of Vauxhall Bridge Road, amid an unprepossessing 1960s Lillington Gardens housing estate. The red-and-black brickwork patterning on the exterior is exceptional, but pales in comparison to the red, black, cream and magenta tiling inside. The capitals of the church's rounded pillars hide biblical scenes amidst their acanthus-leaf foliage, and the font boasts similarly rich adornments, while above the chancel arch there's a wonderfully colourful fresco by G.F. Watts.

Westminster Cathedral

Victoria St • **Campanile** Mon–Fri 9.30am–5pm, Sat & Sun 9.30am–6pm • £5 **Cathedral** Mon–Fri 7am–7pm, Sat 8am–7pm, Sun 8am–8pm • Free • ☎ 020 7798 9055, ⓦ westminstercathedral.org.uk • ⊖ Victoria

Set back from the stark 1960s architecture of Victoria Street, you'll find one of London's most surprising churches, the stripy neo-Byzantine concoction of the Roman

1

THE SECRET SERVICE

The green-and-beige postmodernist ziggurat across the water is Vauxhall Cross, the indiscreet Secret Intelligence Service or **MI6 headquarters** (Ⓦ sis.gov.uk), designed in the 1990s by Terry Farrell. It has featured in several Bond films and is connected by tunnel to Whitehall. Such conspicuousness comes at a price, however, and in 2000, the building, known as "Legoland" to those who work there, was hit by a rocket attack courtesy of some dissident Irish-republican terrorists. **MI5** (Ⓦ mi5.gov.uk), the UK's domestic Security Service, occupies the much more anonymous Thames House on the corner of MIllbank and Horseferry Road.

Catholic **Westminster Cathedral**. Begun in 1895, it's one of the last and wildest monuments to the Victorian era: constructed from more than twelve million terracotta-coloured bricks, decorated with hoops of Portland stone, it culminates in a magnificent tapered campanile which rises to 273ft. From the small piazza to the northwest, you can admire the cathedral and the neighbouring mansions on Ambrosden Avenue, with their matching brickwork.

The **interior** is still only half-finished, and the domed ceiling of the nave – the widest in the country – remains an indistinct blackened mass, free of all decoration. To get an idea of what the place will look like when it's eventually completed, explore the series of **side chapels** – in particular the Holy Souls Chapel, the first one in the north aisle – whose rich, multicoloured decor makes use of over one hundred different marbles from around the world. Further down the north aisle is the Chapel of St George and the English Martyrs, where lies the enshrined body of St John Southworth, who was hanged, drawn and quartered as a traitor at Tyburn in 1654. Be sure, too, to check out the striking baldachin, held up by mustard-yellow pillars, and the low-relief Stations of the Cross sculpted by the controversial Eric Gill during World War I. The view from the **campanile** is definitely worth taking in as well, especially as you don't even have to slog up flights of steps, but can simply take a lift; the entrance is in the north aisle.

North of Victoria Street

The one tower block north of Victoria Street that deserves special mention is the Metropolitan Police headquarters, **New Scotland Yard**, on Broadway. The revolving sign alone should be familiar from countless TV news reports, although in 2015 the sign will move (along with the Met) to a new HQ on Victoria Embankment. Further up Broadway, at no. 55, is the austere **Broadway House**, home to the city's public transport body, Transport for London (TfL) and St James's Park tube station, and the tallest building in London when it was built in 1929 by Charles Holden. The building's exterior nude statues by, among others, Eric Gill, Henry Moore and Jacob Epstein, gained a certain notoriety at the time, in particular the boy figure in *Day*, whose penis had to be shortened to appease public opinion.

Round the corner, standing on its own in Caxton Street, is the former **Blewcoat School** (now a National Trust shop), a lovely little red-brick building built in 1709 by a local brewer as a charity school for the poor and used as such until 1926; a statue of a blue-coated charity boy still stands above the doorway.

There's more delightful Queen Anne architecture just to the north in **Queen Anne's Gate** and **Old Queen Street**, two exquisite streets, originally separated by a wall, whose position is indicated by a weathered statue of Queen Anne herself. Queen Anne's Gate is the older and more interesting of the two, each of its doorways surmounted by a rustic wooden canopy with pendants in the shape of acorns. It's worth walking round the back of the houses on the north side to appreciate the procession of elegant bow windows that look out on to St James's Park.

St James's

An exclusive little enclave sandwiched between St James's Park and Piccadilly, St James's was laid out in the 1670s close to the royal seat of St James's Palace. Even today, regal and aristocratic residences overlook nearby Green Park and the stately avenue of The Mall; gentlemen's clubs cluster along Pall Mall and St James's Street; and jacket-and-tie restaurants and expense-account shops line St James's and Jermyn Street. Hardly surprising, then, that most Londoners rarely stray into this area, though plenty of folk frequent St James's Park, with large numbers heading for the Queen's chief residence, Buckingham Palace. If you're not in St James's for the shops, the best time to visit is on a Sunday, when it's quieter, the nearby Mall is closed to traffic, and the royal chapels, plus Spencer House, the one accessible Palladian mansion, are open to the public.

St James's Park

St James's Park is the oldest of London's royal parks, having been drained and turned into a deer park by Henry VIII. It was redesigned and opened to the public by Charles II, who used to stroll through the grounds with his mistresses and courtiers, feed the ducks and even take a dip in the canal. By the eighteenth century, when some 6500 people had access to night keys for the gates, the park had become something of a byword for robbery and prostitution: diarist James Boswell was among those who went there specifically to be accosted "by several ladies of the town". The park's current landscaping was devised by Nash in the 1820s in an elegant style that established a blueprint for later Victorian city parks.

Today, the banks of the tree-lined lake are a favourite picnic spot for the civil servants of Whitehall and an inner-city reserve for wildfowl. James I's two crocodiles have left no descendants, alas, but the pelicans (which have resided here ever since a pair was presented to Charles II by the Russian ambassador) can still be seen at the eastern end of the lake, and there are exotic ducks, swans and geese aplenty. From the bridge across the lake there's a fine view over to Westminster and the jumble of domes and pinnacles along Whitehall – even the dull east facade of **Buckingham Palace** looks majestic from here.

The Mall

St James's Park, Charing Cross or Westminster

The tree-lined sweep of **The Mall** – London's nearest equivalent to a Parisian boulevard (minus the cafés) – is at its best on Sundays, when it's closed to traffic. It was laid out in the first decade of the twentieth century as a memorial to Queen Victoria, and runs along the northern edge of St James's Park. The bombastic **Admiralty Arch** (currently being converted into a hotel) was erected to mark the entrance at the Trafalgar Square end of The Mall, while at the other end stands the ludicrous **Victoria Memorial**, Edward VII's overblown 2300-ton marble tribute to his mother: *Motherhood* and *Justice* keep Victoria company around the plinth, which is topped by a gilded statue of *Victory*, while the six outlying allegorical groups in bronze confidently proclaim the great achievements of her reign.

The Mall's most distinctive building is John Nash's **Carlton House Terrace**, whose graceful, cream-coloured Regency facade lines the north side of The Mall from Admiralty Arch. Among other things, it serves as the unlikely home of the **Institute of Contemporary Arts** or **ICA** (Wed noon–11pm, Thurs–Sat noon–1am, Sun noon–9pm; free; ☎020 7930 3647, ⊛ica.org.uk), London's official headquarters of the avant-garde, so to speak, which moved here in 1968 and has put on a programme of regularly provocative exhibitions, films, talks and performances ever since. A little further down the terrace, there are statues of George VI, erected in 1955, and his wife, the Queen Mum, erected in 2009 but depicted at the age she would have been when her husband died – on either side bronze reliefs depict the couple visiting the East End during the Blitz and having a day out at the races.

Wellington Barracks, Guards' Chapel and Museum

Birdcage Walk • Museum Daily 10am–4pm • £5 • ☎ 020 7414 3271, ⊛ theguardsmuseum.com • St James's Park

Named after James I's aviary, which once stood here, Birdcage Walk runs along the south side of St James's Park, with the Neoclassical facade of the **Wellington Barracks**, built in 1833 and fronted by a parade ground, occupying more than half its length. Of the various buildings here it's the modernist lines of the **Guards' Chapel** that come as the biggest surprise. Hit by a V1 rocket bomb on the morning of Sunday, June 18, 1944 – killing 121 worshippers – the chapel was rebuilt in the 1960s. Inside, it's festooned with faded military flags, and retains the ornate Victorian apse, with Byzantine-style gilded mosaics, from the old chapel.

In a bunker opposite is the **Guards' Museum**, which displays the glorious scarlet-and-blue uniforms of the Queen's Foot Guards (see p.48). The museum also explains the

Guards' complicated history, and gives a potted military history of the country since the Civil War. Among the exhibits are a lock of Wellington's hair and a whole load of war booty, from Dervish prayer mats plundered from Sudan in 1898 to items taken from an Iraqi POW during the first Gulf War. The museum also displays (and sells) an impressive array of toy soldiers.

2 Buckingham Palace

The Mall • Late July to Aug daily 9.30am–7pm, Sept 9.30am–6.30pm • State Rooms £19; State Rooms & Garden Highlights £27.75; booking fee & postage £2.45 per ticket • ☎ 020 7766 7300, ⓦ royalcollection.org.uk • ⊖ Green Park

The graceless colossus of **Buckingham Palace**, popularly known as "Buck House", has served as the monarch's permanent London residence only since Queen Victoria's reign. It began its days in 1702 as the Duke of Buckingham's city residence, built on the site of a notorious brothel, and was sold by the duke's son to George III in 1762. The building was overhauled by Nash in the late 1820s for the Prince Regent, and again by Aston Webb in 1913 for George V, producing a palace that's about as bland as it's possible to be.

For ten months of the year there's little to do here, with the Queen in residence and the palace closed to visitors – not that this deters the crowds who mill around the railings all day, and gather in some force to watch the **Changing of the Guard** (see box, p.48), in which a detachment of the Queen's Foot Guards marches to appropriate martial music from St James's Palace (unless it rains, that is). If the Queen is at home, the Royal Standard flies from the roof of the palace and four guards patrol; if not, the Union flag flutters aloft and just two guards stand out front.

Traditionally, unless you were one of the select thirty thousand society debutantes attending a "coming out" party, you had little chance of ever seeing inside Buckingham Palace. The debutantes were given the boot in 1958 and more democratic garden parties were established. Since 1993, however, the hallowed portals have been grudgingly opened for two months of the year. **Timed tickets** can be purchased online or from the box office on the south side of the palace; queues vary enormously, but you may have some time to wait before your allocated slot.

The interior

Of the palace's 775 rooms you get to see around twenty of the grandest ones, but with the Queen and her family in Scotland, there's usually very little sign of life. The visitors' entrance is via the **Ambassadors' Court** on Buckingham Palace Road, which lets you into the enormous **Quadrangle**, from where you can see the Nash portico, built in warm Bath stone, that used to overlook St James's Park.

Through the courtyard, you hit the **Grand Hall**, decorated like some gloomy hotel lobby, from where Nash's rather splendid winding, curlicued **Grand Staircase**, with its floral gilt-bronze balustrade and white plaster friezes, leads past a range of very fine royal portraits, all beautifully lit by Nash's glass dome. Beyond, the small Guard Room leads into the **Green Drawing Room**, a blaze of unusually bright green silk walls, framed by lattice-patterned pilasters, and a heavily gilded coved ceiling. It was here that the Raphael Cartoons used to hang, until they were permanently loaned to the V&A.

The scarlet and gold **Throne Room** features a Neoclassical plaster frieze in the style of the Elgin Marbles, depicting the Wars of the Roses. The thrones themselves are disappointingly un-regal – just two pink his 'n' hers chairs initialled ER and P – whereas George IV's outrageous sphinx-style chariot seats, nearby, look more the part.

From the Picture Gallery to the Ballroom

Nash originally designed a spectacular hammerbeam ceiling for the **Picture Gallery**, which stretches right down the centre of the palace. Unfortunately, it leaked and was eventually replaced in 1914 by a rather dull glazed ceiling. Still, the paintings on show here are

excellent and include several Van Dycks, two Rembrandts, two Canalettos, a Poussin, a de Hooch and a wonderful Vermeer. Further on, in the East Gallery, check the cherub-fest in the grisaille frieze, before heading into the palace's rather overwrought **Ballroom**. It's here that the Queen holds her State Banquets, where the annual Diplomatic Reception takes place, and where folk receive their honours and knighthoods.

The west facade rooms

Having passed through several smaller rooms, you eventually reach the **State Dining Room**, whose heavily gilded ceiling, with its three saucer domes, is typical of the suite of rooms that overlooks the palace garden. Next door lies Nash's not very blue, but incredibly gold, **Blue Drawing Room**, lined with flock wallpaper interspersed with thirty fake onyx columns. The room contains one of George IV's most prized possessions, the "Table of the Grand Commanders", originally made for Napoleon, whose trompe-l'oeil Sèvres porcelain top features cameo-like portraits of military commanders of antiquity.

Beyond the domed **Music Room** with its enormous semicircular bow window and impressive parquet floor, the **White Drawing Room** features yet another frothy gold and white Nash ceiling and a superb portrait of Queen Alexandra, wife of Edward VII. This room is also the incongruous setting for an annual royal prank: when hosting the reception for the diplomatic corps, the Queen and family emerge from a secret door behind a mirror to greet the ambassadors. Before you leave the palace, be sure to check out the Canova sculptures: *Mars and Venus* at the bottom of the Ministers' Staircase, and the pornographic *Fountain Nymph with Putto* in the Marble Hall.

If you've booked for the Garden Highlights Tour, you'll now get shown round the Queen's splendiferous herbaceous border, rose garden and veg patch, plus the wisteria-strewn summer house and the tennis court where George VI and Fred Perry used to knock up in the 1930s. There's a **café** overlooking the gardens if you want to linger longer before being ejected onto busy Grosvenor Place, a long walk from the Mall.

Queen's Gallery

Daily 10am–5.30pm • £9 • ☎ 020 7766 7301 • ⊖ Victoria

A modern Doric portico on the south side of the palace forms the entrance to the **Queen's Gallery**, which puts on temporary exhibitions drawn from the **Royal Collection**, a superlative array of art that includes works by Michelangelo, Raphael, Holbein, Reynolds, Gainsborough, Vermeer, Van Dyck, Rubens, Rembrandt and Canaletto, as well as the world's largest collection of Leonardo drawings, the odd Fabergé egg and heaps of Sèvres china. The Queen holds the Royal Collection, which is three times larger than the National Gallery, "in trust for her successors and the nation" – note the word order. However, with over seven thousand works spread over the numerous royal palaces, the Queen's Gallery and other museums and galleries around the country, you'd have to pay a king's ransom to see the lot.

Royal Mews

Feb, March & Nov Mon–Sat 10am–4pm; April–Oct daily 10am–5pm • £8.50 • ☎ 020 7766 7302 • ⊖ Victoria

On the south side of the palace, along Buckingham Palace Road, you'll find the **Royal Mews**, built by Nash in the 1820s. The horses – or at least their backsides – can be viewed in their luxury stables, along with an exhibition of equine accoutrements, but it's the royal carriages, lined up under a glass canopy in the courtyard, that are the main attraction. The most ornate is the **Gold State Coach**, made for George III in 1762, smothered in 22-carat gilding and panel paintings by Cipriani, and weighing four tons, its axles supporting four life-size Tritons blowing conches. Eight horses are needed to pull it and the whole experience apparently made Queen Victoria feel quite sick; since then it has only been used for coronations and jubilees. The mews also house the Royal Family's fleet of five Rolls Royce Phantoms and three Daimlers, none of which is obliged to carry numberplates.

THE ROYAL FAMILY

The popularity of the **royal family** to foreign tourists never seems to flag, but at home it has always waxed and waned. The Queen herself, in one of her few memorable Christmas Day speeches, accurately described 1992 as her **annus horibilis** (or "One's Bum Year" as the *Sun* put it). That was the year that saw the marriage break-ups of Prince Charles and Prince Andrew, the divorce of Princess Anne, and ended with the fire at Windsor Castle. The royals decided to raise some of the money by opening Buckingham Palace to the public for the first time (and by cranking up the admission charges on all the royal residences).

To try and deflect some of the bad publicity from that year, the Queen agreed to reduce the number of royals paid out of the state coffers, and, for the first time in her life, pay **taxes** on her personal fortune. The death of Princess Diana in 1997 was a low point for the royals, but their ratings have improved steadily since the new millennium, partly because the family have got much better at PR. Efficiencies and cost-cutting have also taken place, though public subsidy is still considerable, with around £30 million handed over each year in the Sovereign Grant and millions more spent on **luxuries** such as the Royal Squadron (for air travel) and the Royal Train.

Boosted by the hysteria around the **wedding** of Prince William and Kate Middleton (not to mention the arrival of a new heir to the throne), and the Queen's **Diamond Jubilee** (which coincided with the 2012 Olympics), the Windsors are currently riding high on a wave of good publicity at home. Modernizing continues apace, with female heirs to the throne no longer passed over in preference of younger males, and marriage to a Roman Catholic no longer an issue, although the sovereign still has to be a full-blooded Protestant. However, with none of the mainstream political parties advocating scrapping the monarchy, the royal soap opera looks safe to run for many years to come.

Pall Mall

Running west from Trafalgar Square to St James's Palace, the wide thoroughfare of **Pall Mall** is renowned for its gentlemen's clubs, whose discreet Italianate and Neoclassical facades, fronted by cast-iron torches, still punctuate the street. It gets its bizarre name from the game of *pallo a maglio* (ball to mallet) – something like modern croquet – popularized by Charles II and played here and on The Mall. Crowds gathered here in 1807 when it became London's first gas-lit street – the original lampposts (erected to reduce the opportunities for crime and prostitution) are still standing.

Lower Regent Street

Lower Regent Street, a quarter of the way down Pall Mall, was the first stage in John Nash's ambitious plan to link the Prince Regent's magnificent Carlton House with Regent's Park. Like so many of Nash's grandiose schemes, it never quite came to fruition, as George IV, soon after ascending the throne, decided that Carlton House – the most expensive palace ever to have been built in London – wasn't quite luxurious enough, and had it pulled down. Its Corinthian columns now support the main portico of the National Gallery.

Waterloo Place

Lower Regent Street opens into **Waterloo Place**, which Nash extended beyond Pall Mall once Carlton House had been demolished. At the centre of the square stands the **Crimean War Memorial**, fashioned from captured Russian cannons in 1861, and commemorating the 2152 Foot Guards who died during the Crimean War. The horrors of that conflict were witnessed by Florence Nightingale (see p.220), whose statue – along with that of Sidney Herbert (Secretary at War at the time) – was added in 1914.

South of Pall Mall, Waterloo Place is flanked by St James's two grandest gentlemen's clubs: the former **United Services Club** (now the Institute of Directors), to the east, and the **Athenaeum**, to the west. Their almost identical Neoclassical designs are by Nash's protégé Decimus Burton: the better-looking is the Athenaeum, its portico sporting a garish gilded statue of the goddess Athena and, above, a Wedgwood-type frieze inspired by the Elgin Marbles, which had just arrived in London. The Duke of Wellington was a regular at the United Services Club, and the horse blocks – confusingly positioned outside the Athenaeum – were designed so the duke could mount his steed more easily.

Appropriately enough, an equestrian statue of that eminently clubbable man **Edward VII** stands between the two clubs. More statues line the railings of nearby Waterloo Gardens: **Captain Scott** was sculpted by the widow he left behind after failing to complete the return journey from the South Pole; New Zealander **Keith Park**, the World War I flying ace and RAF commander who organized the fighter defence of London and southeast England during the Battle of Britain, was erected in 2010.

Duke of York's Column

To the south of Waterloo Place, overlooking St James's Park, is the **Duke of York's Column**, erected in 1833, ten years before Nelson's more famous one. The "Grand Old Duke of York", second son of George III, is indeed the one who marched ten thousand men "up to the top of the hill and…marched them down again" in the famous nursery rhyme. The 123ft column was paid for by stopping one day's wages of every soldier in the British Army, and it was said at the time that the column was so high because the duke was trying to escape his creditors, since he died £2 million in debt.

Carlton House Terrace

Having pulled his old palace down, George IV had Nash build **Carlton House Terrace**, whose monumental facade now looks out onto St James's Park. No. 4, by the exquisitely tranquil Carlton Gardens, was handed to de Gaulle for the headquarters of the Free French during World War II; nos. 7–9, by the Duke of York steps, served as the German embassy until World War II. Albert Speer designed the interior under the Nazis, while outside a tiny grave for *ein treuer Begleiter* (a true friend) lurks behind the railings near the column – it holds the remains of **Giro**, the Nazi ambassador's pet Alsatian, accidentally electrocuted in February 1934.

St James's Square

Around the time of George III's birth at no. 31 in 1738, **St James's Square** boasted no fewer than six dukes and seven earls, and over the decades it has maintained its exclusive air: no. 10 was occupied in turn by prime ministers Pitt the Elder, Lord Derby and Gladstone; at no. 16 you'll find the silliest-sounding gentlemen's club, the East India, Devonshire, Sports and Public Schools' Club; no. 4 was home to Nancy Astor, the first woman MP to take her seat in parliament, in 1919; while no. 31 was where Eisenhower formed the first Allied HQ during World War II. The narrowest house on the square (no. 14) is the **London Library**, a private library founded in 1841 by Thomas Carlyle, who got sick of waiting up to two hours for books to be retrieved from the British Library shelves only to find he couldn't borrow them (he used to steal them instead).

The square is no longer residential and, architecturally, it's not quite the period piece it once was, but its proportions remain intact, as do the central **gardens**, which feature an equestrian statue of **William III**, depicted tripping over on the molehill that killed him at Hampton Court. In the northeastern corner, there's a memorial marking the spot where police officer **Yvonne Fletcher** was shot dead in 1984, during a demonstration by Libyan dissidents outside what was then the Libyan embassy, at no. 5. Following the shooting, the embassy was besieged by armed police for eleven days, but in the end the diplomats were simply expelled and no one has ever been charged.

Schomberg House
80–82 Pall Mall

The unusual seventeenth-century mansion of **Schomberg House** is one of the few to stand out on Pall Mall, thanks to its Dutch-style red brickwork and elongated caryatids. In 1769, the house was divided into three, and the artist, Thomas Gainsborough, who was at the height of his fame, lived in no. 80, the western portion, until his death in 1788. Next door, at no. 81, a Scottish quack doctor, James Graham, ran his Temple of Health and Hymen, where couples having trouble conceiving could try their luck in the "grand celestial bed" for £50 a night (a fortune in those days).

79 Pall Mall

Charles II housed **Nell Gwynne** at 79 Pall Mall, and even gave her the freehold, so that the two of them could chat over the garden wall, which once backed onto the grounds of St James's Palace. It was from one of the windows overlooking the garden that Nell is alleged to have dangled her 6-year-old, threatening to drop him if Charles didn't acknowledge paternity and give the boy a title, at which Charles yelled out "Save the Earl of Burford!"; another, more tabloid-style version of the story alleges that Charles was persuaded only after overhearing Nell saying "Come here, you little bastard", then excusing herself on the grounds that she had no other name by which to call him.

Marlborough House

Pall Mall · Visits by guided tour only, of groups of 15 or more · ☎ 020 7747 6500, ⓦ thecommonwealth.org · ⊖ Green Park

Marlborough House itself is hidden from Marlborough Road by a high, brick wall, and only partly visible from The Mall. Queen Anne sacrificed half her garden in granting this land to her lover, Sarah Jennings, Duchess of Marlborough, in 1709. The duchess, in turn, told Wren to design her a "strong, plain and convenient" palace, only to sack him later and finish the plans off herself. The highlight of the interior is the **Blenheim Saloon**, with its frescoes depicting the first duke's eponymous victory, along with ceiling paintings by Gentileschi transferred from the Queen's House in Greenwich. The royals took over the building in 1817, though the last one to live here was Queen Mary, wife of George V. Since 1965, the palace has been the headquarters of the Commonwealth Secretariat, and can only be visited on a guided tour.

THE GENTLEMEN'S CLUBS

The **gentlemen's clubs** of Pall Mall and St James's Street remain the final bastions of the male chauvinism and public-school snobbery for which England is famous. Their origins lie in the coffee- and chocolate-houses of the eighteenth century, though the majority were founded in the post-Napoleonic peace of the early nineteenth century by those who yearned for the life of the officers' mess; drinking, whoring and gambling were the major features of early club life. **White's** – the oldest of the lot, and with a list of members that still includes numerous royals (Prince Charles held his [first] stag party here) – used to be the unofficial Tory party headquarters, renowned for its high gambling stakes, while, opposite, was the Whigs' favourite club, **Brooks's**. Bets were wagered over the most trivial of things to relieve the boredom – "a thousand meadows and cornfields were staked at every throw" – and in 1755 one MP, Sir John Bland, shot himself after losing £32,000 in one night.

In their day, the clubs were also the battleground of sartorial elegance, particularly **Boodle's**, in whose bay window the dandy-in-chief Beau Brummell set the fashion trends for the London upper class and provided endless fuel for gossip. It was said that Brummell's greatest achievement in life was his starched neckcloth, and that the Prince Regent himself wept openly when Brummell criticized the line of his cravat. More serious political disputes were played out in clubland, too. The **Reform Club** on Pall Mall, from which Phileas Fogg set off in Jules Verne's *Around the World in Eighty Days*, was the gathering place of the liberals behind the 1832 Reform Act, and remains one of the more "progressive" – it was one of the first to admit women as members in 1981. The Tories, led by Wellington, countered by starting up the **Carlton Club** for those opposed to the Act – bombed by the IRA in 1990, it's still the leading Conservative club, and only admitted women as full members in 2008 (Mrs Thatcher was made an honorary member).

St James's Palace

St James's Palace was built on the site of a lepers' hospital which Henry VIII bought in 1532. Bloody Mary died here in 1558 (her heart and bowels were buried in the Chapel Royal), and it was here that Charles I chose to sleep the night before his execution, so as not to listen to his scaffold being erected. When Whitehall Palace burnt down in 1698, St James's became the principal royal residence and even today it remains the official residence, with every ambassador to the UK accredited to the "Court of St James's", even though the monarchy moved over to Buckingham Palace in 1837. The main red-brick gate-tower, which looks out on to St James's Street, is a survivor from Tudor times; the rest of the modest, rambling, crenellated complex was restored and remodelled by Nash, and now provides a home for Princess Anne and Princess Alexandra and for the staff of princes William and Harry.

Chapel Royal

Open for services only: Oct to Easter Sun 8.30am & 11.15am · ⊖ Green Park

St James's Palace is off-limits to the public, with the exception of the **Chapel Royal**, which is accessed from Cleveland Row. Charles I took Holy Communion in the chapel on the morning of his execution, and here, too, the marriages of William and Mary, George III and Queen Charlotte, Victoria and Albert and George V and Queen Mary took place. One of the few remaining sections of Henry VIII's palace, it was redecorated in the 1830s, though the gilded strap-work ceiling matches the Tudor original erected to commemorate the brief marriage of Henry and Anne of Cleves (and thought to have been the work of Hans Holbein). The chapel's musical pedigree is impressive, with Tallis, Byrd, Gibbons and Purcell all having worked here as organists. Purcell even had rooms in the palace, which the poet Dryden used to use in order to hide from his creditors.

Queen's Chapel

Open for services only: Easter to July Sun 8.30am & 11.15am · ⊖ Green Park

Despite being on the other side of Marlborough Road, the **Queen's Chapel** is officially part of St James's Palace. A perfectly proportioned classical church, it was designed by Inigo Jones (with Gibbons and Wren helping with the decoration) for the Infanta of Spain, intended child bride of Charles I, and later completed for his French wife, Henrietta Maria, who was also a practising Catholic. A little further down Marlborough Road is the glorious Art Nouveau memorial to **Queen Alexandra** (wife of Edward VII), the last work of Alfred Gilbert (of Eros fame), comprising a bronze fountain crammed with allegorical figures and flanked by robust lampposts.

Clarence House

Aug Mon–Fri 10am–4pm, Sat & Sun 10am–5.30pm · £9 · ☎ 020 7766 7303, ⓦ royalcollection.org.uk · ⊖ Green Park

John Nash was also responsible for **Clarence House**, which is attached to the southwest wing of St James's Palace. Built in the 1820s for William IV and used as his principal residence, it was occupied by various royals until the death of George VI, after which it became the home of the Queen Mother, George's widow for nearly sixty years. It's currently the official London home of Charles and Camilla (ⓦ princeofwales.gov.uk), but a handful of rooms can be visited over the summer when the royals are in Scotland. Visits (by guided tour) must be booked in advance, as they are extremely popular. The rooms are pretty unremarkable, so apart from a peek behind the scenes in a working royal palace, or a few mementoes of the Queen Mum, the main draw is the twentieth-century British paintings on display by the likes of Walter Sickert and Augustus John.

St James's Street and Jermyn Street

St James's Street and **Jermyn Street** (pronounced "German Street"), have been, along with Savile Row in Mayfair, the spiritual home of English gentlemen's fashion since the

HIDDEN GEMS: SHOPS AND SIGNAGE

As you stroll along St James's and Jermyn streets keep an eye out for some of the unique shops and signs – antiquated epithets are part of Jermyn Street's quaint appeal – including:

Berry Brothers 3 St James's St. The oldest wine merchants in the world, with acres of cellars, and a sloping wooden floor of great antiquity.

James Lock & Co 6 St James's St. The first hatters to sell a bowler hat, they have the Duke of Wellington's hat on display, alongside a replica of the cocked hat they made for Nelson.

Fox of St James 19 St James's St. Fox supplied Winston Churchill with his cigars and Oscar Wilde with Sobranie cigarettes – there's a small museum inside and a smoking room for sampling the wares.

Turnbull & Asser 71–72 Jermyn St. Describe themselves as "Hosiers & Glovers".

Bates the hatters, housed within the shirtmakers **Hadditch & Key**, 73 Jermyn St. Bates still displays Binks, the stray cat which entered the shop in 1921 and never left, having been stuffed, sporting a cigar and top hat, and in a glass cabinet.

Taylor 74 Jermyn St. These barber's are dubbed "Gentlemen's Court Hairdresser".

Foster & So 85 Jermyn St. A shoe shop that styles themselves as "Bootmakers since 1840".

Floris 89 Jermyn St. Renowned for covering up the Royal Family's body odour with its ever-so-English fragrances.

Paxton & Whitfield 93 Jermyn St. Boasts an unrivalled selection of cheeses.

advent of the clubs (see box, p.73). The window displays and wooden-panelled interiors (see box above) still evoke an age when mass consumerism was unthinkable, and when it was considered that gentlemen "should either be a work of art or wear a work of art", as Oscar Wilde put it.

Green Park

Green Park was established by Henry VIII on the burial ground of the old lepers' hospital that became St James's Palace. It was left more or less flowerless – hence its name (officially "The Green Park") – and, apart from the springtime swathes of daffodils and crocuses, it remains mostly meadow, shaded by graceful London plane trees. In its time, however, it was a popular place for duels (banned from neighbouring St James's Park), ballooning and fireworks displays. One such display was immortalized by Handel's *Music for the Royal Fireworks*, performed here on April 27, 1749, to celebrate the Peace of Aix-la-Chapelle, which ended the War of the Austrian Succession – over ten thousand fireworks were let off, setting fire to the custom-built Temple of Peace and causing three fatalities. The music was a great success, however.

Along the east side of the park runs the wide, pedestrian-only **Queen's Walk**, laid out for Queen Caroline, wife of George II, who had a little pavilion built nearby. At its southern end, there's a good view of **Lancaster House** (closed to the public), a grand Neoclassical palace built in rich Bath stone in the 1820s by Benjamin Wyatt, and used for government receptions and conferences since 1913.

Spencer House

St James's Place • Feb–July & Sept–Dec Sun 10.30am–5.45pm • £12, no under-10s • ☎020 7499 8620, ⓦspencerhouse.co.uk • ⊖ Green Park

A sign in the garden backing onto Queen's Walk announces Princess Diana's ancestral home, **Spencer House**, one of London's finest Palladian mansions. Erected in the 1750s, its best-looking facade looks out over Queen's Walk to Green Park, though access is from St James's Place. Inside, tour guides take you through nine of the state rooms, returned to something like their original condition by current owners, the Rothschilds. The Great Room features a stunning coved and coffered ceiling in green, white and gold, while the adjacent Painted Room is a feast of Neoclassicism, decorated with murals in the "Pompeian manner". The most outrageous decor, though, is in Lord Spencer's Room, with its astonishing gilded palm-tree columns.

Mayfair

Although shops, offices, embassies and hotels outnumber aristocratic pieds-à-terre nowadays, the social cachet of the luxury apartments and mews houses of Mayfair has remained much the same. This is, after all, where the fictional Bertie Wooster – the perfect upper-class Englishman – and his faithful valet Jeeves, of P.G. Wodehouse's interwar novels, lived. Piccadilly may not be the fashionable promenade it once was, but a whiff of exclusivity still pervades Bond Street and its tributaries, where designer clothes emporia jostle for space with jewellers, bespoke tailors and fine art dealers. Most Londoners, however, stick to Regent and Oxford streets, home to the flagship branches of the country's most popular chain stores and heart of the West End in terms of shopping.

Along with neighbouring St James's and Marylebone, **Mayfair** emerged in the eighteenth century as one of London's first real residential suburbs. Sheep and cattle were driven off the land by the area's big landowners (the largest of whom were the Grosvenor family, whose head is the Duke of Westminster, Britain's richest man) to make way for London's first major planned development: a web of brick-and-stucco terraces and grid-plan streets feeding into a trio of grand, formal squares, with mews and stables round the back. The name comes from the infamous fifteen-day fair, which bit the dust in 1764 after the newly ensconced wealthy residents complained of the "drunkenness, fornication, gaming and lewdness". Mayfair quickly began to attract aristocratic London away from hitherto fashionable Covent Garden and Soho, and set the westward trend for upper-middle-class migration.

Piccadilly Circus

Tacky and congested it may be, but for many visitors, Piccadilly Circus is up there with Trafalgar Square as a candidate for London's city centre. A much-altered product of Nash's grand 1812 **Regent Street** plan, and now a major bottleneck, with traffic from Piccadilly, Shaftesbury Avenue and Regent Street all converging, it's by no means a picturesque place, and is probably best seen at night, when the spread of illuminated signs (a feature since the Edwardian era) gives it a touch of Times Square dazzle, and when the human traffic flow is at its most frenetic.

3

As well as being the gateway to the West End, this is also prime tourist territory, thanks mostly to the celebrated Shaftesbury Memorial, popularly known as **Eros**. The fountain's aluminium archer is one of London's top tourist attractions, a status that baffles all who live here – when it was first unveiled in 1893, it was so unpopular that the sculptor, Alfred Gilbert, lived in self-imposed exile for the next thirty years. The figure depicted is not Eros, but his lesser-known brother Anteros, who was the god of requited love, although in this case he commemorates the selfless philanthropic love of the Earl of Shaftesbury, a Bible-thumping social reformer who campaigned against child labour.

Behind Eros, it's worth popping in to **The Criterion** restaurant, at no. 224 Piccadilly, just for a drink, so you can soak in probably the most spectacular Victorian interior in London, with its Byzantine-style gilded mosaic ceiling.

Trocadero

Piccadilly Circus · Daily 10am–midnight, Fri & Sat until 1am · ☎ 020 7439 1719, Ⓦ londontrocadero.com · ⊖ Piccadilly Circus

Just east of the Circus, **Trocadero** was originally an opulent restaurant, from 1896 until its closure in 1965. Since then, millions have been poured into this glorified amusement arcade, casino and multiplex cinema, in an unsuccessful attempt to find a winning formula. Much of the building is currently being gutted and redeveloped to include London's first Tokyo-style pod hotel, with over 580 windowless rooms.

Ripley's Believe It or Not!

Piccadilly Circus · Daily 10am–10.30pm · £25 · ☎ 020 3238 0022, Ⓦ ripleyslondon.com · ⊖ Piccadilly Circus

Next door to Trocadero, in what was once the London Pavilion music hall, is the world's largest branch of **Ripley's Believe It or Not!**, which bills itself as an odditorium. It's half waxworks, half old-fashioned Victorian freak show, with a mirror maze and laser maze thrown in for good measure. Delights on display include shrunken heads and dinosaur eggs, a chewing gum sculpture of the Fab Four and Tower Bridge rendered in 264,345 matchsticks. Book online to save a few pounds off the stratospheric admission charge.

Regent Street

Regent Street was drawn up by John Nash in 1812 as both a luxury shopping street and a triumphal way between George IV's (now demolished) Carlton House and

Regent's Park to the north. It was the city's first stab at slum clearance, creating a tangible borderline to shore up fashionable Mayfair against the chaotic maze of neighbouring Soho. Today, it's still possible to admire the stately intentions of Nash's plan, even though the original arcading of the **Quadrant**, which curves westwards from Piccadilly Circus, is no longer there.

Regent Street enjoyed eighty years as Bond Street's nearest rival, before the rise of the city's middle classes ushered in heavyweight stores catering for the masses. Two of the oldest established stores can be found close to one another on the east side of the street: **Hamleys**, which claims to be the world's largest toy shop, and **Liberty**, the department store that popularized Arts and Crafts designs. Liberty's famous mock-Tudor entrance, added in the 1920s, is round the corner on Great Marlborough Street – inside there's a central roof-lit well, surrounded by wooden galleries carved from the timbers of two old naval battleships.

● SHOPS							● CAFÉS	
& Other Stories	6	Fortnum & Mason	13	Liberty	7	Vivienne Westwood	9	Claridge's	3
Alexander McQueen	12	Hamleys	8	Marks & Spencer	1	Waterstones	15	Fortnum & Mason	11
Browns	3	Hatchard's	14	Selfridges	2	Wolf and Badger	10	MoCafé	7
Dover Street Market	11	John Lewis	4	Topshop	5			The Ritz	9

● RESTAURANTS	
Kiku	8
Little Social	4
Rasa W1	2
Truc Vert	1
Wild Honey	5

■ PUBS & BARS	
Audley	1
The Windmill	2
Ye Grapes	3

Tibits — 6
The Wolseley — 10

> **MONOPOLY**
>
> Although **Monopoly** was patented during the Depression by an American, Charles Darrow, it was the British who really took to the game, and the UK version was the one used in the rest of the world outside of the US. In 1935, to choose appropriate streets and stations for the game, the company director of Waddington's in Leeds sent his son, Norman Watson, and his secretary, Marjorie Phillips, on a day-trip to London. They came up with an odd assortment, ranging from the bottom-ranking Old Kent Road (still as tatty as ever) to an obscure dead-end street in the West End (Vine Street), and chose only northern train stations. All the properties have gone up in value since the board's inception (six zeros need to be added to most), but Mayfair and Park Lane (its western border), the most expensive properties, are still aspirational addresses.

Piccadilly

Piccadilly apparently got its name from a local resident who manufactured the ruffs or "pickadills" worn by the dandies of the late seventeenth century. Despite its fashionable pedigree, it's no place for promenading in its current state, with traffic careering down it nose to tail most of the day and night. Infinitely more pleasant places to window-shop are the **nineteenth-century arcades**, built to protect shoppers from the mud and horse dung on the streets, but now equally useful for escaping exhaust fumes.

Waterstones and Hatchard's

One of the most striking shops on Piccadilly, at nos. 203–206, is the sleek modernist 1930s facade of Simpsons department store, now the multistorey flagship bookstore of **Waterstones**. While Piccadilly may not be the shopping heaven it once was, it still harbours several old firms that proudly display their royal warrants. London's oldest bookshop, **Hatchard's**, at no. 187, was founded in 1797, as a cross between a gentlemen's club and a library, with benches outside for servants and daily papers inside for the gentlemen to peruse. Today, it's a sister branch of Waterstones, elegant still, but with its old traditions marked most overtly by an unrivalled section on international royalty.

St James's Church

197 Piccadilly • ☎ 020 7734 4511, ⓦ sjp.org.uk • ⊖ Piccadilly Circus

Halfway along the south side of Piccadilly stands **St James's Church**, Wren's favourite parish church (he built it himself). The church has rich furnishings, with the limewood reredos, organ-casing and marble font all by the master sculptor **Grinling Gibbons**. St James's is a radical campaigning church, which runs a daily craft market (Tues–Sat) and a café at the west end of the church; it also puts on top-class, free lunchtime concerts and regularly displays contemporary outdoor sculptures in the churchyard.

Fortnum & Mason

181 Piccadilly • Mon–Sat 10am–8pm, Sun noon–6pm • ☎ 020 7734 8040, ⓦ fortnumandmason.com • ⊖ Green Park or Piccadilly Circus

One of Piccadilly's oldest institutions is **Fortnum & Mason**, the food emporium established in 1707 by Hugh Mason (who used to run a stall at St James's market) and William Fortnum (one of Queen Anne's footmen). Over the main entrance, the figures of its founders bow to each other on the hour as the clock clanks out the Eton school anthem – a kitsch addition from 1964. The store is most famous for its opulent food hall and its picnic hampers, first introduced as "concentrated lunches" for hunting and shooting parties, and now *de rigueur* for Ascot, Glyndebourne, Henley and other society events. Fortnum's is credited with the invention of the Scotch egg in 1851, and was also the first store in the world to sell Heinz baked beans in 1886.

Albany

One palatial Piccadilly residence that has avoided redevelopment is **Albany**, a plain, H-shaped Georgian mansion, designed by William Chambers, neatly recessed behind

---

THE SUMMER EXHIBITION

The most famous event in the Royal Academy's calendar is the **Summer Exhibition**, which has been held annually since 1769, and runs from June to mid-August. It's an odd event: anyone can enter paintings in any style. Around ten thousand entries are surveyed (at considerable speed) by the RA's Hanging Committee (great name) and around one thousand lucky winners get hung, in extremely close proximity, and sold. In addition, the eighty "Academicians" are allowed to display up to six of their own works – no matter how awful. The result is a bewildering display, which gets annually panned by the critics. However, with thirty percent of the purchase price going to the RA, it generates at least £2 million in income.

---

its own iron railings and courtyard, next door to the Royal Academy. Built in the 1770s for Lord Melbourne, it was divided in 1802 into a series of self-contained bachelor "sets" for members of the nearby gentlemen's clubs too drunk to make it home. Only those who had no connections with trade, and did not keep a musical instrument or a wife, were permitted to live here, and over the years they have been occupied by such literary figures as Byron, Gladstone, J.B. Priestley, Aldous Huxley, Patrick Hamilton and Graham Greene.

Royal Academy of the Arts

Burlington House, Piccadilly • Daily 10am–6pm, Fri until 10pm • £10–15 • John Madejski Fine Rooms guided tours Tues 1pm, Wed–Fri 1 & 3pm, Sat 11.30am; free • ☎ 020 7300 8000, ⓦ royalacademy.org.uk • ⊖ Green Park

The **Royal Academy of Arts** occupies Burlington House, one of the few survivors from the ranks of aristocratic mansions that once lined the north side of Piccadilly. Rebuilding in the nineteenth century destroyed the original curved colonnades beyond the main gateway, but the complex has kept the feel of a Palladian *palazzo*. The academy itself was the country's first formal art school, founded in 1768 by a group of painters including Thomas Gainsborough and Joshua Reynolds. Reynolds went on to become the academy's first president, and his statue now stands in the courtyard, palette in hand ready to paint the cars hurtling down Piccadilly.

The academy's alumni range from Turner and Constable to Hockney and Tracey Emin, though the college has always had a conservative reputation for both its teaching and its shows. As well as hosting exhibitions, the RA has a small selection of works from its permanent collection in the white and gold **John Madejski Fine Rooms**. Highlights include a Rembrandtesque self-portrait by Reynolds, plus works by the likes of Constable, Hockney and Stanley Spencer. To see the gallery's most valuable asset, Michelangelo's marble relief, the *Taddei Tondo*, head for the narrow glass atrium of Norman Foster's Sackler Galleries, at the back of the building.

The Wolseley and the Ritz

On the south side of Piccadilly, on the corner of Arlington Street, **The Wolseley** is a superb Art Deco building, originally built as a Wolseley car showroom in the 1920s, now a café (see p.367). The most striking original features are the zigzag inlaid marble flooring, the chinoiserie woodwork and the giant red Japanese lacquer columns. Across St James's Street, with its best rooms overlooking Green Park, stands the **Ritz Hotel**, famous for its afternoon teas (see p.377) and a byword for decadence since it first wowed Edwardian society in 1906. The hotel's design, with its two-storey French-style mansard roof and long arcade, was based on the rue de Rivoli in Paris.

Burlington Arcade

Mon–Wed & Fri 8am–6.30pm, Thurs 8am–7pm, Sat 9am–6.30pm, Sun 11am–5pm • Free • ⓦ burlington-arcade.co.uk • ⊖ Green Park

Along the side of the Royal Academy runs the **Burlington Arcade**, London's first shopping arcade, built in 1819 for Lord Cavendish, then owner of Burlington House, to prevent commoners throwing rubbish into his garden. Today, it's London's longest and most expensive nineteenth-century arcade, lined with mahogany-fronted luxury shops, including Linley, run by the Queen's nephew. Upholding Regency decorum, it's still illegal to whistle, sing, hum, hurry or carry large packages or open umbrellas on this small stretch, and the arcade's beadles (known as Burlington Berties), in their Edwardian frock coats and gold-braided top hats, take the prevention of such criminality very seriously.

Piccadilly and Princes arcades

ⓦ piccadillyarcade.com, ⓦ princesarcade.com • ⊖ Green Park or Piccadilly Circus

Neither of Piccadilly's other two arcades can hold a torch to the Burlington, though they are still worth exploring if only to marvel at the strange mixture of shops. The finer of the two is the **Piccadilly Arcade**, an Edwardian extension to the Burlington on the south side of Piccadilly, whose squeaky-clean bow windows display, among other items, Russian icons, model soldiers and buttons and cufflinks supplied to Prince Charles. The **Princes Arcade**, to the east, exudes a more discreet Neoclassical elegance and contains Prestat, purveyors of handmade, hand-packed chocolates and truffles to the Queen.

Bond Street

Bond Street runs more or less parallel to Regent Street, extending north from Piccadilly all the way to Oxford Street. It is, in fact, two streets rolled into one: the southern half, laid out in the 1680s, is known as **Old Bond Street**; its northern extension, which followed less than fifty years later, is known as **New Bond Street**. In contrast to their international rivals, rue de Rivoli and Fifth Avenue, both Bond streets are pretty unassuming architecturally – a mixture of modest Georgian and Victorian townhouses – but the shops that line them are among the flashiest in London.

Bond Street shops

Unlike its overtly masculine counterpart, Jermyn Street (see p.74), **Bond Street** caters for both sexes, and although it has its fair share of old-established names, it's also home to flagship branches of multinational **designer clothes** outlets like Prada, D&G, Versace, Chanel and so on. This designer madness also spills over into **Conduit Street**, home to Issey Miyake, Vivienne Westwood and Moschino, not to mention Rigby & Peller, corsetieres to the Queen, as well as into neighbouring Dover Street, where Comme des Garçons have a vast indoor fashion bazaar at nos. 17–18.

Bond Street also has its fair share of perfumeries and **jewellers**, many of them long-established outlets that have survived the vicissitudes of fashion, and some, like De Beers, relatively recent arrivals. One of the most famous is **Asprey**, founded in 1781 by a family of Huguenot craftsmen, and now jewellers to the royals. The facade of the store, at no. 167, features a wonderful parade of arched windows, flanked by slender Corinthian wrought-iron columns. Close by is *Allies*, a popular double statue of **Winston Churchill and President Roosevelt**, enjoying a chat on a bench – you can squeeze between the two of them, in the space where Stalin should be, for a photo opportunity.

Auction houses and art galleries

In addition to fashion, Bond Street is renowned for its **auction houses** (see box, p.82) and **art galleries**, although the latter are actually outnumbered by those on neighbouring **Cork Street**. The main difference between the two is that the Bond Street dealers are basically heirloom offloaders, where you might catch an Old Master or an Impressionist masterpiece, whereas Cork Street galleries and others dotted throughout Mayfair – such as the Mason's Yard outpost of White Cube (see p.234) – show largely contemporary art.

3

AUCTION HOUSES

A very Mayfair-style entertainment lies in visiting the area's trio of auction houses. **Sotheby's**, 34–35 New Bond St (☎020 7293 5000, ⓦsothebys.com), was founded in 1744 and is the oldest of the three (and the fourth oldest in the world), though its pre-eminence only really dates from the last war. Above the doorway of Sotheby's is London's oldest outdoor sculpture, an Egyptian statue dating from 1600 BC. **Bonhams**, founded in 1793 (and now merged with Phillips), is at 101 New Bond St (☎020 7447 7447, ⓦbonhams.com); and **Christie's**, founded in 1766, and now the world's largest auction house, is actually over in St James's at 8 King St (☎020 7839 9060, ⓦchristies.com).

Viewing takes place from Monday to Friday, and also occasionally at the weekend, and entry to the galleries is free of charge, though if you don't buy a catalogue, the only information you'll glean is the lot number. Thousands of the works that pass through the rooms are of museum quality, and, if you're lucky, you might catch a glimpse of a masterpiece in transit between private collections. Anyone can attend the auctions themselves, though remember to keep your hands firmly out of view unless you're bidding.

Sotheby's is probably the least intimidating: there's an excellent **café**, and staff offer free valuations, if you have an heirloom of your own to check out. There's always a line of people unwrapping items under the polite gaze of valuation staff, who call in the experts if they see something that sniffs of real money. Only Bonhams remains British-owned; Christie's and Sotheby's, once quintessentially English institutions, are now under French and US control.

Smythson

40 New Bond St • Mon–Wed & Fri 9.30am–6pm, Thurs 10am–7pm, Sat 10am–6pm • ⓦsmythson.com • ⊖ Bond Street

One Bond Street institution you can feel free to walk into is **Smythson**, the bespoke stationers, founded in 1887, who made their name printing Big Game books for colonialists to record what they'd bagged out in Africa and India. At the back of the shop is a small octagonal museum encrusted with shells and mirrors, and a few artefacts: photos and replicas of the book of condolence Smythson created for JFK's funeral, and the cherry calf-and-vellum diary given to Princess Grace of Monaco as a wedding gift.

Albemarle Street

Running parallel to Bond Street to the west, is **Albemarle Street**, connected by the **Royal Arcade**, a short High Victorian shopping mall with tall arched bays and an elegant glass roof, with garish orange-and-white plasterwork entrances at either end. It was designed so that the wealthy guests of nearby **Brown's** hotel could have a sheltered and suitably elegant approach to the shops on Bond Street. Apart from being a posh hotel opened in the 1830s by James Brown, Byron's former valet, *Brown's* is famous as the place where the country's first telephone call was placed by **Alexander Graham Bell** in 1876, though initially he got a crossed line with a private telegraph wire. Also in Albemarle Street, at no. 50, are the offices of **John Murray**, the publishers of Byron and of the oldest British travel guides. It was here in 1824 that Byron's memoirs were burnt to cinders, after Murray persuaded Tom Moore, to whom they had been bequeathed, that they were too scurrilous to publish.

Royal Institution

21 Albermarle St • Mon–Fri 9am–6pm • Free • ☎020 7409 2992, ⓦrigb.org • ⊖ Green Park

The weighty Neoclassical facade at 21 Albermarle Street heralds the **Royal Institution**, a scientific body founded in 1799 "for teaching by courses of philosophical lectures and experiments the application of science to the common purposes of life". The RI is best known for its six Christmas Lectures, begun by Michael Faraday and designed to popularize science among schoolchildren, but it also houses an enjoyable interactive **museum** aimed at both kids and adults. In the basement, you can learn about the ten chemical elements that have been discovered at the RI, and about the famous experiments that have taken place here: Tyndall's blue-sky tube, Humphry Davy's early lamps and

Faraday's explorations into electromagnetism – there's even a reconstruction of Faraday's lab from the 1850s. The ground floor has displays on the fourteen Nobel Prize winners who have worked at the RI, while on the first floor, you can visit the semicircular hall where the Christmas Lectures take place and see some of the apparatus used in lectures over the decades. There's also a great café-bar-restaurant on the ground floor.

Savile Row

Running parallel with New Bond Street, to the east, **Savile Row** has been *the* place to go for bespoke tailors since the early nineteenth century. Gieves & Hawkes, at no. 1, were the first to establish themselves here back in 1785, with Nelson and Wellington among their first customers – they made the military uniform worn by Prince William at his wedding. More modern in outlook, Kilgour, at no. 8, famously made Fred Astaire's morning coat for *Top Hat*, helping to popularize Savile Row tailoring in the US. Henry Poole & Co, who moved to no. 15 in 1846 and has cut suits for the likes of Napoleon III, Dickens, Churchill and de Gaulle, invented the short smoking jacket (originally designed for the future Edward VII), later popularized as the "tuxedo".

Savile Row also has connections with the pop world. **The Beatles** used to buy their suits from Tommy Nutter's House of Nutter established in 1968 at no. 35, and in the same year set up the offices and recording studio of their record label **Apple** at no. 3, until the building's near physical collapse in 1972. On January 30, 1969, The Beatles gave an impromptu gig (their last live performance) on the roof here, stopping traffic and eventually attracting the attentions of the local police – as captured on film in *Let It Be*. More recently feathers have been ruffled in the street by the arrival of the American label, Abercrombie & Fitch, at the southern end of Savile Row, with its trademark semi-nude shop assistants.

Mayfair's squares

Mayfair has three showpiece Georgian squares: **Hanover**, the most modest of the three, **Berkeley,** and **Grosvenor**, the most grandiose, named after the district's two big private landowners. Planned as purely residential, all have suffered over the years, and have nothing like the homogeneity of the Bloomsbury squares. Nevertheless, they are still impressive urban spaces, and their social lustre remains more or less untarnished. Each one is worth visiting, and travelling between them gives you a chance to experience Mayfair's backstreets and, en route, visit one or two hidden sights.

St George's Church, Hanover Square

1–2 Hanover Square • Mon–Fri 8am–4pm, Wed till–6pm, Sun 8am–noon • Free • ⓦ stgeorgeshanoversquare.org • ⊖ Bond Street

At the very southern tip of **Hanover Square** stands the Corinthian portico of **St George's Church**, the first of its kind in London when it was built in the 1720s. Nicknamed "London's Temple of Hymen", it has long been Mayfair's most fashionable church for weddings. Among those who tied the knot here are the Shelleys, Benjamin Disraeli, Teddy Roosevelt and George Eliot. The composer, Handel, a confirmed bachelor, was a warden here for many years and even had his own pew. North of the church, the funnel-shaped St George Street splays into the square itself, which used to boast the old Hanover Square Rooms venue, where Bach, Liszt, Haydn and Paganini all performed before the building's demolition in 1900.

Handel House Museum

25 Brook St • Tues–Sat 10am–6pm, Thurs till 8pm, Sun noon–6pm • £6 • ☎ 020 7495 1685, ⓦ handelhouse.org • ⊖ Bond Street

The **Handel House Museum**, one block west of Hanover Square, is where the composer Handel lived for 36 years from 1723 until his death. He used the ground floor as a shop where subscribers could buy scores, while on the first floor, there was a rehearsal and performance room, plus a composition room at the back. The museum has few original artefacts, but the house has been redecorated to how it would have looked in Handel's day. Further atmosphere is provided by the harpsichord students who often practise in the rehearsal room; to find out about the regular recitals, visit the website. Access to the house is via the chic, cobbled yard at the back of the house.

Berkeley Square

Berkeley Square is where, according to the music-hall song, nightingales sing (though it's probable they were, in fact, blackcaps). Laid out in the 1730s, only the west side of the square has any surviving Georgian houses to boast of, including Maggs, at no. 50, the oldest antiquarian booksellers in the world – they also sell signatures and famously bought Napoleon's penis in 1916. A few doors up, in the basement of the Georgian mansion at no. 44, is *Annabel's*, the nightclub where Princess Diana and Sarah Ferguson turned up, dressed as a police officer and a traffic warden, and were refused entry on the grounds that no uniforms were allowed inside. What saves the square aesthetically, however, is its wonderful parade of two hundred-year-old **London plane trees**. With their dappled, exfoliating trunks, giant lobed leaves and globular spiky fruits, these pollution-resistant trees are a ubiquitous feature of the city, and Berkeley Square's specimens are among the finest. The square has further royal connections, as the Queen was born just off it, at 17 Bruton St, and then lived at 145 Piccadilly until 1936.

Bourdon House: Alfred Dunhill

2 Davies St • Mon–Sat 10am–7pm • ☎ 020 7853 4440, ⓦ dunhill.com • ⊖ Bond Street

Just north of Berkeley Square, it's possible to see inside **Bourdon House**, a lovely Georgian mansion on the corner of Davies and Bourdon streets. Former private

---

HANDEL AND HENDRIX

Born **Georg Friedrich Händel** (1685–1759) in Halle, Saxony, Handel first visited London in 1710, composing *Rinaldo* in fifteen days flat. The furore it produced – not least when Handel released a flock of sparrows for one aria – made him a household name. The following year he was commissioned to write several works for Queen Anne, eventually becoming court composer to George I, his one-time patron in Hanover.

London quickly became Handel's permanent home: he anglicized his name and nationality and lived out the rest of his life here, producing all the work for which he is now best known, including the *Water Music*, the *Fireworks Music* and his *Messiah*, which failed to enthral its first audiences, but which is now one of the great set pieces of Protestant musical culture. George II was so moved by the *Hallelujah Chorus* that he leapt to his feet and remained standing for the entire performance. Handel himself fainted during a performance in 1759, and died shortly afterwards in his home, now a museum (see p.83); he is buried in Westminster Abbey. Today, Handel's birthday is celebrated with a concert at the Foundling Museum (see p.123), and an annual Handel Festival (ⓦ london-handel-festival.com) takes place annually at St George's Church, Hanover Square (see p.83).

Two centuries later, **Jimi Hendrix** (1942–70) moved into the top-floor flat of 23 Brook St, next door to Handel's old address, and lived there for eighteen months or so. Born in Seattle in 1942, Hendrix was persuaded to fly over to London in 1966 by The Animals. Shortly after arriving, he teamed up with two British musicians, Noel Redding and Mitch Mitchell, and formed The Jimi Hendrix Experience. It was at the beginning of 1969 that Hendrix moved into Brook Street with his girlfriend, Kathy Etchingham; apparently he was much taken with the fact that it was once Handel's residence, ordering Kathy to go and buy some Handel albums for him. It was also in London that Hendrix met his untimely death, on September 18, 1970. At the *Samarkand Hotel* in Notting Hill, after a gig at *Ronnie Scott's* in Soho, Hendrix, with alcohol still in his system, swallowed a handful of sleeping pills, later vomiting in his sleep and slipping into unconsciousness. He was pronounced dead on arrival at St Mary's Hospital, Paddington, and is buried in Seattle.

residence of the Duke of Westminster, the house is now the flagship store of **Alfred Dunhill**. As well as a shop, Dunhill's has a bar, a barber's and a screening room where they show classy masculine documentaries. On the first floor, they display a few items from the days of Dunhill Motorities, gadget suppliers to Rolls Royce, whose slogan was "everything but the motor". This wonderful range made hip flasks disguised as books, "Bobby Finders" for detecting police cars, in-car hookahs and even a motorist's pipe with a windshield for open-top toking.

Grosvenor Square

Grosvenor Square is the largest of Mayfair's squares. Its American connections go back to 1785, when John Adams (future US President) established the first American embassy in a house in the northeast corner. During World War II, it was known as "Little America" – General Eisenhower, whose statue stands in the square, ran the D-Day campaign from no. 20. As well as Eisenhower, there are statues of Roosevelt and Reagan, and a memorial garden dedicated to the 67 British victims of 9/11. The entire west side of the square is occupied by the monstrous, heavily guarded **US Embassy**, built in 1960. The embassy is watched over by a giant gilded aluminium eagle and has been the victim of numerous attacks over the decades. The first major incident occurred in 1967 when Spanish anarchists machine-gunned the embassy in protest against US collaboration with Franco. The most famous (and violent) protest took place in 1968, when a demonstration against US involvement in Vietnam turned into a riot. Mick Jagger, so the story goes, was innocently signing autographs in his Bentley at the time, and later wrote *Street Fighting Man*, inspired by what he witnessed. Most weeks, there's some group or other camped out objecting to US foreign policy – in fact, American security concerns are such that in 2016, the embassy will move to a purpose-built $1 billion complex near Vauxhall.

3

Claridge's

49 Brook St • ☎ 020 7629 8860, ⓦ claridges.co.uk • ⊖ Bond Street

Claridge's started out in 1812 as *Mivart's Hotel* in a small terraced house, but has grown considerably larger since those days. The current building dates from 1898, has over two hundred rooms, a Gordon Ramsay restaurant, and still attracts Hollywood and pop glitterati from Brad Pitt to U2. Its royal connections are also second to none. Most famously, King Peter II of Yugoslavia spent most of World War II in exile at the hotel – suite 212 was ceded to Yugoslavia for a day on June 17, 1945 so that his son and heir, Crown Prince Alexander, could be born on Yugoslav soil. A room in the hotel, painted "whorehouse pink", served as General Eisenhower's initial wartime pied-à-terre, and it was also the wartime hangout of the OSS, forerunner of the CIA. It was here in 1943 that Szmul Zygielbojm, from the Polish government-in-exile, was told that Roosevelt had refused his request to bomb the rail lines leading to Auschwitz; the following day he committed suicide.

Grosvenor Chapel

24 South Audley St • Mon, Tues, Thurs & Fri 9am–1pm • Free • ☎ 020 7499 1684, ⓦ grosvenorchapel.org.uk • ⊖ Bond Street or Green Park

American troops stationed in Britain used to worship at the **Grosvenor Chapel**, two blocks south of *Claridge's* on South Audley Street, a simple classical building that formed the model for early settlers' churches in New England and is still popular with the American community. The church's most illustrious corpse is radical MP John Wilkes ("Wilkes and Liberty" was the battle cry of many a mid-eighteenth-century riot). The interior comes as something of a surprise, however, as it was redesigned in Anglo-Catholic style by Ninian Comper in 1912, and features an elaborate tableau of gilded statuary: Christ crucified is flanked by Mary and one of the disciples, with two angels kneeling below with chalices ready to catch the sacred blood.

THE CATO STREET CONSPIRACY

Modern British history is notably short on political assassinations: one prime minister, no kings or queens and only a handful of MPs. One of the most dismal failures was the 1820 **Cato Street Conspiracy**, drawn up by sixteen revolutionaries in an attic off the Edgware Road in Marylebone. Their plan was to decapitate the entire Cabinet as they dined with Lord Harrowby at 44 Grosvenor Square. Having beheaded the Home Secretary and another of the ministers, they then planned to sack Coutts Bank, capture the cannon on the Artillery Ground, take Gray's Inn, Mansion House, the Bank of England and the Tower, torching the barracks in the process, and proclaiming a provisional government.

As it turned out, one of the conspirators was an *agent provocateur*, and the entire mob was arrested in the Cato Street attic on the night of the planned coup, February 23, 1820. In the melee, one Bow Street Runner was killed but eventually eleven of the conspirators were arrested and charged with high treason. Five of the ringleaders were hanged at Newgate, and another five were transported to Australia. Public sympathy for the uprising was widespread, so the condemned were spared being drawn and quartered, though they did have their heads cut off afterwards. (The hangman was later attacked in the streets and almost castrated.)

Mount Street Gardens: Church of the Immaculate Conception

Farm St • Daily 8am–7pm • Free • ☎ 020 7493 7811, ⓦ farmstreet.org.uk • ⊖ Bond Street or Green Park

Built in ostentatious neo-Gothic style in the 1840s, the **Church of the Immaculate Conception Farm Street** is the London stronghold of the Jesuits, and as such is a fascinating and unusual church. Every surface is covered in decoration, but the reredos of gilded stone by Pugin (of Houses of Parliament fame) is particularly impressive. Behind the chapel are the beautifully secluded **Mount Street Gardens**, dotted with two hundred-year-old plane trees and enclosed by nineteenth-century red-brick mansions.

Oxford Street

As wealthy Londoners began to move out of the City during the eighteenth century, in favour of the newly developed West End, so **Oxford Street** – the old Roman road to Oxford – gradually replaced Cheapside as London's main shopping street. Today, despite successive recessions and sky-high rents, this hotchpotch of shops, over a mile long, is still one of the world's busiest streets, its Christmas lights switched on by the briefly famous, and its traffic controllers equipped with loud-hailers to prevent the hordes of Christmas shoppers from losing their lives at the busy road junctions. The stretch west of Oxford Circus is slightly more upmarket; east of Oxford Circus, the street forms a scruffy border between Soho and Fitzrovia.

Selfridges

400 Oxford St • Mon 9.30am–7pm, Tues 11am–9pm, Wed–Sat 9.30am–9pm, Sun 11.30am–6.15pm • ⓦ selfridges.com • ⊖ Bond Street

The one long-standing landmark on Oxford Street is **Selfridges**, a huge Edwardian department store fronted by giant Ionic columns, with the Queen of Time riding the ship of commerce and supporting an Art Deco clock above the main entrance. Opened in 1909 by Chicago millionaire Harry Gordon Selfridge, Selfridges is the second largest shop in London (after Harrods), and is credited with selling the world's first television set, as well as introducing the concept of the "bargain basement", "the customer is always right", the irritating "only ten more shopping days to Christmas" countdown and the nauseous bouquet of perfumes from the cosmetics counters, strategically placed at the entrance to all department stores. Selfridge himself was a big spender and eventually died in Putney in poverty in 1947 at the age of 90. Today, while Harrods may have the snob value and the longer pedigree, it's a conservative institution compared to Selfridges, which keeps reinventing itself and successfully remains ahead of the field, particularly in fashion – the window displays alone are worth the journey here.

MARYLEBONE HIGH STREET

Marylebone

Marylebone may not have quite the social pedigree of neighbouring Mayfair, but it's still a wealthy and aspirational area. Compared to the brashness of Oxford Street, which forms its southern border, Marylebone's backstreets are a pleasure to wander, especially the chi-chi village-like quarter around Marylebone High Street. This is where the city's leading private specialists in medicine and surgery have had their practices since they gravitated here in the nineteenth century. And it was here that The Beatles (and many others since) took up residence when they hit the big time in the 1960s. The area's more conventional sights include the free art gallery and aristocratic mansion of the Wallace Collection, Sherlock Holmes' old stamping ground around Baker Street and the massively touristy Madame Tussauds.

Marylebone was once the outlying village of St Mary-by-the-Bourne (the bourne in question being the Tyburn stream) or St Marylebone (pronounced "marra-le-bun"), and when Samuel Pepys walked through open countryside to reach its pleasure gardens in 1668, he declared it "a pretty place". During the course of the next century, the gardens were closed and the village was swallowed up as its chief landowners – among them the Portlands and the Portmans – laid out a mesh of uniform Georgian streets and squares, much of which survives today.

Langham Place

North of Oxford Circus, Regent Street forms the eastern border of Marylebone, but stops abruptly at **Langham Place**, which formed an awkward twist in John Nash's triumphal route to Regent's Park in order to link up with the pre-existing Portland Place. Nash's solution was to build his unusual All Souls Church, now the only Nash building left in this star-studded chicane that's home to the BBC's Broadcasting House and the historic Langham Hotel.

All Souls Church

Langham Place • Mon–Sat 9.30am–5.30pm, Sun 9am–2pm & 5.30–8.30pm • Free • ☎ 020 7580 3522, ⓦ allsouls.org • ⊖ Oxford Circus

John Nash's simple and ingenious little **All Souls Church** was built in warm Bath Stone in the 1820s, and is the architect's only surviving church. The unusual circular Ionic portico and conical stone spire, which caused outrage in its day, are cleverly designed to provide a visual full stop to Regent Street and lead the eye round into Portland Place and ultimately to Regent's Park.

Broadcasting House

Langham Place • Guided tours Sun; £13.50; no under-9s • ☎ 0370 901 1227, ⓦ bbc.co.uk/tours • ⊖ Oxford Circus

Behind All Souls lies the totalitarian-looking Art Deco **Broadcasting House**, BBC radio headquarters since 1932. The figures of Prospero and Ariel (pun intended) above the entrance are by Eric Gill, who caused a furore by sculpting Ariel with overlarge testicles, and, like Epstein a few years earlier at Broadway House, was forced in the end to cut the organs down to size. Broadcasting House has recently undergone a £1-billion refurbishment and is now the headquarters of BBC News (both TV and radio) and you can sign up for a guided tour (1hr 30min) to see the state-of-the-art open-plan newsroom, the Radio Theatre and some of the studios.

Langham Hotel

Opposite Broadcasting House stands the **Langham Hotel**, built in grandiose Italianate style and opened by the Prince of Wales in 1865 as the city's most

---

DOCTORS AND DENTISTS

Harley Street was an ordinary residential Marylebone street until the nineteenth century when doctors, dentists and medical specialists began to colonize the area in order to serve London's wealthier citizens. Private medicine survived the threat of the postwar National Health Service, and the most expensive specialists and hospitals are still to be found in the streets around here.

The national dental body, the **British Dental Association (BDA)** has its headquarters at nearby 64 Wimpole St, and a **museum** (Tues & Thurs 1–4pm; free; ☎ 020 7935 4549, ⓦ bda.org; ⊖ Bond Street) displaying the gruesome contraptions of early dentistry, and old prints of agonizing extractions. Although dentistry is traditionally associated with pain, it was, in fact, a dentist who discovered the first anaesthetic.

HIDDEN GEMS: MARYLEBONE

Alfie's Antique Market See p.433
Daunt Books See p.429
Lunchtime concerts at the Royal Acadamy See p.94
RIBA bookshop and café See p.90

Tapa Room at Providores See p.368
Tours of Broadcasting House See opposite
Wigmore Hall See p.414
The Wallace Collection See p.90

modern hotel, with over one hundred water closets. It features in several Sherlock Holmes mysteries, and its former guests have included Antonín Dvořák (who courted controversy by ordering a double room for himself and his daughter to save money), exiled emperors Napoleon III and Haile Selassie, Oscar Wilde and the writer Ouida (aka Marie Louise de la Ramée), who threw outrageous parties for young Guards officers and wrote many of her bestselling romances in her dimly lit hotel boudoir. Following World War II, it was taken over by the BBC and used to record legendary shows such as *The Goons*, only returning to use as a luxury hotel in 1991.

Portland Place

After the chicane around All Souls, you enter **Portland Place**, laid out by the Adam brothers in the 1770s and incorporated by Nash in his grand Regent Street plan. Once the widest street in London, it's still a majestic avenue, still lined here and there with Adam-style houses, boasting wonderful fanlights and iron railings. At the northern end of Portland Place, Nash originally planned a giant "circus" as a formal entrance to Regent's Park (see p.283). Only the southern half – two graceful arcs of creamy terraces known collectively as **Park Crescent** – was completed, now cut off from the park by busy Marylebone Road.

Chinese Embassy

Several embassies occupy properties on Portland Place, but the most prominent is the **Chinese Embassy** at no. 49, opposite which there's usually a small group of protesters permanently positioned objecting either to Chinese suppression of Falun Gong or its policies in Tibet. It was here in 1896 that the exiled republican leader Sun Yat-sen was kidnapped and held incognito, on the orders of the Chinese emperor. Eventually Sun managed to send a note to a friend, saying "I am certain to be beheaded. Oh woe is me!". When the press got hold of the story, Sun was finally released; he went on to found the Chinese Nationalist Party and became the first president of China in 1911.

Royal Institute of British Architects (RIBA)

66 Portland Place · Mon, Wed & Thurs 8am–7pm, Tues 8am–9pm, Fri 8am–6pm, Sat 9am–5pm; exhibitions Mon–Sat 10am–5pm · Free · ☎ 020 7580 5533, ⓦ architecture.com · ⊖ Regent's Park or Great Portland Street

The **Royal Institute of British Architects** or RIBA at no. 66 is arguably the finest building on Portland Place, with its sleek Portland-stone facade built in the 1930s amid the remaining Adam houses. The main staircase remains a wonderful period piece, with its etched glass balustrades and walnut veneer, and with two large black marble columns rising up on either side. You can view the interior en route to the institute's excellent ground-floor bookshop, first-floor exhibition galleries and café.

Wallace Collection

Manchester Square · Daily 10am–5pm · Free · ☎ 020 7563 9500, ⓦ wallacecollection.org · ⊖ Bond Street

It comes as a great surprise to find the miniature eighteenth-century French chateau of Hertford House in the quiet Georgian streets just to the north of busy Oxford Street. Even more remarkable is the house's splendid **Wallace Collection** within, a public museum and art gallery combined, which boasts paintings by Titian, Rembrandt and Velázquez, the finest museum collection of Sèvres porcelain in the world and one of the finest displays of Boulle marquetry furniture, too. The collection was originally bequeathed to the nation in 1897 by the widow of Richard Wallace, an art collector and the illegitimate son of the fourth Marquess of Hertford. The museum has preserved the feel of a grand stately home, an old-fashioned institution with exhibits piled high in glass cabinets and paintings covering every inch of wall space. However, it's the combined effect of the exhibits set amid superbly restored eighteenth-century period fittings – and a bloody great **armoury** – that makes the place so remarkable. Labelling is deliberately terse, so as not to detract from the aristocratic ambience, but there are information cards in each room, free highlights tours most days (11.30am & 2.30pm) and themed audioguides available (for a fee).

Ground floor

The ground-floor rooms begin with the **Front State Room**, to the right as you enter, where the walls are hung with several fetching portraits by Reynolds, and Lawrence's

WALLACE COLLECTION >

typically sensuous portrayal of the author and society beauty, the Countess of Blessington, which went down a storm at the Royal Academy in 1822. The decor of the **Back State Room** is a riot of Rococo, and houses the cream of the house's gaudily spectacular Sèvres porcelain. Centre stage is a period copy of Louis XV's desk, which was the most expensive piece of eighteenth-century French furniture ever made. On the other side of the adjacent Dining Room, in the **Billiard Room**, you'll find an impressive display of outrageous, gilded oak and ebony Boulle marquetry furniture. From the Dining Room, with its Canalettos, you can enter the covered courtyard, home to *The Wallace Restaurant*, and head down the stairs to the temporary exhibition galleries and the **Conservation Gallery** where folk of all ages can try on some medieval armour.

Back on the ground floor, the **Sixteenth-Century Gallery** displays a wide variety of works ranging from *pietre dure*, bronze and majolica to Limoges porcelain and Venetian glass. In the **Smoking Room**, a small alcove at the far end survives to give an idea of the effect of the original Minton-tiled decor Wallace chose for this room. The next three rooms house the extensive **European Armoury** bought *en bloc* by Wallace around the time of the Franco-Prussian War. (It was in recognition of the humanitarian assistance Wallace provided in Paris during that war that he received his baronetcy.) A fourth room houses the **Oriental Armoury**, collected by the fourth Marquess of Hertford, including a cabinet of Asante gold treasure, a sword belonging to Tipu Sultan and one of the most important Sikh treasures in Britain, the sword of Ranjit Singh (1780–1839).

First floor

The main staircase, with its incredible Parisian wrought-iron balustrade and its gilded, fluted columns, is overlooked by **Boucher**'s sumptuous mythological scenes. In the gloriously camp pink **Boudoir**, off the landing and conservatory, you'll find Reynolds' doe-eyed moppets, while the adjacent passageway boasts an unbelievably rich display of gold snuff boxes and miniatures. The **Study** features more Sèvres porcelain, Greuze's soft-focus studies of kids and a lovely portrait by Elisabeth Vigée-Lebrun, one of the most successful portraitists of pre-Revolutionary France. Next door, in the sky-blue **Oval Drawing Room**, one of Fragonard's coquettes flaunts herself to a smitten beau in *The Swing*, alongside more Boucher nudes – the soft porn of the *ancien régime*. There's plenty more Rococo froth in the other rooms on this floor, plus classic Grand Tour vistas from Canaletto and Guardi in the **West Room**.

In addition to all this French finery a good collection of Dutch paintings hangs in the **East Galleries**, including de Hooch's *Women Peeling Apples*, oil sketches by Rubens and landscapes by Ruisdael, Hobbema and Cuyp. On the opposite side of the house, the **West Galleries** feature works by the British landscape artist Richard Parkes Bonington and Delacroix, his great friend and admirer.

Great Gallery

Finally, you reach the largest room in the house, the **Great Gallery**, specifically built by Wallace to display his finest paintings, including works by Murillo and Poussin, several vast Van Dyck portraits, Rubens' *Rainbow Landscape* and **Frans Hals'** *Laughing Cavalier*. Here, too, are *Perseus and Andromeda*, a late work by **Titian**, and **Velázquez**'s *Lady with a Fan*. At one end of the room are three portraits of the actress Mary Robinson as Perdita: one by Romney, one by Reynolds and, best of the lot, **Gainsborough**'s deceptively innocent portrayal, in which she insouciantly holds a miniature of her lover, the 19-year-old Prince of Wales (later George IV), who is portrayed in a flattering full-length portrait by Lawrence. Look out, too, for **Rembrandt**'s affectionate portrait of his teenage son, Titus, who helped administer his father's estate after bankruptcy charges and pre-deceased his father at the age of just 28.

Marylebone High Street

Marylebone High Street is all that's left of the village street that once ran along the banks of the Tyburn stream. It's become considerably more upmarket since those bucolic days, though the pace of the street is leisurely by central London standards. A couple of shops, in particular, deserve mention: the branch of *Patisserie Valerie*, at no. 105, is decorated inside with the same mock-Pompeian frescoes that adorned it when it was founded as *Maison Sagne* in 1921 by a Swiss pastry-cook; Daunt, a purpose-built bookshop from 1910, at no. 83, specializes in travel books, and has a lovely, long, galleried hall at the back, with a pitched roof of stained glass.

St James's Church, Spanish Place

22 George St • Mon–Fri 7am–7pm, Sat 10am–7pm, Sun 8am–8pm • ☎ 020 7935 0943, Ⓦ sjrcc.org.uk • ⊖ Bond Street or Baker Street

Despite its name, **St James's Church, Spanish Place,** is actually tucked away on neighbouring George Street, just off Marylebone High Street. A Catholic chapel was built here in 1791 thanks to the efforts of the chaplain at the Spanish embassy, though the present neo-Gothic building dates from 1890. Designed in a mixture of English and French Gothic, the interior is surprisingly large and richly furnished, from the white marble and alabaster pulpit to the richly gilded heptagonal apse. The Spanish connection continues to this day: Spanish royal heraldry features in the rose window, and there are even two seats reserved for the royals, denoted by built-in gilt crowns high above the choir stalls.

Baker Street

4

Running north–south through Marylebone, **Baker Street** is a fairly nondescript one-way highway. Despite its unprepossessing nature, its associations with the fictional detective Sherlock Holmes are, naturally, fully exploited. At the northern edge of Marylebone, Baker Street is bisected by the six-lane highway of **Marylebone Road**. Built as the New Road in the 1750s, to provide London with its first bypass, it remains one of London's major traffic arteries, and is no place for a casual stroll. There are, however, a couple of minor sights, such as **St Marylebone Church** and the **Royal Academy of Music**, and one major tourist trap, **Madame Tussauds**, that are all an easy stroll from Baker Street tube.

Madame Tussauds

Marylebone Rd • Mon–Fri 9.30am–5.30pm, Sat & Sun 9am–6pm • £30 • ☎ 0871 894 3000, Ⓦ madametussauds.com • ⊖ Baker Street

The wax models at **Madame Tussauds** have been pulling in the crowds ever since the good lady arrived from France in 1802 bearing the sculpted heads of guillotined aristocrats (she was lucky to escape the same fate – her uncle, who started the family business, was less fortunate). The entrance fee might be extortionate and the likenesses dubious, but London's biggest queues form here – to avoid joining them (and to save money), book online, or whizz round after 5pm for half-price.

There are **photo opportunities** galore in the first few sections, which are peppered with contemporary celebrities from the BBC to Bollywood. Look out for the diminutive Madame Tussaud herself, and the oldest wax model, Madame du Barry, Louis XV's mistress, who gently respires as Sleeping Beauty – in reality she was beheaded in the French Revolution. The **Chamber of Horrors** is irredeemably tasteless, and – in the section called "Scream" – features costumed actors who jump out at you in the dark (you can opt out of this). All the "great" British serial killers are here, and it remains the murderer's greatest honour to be included. There's a reconstruction of John Christie's hanging, a tableau of Marat's death in the bath and the very guillotine that lopped off Marie Antoinette's head, just for good measure.

Tussauds also features the **Spirit of London**, an irreverent five-minute romp through the history of London in a miniaturized taxicab, taking you from Elizabethan times to

MARYLEBONE STATION

Probably London's most discreet train terminal, **Marylebone Station** is hidden in the backstreets north of Marylebone Road on Melcombe Place, where a delicate and extremely elegant wrought-iron canopy links the station to the former *Great Central Hotel* (now *The Landmark*). Opened in 1899, Marylebone was the last and most modest of the Victorian terminals, originally intended to be the terminal for the Channel tunnel of the 1880s, a scheme abandoned after only a mile or so of digging, when Queen Victoria got nervous about foreign invasions. The station enjoyed a brief moment of fame after appearing in the opening sequence of The Beatles film *A Hard Day's Night* and now serves the Birmingham and Buckinghamshire commuter belt.

a postmodern heritage nightmare of tourist tat (not unlike much of London today). The tour of Tussauds ends with a short hi-tech "experience", often inspired by a recent Hollywood flick, including a 4D 360-degree film projected onto the ceiling of the domed auditorium of the former London Planetarium.

Sherlock Holmes Museum

239 Baker St · Daily 9.30am–6pm · £8 · ☎ 020 7224 3688, ⓦ sherlock-holmes.co.uk · ⊖ Baker Street

Baker Street, which cuts across Marylebone Road, is synonymous with London's languid super-sleuth, Sherlock Holmes, who lived at no. 221b. The detective's address was always fictional, although the most likely inspiration was, in fact, no. 21, at the south end of the street. However, the statue of Holmes's creator, Arthur Conan Doyle, is at the north end of the street, outside Baker Street tube, round the corner from the **Sherlock Holmes Museum**, at no. 239 (the sign on the door says 221b). Unashamedly touristy – you can have your photo taken in a deerstalker – the museum is nevertheless a competent exercise in period reconstruction, stuffed full of Victoriana and life-size models of characters from the books.

St Marylebone Church

Marylebone Rd · ☎ 020 7935 7315, ⓦ stmarylebone.org · ⊖ Baker Street or Regent's Park

Completed in 1817, **St Marylebone Church** is only open fitfully for services and recitals, though the church's most attractive feature – the gilded caryatids holding up the beehive cupola on top of the tower – is visible from Marylebone High Street. It was at this church that **Elizabeth Barrett** and **Robert Browning** were secretly married in 1846 (there's a chapel dedicated to Browning), after which Elizabeth – six years older than Robert, an invalid, morphine addict and virtual prisoner in her father's house on Wimpole Street – returned home and acted as if nothing had happened. A week later the couple eloped to Italy, where they spent most of their married life. The church crypt houses a small chapel, a healing centre, an NHS health centre and a café.

Royal Academy of Music

Marylebone Rd · Mon–Fri 11.30am–5.30pm, Sat noon–4pm · Free · ☎ 020 7873 7373, ⓦ ram.ac.uk · ⊖ Baker Street or Regent's Park

On the other side of Marylebone Road from St Marylebone Church stands the **Royal Academy of Music**, which was founded in 1823 and has taught the likes of Arthur Sullivan, Harrison Birtwistle, Dennis Brain, Evelyn Glennie, Elton John, Michael Nyman and Simon Rattle. As well as putting on free lunchtime and evening concerts, the academy houses a small **museum** at 1 York Gate. Temporary exhibitions are held on the ground floor, while in the String Gallery on the first floor, there's a world-class collection of Cremonese violins including several by Stradivari. The exhibition on the second floor in the Piano Gallery follows the development of the grand piano in England and gives you a peek into the resident luthier's workshop. Listening-posts on each floor allow you to experience the instruments in live performance.

Soho and Fitzrovia

Bounded by Regent Street to the west, Oxford Street to the north and Charing Cross Road to the east, Soho is very much the heart of the West End. It was the city's premier red-light district for centuries and retains an unorthodox and slightly raffish air that's unique for central London. It has an immigrant history as rich as that of the East End and a louche nightlife that has attracted writers and revellers of every sexual persuasion since the eighteenth century. Conventional sights in Soho are few and far between, yet there's probably more street life here than anywhere else in the city centre. Most folk head to Soho to go to the cinema or theatre, and to have a drink or a bite to eat in the innumerable bars, cafés and restaurants that pepper the tiny area and Fitzrovia, the quieter Soho spillover, north of Oxford Street.

5

Soho

Soho's historic reputation for tolerance made it an obvious place of refuge from dour, postwar Britain. **Jazz** and skiffle proliferated in the 1950s, folk and **rock** in the 1960s, and punk at the end of the 1970s. London's artistic (and alcoholic) cliques still gather here and the **media**, film and advertising industries have a strong presence. The area's most recent transformation has seen it become London's most high-profile gay quarter, especially around **Old Compton Street**. The attraction, though, remains in the unique mix of people who drift through Soho. There's nowhere else in the city where such diverse slices of London come face to face: businessmen, drunks, theatregoers, fashion victims, market-stallholders, pimps, prostitutes and politicians. Take it all in, and enjoy – for better or worse, most of London is not like this.

Leicester Square

A short hop east of Piccadilly Circus, most Londoners tend to avoid **Leicester Square** unless they're heading for one of the cinemas. In the eighteenth century, this fairly pleasant leafy square was home to the fashionable "Leicester House set", headed by successive Hanoverian princes of Wales who didn't get on with their fathers at St James's. Busts of celebrities from those days can be found in the gardens, though most people are more impressed by the statues of Shakespeare and Charlie Chaplin. By night – and especially at weekends – Leicester Square resembles city centres across the country, a playground for the drunk and underdressed.

The square has been an **entertainment zone** since the mid-nineteenth century, when it boasted Turkish baths and music halls such as the grandiose Empire, now a cinema that's a favourite for red-carpet premieres and, close by, the Hippodrome – designed by Frank Matcham in 1900 – now the UK's biggest casino. Purpose-built movie houses moved in during the 1930s, a golden age evoked by the sleek black lines of the Odeon on the east side, and maintain their grip on the area.

Notre-Dame de France

5 Leicester Place • Mon–Fri noon–6pm, Sun 10am–6pm • Free • ☎ 020 7437 9363, ⓦ ndfchurch.org • ⊖ Leicester Square

One little-known sight, north of Leicester Square, is the modern Catholic church of **Notre-Dame de France**, heralded by an entrance flanked by two pillars decorated with

---

SOHO'S WHO'S WHO

When **Soho** – named after the cry that resounded through the district when it was a popular place for hunting hares – was built over in the seventeenth century, its streets were among the most sought-after addresses in the capital. Princes, dukes and earls built their mansions around Soho and Leicester squares, which became the centre of high-society nightlife, epitomized by the wild masquerades organized by Viennese prima donna Theresa Cornelys (who had a daughter by Casanova), which drew "a riotous assembly of fashionable people of both sexes", a traffic jam of hackney carriages and a huge crowd of onlookers. By the end of the eighteenth century, however, the party was over, the rich moved west, and Soho began its inexorable descent into poverty and overcrowding. Even before the last aristocrats left, Soho had become one of the city's main dumping grounds for **immigrants**. French Huguenots were followed by Italians, Irish, Jews and eventually the Chinese.

For several centuries, Soho has also been a favourite haunt of the capital's creative bohos, **literati** and rebels. It was at Soho's *Turk's Head* coffee shop, in 1764, that Joshua Reynolds founded "The Club", to give Dr Johnson unlimited opportunities for talking. Thomas de Quincey turned up in 1802, and was saved from starvation by a local prostitute, an incident later recalled in his *Confessions of an English Opium Eater*. Wagner arrived destitute in 1839, Marx lived in poverty here after the failure of the 1848 revolution, and Rimbaud and Verlaine pitched up after the fall of the Paris Commune in 1871. "Such noise and chaos. Such magnificent and terrible abandon. It's like stepping into the future", wrote Verlaine.

5

THE SWISS CORNER

For no particularly good reason, the area in the northwest corner of Leicester Square has a Swiss theme to it. The impetus was the building of the Swiss Centre – a sort of trade centre-cum-tourist office – in 1968 and the renaming of the area as Swiss Court. After forty years of alpine theming, the much unloved Swiss Centre was finally demolished in 2008, leaving behind a slightly surreal **Swiss glockenspiel**. This tall steel structure is topped by a Swiss railway clock and features a glass drum decorated with the 26 cantonal flags which lower on the hour (Mon–Fri noon & 5–8pm, Sat & Sun 2–4pm), to sound a 27-bell carillon, thus revealing a procession of Helvetic cows and peasants making their way up the mountain.

---

biblical reliefs. The main point of interest within the unusual circular interior is the Chapelle de la Vierge Marie, which contains a series of simple frescoes of the Annunciation, Crucifixion and Assumption by Jean Cocteau from 1960 and an altar mosaic of the Nativity by Boris Anrep (originally covered by a new panel by Cocteau much to Anrep's annoyance).

Chinatown

Hemmed in between Leicester Square and Shaftesbury Avenue, **Chinatown**'s self-contained jumble of **shops**, **cafés** and **restaurants** makes up one of London's most distinct ethnic enclaves. Only a minority of the capital's Chinese live in the three small blocks of Chinatown, with its ersatz touches – telephone kiosks rigged out as pagodas and formal entrances or *paifang* – yet the area remains a focus for the community, a place to do business or the weekly shopping, celebrate a wedding or just meet up on Sundays for dim sum. Most Londoners come to Chinatown simply to eat, but if the mood takes you, you can easily while away several hours sorting through the Chinese trinkets, ceramics and ornaments in the various arts and crafts shops, or amassing the perfect ingredients for a demon stir-fry.

The first Chinese immigrants were sailors who arrived here from the late eighteenth century onwards on the ships of the East India Company. London's first Chinatown grew up around the docks at Limehouse and eventually boasted over thirty Chinese shops and restaurants. Predominantly male, this closed community achieved a quasi-mythical status in Edwardian minds as a hotbed of criminal dives and opium dens, a reputation exploited in Sax Rohmer's novels (later made into films) featuring the evil Doctor Fu Manchu. Wartime bomb damage, postwar demolition and protectionist union laws all but destroyed Limehouse Chinatown. However, following the Communist takeover in China, a new wave of Chinese refugees began to buy up cheap property around **Gerrard Street**, eventually establishing the nucleus of today's Chinatown.

Charing Cross Road

Created in the 1880s as part of the Victorians' slum clearance drive, **Charing Cross Road** has historically always been liberally peppered with **bookshops**. One of the first to open here, in 1906, was **Foyles**, a vast book emporium, now at nos. 107–109, where Éamon de Valera, George Bernard Shaw, Walt Disney and Arthur Conan Doyle were all once regular customers. Once famous for its antiquated system for selling books that required customers to queue three times, it's now a much more vibrant place, with a busy café and regular live jazz and classical music gigs.

Two of the nicest places for secondhand-book browsing are **Cecil Court** and **St Martin's Court**, connecting the southern end of Charing Cross Road and St Martin's Lane. These short, civilized, late-Victorian paved alleys boast specialist bookshops, such as the Italian Bookshop and Watkins Books, home of the occult, plus various antiquarian dealers selling modern first editions, old theatre posters, coins and notes, cigarette cards, maps and children's books.

5

Coliseum
St Martin's Lane • ☎ 020 7845 9300, ⓦ eno.org • ⊖ Leicester Square or Charing Cross

At the southern end of St Martin's Lane stands the **Coliseum**, an extravagant variety theatre built in 1904 by Frank Matcham, where the likes of Lillie Langtry, Sarah Bernhardt and the Ballets Russes all performed. Now home to the English National Opera (see p.415), it remains London's largest theatre, its cutest feature the revolving illuminated globe that crowns the building.

Shaftesbury Avenue
Sweeping through the southern part of Soho, the gentle curve of **Shaftesbury Avenue** is the heart of the West End's **Theatreland**, with theatres and cinemas along its entire length. Built in the 1870s, ostensibly to relieve traffic congestion but with the dual purpose of destroying the slums that lay in its path, the street was ironically named after Lord Shaftesbury, whose life had been spent trying to help the likes of those dispossessed by the road. The most impressive theatre architecturally is the grandiose terracotta **Palace Theatre**, overlooking Cambridge Circus, which opened in 1891 as the Royal English Opera House; it folded after just one year, and, since the 1920s, has mostly hosted musicals. Just off Cambridge Circus, hidden away down West Street, is St Martin's Theatre, where Agatha Christie's record-breaking murder-mystery *The Mousetrap* has been on nonstop since 1952, notching up over 24,000 performances.

Old Compton Street
If Soho had an official main drag, it would be **Old Compton Street**, which runs parallel with Shaftesbury Avenue, and forms the heart of Central Soho. The shops, boutiques and cafés in the narrow surrounding streets are typical of the area and a good barometer of the latest Soho fads. Several places have survived the vicissitudes of fashion, including the original *Patisserie Valerie*, opened by the Belgian-born Madame Valerie in 1926, the Algerian Coffee Store, the Italian deli, I Camisa & Son, The Vintage House off-licence, and Gerry's, whose spirit-window display is a paean to alcohol.

The liberal atmosphere of Soho has made it a permanent fixture on the **gay scene** since the last century: gay servicemen frequented the *Golden Lion*, on Dean Street, from World War II until the end of National Service, while a succession of gay artists found refuge here during the 1950s and 1960s. Nowadays the scene is much more upfront, with every type of gay business jostling for position on and off Old Compton Street.

Greek Street
The streets off Old Compton Street are lined with Soho institutions past and present, starting in the east with **Greek Street**, named after the Greek church that once stood nearby. South of Old Compton Street, at no. 29, stands *Maison Bertaux*, London's oldest French patisserie, founded in 1871. The *Coach and Horses*, one door down at no. 29, was lorded over for years by the boozy gang of writer Jeffrey Bernard, painter Francis Bacon and jazz man George Melly, as well as the staff of the satirical magazine, *Private Eye*.

HIDDEN GEMS: QUINTESSENTIAL SOHO

Algerian Coffee Stores See p.431	**The French House** See p.387
Bar Italia See p.369	**Maison Bertaux** See p.369
Cecil Court bookshops See opposite	**Society Club** See p.430
Ronnie Scott's See p.402	**Vintage House** See p.432

CENTRAL SOHO

CAFÉS
Bar Italia	8
Beatroot	5
Breakfast Club	1
Fernandez & Wells	2
Maison Bertaux	11
Patisserie Valerie	10

RESTAURANTS
Bar-shu	13
Bocca di Lupo	16
Four Seasons	18
Koya	6
Leong's Legend	17
Misato	21
Mr Kong	19
New World	15
One Leicester Street	20
Quo Vadis	4
Spuntino	14
Stockpot	7
Tonkotsu	9
Yalla Yalla	12
Yauatcha	3

SHOPS
Absolute Vintage	2
Algerian Coffee Stores	11
Any Amount of Books	16
Berwick Street Market	7
Blackwell's	8
Foyles	5
Gerry's	12
Gosh!	9
I. Camisa & Son	13
Kokon to Zai	4
Loon Fung Supermarket	15
Paul A Young	3
Quinto	14
Sister Ray	1
Society Club	6
Vintage House	10

PUBS & BARS
Blue Posts	28
Dog & Duck	9
French House	23
Phoenix Artist Club	10

MUSIC VENUES
Borderline	6
Jazz@Pizza Express	3
Ronnie Scott's	12

CLUBS
Café de Paris	30
Madame Jojo's	18
Moonlighting	11

GAY AND LESBIAN VENUES
The Admiral Duncan	17	G-A-Y Late	5
Balans	14	Green Carnation	7
Candy Bar	4	Ku Bar	16, 29
Circa	8	Manbar	27
Comptons of Soho	22	Rupert Street	26
Duke of Wellington	24	Shadow Lounge	20
The Edge	2	Star at Night	1
Escape	19	Village Soho	21
Freedom	15	The Yard	25
G-A-Y Bar	13		

ACCOMMODATION
Dean Street Townhouse	3	Nadler Soho	1
Hazlitt's	2	One Leicester Street	4

5

SOHO ON RECORD

Soho has been a popular meeting point for the capital's up-and-coming pop stars since the late 1950s, when the likes of Cliff Richard, Tommy Steele and Adam Faith used to hang out at the **2 i's coffee bar**, 59 Old Compton St, and perform at the rock'n'roll club in the basement. Marc Bolan, whose parents ran a market stall on Berwick Street, also worked at the café in the early 1960s. The Rolling Stones first met in a pub on Broadwick Street in early 1962 and, by the mid-1960s, were playing Soho's premier rock venue, the **Marquee**, originally at 90 Wardour St. David Bowie performed there (as David Jones) in 1965, Pink Floyd played their "Spontaneous Underground" sessions the following year, Led Zeppelin had their first London gig there in 1968 and Phil Collins worked for some time as a cloakroom attendant.

In November 1975, The Sex Pistols played their first gig at **St Martin's School of Art** (now Foyles) on Charing Cross Road, during which Sid Vicious (in the audience, and not the band, at the time) made his contribution to dance history when he began to "pogo". The classic punk venue, however, was the **100 Club** on Oxford Street, where the Pistols, The Clash, Siouxsie, The Damned and The Vibrators all played. The Pistols used to rehearse in the studios on **Denmark Street**, London's own version of New York's Tin Pan Alley, off Charing Cross Road (still lined with music shops). The Rolling Stones, The Kinks and Genesis all recorded songs there, and Elton John got his first job at one of the street's music publishers in 1963. There's a whiff of Soho's pop music past still in **Berwick Street**, where a cluster of independent and secondhand record shops survive on either side of the market.

Frith Street

Frith Street is home to **Ronnie Scott's**, London's longest-running jazz club, founded in 1958 and still pulling in the big names. Opposite is *Bar Italia*, a tiny, quintessentially Italian café established in 1949, whose late-night hours make it a clubbers' favourite. It was in this building, appropriately enough for such a media-saturated area, that **John Logie Baird** made the world's first public television transmission in 1926. Next door, a plaque recalls that the 7-year-old Mozart stayed here in 1763, having wowed George III and London society.

Soho Square

Soho Square is one of the few patches of green amid the neighbourhood's labyrinth of streets and alleys. It began life as a smart address, surrounded by the houses of the nobility and centred on an elaborate fountain topped by a statue of Charles II. Charles survives, if a little worse for wear, on one of the pathways, but the fountain is now an octagonal, mock-Tudor garden shed. As for the buildings around the square, they are a typical Soho mix: 20th Century-Fox; the Victorian Hospital for Sick Women (now a walk-in health centre); Paul McCartney's discreet corporate headquarters, MPL; and the British Board of Film Classification (the national guardians of film censorship).

There are also two square red-brick churches. The most prominent is the Italianate **St Patrick's**, on the east side of the square, first consecrated in 1792 and thus the first Catholic church built in England after the Reformation; the current building dates from the 1890s and serves the Irish, Italian and Chinese communities. Concealed on the north side of the square, the **Église Protestante**, also from the 1890s, is the sole survivor of London's once numerous Huguenot churches; the 1950 tympanum relief depicts the French refugees crossing the Channel and being granted asylum by Edward VI.

Dean Street

One block west of Frith Street runs **Dean Street**, once home to *The Colony Room*, a private drinking club that was at the heart of Soho's postwar bohemian scene, and still home to the members-only *Groucho Club*, at no. 45, where today's literati and media types preen themselves. Nearby, at no. 49, *The French House* is an open-to-all

5

bohemian landmark, where the most popular drink is Ricard, and they only serve beer in halves. Opened by a German as the *York Minster* pub, it was bought by a Belgian, Victor Berlemont, in 1914, when the German owner was deported, and transformed into a French émigré haunt. Dylan Thomas and Brendan Behan were both regulars, and during World War II it was frequented by de Gaulle and the Free French forces.

Soho's most famous Jewish immigrant was **Karl Marx**, who in 1850 moved into two "evil, frightful rooms" on the top floor of no. 28, with his wife and maid (both of whom were pregnant by him) and four children, having been evicted from his first two addresses for failing to pay the rent. There's a plaque commemorating his stay (with incorrect dates), and the waiters at *Quo Vadis* restaurant below will show diners round the rooms on request (☎020 7437 9585).

Wardour Street

A kind of dividing line between the busier eastern half of Soho and the marginally quieter western zone, **Wardour Street** is largely given over to the media industry. Just north of Shaftesbury Avenue, there's a small park laid out on what used to be **St Anne's Church**, bombed in the last war, with only its tower now standing – the ashes of Dorothy L. Sayers, who was a churchwarden for many years, are buried under the tower.

Brewer Street

West of Wardour Street, along **Brewer Street**, the sex industry has a long history and retains a foothold. It was at the **Windmill Theatre**, on nearby Great Windmill Street, that the famous "Revuedeville" shows, featuring static nude performers (movement was strictly forbidden by the censor), were first staged in the 1930s. The shows continued pretty much uninterrupted right through World War II – the subject of the 2005 film *Mrs Henderson Presents* – eventually closing in 1964. Meanwhile, back on Brewer Street, the **Raymond Revuebar** opened in 1952 as a "World Centre of Erotic Entertainment", finally succumbing, in 2004, to competition from the slick **lap-dancing clubs** that now prevail.

SOHO VICE

Prostitution is nothing new to Soho. Way back in the seventeenth and eighteenth centuries, prince and prole alike used to come here (and to Covent Garden) for paid sex. Several prominent courtesans were residents of Soho, their profession recorded as "player and mistress to several persons", or, lower down on the social scale, "generally slut and drunkard; occasionally whore and thief". *Hooper's Hotel*, a high-class Soho brothel frequented by the Prince of Wales, even got a mention in the popular, late eighteenth-century book *The Mysteries of Flagellation*. By Victorian times, the area was described as "a reeking home of filthy vice", where "the grosser immorality flourishes unabashed from every age downwards to mere children". And it was in Soho that Prime Minister Gladstone used to conduct his crusade to save prostitutes – managing "to combine his missionary meddling with a keen appreciation of a pretty face", as one perceptive critic observed.

By World War II, **organized gangs**, like the notorious Messina Brothers from Malta, controlled a huge vice empire in Soho, later taken over by one of their erstwhile henchmen, Bernie Silver, Soho's self-styled "Godfather". In the 1960s and 1970s, the sex trade threatened to take over the whole of Soho, aided and abetted by the police themselves, who were involved in a massive protection racket. The complicity between the gangs and the police was finally exposed in 1976, when ten top-ranking Scotland Yard officers were charged with bribery and corruption on a massive scale and sentenced to prison for up to twelve years. (Silver himself had been put inside in 1974.) The combined efforts of the Soho Society and Westminster Council has enormously reduced the number of sex establishments, but, with the rise of the lap-dancing club, the area's vice days are not quite over yet.

ART AND HERESY IN SOHO

The streets around Poland Street have more than their fair share of artistic and heretical associations. A blue plaque at 74 Broadwick St records that **William Blake** was born there in 1757, above his father's hosiery shop, and where, from the age of 9, he had visions of "messengers from heaven, daily and nightly". He opened a print shop of his own next door to the family home, and later moved nearby to 28 Poland St, where he lived six years with his "beloved Kate" and wrote perhaps his most profound work, *The Marriage of Heaven and Hell*, among other poems. Poland Street was also **Shelley's** first halt after having been kicked out of Oxford in 1811 for distributing *The Necessity of Atheism*, and **Canaletto** ran a studio just south on Beak Street for a couple of years while he sat out the Seven Years' War in exile in London. And it was in the *Old King's Arms* pub on Poland Street in 1781 that the **Ancient Order of Druids** was revived.

Berwick Street

ⓦ berwickstreetlondon.co.uk • ⊖ Piccadilly Circus

Pop down Walker's Court, off Brewer Street, past the triple-X-rated film shops, and you come out into **Berwick Street** where the unlikely sight of one of the capital's traditional fruit and veg markets greets you (see p.433). The street itself is no beauty spot but the barrow displays are works of art in themselves. On either side, and round the corner in Broadwick Street, you'll find some of London's best specialist record shops like Sister Ray (see p.432) and Reckless Records.

Broadwick Street

It was a water pump on **Broadwick Street** that caused the deaths of some five hundred Soho residents in the **cholera epidemic** of 1854. Dr John Snow, Queen Victoria's obstetrician, traced the outbreak to the pump, thereby proving that the disease was waterborne rather than airborne, as previously thought. No one believed him, however, until he removed the pump handle and effectively stopped the epidemic. The original pump stood outside the pub now called the *John Snow*, on which there's a commemorative plaque and an easily missed red-granite kerbstone.

Carnaby Street

Until the 1950s, **Carnaby Street** was a backstreet on Soho's western fringe, occupied, for the most part, by sweatshop tailors who made up the suits for nearby Savile Row in Mayfair. Then, in 1954, Bill Green opened a shop in neighbouring Newburgh Street, selling outrageous clothes to the gay men who were hanging out at the local baths. He was followed by **John Stephen**, a Glaswegian grocer's son, who opened His Clothes in Beak Street. In 1960, Stephen moved his operation to Carnaby Street and within a couple of years owned a string of trendy boutiques catering for the new market in flamboyant men's clothing, including the wonderfully named I Was Lord Kitchener's Valet. By 1964 – the year of the official birth of the Carnaby Street myth – Mods, West Indian Rude Boys and other "switched-on people", as the *Daily Telegraph* noted, had begun to hang out in Carnaby Street. By the time Mary Quant sold her first miniskirt here, the area had become the heart of London's **Swinging Sixties**, its street sign the capital's most popular postcard. A victim of its own hype, Carnaby Street quickly declined into an avenue of overpriced tack. Nowadays, it's pedestrianized and smart again, but dominated by chains – for any sign of contemporary London fashion, you need to go round the corner to **Fouberts Place**, **Newburgh Street** and Kingly Court or head over to East London.

Photographers' Gallery

16–18 Ramillies St • Mon–Sat 10am–6pm, Thurs till 8pm, Sun 11.30am–6pm • Free • ☎ 020 7087 9300, ⓦ thephotographersgallery .org.uk • ⊖ Oxford Circus

Established in 1971, the **Photographers' Gallery** was the first independent gallery devoted to photography in London, and is now the city's largest public photographic

5

gallery. This former warehouse hosts three floors of exhibitions that change regularly and are invariably worth a visit, as are the bookshop and café. There's also a **camera obscura** on the third floor (Fri–Sun 11am–1pm).

Fitzrovia

Fitzrovia is the very much quieter northern extension of Soho, beyond Oxford Street. Like its neighbour, it has a raffish, cosmopolitan history, attracting its fair share of writers and bohemians over the last hundred years or so, including the Pre-Raphaelites and members of the Bloomsbury Group. That said, it's a lot less edgy than Soho, with just two real sights to visit – an ornate Victorian church on Margaret Street and Pollock's Toy Museum – and one unavoidable landmark, the former Post Office Tower.

All Saints, Margaret Street

Margaret St • Mon–Sat 7.30am–7pm, Sun 8am–7.30pm • ⓦ allsaintsmargaretstreet.org.uk • ⊖ Oxford Circus

Few London churches are as atmospheric as **All Saints, Margaret Street**, built by William Butterfield in the 1850s. Patterned brickwork characterizes the entire ensemble of clergy house, choir school (Laurence Olivier sang here as a boy) and church, set around a small courtyard entered from the street through a pointed arch. The church interior – one of London's gloomiest – is best visited on a sunny afternoon when the light pours in through the west window, illuminating the fantastic polychrome marble and stone which decorates the place from floor to ceiling. Several of the walls are also adorned with Pre-Raphaelite Minton-tile paintings, the east window is a neo-Byzantine quasi-iconostasis with saintly images nestling in gilded niches, and the elaborate pulpit is like the entire church in miniature. Surrounded by such iconographical clutter, you would be forgiven for thinking you were in a Catholic church – but then that was the whole idea of the Victorian High Church movement, which sought to re-Catholicize the Church of England without actually returning it to the Roman fold.

Charlotte Street

Fitzrovia's main street, **Charlotte Street** is lined with lively cafés and restaurants, but its real heyday was in the 1930s, when it was home to the *Tour Eiffel*, where Wyndham Lewis and Ezra Pound launched the Vorticist magazine *Blast*. *L'Étoile*, further up, was patronized by the likes of Dylan Thomas and T.S. Eliot, while *Bertorelli's* was where Eliot, John Berger and Christopher Isherwood used to meet at the Wednesday Club in the 1950s. The same crowd would get plastered in the nearby *Fitzroy Tavern* – from which the area got its sobriquet – along with rather more outrageous bohemians, like the hard-drinking Nina Hamnett, the self-styled "Queen of Bohemia", who used to boast that Modigliani once told her she had the best tits in Europe.

Pollock's Toy Museum

1 Scala St • Mon–Sat 10am–5pm • £3 • ☎ 020 7636 3452, ⓦ pollockstoymuseum.com • ⊖ Goodge Street

Housed above a wonderful toy shop in the backstreets of Fitzrovia is the highly atmospheric, doll's-house-like **Pollock's Toy Museum**. Its collections include a fine example of the Victorian paper theatres popularized by Benjamin Pollock, who sold them under the slogan "a penny plain, two pence coloured". The other exhibits range from vintage teddy bears to Sooty and Sweep, and from Red Army soldiers to wax dolls, filling every nook and cranny of the museum's six tiny, rickety rooms and the stairs – be sure to look out for the dalmatian, Dismal Desmond.

Post Office Tower

Exploring Fitzrovia, it's impossible to ignore the looming presence of the former **Post Office Tower** (officially known as the BT Tower), a glass-clad pylon on Cleveland Street,

5

> ### CROSSRAIL
>
> Near where Tottenham Court Road tube station used to be, there's now a very large hole in the ground – just one of several prominent sites across London due to the £15 billion **Crossrail** project. Aimed at relieving congestion on the tube, Crossrail will provide a super-fast method of crossing the city from east to west (and vice versa) by digging a thirteen-mile long, deep-bore tunnel, reducing travel time between Paddington and Liverpool Street stations to just ten minutes. The development around the new station at Tottenham Court Road alone is going to cost around £1 billion, and the first trains are due to run in 2018. If you want to learn more about the project, visit ⓦ crossrail.co.uk or head for the **Visitor Centre** (Tues & Thurs noon–8pm) at 16–18 St Giles High St.

designed in the early 1960s by a team of bureaucrats in the Ministry of Works. The city's tallest building until the NatWest Tower (now Tower 42) topped it in 1981, it's still a prominent landmark north of the river. Sadly, after a bomb attack in 1971, the tower closed to the public, and the revolving restaurant followed in 1980.

Fitzroy Square

Near the top of Fitzroy Street is **Fitzroy Square**, a Bloomsbury-style square begun by the Adam brothers in the 1790s and faced, initially, with light Portland stone, rather than the ubiquitous dark Georgian brickwork, but completed in stucco, some forty years later. Traffic is excluded, but few pedestrians come here either – except those hobbling to the London Foot Hospital – yet it's a square rich in artistic and revolutionary associations.

The painter **Ford Madox Brown** had fortnightly singsongs at no. 37 with his Pre-Raphaelite chums, and guests such as Turgenev and Liszt. **Virginia Woolf**'s blue plaque is at no. 29 (a house previously lived in by George Bernard Shaw): her Bloomsbury mates considered it a disreputable neighbourhood when she moved with her brother in 1907 (after first checking with the police). In 1913, artist Roger Fry set up his **Omega Workshops** at no. 33, padding the walls with seaweed to keep out the noise. In the 1890s the square was home to the **International Anarchist School for Children**, run by 60-year-old French anarchist Louise Michel. The police eventually raided the building and closed down the school after finding bombs hidden in the basement.

A revolutionary of more international fame – the Venezuelan adventurer **General Francisco de Miranda** (1750–1816) – is commemorated with a statue at the eastern corner of the London Foot Hospital, situated on the southern side of the square. De Miranda lived nearby for a few years at 58 Grafton Way, and in 1810 he met up in Fitzrovia with fellow revolutionary Simón Bolívar; de Miranda ended his days in a Spanish prison, while Bolívar went on to liberate much of South America.

Tottenham Court Road

It's been centuries since there was a stately mansion – the original Tottenham Court – at the northern end of **Tottenham Court Road**, which consistently makes a strong challenge for London's least prepossessing, central shopping street. A rash of stores flogging discount-priced electrical equipment pack out the southern end, while furniture-makers – the street's original vendors – from Habitat and Heal's to cheap sofa outlets, pepper its northern stretch.

The British Museum

Housed in London's grandest Greek Revival building, fronted by a giant Ionic colonnade and portico designed by Robert Smirke in the 1820s, the British Museum is one of the great museums of the world. With over seventy thousand exhibits ranged over several miles of galleries, it boasts one of the largest collections of antiquities, prints and drawings housed under one roof – over thirteen million objects (and growing). Its assortment of Roman and Greek art is unparalleled, its Egyptian collection is the best outside Egypt and there are fabulous treasures from Anglo-Saxon and Roman Britain, from Africa, China, Japan, India and Mesopotamia. You'll clearly never manage to see everything in one visit, so the best advice is to concentrate on a couple of areas of interest, or else sign up with one of the museum's excellent guided tours of a single room.

The origins of the BM (as it's known) lie in the seventy thousand curios – from fossils and flamingo tongues to "maggots taken from a man's ear" – collected by **Hans Sloane**, a Chelsea physician who bequeathed them to George II in 1753 for £20,000. The king couldn't (or wouldn't) pay, so the collection was purchased by an unenthusiastic government to form the world's first public secular museum, housed in a mansion bought with the proceeds of a dubiously conducted public lottery. Soon afterwards, the BM began to acquire the antiquities that have made it, in many ways, the world's largest museum of plundered goods. The "robberies" of Lord Elgin are only the best known; countless others engaged in sporadic looting throughout the Empire and the BM itself sent out archeologists to strip classical sites bare. Despite calls from countries around the world for the return of their national treasures, the BM looks unlikely to shift its stance.

The BM can get very crowded, particularly at weekends, so get here as early as possible. It's all a far cry from the museum's beginnings in 1759, when it was open for just three hours a day, entry was by written application and tickets for "any person of decent appearance" were limited to ten per hour. Nowadays, the BM can tire even the most ardent museum lover. J.B. Priestley, for one, wished "there was a little room somewhere in the British Museum that contained only about twenty exhibits and good lighting, easy chairs and a notice imploring you to smoke". Short of such a place, the best advice is to visit the Enlightenment gallery and the adjacent room 2, tick off one or two of the **highlights** (see box, p.109), or concentrate on one or two sections.

6

INFORMATION AND TOURS

Opening hours Daily 10am–5.30pm, Fri until 8.30pm.

Admission Free except for large special exhibitions – for these, tickets cost £12–15 and are best bought in advance as they often sell out.

Contact details ☎ 020 7323 8000, ⊕ britishmuseum.org.

Tube Tottenham Court Road, Russell Square or Holborn.

Orientation There are two entrances: the main one on Great Russell St and a back entrance on Montague Place. You can pick up a museum plan from the main information desk in the Great Court, but even equipped with a plan, it's easy to get confused – don't hesitate to ask the helpful and knowledgeable museum staff.

Tours Regular daily guided tours, known as eyeopener tours (30–40min; free), concentrate on just one room, as do Friday evening Spotlight tours (20min; free). A Highlights tour costs £12 (daily 11.30am & 2pm; 1hr 30min). Look out, too, for the Hands on desks in some galleries, where you can handle some artefacts. Another option is to pick up a multimedia guide (available daily 10am–4.30pm; £5).

Eating The museum's best café and restaurant is the *Gallery Café* beyond room 12; the *Court Café* in the Great Court itself is more snacky, though it has a spectacular setting; the *Court Restaurant* on the upper floor is pricier, and best booked in advance (☎ 020 7323 8990).

Ancient Greece and Rome

The BM's **Ancient Greece and Rome galleries** make up the largest section in the museum. The ground floor (rooms 11–23) is laid out along broadly chronological lines, from the Bronze Age to Hellenistic times; the upper floor (rooms 69–73) concentrates on the Roman Empire.

THE GREAT COURT

At the centre of the British Museum is the spectacular **Great Court** – the largest covered square in Europe – with its startling glass-and-steel curved roof, designed in 2000 by Norman Foster. At the centre of the Great Court, newly encased in stone, is the domed, Round **Reading Room**, designed by Sydney Smirke, Robert's younger brother, in 1857 to house the British Library. Numerous writers from Oscar Wilde to Virginia Woolf, have frequented the library, and it was here at padded leather desk O7 that Karl Marx wrote *Das Kapital*. Since the British Library moved out (see p.127), the BM have been using the place to stage temporary exhibitions, but when the new Conservations and Exhibitions Centre, on the north side of the museum, opens in 2014, the Reading Room should once again be open to the public – and spectacular it is, too.

Classical Greece

The twin half-columns that once flanked a beehive tomb at Mycenae now herald the beginning of the Greek antiquities. There's a lot of fabulous stuff in the first few rooms, but the real highlights begin in room 15, whose centrepiece is the marble relief from the **Harpy Tomb**, an imposing 30ft funerary pillar from Xanthos in Turkey. Its name derived from the strange birdwomen which appear on two sides of the relief, carrying children in their arms.

The most important monument from Xanthos can be seen, partially reconstructed, in room 17. The fourth-century BC **Nereid Monument** is a mighty temple-like chieftain's tomb, fronted with Ionic columns interspersed with figures, once identified as Nereids (sea nymphs), now thought to be Aurae, or wind goddesses. The monument was brought back from the BM's first overseas excavations in 1842 by Charles Fellows, along with the greater part of the site's moveable art (including the Harpy Tomb relief).

Elgin Marbles

Dull is the eye that will not weep to see
Thy walls defaced, thy mouldering shrines removed
By British hands, which it had best behoved
To guard those relics ne'er to be restored.
Curst be the hour when from their isle they roved,
And once again thy hapless bosom gored,
And snatch'd thy shrinking gods to northern climes abhorred!   *Childe Harold's Pilgrimage*, Lord Byron

The large, purpose-built room 18 houses the museum's most famous relics, the **Parthenon sculptures**, better known as the **Elgin Marbles**, after Lord Elgin, who removed them from the Parthenon in Athens between 1801 and 1812. As British ambassador, Elgin claimed he had permission from the Ottoman authorities (who ruled Greece at the time) to remove them. There were justifications for Elgin's action – a Venetian missile had caused considerable damage in 1687 when it landed on a pile of gunpowder the Turks had thoughtfully stored there – though Byron was not the only one to protest at the time. The Greek government has asked for the sculptures to be sent back so they can be displayed, along with the rest of the sculptures, at the Acropolis Museum in Athens – so far, to no avail.

The frieze and the statues

Despite their grand setting (and partly due to all the hype), first impressions of the marble friezes, carved between 447 and 432 BC under the supervision of the sculptor **Pheidias**, can be a little disappointing. The long, repetitive queues of worshippers lack the vigorous immediacy of high-relief sculptural friezes. To prepare yourself, head into the adjacent interpretive rooms to learn more about the context of the marbles. The main frieze, for example, would actually have been situated virtually out of sight behind the first set of columns, and would originally have been picked out in red, blue and gold paint.

Next, head into the main room for the traffic jam of horsemen on the north frieze, which exhibits superb compositional dexterity – it's worth remembering that the frieze is carved to a depth of only two inches, yet manages to convey a much greater feeling of

---

THE BM HIGHLIGHTS

Assyrian reliefs Ground floor, rooms 7–10
African galleries Lower floor, room 25
Egyptian mummies Upper floor, rooms 62–63
Elgin Marbles Ground floor, room 18

Enlightenment Ground floor, room 1
Lewis chessmen Upper floor, room 40
Rosetta Stone Ground floor, room 4
Sutton Hoo Treasure Upper floor, room 41

6

> **GREEK VASES**
>
> The BM boasts an exhausting array of **Greek vases**: Mycenaean vases (1300 BC) in room 12 and Geometric (around 800 BC) and Athenian black-figure vases (around 600 BC) in room 13. Among the red-figure vases from Greece's Classical age (500 BC onwards) in rooms 14 and 15, check out the satyrs balancing wine coolers on their erect penises (room 15, cabinet 7). There are further hoards of mostly red-figure vases in room 19 and the mezzanine gallery in room 20, not to mention various examples dotted about rooms 68–73 and in the Enlightenment gallery (room 1).

perspective. Another superlative slice stands directly opposite, where the oxen are being led to the gods (said to have inspired Keats to write *Ode on a Grecian Urn*). At each end of the room are the freestanding pedimental sculptures: the figures from the east pediment, which depict the extraordinary birth of Athena – she emerged full-grown and armed from the head of Zeus – are the more impressive, though most are headless.

Tomb of Payava
Two of Lord Elgin's even less defensible appropriations stand forlornly in room 19: a single Ionic column and one of the six caryatids from the portico of the **Erechtheum**, on the Acropolis. Further on, in room 20, is another large relic from Xanthos, the partially reconstructed **Tomb of Payava**, built during the incumbent's lifetime in the fourth century BC; the reliefs on the tomb's steep roof would have been out of view of earthbound mortals, and are best viewed from the mezzanine (room 20a) – if it's open.

Wonders of the Ancient World
Room 21 contains fragments from one of the Seven Wonders of the Ancient World: two huge figures, an Amazonian frieze and a marble horse the size of an elephant from the self-aggrandizing tomb of **King Mausolus at Halikarnassos** (source of the word "mausoleum") from the fourth century BC. However, the real gem is the sculpted column drum, decorated in high relief, in room 22, from another Wonder, the colossal **Temple of Artemis at Ephesus**. The rest of the room is devoted to Hellenistic culture and features a fabulously delicate, gold oak wreath with a bee and two cicadas.

The upper floors
The remainder of the Greek and Roman collection is situated on the **upper floors** (rooms 69–73), best approached from the west stairs, which are lined with rich **mosaics**. For the most part, the best stuff is displayed in room 70, and includes a dazzling display of silverware from Roman Gaul and an intriguing, warty, crocodile-skin suit of armour worn by a Roman follower of the Egyptian crocodile cult (cabinet 18). Don't miss the first-century AD silver **Warren Cup** (cabinet 12a), whose graphic depictions of gay sex were deemed too risqué to be shown to the public until the 1990s. Next to it stands the **Portland Vase**, made from cobalt-blue blown glass, and decorated with opaque white cameos. The vase was famously smashed into over two hundred tiny pieces by a drunken Irishman in 1845, for which he was fined £3.

Middle East
The **Middle Eastern collection** covers all the lands east of Egypt and west of India. The majority of exhibits on the ground floor (rooms 6–10) come from the Assyrian Empire, centred on modern-day Iraq; upstairs (rooms 52–59) you'll find more rich pickings from Mesopotamia and the surrounding region; in the north wing of the building, on the ground floor, is a room devoted to Islam (room 34).

Assyrian sculpture and reliefs

A colossal guardian lion, smothered in inscriptions, signals the beginning of the BM's remarkable collection of **Assyrian sculptures and reliefs** (room 6). Close by stands a small black obelisk carved with images of foreign rulers paying tribute to Shalmaneser III (858–824 BC), interspersed with **cuneiform inscriptions**, the world's oldest written language. Ahead lies the Egyptian sculpture gallery (room 4), but to continue with Assyria, turn left and pass between the two awesome five-legged, human-headed winged lions that once flanked the doorway of the throne room in the palace in Nimrud (now in northern Iraq), built by Ashurnasirpal II (883–859 BC). Beyond is a full-scale reconstruction of the colossal wooden **Balawat Gates** from the palace of Shalmaneser III, bound together with bronze strips decorated with low-relief friezes, depicting the defeat and execution of Shalmaneser's enemies.

Nimrud and Nineveh reliefs

The vast corridor of **Nimrud reliefs**, in room 7, were originally brightly coloured, appearing rather like stone tapestries, and adorned the interior of Ashurnasirpal II's palace. There are some great snapshots of Assyrian life – a review of prisoners, a bull hunt and so on – but the most memorable scene, located towards the middle of the room, is of the soldiers swimming across the sea on inflated animal bladders. The **Nineveh reliefs** in room 9 record the stupendous effort involved in transporting some gargantuan winged bulls from their quarry to the palace of Sennacherib (704–681 BC). The Assyrians moved these carved beasts in one piece; not so the British, who cut the two largest winged bulls into four pieces before transporting them – the joins are still visible on the pair, which now stand at the northern entrance to room 10.

Room 10 itself is lined with even more splendid Assyrian friezes from Sennacherib's palace in Nineveh. On one side (10b) the reliefs portray the chaos and carnage during the capture of Lachish (a city in modern-day Israel); the friezes were damaged, and Sennacherib's face smashed in, by Babylonian soldiers when the Assyrian capital later fell to its southern neighbours in 612 BC. On the other side (10a) are the **royal lion hunts** of Ashurbanipal (668–631 BC), which involved rounding up the beasts before letting them loose, one at a time, in an enclosed arena for the king's sport, a practice that effectively eradicated the species in Assyria; the succession of graphic death scenes features one in which the king slaughters the cats with his bare hands.

Mesopotamia

Upstairs, in room 59, are the Neolithic **Ain Ghazal statues**, the oldest large-scale representations of humans in the world, dating from the eighth millennium BC. Further on, in room 56, are some more of the BM's oldest artefacts, dating from Mesopotamia in the third millennium BC. The most extraordinary treasures hail from Ur, the first great city on earth, (now in Iraq): the enigmatic **Ram in the Thicket** (cabinet 17), a deep-blue lapis lazuli and white shell statuette of a goat on its hind legs, peering through gold-leaf branches; beside it, the equally mysterious **Standard of Ur**, a small hollow box showing scenes of battle on one side, with peace and banqueting on the other, all fashioned in shell, red limestone and lapis lazuli, set in bitumen; and the **Royal Game of Ur** (cabinet 16), one of the earliest known board games.

In room 55, a selection of tablets scratched with infinitesimal cuneiform script includes lists, receipts, spells and prescriptions, the **Flood Tablet** (cabinet 8), a fragment of the Epic of Gilgamesh, the world's oldest story, and, in room 52, the **Cyrus Cylinder** (cabinet 4), recounting the Persian leader's capture of Babylon in 539 BC. Also in room 52, there's the **Oxus Treasure** (cabinet 3), the most important surviving hoard of Persian goldwork from the Achaemenid Empire (550–330 BC), discovered in Tajikistan in 1877 and eventually picked up from the bazaar in Rawalpindi. The most celebrated pieces are the miniature four-horse chariot and the pair of armlets sprouting fantastical horned griffins.

Islam

The museum's fairly modest **Islamic collection** is tucked away in room 34, by the Montague Place entrance. Among the highlights are the **Damascus and Iznik ceramics** in greens, tomato-reds and no fewer than five shades of blue. Also worth seeking out at the far end of the room, are the medieval astrolabes, celestial globes and a **geomantic instrument** used to tell the future. The most striking exhibit is a naturalistic **jade terrapin**, discovered in Allahabad in 1600; close by is a silver-filigree cosmetic box said to be from Tipu Sultan's palace, and a couple of jade Mughal hookah bases encrusted with lapis lazuli and rubies set in gold.

6

Ancient Egypt

The BM's collection of **Egyptian antiquities**, ranging from Pre-dynastic times to Coptic Egypt, is one of the finest in the world, rivalled only by Cairo's; the highlights are the **Rosetta Stone**, the vast hall of Egyptian **sculpture** (room 4) and the large collection of **mummies** (rooms 61–66).

Egyptian sculpture

On the ground floor, just past the entrance to the Assyrian section (see opposite), two black-granite statues of **Amenophis III**, also known as Amenhotep III (c.1417–1379 BC), whose rule coincided with the zenith of Egyptian power, guard the entrance to the BM's large hall of **Egyptian sculpture** (room 4). The name "Belzoni", scratched behind the left heel of the larger statue, was carved by the Italian circus strongman responsible for dragging some of the heftiest Egyptian treasures to the banks of the Nile. Further on, a colossal pink-speckled granite head of Amenophis III stands next to his enormous dislocated arm. Nearby are four black granite statues of the goddess Sakhmet, the half-lion, half-human bringer of destruction, who was much loved by Amenophis III – each sports solar discs and clutches the *ankh*, the Egyptian symbol of life.

North of here, another giant head and shoulders, comprised of two-coloured granite, bears the hole drilled by Napoleon's soldiers in an unsuccessful attempt to remove it from the mortuary temple of Ramesses II – it was this relic that inspired Shelley's poem *Ozymandias*. Moving towards the end of the room, make sure you seek out the bronze Gayer-Anderson cat goddess **Bastet**, with gold nose- and earrings, and the colossal granite scarab beetle by the exit.

The mummies and other funerary art

Upstairs in room 61, eleven large fragments of the colourful wall-paintings from the **tomb-chapel of Nebamun** from 1350 BC are displayed, depicting the idealized life of wealthy Egyptians of the period. Next door, in room 62, is the popular **Egyptian mummy**

THE ROSETTA STONE

There's usually a little huddle of people in the centre of the Egyptian sculpture hall crowded round the **Rosetta Stone**, officially the most visited object in the BM. This slab of dark granodiorite, found in Rashid (Rosetta) in the Nile delta in 1799 by French soldiers, is inscribed with a decree extolling the virtues of the Greek pharoah Ptolemy V in 196 BC. What made the Rosetta Stone so famous, however, was that it was the same text written in two different languages and three different scripts: Ancient Greek at the bottom, demotic Egyptian script in the middle and, most importantly of all, **Egyptian hieroglyphs** at the top. It was surrendered to the Brits in 1801, after they had defeated the French at Alexandria, and brought to the BM, where it has been on more or less continuous display since 1802. However, it was a French professor, Champollion, who eventually unlocked the secret of Egyptian hieroglyphs, and produced an accurate translation some twenty years later. A full-size replica, displayed as the Stone used to be, is on display in the Enlightenment gallery –it's free to touch and free from crowds.

collection, including numerous mummified corpses, embalmed bodies, and inner and outer **coffins** richly decorated with hieroglyphs. In cabinet 29, there are mummies of animals, including cats, apes, crocodiles, falcons and an eel, along with their highly ornate coffins. Also on display, in cabinet 23, are colourful funerary **amulets**, which were wrapped with the mummy, and **scarabs**, which were placed on the chest of the mummy to prevent the deceased's heart from bearing witness against him or her after death. And don't miss the diminutive, glazed turquoise hippo, one of the museum's most popular items (cabinet 23). In room 63, you can view the varied contents of Egyptian tombs: food, drink, clothing, furniture, weapons and dozens of **shabti figures** (cabinet 16) designed to perform any task the gods might require in the afterlife. There are also miniature boats to provide transport in the afterlife, beer brewers, butchers and even an entire model granary.

At this point, pop into room 66 to admire the joyful depiction of the Battle of Adwa (1896), when **Ethiopia** trounced Italy, the nearby Falasha (Jewish) dolls and the "chestlet" of beetle wings. Lastly, the five thousand-year-old sand-preserved corpse in room 64 (cabinet 15) always comes in for ghoulish scrutiny, and there's a limestone building block (cabinet 14) from the Great Pyramid of Khufu (Cheops), another of the Seven Wonders of the Ancient World.

Europe

The BM fulfils its less controversial role as national treasure house of antiquities in the **Europe** section on the upper floor (rooms 40–51). Here, you'll find a vast range of exhibits from Iron Age jewellery to twentieth-century objets d'art.

Prehistoric/Roman Britain

One of the BM's most sensational finds is the **Mold Gold Cape**, a remarkable paper-thin gold garment from the Bronze Age, found in north Wales and now centre stage in room 51. Look out, too, for the well-preserved leathery half-corpse **Lindow Man**, in room 50, thought to have been clubbed and garrotted during a Druid sacrificial ceremony. Several impressive Iron Age treasure troves are also displayed in room 50, among them the **Snettisham Treasure** (cabinet 19) of gold and silver torcs (neck-rings). Room 49 displays finds from **Roman Britain**, many, like the bronze head (and hand) of the Roman emperor Hadrian (cabinet 14), dredged out of the Thames. The most impressive display is the fourth-century AD **Mildenhall Treasure** (cabinet 22), a 28-piece silver tableware set, whose Great Dish is decorated with Bacchic images in low relief.

Europe: Dark Ages to Medieval

Visitors entering room 40 are greeted by the incredible, fourteenth-century French **Royal Gold Cup** (cabinet 2), given by James I to the Constable of Castille, only to find its way back to England in later life – the scenes enamelled on its surface depict the gruesome story of St Agnes. Beyond lie the celebrated **Lewis chessmen** (cabinet 5), wild-eyed, thick-set, twelfth-century Scandinavian figures carved from walrus ivory, discovered in 1831 by a crofter in the Outer Hebrides. Room 41 houses the Anglo-Saxon **Sutton Hoo Treasure**, which includes silver bowls, gold jewellery and an iron helmet bejewelled with gilded bronze and garnets, all buried along with a forty-oar open ship in East Anglia around 625 AD, and discovered by accident in 1939.

Europe: Renaissance to Modern

Room 47 kicks off the **European nineteenth-century** section, and reflects the era's eclectic tastes, with everything from quasi-medieval jewellery to Neoclassical porcelain vases, much of it inspired by the BM itself. Look out for the Arts and Crafts De Morgan and Minton tiles (cabinet 12) and Christopher Dresser's outstanding geometric metalwork (cabinet 15). In room 48, the best of the museum's **twentieth-century exhibits** are displayed, including stunning examples of iridescent Tiffany glass, a copper vase by Frank Lloyd Wright and a lovely, chequered oak clock with a mother-of-pearl face, designed by Charles Rennie Mackintosh. There's also usually an impressive array of avant-garde Russian ceramics celebrating the achievements of the 1917 revolution.

Renaissance and Baroque art fills room 46, with a bafflingly wide range of works from all over Europe (though much of it of British origin). Highlights include a collection of eighteenth-century Huguenot silver, two pure-gold ice pails that belonged to Princess Diana's family and the Armada Service, a Tudor silver dining set.

Room 45 contains the **Waddesdon Bequest**, curiosities amassed by Baron Rothschild in the nineteenth century: a mixed bag of silver gilt, enamelware, glassware and hunting rifles. Two of the finest works are the Holy Thorn Reliquary (cabinet 1), with its wonderfully macabre depiction of the Resurrection, and a Flemish sixteenth-century boxwood altarpiece of Christ's Life and Passion (cabinet 8), just six inches high and carved with staggering detail.

King's Library – Enlightenment

The **Enlightenment gallery** (room 1) runs the length of the east wing. Built to house George III's library (now in the British Library in St Pancras), it's like a snapshot of the BM of old, lined with antique display cases stuffed with books and artefacts, illustrating the magpie tastes of the eighteenth-century colonial collector, epitomized by Hans Sloane himself, the BM's founder.

Sloane's own collection features everything from priapic statuettes to a black obsidian mirror used by the magician, John Dee, to conjure up spirits (case 20). And he was not alone in falling for the bizarre and magical to augment his "cabinet of curiosities": the rhino-horn cup which protected the drinker from poison and the Japanese "merman" (opposite case 14) – a dried monkey sewn onto a fish tail – are not atypical. Displayed here, too, are some of the museum's earliest acquisitions, brought back from the far reaches of the expanding British Empire: a piece of bark cloth made by Fletcher Christian's Tahitian partner (case 22); Tipu Sultan's sword and ring, and a whole variety of Javanese puppets and dolls (case 23) collected by Stamford Raffles.

Don't neglect to pop into adjacent room 2, where some of the museum's **oldest exhibits** are usually displayed, like the thirteen thousand-year-old ivory sculpture of swimming reindeer and the eleven thousand-year-old sculpture of two lovers entwined, found in the Judean desert.

Americas

The BM's two American galleries lie to the side of the **Living and Dying gallery** (room 24), which features Hoa Hakananai'a, the giant basalt **Easter Island statue** (originally

---

TIME AND MONEY

The BM has a number of themed rooms, the largest of which is the Enlightenment gallery on the ground floor (see above). On the upper floor, **clocks and watches** (rooms 38 & 39) resound to the tick-tocks and chimes of every type of timepiece from pocket watches to grandfather clocks. One of the best party pieces is the Polish clock from 1600 (room 38), featuring a cow that produced liquid from its udders on the hour, and the spectacular ship from 1585 (room 39), whose concealed organ would announce a banquet.

The **money** gallery (room 68) traces the history of filthy lucre from the use of grain in Mesopotamia around 2000 BC, through the advent of coins in around 600 BC in Lydia in Asia Minor to the plastic money of today. The prize for the largest denomination bill goes to the 1946 one hundred million billion *pengö* note from Hungary (cabinet 16). In the centre of the room, there's a geometric lathe for old £1 notes (cabinet 14), a wonderful Tiffany-designed National Cash Register till (cabinet 17) and a hoard of fake Roman coins and fake £1 coins (cabinet 10). Plus ca change.

painted red and white), and four modern apocalyptic papier-mâché skeletons from the Mexican Day of the Dead festival. Close by is the famous crystal skull, thought to have been Aztec when the BM bought it in 1897, but now known to be a fake.

Next door is the **North American gallery** (room 26), whose precise exhibits change regularly, due to the delicate, organic nature of the materials used. However, you can be sure to find feather headdresses, masks, basketry, bead and shell currency and zoomorphic stone pipes. From the Arctic, there are Inuit furs and skins, including a caribou-skin parka and bone sled, and from the Southwest, the ever-popular Pueblo pottery made by the Hopi.

The **Mexican gallery** (room 27) covers Mexican art from the second millennium BC to the sixteenth century AD. The centrepiece is an Aztec fire serpent, Xiuhcoatl, carved in basalt: on one side is a collection of Huaxtec female deities in stone, sporting fan-shaped headdresses; on the other are an Aztec stone rattlesnake, the squatting figure of the sun-god, Xochipili, and the death-cult god, Mictlantecuhtli. A series of limestone Mayan reliefs from Yaxchilan, depicting blood-letting ceremonies, lines one wall and, elsewhere, there are some exquisite fifteenth-century turquoise mosaic masks and figurines.

Africa

The BM's **Africa** collection is housed on the lower floor (room 25). As you enter, you'll see the "Throne of Weapons", made in Mozambique from decommissioned weapons, as is the "Tree of Life" further on. Nearby there are **woodcarvings** from a whole range of African cultures: everything from carved gods from Mali to backrests from the Congo. Further to the left, you'll find the Yoruba royal palace doors, carved in high relief and depicting, among other things, lazy British imperialists arriving on a litter to collect taxes. And don't miss the incredible display of throwing knives from central Africa in the next door gallery.

To the right, there's a section on **masquerades**, with elaborate crocodile, buffalo, warthog and hippo masks from the last two centuries, and a video of contemporary initiation ceremonies in Nigeria. Perhaps the most famous of the BM's African exhibits are the so-called "**Benin Bronzes**", looted by the British in 1897. Confusingly, these are neither bronzes (they are, in fact, brass), nor from modern-day Benin, but from the former Benin Empire within modern-day Nigeria. Among the most impressive are the fifty or so ornate sixteenth-century brass plaques, nine hundred of which once decorated the royal palace in Benin City. Other Benin exhibits, such as the eye-catching ivory leopards studded with copper gun caps, were actually commissioned by Europeans.

Asia

The BM's Chinese collection is unrivalled in the West, and the Indian sculpture is easily as good as anything at the V&A. The Asian galleries (rooms 33, 67 & 92–95) are in the museum's north wing, by the Montague Place entrance.

China

The **Chinese collection** occupies one half of room 33. Immediately striking are the large pieces of garishly glazed **three-colour statuary**, particularly the three seated sages at the far end of the room, and the central cabinet of horses, camels, kings, officials and fabulous beasts. However, take time for the smaller pieces: the miniature landscapes (cabinet 56), popular among bored Chinese bureaucrats, or the incredible array of **snuff bottles** (cabinet 54), made from lapis lazuli, jade, crystal, tortoiseshell, quartz and amber. The Chinese invented **porcelain**, and there's a whole range on display here, but for an even more impressive collection of Chinese ceramics, head for room 95 (see opposite). Lastly, don't miss the **Chinese jade**, on display in the adjacent corridor (room 33b).

South and Southeast Asia

The other half of room 33 starts with a beautiful gilt-bronze statue of Tara, the goddess of good fortune, who was born from one of the tears wept by Avalokiteshvara (who embodies compassion and stands on the east side of the marble well). She heralds the beginning of the **South and Southeast Asian** antiquities, a bewildering array of artefacts from places as far apart as India and Indonesia. It's worth seeking out cabinet 55 with its Tibetan depictions of tantric sex, its *dakinis* (fierce minor goddesses who dance on demons) and Chitipati, lord of the graveyard. Cabinet 39 features a whole set of ivory figures from Kandy, representing the local royal family and officials, including the all-important umbrella-bearer. Beyond are larger-scale **Indian stone sculptures**, featuring a bevy of intimidating goddesses such as Durga, depicted killing a buffalo demon with her eight hands (cabinet 25).

6

Korea

The centrepiece of the BM's Korea gallery (room 67), up the north stairs from room 33, is a nail-free reconstruction of a *sarangbang* or scholar's study, a serene, minimalist space set aside for the gentleman of the house. Among the other exhibits, which range from illuminated Buddhist manuscripts to contemporary Korean objets d'art, look out for the bamboo fans (cabinet 21), used by dapper Korean gentlemen, their woven horsehair hats (cabinet 19) and the *paduk* gaming board (better known in the West as Go). There's a seventeenth-century white porcelain "full-moon" jar, admired for both its irregularity and its Confucian austerity.

Chinese ceramics – Sir Percival David Collection

Next door is an entire room given over to **Chinese ceramics** (room 95), with nearly 1700 objects on display, dating from the third to the twentieth centuries, which once formed the largest private collection in the world. A few star exhibits get labels, like the "David vases", by the entrance, from 1351, in the blue-and-white Ming style that became so popular in Europe – touch-screen computers will help you identify the rest. What is so striking about many of the pieces is their apparent modernity – the bold single-colour porcelain wares at the far side of the room wouldn't look out of place in the 1960s, though in fact they date from the Ming and Qing dynasties. Among the most celebrated Chinese ceramics are the *Ru* wares whose "crackling" glaze was seen as a merit rather than a defect from the Song dynasty onwards.

Japan

The sensitive materials used in Japanese art mean that the items on display in the **Japan** (rooms 92–94) galleries change frequently. What you get is an educational sample laid out chronologically from the Neolithic Jomon period to the manga culture of contemporary Japan. In between, you get to inspect colourful Buddhist scrolls, Shinto shrines, nineteenth-century woodblock prints by artists such as Hokusai and Hiroshige, examples of *netsuke* (ornamental toggles) and *inro* (cases for holding small objects). Centre stage, there's a wonderfully ornate suit of Samurai armour, complete with the sort of horned helmet and mask that Darth Vadar might wear. There's also a section on the traditional tea ceremony alongside a reconstructed tea house, where the museum puts on regular demonstrations.

PRINTS AND DRAWINGS

The sheer volume of the BM's **prints and drawings** – two million prints and fifty thousand drawings – means there's only space for a changing display in room 90. However, with an incredible collection of drawings by Leonardo, Raphael, Michelangelo, Rubens and Rembrandt, plus prints by Dürer and works by Hogarth, Constable, Turner and Blake – to mention but a few – the exhibitions are always worth exploring.

THE BRITISH LIBRARY

Bloomsbury

Bloomsbury was built over in grid-plan style from the 1660s onwards, and the formal, bourgeois Georgian squares remain the area's main distinguishing feature. In the last century, Bloomsbury acquired the reputation it continues to hold, as the city's most learned quarter, dominated by the dual institutions of the British Museum (see p.106) and London University. Today, the British Museum is clearly Bloomsbury's main draw, but the real pleasure in Bloomsbury is simply strolling through its leafy squares, which provide some of the nicest picnic spots in central London. Only in its northern border, formed by busy Euston Road, does the character of the area change dramatically, with the hustle and bustle of the mainline train stations of St Pancras and King's Cross.

South of the British Museum

Over the years, there have been moves to demolish the small grid of Georgian streets to the south of the British Museum to give the BM (as it's known) a more triumphal approach. Thankfully, none have come to fruition and **Museum Street** and **Bury Place** remain a pleasure to explore, thriving on a mixture of antiquarian and secondhand print and book shops, and cafés and sandwich shops which feed the museum hordes. It's worth looking in at **Jarndyce**, the booksellers at 46 Great Russell St, whose left window is renowned for its display of bizarre antiquarian books, with titles such as *Correctly English in Hundred Days* and *The Art of Faking Exhibition Poultry*.

Cartoon Museum

35 Little Russell St · Tues–Sat 10.30am–5.30pm, Sun noon–5.30pm · £5.50 · ☎ 020 7580 8155, ⓦ cartoonmuseum.org · ➜ Tottenham Court Road

As well as putting on excellent temporary exhibitions, the **Cartoon Museum** also has a permanent display of over two hundred works spanning two centuries, beginning with Hogarth's moralistic engravings and the caricatures of Gillray, Rowlandson and Cruickshank. The emphasis is very much on British cartoons from the likes of *Punch*, one of the earliest and longest-lasting satirical magazines, to *Private Eye*, which helped launch the careers of, among others, Ralph Steadman and Gerald Scarfe. The comic strips range from Ally Sloper, Britain's first regular comic-strip character who appeared in 1884, through D.C. Thompson (publisher of *Beano*), to *Viz*, the country's best-selling comic ever, which at its peak sold over a million copies each edition.

Church of St George's Bloomsbury

Bloomsbury Way · Daily 1–4pm · ☎ 020 7242 1979, ⓦ stgeorgesbloomsbury.org.uk · ➜ Tottenham Court Road or Holborn

A couple of blocks south of the BM is Hawksmoor's **Church of St George's Bloomsbury**, built in 1730 to serve Bloomsbury's respectable new residents. Its main point of interest is the unusual steeple – Horace Walpole called it "a masterpiece of absurdity" – a stepped pyramid based on Pliny's description of the tomb of Mausolus at Halikarnassos (fragments of which now reside in the BM), with lions and unicorns clinging precariously to the base. The tower is topped by a statue of the unpopular German-speaking monarch, George I, dressed in a Roman toga. The interior is tall, wide and gleaming white, with a large clerestory, its best features the flaming pentecostal tongues on the keystones and the unusual semicircular apse, complete with a scallop-shell recess. There's an interesting multimedia exhibition on Hawksmoor and Bloomsbury in the crypt (phone ahead to check it's open).

Bloomsbury Square

Laid out in 1665, **Bloomsbury Square** was the first of the city's open spaces to be officially called a "square". John Evelyn thought it "a noble square or piazza – a little towne", but sadly little remains of its original or later Georgian appearance. At the south end of the square you'll find **Sicilian Avenue**, a beautifully preserved architectural set piece from 1910. This unusually continental promenade leads diagonally onto Southampton Row and is separated from the main roads by slender Ionic screens. On Southampton Row itself, you can see the only **tram lines** left uncovered in central London from what was, between World Wars I and II, the world's largest tram system: to catch a glimpse, you must dodge the traffic and peek through the wrought-iron railings to the tracks as they descend into the former Kingsway tram subway.

Bedford Square

The most handsome of the Bloomsbury squares is **Bedford Square**, to the west of the BM. Some of Bloomsbury's best-known publishing houses had their offices here until the 1980s – now it's home to Bloomsbury, publishers of Harry Potter. Architecturally, what you see now is pretty much as it was in the 1770s when it was built by the Russells (who still own it), though the gates which sealed the square from traffic have unfortunately been removed, as have all but one of the mews that once accommodated the coaches and servants of the square's wealthy inhabitants. Today, it's a perfect example of eighteenth-century symmetry and uniformity: each doorway arch is decorated with rusticated Coade stones; each palatial facade of the square is broken only by the white-stuccoed central houses; and the central garden is for residents only.

BLOOMSBURY

ACCOMMODATION	
Arosfa Hotel	9
Astor Museum Inn	12
Clink 261 Hostel	6
Clink 78 Hostel	8
Generator	7
Great Northern Hotel	1
Jesmond Hotel	11
Morgan Hotel	13
Passfield Hall	5
Ridgemount Hotel	10
Rough Luxe	4
St Pancras Renaissance	2
St Pancras YHA	3

● SHOPS	
Arthur Probsthain	4
Bookmarks	6
Gay's the Word	2
London Review Bookshop	5
Persephone Books	3
School of Life	1

■ PUBS & BARS	
Bar Pepito	4
The Duke	10
Euston Tap	5
The Lamb	9
Museum Tavern	11
Parcel Yard	2
The Queen's Head	7

■ GAY & LESBIAN VENUES	
Central Station	3
New Bloomsbury Set	8

■ MUSIC VENUE	
King's Place	1

■ CLUB	
Scala	6

● CAFÉS	
Abeno	6
Bloomsbury Coffee House	3
Hummus Bros	5

● RESTAURANTS	
Caravan	1
Diwana Bhel Poori House	2
GAIL's Kitchen	4

Architectural Association

36 Bedford Square · Term time Mon–Fri 10am–7pm, Sat 11am–5pm · ☎ 020 7887 4000, Ⓦ aaschool.ac.uk · ⊖ Tottenham Court Road

The best way to get a look inside one of Bedford Square's Georgian mansions is to head for the **Architectural Association**, which occupies eight houses on the west side of the square. The public can visit the AA's occasional exhibitions, its basement bookshop and the studenty café-bar on the first floor, with a roof terrace open in fine weather.

Building Centre

26 Store St · Mon–Fri 9.30am–6pm, Sat 10am–5pm · Free · ☎ 020 7692 4000, Ⓦ buildingcentre.co.uk · ⊖ Goodge Street

If you've got even a passing interest in London's architecture and planning, it's a good idea to pop into the **Building Centre**, which has a café and a bookshop and which stages topical exhibitions on the future of London's built environment. Its centrepiece is a vast 1:1500 model of London, including the latest City skyscrapers and the Olympic Park.

Russell Square

The largest Bloomsbury square – indeed one of the largest in London – is **Russell Square**, to the northeast of the BM. Apart from its monumental scale, little remains of the Georgian scheme, though the gardens, with their gargantuan plane trees, are good for a picnic, and there's a café in the northeastern corner. The Bloomsbury figure most closely associated with the square is T.S. Eliot, who worked at no. 24, then the offices of Faber & Faber, from 1925 until his death in 1965. The only architectural curiosity is the **Russell Hotel**, on the eastern side; twice as high as everything around it, it's a no-holds-barred Victorian terracotta fancy, concocted in a bewildering mixture of styles in 1898 by Fitzroy Doll.

Gordon Square

Gordon Square is owned by the University of London, which surrounds it on three sides, and open to the public. With its winding paths and summer profusion of roses, it remains one of Bloomsbury's quietest sanctuaries and is predictably popular with students. Between the wars, it was at the centre of the Bloomsbury Group (see p.122): on the east side, where the Georgian houses stand intact, plaques mark the residences of writer Lytton Strachey (no. 51) and economist John Maynard Keynes (no. 46), while another (no. 50) commemorates the group as a whole.

Church of Christ the King

Gordon Square · Mon–Fri 8am–4pm · Free · ☎ 020 7388 3588, Ⓦ fifparish.com · ⊖ Euston Square or Goodge Street

Looking like a miniature cathedral, in the southwest corner of the square, stands the strangely towerless **Church of Christ the King**, built in neo-Gothic style in the 1850s. The five-bay nave is cathedralesque – the nave of Westminster Abbey is only 13ft taller – with a hammerbeam roof, full triforium and clerestory; the unbuilt spire was to have been nearly 150ft high. It was built for (and still belongs to) the Catholic Apostolic Church, a prayer sect within the Anglican Church who were utterly convinced that the Second Coming was imminent (and who were renowned for elaborate rituals, for speaking in tongues and for miraculous healing). It's currently the home of Forward in Faith, the conservative wing of the Church of England.

Tavistock Square

One block east of Gordon Square is **Tavistock Square**, laid out by Thomas Cubitt in the early nineteenth century. Though the west side of the square survives intact, the house on the south side at no. 52, where the Woolfs lived from 1924 until shortly before Virginia's suicide in 1941, and from which they ran the Hogarth Press, is no longer standing. It was here that Woolf wrote her most famous novels – *To the Lighthouse, Mrs Dalloway, Orlando* and *The Waves* – in a little studio decorated by her sister Vanessa and Duncan Grant. At the centre of the square's gardens is a statue of **Mahatma Gandhi**, who studied law at UCL, and whose presence has transformed the square into something of a garden for peace, with trees and benches dedicated to the cause. That peace, however, was shattered on the morning of **July 7, 2005**, when a suicide bomber blew himself up on bus #30 as it approached the northeast corner of the square, killing thirteen people. The blast occurred shortly after three tube trains had been hit by bombs (see p.461) – a plaque on the BMA building commemorates the victims.

Woburn Walk

A short distance up Upper Woburn Place from Tavistock Square, not far from where the July 7, 2005, blast occurred, is the beautifully preserved Georgian terrace of **Woburn Walk**, designed in 1822 by Cubitt as London's first purpose-built pedestrianized shopping street. **W.B. Yeats** moved into no. 5 in 1895, shortly afterwards losing his virginity at the age of 31 to fellow writer Olivia Shakespear. He and Olivia went to Heal's to order a bed before consummating the relationship, and Yeats found the experience (of ordering the bed) deeply traumatic, as "every inch added to the expense". The same address was later occupied by the unrequited love of Yeats' life, Irish nationalist Maud Gonne, reputedly the most beautiful woman in Ireland, with, in Yeats' own words, "the carriage and features of a goddess".

Coram's Fields

Guilford Street · Daily 9am–7pm or dusk · Free · ☎ 020 7837 6138, ⓦ coramsfields.org · ⊖ Russell Square

Halfway along Guilford Street stands the old entrance to the **Foundling Hospital**, established in 1739 by **Thomas Coram**, a retired sea captain. Coram campaigned for nearly twenty years to obtain a royal charter for the hospital, having been shocked by

---

THE BLOOMSBURY GROUP

The **Bloomsbury Group** were essentially a bevy of upper-middle-class friends who lived in and around Bloomsbury, at that time "an antiquated, ex-fashionable area", in the words of Henry James. The group revolved around siblings Virginia, Vanessa, Thoby and Adrian Stephen, who moved into 46 Gordon Square in 1904. Thoby's Thursday-evening gatherings and Vanessa's Friday Club for painters attracted a whole host of Cambridge-educated types who subscribed to Oscar Wilde's theory that "aesthetics are higher than ethics". Their diet of "human intercourse and the enjoyment of beautiful things" was hardly revolutionary, but their behaviour, particularly that of the two sisters – unmarried, unchaperoned, intellectual and artistic – succeeded in shocking London society, especially through their louche sexual practices (most of the group swung both ways).

All this, though interesting, would be forgotten were it not for their individual work. In 1922, Virginia declared, without too much exaggeration, "Everyone in Gordon Square has become famous": Lytton Strachey was the first to make his name with a series of unprecedentedly frank biographies; Vanessa, now married to the art critic Clive Bell, became involved in Roger Fry's prolific design firm, **Omega Workshops**; and the economist John Maynard Keynes became an adviser to the Treasury. (He later went on to become the leading economic theorist of his day.) The group's most celebrated figure, Virginia, now married to Leonard Woolf, had become an established novelist; she and Leonard had also founded the **Hogarth Press**, which published T.S. Eliot's *Waste Land* in 1924.

Eliot was just one of a number of writers, such as Aldous Huxley, Bertrand Russell and E.M. Forster, who were drawn to the Bloomsbury set, but others, notably D.H. Lawrence, were repelled by the clan's narcissism and narrow-mindedness. Whatever their limitations, the Bloomsbury Group were certainly Britain's most influential intellectual coterie of the interwar years, and their appeal shows little sign of waning.

the number of dead or dying babies left by the wayside on the streets of London during the gin craze. (At the time, 75 percent of London's children died before they were 5.) All that remains of the original eighteenth-century buildings is the whitewashed loggia which forms the border to **Coram's Fields**, an inner-city haven for children, with swings and slides, plus a whole host of hens, goats, rabbits, ducks and a sheep. There's a seasonal veggie **café** (March–Nov daily 10am–5pm), but adults are not allowed into the grounds unless accompanied by a child.

Foundling Museum

40 Brunswick Square · Tues–Sat 10am–5pm, Sun 11am–5pm · £7.50 · ☎ 020 7841 3600, Ⓦ foundlingmuseum.org.uk · ⊖ Russell Square

The **Foundling Museum**, north of Coram's Fields, tells the fascinating story of the Foundling Hospital. As soon as it opened, it was besieged, and forced to introduce a ballot system, with around a third of the applicants accepted. After 1801 only illegitimate children were admitted, and even then only after the mother had given a verbal statement confirming that "her good faith had been betrayed, that she had given way to carnal passion only after a promise of marriage or against her will". Among the most tragic exhibits are the tokens left by the mothers in order to identify the children should they ever be in a position to reclaim them: these range from a heart-rending poem to a simple enamel pot label reading "ale".

One of the hospital's governors – he even fostered two of the foundlings – was the artist **William Hogarth**, who established London's first-ever public art gallery at the hospital to give his friends somewhere to display their works and to attract potential benefactors. As a result the museum boasts works by artists such as Gainsborough and Reynolds, as well as Hogarth's splendid *March of the Guards to Finchley*. Upstairs, the original Georgian **Court Room**, where the governors still hold their meetings, has been faithfully reconstructed, with all its fine stuccowork. The fireplace features a wonderful relief depicting the trades of navigation and agriculture, into which the foundling boys were apprenticed at the age of ten before being sent out to the colonies. (The girls went into service.) On the top floor, there's a room dedicated to **Georg Friedrich Handel**, who gave annual charity performances of the *Messiah*, wrote an anthem for the hospital (basically a rehash of the *Hallelujah Chorus*) and donated an organ for the chapel, the keyboard of which survives. Today, the museum continues to put on regular concerts and family events and puts on special exhibitions in the basement.

Charles Dickens Museum

48 Doughty St · Daily 10am–5pm · £8 · ☎ 020 7405 2127, Ⓦ dickensmuseum.com · ⊖ Russell Square

Despite its plethora of blue plaques, Bloomsbury boasts just one literary museum, the **Charles Dickens Museum**, the only one of the writer's fifteen London addresses to survive intact. Doughty Street was a well-to-do gated Georgian street when Dickens – flushed with the success of his first two published works – moved here in 1837 soon after his marriage to Catherine Hogarth. The family lived in this light and airy house for two years, during which time he wrote *Oliver Twist* and *Nicholas Nickleby*. Catherine gave birth to two children in the bedroom here, and her younger sister died tragically in Dickens' arms. Much of the house's furniture belonged, at one time or another, to Dickens, and the house also owns the earliest known portrait of the writer (a miniature painted by his aunt in 1830). The museum also owns the adjacent house, no. 49, where they stage special exhibitions, house the bookshop and have a lovely café with free wi-fi.

London University

London only organized its own **University** in 1826, but it was the first in the country to admit students regardless of race, class, religion or gender. The university started life in Bloomsbury, but it wasn't until after World War I that it really began to take over the

CHARLES DICKENS

Few cities are as closely associated with one writer as London is with **Charles Dickens** (1812–70). The recurrent motifs in his novels have become the clichés of Victorian London – the fog, the slums and alleys, the prisons and workhouses and, of course, the stinking river. Drawing on his own personal experience, he was able to describe the workings of the law and the conditions of the poor with an unrivalled accuracy.

Born in Portsmouth, the second of eight children, Dickens spent a happy early childhood mostly in Chatham, Kent. This was cut short at the age of 12 when his father was imprisoned in Marshalsea debtors' prison, and Charles was forced to work in a boot-blacking factory on the site of Charing Cross Station. The experience scarred him for life – he was hurt further when his mother forced him to keep the job even after his father's release – and was no doubt responsible for Dickens' strong philanthropic convictions. After two years as a solicitor's clerk at Gray's Inn, he became a parliamentary reporter and wrote *Sketches by Boz* (Dickens' journalistic pen name) and *The Pickwick Papers*, the two works that propelled him to fame in 1836.

The same year he married **Catherine Hogarth**, and there followed ten children – "the largest family ever known with the smallest disposition to do anything for themselves", as Dickens later described them – and fifteen novels, each published in monthly (or weekly) instalments, which were awaited with bated breath by the Victorian public. Then in 1857, at the peak of his career, Dickens fell in love with the actress, **Ellen Ternan**; Dickens was 45, Ternan just 18. His subsequent separation from his wife, and his insistence that she leave the family house (while her sister Georgina and most of the children stayed), scandalized society and forced the author to retreat to Kent.

Dickens died at his desk at the age of 58, while working on *The Mystery of Edwin Drood*. According to his wishes, there was no public announcement of his burial, though he was interred in Westminster Abbey (at Queen Victoria's insistence) rather than in Rochester (as he had requested). The twelve people present at the service were asked not to wear a black bow, long hatband or any other accessories of the "revolting absurdity" of Victorian mourning.

If you're on the **Dickens trail**, there are one or two other sights worth checking out: the **Old Curiosity Shop** (see p.145), on Lincoln's Inn Fields, the (possible) inspiration for Dickens' novel of the same name; the atmospheric **Inns of Court** (see p.143), which feature in several Dickens novels; **"Nancy's Steps"**, where Nancy tells Rose Maylie Oliver's story in *Oliver Twist*, on the west side of London Bridge on the South Bank; and the evocative dockland area of **Shad Thames** (see p.235), where Bill Sykes has his hide-out.

area. Nowadays, the various colleges and institutes have spread their tentacles to form an almost continuous academic swathe from the British Museum all the way to Euston Road, occupying some 180 buildings. Despite this, the university's piecemeal development has left it with only a couple of distinguishing landmarks in the form of **Senate House** and **University College**. Several of the university departments run their own small, specialist **museums and galleries**, scattered across the campus.

Senate House

Looming over central Bloomsbury is the skyscraper of **Senate House**, a "bleak, blank, hideous" building, according to Max Beerbohm, now housing the university library. Designed with discreet Art Deco touches by Charles Holden in 1932, and austerely clad in Portland stone, it's best viewed from Malet Street. During the war it served as the Ministry of Information, where the likes of Evelyn Waugh, Graham Greene, Dorothy L. Sayers and George Orwell worked. Orwell later modelled the Ministry of Truth in *1984* on it: "an enormous pyramidal structure of glittering white concrete, soaring up, terrace after terrace, 300 metres into the air".

SOAS (School of Oriental and African Studies)

Thornhaugh St • Galleries Tues–Sat 10.30am–5pm, Thurs till 8pm • Free • ☎ 020 7898 4046, ⓦ soas.ac.uk • ⊖ Russell Square

To the north of Senate House, the **School of Oriental and African Studies**, or **SOAS**, puts on fascinating temporary exhibitions of photography, sculpture and art at the rather snazzy **Brunei Gallery**, funded by the immensely rich Sultan of Brunei. In addition, there's a small permanent display of the **Treasures of SOAS**, a mere snapshot of their collection, but containing an incredible range of artefacts from a Korean "moon jar" to a fortune-teller's book from Thailand. The school's prize possession, though, is a sixteenth-century illustrated Mughal manuscript of *Anvar-i Suhayli*, a Persian adaptation of the Panchatantra, a set of Indian animal fables. There's also a tiny but excellent bookshop and a café on the ground floor, and a secluded Zen-like Japanese **roof garden** dedicated to Forgiveness.

Petrie Museum of Egyptian Archeology

Malet Place • Tues–Sat 1–5pm • Free • ☎ 020 7504 2884, ⓦ ucl.ac.uk • ⊖ Euston Square or Goodge Street

The **Petrie Museum**, next door to the Science Library, has a handful of rooms jam-packed with Egyptian antiquities, the bulk of them from excavations carried out from the 1880s onwards by Flinders Petrie, UCL's first Professor of Egyptology. The first large room is crammed with objects, including huge slabs of stonework – look out for Min, the god of fertility, depicted with a particular type of lettuce which, when rubbed, secreted a milky substance. Other cabinets are crammed full of tiny objects including weights and measures, *shabti* figures, combs, bottle stoppers, sandals, legs from a toy table, a mummified bird and a pair of tweezers. At the back of the room is the richly decorated wooden coffin of Nairytisitnefer from 750 BC, while down the back stairs are frog amulets, ivory spoons and a giant sandstone jackal's paw. To the nonspecialist, the adjacent room appears to contain little more than broken bits of pottery (a speciality of Professor Petrie's). Look more closely, however, and you'll also find the world's oldest dress, an understandably ragged, pleated garment worn by an Ancient Egyptian teenager around 3000 BC. More intriguing still is the very revealing bead-net dress made for a 12-year-old, from around 2400 BC.

Grant Museum of Zoology

21 University St • Mon–Fri 1–5pm • Free • ☎ 020 3108 2052, ⓦ ucl.ac.uk • ⊖ Warren Street or Euston Square

Another museum piled high with exhibits – in this case skeletons – is the **Grant Museum of Zoology**, named after Robert E. Grant (1793–1874), the university's first Professor of Zoology and Comparative Anatomy, a pre-Darwinian transmutationist who always wore full evening dress when delivering lectures and later risked his career by teaching evolution at UCL. Among the numerous specimens here, don't miss the jar of pickled moles, the walrus penis bone and the skeletons of a dugong, a dodo, a quagga (an extinct zebra) and a thylacine (an extinct marsupial wolf).

University College London (UCL)

Gower St • Art Museum Mon–Fri 1–5pm • Free • ☎ 020 7679 2540, ⓦ ucl.ac.uk • ⊖ Euston Square

The oldest part of **University College London** is the rather prosaically named **Main Building**, William Wilkins' Neoclassical edifice from the 1820s, with its handsome Corinthian portico and fine quadrangle, set back (and well hidden) from busy Gower

---

JEREMY BENTHAM'S SKELETON

Also in the south cloisters of UCL's Main Building is the philosopher **Jeremy Bentham** (1748–1832), one of the university's founders. Bentham bequeathed his fully clothed skeleton so that he could be posthumously present at board meetings of the University College Hospital governors, where he was duly recorded as "present, but not voting". Bentham's **Auto-Icon**, topped by a wax head and wide-brimmed hat, is in "thinking and writing" pose as the philosopher requested, and can be seen in a hermetically sealed mahogany booth. Close by is a pair of watchful Ancient Egyptian lions, reconstructed from several thousand fragments belonging to the Petrie Museum (see above).

Street. UCL is home to one of London's most famous art schools, the **Slade**, which puts on small, but excellent temporary exhibitions drawn from its collection of over ten thousand works of art, by the likes of Dürer, Rembrandt, Turner and Constable, as well as works by former students, such as Stanley Spencer, Paul Nash, Gwen John, Augustus John and Raymond Briggs. These are held at the **UCL Art Museum**, situated in the south cloister of the main quadrangle.

There's more artwork on display in the octagon beneath the Main Building's central dome, in an area known as the **Flaxman Gallery** – follow the signs to the library and ask the guards to let you through. John Flaxman (1755–1826) made his name producing Neoclassical funerary sculpture – his works feature prominently in Westminster Abbey and St Paul's – and the walls here are filled with scaled-down, high-relief, plaster models worked on by Flaxman himself for his marble monuments. The gallery's centrepiece is a dramatic, full-size plaster model of *St Michael Overcoming Satan*.

7 Euston

The northern boundary of Bloomsbury is defined by **Euston Road**, which was laid out in 1756 as part of the "New Road", the city's first bypass. This was the northern limit of London until the mid-nineteenth century when rival companies built Euston, King's Cross and St Pancras, termini serving the industrial boom towns of the north of England. Since those days, Euston Road has had some of the city's best and worst architecture foisted on it, which, combined with the current volume of traffic, makes this an area where it pays to be selective.

Amidst all the hubbub of Euston Road, it's easy to miss the depressingly functional **Euston Station**, descendant of London's first great train terminus, originally built with just two platforms way back in 1837. Philip Hardwick's original Neoclassical ensemble – including the famous Euston Arch – was demolished in the face of fierce protests in the 1960s – British Rail claimed it needed the space in order to lengthen the platforms, which it never did. All that remains of old Euston are the sad-looking lodge-houses, though there are moves afoot to rebuild the arch if and when the new high-speed link to Birmingham, HS2, arrives at the overstretched station.

Wellcome Collection

183 Euston Rd · Tues–Sat 10am–6pm, Thurs till 10pm, Sun 11am–6pm · Free · ☎ 020 7611 2222, Ⓦ wellcomecollection.org · ⊖ Euston or Euston Square

Despite its unpromising location, the **Wellcome Collection** puts on thought-provoking temporary exhibitions on topical scientific issues on the ground floor, where there's also an excellent café and bookshop. The permanent collection, on the first floor, is also worth a visit, beginning with **Medicine Now**, which focuses on contemporary medical questions such as the body, genomes, obesity and malaria. Each subject has an "art cube" displaying contemporary artists' responses to the issues: a world map traced out in mosquitoes by Alastair Mackie; Chris Drury's collage of maps and an echocardiogram; and a giant jelly baby "clone" by Mauro Perucchetti. Next door, **Medicine Man** showcases the weird and wonderful collection of historical and scientific artefacts amassed by American-born pharmaceutical magnate Henry Wellcome (1853–1936). These range from Florence Nightingale's moccasins and Napoleon's toothbrush to a sign for a Chinese doctor's hung with human teeth, from erotic figurines and phallic amulets to Inuit snow goggles and a leper clapper – in other words, this section is an absolute must.

St Pancras New Church

Euston Rd · Mon–Fri 8am–6pm · Free · ☎ 020 7388 1461, Ⓦ stpancraschurch.org · ⊖ Euston

Euston Road's oldest edifice is **St Pancras New Church**, built at enormous expense in the 1820s on the corner of Upper Woburn Place. The first Greek Revival edifice in London, it is notable for its octagonal tower, based on the Tower of the Winds in Athens, and for the caryatids, tacked onto the east end, which are modelled on the Erechtheion on the Acropolis – though the Euston Road ladies had to be truncated at the waist after they were found to be too tall. The best time to visit the interior, which features a dramatically lit Ionic colonnade in the apse, and some lovely Victorian stained glass, is during one of the free Thursday lunchtime recitals. There are also regular art exhibitions held in the atmospheric **Crypt Gallery** (Ⓦcryptgallery.org.uk), with access from Duke's Road.

King's Cross St Pancras

The area around **King's Cross** and **St Pancras** stations is always buzzing with buses, cars, commuters, tourists and, with the massive ongoing development behind King's Cross Station, construction workers. Architecturally, it's dominated by **St Pancras Station**, the most glorious of London's red-brick Victorian edifices, which overshadows its two neighbours: workaday **King's Cross Station** and the red-brick brutalist **British Library**, home to some of the nation's most precious books and documents.

British Library

96 Euston Rd • Mon–Fri 9.30am–6pm, Tues till 8pm, Sat 9.30am–5pm, Sun 11am–5pm • ☎ 020 7412 7332, Ⓦ bl.uk •
⊖ King's Cross St Pancras

As one of the country's most expensive public buildings, the **British Library** took flak from all sides during its construction: few readers wanted to move out of the splendid Round Reading Room in the British Museum, where the library had been since the 1850s; the number of extra readers' seats was negligible and the shelving inadequate; and, to top it all, the design was criticized by Prince Charles, who compared it to an academy for secret policemen. Yet, while it's true that Colin St John Wilson's penchant for red-brick brutalism is horribly out of fashion, the library has proved popular both with the scholars who use it and the public who visit the superb galleries.

The **piazza** features Eduardo Paolozzi's giant statue of Isaac Newton bent double over his protractor, inspired by William Blake – just one of a number of specially commissioned artworks. Look out, too, for Bill Woodrow's *Book, Ball & Chain* sofa and R.B. Kitaj's unsettling giant tapestry, *If not, not*, both in the main foyer, and Patrick Hughes' optical illusion, *Paradoxymoron*, near the basement cloakroom. The spiritual heart of the building is a multistorey glass-walled tower housing the vast **King's Library**, collected by George III and donated by George IV in 1823. The library puts on a wide variety of events, including talks, films and occasional live performances, and has several cafés, a restaurant and free wi-fi.

John Ritblat Gallery; Treasures of the British Library

The dimly lit **John Ritblat Gallery** is where the BL's ancient manuscripts, maps and precious books are permanently displayed. The sheer variety of sacred texts displayed is overwhelming, from illuminated Torahs to richly decorated Qur'ans (Korans), from a tiny palm-leaf glorification of the Hindu goddess Jagannatha in the shape of a cow to folding books on the life of the Buddha. The richly illustrated **Lindisfarne Gospels**, begun in 698 AD, is always on display, as is the fourth century AD Codex Sinaiticus, one of the earliest Greek Bibles in the world, and the thousand-year-old manuscript of the Anglo-Saxon epic poem Beowulf. In the section on printing, you can see the world's earliest-dated printed document, along with the **Gutenberg Bible**, from 1454–55, the first Bible printed using movable type (and therefore capable of being mass-produced).

The most famous of the **historical documents** is the **Magna Carta**, King John's agreement with his rebellious barons in 1215, on display in a room of its own. Other exhibits change from time to time, and could be anything from Thomas More's last letter to Henry VIII to Lenin's application for a British Library pass. Among the **literature**, there's Shakespeare's First Folio from 1623, Jane Austen's notebooks and writing desk and the touchingly beautiful handwritten and illustrated copy of *Alice in Wonderland* given by

Lewis Carroll to Alice Liddell. You can also hear recordings of several authors reading extracts from their works. Similarly, in the **music** section, which contains oddities such as Mozart's marriage contract and Beethoven's tuning fork, you can listen to works by Bach and The Beatles while perusing Purcell's autographed score.

The other galleries

The BL has several galleries in which it stages temporary exhibitions (occasionally with an entrance charge), employing more of the library's wonderful texts, supplemented by items from the British Museum. Stamp lovers should make their way up to the BL's gargantuan **Philatelic Collections**, made up of over eight million items, eighty thousand of which are displayed in vertical pull-out drawers just outside the John Ritblat Gallery. The Tapling Collection kicks off the proceedings, as it did when it was bequeathed in 1891, and in drawer number one you'll find the famous "Penny Black", the birthmark of modern philately. After that you get a world tour of stamps from long-forgotten mini-kingdoms such as Mecklenburg-Schwerin and Nowanugger. Those with a political interest should head for the Bojanowicz Collection, which covers Polish stamps from 1939 to 1946, including ones from the German and Russian occupations, and even POW and displaced persons' camps. Real boffins should head for the Turner Collection of railway letter stamps from the likes of the Pembroke & Tenby Railway.

St Pancras Old Church

Pancras Rd • Daily 9am to dusk • Free • ☎ 020 7387 4193, ⓦ oldstpancrasteam.wordpress.com • ⊖ King's Cross St Pancras

Allegedly the first parish church built in London, **St Pancras Old Church** lies hidden and neglected behind iron railings on raised ground behind the British Library, up Midland Road. Apart from a little exposed Norman masonry and the sixth-century Roman altar stone, most of the church dates from the nineteenth century. The **churchyard**, which is overlooked by the lugubrious former Victorian workhouse (now the Hospital for Tropical Diseases), was partially destroyed by the arrival of the railway, with the majority of graves being heaped around an ash tree under the supervision of the writer (then architect) Thomas Hardy. **John Soane's mausoleum** from 1816 still stands in its original location, to the north of the church – designed initially for his wife, it was the inspiration for Giles Gilbert Scott's red phone box design, along with the mausoleum at Dulwich Picture Gallery (see p.312). Also originally buried here was Britain's great protofeminist, **Mary Wollstonecraft**, who died a few days after giving birth to her daughter, Mary. At the age of 16, the younger Mary was spotted visiting her mother's grave by the poet Percy Bysshe Shelley, who immediately declared his undying love, before eloping with her to Italy – both Marys are now buried in Bournemouth.

A list of the graveyard's most illustrious corpses is inscribed on the monumental sundial erected by Baroness Burdett-Coutts, below which sit four beasts, two of which are based on her collie dog – there's also a map of the prominent graves by the entrance.

THE GERMAN GYMNASIUM AND THE GASHOLDERS

King's Cross is undergoing its biggest ever transformation, and although a whole host of lovely old buildings have bitten the dust, around twenty venerable structures have survived, among them the **German Gymnasium** on St Pancras Road, built in the 1860s and now set to house a restaurant. To the east of here, King's Boulevard slopes up past Google's new UK headquarters, over the canal to the old Granary building which houses the campus for the **University of the Arts**, complete with dancing fountains, and, in the reception area, a model of the development and a visitor centre (Mon, Thurs & Fri 10am–5pm, Tues & Wed noon–5pm, Sat 11am–5pm), from which you can take a guided tour of the area (book on ☎020 3479 1795). Look out, too, for the brooding skeletal **gasholders**, Victorian monsters that hark back to an era when nothing was too lowly to be given Neoclassical decoration – viz George Gilbert Scott's ornate **St Pancras Waterpoint**, just beyond Camley Street Natural Park (see opposite).

St Pancras Station

Euston Rd • For guided tours contact the hotel's historian Royden Stock on ☎ 07778 932359 • £20 • ⊖ King's Cross St Pancras

Among London's greatest Victorian follies is the former *Midland Grand Hotel*, whose majestic sweep of lancets, dormers and chimneypots forms the facade of **St Pancras Station**, London's Eurostar terminus. Completed in 1876 by George Gilbert Scott, this masterpiece of neo-Gothic architecture enjoyed a brief heyday in the 1890s when the ratio of staff to guests was 3:1, but with few private bathrooms and no central heating, the hotel couldn't survive long into the modern age. For fifty years from 1935, it languished as underused railway offices, but now houses private apartments and rooms belonging to the luxury *St Pancras Renaissance London Hotel*.

King's Cross Station

Compared to St Pancras, **King's Cross Station**, opened in 1852 as the terminus for the Great Northern Railway, is a mere shed (albeit a smartly refurbished shed). Legend has it that Boudicca's bones lie under platform 9 – the area used to be known as Battle Bridge, and was believed to have been the site of the final set-to between the Iceni and the Romans. More famously, the fictional **Harry Potter** and his wizarding chums leave for school on the Hogwarts Express each term from platform 9¾. (The scenes from the films were, in fact, shot between platforms 4 and 5, but a station trolley half-submerged into the wall provides a photo opportunity in the new semi-circular concourse to the west, and there's an HP shop close by.)

7

Camley Street Natural Park

12 Camley St • Daily except Sat: April–Sept 10am–5.30pm; Oct–March 10am–4.30pm • Free • ☎ 020 7833 2311, Ⓦ wildlondon.org.uk • ⊖ King's Cross St Pancras

The oasis among all the King's Cross redevelopment is **Camley Street Natural Park**, transformed from a rubbish dump into a canalside wildlife haven, and run by the London Wildlife Trust. Pond, meadow and woodland habitats have been re-created and provide a natural environment for birds, butterflies, frogs, newts, toads and even the odd heron, plus a rich variety of plant life.

Kings Place

90 York Way • ☎ 020 7520 1490, Ⓦ kingsplace.co.uk • ⊖ King's Cross St Pancras

A definite plus in the King's Cross redevelopment has been the arrival of **Kings Place**, the glassy new arts centre overlooking the Regent's Canal. As well as housing two state-of-the-art concert halls – home to the London Sinfonietta and the Orchestra of the Age of Enlightenment – the venue puts on art exhibitions, talks and events and has a swanky canalside café and restaurant to boot. The most famous residents, however, are *The Guardian* and *The Observer* newspapers, which occupy the southern part of the building.

London Canal Museum

12–13 New Wharf Rd • Tues–Sun 10am–4.30pm; first Thurs in month till 7.30pm • £4 • ☎ 020 7713 0836, Ⓦ canalmuseum.org.uk • ⊖ King's Cross St Pancras

Packed with traditional narrowboats, Battlebridge Basin, behind Kings Place, is a thoroughly appropriate location for the **London Canal Museum**. The museum testifies to the hard life boat families endured and includes a restored "butty" (an engine-less narrowboat used for storage) and some of the unusual Measham Ware pottery and crockery that was popular with canal-boat families. Other exhibits relate to the building itself, built as an icehouse by Swiss-Italian entrepreneur Carlo Gatti, London's main ice trader in the nineteenth century. Gatti single-handedly popularized ice cream in London, supplying most of the city's vendors, who became known as "Hokey-Pokey Men" – a corruption of the street cry *Ecco un poco*, "Just try a little". Upstairs there's video footage of the canal from the 1920s and the 1990s.

COVENT GARDEN PIAZZA

Covent Garden and the Strand

Covent Garden's transformation from a workaday fruit and vegetable market into a fashionable *quartier* is one of the most miraculous and successful developments of the 1980s. More mainstream and commercial than neighbouring Soho, it's also a lot more popular thanks to the buskers, street entertainers and human statues that make the traffic-free Covent Garden Piazza an undeniably lively place to be. As its name suggests, the Strand, on the southern border of Covent Garden, once lay along the riverbank until the Victorians created the Embankment to shore up the banks of the Thames. One showpiece river palace, Somerset House, remains, its courtyard graced by a lovely fountain in summer, and its chambers home to the Courtauld Gallery's superb collection of Impressionist and Post-Impressionist paintings.

Covent Garden

Covent Garden has come full circle: what started out in the seventeenth century as London's first luxury neighbourhood is once more an aspirational place to live, work and shop. Boosted by buskers and street entertainers, the piazza is now one of London's major tourist attractions, and the streets to the north – in particular, Long Acre, Neal Street and Floral Street – are home to fashionable clothes and shoe shops.

Most visitors are happy enough simply to wander around watching the street life, having a coffee and doing a bit of shopping, but there are a couple of specific sights worth picking out. One of the old market buildings houses the enjoyable **London Transport Museum**, while another serves as the public foyer for the **Royal Opera House** and boasts a great roof terrace overlooking the piazza.

The piazza

Covent Garden's **piazza** – London's oldest planned square – was laid out in the 1630s, when the Earl of Bedford commissioned Inigo Jones to design a series of graceful Palladian-style arcades based on the main square in Livorno, Tuscany, where Jones had helped build the cathedral. Initially it was a great success, its novelty value alone attracting a plutocratic clientele, but over time the tone of the place fell as the **market** (set up in the earl's back garden) expanded and theatres, coffee houses and brothels began to proliferate.

By the onset of the nineteenth century, the market dominated the area, and so in the 1830s a proper market hall was built in the middle of the piazza in the Greek Revival style. A glass roof was added in the late Victorian era, but otherwise the building stayed unaltered until the market's closure in 1974, and only public protests averted yet another office development. Instead, the elegant market hall and its environs were restored to house shops, restaurants and arts-and-crafts stalls. In its early days, the area had an alternative hippy vibe, a legacy of the area's numerous squats. Nowadays, upmarket chain stores occupy much of the market hall and the arcades, with the world's largest Apple Store, on the north side of the piazza, a sign of the how far the area has come from its origins.

8

St Paul's Church

Covent Garden Piazza • Mon–Fri 8.30am–5pm, Sat times vary, Sun 9am–1pm • ☎ 020 7836 5221, Ⓦ actorschurch.org •
⊖ Covent Garden or Leicester Square

Covent Garden piazza is overlooked from the west by **St Paul's Church**. The Earl of Bedford allegedly told Inigo Jones to make St Paul's no fancier than a barn, to which

---

COFFEE HOUSES AND BROTHELS

By the eighteenth century the piazza was known as "the great square of Venus", home to dozens of gambling dens, bawdy houses and so-called "bagnios". Some bagnios were plain Turkish baths, but many doubled as **brothels**, where courtesans stood in the window and, according to one contemporary, "in the most impudent manner invited passengers from the theatres into the houses".

London's most famous **coffee houses** were concentrated here, too, attracting writers such as Sheridan, Dryden and Aphra Behn. The rich and famous frequented places like the piazza's *Shakespeare's Head*, whose cook made the best turtle soup in town, and whose head waiter, John Harrison, was believed to be the author of the anonymously published "Who's Who of Whores", *Harris's List of Covent Garden Ladies*, which sold over a quarter of a million copies in its day.

The *Rose Tavern*, on Russell Street (immortalized in Hogarth's *Rake's Progress*), was one of the oldest brothels in Covent Garden – Pepys mentions "frigging with Doll Lane" at the *Rose* in his diary of 1667 – and specialized in "Posture Molls", who engaged in flagellation and striptease, and were deemed a cut above the average whore. Food was apparently excellent, too, and despite the frequent brawls, men of all classes, from royalty to ruffians, made their way there.

the architect replied, "Sire, you shall have the handsomest barn in England". It's better known nowadays as the **Actors' Church**, and is filled with memorials to thespians from Boris Karloff to Gracie Fields. The cobbles in front of the church's Tuscan portico – where Eliza Doolittle was discovered selling violets by Henry Higgins in George Bernard Shaw's *Pygmalion* – are now a legalized venue for buskers and street performers, who must audition for a slot.

The piazza's history of entertainment goes back to May 1662, when the first recorded performance of Punch and Judy in England was staged by Italian puppeteer Pietro Gimonde, and witnessed by Pepys. To celebrate this a **Punch and Judy Festival,** called May Fayre, is held on the second Sunday in May, in the gardens behind the church; for the rest of the year the **churchyard** provides a tranquil respite from the activity outside.

COVENT GARDEN & THE STRAND

ACCOMMODATION
Covent Garden Hotel	6
The Fielding	3
Grosvenor House Studios	2
High Holborn Residence	1
The Savoy	4
Seven Dials Hotel	5

CAFÉS
Canela	15
Food for Thought	14
Homeslice Pizza	11
Kastner & Ovens	3
Monmouth Coffee Company	12
Poetry Café	1
Rock & Sole Plaice	13
Spud	7

RESTAURANTS
Dishoom	5
Green Man & French Horn	9
Hawksmoor	2
J. Sheekey	6
Kopapa	16
Masala Zone	4
Opera Tavern	8
Terroirs	10

SHOPS
The Natural Shoe Store	9
Neal's Yard Dairy	7
Paul Smith	3
Pollock's Toyshop	5
Rokit	1
Stanfords	4
Tatty Devine	2
The Tea House	8
The VIVOBAREFOOT Experience	6

PUBS & BARS
Cross Keys	2
Gordon's	9
Harp	5
Lamb & Flag	3
Princess Louise	1
The Salisbury	4

GAY & LESBIAN VENUES
Halfway 2 Heaven	7
Heaven	6
Retro Bar	6

London Transport Museum

Covent Garden Piazza • Daily 10am–6pm, Fri from 11am • Adults £15, under-16s free • ☎ 020 7379 6344, ⓦ ltmuseum.co.uk • ⊖ Covent Garden

A former flower-market shed on the piazza's east side houses the ever-popular **London Transport Museum**. A sure-fire hit for families with kids under 10, it's a must-see for any transport enthusiast, though restrictions of space mean that there are only a handful of large exhibits.

Still, the story of London's transport is a fascinating one – to follow it chronologically, head for Level 2, where you'll find a replica 1829 Shillibeer's Horse Omnibus, which provided the city's first regular **horse-bus** service, and a double-decker horse-drawn tram, introduced in the 1870s. Level 1 tells the story of the world's first underground system and contains a lovely 1920s Metropolitan Line carriage, fitted out in burgundy and green with pretty, drooping lamps.

Down on the ground floor, the museum's one double-decker electric **tram** is all that's left to pay tribute to the world's largest tram system, which was dismantled in 1952. Look out, too, for the first **tube** train, from the 1890s, whose lack of windows earned it the nickname "the padded cell". Most of the interactive stuff is aimed at kids, but visitors of all ages should check out the tube driver simulator.

A good selection of London Transport's stylish **maps and posters** are usually on display, many commissioned from well-known artists, and you can buy copies at the shop on the way out. Real transport enthusiasts should check out the reserve collection at the **Museum Depot** in Acton (details on the website), which is open occasional weekends throughout the year.

8

London Film Museum

45 Wellington St • Daily 10am–6pm • Free • ☎ 020 3617 3010, ⓦ londonfilmmuseum.com • ⊖ Covent Garden

Such is the success of the main branch of the **London Film Museum** in County Hall that this satellite museum has opened on the site of the former Theatre Museum. The exhibition is basically a celebratory history of the era of celluloid, which is drawing to a close. It begins with the early experiments in cinema from magic lantern to stereoscopes, and features some of the earliest silent moving pictures ever made. The rest of the displays concentrate on the history of London in film, and are grouped into themed sections – Literary London, Gas-lit London, Wartime London and so on. There are plenty of film clips and stills to keep you amused, but only a handful of artefacts to look at, from Fagin's gloves and hat to Ali G's orange shellsuit.

Bow Street

Covent Garden's dubious reputation was no doubt behind the opening of **Bow Street** magistrates' office in 1748. The first two magistrates were Henry Fielding, author of *Tom Jones*, and his blind half-brother John – nicknamed the "Blind Beak" – who, unusually for the period, refused to accept bribes. Finding "lewd women enough to fill a mighty colony", Fielding set about creating London's first police force, the **Bow Street Runners**. Never numbering more than a dozen, they were employed primarily to combat prostitution, and they continued to exist a good ten years after the establishment of the uniformed Metropolitan Police in 1829. Bow Street police station and magistrates court (both now closed) had the honour of incarcerating Oscar Wilde after he was arrested for "committing indecent acts" in 1895 – he was eventually sentenced to two years' hard labour. In 1908 Emmeline Pankhurst appeared here, charged with leafleting supporters to "rush" the House of Commons, and, in 1928, Radclyffe Hall's lesbian novel *The Well of Loneliness* was deemed obscene by Bow Street magistrates and remained banned in this country until 1949.

Royal Opera House

Bow St • Foyer: daily 10am–3.30pm • Several tours including backstage tours (1hr 15min) take place regularly and can be booked in advance: Mon–Fri 10.30am, 12.30pm & 2.30pm, Sat 10.30am, 11.30am, 12.30pm & 1.30pm • £12 • ☎ 020 7304 4000, ⓦ roh.org.uk • ⊖ Covent Garden

The main entrance to the **Royal Opera House** – a splendid Corinthian portico – stands opposite the former Bow Street magistrates' court. The original theatre witnessed the premieres of Goldsmith's *She Stoops to Conquer* and Sheridan's *The Rivals* before being destroyed by fire in 1808. To offset the cost of rebuilding, ticket prices were increased; riots ensued for 61 performances until the manager finally backed down. The current building dates from 1858, and is the city's main opera house, home to both the Royal Ballet and Royal Opera. A covered passageway connects the piazza with Bow Street, and allows access to the ROH box office, and upstairs to the beautiful Victorian wrought-iron-and-glass **Floral Hall**. Continuing up the escalators, you reach the *Amphitheatre* bar-restaurant, with a fine terrace overlooking the piazza.

Drury Lane

One block east of Bow Street runs **Drury Lane**, nothing to write home about in its present condition, but in Tudor and Stuart times a very fashionable address. During the Restoration, it became a permanent fixture in London's theatrical and social life, but by the eighteenth century, it had become a notorious slum rife with prostitution. Nevertheless, it was at no. 179 that J Sainsbury (founder of the supermarket chain) opened his first food store in 1869 – "Quality perfect, prices lower" – and it is here, of course, that the Muffin Man lives in the children's nursery rhyme.

Theatre Royal, Drury Lane

Drury Lane • ⊖ Covent Garden

The most famous building in the street is the **Theatre Royal, Drury Lane** first established here in 1663 – the current theatre (the fourth on the site) dates from 1812, faces onto Catherine Street and currently churns out Andrew Lloyd Webber musicals. It was at the original theatre that women were first permitted to appear on stage in England

---

COVENT GARDEN'S SHOPPING STREETS

Apple may have arrived on the piazza, but the shopping streets to the north still hold one or two surprises. **Floral Street**, a quiet cobbled backstreet, running east–west one block north of the piazza, is a good place to start. At the eastern end is a strange helix-shaped walkway connecting the Royal Ballet School with the Royal Opera House. In the western half you can inspect the tongue-in-cheek window displays of three adjoining shops run by top-selling British designer Paul Smith (nos. 40–44). Another quirky outlet is the shop entirely dedicated to Tintin, the Belgian boy-detective (no. 34). Meanwhile, squeezed beside a very narrow alleyway off Floral Street is the **Lamb and Flag**, the pub where the Poet Laureate, John Dryden, was beaten up in December 1679 by a group of thugs, hired most probably by his rival poet, the Earl of Rochester, who mistakenly thought Dryden was the author of an essay satirizing him.

One block north, **Long Acre** has long been Covent Garden's main shopping street, though it originally specialized in coach manufacture. The most famous shop on the street is **Stanfords**, the world's oldest and largest map shop (see p.430), packed to the rafters with Rough Guides. Look out, too, for **Carriage Hall**, an old stabling yard originally used by coachmakers (now converted into shops), surrounded by cast-iron pillars and situated between Long Acre and Floral Street. Running north from Long Acre, **Neal Street** features some fine Victorian warehouses, complete with stair towers for loading and shifting goods between floors, from the days of the fruit, vegetable and flower market. The street is currently dominated by shoe stores, with only a few alternative shops left: *Food for Thought*, the veggie café founded in 1971, is a rare survivor, as is **Neal's Yard**, a tiny little courtyard off Shorts Gardens, stuffed with cafés and prettily festooned with flower boxes and ivy.

(their parts having previously been played by boys), but critics were sceptical about their competence at portraying the fairer sex and thought their profession little better than prostitution – most had to work at both to make ends meet (as the actress said to the bishop). The scantily clad women who sold oranges to the audience were considered even less virtuous, the most famous being **Nell Gwynne** who from the age of 14 was playing comic roles on stage. At the age of 18, she became Charles II's mistress, the first in a long line of Drury Lane actresses who made it into royal beds.

It was also at the Theatre Royal that **David Garrick**, as actor, manager and part-owner from 1747, revolutionized the English theatre, treating the text with more reverence than had been customary, insisting on rehearsals and cutting down on improvisations. The rich, who had previously occupied seats on the stage itself, were confined to the auditorium, and the practice of refunding those who wished to leave at the first interval was stopped. However, an attempt to prevent half-price tickets being sold at the beginning of the third act provoked a riot and had to be abandoned. Despite Garrick's reforms, the Theatre Royal remained a boisterous and often dangerous place of entertainment: George III narrowly escaped an assassination attempt, and ordered the play to continue after the assassin had been apprehended, and the orchestra often had cause to be grateful for the cage under which they were forced to play. The theatre has one other unique feature: two royal boxes, instigated in order to keep George III and his son, the future George IV, apart, after they had a set-to in the foyer.

Freemasons' Hall

60 Great Queen St • Mon–Fri 10am–5pm • Free • Guided tours Mon–Fri usually 11am, noon, 2, 3 & 4pm; free • ☎ 020 7395 9257, ⓦ freemasonry.london.museum • ⊖ Covent Garden

Looking east off Drury Lane, down Great Queen Street, it's difficult to miss the austere, Pharaonic mass of the **Freemasons' Hall**, built as a memorial to all the Masons who died in World War I. Whatever you may think of this reactionary, secretive, male-dominated organization, the interior is worth a peek for the **Grand Temple** alone, whose pompous, bombastic decor is laden with heavy symbolism. To see the Grand Temple, sign up for one of the **guided tours** and bring some ID with you. The Masonically curious might also take a look at the shop, which sells Masonic merchandise – aprons, wands, rings and books about alchemy and the cabbala – as do several outlets on Great Queen Street.

The Strand

As its name suggests the **Strand** – the main road from Westminster to the City – once ran along the banks of the River Thames. From the twelfth century onwards, it was famed for its riverside residences, owned by bishops, noblemen and courtiers, which lined the south side of the street, each with their own river gates opening onto the Thames. In the late 1860s, the Victorians built the **Embankment**, simultaneously relieving congestion along the Strand, cutting the aristocratic mansions off from the river and providing an extension for the tube and a new sewerage system. By the 1890s, the mansions on the Strand were outnumbered by **theatres**, giving rise to the music-hall song *Let's All Go Down the Strand* (have a banana!), and prompting Disraeli to declare it "perhaps the finest street in Europe". A hundred years later, several theatres survive, from the sleek Art Deco Adelphi to the Rococo Lyceum, but the only surviving Thames palace is **Somerset House**, which houses gallery and exhibition space, and boasts a wonderful fountain-filled courtyard.

Charing Cross Station

The Strand begins at **Charing Cross Station**, fronted by the French Renaissance-style *Charing Cross Hotel*, built in the 1860s. Standing rather forlorn, in the station's cobbled forecourt, is a Victorian version of the medieval **Charing Cross**, removed from nearby Trafalgar Square by the Puritans. The original thirteenth-century cross was the last of twelve erected by Edward I, to mark the overnight stops on the funeral procession of his wife, Eleanor of Castile, from Lincoln to Westminster in 1290.

Zimbabwe House

Opposite Charing Cross Station, on the corner of Agar Street, is the Edwardian-era former British Medical Association building, now **Zimbabwe House**, housing the Zimbabwean embassy, outside which there are now regular protests against the Mugabe regime. Few passers-by even notice the eighteen naked figures by Jacob Epstein that punctuate the second-floor facade, but at the time of their unveiling in 1908, they caused enormous controversy – "a form of statuary which no careful father would wish his daughter and no discriminating young man his fiancée to see", railed the press. When the Southern Rhodesian government bought the building in 1937 they pronounced the sculptures to be a health and safety hazard to passers-by, and hacked at the genitals, heads and limbs of all eighteen, which remain mutilated to this day.

The Savoy

Strand • ☎ 020 7836 4343, ⓦ fairmont.com/savoy-london • ⊖ Charing Cross or Embankment

On the south side of the Strand, the blind side street of Savoy Court – the only street in the country where the traffic drives on the right – leads to **The Savoy**, one of London's grandest hotels, built in 1889 by Richard D'Oyly Carte. César Ritz was the original manager, Auguste Escoffier the chef, who went on to invent the *pêche Melba* at the hotel. The hotel's *American Bar* introduced cocktails into Europe in the 1930s, Guccio Gucci started out as a dishwasher here and the list of illustrious guests is endless: Monet and Whistler both painted the Thames from one of the south-facing rooms, Sarah Bernhardt nearly died here and Strauss the Younger arrived with his own orchestra. It's worthwhile strolling up Savoy Court to check out the hotel's Art Deco foyer, the polygonal glass fish fountain and the silver and gold statue of John of Gaunt, whose medieval palace stood on the site (see below). The adjacent **Savoy Theatre**, with its outrageous 1930s silver and gold fittings, was originally built in 1881 to showcase Gilbert and Sullivan's comic operas, witnessing eight premieres, including *The Mikado* – the theatre's profits helped fund the building of the hotel.

8

Savoy Chapel

Savoy Hill • Mon–Thurs 9.30am–4pm, Sun 9am–1pm • Free • ☎ 020 7836 7221, ⓦ duchyoflancaster.co.uk • ⊖ Charing Cross or Embankment

Nothing remains of John of Gaunt's medieval Savoy Palace, which stood here until it was burnt down in the 1381 Peasants' Revolt, though the **Savoy Chapel** (or The Queen's Chapel of the Savoy to give its full title), hidden round the back of the hotel down Savoy Street, dates from the time when the complex was rebuilt as a hospital for the poor in 1512. The chapel is much altered, but it became a fashionable venue for weddings when the hotel and theatre were built next door – all three were the first public buildings in the world to be lit by electricity. And talking of lighting, don't miss the **Patent Sewer Ventilating Lamp**, erected in the 1880s halfway down Carting Lane, and still powered by methane collected in a U-bend in the sewers below.

Victoria Embankment

To get to the **Victoria Embankment**, from the Strand, head down Villiers Street, beside Charing Cross Station. Completed in 1870, the embankment was the inspiration of engineer **Joseph Bazalgette**, who used the reclaimed land for a new tube line, new sewers, and a new stretch of riverside parkland – now filled with an eclectic mixture of statues and memorials from Robbie Burns to the Imperial Camel Corps. The 1626 **York Watergate**, in the Victoria Embankment Gardens to the east of Villiers Street, gives you an idea of where the banks of the Thames used to be: the steps through the gateway once led down to the river.

Cleopatra's Needle

London's oldest monument, **Cleopatra's Needle**, languishes little noticed on the Thames side of the busy Victoria Embankment, guarded by two Victorian sphinxes (facing the wrong way). In fact, the 60ft-high, 180-ton stick of granite has nothing to do with Cleopatra – it's one of a pair erected in Heliopolis (near Cairo) in 1475 BC (the other one is in New York's Central Park) and taken to Alexandria by Emperor Augustus fifteen years after Cleopatra's suicide. This obelisk was presented to Britain in 1819 by the Turkish viceroy of Egypt, but nearly sixty years passed before it made the treacherous voyage, in its own purpose-built boat, all the way to London. It was erected in 1878 above a time capsule containing, among other things, the day's newspapers, a box of hairpins, a railway timetable and pictures of the country's twelve prettiest women.

Royal Society of Arts (RSA)

6–8 John Adam St • Tours by appointment only • ☎ 020 7930 5115, ⓦ thersa.org • ⊖ Charing Cross or Embankment

Founded in 1754, the "Society for the encouragement of Arts, Manufactures and Commerce", better known now as the Royal Society of Arts or **RSA**, moved into a purpose-built, elaborately decorated house designed by the Adam brothers in 1774. The building contains a small display on the Adelphi and retains several original Adam ceilings and chimneypieces. The highlight, however, is The Great Room, with six paintings on *The Progress of Human Knowledge and Culture* by James Barry, forming a busy, continuous pictorial frieze around the room, punctuated by portraits of two early presidents by Reynolds and Gainsborough. The RSA is one of a number of Adam houses that survive from the magnificent riverside development built between 1768 and 1772 by the Adam brothers and known as the **Adelphi**, which was, for the most part, demolished in 1936.

Benjamin Franklin House

36 Craven St • Architectural tours Mon noon, 1, 2, 3.15 & 4.15pm Historical Experience Wed–Sun noon, 1, 2, 3.15 & 4.15pm • £7 •
☎ 020 7925 1405, ⓦ benjaminfranklinhouse.org • ⊖ Charing Cross or Embankment

From 1757 to 1775, **Benjamin Franklin** (1706–90) had "genteel lodgings" here. While Franklin was espousing the cause of the British colonies (as the US then was), the house served as the first de facto American embassy; eventually, he returned to America to help draft the Declaration of Independence and frame the US Constitution. On Mondays, the emphasis is on the **Benjamin Franklin House**'s architecture and restoration, as well as Franklin's own story. For the Historical Experience, a costumed guide and a series of impressionistic audiovisuals transport visitors back to the time of Franklin, who lived here with his "housekeeper" in cosy domesticity, while his wife and daughter languished in Philadelphia.

Aldwych

The wide crescent of **Aldwych**, forming a neat "D" on its side with the eastern part of the Strand, was driven through the slums of this zone in the early twentieth century. A confident ensemble occupies the centre, with the enormous Australia House and India House sandwiching **Bush House**, home of the BBC's World Service from 1940 to 2012. Despite its thoroughly British associations, Bush House was actually built by the American speculator Irving T. Bush, whose planned trade centre flopped in the 1930s. The giant figures on the north facade and the inscription, "To the Eternal Friendship of English-Speaking Nations", thus refer to the friendship between the US and Britain, and are not, as many people assume, the World Service's declaratory manifesto.

Not far from these former bastions of Empire, up Houghton Street, lurks that erstwhile hotbed of left-wing agitation, the **London School of Economics**. Founded in 1895, the LSE gained a radical reputation in 1968, when a student sit-in protesting against the Vietnam War ended in violent confrontations that were the closest London came to the heady events in Paris that year. Famous alumni include Carlos the Jackal, Cherie Booth (wife of ex-Prime Minister Tony Blair) and Mick Jagger.

Somerset House

Strand • **Fountain Court** Daily 7.30am–11pm • Free **Riverside terrace** Daily 8am–6pm • Free Guided tours Thurs 1.15 & 2.45pm, Sat 1.15, 2.15, 3.15 & 4.15pm • Free **Embankment galleries** Daily 10am–6pm • £6 • ☎ 020 7845 4600, ⓦ somersethouse.org.uk • ⊖ Temple or Covent Garden

Somerset House is the sole survivor of the grandiose river palaces that once lined the Strand, its four wings enclosing a large courtyard rather like a Parisian *hôtel*. Although it looks like an old aristocratic mansion, the present building was, in fact, purpose-built in 1776 by William Chambers, to house governmental offices (including the Navy Office). Nowadays, Somerset House's granite-paved courtyard is a great place to relax thanks to its fab 55-jet **fountain** that spouts straight from the cobbles, and does a little syncopated dance every half-hour (daily 10am–11pm). The courtyard is also used for open-air performances, concerts, installations and, in winter, an ice rink.

The north wing houses the permanent collection of the **Courtauld Institute**, best known for its outstanding Impressionist and Post-Impressionist paintings. The south wing has a lovely riverside terrace with a café-restaurant and the **Embankment Galleries**, which host innovative special exhibitions on contemporary art and design. Before you head off to one of the collections, however, make sure you go and admire the Royal Naval Commissioners' superb gilded eighteenth-century barge in the **King's Barge House**, below ground level in the south wing.

Courtauld Gallery

8

Somerset House, Strand • Daily 10am–6pm, occasional Thurs until 9pm • £6 (Mon £3) • ☎ 020 7848 2526, ⓦ courtauld.ac.uk • ⊖ Temple or Covent Garden

Founded in 1931 as part of the University of London, the Courtauld Institute was the first body in Britain to award degrees in art history as an academic subject. It's most famous, however, for the **Courtauld Gallery**, which displays its priceless art collection, whose virtue is quality rather than quantity. Best known for its superlative Impressionist and Post-Impressionist works, the Courtauld also owns a fine array of earlier works by the likes of Rubens, Botticelli, Bellini and Cranach the Elder and gives regular talks throughout the year.

The displays currently start on the **ground floor** with a small room devoted to medieval religious paintings. Next, you ascend the beautiful, semicircular **staircase** to the first-floor galleries, whose exceptional plasterwork ceilings recall their original use as the learned societies' meeting rooms. This is where the cream of the Courtauld's collection is currently displayed: rehangings have become more frequent, however, so ask if you can't find a particular painting.

The first floor galleries

To follow the collection chronologically, start in room 2, where you'll find two splendid fifteenth-century Florentine *cassoni* (chests), with their original backrests, and a large **Botticelli** altarpiece commissioned by a convent and refuge for repentant prostitutes; hence Mary Magdalene's pole position below the Cross. You can also admire **Lucas Cranach the Elder**'s *Adam and Eve*, one of the highlights of the collection, with the Saxon painter revelling in the visual delights of Eden. Works by **Rubens** dominate room 3, ranging from oil sketches for church frescoes to large-scale late works, plus a winningly informal portrait of his close friend Jan Brueghel the Elder and family. Also in this room hangs **Pieter Bruegel the Elder**'s *Landscape with Flight into Egypt*, a small canvas once owned by Rubens. Further on, there are works by Goya, Reynolds, Romney, Tiepolo and an affectionate portrait by **Gainsborough** of his wife, painted in his old age.

The cream of the gallery's **Impressionist** works occupy the next few rooms, with room 5 devoted to **Cézanne** and featuring his characteristically lush landscapes and one of his series of *Card Players*. The works in room 6 are all by artists who took part in the first Impressionist exhibition in Paris in 1874, and include **Renoir**'s *La Loge*, a **Monet** still-life, and a view of Lordship Lane by **Pissarro** from his days in exile in London. Also on display are a small-scale version of **Manet**'s bold *Déjeuner sur l'herbe*, and his atmospheric *A Bar at the Folies-Bergère*, a nostalgic celebration of the artist's love affair with Montmartre, painted two years before his death. In room 7, **Gauguin**'s Breton peasants *Haymaking* contrasts with his later Tahitian works, including the sinister *Nevermore*. And there are works by **Van Gogh** including his *Self-Portrait with Bandaged Ear*, painted shortly after his remorseful self-mutilation, following his attempted attack on his flatmate Gauguin. Look out, too, for **Picasso**'s *Child with a Dove*, from 1901, which heralded his "Blue Period".

Second floor: twentieth-century works

The **second floor** is used primarily to display the Courtauld's twentieth-century works, which bring a wonderful splash of colour and a hint of modernism to the galleries. There isn't the space to exhibit the entire collection, so it's impossible to say for definite which paintings will be on show at any one time. Room 8 is home to paintings, sketches and sculptures by **Edgar Degas**, while in room 9, you hit the bright primary colours of the Courtauld's superb collection of **Fauvist** paintings, by the likes of Derain, Vlaminck, Braque, Dufy and Matisse, which spill over into room 10. You'll also find *Yellow Irises*, a rare early Picasso from 1901, and one of **Modigliani**'s celebrated nudes.

The Courtauld owns a selection of works by **Roger Fry**, who helped organize the first Impressionist exhibitions in Britain, and went on to found the Omega Workshops in 1913 with Duncan Grant. Fry also bequeathed his private collection to the Courtauld, including several paintings by Grant, his wife Vanessa Bell and Fry himself. There's a room devoted to British artists from the 1930s like Ben Nicolson, Barbara Hepworth and Ivon Hitchens, and at least one room with works by the likes of Kokoschka, Jawlensky, Kirchner, Delaunay and Léger, and an outstanding array of works by **Kandinsky**, the Russian-born artist who was 30 when he finally decided to become a painter and move to Munich. He's best known for his pioneering abstract paintings, such as *Improvisation on Mahogany* from 1910, where the subject matter begins to disintegrate in the blocks of colour.

King's College

Strand • ☎ 020 7848 2343, Ⓦ kcl.ac.uk • ⊖ Temple or Covent Garden

Adjacent to Somerset House, the ugly concrete facade of **King's College** (part of the University of London) conceals Robert Smirke's much older buildings, which date from its foundation in 1829. Rather than entering the college itself, stroll down Surrey Street and turn right down Surrey Steps, which are in the middle of the old *Norfolk Hotel*, whose terracotta facade is worth admiring. This should bring you out at one of the most unusual sights in King's College: the **"Roman" Bath**, a 15ft-long tub (actually dating from Tudor times at the earliest) with a natural spring that produces 2000 gallons a day. It was used in Victorian times as a cold bath (Dickens himself used it and David Copperfield "had many a cold plunge" here). The bath is visible through a window (daily 9am–dusk; ☎ 020 7641 5264), but you can only get a closer look by appointment.

St Mary-le-Strand

Strand • Tues–Thurs 11am–4pm, Sun 10am–1pm • Free • ☎ 020 7836 3126, Ⓦ stmarylestrand.org, • ⊖ Temple or Covent Garden

St Mary-le-Strand, completed in 1724 in Baroque style and topped by a delicately tiered tower, was the first public building of James Gibbs, who went on to design St Martin-in-the-Fields. Nowadays, the church sits ignominiously amid the traffic hurtling westwards down the Strand, though even in the eighteenth century, parishioners complained of the noise from the roads, and it's incredible that recitals are still given here. The entrance is flanked by two lovely magnolia trees, and the interior has a particularly rich plastered ceiling in white and gold. It was in this church that Bonnie Prince Charlie allegedly renounced his Roman Catholic faith and became an Anglican, during a secret visit to London in 1750.

St Clement Danes

Strand • Daily 9am–4pm • Free • ☎ 020 7242 8282, ⓦ raf.mod.uk/stclementdanes • ⊖ Temple or Covent Garden

St Clement Danes, designed by Wren, occupies a traffic island in the Strand. Badly burnt out in the Blitz (the pock marks are still visible in the exterior north wall), the church was handed over to the RAF, who turned it into a memorial to those killed in World War II. Glass cabinets in the west end of the church contain some poignant mementoes, such as a wooden cross carved from a door hinge in a Japanese POW camp. The nave and aisles are studded with over eight hundred squadron and unit badges, while heavy tomes set in glass cabinets record the 120,000 RAF service personnel who died. The church's carillon plays out various tunes, including the nursery rhyme *Oranges and Lemons* (daily 9am, noon, 3, 6 & 9pm), though St Clement's Eastcheap in the City is more likely to be the church referred to in the rhyme.

In front of the church, the statue of **Gladstone**, with his four female allegorical companions, is flanked by two air chiefs: **Lord Dowding**, the man who oversaw the Battle of Britain, and "**Bomber**" **Harris**, architect of the saturation bombing of Germany which killed five hundred thousand civilians (and over 55,000 Allied airmen commemorated on the plinth). Although Churchill was ultimately responsible, the opprobrium was left to fall on Harris, who was denied the peerage all the other service chiefs received, while his forces were refused a campaign medal. The statue was unveiled somewhat insensitively, in 1992, on the anniversary of the bombing of Cologne.

Twinings

216 Strand • Mon–Fri 8.30am–7.30pm, Sat 10am–5pm, Sun 10am–4pm • ☎ 020 7383 1359, ⓦ twinings.com • ⊖ Temple, Chancery Lane or Covent Garden

In 1706, Thomas Twining, tea supplier to Queen Anne, bought Tom's Coffee House and began serving tea as well as coffee, thereby effectively opening the world's first tearoom. A branch of **Twinings**, which sells limited edition long leaf tea, still occupies the site and its slender Neoclassical portico features two reclining Chinamen, dating from the time when all tea came from China. At the back of the shop is a small **museum** with a fine display of ornate caddies, photos of the Twining family and some historic packaging and advertising.

Lloyd's Bank (Law Courts branch)

222 Strand • Mon, Tues, Thurs & Fri 9am–5pm, Wed 10am–5pm • ⊖ Temple, Chancery Lane or Covent Garden

Much of the extravagant decor of the short-lived *Palsgrave Restaurant*, which was built at 222 Strand in 1883, is preserved in **Lloyds TSB**'s Law Courts branch. The foyer features acres of Doulton tiles, hand-painted in blues and greens, and a flying-fish fountain that was originally supplied with fresh water from an artesian well sunk 238ft below the Strand. The interior of walnut and sequoia wood panelling is worth a look, too, and features ceramic portrait panels. The Law Courts themselves stand opposite (see p.142).

ROYAL COURTS OF JUSTICE

Holborn and the Inns of Court

Strategically placed between the royal and political centre of Westminster and the mercantile and financial might of the City, Holborn (pronounced "Ho-bun") became the hub of the English legal system in the thirteenth century. Hostels, known as Inns of Court, were established where lawyers could eat, sleep and study law. Hidden away from the general hubbub of London, the Inns make for an interesting stroll, their archaic, cobbled precincts exuding the rarefied atmosphere of an Oxbridge college, and sheltering one of the city's oldest churches, the twelfth-century Temple Church. Elsewhere, Holborn boasts two of London's most enjoyable small museums: the Sir John Soane's Museum, with its architectural illusions and eclectic array of curios, and the Hunterian Museum, home of freakish medical curiosities.

Temple

9

Temple, the largest of the Inns of Court, was once the headquarters of the Knights Templar, a military order of monks whose job was to protect pilgrims en route to Jerusalem. The Templars became very powerful, the Crown took fright and the order was suppressed in 1307, with the land passing to another order, the Knights Hospitaller. Legal London already had a foothold here by this point, so when the monks left during the Reformation, the lawyers simply took over the whole precinct. Temple actually consists of two Inns – **Middle Temple** and **Inner Temple** – both of which lie south of the Strand and Fleet Street. It's difficult to tell which Inn you're in, unless you check the coat of arms on each building: the Lamb of God (for Middle Temple) and the Pegasus (for Inner Temple). Nevertheless, the maze of courtyards and passageways is fun to explore – especially after dark, when Temple is gas-lit – and a welcome haven from London's traffic. There are several points of access, simplest of which is Devereux Court, which leads south off the Strand, but at the weekend you can usually only enter from Tudor Street to the east.

Middle Temple Hall

Mon–Fri 10–11.30am & 3–4pm, though sometimes closed for events • Free • ☎ 020 7427 4800 • ⊖ Temple or Blackfriars

Medieval students ate, attended lectures and slept in the **Middle Temple Hall**, on Fountain Court, and it remains the Inn's main dining room. The present building was constructed in the 1560s and provided the setting for many Elizabethan masques and plays – including Shakespeare's *Twelfth Night*, which was premiered here in 1602. The hall is worth a visit for its fine hammerbeam roof, wood panelling and decorative Elizabethan screen, and the small wooden table said to have been carved from the hatch from Francis Drake's ship, the *Golden Hind*.

Temple Church

Mon–Fri 11am–1pm & 2–4pm, but times vary • £4 • ☎ 020 7353 3470, ⓦ templechurch.com • ⊖ Temple or Blackfriars

Despite wartime damage, the original round **Temple Church** – built by the Templars in 1185 and modelled on the Church of the Holy Sepulchre in Jerusalem – still stands. The interior features striking Purbeck marble piers, recumbent marble effigies of medieval knights and tortured grotesques grimacing in the spandrels of the blind arcading. At the northwestern corner of the choir, behind the decorative altar tomb of Edmund Plowden, builder of Middle Temple Hall, stairs lead up to a cell, less than 5ft long, in which disobedient knights were confined. The church makes an appearance in both the book and the film of *The Da Vinci Code* by Dan Brown.

Inner Temple

Garden May–Sept: Mon–Fri 12.30–3pm • Free • ⓦ innertemple.org.uk • ⊖ Temple or Blackfriars

The millennium column, to the south of Temple Church, marks the point where the Great Fire of 1666 was extinguished; it's topped by a diminutive statue of two

---

THE INNS

Even today, every aspiring barrister in England and Wales must belong to one of the four Inns – **Inner Temple**, **Middle Temple**, **Lincoln's Inn** and **Gray's Inn** – in order to qualify and be "called to the Bar". It's an old-fashioned system of patronage (you need contacts to get accepted at one of the Inns) and one that has done much to keep the judiciary overwhelmingly white, male, public school- and Oxbridge-educated. The most bizarre stipulation is that to qualify as a barrister, you must attend a dozen formal dinners. Dress code is strict – "dark lounge suit, plain collar and sober tie/white blouse" or "genuine ethnic dress" – although the meals are heavily subsidized: under £20 for a four-course meal with wine and port. Back in medieval times, aspiring lawyers would take part in mock courts and dine together in the main halls. Today, while the barristers' professional training is conducted by private law schools, the dinners live on.

9

knights sharing a horse, emphasising the vow of poverty taken by the Knights Templar. **Inner Temple Hall**, to the south of the column, is a postwar reconstruction, as is clear from the brickwork. This was the Inn Mahatma Gandhi belonged to in 1888, when he was studying law, living as a true Englishman, dressing as a dandy, dancing, taking elocution lessons and playing the violin, while his close associate Jawaharlal Nehru spent two even wilder years here a decade or so later, gambling, drinking and running up considerable debts. The public are also permitted to explore the **Inner Temple Garden**, which slopes down to the Embankment and is

HOLBORN & THE INNS OF COURT

PUBS & BARS	
Bounce	2
Old Bank of England	4
Seven Stars	3
Ye Olde Mitre	1

9

where Shakespeare set the fictional scene of the plucking of red and white roses in *Henry VI Part One*.

Royal Courts of Justice

Strand · Mon–Fri 9.30am–4.30pm; no cameras allowed · Free · Guided tours Mon–Fri · £12 · ☎ 020 7947 6000 · ⊖ Temple

On the north side of the Strand, the **Royal Courts of Justice** are home to the Court of Appeal and the High Court, where the most important civil cases are tried (criminal cases are heard at the Old Bailey). The main portal and steps of this daunting Gothic Revival complex, designed in the 1870s, often features in the news, as this is also where libel disputes and high profile divorce cases are heard. In the intimidating Main Hall, where bewigged barristers are busy on their mobiles, you can pick up a plan and a short guide to the complex, while the glass cabinets in the centre of the hall list which cases are being heard and where. In the minstrels' gallery, there's a small exhibition on the history of legal dress codes.

Lincoln's Inn Fields

To the north of the Law Courts lies **Lincoln's Inn Fields**, London's largest square. Originally simply pasture land and a playground for Lincoln's Inn students, it was used as a place of execution in Tudor times, would-be assassin Anthony Babington and his Catholic accomplices being hanged, drawn and quartered here for high treason in 1586. Laid out in the early 1640s, the square's most arresting statue is that of Margaret MacDonald (wife of the first Labour prime minister Ramsay MacDonald, who lived and died at no. 3), amid a brood of nine children (she herself had six), commemorating her social work among the young. In the southwest corner of the square is one of London's few surviving timber-framed buildings, the sixteenth-century **Old Curiosity Shop** in Portsmouth Street (currently a shoe shop), which claims to be the inspiration for Dickens' sentimental tale of the same name.

Hunterian Museum

Lincoln's Inn Fields · Tues–Sat 10am–5pm · Free · ☎ 020 7869 6560, ⓦ rcseng.ac.uk · ⊖ Holborn

The **Hunterian Museum** is on the first floor of the imposing Royal College of Surgeons building on the south side of Lincoln's Inn Fields. First opened in 1813, the museum contains the unique specimen collection of the surgeon-scientist John Hunter (1728–93). The centrepiece of the museum is the Crystal Gallery, a wall of jars of pickled skeletons and body pieces – from the gall bladder of a puffer fish to the thyroid of a dromedary – prepared by Hunter himself. Among the most prized exhibits are the skeleton of the "Irish giant", Charles Byrne (1761–83), who was seven feet ten inches tall, and the Sicilian dwarf Caroline Crachami (1815–24), who stood at only one foot ten and a half inches when she died at the age of 9. You'll find Crachami in the McCrae Gallery, where a series of gruesome dental instruments herald the odontological collection. Upstairs, you can have a go at simulated minimal-access surgery, and examine Joseph Lister's cumbersome carbolic-acid spray machine, known as the "donkey engine", with which he pioneered antiseptic surgery, performing operations obscured in a cloud of phenol (he even conducted a foggy operation on Queen Victoria – who had an abscess in the royal armpit – accidentally spraying her in the face in the process).

Sir John Soane's Museum

13 Lincoln's Inn Fields · Tues–Sat 10am–5pm, candle-lit eve first Tues of month 6–9pm (the museum is very popular and you may have to queue) · Free · Guided tours Tues & Fri 11.30am, Wed & Thurs 3.30pm, Sat 11am; £10 · ☎ 020 7405 2107, ⓦ soane.org · ⊖ Holborn

A group of buildings on the north side of the square houses the fascinating **Sir John Soane's Museum**. Soane (1753–1837), a bricklayer's son who rose to be architect of the Bank of England, gradually bought up three adjoining Georgian properties here

9

between 1792 and 1824, altering them to serve not only as a home but also as a place to stash his large collection of art and antiquities. No. 13, the central house with the stone loggia, is arranged much as it was in his lifetime, with an ingenious ground plan and an informal, treasure-hunt atmosphere. Few of Soane's projects were actually built, and his home remains the best example of what he dubbed his "poetry of architecture", using mirrors, domes and skylights to create wonderful spatial ambiguities.

The most unusual part of the house is the colonnaded **monument court**, built over the former stables at the back of the house. All around are antique busts and masonry; above is the wooden chamber on stilts from which Soane supervised his students. To your right is the **picture room**, whose false walls swing back to reveal another wall of pictures, which itself opens to reveal a window and a balcony looking down onto the crypt. The star paintings are **Hogarth**'s satirical *Election* series and his merciless morality tale *The Rake's Progress*.

The flagstoned **crypt** features a "monk's parlour", a Gothic folly dedicated to a make-believe padre, Giovanni, complete with tomb (containing Soane's wife's dog, Fanny), cloister and eerie medieval casts and gargoyles. The hushed sepulchral chamber continues the morbid theme with its wooden mummy case, a model of an Etruscan tomb (complete with skeleton) and the tombstones of Soane's wife and son. You then emerge into the colonnaded atrium, home to an Egyptian **sarcophagus**, rejected by the British Museum and bought by Soane.

Back on the ground floor, make your way to the **breakfast parlour**, which features all Soane's favourite architectural features: coloured skylights, a canopied dome and ranks of tiny convex mirrors. A short stroll up the beautiful cantilevered staircase brings you to the first-floor **drawing rooms**, whose airiness and bright colour scheme come as a relief after the ancient clutter of the downstairs rooms.

Lincoln's Inn

Lincoln's Inn Fields • Inn Mon–Fri 7am–7pm; Chapel Mon–Fri noon–2.30pm; Gardens Mon–Fri noon–2.30pm • Free • First Fri of month guided tour 2pm; £5 • ☎ 020 7405 1393, ⓦ lincolnsinn.org.uk • ⊖ Holborn

Lincoln's Inn, on the east side of Lincoln's Inn Fields, is in many ways the prettiest of the Inns of Court – famous alumni include Thomas More, Oliver Cromwell and Margaret Thatcher. The oldest building is the fifteenth-century Old Hall (by appointment only), where the lawyers used to live and where Dickens set the case Jarndyce versus Jarndyce, the opening scene in *Bleak House*.

Beyond the Old Hall is the sixteenth-century **gatehouse** – best viewed from Chancery Lane – impressive for its age and bulk, not to mention its characteristic diamond-patterned brickwork. Adjacent is the **chapel**, built in 1620, with its unusual fan-vaulted open undercroft; on the first floor, the nave, rebuilt in 1880, hit by a Zeppelin in World War I and much restored since, still boasts its original ornate pews. North of the chapel lie the Palladian **Stone Buildings**, best appreciated from the manicured lawns of the Inn's gardens; the strange miniature castle near the garden entrance is the gardeners' tool shed, a creation of George Gilbert Scott, designer of St Pancras Station.

Chancery Lane

Running along the eastern edge of Lincoln's Inn is legal London's main thoroughfare, **Chancery Lane**, home of the Law Society (the solicitors' regulatory body for England and Wales) and lined with shops where barristers, solicitors and clerks can buy their wigs, gowns, legal tomes, stationery and champagne.

London Silver Vaults

Chancery Lane • Mon–Fri 9am–5.30pm, Sat 9am–1pm • Free • ☎ 020 7242 3844, ⓦ thesilvervaults.com • ⊖ Chancery Lane

On the east side of Chancery Lane are the **London Silver Vaults**, which began life in 1876 as the Chancery Lane Safe Deposit for London's wealthy elite, but now house a strange, claustrophobic lair of subterranean shops selling every kind of silverware – mostly antique, mostly English and often quite tasteless.

Gray's Inn

South Square · Mon–Fri 10am–4pm; gardens open to the public weekday lunchtimes · Free · ☎ 020 7458 7800, ⓦ graysinn.info ·
⊖ Chancery Lane

The last of the four Inns of Court, **Gray's Inn** lies hidden away off High Holborn, at the top of Chancery Lane; access is next to the venerable *Cittie of Yorke* pub. Established in the fourteenth century, the Inn took its name from the de Grey family, who owned the original mansion used as student lodgings; most of what you see today, however, was rebuilt after the Blitz. The **Hall** (by appointment only), with its fabulous Tudor screen and stained glass, witnessed the premiere of Shakespeare's *Comedy of Errors* in 1594. The north side of the Inn, taken up by the wide green expanse of **Gray's Inn Gardens**, is entirely and impressively visible through its wrought-iron railings from Theobald's Road.

Holborn

Confusingly, **Holborn** is also the name of a street – an eastern continuation of High Holborn – with two remarkable buildings, one on either side of the road. The first, on the south side, is **Staple Inn**, a former Inn of Chancery (a less prestigious version of the Inns of Court). Its overhanging half-timbered facade and gables date from the sixteenth century and are the most extensive in the whole of London; they survived the Fire, but had to be extensively rebuilt after the Blitz. More or less opposite stands the palatial, terracotta-red **Prudential Assurance Building**, begun in 1879 by Alfred Waterhouse. This fortress of Victorian capitalism has its very own Bridge of Sighs, harbours a dramatic memorial to the Prudential men who fell in World War I (plus a more sober one for World War II) and retains much of its original Doulton-tiled interior. At the eastern end of Holborn lies **Holborn Circus**, a vast traffic intersection centred on London's politest statue, in which a cheerful Prince Albert doffs his hat to passers-by.

Ely Place

Just off Charterhouse Street, which runs northeast from Holborn Circus, is the cul-de-sac of **Ely Place**, named after the Bishop of Ely, whose London residence used to stand here from 1290 to 1772. John of Gaunt lived in the bishop's palace for a while after his own house on the Strand was burnt down in the 1381 Peasants' Revolt. It's from Ely Place that Shakespeare has John of Gaunt say his "this sceptre'd isle" speech in *Richard II*, and the strawberries produced by the palace gardens get a positive recommendation in *Richard III* – a strawberry fair is held each June in honour of this. The street remained technically part of Cambridgeshire until the 1930s, and even today it is gated and guarded by a beadle, lodge and wrought-iron gates.

St Etheldreda's Church

14 Ely Place · Mon–Sat 8am–5pm, Sun till 12.30pm · Free · ☎ 020 7405 1061, ⓦ stetheldreda.com · ⊖ Chancery Lane

All that remains of the bishop's palace now is **St Etheldreda's Church**, the bishop's former private chapel, halfway down the street on the left. Built in the thirteenth century, the chapel was bought by the Roman Catholic Rosminian Order in 1874. The Upper Church, though much restored, retains much of its medieval masonry, and features two spectacularly huge postwar stained-glass windows; the west window depicts several English Catholic martyrs, including the Carthusian Prior John Haughton, whose statue also occupies the first niche on the south wall. The atmospherically gloomy medieval crypt contains a model of the pre-Reformation church complex.

CLERKENWELL GREEN

Clerkenwell

Situated slightly uphill from the City and, more importantly, outside its jurisdiction, Clerkenwell (pronounced "Clark-unwell") began life as a village serving the various local monastic foundations. In the nineteenth century, the district's population trebled, mostly through Irish and Italian immigration, and the area acquired a reputation for radicalism exemplified by the Marx Memorial Library, where the exiled Lenin plotted revolution. Nowadays, Clerkenwell is a typical London mix of Georgian and Victorian townhouses, housing estates, old warehouses, loft conversions and art studios. It remains off the conventional tourist trail, but since the 1990s, it has established itself as one of the city's most vibrant and fashionable areas, with a host of shops, cafés, restaurants and pubs.

Following the Great Fire, Clerkenwell was settled by craftsmen, including newly arrived French Huguenots, excluded from the City guilds. At the same time, the springs that give the place its name were rediscovered (and are still visible through the window of 14–16 Farringdon Lane), and Clerkenwell became a popular **spa resort** for a century or so. During the nineteenth century, the district's springs and streams became cholera-infested sewers, and the area became an overpopulated **slum area**, home to three prisons and the setting for Fagin's Den in Dickens' *Oliver Twist*. Victorian slum clearances and wartime bombing took their toll, the population declined and by the 1980s, the area's traditional trades – locksmithing, clockmaking, printing and jewellery – all but disappeared. Nowadays, the area is characterized by media and design companies (particularly architects), with trendy bars and restaurants catering for the area's loft-dwelling residents.

10

Hatton Garden

Ⓦ hatton-garden.net

Hatton Garden, connecting Holborn Circus (see p.147) with Little Italy (see p.151), is no beauty spot, but, as the centre of the city's **diamond and jewellery trade** since medieval times, it's an intriguing place to visit during the week. There are over fifty shops and, as in Antwerp and New York, ultra-orthodox Hasidic Jews dominate the business here as middlemen. Near the top of Hatton Garden, there's a plaque commemorating **Hiram Maxim** (1840–1916), the American inventor who perfected the automatic gun named after him in the workshops at no. 57.

East of Hatton Garden, off Greville Street, lies **Bleeding Heart Yard**, a key location in Dickens' *Little Dorrit*. The name refers to the gruesome 1626 murder of Lady Hatton, who sold her soul to the devil, so the story goes. One night, during a ball at nearby Hatton House, the devil came to collect, and all trace of her vanished except her heart, which was found bleeding and throbbing on the pavement.

Parallel to Hatton Garden, take a wander through **Leather Lane Market**, a weekday lunchtime market selling everything from fruit and veg to clothes and electrical gear.

Mount Pleasant and the British Postal Museum

Rosebery Ave · Postal Museum Mon–Fri 10am–5pm, Thurs till 7pm, plus second Sat of month 10am–5pm (closed the following Mon) · Free · ☎ 020 7239 2570, Ⓦ postalheritage.org.uk · ⊖ Farringdon

Halfway up Rosebery Avenue – built in the 1890s to link Clerkenwell Road with Islington to the north – stands **Mount Pleasant**, opened in 1889 and at one time the largest sorting office in the world. A third of all inland mail passes through here, and originally much of it was brought by the post office's own underground railway network, **Mail Rail** (Ⓦ mailrail.co.uk). Opened in 1927 and similar in design to the tube, the railway was fully automatic, sending driverless trucks between London's sorting offices and train stations at speeds of up to 35mph. Unfortunately, all 23 miles of this 2ft-gauge railway were mothballed in 2003. Philatelists, meanwhile, should head to the **British Postal Museum**, by the side of the sorting office on Phoenix Place, which puts on small exhibitions drawn from its vast archive.

Exmouth Market

Food market Mon–Fri noon–3pm · Ⓦ exmouth-market.com · ⊖ Farringdon

Opposite Mount Pleasant is **Exmouth Market**, the heart of today's vibrant Clerkenwell. Apart from a surviving pie-and-mash shop, the street is now characterized by modish shops, bars and restaurants, and a small **foodie market**, at its busiest towards the end of the week. A blue plaque at no.56 pays tribute to **Joey Grimaldi** (1778–1837), son of Italian immigrants and the "Father of Clowns", who first appeared on stage at nearby

Sadler's Wells at the age of 3. Close by, the street's **Church of the Holy Redeemer** sports a fetching Italianate campanile, while the groin-vaulted interior features a large baldachin and stations of the cross – yet despite appearances, it belongs to the Church of England.

Sadler's Wells

Rosebery Ave • 🌐 sadlerswells.com • 🔵 Angel

Clerkenwell's days as a fashionable spa began when Thomas Sadler rediscovered a medicinal well in his garden in 1683 and established a music house to entertain visitors. The well has since made a comeback at the **Sadler's Wells Theatre** on Rosebery Avenue, the seventh theatre here since 1683, and now one of London's main dance venues. A borehole sunk into the old well provides all non-drinking supplies, helps cool the building and produces bottled drinking water for the punters.

LITTLE ITALY

In the late nineteenth century, London experienced a huge influx of Italian immigrants who created their own **Little Italy** in the triangle of land now bounded by Clerkenwell Road, Rosebery Avenue and Farringdon Road; craftsmen, artisans, street performers and musicians were later joined by ice-cream vendors, restaurateurs and political refugees. Between the wars the population peaked at around ten thousand, crammed into overcrowded, insanitary slums. The old streets have long been demolished, and few Italians live here these days; nevertheless, the area remains a focus for a community that's now spread right across the capital.

The main point of reference is **St Peter's Italian Church** (☎020 7837 1528, ⓦitalianchurch .org.uk), a surprisingly large, bright, basilica-style church built in 1863 and still the favourite venue for Italian weddings and christenings, as well as for Sunday Mass. It's rarely open outside of daily Mass, though you can view the World War I memorial in the main porch, and, above it, the grim memorial to seven hundred Anglo-Italian internees who died aboard the *Arandora Star*, a POW ship which sank en route to Canada in 1940. St Peter's is the starting point of the annual Italian Procession, begun in 1883 and a permanent fixture on the Sunday nearest July 16 (see p.25).

A few old-established Italian businesses survive, too: the Scuola Guida driving school at 178 Clerkenwell Rd, and the deli, G. Gazzano & Son, at 167–169 Farringdon Rd. There's also a plaque to **Giuseppe Mazzini** (1805–72), the chief protagonist in Italian unification, above the barbers at 10 Laystall St. Mazzini lived in exile in London for many years and was very active in the Clerkenwell community, establishing a free school for Italian children in Hatton Garden.

10

Islington Museum

245 St John St • Daily except Wed & Sun 10am–5pm • Free • ☎ 020 7527 2837 • ⊖ Angel or Farringdon

If you're keen to learn some more about Clerkenwell, Finsbury or the wider borough of Islington (see p.288), it's worth seeking out the **Islington Museum**, housed in the basement of the Finsbury Library (access is down the steps on the north side). There's a dressing-up box for the kids and some fascinating sections on the area's radical politics for the adults. Highlights include the bust of Lenin, part of a memorial designed by Lubetkin, that was erected in 1942 in Holford Square (see p.153), but had to be removed after the war, after it was targeted by Fascists; you can also view some of the library books embellished by Joe Orton and Kenneth Halliwell (see p.290).

Clerkenwell Green

There hasn't been any green on **Clerkenwell Green** for at least three centuries. By contrast, poverty and overcrowding were the main features of nineteenth-century Clerkenwell, and the Green was well known in the press as "the headquarters of republicanism, revolution and ultra-non-conformity" and a popular spot for **demonstrations**. The most violent of these was the "Clerkenwell Riot" of 1832, when a policeman was stabbed to death during a clash between unemployed demonstrators and the newly formed Metropolitan Police Force. In 1871, a red flag was flown from a lamppost on the Green in support of the Paris Commune. London's first **May Day** march set off from here in 1890, and the tradition continues to this day. In 1900, the Labour Party was founded at a meeting on nearby Farringdon Road; in 1903 Lenin and Stalin first met at the *Crown & Anchor* (now the *Crown Tavern*); the Communist Party had its headquarters close by on St John Street for many years; and the Party's *Daily Worker* (and later *Morning Star*), *The Guardian* and *The Observer* were all printed on Farringdon Road.

Marx Memorial Library

37a Clerkenwell Green • Mon–Thurs 1–2pm or by appointment; closed Aug • Free • ☎ 020 7253 1485, ⓦ marx-memorial-library.org • ⊖ Farringdon

The oldest building on the Green is the former Welsh Charity School, at no. 37a, built in 1738 and now home to the **Marx Memorial Library**. Headquarters of the left-wing

10

THE PEOPLE'S REPUBLIC OF FINSBURY

The Borough of Finsbury was subsumed into Islington in 1965, but the former **Finsbury Town Hall** (now a dance academy) still stands, an attractive building from 1899, whose name is spelt out in magenta glass on the delicate wrought-iron canopy that juts out into Rosebery Avenue. As the plaque outside states, the district was the first to boast an Asian MP, **Dadabhai Nairoji**, who was elected (after a recount) as a Liberal MP in 1892 with a majority of five. In keeping with its radical pedigree, the borough went on to elect several Communist councillors and became known popularly as the "People's Republic of Finsbury". The council commissioned Georgian-born Berthold Lubetkin to design the modernist **Finsbury Health Centre** on Pine Street, off Exmouth Market, described by Jonathan Glancey as "a remarkable outpost of Soviet thinking and neo-Constructivist architecture in a part of central London wracked with rickets and TB". Lubetkin's later **Spa Green Estate**, the council flats further north on the opposite side of Rosebery Avenue from Sadler's Wells, featured novelties such as rubbish shutes and an aerofoil roof to help tenants dry their clothes.

London Patriotic Society from 1872, and later the Social Democratic Federation's Twentieth Century Press, this is where **Lenin** edited seventeen editions of the Bolshevik paper *Iskra* in 1902–03. The library itself, founded in 1933 in response to the book burnings in Nazi Germany, is open to members only. However, visitors are welcome to view the "workerist" *Hastings Mural* from 1935, and the poky little back room where Lenin worked on *Iskra*. Stuffed with busts, the latter is maintained as a kind of shrine, and there's a copy of Rodchenko's red-and-black chess set for good measure, too.

St James's Church

Clerkenwell Close • Mon–Fri 9.30am–5.30pm • Free • ☎ 020 7251 1190, ⓦ jc-church.org • ⊖ Farringdon

The area north of Clerkenwell Green was once occupied by the Benedictine nunnery of St Mary. The buildings have long since vanished, though the current church of **St James** on Clerkenwell Close, from 1792, is the descendant of the convent church. A plain, galleried building decorated in Wedgwood blue and white, its most interesting features are the twin staircases for the galleries at the west end, both of which were fitted with wrought-iron guards to prevent parishioners from glimpsing any ladies' ankles as they ascended.

St John's Gate

St John's Lane • Mon–Sat 10am–5pm • Free • ☎ 020 7324 4005, ⓦ museumstjohn.org.uk • ⊖ Farringdon

St John's Gate was built in Kentish ragstone in 1502 as the southern entrance to the Priory of the Order of St John of Jerusalem, the oldest of Clerkenwell's religious establishments. The Knights of St John, or Knights Hospitaller, were responsible for the defence of the Holy Land, and the Clerkenwell priory was established as the order's headquarters in the 1140s. The priory was sacked by Wat Tyler's poll-tax rebels in 1381 on the lookout for the prior, Robert Hales, who was responsible for collecting the tax; Hales was eventually discovered at the Tower, dragged out and beheaded on Tower Hill. Following the Reformation, the Knights moved to Malta, and the Gate housed the Master of Revels, the Elizabethan censor, and later a Latin-speaking coffee house run by Richard Hogarth, father of the painter, William. Today, the gatehouse is the headquarters of the **St John Ambulance**, a voluntary first-aid service, established in 1877.

The main room of the gatehouse **museum** traces the development of the Order before its expulsion in 1540 by Henry VIII. There's masonry from the old priory, crusader coins and a small arms collection salvaged from the knights' armoury on Rhodes. The museum's other gallery tells the story of the St John Ambulance, featuring a display of early uniforms and equipment. And if you're lucky, there'll be a uniformed nurse on hand to bring the exhibition to life.

Crypt of the Grand Priory Church

Guided tours Tues, Fri & Sat 11am & 2.30pm • £5 donation requested

Of the original twelfth-century church, all that remains is the **Norman crypt**, which contains two outstanding monuments: a sixteenth-century Spanish alabaster effigy of a Knight of St John, and the emaciated effigy of the last prior, who died of a broken heart in 1540 following the Order's dissolution. Above ground, the curve of the church's walls – it was circular, like Temple Church – is traced out in cobblestones on St John's Square. To visit the Grand Priory Church, you must take a **guided tour**, which also allows you to explore the gatehouse, including the mock-medieval Chapter Hall.

10

Charterhouse

Charterhouse Square • By guided tour only April–Aug by appointment • £10 • ☎ 020 7253 9503, ⓦ thecharterhouse.org • ❸ Barbican or Farringdon

In the southeast corner of Clerkenwell lies **Charterhouse**, founded in 1371 as a Carthusian monastery. The Carthusians were the most respected of the religious orders in London and the only one to put up any significant resistance to the Dissolution of the Monasteries, for which the prior was hanged, drawn and quartered at Tyburn, and his severed arm nailed to the gatehouse as a warning to the rest of the community. The gatehouse, on Charterhouse Square, which retains its fourteenth-century oak doors, is the starting point for the excellent, exhaustive two-hour **guided tours**.

Very little remains of the original buildings, as the monastery was rebuilt as a Tudor mansion after the Dissolution. The monks lived in individual cells, each with its own garden and were only allowed to speak to one another on Sundays; three of their tiny cells can still be seen in the west wall of **Preachers' Court**. The larger of the two enclosed courtyards, **Masters' Court**, retains the wonderful Great Hall, which boasts a fine Renaissance carved screen and a largely reconstructed hammerbeam roof, as well as the Great Chamber where Elizabeth I and James I were once entertained. The **Chapel**, with its geometrical plasterwork ceiling, is half-Tudor and half-Jacobean, and contains the marble and alabaster tomb of **Thomas Sutton**, whose greyhound-head emblem crops up throughout the building. It was Sutton, deemed "the richest commoner in England" at the time, who bought the place in 1611 and converted it into a charity school for boys (now the famous public school in Surrey) and an **almshouse** for gentlemen – known as "brothers" – forty of whom continue to be cared for here.

LENIN IN CLERKENWELL

Virtually every Bolshevik leader spent at least some time in exile in London at the beginning of the twentieth century, to avoid the attentions of the Tsarist secret police. **Lenin** (1870–1924) and his wife, Nadezhda, arrived in April 1902 and found unfurnished lodgings at 30 Holford Square, off Great Percy Street, under the pseudonyms of Mr and Mrs Jacob Richter. Like Marx, Lenin did his studying in the British Library – L13 was his favourite desk.

The couple also entertained other exiles – including **Trotsky**, whom Lenin met for the first time at Holford Square in October 1902 – but Lenin's most important job was his editing of *Iskra* with Yuli Martov (later the Menshevik leader) and Vera Zasulich (one-time revolutionary assassin). The paper was set in Cyrillic script at a Jewish printer's in the East End and run off on the Social Democratic Federation presses on Clerkenwell Green.

In May 1903, Lenin left to join other exiles in Geneva, though over the next eight years he visited London on five more occasions. The Holford Square house was destroyed in the Blitz, so, in 1942, the local council erected a (short-lived) **monument** to Lenin (now in the Islington Museum). A blue plaque at the back of the hotel on the corner of Great Percy Street commemorates the site of 16 Percy Circus, where Lenin stayed in 1905.

BANK OF ENGLAND

The City

The City is where London began. It was here, nearly two thousand years ago that the Romans first established a settlement on the Thames; later the medieval city emerged as the country's most important trading centre; and it remains one of the world's leading financial hubs. When you consider what's happened here, it's amazing that anything has survived. Yet there are Roman remains, Wren's spires still punctuate the skyline, as does his masterpiece, St Paul's Cathedral. Other relics, such as the City's few remaining medieval alleyways are less conspicuous, and even the locals have problems finding the Museum of London and the Barbican arts complex. By contrast, the City's modern architecture is difficult to miss, from Richard Rogers' mould-breaking Lloyd's Building and Norman Foster's eye-catching Gherkin to the latest batch of skyscrapers.

The City currently stretches from Temple Bar in the west to the Tower of London in the east – administrative boundaries only slightly larger than those marked by the Roman walls and their medieval successors. However, in this **Square Mile** (as the City is often called) you'll have to dig hard to find leftovers of London's early days: four-fifths of the area burnt down in the Great Fire. What you see on the ground is mostly the product of three fairly recent building phases: the Victorian construction boom; the rapid reconstruction that followed the Blitz; and the building frenzy that began in the late1980s, and which has since seen over half the City's office space rebuilt.

The biggest change of all, though, has been in the City's **population**. Until the eighteenth century, the vast majority of Londoners lived and worked in or around the City; nowadays, while more than 350,000 commuters spend Monday to Friday here, only ten thousand actually live here, mostly cooped up in the Barbican complex. The result of this shift is that the City is only fully alive during office hours, with many pubs, restaurants and even some tube stations and tourist sights closing at the weekend.

11

Fleet Street

Fleet Street offers one of the grandest approaches to the City, thanks to the view across to Ludgate Hill and beyond to St Paul's Cathedral, but it's best known for its associations with the printed press and particularly the newspaper industry (see box, p.158).

Temple Bar

Temple Bar, at the western end of Fleet Street, is the latest in a long line of structures marking the boundary between the City of Westminster and the City of London. It began as a simple chain between two posts, but a Wren-designed triumphal arch stood here by the 1670s. The heads of executed traitors were displayed on the arch until the mid-eighteenth century – one could even rent a telescope for a closer look. Then, in 1878, the arch was removed to ease traffic, exiled for over a century to a park in Hertfordshire, only to be re-erected recently near St Paul's (see p.163). The current monument, topped by a winged dragon, marks the spot where the sovereign must ask for the Lord Mayor's permission to enter the City, a tradition that began when Elizabeth I passed through on her way to St Paul's to give thanks for the defeat of the Spanish Armada.

St Dunstan-in-the-West

186a Fleet St • Mon–Fri 9.30am–5pm • ☎ 020 7405 1929, ⓦ stdunstaninthewest.org • ⊖ Temple or Blackfriars

The church of **St Dunstan-in-the-West**, with a distinctive neo-Gothic tower and lantern, from the 1830s, dominates the top of Fleet Street. To the side is the much earlier clock temple, erected in 1671 by the parishioners in thanks for escaping the Great Fire, which stopped just short of the church; inside the temple, the legendary British giants Gog and Magog, in gilded loincloths, nod their heads and clang their bells on the hour.

THE CORPORATION

The one unchanging aspect of the City is its special status, conferred on the area by William the Conqueror to win favour with London's powerful burghers, and extended and reaffirmed by successive rulers ever since. Even today, with its own Lord Mayor, its Beadles, Sheriffs and Aldermen, its separate police force and its select electorate of freemen and liverymen, the City is an anachronistic, one-party mini-state. It's run by the **City of London Corporation** (ⓦ cityoflondon.gov.uk), an unreconstructed old-boys network whose medievalist pageantry camouflages the very real power and wealth that it holds. Its anomalous status is all the more baffling when you consider that the area was an early bastion of British democracy: it was the City that traditionally stood up to bullying sovereigns.

THE CITY

0   200
yards

CLERKENWELL ROAD

CLERKENWELL

Charterhouse

CHARTERHOUSE SQUARE

COWCROSS ST
Farringdon

Barbican

Barbican Arts Centre

BARBICAN

St Giles

Museum of London

LONDON WA

Smithfield Market

St Bartholomew-the-Great

HOLBORN

HOLBORN CIRCUS

St Andrew

HOLBORN VIADUCT

St Sepulchre

St Bartholomew's Hospital

St Botolph

Postman's Park

Goldsmiths' Hall

GRESHAM STREET

City Thameslink

NEWGATE STREET

St Vedast

St Lawre Jev

BREAM BUILDINGS

NEW STREET SQUARE

Old Bailey

St Paul's

CHEAPSIDE

St Mary le-Bow

GOUGH SQUARE

Dr Johnson's House

FLEET STREET

St Dunstan-in-the-West

City Thameslink

LUDGATE HILL

St Bride

LUDGATE CIRCUS

St Martin Ludgate

Temple Bar

PATERNOSTER SQUARE

St Paul's Cathedral

One New Change

WATLING STREET

Temple Bar

St Paul's Churchyard

CANNON STREET

Apothecaries' Hall

Church of Scientology

College of Arms

Mansion House

St Nicholas Cole Abbey

TEMPLE

St Andrew-by-the-Wardrobe

QUEEN VICTORIA STREET

St Benet

VICTORIA EMBANKMENT

Blackfriars

Blackfriars Station

UPPER THAMES STREET

Vintners' Hall

Blackfriars Millennium Pier

RIVERSIDE WALK

River Thames

Bankside Pier

BANKSIDE

Tate Modern

PARK STREET

SUMNER STREET

PUBS & BARS
The Black Friar   7
Jamaica Wine House   5
The Lamb Tavern/
  Old Tom's Bar   6
The Old Bell   4
Viaduct Tavern   2
Ye Old Cheshire Cheese   3

MUSIC VENUE
Barbican   1

ACCOMMODATION
Andaz   1
Apex City of London Hotel   6
Apex London Wall   2
Doubletree by Hilton London
  – Tower of London   5
The King's Wardrobe   4
YHA St Paul's   3

CAFÉ
De Gustibus   3

RESTAURANTS
Duck and Waffle   1
L'Anima   2

11

THE FLEET STREET PRESS

Fleet Street's associations with the printed press began in 1500, when Wynkyn de Worde, William Caxton's apprentice (and the first man to print italics), moved the Caxton presses from Westminster to Fleet Street to be close to the lawyers of the Inns of Court (his best customers) and to the clergy of St Paul's, London's largest literate group. In 1702, the world's first daily newspaper, the now defunct **Daily Courant**, began publishing here, and by the nineteenth century, all the major national and provincial dailies had moved their presses to the area. Then in 1985, Britain's first colour tabloid, *Today*, appeared, using computer technology that rendered the Fleet Street presses obsolete. It was left to media tycoon Rupert Murdoch to take on the printers' unions in a bitter year-long dispute that changed the newspaper industry for ever.

The press headquarters that once dominated the area have all now relocated, leaving just a handful of small publications and a few architectural landmarks to testify to five hundred years of printing history. The former **Daily Telegraph** building, at nos. 135–141, is one of London's few truly Art Deco edifices, built in a Greco-Egyptian style in 1928, with a striking polychrome clock and a great stone relief above the doorway depicting Mercury's messengers sending news around the world. It was upstaged a few years later, however, by the city's first glass curtain-wall construction, the former **Daily Express** building at no. 127, with its sleek black Vitrolite facade. It's worth peering inside the cinema-like foyer, which features a silver-leaf sunburst ceiling, ocean-wave floor tiles, shiny silver serpent handrails and remarkable chrome and gold relief panels extolling the British Empire.

There's a tiled wall in Magpie Alley, off Bouverie Street, which illustrates the history of Fleet Street's presses, and some metal information panels nearby in the windows of the old *Daily Mail* building at Ashentree Court, off Whitefriars Street. Another account of Fleet Street's history is the exhibition in the crypt of **St Bride's Church** (Mon–Fri 9am–6pm, Sat 11am–3pm, Sun 10am–6.30pm; free; ☎020 7427 0133, ⊕stbrides.com), the "journalists' and printers' cathedral", situated behind the former Reuters building. The church also boasts Wren's tallest, and most exquisite, spire (said to be the inspiration for the traditional tiered wedding cake).

The statue of Queen Elizabeth I, in a niche in the vestry wall, and the crumbling statues of the legendary King Lud and his two sons in the porch, originally stood over Ludgate, the City gateway that once stood halfway up Ludgate Hill. The church's unusual, octagonal, neo-Gothic interior features a huge wooden iconostasis, used during the regular Romanian Orthodox services.

Dr Johnson's House

17 Gough Square • Mon–Sat: May–Sept 11am–5.30pm; Oct–April 11am–5pm • £4.50 • ☎020 7353 3745, ⊕drjohnsonshouse.org • ⊖ Blackfriars

Numerous narrow alleyways lead off the north side of Fleet Street beyond Fetter Lane, concealing legal chambers and offices. Two of the narrow alleyways that lead north off Fleet Street – Bolt Court and Hind Court – eventually open out into cobbled Gough Square, which features a statue of Dr Johnson's cat, Hodge, enjoying an oyster. The square's one authentic eighteenth-century building is **Dr Johnson's House,** where the great savant, writer and lexicographer lived from 1748 to 1759 while compiling the 41,000 entries for his very successful English dictionary.

Johnson rented the house on Gough Square with the £1575 advance he received for the dictionary. Despite his subsequent fame, Johnson was in and out of debt all his life – his bestselling romance, *Rasselas*, was written in less than a week to raise funds for his mother's funeral. The house itself is a lovely Georgian period piece peppered with quotes by the great man and portraits of his contemporaries, including Johnson's servant Francis Barber, to whom he left most of his wordly goods. On the second floor, you can watch a film on Johnson's life, after which you get to see the open-plan attic, in which Johnson and his six clerks put together the dictionary, and where kids can try on some replica Georgian garb.

Ludgate Circus

Fleet Street terminates at **Ludgate Circus**, built in the 1870s to replace a bridge over the **River Fleet**, which had already been buried under the roads after a drunken butcher got stuck in the river mud and froze to death. The Fleet originally marked the western boundary of the walled City, and was once an unmissable feature of the landscape, as the tanneries and slaughterhouses of Smithfield, to the north, used to turn the water red with entrails. The Fleet's western bank was the site of the notoriously inhumane **Fleet Prison**, where the poet John Donne was imprisoned in 1601 for marrying without his father-in-law's consent. Until 1754, Fleet Prison was renowned for its clandestine "**Fleet Marriages**", performed by priests (or impostors) who were imprisoned there for debt. These marriages, in which couples could marry without a licence, attracted people of all classes, and took place in the prison chapel until 1710, when they were banished to the neighbouring taverns, the fee being split between clergyman and innkeeper.

St Paul's Cathedral

11

Cathedral Mon–Sat 8.30am–4.30pm; galleries Mon–Sat 9.30am–4.15pm • £16 (£14.50 online) • ☎ 020 7236 4128, Ⓦ stpauls.co.uk • ⊖ St Paul's

The enormous lead-covered dome of **St Paul's Cathedral** has dominated the City skyline since it was built after the Great Fire – and remains so despite the encroaching tower blocks. Its showpiece west facade is particularly magnificent, fronted by a wide flight of steps, a double-storey portico and two of London's most Baroque towers. While it can't compete with Westminster Abbey for celebrity corpses, pre-Reformation sculpture, royal connections and sheer atmosphere, St Paul's is nevertheless a perfectly calculated architectural space, a burial place for captains rather than kings, artists not poets, and a popular wedding venue for the privileged few (including Charles and Diana).

The current building is the fifth on this site, its immediate predecessor being **Old St Paul's**, a huge Gothic cathedral built by the Normans, whose 489ft spire (destroyed by lightning in 1561) was one of the wonders of medieval Europe. St Paul's was just one of over fifty church commissions Christopher Wren received in the wake of the Great Fire. Hassles over his initial plans, and wrangles over money plagued the project throughout, but Wren remained unruffled and the world's first Protestant

SAMUEL PEPYS

Born to a humble tailor and a laundress in Salisbury Court, off Fleet Street, **Samuel Pepys** (1633–1703) was baptized in St Bride's (see opposite) and buried in St Olave's, having spent virtually his entire life in London. Family connections secured an education at St Paul's School, a scholarship to Cambridge and a career in the civil service. He was an MP, served as Secretary to the Admiralty, and was instrumental in the establishment of a professional British navy. In 1679 he was imprisoned for six weeks in the Tower on suspicion of treason, but returned to office, only to be forced out again in 1689, following the overthrow of James II.

Of course, it's not Pepys' career, but his **diaries**, written between 1660 and 1669, that have immortalized him. This rollicking journal includes eyewitness accounts of the Restoration, the Great Plague and the Great Fire, giving an unparalleled insight into London life at the time. Ultimately, Pepys emerges from the pages, warts and all, as an eminently likeable character, who seems almost imperturbable – he gives as much space to details of his pub meals as he does to the Great Fire, and finishes most entries with his catchphrase "and so to bed".

Pepys was also a notorious womanizer, detailing his philanderings in his diary in a mixture of Spanish, Italian and French so as to avoid detection by his French Huguenot wife. Nevertheless he was caught *in flagrante* with his maid, and his slow reconciliation with his spouse is recorded in a novelist's detail, the diary ending in 1669 as they sail off to the Continent to patch things up. In the event, his wife died later that year and he never remarried. Pepys bequeathed his vast library to his old college in Cambridge, where his diaries lay undiscovered until the nineteenth century, when they were finally published (with the erotic passages omitted) in 1825.

11

THE CITY'S CHURCHES

The City of London is crowded with **churches**, the majority of them built or rebuilt by Christopher Wren after the Great Fire. Prompted by the decline in the City's population, the Victorians demolished a fair few, but over forty remain intact. The **opening times** given in the text should be taken with a pinch of salt, since most rely on volunteers to keep their doors open. As a general rule, weekday lunchtimes are the best time to visit, since many City churches put on free lunchtime concerts. Below is a list of the six most interesting:

St Bartholomew-the-Great Cloth Fair. This is the oldest surviving pre-Fire church in the City and by far the most atmospheric. It was also the first church in the country to charge an entrance fee. See p.167.

St Mary Abchurch Abchurch Lane. Uniquely for Wren's City churches, the interior features a huge, painted, domed ceiling, plus the only authenticated Gibbons reredos. See p.174.

St Mary Aldermary Bow Lane/Queen Victoria St. Wren's most successful stab at Gothic, with fan vaulting in the aisles and a panelled ceiling in the nave. See p.164.

St Mary Woolnoth King William St. Hawksmoor's only City church, sporting an unusually broad, bulky tower and a Baroque clerestory that floods the church with light from its semicircular windows. See p.173.

St Olave Hart Street. Built in the fifteenth century, and one of the few pre-Fire Gothic churches in the City. See p.179.

St Stephen Walbrook Walbrook. Wren's dress rehearsal for St Paul's, with a wonderful central dome and plenty of original woodcarving. See p.173.

cathedral was officially completed in 1710 under Queen Anne, whose statue stands below the steps. The cathedral achieved iconic status during the **Blitz**, when it stood defiantly unscathed amid the carnage (as in the famous wartime propaganda photo), and a monument to the south of the cathedral commemorates both the **St Paul's Watch** –volunteers who patrolled the cathedral roof every night to combat the incendiary bombs – and all those firefighters who have died since while carrying out their duties.

INFORMATION AND TOURS

Entry Admission charges are nothing new at St Paul's – they were first introduced in 1709, before the cathedral was even finished. Once inside, pick up a free plan, and simply ask the vergers if you're having trouble locating a particular monument; alternatively, multimedia guides are available free of charge.

Tours Introductory talks run regularly throughout the day, and there are longer guided tours (1hr 30min) that allow you access to one or two areas off limits to the public, setting off at 10.45am, 11.15am, 1.30pm and 2pm. If you're in a group of five or more, you can also pay an extra £8 each to go on a full-on behind-the-scenes triforium tour (Mon & Tues 11.30am & 2pm, Fri 2pm; book in advance on ☎020 7246 8357).

Services It's worth attending one of the cathedral's services, if only to hear the choir, who perform during most evensongs (Mon–Sat 5pm), and on Sundays at 10.15am, 11.30am and 3.15pm. Strictly speaking, on Sundays St Paul's is only open for services and consequently there's no admission charge. However, in between services, you're free to wander round the cathedral and crypt (though not the galleries).

The interior

Queen Victoria thought the **nave** "dirty, dark and undevotional", though since the destruction of the stained glass in the Blitz, it is once again light and airy, as Wren intended. Burials are confined to the crypt, and memorials were only permitted after 1790 when overcrowding at Westminster Abbey had become intolerable. Unfortunately, what followed was a series of overblown funerary monuments to the military heroes of the Napoleonic Wars. Some are simply ludicrous, like the virtually naked statue of Captain Burges, in the south aisle, holding hands with an angel over a naval cannon; others are more offensive, such as the monument to Thomas Fanshaw Middleton, first Protestant Bishop of India, depicted baptizing "heathen" locals. The best of the bunch are Flaxman's **Nelson** memorial, in the south transept, with its seasick lion, and, in the north aisle, the bombastic bronze and marble monument – the cathedral's largest – to

the **Duke of Wellington**, begun in 1857 but only topped with the statue of the duke astride his faithful steed, Copenhagen, in 1912. Both men are buried in the crypt.

The best place from which to appreciate the glory of St Paul's is beneath the **dome**, which was decorated (against Wren's wishes) by Thornhill's monochrome trompe-l'oeil frescoes, now rather upstaged by the adjacent gilded spandrels. St Paul's most famous work of art, however, hangs in the north transept: the crushingly symbolic *Light of the World* by the Pre-Raphaelite **Holman Hunt**, depicting Christ knocking at the handleless, bramble-strewn door of the human soul, which must be opened from within. The original is actually in Keble College, Oxford, though this copy was executed by the artist himself, some fifty years later in 1900.

The chancel

By far the most richly decorated section of the cathedral is the **chancel**, in particular the spectacular, swirling, gilded Byzantine-style mosaics of birds, fish, animals and greenery, from the 1890s. The intricately carved oak and limewood choir stalls, and the imposing organ case, are the work of Grinling Gibbons. The north choir-aisle contains Henry Moore's *Mother and Child* sculpture and allows you to admire Jean Tijou's ornate black-and-gold **wrought-iron gates** that separate the aisles from the high altar. The latter features an extravagant Baroque baldachin, held up by barley-sugar columns and wrapped round with gilded laurel, created after the war to a design by Wren. Behind the high altar stands the **American Memorial Chapel**, dedicated to the 28,000 Americans based in Britain who lost their lives in World War II (check out the space rocket hidden in the carved wooden foliage of the far right-hand panel, a tribute to America's postwar space exploration). Leaving via the south choir-aisle, you'll find the upstanding shroud of **John Donne**, poet, preacher and one-time Dean of St Paul's, the only complete effigy to have survived from Old St Paul's.

The galleries

From the south transept, a series of stairs lead to the dome's three **galleries**, and they're well worth the climb. The initial 259 steps take you to the **Whispering Gallery**, so called because of its acoustic properties – words whispered to the wall on one side are audible 100ft away on the other, though it's often so busy you can't hear much above the hubbub. Another 119 steps up bring you to the exterior **Stone Gallery**, around the base of the dome, while the final 152 steel steps take you inside the dome's inner structure to the **Golden Gallery**, just below the golden ball and cross which top the cathedral. The views of the City and along the Thames are surprisingly good – you should be able to identify the distinctive white facade of Wren's London house, next to the Globe Theatre, from which he could contemplate his masterpiece. Before you ascend the last flight of stairs, be sure to look through the peephole in the floor, onto the monochrome marble floor beneath the dome, a truly terrifying sight.

The crypt

The entrance to the cathedral's vast **crypt** is on your left as you leave the south choir-aisle. The whitewashed walls make this one of the least atmospheric mausoleums you could imagine – a far cry from the nineteenth century, when visitors were shown around the tombs by candlelight.

The crypt boasts as many painters and architects as Westminster Abbey has poets, most of them stuffed into the southern aisle, known as **Artists' Corner**. Appropriately enough, it was Wren himself who started the trend, with a tomb inscribed: "*lector, si monumentum requiris, circumspice*" (reader, if you seek his monument, look around). Close to Wren are the graves of Reynolds, Turner, Millais, Holman Hunt, Lord Leighton and Alma-Tadema; nearby there's a bust of Van Dyck, whose monument perished along with Old St Paul's. Over in the north aisle is the grave of Alexander Fleming, the discoverer of penicillin.

PATERNOSTER SQUARE

The Blitz destroyed the area immediately to the north of St Paul's, including Paternoster Row, which had been the centre of the book trade since 1500. The postwar office complex that replaced it was torn down in the 1980s and supplanted by the softer, post-classical development of **Paternoster Square**, centred on a Corinthian column topped by a gilded urn, and, since 2004, home to the London Stock Exchange. One happy consequence of the square's redevelopment is that **Temple Bar**, the last surviving City gateway which once stood at the top of Fleet Street (see p.155), found its way back to London after a century of languishing in a park in Hertfordshire. Designed by Wren himself, the triumphal arch now forms the entrance to Paternoster Square from St Paul's, with the Stuart monarchs, James I and Charles II, and their consorts, occupying the niches.

The crypt's two star tombs – those of **Nelson** and **Wellington** – occupy centre stage. Wellington's porphyry and granite monstrosity is set in its own mini-chapel, surrounded by memorials to illustrious British field marshals, while Nelson lies in a black marble sarcophagus originally designed for Cardinal Wolsey and later intended for Henry VIII and his third wife, Jane Seymour. As at Trafalgar Square, Nelson lies close to later admirals Jellicoe and Beatty (the last person to be buried in the cathedral, in 1936). Beyond are the cathedral shop, a café and the exit.

St Paul's Churchyard

St Paul's Churchyard, to the northeast of the cathedral, was also destroyed in the Blitz. The churchyard's most arresting feature now is a column, erected in 1910, topped by a gilded statue of St Paul, and diplomatically inscribed "amid such scenes of good and evil as make up human affairs, the conscience of the church and nation through five centuries found public utterance". This is a reference to **Paul's Cross**, a polygonal open-air pulpit – its groundplan is marked out in the paving – from which official proclamations and religious speeches were made. Heretics were regularly executed on this spot, and in 1519 Luther's works were publicly burnt here, before Henry VIII changed sides and demanded the "preaching down" of papal authority from the same spot. The cross was destroyed by the Puritans in 1643.

Cheapside

It's difficult to believe that **Cheapside**, which connects St Paul's with Bank, was once London's foremost shopping street, the widest thoroughfare in the City, and site of the medieval marketplace. Nowadays only the names of the nearby streets – Bread Street, Milk Street, Honey Lane, Poultry – recall its former prominence, which faded when the shops and their customers moved to the West End from the eighteenth century onwards.

One New Change

1 New Change • Mon–Fri 10am–7pm, Sat 10am–6pm, Sun noon–6pm • ⓦ onenewchange.com • ⊖ St Paul's

Commerce has recently returned to Cheapside in the form of **One New Change**, an uncompromisingly modern building by Jean Nouvel, whose opaque brown glass facade is reminiscent of a Stealth bomber. Even if you've no interest in the formulaic franchises which fill this multistorey shopping mall, it has one great thing going for it: a sixth-floor, sun-trap roof terrace that's open to the public, has a few mosaics by Boris Anrep and views over to St Paul's, Tate Modern and the Shard.

St Mary-le-Bow

Cheapside • Mon–Thurs 7am–6pm, Fri 7am–4pm • ☎ 020 7248 5139, ⓦ stmarylebow.co.uk • ⊖ St Paul's

One of the distinguishing features of Cheapside is Wren's church of **St Mary-le-Bow**, whose handsome tower features a conglomeration of pilasters, a circular colonnade, a

11

DICK WHITTINGTON

The City's Lord Mayor is elected on an annual basis, and the most famous Lord Mayor of the lot is **Dick Whittington** (c.1350–1423) of pantomime fame. The third son of a wealthy Gloucestershire family, Whittington was an apprentice mercer, dealing in silks and velvets, who rose to become one of the richest men in the City by the age of just 21. He was an early philanthropist, establishing a library at Greyfriars' monastery and a refuge for single mothers at St Thomas's Hospital, and building one of the city's first public lavatories, a unisex 128-seater known as "Whittington's Night Soil House of Easement". The pantomime story appeared some two hundred years after Whittington's death, though quite how he became the fictional ragamuffin who comes to London after hearing the streets are paved with gold, no one seems to know. Traditionally, Whittington is leaving London with his knapsack and cat, when he hears the Bow Bells ring out "Turn again, Whittington, thrice Lord Mayor of London" (he was, in fact, mayor on four occasions and was never knighted as the story claims). The theory on the cat is that it was a common name for a coal barge at the time, and Whittington is thought to have made much of his fortune in the coal trade. There's a statue on Highgate Hill commemorating the very spot where Dick allegedly heard the Bow Bells, and a stained-glass window in St Michael Paternoster Royal, on Skinner's Lane, near where he lived.

---

granite obelisk and a dragon weather vane. The tower also contains postwar replicas of the famous "Bow Bells", which sounded the 9pm curfew for Londoners from the fourteenth to the nineteenth centuries, and within whose earshot all true Cockneys are born. The original interior was totally destroyed in the Blitz and is a postwar re-creation, but the church's medieval crypt survived and is home to the atmospheric *Café Below* (see p.376).

St Mary Aldermary

Bow Lane • Mon–Fri 9am–4.45pm • ☎ 020 7248 9902, ⓦ stmaryaldermary.co.uk • ⊖ Mansion House or Bank

At the southern end of Bow Lane lies the church of **St Mary Aldermary**, whose interior is a rare foray into the perpendicular Gothic style by Wren, based on the original church – the plaster fan-vaults and saucer domes in the aisles are the highlight and, as a bonus, there's now a great café called *Host* in the nave. **Bow Lane** itself is a lovely, narrow, pedestrianized street redolent of the pre-Fire City, jam-packed at weekday lunchtimes with office workers heading for its sandwich bars and pubs.

Blackfriars

Most folk heading south from St Paul's are aiming for the **Millennium Bridge** (see p.227), to cross over the river to Tate Modern and Bankside. However, instead of simply heading for the bridge, it's worth taking time to venture into the backstreets and alleyways, or go for a stroll along the **Riverside Walk** which now extends all the way from Blackfriars railway bridge to Tower Bridge.

Blackfriars, the district between Ludgate Hill and the river, is named after the Dominican monastery that stood here until the Dissolution. The monks' old refectory became Blackfriars Theatre, where Shakespeare and his fellow actors performed in the winter months. Although the area was destroyed in the Great Fire, it suffered little from wartime bombing and remains a warren of alleyways, courtyards and narrow streets, conveying something of the plan of the City before the Victorians, the German bombers and the 1960s brutalists did their worst. The best place to go for a taste of the monastic is *The Black Friar*, 174 Queen Victoria St, which boasts a fantastically ornate **Arts and Crafts** pub interior (see p.390).

Church of Scientology

146 Queen Victoria St • Mon–Fri 9.30am–10pm, Sat & Sun 9.30am–6pm • Free • ☎ 020 7246 2700, ⓦ scientology-london.org • ⊖ Blackfriars

Built in the 1860s for the British and Foreign Bible Society, the London headquarters of the Church of Scientology look like an Italian *palazzo*. If you're prepared to put up with the slightly creepy attendants, the building itself is worth admiring, and there's a whole exhibition on **L. Ron Hubbard**, the American pulp-fiction writer and hypnotist who founded the Scientology cult.

College of Arms

Queen Victoria St • Mon–Fri 10am–4pm • Free • ☎ 020 7248 2762, ⓦ college-of-arms.gov.uk • ⊖ Blackfriars or Mansion House

Originally built round a courtyard in the 1670s, the red-brick mansion of the **College of Arms** was opened up to the south with the building of Queen Victoria Street in the 1870s. The college is the headquarters of heraldry in England, and even today is in charge of granting coats of arms to those who can prove they've been "a benefit to the community". The Earl Marshal's Court – featuring a gallery, copious wooden panelling and a modest throne – is the only room open to the public, unless you apply to trace your family or study heraldry in the college library.

Old Bailey

11

Old Bailey • Mon–Fri 10am–1pm & 2–5pm • Free • ☎ 020 7248 3277, ⓦ cityoflondon.gov.uk • ⊖ St Paul's

The Central Criminal Court is better known as the **Old Bailey**, after the street on which it stands, which used to run along the medieval city walls. The court's pompous, domed, Edwardian building – "Defend the Children of the Poor & Punish the Wrongdoer" the entrance proclaims – is topped by a gilded statue of Justice, depicted without blindfold, holding her sword and scales. The country's most serious criminal cases are heard here, and have included, in the past, the trials of Lord Haw-Haw, the Kray Twins, the Angry Brigade (see p.292), plus all Britain's multiple murderers. You can watch the proceedings from the visitors' gallery (no under-14s), but you're not allowed to take anything into the court (and that includes mobiles) and there's no cloakroom. Sadly, visitors do not get to see the Grand Hall, with its swirling marble floor and walls, succession of domes and grandiloquent frescoes.

The site of the Old Bailey was originally occupied by **Newgate Prison**, which began life as a small lock-up above the medieval gateway of Newgate. Burnt down in the

---

PUBLIC EXECUTIONS AND BODY SNATCHERS

After 1783, when hangings at Tyburn were stopped, **public executions** at Newgate began to draw crowds of one hundred thousand and more. The last public beheading took place here in 1820 when five Cato Street Conspirators (see p.86) were hanged and decapitated with a surgeon's knife. It was in hanging, however, that Newgate excelled, its most efficient gallows dispatching twenty criminals simultaneously. Unease over the "robbery and violence, loud laughing, oaths, fighting, obscene conduct and still more filthy language" that accompanied public hangings drove the executions inside the prison walls in 1868. The night before an execution, a handbell was tolled outside the condemned's cell, while the jailer recited the Newgate verse that ended: "All you that in the condemned hole do lie/Prepare you, for tomorrow you shall die… And when St Sepulchre's bell in the morning tolls/The Lord above have mercy on your souls." Until Newgate got its own bell, the "Great Bell of Old Bailey" was in the church of **St Sepulchre** (Mon–Fri 11am–3pm; ⓦ st-sepulchre.org.uk), and tolled the condemned to the scaffold at eight in the morning. The handbell and verse are displayed inside the church, opposite the Old Bailey.

The bodies of the executed were handed over to the surgeons of St Bartholomew's for dissection, but body snatchers also preyed on non-criminals buried in St Sepulchre churchyard. Such was the demand for corpses that relatives were forced to pay a nightwatchman to guard the graveyard in a specially built watch-house – still visible to the north of the church – to prevent the "Resurrection Men" from retrieving their quarry. Successfully stolen stiffs were taken to the nearby *Fortune of War* tavern, which stood on Pie Corner, by Cock Lane, to be sold to the surgeons. Today, Pie Corner is marked by a gilded overfed cherub known as **Fat Boy**, who commemorates the "staying of the Great Fire" of 1666, which, when it wasn't blamed on the Catholics, was ascribed to the sin of gluttony, since it had begun in Pudding Lane and ended at Pie Corner.

1780 Gordon Riots, it was rebuilt as "a veritable Hell, worthy of the imagination of Dante", as one of its more famous inmates, Casanova, put it. Earlier well-known temporary residents included Thomas Malory, who wrote *Le Morte d'Arthur* while imprisoned here for murder (among other things); Daniel Defoe, who was put inside for his *The Shortest Way with Dissenters*; Ben Jonson, who served time for murder; and Christopher Marlowe, who was on a charge of atheism.

Smithfield

The ground was covered, nearly ankle-deep with filth and mire; a thick steam perpetually rising from the reeking bodies of the cattle, and mingling with the fog.   *Oliver Twist*, Charles Dickens

Originally open ground outside the City walls, **Smithfield** is a corruption of "Smooth Field". It was used as a horse fair in Norman times, and later became the site for **Bartholomew Fair**, established in 1133 by Rahere, prior and founder of St Bartholomew's priory and hospice to raise funds. Rahere himself used to perform juggling tricks, while Pepys reports seeing a horse counting sixpences and, more reliably, a puppet show of Ben Jonson's play *Bartholomew Fair*. Predictably enough, it was the Victorians who closed it down to protect public morals.

The meat **market**, with which Smithfield is now synonymous, grew up as a kind of adjunct to the fair. Live cattle continued to be herded into Smithfield until 1852, when the fair was suppressed and the abattoirs moved out to Islington. A new covered market hall was erected in 1868, along with the "Winkle", a spiral ramp at the centre of West Smithfield, linked to the market's very own (now defunct) tube station. Smithfield subsequently tripled in size and remains London's main meat market – the action starts around 4am and is all over by noon.

St Bartholomew's Hospital

West Smithfield • Museum Tues–Fri 10am–4pm • Free • Guided tours Fri 2pm; £5 • ☎ 020 3465 5798 • ⓦ www.bartsandthelondon .nhs.uk • ⊖ St Paul's

St Bartholomew's Hospital – affectionately known as Bart's – is the oldest hospital in London. It began as an Augustinian priory and hospice in 1123, founded by Rahere, courtier, clerk and even court jester to Henry I, on the orders of St Bartholomew, who appeared to him in a vision while he was in malarial delirium on a pilgrimage to Rome. The priory was dissolved by Henry VIII, but in 1546, with just two weeks left to live, the king agreed to re-found the hospital.

The **Henry VIII Gate**, built in 1702, features a statue of the king, with a lame man on the right and a diseased man on the left lounging on the broken pediment above.

BLOOD AND GUTS AT SMITHFIELD

Blood was spilled at **Smithfield** long before the meat market was legally sanctioned here in the seventeenth century. The Scottish hero, William Wallace, was dragged behind a horse from the Tower, then hanged, drawn and quartered here in 1305. Most famously, during the 1381 Peasants' Revolt, the poll-tax rebels under **Wat Tyler** assembled here to negotiate with the boy-king Richard II. At the meeting, Lord Mayor Walworth pulled Tyler from his horse and stabbed him, after which he was bustled into St Bartholomew's for treatment, only to be dragged out by the king's men and beheaded.

Smithfield subsequently became a regular venue for **public executions**. The Bishop of Rochester's cook was boiled alive in 1531, after being found guilty of poisoning, but the local speciality was **burnings**. These reached a peak during the reign of "Bloody" Mary in the 1550s, when hundreds of Protestants were burnt at the stake for their beliefs, in revenge for the Catholics who had suffered a similar fate under Henry VIII and Edward VI; a plaque on the side of Bart's commemorates some of those who died.

Further along, you can make out shrapnel marks left from a 1916 Zeppelin air raid. Behind the Henry VIII Gate stands the church of **St Bartholomew-the-Less** (daily 7am–8pm), sole survivor of the priory's four chapels. The tower and vestry are fifteenth century, the octagonal interior is neo-Gothic, though it does contain a Tudor memorial to Elizabeth I's surgeon. Beyond the church lies three-quarters of **The Square** created for the hospital by James Gibbs in the mid-eighteenth century, with the **Great Hall** on the north side, accessed by the **Grand Staircase**, its walls decorated with biblical murals that were painted free of charge by Hogarth, who was born and baptized nearby and served as one of the hospital's governors.

You can get a glimpse of the hospital's Grand Staircase from inside **St Bartholomew's Museum**, on the left, under the archway into the courtyard. Among the medical artefacts, there are some fearsome amputation instruments, a pair of leather "lunatic restrainers", some great jars with labels such as "poison – for external use only", and a cricket bat autographed by W.G. Grace, who was a student at Bart's in the 1870s. To see the Great Hall join one of the fascinating weekly **guided tours**, which take in the surrounding area as well; the meeting point is the Henry VIII Gate.

11

St Bartholomew-the-Great

Cloth Fair • Mon–Fri 8.30am–5pm, Sat 10.30am–4pm, Sun 8.30am–8pm; mid-Nov to mid-Feb Mon–Sat closes 4pm • £4 • ☎ 020 7606 5171, ⓦ greatstbarts.com • ⊖ Barbican

Hidden in the backstreets north of the hospital, **St Bartholomew-the-Great** is London's oldest and most atmospheric parish church. Begun in 1123 as the main church of St Bartholomew's priory and hospice, it was partly demolished in the Reformation, and gradually fell into ruins: the cloisters were used as a stable, there was a boys' school in the triforium, a coal and wine cellar in the crypt, a blacksmith's in the north transept and a printing press (where Benjamin Franklin once worked) in the Lady Chapel. From 1887, Aston Webb restored what remained, and added the chequered patterning and flintwork that now characterizes the exterior. Much beloved of film companies, it is one of the few parish churches in the country to charge an entrance fee.

To get an idea of the scale of the original church, approach it through the half-timbered Tudor **gatehouse**, on Little Britain Street. A wooden statue of St Bartholomew stands in a niche; below is the thirteenth-century arch that once formed the entrance to the nave. The churchyard now stands where the nave itself would have been, and one side of the **cloisters** survives to the south, now housing the delightful *Cloister Café* (closed Sat). The rest of the church is a confusion of elements, including portions of the transepts and, most impressively, the **chancel**, where thick Norman pillars separate the main body from the ambulatory. There are various pre-Fire monuments, the most prominent being the tomb of Rahere (see opposite), which shelters under a fifteenth-century canopy north of the altar, with an angel at his feet and two canons kneeling beside him reading from the prophets. Beyond the ambulatory lies the large Lady Chapel, mostly nineteenth century, though with original stonework here and there.

Barbican

Silk St • Arts Centre Mon–Sat 9am–11pm, Sun noon–11pm • Free • ☎ 020 7638 8891, ⓦ barbican.org.uk • ⊖ Barbican

The City's only large residential complex is the concrete brutalist ghetto of the **Barbican**, built on the heavily bombed Cripplegate area. It's a classic 1970s urban dystopia, a maze of pedestrian walkways and underground car parks, pinioned by three 400ft tower blocks. At the centre of the complex is the **Barbican Arts Centre**, home to the London Symphony Orchestra, two performance spaces, a three-screen cinema, a rooftop garden, a public library and an art gallery. Sadly, the arts centre's obtusely confusing layout continues to prove user-repellent; just finding the main entrance on Silk Street is quite a feat, even for Londoners.

St Giles-without-Cripplegate

Fore St • Mon–Fri 11am–4pm • Free • ☎ 020 7638 1997, ⓦ stgilescripplegate.com • ⊖ Barbican

The Barbican's solitary prewar building is the heavily restored early Tudor church of **St Giles-without-Cripplegate**, now bracketed between a pair of artificial lakes, and overlooking an impressive corner bastion of the old Roman fort. It was in this church that Oliver Cromwell was married in 1620 and John Milton buried in 1674 – he was subsequently exhumed in 1793, his teeth knocked out as souvenirs and his corpse exhibited to the public until the novelty wore off.

Museum of London

150 London Wall • Daily 10am–6pm • Free • ☎ 020 7001 9844, ⓦ museumoflondon.org.uk • ⊖ Barbican or St Paul's

Hidden in the southwestern corner of the Barbican complex is the **Museum of London**, whose permanent galleries are basically an educational trot through London's past from prehistory to the present day, illustrated by the city's major archeological finds and some great scale models. The real strength of the museum, however, lies in the excellent temporary exhibitions, gallery tours, lectures, walks and videos it organizes throughout the year.

London until 1666

The permanent displays start on floor E (where visitors enter), with a section on **London before London**. Here, you'll find a cave-bear skull from half a million years ago, Neolithic flint tools, not to mention a lion skull, a hippo's tooth, an auroch's skull and an elephant's foot. The **Roman London** section includes the Bucklersbury mosaic floor, displayed in a mock-up of a wealthy Roman dining room, gold coins, marble busts from the Temple of Mithras (see p.174) and mock-up Roman shop displays. Highlights in the **Medieval London** section include a reconstructed Saxon home, a model of Old St Paul's and a wonderfully over-the-top video on the Black Death. Look out, too, for the Cheapside Hoard, found by workmen in 1912, and containing the finest collection of Elizabethan and Jacobean jewels in the world.

Modern London

The museum's post-1666 galleries are all on the ground floor (L2), and begin with **Expanding City**, which includes revealing sections on how slavery helped increase the city's wealth, an original Newgate Prison door and a recreation of a pleasure garden. The **People's City** section traces the history of the suffragette movement and the political struggles of the 1930s and features one of the most popular sections, the **Victorian Walk**, with several streets of reconstructed period shops from a toyshop to a barber's. You can relax in a mock-up interwar cinema and watch old footage of prewar London, admire the wonderful Art Deco bronze lifts from Selfridges, or play on the interactive Charles Booth map which plotted the city's poverty in 1889.

The postwar section features snapshots from each decade: a model of the Skylon from the 1951 Festival of Britain, some groovy Swinging Sixties clothes, punk and Silver

---

POSTMAN'S PARK

Opposite the former General Post Office building, south of the Museum of London, lies **Postman's Park**, one of the most curious and little-visited corners of the City. Here, in 1900, in the churchyard of St Botolph, Aldersgate, the painter and sculptor George Frederick Watts paid for a national memorial to "heroes of everyday life", a patchwork wall of majolica tiles protected by a canopy and inscribed with the names of ordinary folk who had died in the course of some act of bravery. It exhibits the classic Victorian sentimental fascination with death, and makes for macabre but compelling reading: "Drowned in attempting to save his brother after he himself had just been rescued" or "Saved a lunatic woman from suicide at Woolwich Arsenal station, but was himself run over by the train". In 2009, the first new addition for 78 years was added to the wall.

LONDON'S WALLS

London was a bona fide **walled city** from the time of the Romans until the Great Fire of 1666. For another hundred years, it still had its **seven gateways** – the last one, Temple Bar, was only removed in 1878, and now stands near St Paul's Cathedral. Sections of wall were still being dismantled in the eighteenth and nineteenth centuries, and, if you know where to look, there are still several substantial slices of the city walls in situ today.

In 120 AD, the Romans built a grid-plan **military fort** to house around one thousand soldiers, just east of the Museum of London – the wall is visible from the museum, and one of the corner bastions (complete with section of moat) can be seen from St Giles Cripplegate in the Barbican. However, it wasn't until 200 AD that the Romans threw up a proper two-mile long curtain wall, 20ft high and 9ft thick. The walls fell into decay in Saxon times, but were repaired and restored in the medieval and Tudor periods. On **Noble Street**, just southeast of the museum, one of the most interesting sections came to light after the Blitz, showing where the new city walls joined the older wall of the military fort.

There's an official **London Wall Walk**, which starts outside Tower Hill tube, by the remains of the medieval Postern Gate, although the only other really impressive sections of wall are in nearby Cooper's Row (see p.187).

11

Jubilee memorabilia from 1977. There's a great section paying tribute to London's ethnic diversity and a vast model of some 1990s squats on Hackney's London Fields. Finally, you reach the space reserved for the **Lord Mayor's Coach**, which rivals the Queen's in sheer weight of gold decoration. Built in 1757, it's still used to parade the new Lord Mayor at the annual Lord Mayor's Show (see p.26).

Guildhall

Gresham St • Daily 10am–5pm; Oct–April closed Sun • Free • ☎ 020 7606 3030, ⓦ cityoflondon.gov.uk • ⊖ Bank

Despite being the seat of the City governance for over eight hundred years, **Guildhall** doesn't exactly exude municipal wealth. Nevertheless, it's worth popping inside the **Great Hall** which miraculously survived both the Great Fire and Blitz – you must approach from the reception on the west side of the courtyard, not the quasi-Indian porch, tacked on by George Dance the Elder in the eighteenth century, to the north. The hall is lined with statues of worthies and is still used for functions, though only the walls survive from the original fifteenth-century building, which was the venue for several high-treason trials, including those of Lady Jane Grey and her husband, Lord Dudley, and, three years later, Archbishop Cranmer. As you leave, be sure to check out the crazy pagan giants Gog and Magog, who look down from the minstrels' gallery, and who feature every year in the Lord Mayor's Show (see p.26).

Guildhall Art Gallery

Mon–Sat 10am–5pm, Sun noon–4pm • Free • ☎ 020 7332 3700, ⓦ cityoflondon.gov.uk • ⊖ Bank

Occupying the eastern side of the Guildhall courtyard is the **Guildhall Art Gallery**. Some of the best works are the Pre-Raphaelite pictures displayed in the first gallery you enter: **Holman Hunt**'s *The Eve of St Agnes* (inspired by Keats' poem), painted while he was still a student, and bought by the gallery's first director out of his own pocket; **Rossetti**'s *La Ghirlandata*, a typically lush portrait, in intense blues and greens, of a model who's a dead ringer for Jane Morris, with whom the artist was infatuated; **Millais**' two portraits of his daughter Effie in her Sunday best – *My First Sermon*, in which she sits attentively listening, and *My Second Sermon*, when the novelty has worn off and she has dozed off.

Also hiding up here is **Constable**'s full-sized oil sketch of *Salisbury Cathedral*, characterized by loose brushwork and an air of foreboding, and a marble statue of **Margaret Thatcher**, now surrounded by a protective glass cabinet after the head was knocked off by a protester in 2002.

The Copley painting, London pictures and Victorian galleries

The layout of the entire gallery is designed around the gigantic and very dramatic painting *The Defeat of the Floating Batteries at Gibraltar, September 1782* by **John Singleton Copley**, depicting the Brits magnanimously saving the drowning enemy from flaming barques. Commissioned by the Corporation, poor old Copley had to redo the entire thing when the garrison officers insisted on having more prominence.

One of the gallery's strengths is its wide range of **London** pictures – depicting City ceremonies, bygone vistas of old London, postwar bomb sites and so on – which you'll find sprinkled throughout the collection. On the ground floor, you'll also find a small sample of works by the English artist **Matthew Smith** (1879–1959), who was heavily influenced by Cézanne's late works and Matisse's Fauvist phase. Confusingly, it's in the **Victorian galleries** that you'll find one of the 22 portraits, commissioned

GUILDHALL TO CANNON STREET

by the Corporation, of the Fire Judges who assessed property claims in the wake of the Great Fire.

Roman amphitheatre

During the gallery's construction in the 1990s, a **Roman amphitheatre**, dating from around 120 AD, was discovered in the Guildhall courtyard. The foundations of the eastern entrance are all that remain, displayed in the basement, but they give you a hint of the vast size of the original arena, which would have held up to six thousand. (The outline of the amphitheatre is marked out on the pavement in the courtyard.)

Clockmakers' Museum

Aldermanbury • Mon–Sat 9.30am–4.45pm • Free • ☎ 020 7332 1868, ⓦ clockmakers.org • ⊖ Bank

Access to the **Clockmakers' Museum**, run by the Worshipful Company of Clockmakers, is from Aldermanbury, on the west side of Guildhall. Here, you'll find everything from Tudor pocket watches to grandfather clocks, which ring out in unison on the hour. Highlights include an orrery clock, a rolling ball clock (of the kind invented by William Congreve), a water clock, the ghoulish skull watch, once believed to have been given by Mary Queen of Scots to her maid-of-honour, and the watch used by Edmund Hillary on Everest. Of particular interest is the collection of marine chronometers including the earliest known clock made by **John Harrison** (1693–1776), along with his brother, when he was only 20. Pride of place, though, goes to H5, which looks like an oversized pocket watch, was tested by George III himself at Richmond observatory, and won Harrison the Longitude Prize (see p.320).

11

St Lawrence Jewry

Mon–Fri 8am–4pm • Recitals Mon & Tues 1pm • ☎ 020 7600 9478, ⓦ stlawrencejewry.org.uk • ⊖ Bank

Across the courtyard from the Guildhall stands Wren's church of **St Lawrence Jewry**, whose smart interior reflects its role as the official City of London Corporation church. Opened in 1677 in the presence of Charles II, but gutted during the Blitz, the church's handsome, wide, open-plan interior is well worth a peek for its richly gilded plasterwork ceiling. The church's gilded gridiron weathervane recalls St Lawrence's martyrdom – he was slow-roasted, but still managed to crack jokes, hence why he's the patron saint of comedians. The name "Jewry" recalls the site of London's **Jewish ghetto**. Old Jewry, the street two blocks east, was the nucleus of the community, who suffered a bloody expulsion on the orders of Edward I.

Bank and around

Bank lies at the heart of the City's financial district and is the busy meeting point of eight streets. It's an impressive architectural ensemble, overlooked by a handsome collection of Neoclassical buildings – among them the Bank of England, the Royal Exchange and Mansion House – each one faced in Portland stone.

Royal Exchange

Mon–Fri: shops 10am–6pm; cafés, bars and restaurants 8am–11pm • ⓦ theroyalexchange.co.uk • ⊖ Bank

By far the most graceful of Bank's buildings is the **Royal Exchange**, first built in 1570 at the personal expense of the fabulously wealthy businessman, Thomas Gresham (his gilded grasshopper flies from the roof), as a meeting place for City merchants. The current building, fronted by a massive eight-column portico and a very convenient set of steps for lunching office workers, is the third on the site and was built in the 1840s. Nowadays, the building is filled with expense account shops, but it's still worth exploring the inner courtyard, with its beautifully tiled floor, glazed roof and half-columns in three classical orders. The swish *Grand Café* occupies both the courtyard and the mezzanine floor, from which you can view a series of frescoes illustrating the history of the City.

11

THE CITY LIVERY COMPANIES

The hundred or so **City Livery Companies** in the Square Mile are descended from the craft guilds of the Middle Ages, whose purpose was to administer apprenticeships and take charge of quality control, in return for which they were granted monopolies. Over time, the guilds grew prodigiously wealthy, built themselves ever more opulent halls and staged lavish banquets at which they would wear elaborate "livery" (or uniforms). Most – though not all – of the old guilds now have very little to do with their original trade, though this is not the case with the guilds that have been formed in the last hundred years. It's fair to say the livery companies remain deeply undemocratic and anomalous, but their prodigious wealth and charitable works have helped pacify the critics. As with the Freemasons, the elaborate ceremonies serve to hide the very real power that these companies still hold. Liverymen dominate the Court of Common Council, the City's ruling body, and as Aldermen, they take it in turns to be first a Sheriff, and eventually Lord Mayor – a knighthood is virtually guaranteed.

The City boasts numerous Livery Company halls, many with enticing names such as the Tallow Chandlers and Cordwainers. Few survived the Great Fire, fewer still the Blitz, but a handful are worth visiting for their ornate interiors. The problem is gaining **admission**. The City tourist office (☎ 020 7332 1456) has tickets to some halls; other halls will allow you to join a pre-booked group tour for around £5–10 per person. It's not something you can do on the spur of the moment, though some Livery halls are used during the City of London Festival and others are open on Open House weekend (see p.26). Below is a selection of the most interesting Livery halls:

Apothecaries' Hall Blackfriars Lane ☎ 020 7236 1189, ⓦ apothecaries.org; ⊖ Blackfriars. The seventeenth-century courtyard is open to the public, but entry to the magnificent staircase and the Great Hall – with its musicians' gallery, portrait by Reynolds and collection of leech pots – is by appointment only.
Fishmongers' Hall London Bridge ☎ 020 7626 3531, ⓦ fishhall.org.uk; ⊖ Monument. A prominent Greek Revival building on the riverfront, with a grand staircase hall, and the very dagger with which Mayor Walworth stabbed Wat Tyler (see p.448).
Goldsmiths' Hall Foster Lane ☎ 020 7606 7010, ⓦ thegoldsmiths.co.uk; ⊖ St Paul's. One of the easiest to visit as there are regular exhibitions allowing you to see the sumptuous central staircase built in the 1830s.

Skinners' Hall 8 Dowgate Hill ☎ 020 7236 5629, ⓦ skinnershall.co.uk; ⊖ Cannon Street. The seventeenth-century staircase and courtroom survive, while the wood-panelled hall contains a wonderful series of Frank Brangwyn murals from 1902.
Tallow Chandlers' Hall 4 Dowgate Hill ☎ 020 7248 4726, ⓦ tallowchandlers.org; ⊖ Cannon Street. Set back from the street around an attractive courtyard, the Tallow Chandlers Hall retains its seventeenth-century courtroom, complete with original seating.
Vintners' Hall 68 Upper Thames St ☎ 020 7236 1863, ⓦ vintnershall.co.uk; ⊖ Mansion House. The oldest hall in the City, dating from 1671, with a period-piece staircase with "fabulously elaborate balusters".

Mansion House

Guided tours Tues 2pm; closed Aug • £7 • ☎ 020 7937 9307, ⓦ cityoflondon.gov.uk • ⊖ Bank

Mansion House, the Lord Mayor's sumptuous Neoclassical lodgings during his or – on the odd, rare occasion – her term of office, is open to the public once a week. Designed in 1753 by George Dance the Elder, the building's grandest room is the columned **Egyptian Hall**, with its high, barrel-vaulted, coffered ceiling. Also impressive is the vast collection of gold and silver tableware, the mayor's 36-pound gold mace and the pearl sword given by Elizabeth I and held out to the sovereign on visits to the City. Scattered about the rooms are an impressive array of Dutch and Flemish paintings by the likes of Hals, Ruisdael, Cuyp, Hobbema and de Hooch. Places are allocated on a first-come, first-served basis, so turn up at the Walbrook entrance in good time.

Bank of England

Threadneedle St • Mon–Fri 10am–5pm • Free • ☎ 020 7601 5545, ⓦ bankofengland.co.uk • ⊖ Bank

Established by William III in 1694 to raise funds for his costly war against France, the **Bank of England** – the so-called "Grand Old Lady of Threadneedle Street" – wasn't erected on its present site until 1734. The bank was attacked during the 1780 Gordon

Riots, but never sacked thanks to the bank's clerks, who melted down their inkwells into bullets. Subsequently a detachment of the Foot Guards, known as the Bank Picquet, was stationed overnight here until 1973. Security remains pretty tight at the bank, which still acts as a giant safe-deposit box, storing the official gold reserves of many of the world's central banks, as well the UK's, in its basement vaults.

The windowless, outer curtain wall, which wraps itself round the 3.5-acre island site, is pretty much all that remains of John Soane's late eighteenth-century design. However, you can view a reconstruction of Soane's Bank Stock Office, with its characteristic domed skylight, in the **museum**, whose entrance is on Bartholomew Lane. The exhibition traces the history of the bank, banknotes and banking in general. Beyond, beneath a reconstruction of Herbert Baker's interwar rotunda (wrecked in the Blitz), you can caress a 13kg gold bar, worth over £250,000, and, elsewhere, view specimens of every note issued by the Royal Mint over the centuries (including a million pound note).

St Mary Woolnoth

King William St • Mon–Fri 9.30am–4.30pm • Free • ⊖ Bank

Hidden from the bustle of Bank itself, a short distance down King William Street, stands **St Mary Woolnoth**, one of Nicholas Hawksmoor's six idiosyncratic London churches. The main facade is very imposing, with its twin turrets, Doric pillars and heavy rustication. Inside, in a cramped but lofty space, Hawksmoor manages to cram in a cluster of three big Corinthian columns at each corner, which support an ingenious lantern lit by semicircular clerestory windows. The most striking furnishing is the altar canopy, held up by barley-sugar columns and studded with seven golden cherubic faces. The church's projecting clock gets a brief mention in T.S. Eliot's *The Waste Land*, and the quote is commemorated in the southeast corner of the church.

St Stephen Walbrook

39 Walbrook • Mon–Fri 10am–4pm • Free • ⓦ ststephenwalbrook.net • ⊖ Bank

Named after the nearby shallow stream which provided Roman London with its fresh water, the church of **St Stephen Walbrook** is the Lord Mayor's official church and Wren's most spectacular after St Paul's. Faced with a fairly cramped site, Wren created a church of great space and light, with sixteen Corinthian columns arranged in clusters around a central coffered dome, which many regard as a practice run for his cathedral. The furnishings are mostly original, but the modern beech-wood pews jar, as does Henry Moore's altar, an amorphous blob of Travertine stone – nicknamed "The Camembert". The Samaritans were founded here by the local rector in 1953, and their first helpline telephone serves as a memorial in the church's southwest corner.

FROM COFFEE HOUSE TO BOARDROOM

Several of the City's most important institutions have their origins in the **coffee houses** which sprung up in the second half of the seventeenth century. The first coffee house in London was established in St Michael's Alley, off Cornhill, in 1652 by **Pasqua Rosée**, the Armenian servant of a merchant who traded in Turkey. It was an instant success and in less than a century, there were literally hundreds of rival establishments, as the coffee house became the place the City's wheelers and dealers preferred to conduct their business. **Richard Lloyd's** coffee house – perhaps the best known – was where London's sailors, merchants and ship owners went for the latest maritime news, eventually evolving into Lloyd's Register of Shipping and Lloyd's of London insurance market. Meanwhile, **Jonathan's**, in Exchange Alley, posted up the price of stocks and commodities, attracting dealers who'd been ejected from the nearby Royal Exchange for rowdiness, and eventually became the London Stock Exchange.

> ### LONDON STONE
>
> Bank may have a good claim to being the heart of the City, or perhaps Guildhall as the administrative core, but London's real omphalos, its geomantic centre, is the **London Stone**, a small block of limestone lodged behind an iron grille set low into the exterior wall of 111 Cannon St, at the corner of St Swithin's Lane. Whatever your reaction to this bizarre relic, it has been around for some considerable time, certainly since the 1450 Peasants' Revolt, when the Kentish rebel Jack Cade struck it, declaring himself "Lord of the City".

St Mary Abchurch
Abchurch Lane, off King William St • Mon–Fri 11am–3pm • ⊖ Cannon Street

St Mary Abchurch is set in its own courtyard (the paved-over former graveyard), but nothing about the dour red-brick exterior prepares you for Wren's spectacular interior, which is dominated by a vast dome fresco painted by a local parishioner and lit by oval lunettes, with the name of God in Hebrew centre stage. The lime-wood reredos, festooned with swags and garlands, and decorated with gilded urns and a pelican, is a Grinling Gibbons masterpiece.

Temple of Mithras
The remains of a **Temple of Mithras** were discovered beside the old stream of the Walbrook in 1954 during the construction of an office block on Queen Victoria Street. Mithraism was a male-only cult popular among the Roman legions before the advent of Christianity. Its Persian deity, Mithras, is always depicted slaying a cosmic bull, while a scorpion grasps its genitals and a dog licks its wounds – the bull's blood was seen as life-giving, and initiates had to bathe in it. The site is currently being redeveloped once more – this time as Bloomberg's Norman Foster-designed European headquarters – and the temple is due to be returned to its original site. In the meantime, the reconstruction in the Museum of London gives you a good idea of what the place was once like.

Bishopsgate to the Tower

Financial institutions predominate in the easterly section of the Square Mile, many of them housed in the brashest of the City's new architecture. **Bishopsgate**, named after one of the seven gates in the old City walls, is dominated by bombastic skyscrapers such as the angular, glass-clad Broadgate Tower, at the northern end, Heron Tower, halfway along, and the Pinnacle – which aims to be the City's tallest skyscraper, at the southern end. The area's two most original architectural works are modest by comparison: the groundbreaking **Lloyd's Building** and the unmissable **Gherkin**. These, plus the Victorian splendour of **Leadenhall Market**, the oldest **synagogue** in the country, several pre-Fire churches and Wren's famous **Monument** to the Great Fire make for an especially interesting sector of the City to explore.

Liverpool Street Station
Built in 1874 **Liverpool Street Station** stands on the site of the old Bethlem Royal Hospital (or Bedlam), the infamous lunatic asylum, where the public could pay a penny and laugh at the inmates. Liverpool Street is now the City's busiest terminus, renowned for its vibrantly painted wrought-iron Victorian arches. The station's Liverpool Street entrance features the **Kindertransport memorial**, erected in 2003 and depicting some of the nearly ten thousand Jewish children who arrived at the station from central Europe, without their parents, shortly before war broke out.

Adjoining Liverpool Street Station, to the west, are the traffic-free piazzas of the very successful 1980s **Broadgate** complex. *Fulcrum*, Richard Serra's 55ft-high rusting steel sheets, acts as a kind of gateway to the **Broadgate Circle**, whose arena is used as an open-air ice rink in winter and as a performance space in summer. Continuing north to **Exchange Square**, you'll find a cascading waterfall, the hefty *Broadgate Venus* by Fernando Botero, and Xavier Corbero's *Broad Family* of obelisks, one of whose "children" reveals a shoe.

Bishopsgate Institute

230 Bishopsgate • Mon–Fri 9am–8.30pm, Sat 10am–5.30pm • Free • ☎ 020 7392 9200, ⓦ bishopsgate.org.uk • ⊖ Liverpool Street

Across the road from Liverpool Street Station is the faïence facade of the diminutive **Bishopsgate Institute**, a graceful Art Nouveau building designed by Harrison Townsend. Townsend went on to design the excellent Whitechapel Art Gallery (see p.198) and the wonderful Horniman Museum (see p.313). Opened in 1895, the institute houses a public library and puts on courses and talks throughout the year.

St Ethelburga's

78 Bishopsgate • Fri 11am–3pm • Free • ☎ 020 7496 1610, ⓦ stethelburgas.org • ⊖ Liverpool Street

Hemmed in by office blocks on either side is the "humble rag-faced front" of the pre-Fire church of **St Ethelburga**. All but totally destroyed by an IRA bomb in 1993, the church was totally rebuilt and now houses a Centre for Reconciliation and Peace, hosting regular interfaith events and workshops, and hosting world music gigs. The bare interior retains the nineteenth-century font inscribed with the Greek palindrome "Cleanse my sins, not just my face" and half the tiny garden round the back, houses a polygonal, multi-faith Bedouin tent covered in woven goat's hair.

11

St Helen's

Bishopsgate • Mon–Fri 9.30am–12.30pm • Free • ☎ 020 7283 2231, ⓦ st-helens.org.uk • ⊖ Liverpool Street, Bank, Monument or Aldgate

Another pre-Fire church that suffered extensive damage in the IRA blasts of the 1990s is the late Gothic church of **St Helen**, set back to the east of Bishopsgate. With its undulating crenellations and Baroque bell turret, it's an intriguing building, incorporating the original pre-Reformation Benedictine nunnery church and containing five grand pre-Fire tombs. Since the bomb, the floor level has been raised, the church screens shifted, a new organ gallery added and the seating rearranged to focus on the pulpit, in keeping with the church's current evangelical bent.

The Gherkin

30 St Mary Axe • ⊖ Liverpool Street or Aldgate

Completed in 2003, Norman Foster's glass-diamond-clad **Gherkin** remains one of the most popular of the new rash of brash tall buildings in the City. Most Londoners like it for its cheeky shape, though it's beginning to be hemmed in and upstaged by the skyscrapers it helped encourage. Officially known as **30 St Mary Axe**, the Gherkin sits on the site of the old Baltic Exchange, destroyed in an IRA bomb in 1992 that killed three people, commemorated on a nearby wall. At 590ft, it's actually pretty tall, but at street level it appears a very modest building – you can't go up it, but you can grab a bite to eat on the ground floor.

Lloyd's Building

1 Lime St • Guided tours by appointment; £10 • ☎ 020 7327 6586, ⓦ lloyds.com • ⊖ Bank or Monument

Completed by Richard Rogers in 1986, the **Lloyd's Building**, opposite St Andrew Undershaft, remains probably the City's most innovative and remarkable office block. "A living, breathing machine", it's a vertical version of Rogers and Renzo Piano's Parisian Pompidou Centre, in which the jumble of blue-steel pipes and cables form the outer casing, with glass lifts zipping up and down the exterior. The portico of the previous, much more sedate, Lloyd's Building (c.1925) has been preserved on Leadenhall Street, so the current headquarters represented a bizarre leap into the modern by this most conservative of City institutions – the largest insurance and

CITY SKYSCRAPERS

The economic recession notwithstanding, the City skyline is continuing to sprout a whole new generation of glass-clad **skyscrapers**. From 1980, for thirty years, the City's tallest building was 600ft **NatWest Tower** (now **Tower 42**; ⓦtower42.com) by Richard Seifert (in the shape of the bank's logo), which has a public bar on the 42nd floor (prior booking required). In 2010, this was topped by the **Heron Tower** (ⓦherontower.com), a fairly undistinguished 660ft skyscraper with a 144ft mast at 110 Bishopsgate, designed by Kohn Pedersen Fox – on the plus side, it has a 70,000-litre aquarium in the atrium, a "sky bar" on the 40th floor, accessed via the *Sushisamba* glass lifts, and the restaurant *Duck and Waffle* (see p.376). Rafael Viñoly's 525ft **Walkie Talkie**, 20 Fenchurch St (ⓦ20fenchurchstreet.co.uk), so-called because it's wider at the top than the bottom, includes a free public "sky garden" café and restaurant on the roof. **The Cheesegrater**, Richard Rogers' 737ft tapered office block at 122 Leadenhall St (ⓦtheleadenhallbuilding.com) is remarkable not simply for its triangular shape but also for its giant steel frame and its 90ft-high ground-floor Galleria, which will feature lawns and mature trees and will be open to the public. Kohn Pedersen Fox are also responsible for **The Scalpel**, a twisted 620ft angular shard of glass in Lime Street, due for completion in 2017. The only skyscraper that's failed so far to get off the ground is the **Pinnacle**, 22–24 Bishopsgate (ⓦlondonpinnacle.com), also by Kohn Pedersen Fox, a swirling 945ft helter-skelter of a tower, which has been re-nicknamed "The Stump" after work stopped in 2012 with only seven floors of the concrete core built. If the Pinnacle fails to get built, the City will remain just behind Canary Wharf, and a long way below the country's tallest building, the 1016ft **Shard** over at London Bridge (see p.232).

reinsurance market in the world. Some things never change, though, and the building is still guarded by porters in antiquated waiters' livery, in recognition of Lloyd's origins as Edward Lloyd's coffee house in 1688.

Lloyd's started out in shipping, but the famous **Lutine Bell**, salvaged from a captured French frigate in 1799 and traditionally struck once for bad news, twice for good, now only tolls once to commemorate more general disasters, twice for distinguished guests. The highlights of the interior are the **Underwriting Room**, centred on the aforementioned Lutine Bell, above which an incredible barrel-vaulted glass atrium rises almost 200ft, and the **Adam Room**, a dining room designed by Robert Adam in 1763 for Bowood House, Wiltshire, and now incongruously positioned on the eleventh floor. Dress code for visitors is jacket and tie for men and business-style for women.

Leadenhall Market

Gracechurch St • Market: Mon–Fri 10am–5pm • ⓦleadenhallmarket.co.uk • ⊖ Bank or Monument

Occupying the very site where Roman London's basilica and forum once stood, **Leadenhall Market**'s graceful Victorian cast-ironwork is richly painted in cream and maroon, with each of the four entrances to the covered arcade topped by an elaborate stone arch. Inside, the traders cater mostly for the lunchtime City crowd, their barrows laden with exotic seafood and game, fine wines, champagne and caviar, while the surrounding shops and bars remain busy until the early evening.

Bevis Marks Synagogue

4 Heneage Lane • Mon, Wed & Thurs 10.30am–2pm, Tues & Fri 10.30am–1pm, Sun 10.30am–12.30pm • £4 • Guided tours Wed & Fri 11.15am, Sun 10.45am; free • ☏ 020 7626 1274, ⓦbevismarks.org.uk • ⊖ Aldgate

Hidden away behind a red-brick office block in a little courtyard off Bevis Marks is the Bevis Marks Synagogue. Built in 1701 by Sephardic Jews who had originally fled the Inquisition in Spain and Portugal, this is the country's oldest surviving synagogue, and its roomy, rich interior gives an idea of just how wealthy the community was at the time. Although it seats over six hundred, it's only a third of the size of its prototype in Amsterdam, where many Sephardic Jews initially settled. The Sephardic community has since moved out to Maida Vale and Wembley, and the congregation has dwindled,

though the synagogue's magnificent array of chandeliers makes it very popular for candle-lit Jewish weddings. Close by Bevis Marks, just past Creechurch Lane, a plaque commemorates the even larger **Great Synagogue** of the Ashkenazi Jews, founded in 1690 but destroyed by bombs in 1941.

St Katharine Cree

86 Leadenhall St • Mon–Fri 10.30am–4pm • Free • ⊖ Aldgate

The church of **St Katharine Cree**, completed in 1631, is a rare example of its period, having miraculously escaped the Great Fire of 1666. It's a transitional building with Neoclassical elements, such as the Corinthian columns of the nave and, above, a Gothic clerestory and ribbing. At the east end is a very lovely, seventeenth-century stained-glass Catherine-wheel window. The church was consecrated in 1631 by Bishop Laud, and the "bowings and cringings" he indulged in during the service, were later used as evidence of his Catholicism at his trial and execution for heresy in 1645.

11

London Metal Exchange

56 Leadenhall St • Mon–Fri noon–1.30pm & 3.30–5pm • Free • ☎ 020 7264 5555, ⓦ lme.com • ⊖ Aldgate

The only place in the City where you can still witness the human scrum of share dealing – known as "open-outcry" – is at the **London Metal Exchange**, where metals – and even plastic – but not silver, gold or platinum are traded. The dealing takes place within the Ring, with each metal traded in five-minute bursts – to visit the public viewing gallery, you must phone ahead.

St Botolph-without-Aldgate

Aldgate High St • Tues 11am–3pm, Thurs 10am–3pm • Free • ☎ 020 7283 1670, ⓦ stbotolphs.org.uk • ⊖ Aldgate

St Botolph-without-Aldgate was designed in the 1740s by George Dance the Elder, and stood beside Aldgate, one of the old City gateways, now commemorated by a modern, wooden, latticed "palace on pillars" which stands close by. The church's bizarre interior, remodelled last century, features blue-grey paintwork, gilding on top of white plasterwork, some dodgy modern art, a batik reredos and a stunning, modern stained-glass rendition of Rubens' *Descent from the Cross* on a deep-purple background. Situated at the edge of the East End, this is a famously campaigning church, active on issues like gay priests and social exclusion.

Monument

Fish St Hill • Daily 9.30am–5.30pm • £3 • ☎ 020 7626 2717, ⓦ themonument.info • ⊖ Monument

In the 1670s, Robert Hooke and Christopher Wren's **Monument** commemorating the Great Fire of 1666 (see p.452) used to rise above the rooftops. No longer so prominent on the skyline, this plain 202ft Doric column, crowned with spiky gilded flames, nevertheless remains the tallest isolated stone column in the world; if it were laid out flat it would touch the site of the bakery where the fire started, east of Monument. The bas-relief on the base depicts Charles II and the Duke of York in Roman garb conducting the emergency relief operation. The 311 steps to the gallery at the top – plagued by suicides until a cage was built around it in 1842 – once guaranteed an incredible view; nowadays it's dwarfed by the surrounding buildings.

St Magnus-the-Martyr

Lower Thames St • Tues–Fri 10am–4pm • ☎ 020 7626 4481, ⓦ stmagnusmartyr.org.uk • ⊖ Monument

Not far from the Monument is another Wren edifice, the church of **St Magnus-the-Martyr**, whose octagonal spire used to greet all travellers arriving in the City across old London Bridge. Now it stands forlorn by busy Lower Thames Street, though the Anglo-Catholic interior holds, in T.S. Eliot's words, "an inexplicable splendour of Ionian white and gold". In addition, there's a wooden pier from an old Roman wharf in the porch, and a great model of the old London Bridge in the vestry.

LONDON BRIDGE

Unreal City
Under the brown fog of a winter dawn,
A crowd flowed over London Bridge, so many,
I had not thought death had undone so many.

The Waste Land, T.S. Eliot

At rush hour, you can still see Eliot's "undead" trudging to work across **London Bridge**, which was, until 1750, the only bridge across the Thames. The Romans were the first to build a permanent crossing here, a structure succeeded by a Saxon version that was pulled down by King Olaf of Norway in 1014, and commemorated in the popular nursery rhyme *London Bridge is Falling Down*. It was the medieval bridge, however, that achieved world fame: built of stone and crowded with timber-framed houses, it became one of London's greatest attractions. At the centre stood the richly ornate **Nonsuch House**, decorated with onion domes and Dutch gables, and a chapel dedicated to Thomas Becket; at the Southwark end was the Great Gatehouse, on which the heads of traitors were displayed, dipped in tar to preserve them. The houses were removed in the mid-eighteenth century, and a new stone bridge erected in 1831 – that one now stands near **Lake Havasu** in the Arizona desert, having been bought in the 1960s by a guy who, so the apocryphal story goes, thought he'd purchased Tower Bridge. The present concrete structure – without doubt the ugliest yet – dates from 1972.

11

Old Billingsgate Market

16 Lower Thames St • ☎ 020 7283 2800, �🌐 oldbillingsgate.co.uk • ⊖ Monument

Along the river from St Magnus is **Old Billingsgate Market**, a handsome Victorian market hall that once housed London's chief wholesale fish market, but has since been turned into a corporate events venue. It's difficult now to imagine the noise and smell of old Billingsgate, whose porters used to carry the fish in towers of baskets on their heads, and whose wives were renowned for their bad language even in Shakespeare's day: "as bad a tongue…as any oyster-wife at Billingsgate" (*King Lear*). Next door stands the Neoclassical **Custom House**, from 1825, which has been collecting duties from incoming ships since around 1275, and still houses a department of HM Customs and Revenue.

St Olave

8 Hart St • Mon–Fri 10am–5pm • Free • ☎ 020 7488 4318, �🌐 sanctuaryinthecity.net • ⊖ Tower Hill

Saved from the Fire, but left as an empty shell by the Blitz, the Kentish ragstone church of **St Olave** was dubbed "St Ghastly Grim" by Dickens after the skulls and crossbones and vicious-looking spikes adorning the 1658 entrance to the graveyard on Seething Lane, a short stroll from St Dunstan's. Samuel Pepys lived in Seething Lane for much of his life, and he and his wife, Elizabeth, are both buried here amid the pre-Fire brasses and monuments – Elizabeth's monument was raised by Pepys himself; Pepys' own is Victorian.

All Hallows-by-the-Tower

Byward St • Mon–Fri 8am–5pm, Sat 10am–4pm, Sun 10am–1pm • Guided tours daily 2–4pm • Free • Brassrubbing Mon–Fri 2–4pm; £5 per brass • ☎ 020 7481 2928, �🌐 ahbtt.org.uk • ⊖ Tower Hill

All Hallows-by-the-Tower, another pre-Fire church, only just survived the Blitz – most of the church is a postwar neo-Gothic pastiche wrought in concrete. The furnishings are fascinating, however, and include lots of maritime memorials, model ships, two wings of a Flemish triptych from around 1500, and, best of all, the exquisitely carved Gibbons limewood font cover, in the southwest chapel. Close by is an arch from the original seventh-century church; remains of a tessellated Roman pavement can also be found in the tiny Crypt Museum. All Hallows also has some superb pre-Reformation brasses, and offers brassrubbing.

Tower of London and around

Tower Hill is choked with tourists who flock here to see one of London's most famous landmarks, Tower Bridge and the adjacent Tower of London. Despite all the attendant hype and heritage claptrap, the Tower remains one of London's most remarkable buildings, site of some of the goriest events in the nation's history, and somewhere all visitors and Londoners should explore at least once. Sitting beside the river, at the eastern edge of the old city walls, the Tower is chiefly famous as a place of imprisonment and death, yet it's also been used as a royal residence, armoury, mint, menagerie, observatory and – a function it still serves – a safe-deposit box for the Crown Jewels. And, finally, it's easy to forget that the Tower is, above all, the most perfectly preserved (and restored) medieval fortress in the country.

Begun as a simple watchtower, built by **William the Conqueror** to keep an eye on the City, the Tower had evolved into a palace-fortress by 1100. The inner curtain wall and towers were built under Henry III, while the outer fortifications, and an even wider moat, were added by Edward I, on his return from the Crusades, which means that most of what's visible today was already in place by 1307, the year of Edward's death. The Tower has been besieged on a number of occasions – firstly, in 1191, when the unpopular Bishop Longchamp held out against Richard I's brother, John, but caved in after only three days – but sacked only once, during the 1381 Peasants' Revolt, when the Archbishop of Canterbury, Simon Sudbury, among others, was dragged out and lynched.

The Tower's **first prisoner**, the Bishop of Durham, arrived in 1101, imprisoned by Henry I, and promptly escaped from the window of his cell by a rope, having got the guards drunk. Gruffydd ap Llywelyn Fawr, heir to the Welsh throne, attempted a similar feat from the White Tower in 1244, with less success: "his head and neck were crushed between his shoulders…a most horrid spectacle." – the window he used was subsequently bricked up and can still be seen on the south side of the Tower. Incidentally, the **most famous escapee** from the Tower was the Jacobite 5th Earl of Nithsdale, who, the night before his execution in 1716, managed to get past the guards dressed as his wife's maid (despite his red beard), and lived in poverty and happiness for almost thirty years in exile in Rome.

Following the Restoration in 1660, the general public were admitted to the Tower for the first time to view the **coronation regalia** and the impressive displays of arms and armour – by the end of Victoria's reign, there were half a million visitors to the fortress each year. Nevertheless, during both of the world wars, the Tower was still used to hold prisoners: **Roger Casement**, the Irish nationalist, was held here briefly before his trial and hanging in 1916, and the last VIP inmate was **Rudolf Hess**, Hitler's deputy, who flew secretly into Britain to try to sue for peace in May 1941 and was held in the tower for a few days. The **last execution** took place on August 14, 1941, when Josef Jakobs, a German spy who (like Hess) had broken his ankle while parachuting into Britain, was given the privilege of being seated before the firing squad.

12

INFORMATION AND TOURS

Opening hours March–Oct Mon & Sun 10am–5.30pm, Tues–Sat 9am–5.30pm; Nov–Feb closes 4.30pm.

Admission £22. To avoid queuing (and save some money), buy your ticket online.

Contact details ☎ 020 3166 6000, ⊚ hrp.org.uk.

Tube Tower Hill.

Eating There's a spacious and fairly decent café in the New Armouries building, and plenty of benches on which to picnic. Alternatively, you can obtain a re-entry pass and have lunch outside the Tower.

Tours You can explore the Tower complex independently, or with an audioguide (£4), but it's a good idea to get your bearings by joining up with one of the free, entertaining hour-long guided tours, given at regular intervals by one of the Tower's Beefeaters – it's also the easiest way to visit the Chapel of St Peter-ad-Vincula.

BEEFEATERS

Formed in 1485 by Henry VII as a personal bodyguard, The Tower's forty or so Beefeaters are officially known as **Yeoman Warders** – the nickname "Beefeaters" was coined in the seventeenth century, when it was a term of abuse for a well-fed domestic servant. These self-assured, eminently photogenic guards are best known for their scarlet-and-gold Tudor costumes, but unless it's a special occasion you're more likely to see them in dark-blue Victorian "undress". The Beefeaters have all done at least 22 years' military service, reached at least the rank of sergeant major and are aged between 40 and 55 on appointment. The first-ever woman Beefeater was appointed in 2007; two years on, two of her male colleagues were dismissed for harassing her. All the Beefeaters live in the Tower and one of their many duties is to give theatrically irreverent guided tours to the tourists, which many of them clearly relish.

Bell Tower

Visitors enter the Tower by the Middle Tower and the Byward Tower, in the southwest corner. Two of the first victims of the Reformation – Thomas More and John Fisher – were incarcerated nearby in the **Bell Tower**, from whose dinky wooden belfry a bell still signals the curfew hour (and used to toll to signal an execution). More was initially allowed writing materials, but later they were withdrawn; Fisher was kept in worse conditions ("I decay forthwith, and fall into coughs and diseases of my body, and cannot keep myself in health") and was so weak that he had to be carried to the scaffold on Tower Hill. The 20-year-old future Queen Elizabeth I arrived here in 1554, while her half-sister Queen Mary tried to find incriminating evidence against her. Catholic Mass was performed daily in Elizabeth's cell for the two months of her imprisonment, but she refused to be converted.

TOWER OF LONDON

Traitors' Gate

Most prisoners were delivered through **Traitors' Gate**, on the waterfront, which forms part of **St Thomas's Tower**, now partially reconstructed to re-create the atmosphere of Edward I's **medieval palace**. The King's Bedchamber has a beautiful little oratory in one of the turrets, while in the larger oratory of the Throne Room, in 1471, the "saintly but slightly daft" Henry VI was murdered at prayer, possibly on the orders of Edward IV or Richard III. Not long afterwards, Edward had his brother, the Duke of Clarence, executed in the Tower for high treason, drowned in a butt of malmsey wine (at his own request – according to Shakespeare).

Bloody Tower

The main entrance to the Inner Ward is beneath a 3.5-ton, seven hundred-year-old portcullis, which forms part of the **Bloody Tower**, so called because it was here that the 12-year-old Edward V and his 10-year-old brother, Richard, were accommodated "for their own safety" in 1483 by their uncle, Richard of Gloucester (later Richard III), following the death of their father, Edward IV. Of all the Tower's many inhabitants, few have so captured the public imagination as the **Princes in the Tower**. According to Thomas More, they were smothered in their beds, and buried naked at the foot of the White Tower. In 1674, workmen discovered the skeletons of two young children close to the Tower; they were subsequently buried in Innocents' Corner in Westminster Abbey.

The study of **Walter Raleigh** (see box below) is re-created on the first floor, while his sleeping quarters upstairs, built to accommodate his wife, children and three servants, now house an exhibition on the Princes in the Tower and on the poisoning of the poet **Thomas Overbury**. Confined to the Bloody Tower in 1613 by James I, Overbury was slowly poisoned to death with arsenic concealed within the tarts and jellies sent by the wife of one of the king's favourites, Robert Carr, the Earl of Somerset. Two years later, Carr and his wife were themselves arrested, tried and condemned to death – in the end, they were simply incarcerated in the Tower for five years before being pardoned. The Lieutenant of the Tower was less fortunate, and was hanged for failing to protect his prisoners.

12

White Tower

William the Conqueror's central hall-keep, known as the **White Tower**, is the original "Tower", begun in 1076. Whitewashed (hence its name) in the reign of Henry III, it now sports a Kentish ragstone exterior thanks to Wren, who added the large windows. Of the

---

WALTER RALEIGH

The Bloody Tower's most illustrious inmate – even more famous in his time than the princes – was **Walter Raleigh** (1554–1618), who spent three separate periods in the Tower. His first misdemeanor was in 1591 when he impregnated and secretly married Elizabeth Throckmorton, one of Elizabeth I's ladies-in-waiting, without the Queen's permission. A year later his crime was discovered and he was sent to the Tower (with his wife Bess); his second spell began in 1603, when he was found guilty of plotting against James I. He spent nearly thirteen years here, with his wife and kids, growing and smoking tobacco (his most famous import), composing poetry, concocting potions in his distillery and writing *The Historie of the World*, which outsold even Shakespeare, despite being banned by James I for being "too saucy in censuring princes". When Raleigh complained that the noise of the portcullis kept him awake at night, he was moved to much worse accommodation. In 1616 he was released and sent off to Guyana to discover gold, on condition that he didn't attack the Spanish; he broke his word and was sent straight back to the Tower on his return in 1618. For six weeks he was imprisoned in "one of the most cold and direful dungeons", before being beheaded at Westminster.

tower's four turrets, topped by stylish Tudor cupolas, only three are square: the fourth is rounded in order to encase the main spiral staircase, and for a short while was used by Charles II's royal astronomer, Flamsteed, before he moved to Greenwich. The main entrance to the Tower is the original one, high up in the south wall, out of reach of the enemy, and accessed by a wooden staircase which could be removed during times of siege.

Royal Armouries

The four floors of arms and armour displayed within the tower represent a mere smidgen of the **Royal Armouries** (the majority of which resides in Leeds), originally established by Henry VIII in Greenwich and on display here since the time of Charles II. Among the most striking armour displayed on the ground floor is the colossal garniture of 1540 made for Henry VIII (and famous for its protruding codpiece, which women used to touch to boost their fertility), juxtaposed with boy king Edward VI's tiny suit of armour. Several exotic gifts presented to the royalty reside here, too, including the Japanese shogun armour presented to King James I by the East India Company. The collection takes a lurch into the present day with a polo helmet and knee pads belonging to Prince Charles.

The **Line of Kings**, on the same floor, is a display first recorded in 1660, a sort of Restoration waxworks only in wood, originally depicting the monarchs of England on horseback. Also on show here is a suit of armour for a man six feet nine inches tall (once thought to have been John of Gaunt) and one for a boy just three feet one and a half inches high (possibly Charles I). On the top floor, there's an interesting exhibition on the executions that have taken place within the Tower and on Tower Hill over the years – the block and axe from the last beheading are here (see opposite).

Chapel of St John

Whatever your interests, you should pay a visit to the first-floor **Chapel of St John**, a beautiful Norman structure completed in 1080, making it the oldest intact ecclesiastical building in London. It was here that Henry VI's body was buried following his murder in 1471; that Henry VII's queen, Elizabeth of York, lay in state surrounded by eight hundred candles, after dying in childbirth, and that Lady Jane Grey came to pray on the night before her execution. Today, the once highly decorated

---

ROYAL MENAGERIE

The **Royal Menagerie** began in earnest in 1235 when the Holy Roman Emperor presented three "leopards" to Henry III; the keeper was initially paid sixpence a day for the sustenance of the beasts (they were, in fact, **lions**), and one penny for himself. From the 1330s, they were put on public display in the outer barbican (which became known as the Lion Tower), and joined some years later by a **polar bear** from the King of Norway (who was put on a leash and allowed to catch fish in the Thames) and an **elephant** from the King of France. James I was particularly keen on the menagerie, and used to stage regular animal fights on the green, but the practice was stopped in 1609 when one of the bears killed a child. In 1704, six lions, two leopards, three eagles, two Swedish owls "of great bigness", two "cats of the mountains" and a jackal were recorded. Visitors were advised not to "play tricks" after an orang-utan threw a cannonball at one and killed him.

The menagerie was transferred to the newly founded **London Zoo** in the 1830s, leaving the Tower with just its **ravens**, descendants of early scavengers attracted by waste from the palace kitchens. They have been protected by royal decree since the Restoration, and have their wings clipped so they can't fly away – legend says that the Tower (and therefore the kingdom) will fall if they do, though the Tower was in fact briefly raven-less during the last war after the Tower suffered heavy bombing. While the ravens may appear harmless, they are vicious, territorial creatures best given a wide berth. They live in coops in the south wall of the Inner Ward, are fed raw meat from Smithfield Market, have individual names and even have their own graveyard in the dry moat near the main entrance.

THE TOWER GREEN TEN

Being **beheaded** at Tower Hill (as opposed to being hanged, drawn and quartered) was a privilege of the nobility; being beheaded on Tower Green, the stretch of lawn to the west of the White Tower, was an honour conferred on just ten people. It was an arrangement that suited both parties: the victim was spared the jeering crowds of Tower Hill, and the monarch was spared bad publicity. Among the victims were: Lord Hastings, executed immediately after his arrest on the orders of Richard III, who swore he wouldn't go to dinner until Hastings was beheaded; **Anne Boleyn** (Henry VIII's second wife), accused of incest and adultery, who was dispatched cleanly and swiftly with a French long sword rather than the traditional axe, at her own insistence; 19-year-old **Catherine Howard** (Henry VIII's fifth wife and Anne's cousin), convicted of adultery and beheaded along with her lady-in-waiting, who was deemed an accomplice; 16-year-old **Lady Jane Grey**, who was Queen for just nine days; and the Earl of Essex, one-time favourite of Elizabeth I.

---

blocks of honey-coloured Caen limestone are free of all ecclesiastical excrescences, leaving the chapel's smooth curves and rounded apse perfectly unencumbered.

Tower Green

Despite appearances, the pretty little open space of **Tower Green** was the chief place of execution within the Tower for many centuries – the names of those beheaded here are recorded on an incongruous glass monument at the centre of the green. The bloody, headless corpses of the executed (from Tower Green and Tower Hill) were buried in the Tudor **Chapel of St Peter-ad-Vincula**, to the north, accessible only during the first and last hour the Tower is open, or on the Beefeaters' tours.

On the west side of the green, the **Beauchamp Tower** houses an exhibition on the Tower's prisoners on the ground floor. Beauchamp Tower itself accommodated only the wealthiest prisoners and boasts a better class of graffiti: Lord Dudley, husband of Lady Jane Grey, even commissioned a stonemason to carve the family crest on the first floor.

In the southwest corner of the green is the sixteenth-century **Queen's House** (closed to the public), distinguished by its swirling Tudor timber frames. These were the most luxurious cells in the Tower, and were used to incarcerate the likes of Catherine Howard and Anne Boleyn, who had also stayed there shortly before her coronation. Lady Jane Grey was cooped up here in 1553, and in the following year it was from here she watched the headless torso of her husband, Lord Dudley, being brought back from Tower Hill, only hours before her own execution. In 1688, William Penn, the Quaker and founder of Pennsylvania, was confined to the Queen's House, where he penned his most popular work, *No Cross, No Crown*.

Jewel House

The castellated Waterloo Block or Jewel House, north of the White Tower, now holds the **Crown Jewels**, the major reason so many people flock to the Tower. The Jewels include the world's three largest cut diamonds, but only a few of the exhibits could be described as beautiful – assertions of status and wealth are more important considerations. Queues can be long, and you only get to view the rocks from moving walkways. The vast majority of exhibits postdate the Commonwealth of 1649–60, when most of the royal riches were melted down for coinage or sold off.

Before you reach the walkway, look out for the twelfth-century **Coronation Spoon**, the oldest piece of regalia. The first major piece along the walkway is the Sceptre with the Cross, which contains the world's largest diamond, the 530-carat "First Star of Africa" or **Cullinan I**, followed by **St Edward's Crown**, used in every coronation since the Restoration. The legendary 105.6-carat **Koh-i-Nûr** (Mountain of Light) is set into the

Queen Elizabeth, the Queen Mother's Crown from 1937. The last and most famous crown, set apart from the others, is the **Imperial State Crown**, worn by the Queen on state occasions, and sparkling with 2868 diamonds, 17 sapphires, 11 emeralds, 5 rubies and 273 pearls. The crown contains several very famous jewels: St Edward's Sapphire, taken from the ring of Edward the Confessor and set in the cross atop the crown; the Black Prince's Ruby, on the front cross; and Cullinan II, the 317-carat "Second Star of Africa"; the crown also contains pearls from Elizabeth I's ear-rings.

Salt Tower to the Martin Tower

Visitors can walk along the Tower's eastern walls, starting at the **Salt Tower**, which features more prisoners' graffiti, including a stunningly detailed zodiac carved by Hugh Draper, incarcerated in 1561 on a charge of sorcery. This is where Edward I kept the Scottish King John Baliol prisoner for three years from 1296. Halfway along the walls, the **Constable Tower** contains a small exhibition on the 1381 Peasants' Revolt.

The **Martin Tower**, at the far end of the wall walk, houses a display of crowns with their gems taken out and relates the story of the most famous attempt to steal the Crown Jewels which took place here in 1671, when "Colonel" **Thomas Blood**, an Irish adventurer, made an attempt to make off with the lot, disguised as a parson. He was caught with the crown under his habit, the orb in one of his accomplices' breeches and the sceptre about to be filed in half. Charles II, good-humoured as ever, met and pardoned the felon, and even awarded him a pension and made him welcome at court.

12

Fusiliers' Museum

Last, and probably least, the Tower also contains the **Fusiliers' Museum** which tells the story of the Royal Fusiliers, now part of the Royal Regiment of Fusiliers. The original regiment was founded by James II in 1685 from Tower guards and was called the Ordnance Regiment, as it was their job to escort the artillery. The museum trots through the regiment's various campaigns, displays its medals and spoils from across the Empire, and lists its most famous alumni, although it neglects to mention that East End gangsters, the Kray Twins, were once Fusiliers, and were in fact held prisoner in the Tower overnight in 1952 after having failed to turn up on time for their National Service call-up.

TOWER CEREMONIES

The Ceremony of the Keys is a seven hundred-year-old, seven-minute floodlit ceremony. At 9.53pm daily, the Chief Yeoman Warder, accompanied by the Tower Guard, locks the Tower gates, and as he attempts to return to the Inner Ward, the following exchange then takes place: "Halt. Who comes there?" "The Keys." "Whose Keys?" "Queen Elizabeth's Keys." "Pass then, all's well." Then the Last Post is sounded and the ceremony ends. To find out how to witness this long-running drama, visit the website.

Gun Salutes are fired by the Honourable Artillery Company at 1pm at Tower Wharf on royal birthdays and other special occasions.

The Constable's Dues occurs once a year when a large Royal Navy ship moors alongside the Tower; the ship's captain and his escort march through the Tower and present a barrel of rum to the Constable of the Tower.

The Ceremony of the Lilies and Roses is carried out every year on May 21 by the provosts of Eton and King's College, Cambridge, who place white lilies and roses (their respective emblems) on the spot where King Henry VI, founder of both institutions, was murdered on May 21, 1471.

The Beating of the Bounds ceremony takes place once every three years (including in 2014) on Ascension Day (forty days after Easter), outside the walls of the Tower. It used to be little boys who were beaten, but now it's the 29 stones that mark the limits of the Tower's jurisdiction that are thrashed with willow wands by local children, while the Chief Yeoman Warder gives the order "Whack it, boys! Whack it!"

> ### OFF WITH HIS HEAD!
>
> During the **1381 Peasants' Revolt**, rioters broke into the Tower, dragged out the Lord High Treasurer (the man responsible for the hated poll tax), and hacked him to death on Tower Hill, along with the Archbishop of Canterbury. However, the first official beheading didn't take place until 1388 with the last one in 1747, when the 80-year-old Jacobite **Lord Lovat** was dispatched. Lovat's beheading drew such a crowd that one of the spectators' stands collapsed, killing several bystanders, at which Lovat exclaimed: "The more mischief, the better sport." The Duke of Monmouth, beheaded in 1685 for his rebellion against James II, suffered the most botched execution: it took **Jack Ketch** (who lives on in Punch & Judy shows) five blows of the axe to sever his head, and even then the job had to be finished off with a surgeon's knife. Hangings continued for another thirty-odd years, ending with the execution of two prostitutes and a one-armed soldier arrested for attacking a Catholic-run pub in the 1780 Gordon Riots.

Tower Hill

Perhaps it's fitting that traffic-blighted **Tower Hill** to the northwest of the Tower should be such a god-awful place, for it was here that the Tower's convicted "traitors" were executed. The actual spot for the executions, at what was the country's first permanent scaffold, is marked by a plaque on the west side of Trinity Square Gardens, which names a handful of the 125 executed here.

Close by stands the **Mercantile Marine Memorial**, designed by Edwin Lutyens, smothered with the names of the 12,000 merchant seamen who died in World War I, and subsequently enlarged with a vast, sprawling sunken section commemorating the 24,000 more who died in World War II.

The marine theme is continued in the buildings overlooking the gardens: the gargantuan temple-like former headquarters of the **Port of London Authority** (now a hotel), an Edwardian edifice that exudes imperial confidence, with Neptune adorning the main tower; and, to the east, the elegant Neoclassical former headquarters of **Trinity House** (tours can be booked; £8; ☎020 7481 6900, ⓦtrinityhouse.co.uk), the organization that oversees the upkeep of the lighthouses of England, Wales, the Channel Islands and Gibraltar – check out the reliefs of mermen, cherubs and lighthouses on the main facade, and the splendid gilded nautical weather vane.

Continuing east, you'll find perhaps the most impressive remaining section of London's **Roman walls** (see p.169) behind the *Grange City Hotel*, on Cooper's Row, and in Wakefield Gardens, close to Tower Hill tube station, along with an eighteenth-century copy of a Roman statue of Emperor Trajan, saved from a Southampton scrapyard by a local vicar.

Tower Bridge

Daily: April–Sept 10am–6pm; Oct–March 9.30am–5.30pm · £8 · ☎ 020 7403 3761, ⓦ towerbridge.org.uk · ⊖ Tower Hill

Tower Bridge ranks with Big Ben as the most famous of all London landmarks. Completed in 1894, its neo-Gothic towers are clad in Cornish granite and Portland stone, but conceal a frame of Scottish steel, which, at the time, represented a considerable engineering achievement, allowing a road crossing that could be raised to give tall ships access to the upper reaches of the Thames. The raising of the bascules (from the French for "seesaw") remains an impressive sight, and an event that takes place around a thousand times a year – visit the website for details. If you buy a ticket for the Tower Bridge Exhibition, you get to walk across the elevated walkways linking the summits of the towers, and visit the Tower's Engine Rooms, on the south side of the bridge, where you can see the now-defunct, giant coal-fired boilers which drove the hydraulic system until 1976, and play some interactive engineering games.

STREET ART ON HANBURY STREET, OFF BRICK LANE

The East End

The districts of Whitechapel and in particular Spitalfields, within sight of the City's skyscrapers, represent the old heart of the East End. If you visit just one part of East London, it should be this neighbourhood, which preserves mementoes from each wave of immigration. Most visitors come for the nightlife that has evolved around Brick Lane and Shoreditch, and for the Sunday markets: Spitalfields for fashion and food; Petticoat Lane for cheap clothes; Brick Lane for fashion, accessories and music; Columbia Road for flowers and plants. Further afield, the East End only repays selective sightseeing since Victorian slum clearances, Hitler's bombs and postwar tower blocks have left large areas looking bleak. Of course the one part of the East End that has been totally transformed is the lower Lee Valley, a former industrial area, now home to the Olympic Park.

13

Few places in London have engendered so many myths as the **East End**, a catch-all title that covers just about everywhere east of the City, but has its historic heart closest to the latter. Its name is synonymous with slums, sweatshops and crime, epitomized by antiheroes such as Jack the Ripper and the Kray twins, and with rags-to-riches success stories of a whole generation of Jews who were born in these cholera-ridden quarters and then moved to wealthier pastures. Old East Enders will tell you that the area's not what it was – and it's true, as it always has been. The East End is constantly changing, as newly arrived **immigrants** assimilate and move out.

The first immigrants were **Huguenots**, French Protestants fleeing from religious persecution in the 1680s, who bequeathed the word "refugee" (from the French, *réfugié*). They were welcomed by all except the apprentice weavers whose work they undercut. Some settled in Soho, but the majority settled in Spitalfields, where they were operating thousands of silk looms by the late eighteenth century. Within three generations the Huguenots were almost entirely assimilated, and the **Irish** became the new immigrant population. Irish labourers, ironically enough, played a major role in building the area's Protestant churches, and were crucial to the development of the canals and docks. The threat of cheap Irish labour provoked riots in 1736 and 1769, and their Catholicism made them easy targets during the 1780 Gordon Riots.

It was the influx of **Jews** escaping pogroms in eastern Europe and Russia that defined the character of the East End in the late nineteenth century. The Bishop of Stepney complained in 1901 that his churches were "left like islands in the midst of an alien sea". The same year, the MP for Stepney helped found the East End's first organized racist movement, the British Brothers League, whose ideology foreshadowed the British Union of Fascists, led by Oswald Mosley and famously defeated at the **Battle of Cable Street** (see p.194). The area's Jewish population has now dispersed throughout London, and gentrification has made serious inroads over the last decade or so, though the East End – and the borough of Tower Hamlets in which it resides – remains a deeply deprived area. Despite the millions that have been poured into the nearby Docklands development, and the proximity of the wealth of the City, unemployment, racial tensions and housing problems persist.

Spitalfields

ⓦ visitspitalfields.com

On the eastern edge of the City, **Spitalfields** started life as a cemetery, situated just outside the Roman walls. Its name derives from the medieval priory and hospital (hence "spital") of St Mary which stood here until the Dissolution – the old priory mortuary chapel has been preserved, in an underground vault, to the west of the old market. Nowadays, Spitalfields is continuing to undergo a slow but steady gentrification. The whole area is at its busiest and buzziest on Sundays, when there are no fewer than five **markets** all within a stone's throw of one another.

Spitalfields Market

Thurs & Fri 10am–4pm, Sun 9am–5pm • ⓦ oldspitalfieldsmarket.com • ⊖ Liverpool Street

Originally established back in the seventeenth century in open countryside east of the City, **Spitalfields Market** was once the capital's premier fruit and vegetable market. Since the wholesale market moved out to Stratford in 1991, Spitalfields has become something of a hybrid. In the rather lugubrious Victorian red-brick and green-gabled

---

The East End of London is the hell of poverty. Like an enormous, black, motionless, giant kracken, the poverty of London lies there in lurking silence and encircles with its mighty tentacles the life and wealth of the City and of the West End…   J.H. Mackay, *The Anarchists* (1891)

13

building, a food, vintage clothes and crafts market continues to thrive. Meanwhile, the western, 1920s half of the market has been replaced by an anonymous glass-box mixed offices and shops development designed by Norman Foster. Part of the original facade survives on the north side of Brushfield Street; on the south side, the old fruiterers' shops are occupied by modishly retro businesses, such as Verde & Co, author Jeanette Winterson's deli venture (see p.378).

Christ Church

Commercial St • Mon–Fri 10am–4pm, Sun 1–4pm • ☎ 020 7377 2440, ⓦ ccspitalfields.org • ⊖ Liverpool Street

Christ Church is a characteristically bold church designed by Nicholas Hawksmoor, completed in 1729 and facing Spitalfields Market from across Commercial Street. The church's main features are its huge 225ft-high broach spire and giant Tuscan portico, raised on steps and shaped like a Venetian window (a central arched opening flanked by two smaller rectangles), a motif repeated in the tower and doors. Inside, there's a forest of giant columned bays, a hexagonal, embossed ceiling, with a lion and a unicorn

■ ACCOMMODATION	
40 Winks	1

● CAFÉS	
Frizzante @ City Farm	2
G. Kelly	3

● RESTAURANTS	
Bistrothèque	1
Viajante	4

■ PUBS & BARS	
The Approach	3
Camel	5
Edward VII	1
The George Tavern	6
The Palm Tree	4

● SHOPPING	
Chatsworth Road Market	1
Little Shop of Horrors	2

■ MUSIC VENUE	
Sebright Arms	2

EAST END

EAST END HIDDEN GEMS

13

Silent Nights at Dennis Severs' House
See below
19 Princelet Street See p.196
**Visiting an East End almshouse at the
Geffrye Museum** See p.197

**Experiencing a Victorian classroom
at the Ragged School Museum**
See p.201
Little Shop of Horrors See p.433

playing peekaboo on the top of the chancel beam and, opposite, London's largest Georgian organ. The church's restoration has saved it from falling down; sadly, it's also removed all the atmosphere the old decaying interior once had.

South of Spitalfields Market

South of Spitalfields Market are several reminders of the old Jewish community: the **Soup Kitchen for the Jewish Poor**, on Brune Street, which opened in 1902 and closed in 1992 (the undulating stone lettering with the Christian and Jewish dates of its foundation are still clearly visible), a mural opposite, and the **Sandys Row synagogue**, an old Huguenot chapel converted in 1870 for Dutch Jews and one of the few working synagogues left in the East End. The surrounding network of narrow streets is fascinating to walk around – unique survivors that give a strong impression of the old East End. From the bakery at 12 Widegate St, with its high-relief ceramic friezes, cross Sandys Row and walk down Artillery Passage into **Artillery Lane**, which boasts a superb Huguenot shop front at no. 56. Incidentally, the ballistic connection dates from the reign of Henry VIII, when the Royal Artillery used to hold gunnery practice here.

Petticoat Lane (Middlesex St)

Clothes market Sun 9am–2pm

Further south from Spitalfields Market lies **Petticoat Lane**, heavily bombed in the Blitz and not one of London's prettiest streets, but one with a rich history. The street originally lay outside the City walls, and was known as Hogs Lane; later, the area became known for its secondhand goods market, selling among other things the petticoats that gave the market and street its new name; the authorities then renamed it Middlesex Street in 1830 to avoid the mention of ladies' underwear (though the original name has stuck) and tried to prevent Sunday trading here (it was finally sanctioned by law in 1936). In the Victorian era the market grew into one of London's largest, and by the end of the century it was known as the Jews' Market, and stood at the heart of the Jewish East End, a "stronghold of hard-sell Judaism…into which no missionary dared to set foot", according to novelist Israel Zangwill. It remains the city's number-one cheap new clothes market, with a smaller lunchtime version in the week (Mon–Fri) on neighbouring Wentworth Street.

Dennis Severs' House

18 Folgate St • Mon noon–2pm £7, Mon "Silent Night" 6–9pm £14, Sun noon–4pm £10; Oct–May also Wed 6–9pm £14; occasional Thurs "Exclusive Silent Night" £45 • ☎ 020 7247 4013, ⓦ dennissevershouse.co.uk • ➔ Liverpool Street

You can visit one of Spitalfields' characteristic eighteenth-century terraced houses at 18 Folgate St, where the American artist **Dennis Severs** lived until 1999. Eschewing all modern conveniences, Severs lived under candlelight, decorating his house as it would have been two hundred years ago. The public were invited to share in the experience which he described as like "passing through a frame into a painting". Today, visitors are free to explore the candle-lit rooms and are left with the distinct impression that the resident Huguenot family has literally just popped out: there's the smell of food, lots of clutter and the sound of horses' hooves on the cobbled street outside.

SHOREDITCH, SPITALFIELDS & WHITECHAPEL

● SHOPS

A. Gold	21
Absolute Vintage	17
Backyard Market	12
Beyond Retro	5
Blitz	16
Blondie	14
Brick Lane Market	7
Columbia Road Market	2
Duke of Uke	4
The Laden Showroom	9
Lomography Gallery Store	18
Petticoat Lane Market	22
Rokit	8, 10
Rough Trade	13
Spitalfields Market	20
Sunday UpMarket	15
Tea Rooms Market	11
Taj Stores	19
Tatty Devine	3
Treacle	1
The Vintage Emporium	6

0 — 200 yards

N

■ ACCOMMODATION

Boundary Hotel	2
Hoxton Hotel	1
Shoreditch Rooms	3

● CAFÉS

Brick Lane Beigel Bake	10
The Bridge	4
Café 1001	13
E. Pellicci	7
Fabrique	1
G. Kelly	5
Jones' Dairy	3
Leila's Shop	8
Sông Quê	2
Story Deli	9
Verde and Co	15

■ RESTAURANTS

Chez Elles	16
Clove Club	6
Eyre Brothers	11
Hawksmoor	12
Lahore Kebab House	19
Needoo Grill	18
St John Bread and Wine	14
Tayyabs	17

■ PUBS & BARS

Bar Kick	8
Boundary	13
The Carpenter's Arms	17
Happiness Forgets	5
Indo	22
The Owl & Pussycat	16
Ten Bells	21
Vibe Bar	20
Worship Street Whistling Shop	19

■ GAY & LESBIAN VENUES

East Bloc	4
George & Dragon	7
Joiners Arms	2

■ MUSIC VENUES

The Book Club	14
Cargo	11
Hoxton Square Bar & Kitchen	6
The Macbeth	1
Village Underground	18

■ CLUBS

Bethnal Green Working Men's Club	3
Cargo	10
East Village	11
The Old Blue Last	15
Plastic People	9
Rhythm Factory	23
XOYO	12

13 Brick Lane

Brick Lane gets its name from the brick kilns situated here after the Great Fire to help rebuild the City. By 1900, this was the high street of London's unofficial Jewish ghetto, but from the 1960s, Brick Lane became the heart of the Bangladeshi community. Racism has been a problem for each wave of immigrants, but nowadays it's City developers and bohemian gentrification that are changing the face of the street. For the moment, the southern half of Brick Lane remains pretty staunchly Bangladeshi: bright-coloured sari fabrics line the clothes-shop windows, and, in the evening, waiters from the numerous restaurants try to cajole you into their establishments. Along the northern half of Brick Lane, the pavements are busy with punters heading for the late-night cafés and clubs that have colonized the area.

The changing ethnic make-up of this part of Brick Lane is most clearly illustrated in the **Jamme Masjid** (Great Mosque) on the corner of Fournier Street. Established in 1743 as a Huguenot church, it became a Wesleyan chapel in 1809, the ultra-Orthodox Spitalfields Great Synagogue in 1897, and since 1976 has served as a mosque – it's impossible to miss thanks to the 90ft-high luminous, freestanding metal minaret, topped by a crescent moon, that was erected in 2009. Another example, a little further south, is **Christ Church primary school**, a Church of England school the majority of whose pupils are Muslim; a hundred years ago they were mainly Jewish, as the Star of David on one of the drainpipes testifies.

LONDON'S JEWS

William the Conqueror invited the first **Jews** to England in 1066. After a period of relatively peaceful coexistence and prosperity, the small community increasingly found itself under attack, financially milked by successive monarchs and forced eventually to wear a distinguishing mark or *tabula* on their clothing. The Crusades whipped up further religious intolerance, the worst recorded incident taking place in 1189, when thirty Jews were killed by a mob during the coronation of Richard I. In 1278 Edward I imprisoned the entire community of around six hundred on a charge of "clipping coins" (debasing currency by shaving off bits of silver from coins), executing 267 at the Tower, and finally in 1290 expelling the rest.

For nearly four centuries thereafter, Judaism was outlawed in England. Sephardic (ie Spanish or Portuguese) Jews fleeing the Inquisition began arriving from 1540 onwards, though they had to become, or pretend to be, Christians until 1656, when Oliver Cromwell granted Jews the right to meet privately and worship in their own homes. The Jews who arrived immediately following this **Readmission** were in the main wealthy merchants, bankers and other businessmen. As a beacon of (relative) tolerance and economic prosperity, London quickly attracted further Jewish immigration by poorer Sephardi families and, increasingly, Ashkenazi settlers from eastern and central Europe.

By far the largest influx of **Ashkenazi Jews** arrived after fleeing pogroms that followed the assassination of the Russian Tsar Alexander II in 1881. The more fortunate were met by relatives at the Irongate Stairs by Tower Bridge; the rest were left to the mercy of the boarding-house keepers or, after 1885, found shelter in the Jewish Temporary Shelter. They found work in the sweatshops of the East End: cabinetmaking, shoemaking and, of course, tailoring – by 1901, over 45 percent of London's Jews worked in the garment industry.

Perhaps the greatest moment in Jewish East End history was the **Battle of Cable Street**, which took place on October 4, 1936, when Oswald Mosley and three thousand of his black-shirted fascists attempted to march through the East End. More than twice that number of police tried to clear the way for Mosley with baton charges and mounted patrols, but they were met with a barrage of bricks and stones from some one hundred thousand East Enders chanting the slogan of the Spanish Republicans: "*No pasaran*" (They shall not pass). Eventually the police chief halted the march – and another East End legend was born. A mural on the side of the old Shadwell town hall on Cable Street commemorates the event.

After World War II, more and more Jews moved out to the suburbs of North London, and the largest Orthodox Jewish communities are now to be found in Golders Green and Stamford Hill, with two hundred thousand Jews across the city as a whole.

CLOCKWISE FROM TOP LEFT SPITALFIELDS (P.189); SUNDAY MARKET STALL; CHRIST CHURCH (P.190); COLUMBIA ROAD (P.434) >

13

> ### HOXDITCH
>
> Ever since **Shoreditch** and **Hoxton** became trendy, there's been utter confusion over the name of the area. The problem is that Shoreditch was one of the boroughs that was swallowed up into Hackney, during the local government shake-up in 1965. The old borough of Shoreditch was made up of three main areas: Shoreditch, Hoxton and Haggerston. Strictly speaking, Shoreditch is south of Old Street, and Hoxton north of it, but you'll still find the *Hoxton Hotel* in Shoreditch and the Shoreditch Electric Light Station (now Circus Space) in Hoxton. And as for where Old Street fits into all this….

The Old Truman Brewery

Brick Lane • ⓦ trumanbrewery.com

A red-brick chimney halfway up Brick Lane heralds the **Old Truman Brewery**, founded back in 1666 and once the largest brewery in the world. It's now a creative centre for music, fashion, art and IT and forms the focal point of Brick Lane's current gentrification. In the brewery's **Dray's Lane**, the old stables have been turned into cafés and shops for independent designers and artists; on Sundays, market stalls fill the Up Market and Backyard Market buildings.

19 Princelet Street

Occasional open days • Free • ☏ 020 7247 5352, ⓦ 19princeletstreet.org.uk • ⊖ Liverpool Street

If you want to dig deeper into the area's past, try and visit on one of the open days at **19 Princelet St**, just off Brick Lane, where there's a permanent exhibition on Spitalfields' rich history of immigration – get there early, though, as it's always very popular. This beautifully preserved eighteenth-century silk-weavers' house also houses a wonderfully evocative former synagogue, built by Polish Jews in the 1860s and entirely hidden behind the Georgian facade. The attic was home to the mysterious real-life main character in Rachel Lichtenstein's *Rodinsky's Room* (see p.463).

Shoreditch

Home to artists, designers and architects, **Shoreditch**, to the north of Spitalfields, is now one of the city's most self-consciously artistic enclaves, despite its lack of obvious aesthetic charm. The centre of the area's transformation shifts with the vicissitudes of fashion, but **Redchurch Street**, off Shoreditch High Street, has as good a claim as any street right now. Over in the west, so many web-based companies have started up around **Old Street** tube that the area's main traffic interchange has been renamed "Silicon Roundabout". Shoreditch is, in fact, also rich in historical literary and artistic associations. Situated just outside the City, it was here that James Burbage established the country's **first public theatre** – called simply the Theatre – in 1576 (he later took it down and reassembled it on Bankside as the Globe). There are a couple of specific sights – the **Geffrye Museum** of period interiors and **Wesley's Chapel and House** – but the majority of folk come here for the area's **bars** (see p.391), **clubs** (see p.403) and **art galleries**, such as the David Adjaye-designed **Rivington Place** (ⓦ rivingtonplace.org), the first publicly funded, newly built art gallery for over forty years.

St Leonard's, Shoreditch

Mon–Fri noon–2pm • Free • ☏ 020 7739 2063, ⓦ shoreditchchurch.wordpress.com • ⊖ Old Street or Liverpool Street

The area's most prominent landmark is **St Leonard's**, the Neoclassical church designed by George Dance the Elder in 1740 and situated at the junction of Old Street, Shoreditch High Street and Kingsland Road. It's worth a look inside if you've ever seen the BBC sit-com *Rev*, which is filmed in the church, and also to admire the memorial to Elizabeth Benson on the southeast wall, which depicts two skeletons tearing at the Tree of Life.

Shoreditch Town Hall

380 Old St • ☎ 020 7739 6176, ⓦ shoreditchtownhall.org.uk • ⊖ Old Street

13

The former **Shoreditch Town Hall** is a self-confident Victorian edifice, now host to a whole number of events and exhibitions, particularly cabaret, theatre, comedy and dance, plus the stylish *Clove Club* restaurant (see p.377). The town hall's tower features Progress, torch and battleaxe in hand, and, in the pediment, Hope and Plenty, reclining beside the Shoreditch motto "More Light, More Power", adopted in recognition of the borough's progressive policy of creating power from rubbish incineration. The source of this power, the Shoreditch Electric Light Station, still stands on nearby **Hoxton Market**, sporting the wonderful motto *E pulvere lux et vis* (Out of the dust, light and power). The old refuse destructor now houses Circus Space (ⓦ thecircusspace.co.uk), the country's leading college for jugglers and acrobats.

Geffrye Museum

Kingsland Rd **Museum** Tues–Sat 10am–5pm, Sun noon–5pm • Free **Almshouse** First Sat and first & third Wed of month • £2.50 •
☎ 020 7739 9893, ⓦ geffrye-museum.org.uk • Hoxton Overground

Hoxton's chief attraction is the **Geffrye Museum**, housed in a grandiose enclave of eighteenth-century ironmongers' almshouses, set back from Kingsland Road. In 1911, at a time when the East End furniture trade was centred on Shoreditch, the almshouses were converted into a museum for the "education of craftsmen". The Geffrye remains, essentially, a furniture museum, with the almshouses rigged out as period living rooms of the urban middle class, ranging from the oak-panelled seventeenth century, through refined Georgian to cluttered Victorian. You'll also pass through the original central Georgian **chapel**, with its tiny Neoclassical apse and archetypal stone-coloured wood panelling; round the back of the chapel, an enclosed balcony overlooking the garden serves as a reading room.

Further on is the museum's twentieth-century **extension**, with four "snapshots in time", beginning with an Edwardian drawing room in understated Arts and Crafts style, and finishing off with a minimalist 1990s loft conversion. The extension also houses a pleasant licensed **café-restaurant**, serving inexpensive British food, and hosts excellent temporary exhibitions on the lower ground floor. Out the back, the **gardens** show the transition in horticultural tastes from the seventeenth-century knot gardens to today's patio garden, culminating in a pungent, walled **herb garden** (April–Oct only).

To get a feel of what the living conditions in the **almshouses** were like, one of them has been restored to its original condition and can now be visited on certain days (see above), though numbers are limited and visits are by timed entry only.

Wesley's Chapel and House

49 City Rd • Mon–Sat 10am–4pm, Sun 12.30–1.45pm • Free • ☎ 020 7253 2262, ⓦ wesleyschapel.org.uk • ⊖ Old Street

Striking an unusual note of calm on busy City Road is the largely Georgian ensemble of **Wesley's Chapel and House** set around a cobbled courtyard. A place of pilgrimage for Methodists from all over the world, the chapel was designed in 1778 by George Dance the Younger and heralded the coming-of-age of the followers of **John Wesley** (1703–91), who had started out in a small foundry east of the present building.

The **chapel** forms the centrepiece of the complex, though it is uncharacteristically ornate for a Methodist place of worship, with its powder-pink columns of French jasper and its superb, Adam-style gilded plasterwork ceiling, not to mention the colourful Victorian stained glass depicting, among other things, Wesley's night-time conversion, with his brother still in his dressing gown. The chapel has often attracted well-heeled weddings: one Margaret Hilda Roberts got married to divorcé Denis Thatcher here in 1951, and later paid for the new communion rail.

The **Museum of Methodism** (same hours) in the basement tells the story of Wesley and Methodism, and there's even a brief mention of Mrs Mary Vazeille, the

13

JOHN WESLEY AND METHODISM

The name "**Methodist**" was a term of abuse used by John Wesley's fellow Oxford students, because of the methodical way Wesley and his followers ordered their lives. However, it wasn't until his "conversion" at a Moravian prayer meeting in Aldersgate (marked by a large memorial outside the Museum of London) in 1738, that Wesley decided to become an independent field preacher. "I felt my heart strangely warmed" was his famous description of the experience. More verbal and even physical abuse followed during which Wesley was accused of being, among other things, a papist spy and an illegal gin distiller. Yet despite his lifelong dispute with the Anglican church, despite commissioning preachers, and bequeathing more than 350 Methodist chapels serving over 130,000 worshippers, Wesley himself never left the Church of England and died within it, urging his followers, where possible, to do the same.

41-year-old, insanely jealous, wealthy widow he married, and who eventually left him. Wesley himself lived his last two years in the Georgian **house** to the right of the main gates, and inside you can see bits of his furniture and his deathbed, plus an early shock-therapy machine with which he used to treat members of his congregation. Wesley's **grave** is round the back of the chapel, in the shadow of a modern office block.

Bunhill Fields

City Rd • April–Sept Mon–Fri 7.30am–7pm, Sat & Sun 9.30am–7pm; Oct–March closes 4pm • ⊖ Old Street

Appropriately enough, **Bunhill Fields**, the main burial ground for Dissenters or Nonconformists (practising Christians who were not members of the Church of England), lies across the road from Wesley's Chapel. Following bomb damage in the last war, most of the graveyard is fenced off, though you can still stroll through on the public footpaths under a canopy of giant London plane trees. The three most famous graves have been placed in the central paved area: the simple tombstone of poet and artist **William Blake** stands next to a replica of writer **Daniel Defoe**'s, while opposite lies the recumbent statue of **John Bunyan**, seventeenth-century author of *The Pilgrim's Progress*.

Whitechapel High Street and Road

Whitechapel High Street lies at the heart of the old East End, and – along with its extension, Whitechapel Road – follows the route of the old Roman road from London to Colchester. Starting in the west at Aldgate, the City's eastern gateway, the street is still a good barometer for the current East End and is worth a stroll for a glimpse of London that's only a stone's throw (and yet light years) from the City.

Whitechapel Art Gallery

77–82 Whitechapel High St • Wed–Sun 11am–6pm, Thurs until 9pm • Free • ☎ 020 7522 7888, ⓦ whitechapel.org • ⊖ Aldgate East

The East End institution that draws in more outsiders than any other is the **Whitechapel Art Gallery**, housed in a beautiful, crenellated 1899 Arts and Crafts building by Charles Harrison Townsend. The gallery's facade has been embellished with a smattering of gilded leaves by the sculptor Rachel Whiteread – cast from the original arts-and-craft Tree of Life reliefs on either side – while the gallery's extension to the east into a former library (doubling the gallery's size), sports a modern copper weathervane featuring the philosopher Erasmus seated backwards reading a book. The gallery was founded by one of the East End's many Victorian philanthropists, **Samuel Barnett**. His motives may have been dubious – "The principle of our work is that we aim at decreasing not suffering but sin", he once claimed – but the legacy of his good works is still discernible across the East End. The gallery now puts on innovative exhibitions of contemporary art, and has a great bookshop and café-restaurant.

East London Mosque

82–92 Whitechapel Rd • Mon–Fri 9am–10pm • Free • ☎ 020 7650 3000, ⓦ eastlondonmosque.org.uk • ⊖ Whitechapel

Whitechapel Road boasts the most visible symbol of Muslim presence in the East End, the **East London Mosque**, a gaudy red-brick 1980s building, with a golden dome and minarets, which seats five thousand. Its size completely overwhelms tiny **Fieldgate Street Great Synagogue**, dating from 1899, which lies behind the mosque, and is hemmed in on three sides by its neighbour.

Whitechapel Bell Foundry

33–34 Whitechapel Rd • Mon–Fri 9am–5pm • Free • Guided tours Sat 10am, 1.30 & 4pm; £12; no under-14s • ☎ 020 7247 2599, ⓦ whitechapelbellfoundry.co.uk • ⊖ Whitechapel

On the south side of the street, the **Whitechapel Bell Foundry** occupies the short terrace of Georgian houses on the corner of Fieldgate Street. Big Ben, the Liberty Bell, the Bow Bells and numerous English church bells (including those of Westminster Abbey) all hail from the foundry, established in 1570. Inside, there's a small exhibition on the history of the foundry, which is the oldest manufacturing company in the country.

Whitechapel Market

Mon–Sat 8am–6pm • ⊖ Whitechapel

Whitechapel Road widens halfway along, at the beginning of **Whitechapel Market**, once one of the largest hay markets in London, now given over to everything from nectarines to net curtains, and including a large number of stalls catering for the local Bangladeshi and Somali communities. In the 1890s, this was where casual workers used to gather to be selected for work in the local sweatshops, earning it the Yiddish nickname *Hazer Mark*, or "pig market". The sole reminder of those days is the Edward VII monument at the centre of the market, erected by the local Jewish community in 1911.

ANARCHISTS IN THE EAST END

Founded in 1886 by Charlotte Wilson and Prince Kropotkin, the **Freedom Press** (Mon–Sat noon–6pm, Sun noon–4pm; ☎ 020 7247 9249, ⓦ freedompress.org.uk; ⊖ Aldgate East), a small anarchist bookshop and printing press in Angel Alley, by the side of the Whitechapel Art Gallery, is the lone survivor of an East End tradition of radical politics that reached its height at the end of the nineteenth century. For a roll call of famous anarchists, check out the stainless-steel portrait gallery in Angel Alley. East End anarchism found a strong following among the Jewish community especially, and supporters of the *Arbeter Fraynd* newspaper (whose editor was the wonderfully named Rudolf Rocker) staged atheist demonstrations outside Orthodox synagogues on the Sabbath, as well as making other gestures like ostentatiously smoking and eating ham sandwiches. In 1907, delegates to the Fifth Congress of the Russian Social Democratic Labour Party staged a meeting on the corner of Fulbourne Street attended by, among others, Lenin, Stalin, Trotsky, Gorky, Litvinov and Rosa Luxembourg. The local Jubilee Street Anarchist Club later loaned £1700 to the Bolsheviks, and were paid back in full by the Soviet government after the revolution.

The event for which the anarchists are best remembered, however, is the **Siege of Sidney Street**, which took place in January 1911. A gun battle occurred after a routine police enquiry at the back of a jeweller's on Houndsditch, and left one Russian anarchist and three policemen dead. Over the next few weeks, all but three of the anarchist gang were arrested; following a tip-off, the three were eventually cornered in a building on Sidney Street. A further gun battle ensued: a detachment of Scots Guards and two cannons were deployed, and even the Home Secretary, Winston Churchill, put in an appearance. By lunchtime the house was in flames, leaving two charred bodies in the burnt-out shell. However, the ringleader, nicknamed Peter the Painter, vanished without trace, to join the likes of Jack the Ripper as an East End legend.

13

THE WHITECHAPEL MURDERS

In eight weeks between August and November 1888, five prostitutes were stabbed to death in and around Whitechapel. Few of the letters received by the press and police, which purported to come from the murderer, are thought to have been genuine (including the one which coined the nickname **Jack the Ripper**), and the murderer's identity remains a mystery to this day. At the time, it was assumed he was a Jew, probably a *shochet* (a ritual slaughterman), since the mutilations on the corpses were obviously carried out with some skill. The theory gained ground when the fourth victim was discovered outside the (predominantly Jewish) Working Men's Club off Commercial Road, and for a while it was dangerous for Jews to walk the streets at night for fear of reprisals.

Ripperologists have trawled through the little evidence there is to produce **numerous suspects**, none of whom can be conclusively proven guilty. The most celebrated suspect is the Duke of Clarence, eldest son of the future Edward VII, an easy if improbable target, since he was involved in a scandal involving a male brothel and was a well-known homosexual. Crime writer Patricia Cornwell spent over a million dollars trying (and failing) to prove conclusively that the Ripper was the painter Walter Sickert, who exhibited an unhealthy fascination with the murders. The man who usually tops the lists, however, was a cricket-playing barrister named Druitt whose body was found floating in the Thames some weeks after the last murder, though, as usual, there is no evidence linking him with any of them.

The one **positive outcome** of the murders was that they focused the attention of the rest of London on the squalor of the East End. Philanthropist Samuel Barnett, for one, used the media attention to press for improved housing, streetlighting and policing to combat crime and poverty in the area. Today, the murders continue to be exploited in gory, misogynistic detail by the likes of Madame Tussauds and the London Dungeon, while guided walks retracing the Ripper's steps set off every week throughout the year (see p.33).

Royal London Hospital Museum

Newark St · Tues–Fri 10am–4.30pm · Free · ☎ 020 7377 7608, ⓦ medicalmuseums.org · ⊖ Whitechapel

It was on the nearby Mile End Road that Joseph Merrick, better known as the **Elephant Man**, was discovered in a freak show in 1884 by Dr Treves, and subsequently admitted as a patient to the **Royal London Hospital** on Whitechapel Road. He remained there, on show as a medical freak, and was eventually allowed to live there until his death in 1890, at the age of just 27. There's an interesting twenty-minute documentary on Merrick, and a small section displaying, among other things, the veil and hat he wore, in the **Hospital Museum**, housed in the crypt of an old church on Newark Street. The museum also covers the history of the hospital and of nursing and medicine in general, with a section on Edith Cavell, who trained here before assisting Allied soldiers to escape from occupied Belgium; she was eventually arrested and shot as a spy by the Germans in 1915.

The Blind Beggar

337 Whitechapel Rd · Mon–Sat 11am–11pm, Sun noon–10.30pm · Free · ☎ 020 7347 6195, ⓦ theblindbeggar.com · ⊖ Whitechapel

At the eastern end of Whitechapel Road stands the handsome, gabled entrance to the former **Albion Brewery**, where the first bottled brown ale was produced in 1899. Next door is the former brewery tap, the **Blind Beggar**, the East End's most famous pub since March 9, 1966, when Ronnie Kray walked into the crowded bar and shot gangland rival George Cornell for calling him a "fat poof". This murder spelt the end of the infamous Kray Twins, Ronnie and Reggie, both of whom were sentenced to life imprisonment, though their well-publicized gifts to local charities created a Robin Hood image that still persists.

Bethnal Green and Bow

The East End spreads out east of Whitechapel into the districts of **Bethnal Green**, to the north, and **Bow**, to the east. The Mile End Road is just an extension of Whitechapel

Road, and easily explored on foot, but to reach more mainstream sights such as the **Museum of Childhood**, you'll need to hop on public transport.

Mile End Road

The **Mile End Road** is an extension of Whitechapel Road, and the westernmost section, known as the Mile End Waste, is punctuated at the western end by a bust, and at the eastern by a more dramatic statue, of William Booth, founder of the Salvation Army (see below). There are also two unusual architectural features worth mentioning nearby. The more surprising is the **Trinity Almshouses**, a quaint courtyard of cottages with a central chapel, built in 1695 for "Twenty-eight decay'd Masters and Commanders and the widows of such". Further up, on the same side of the street, stands a large Neoclassical former department store, sporting a central domed tower, its facade of Ionic half-columns sliced in two by a small two-storey shop (currently boarded up) that used to belong to a Jewish watchmaker called **Spiegelhalter**. This architectural oddity is the result of a dispute between Spiegelhalter and his affluent Gentile neighbour, Thomas Wickham, who was forced to build his new store around the watchmaker's shop after he refused to be bought out.

Ragged School Museum

46–50 Copperfield Rd · Wed & Thurs 10am–5pm, first Sun of month 2–5pm · Free · ☎ 020 8980 6405, ⓦ raggedschoolmuseum.org.uk · ➌ Mile End

South of the Mile End Road, on the bombed-out remains of Copperfield Road, the **Ragged School Museum** occupies a Victorian canalside warehouse originally used to store lime juice. Accommodating more than one thousand pupils from 1877 to 1908, this was the largest of London's numerous Ragged Schools, institutions that provided free education and two free meals daily to children with no means to pay the penny a week charged by most Victorian schools. This particular Ragged School was just one of innumerable projects set up by the East End's most irrepressible philanthropist, the diminutive and devout **Dr Thomas Barnardo**, whose tireless work for the children of the East End is the subject of the ground-floor exhibition. Upstairs, there's a reconstructed Victorian schoolroom, where period-dressed teachers, cane in hand, take today's schoolkids through the rigours of a Victorian lesson – the public can experience the same treatment on Sunday openings (2.15 & 3.30pm; £2 donation suggested). On the top floor you can see two contrasting mock-up kitchens from the 1890s and the 1950s. There are also further displays on the nearby docks and local sweatshops, and a canalside café back on the ground floor.

EAST END PHILANTHROPISTS

The poverty of the East End has attracted numerous philanthropists over the years, particularly during the Victorian era, from Dr Barnardo, of Ragged School fame, to Lady Burdett-Coutts, whose fountain still stands in Victoria Park. The most famous of the lot, however, was **William Booth** (1829–1912), a pawnbroker by trade and a Methodist lay preacher. One June evening in 1865, Booth was preaching to the crowds of revellers outside *The Blind Beggar*. Some fellow missioners were so impressed they asked him to lead a series of meetings in a tent they had set up on the Mile End Waste. Booth and his wife then set up the Christian Mission, which eventually led to the foundation, in 1878, of the quasi-military Christian movement known as the **Salvation Army**. In contrast to many Victorian philanthropists, Booth never accepted the divisive concept of the deserving and undeserving poor – "if a man was poor, he was deserving". Booth railed against the laissez-faire economic policies of his era, while attending to the immediate demands of the poor, setting up soup kitchens and founding hostels, which, by the time of his death in 1912, had spread right across the globe. Booth is buried in Abney Park Cemetery (see p.292).

13

Victoria Park

Grove Rd · Daily 6am–dusk · Cambridge Heath train station or Hackney Wick Overground; bus #277 from ⊖ Mile End or bus #8 from ⊖ Liverpool Street

London's first public park (as opposed to royal park) **Victoria Park** was opened in the heart of the East End in 1845, after a local MP presented Queen Victoria with a petition of thirty thousand signatures. The only large open space in the area, "Viccy Park" immediately became a favourite spot for **political rallies**: Chartists congregated here in their thousands in 1848; Suffragette supporters of the ELFS gathered here, under the leadership of Sylvia Pankhurst; it even had its own Speakers' Corner attended by the likes of George Bernard Shaw and William Morris. Since the Anti-Nazi League played here in 1978, it's probably more famous for its regular use for music festivals.

The world's oldest **model boat club**, the Victoria Model Steam Boat Club, founded in 1904, still meets on most summer Sunday mornings at the park's lakes. Look out, too, for the (replica) **Dogs of Alcibiades**, two snarling sculpted beasts based on the Molossian hounds kept by the Athenian statesman and presented by Lady Regnart in 1912. The much larger eastern section of the park contains an extraordinarily lavish Gothic-cum-Moorish **drinking fountain**, decorated with oversized cherubs and paid for by Baroness Burdett-Coutts in 1861 – it hasn't functioned for years. At the park's eastern edge are two alcoves from Old London Bridge, brought here in 1860.

Museum of Childhood

Cambridge Heath Rd · Daily 10am–5.45pm · Free · ☎ 020 8983 5200, ⓦ vam.ac.uk · ⊖ Bethnal Green

The elegant, open-plan wrought-iron hall that houses the **Museum of Childhood** was, in fact, part of the original V&A building, and was transported to the East End from South Kensington in the late 1860s in order to bring art to the poor. The emphasis has changed since those pioneering days, and although the wide range of exhibits means that there's something here for everyone, the museum's most frequent visitors are children, with plenty of hands-on exhibits and special kids' events at weekends and during school holidays.

To the right as you enter, are the clockwork and moving **toys** – bring your 20p pieces for the bigger exhibits – everything from classic robots to a fully functioning model railway, early computer games and wooden toys – there's often a queue for the replica Victorian rocking horse. At the back, the museum has a great collection of marionettes and puppets, which brings you into the doll and figures section, ranging from teddies and Smurfs to Inuit dolls. The most famous exhibits are the remarkable antique **dolls' houses** dating back to 1673: they are displayed upstairs, where you'll also find antique dolls and prams, a play area for very small kids, the ever-popular Wallace the Lion gobbling up the little schoolboy Albert, and a space for temporary exhibitions.

Olympic Park

ⓦ queenelizabetholympicpark.co.uk · ⊖ Stratford, Pudding Mill Lane DLR or Hackney Wick Overground

London is the only city in the world to have hosted the Olympics three times. In 1908, the city saved the day when Vesuvius erupted and Rome had to pull out as host. In 1948, London stepped in at short notice and staged the "Austerity Games", where the athletes were told to bring their own food and were put up in RAF camps. 2012 was an altogether more extravagant affair, with a total spend in excess of £9 billion. The focus of the 2012 Olympics was London's **Olympic Park** – officially now the Queen Elizabeth Olympic Park – situated in a most unlikely East End backwater, on a series of islands formed by the River Lee (or Lea) and various tributaries and canals. Since the Olympics, the whole area has been replanted with swathes of grass, trees and flowers making it a great new park in which to hang out on a sunny day. In addition, the park is also peppered with those Olympic venues that are set to stay put, plus a number of cafés to cater for passing visitors.

13

The centrepiece of the park is the **Olympic Stadium**, surrounded on three sides by the River Lee and the City Mill River; it seated eighty thousand for the Olympics, but the stadium is set to become home to West Ham United football club in 2015, with a reduced capacity of 56,000, but with retractable seating so it can still host athletics events, as well as live music. Standing close to the stadium, with a bird's-eye view of the whole site from its public observation deck, is the **Orbit** tower, a 377ft-high continuous loop of red recycled steel designed by Anish Kapoor, looking like a giant helter skelter (re-opening spring 2014). The most eye-catching Olympic venue is Zaha Hadid's wave-like **Aquatics Centre**, to the east, which cost four times its original estimate, and is expensive to maintain, but at least looks good. The other truly sexy building is the curvy **Velodrome**, with its banked, Siberian pine track and adjacent BMX circuit. At the western edge of the park, the **Copper Box** (used for handball during the Olympics) is now a multi-sports centre and events venue. Overlooking the whole site, the **Olympic Village** – now renamed East Village – at the eastern edge of the park, originally housed seventeen thousand athletes during the Games, and is now being converted into 2800 new homes.

Three Mills Island

A short walk south of the Olympic Park, along the River Lee, you can visit the eighteenth-century architectural ensemble of **Three Mills Island**, an artificial island in the Lee. Despite its name, there are now only two mills remaining, the most distinctive of which is the **Clock Mill**, with its conical oasts – kilns used to dry grain – and its pretty white clock tower.

House Mill

Three Mill Lane • May–Oct Sun 11am–4pm; March, April & Dec first Sun of month • £3 • ☎ 020 8980 4626, ⓦ housemill.org.uk • ⊖ Bromley-by-Bow

Opposite the Clock Mill stands the Dutch-style **House Mill**, built in 1776, around which you can take a guided tour, which explains the milling process and shows you the surviving mill wheels which were driven by the tide. Beyond the mills are later gin-distillery buildings, now converted into television and film studios. There's a café in the Miller's House (open when the House Mill is open and on weekdays).

Abbey Mills

Visible to the northeast of Three Mills Island is the modern **Abbey Mills Pumping Station**, sporting a gleaming metal pitched roof, and, adjacent, its much more famous Victorian predecessor, a glorious Gothic-Italianate edifice nicknamed the "Cathedral of Sewage". The latter was built in the 1860s by Joseph Bazalgette and Edwin Cooper, and was originally flanked by two twin chimneys decorated in Moorish style, which were sadly demolished during World War II. Visible to the southeast of Three Mills are seven ornate, wrought-iron **Victorian gasholders**, built on the site of a rocket factory set up in the 1820s by William Congreve.

Docklands

The architectural embodiment of smash-and-grab capitalism according to its critics or a blueprint for inner-city regeneration to its free-market supporters – the Docklands area has always provoked extreme reactions. Despite the catch-all name, however, Docklands is far from homogeneous. Canary Wharf, with its Manhattan-style skyscrapers, is the most visible landmark, but it's by no means typical; warehouse conversions, industrial-estate sheds, left-over council housing and Costa del Thames apartments in a whole travesty of styles, are more indicative. Travelling through on the Docklands Light Railway (DLR), the area comes over as a fascinating open-air design museum, not a place one would choose to live or work necessarily – it still feels apart from the rest of London – but a spectacular sight nevertheless.

From the sixteenth century onwards the **Port of London** was the trading lynchpin of the British Empire and the key to the city's wealth. The "legal quays" – roughly the area between London Bridge and the Tower – were crowded with as many as 1400 seagoing vessels forced to wait for up to six weeks to be unloaded, with some 3500 cutters, barges and punts jostling between their hulls. It was to relieve such congestion that, from 1802 onwards, London constructed the largest enclosed **cargo-dock system** in the world. Each dock was surrounded by 40ft-high walls, patrolled by its own police force and geared towards a specific cargo. Casual dockers gathered at the dock gates each morning for the "call-on", a human scrummage to get selected for work. This mayhem was only stopped after World War II, when the

Dock Labour Scheme was introduced, and by then it was too late. Since the mid-nineteenth century, competition from the railways eroded the river traffic, and with the development of container ships and the movement of the port to Tilbury in the 1960s, the old city docks began to wind down.

In 1981, the **London Docklands Development Corporation (LDDC)** was set up to regenerate the area, with the unfortunate slogan of "Looks like Venice, works like New York". By the time the LDDC was wound up in 1998, it had achieved more than many thought possible, though it's certainly easy to criticize its approach – ad hoc planning, and a lack of basic amenities, green spaces, civic architecture or public buildings, and consultation with the local community. Today, however, construction

DOCKLANDS

■ **ACCOMMODATION**
Four Seasons Hotel
Canary Wharf   1

● **CAFÉS**
Frizzante at Mudchute   3
Hubbub   2

● **RESTAURANT**
Mem Saheb on Thames   1

■ **PUBS**
The Grapes   1
The Gun   4
Prospect of Whitby   2
Town of Ramsgate   3

THE THAMES PATH

The **Thames Path** is a 184-mile National Trail that runs along, or close to, the riverbank of the Thames from its source to the Thames Barrier. The London section exists on both banks, and is clearly signposted, so you can **walk** the two miles from Tower Bridge, via Wapping and Limehouse to Canary Wharf. And if you're feeling really energetic, you can continue right round the Isle of Dogs to East India Dock near Trinity Buoy Wharf.

14

continues apace, with the end result destined to be, as one critic aptly put it, "a chain of highly polarized ghettos epitomizing the gulf between the rich and poor, home-owner and tenant". For the local community's views, visit ⓦwharf.co.uk.

Wapping

Once famous for its boatyards and its 36 riverside pubs (a handful of which remain), **Wapping** changed forever with the construction of the enclosed docks. Cut off from the East End by the high dock walls, its inhabitants crowded into unsanitary housing, the area became notorious for thieves, attracted by rolling drunk sailors and poorly guarded warehouses. With the destruction wrought during the Blitz and the commercial demise of the docks, Wapping was very rundown by the 1980s and an early candidate for Docklands regeneration. Restoration of existing property rather than demolition and redevelopment has been the rule, so much of Wapping's Victorian atmosphere remains, and, as it's only a short walk from the Tower, this is easily the most satisfying part of Docklands to explore.

St Katharine Docks

ⓦ skdocks.co.uk • ⊖ Tower Hill or Tower Gateway DLR

St Katharine Docks were built in the late 1820s – in the process some 11,300 people were made homeless, and the medieval hospital of St Katharine demolished. The docks specialized in luxury goods such as ivory, spices, carpets and cigars, but were very badly bombed in the Blitz and, in the early 1970s, were turned into a luxury yacht marina.

With little of the original warehouse architecture surviving, the docks' redeeming qualities are the old **swing bridges**, the one or two old sailing ships and Dutch barges that moor here, and the central **Ivory House** warehouse, with its clock tower and wrought-iron colonnade. Built in 1854, at its peak this warehouse received over 200 tons of ivory annually (that's four thousand dead elephants), plus hippopotamus and walrus teeth and even mammoth tusks from Siberia. Halfway along East Smithfield, you can see the original gates with elephants on the pillars, and on the corner of Thomas More Street, a section of the **original dock wall** survives, plus the main entrance to the former London Docks, with two Neoclassical Customs and Excise offices from 1805.

Dickens Inn, an eighteenth-century timber-framed brewery warehouse, was airlifted in 1969 from its original site several hundred yards to the east. At the centre of the docks is the ugly **Coronarium chapel** (now a *Starbucks*), built for Queen Elizabeth II's Silver Jubilee, and as near as possible to the church of St Katharine, which was owned by the Crown.

Tobacco Dock

East from St Katharine Docks down the busy Highway lies **Tobacco Dock**, a huge warehouse built in 1814 and initially used to store tobacco and wine. A fascinating combination of timber and early cast-iron framing, it was converted into a shopping complex in 1990 by postmodernist Terry Farrell, but the place closed soon afterwards and has been a dead mall for decades now. On the south of Tobacco Dock, a tree-lined **canal walk** – all that remains of the huge Western Dock that once stood here – will take you effortlessly down to Wapping High Street.

St George-in-the-East

The Highway • Daily 8am–6pm • ☎ 020 7481 1345, ⓦ stgite.org.uk • Shadwell DLR

Nicholas Hawksmoor's church of **St George-in-the-East**, built in 1726, stands on the north side of the busy Highway. As bold as any of Hawksmoor's buildings, it boasts four "pepperpot" towers above the nave, built to house the staircases to the church's galleries, and a hulking west-end tower topped by an octagonal lantern. Within, it comes as something of a shock to find a miniature modern church squatting in the nave, but that's all the parish could come up with following the devastation of the Blitz.

14

Wapping High Street

If you arrive on **Wapping High Street** expecting the usual parade of shops, you're in for a big surprise. Traditionally, the business of Wapping took place on the river; thus tall brick-built warehouses, most now converted into flats, line the Thames side of the street, while to the north – in a stark contrast typical of Docklands – lie the council estates of the older residents. (Alf Garnett, the dockworker of the 1960s BBC comedy *Till Death Us Do Part*, lived here.) Few tourists make it out here, but it's only a ten-minute walk from St Katharine Docks, and well worth the effort.

Five minutes' walk along the High Street will bring you to **Wapping Pier Head**, former entrance to the London Docks, now grassed over but still flanked by grand, curvaceous Regency terraces built for the officials of the Dock Company (and now home to celebrities such as Helen Mirren). Further east is the unusual neo-Gothic former tea warehouse, **Oliver's Wharf**, a trailblazing apartment conversion from 1972, with a couple of preserved overhead gangways crossing the High Street just beyond. You'll also find one of the few surviving stairs down to the river beside the *Town of Ramsgate* pub (see p.392); beneath the pub are the dungeons where convicts were chained before being deported to Australia.

Wapping Police Station

Further along the High Street from Oliver's Wharf stands **Wapping Police Station**, headquarters of the world's oldest uniformed police force, the Marine Police, founded in 1798 and now a subdivision of the Met. The police boatyard is a 1960s building which features funky, abstract, vertical fibreglass friezes. Down by the riverside here, at the low-water mark, was **Execution Dock**, where for four centuries pirates, smugglers and mutineers were hanged and left dangling until three tides had washed over them – the worst offenders were then tarred and gibbeted further downstream. The most famous felon to perish here was Captain Kidd, pirate-catcher-turned-pirate, hanged in 1701, and left gibbeted in an iron cage by the Thames for twenty years; the last victims were executed for murder and mutiny in 1830.

Wapping Wall

Beyond Wapping station, along **Wapping Wall**, you'll find the finest collection of nineteenth-century warehouses left in the whole of Docklands, beginning with the gargantuan Metropolitan Wharf, its wrought-iron capstan cranes and pulleys still clearly in evidence. At the far end of Wapping Wall is the venerable *Prospect of Whitby* pub (see p.392), and, opposite, the ivy-clad red-brick **London Hydraulic Pumping Station**, built in the 1890s and once chief supplier of hydraulic power to the whole of central London; it now houses **The Wapping Project**, a restaurant and art gallery (ⓦ thewappingproject.com), which puts on occasional exhibitions.

Shadwell Basin

Shadwell Basin, over the swing bridge to the north of the Pumping Station, is one of the last remaining stretches of water that once comprised three interlocking docks, known simply as London Docks and first opened in 1805. Now a watersports centre, it's enclosed on three sides by characteristically gimmicky new housing finished off in primary reds and blues. Rising up majestically behind the houses to the north is **St Paul's** (ⓦstpaulsshadwell.org), the "sea captains' church", with a Baroque tower.

Limehouse

14

East of Wapping, **Limehouse** was a major shipbuilding centre in the eighteenth and nineteenth centuries, hub of London's canal traffic and the site of the city's first **Chinatown**, a district sensationalized in Victorian newspapers as a warren of opium and gambling dens, and by writers such as Oscar Wilde, Arthur Conan Doyle, Sax Rohmer and Dickens: "Down by the docks the shabby undertaker's shop will bury you for next to nothing, after the Malay or Chinaman has stabbed you for nothing at all." Wartime bombing and postwar road schemes all but obliterated Limehouse: the only remnants of the Chinese community are the street names: Canton, Mandarin, Ming and Pekin among them. London's contemporary Chinatown is in Soho (see p.98). **Narrow Street**, the main thoroughfare, is sleepier than Wapping High Street, and famous primarily for its pub *The Grapes*, currently owned by the actor Ian McKellen. On the shoreline (and visible from the pub terrace) is one of Antony Gormley's statues, who is standing on a mooring pile and appears to be walking on water at high tide.

St Anne's Church

Newell St · Open for Sun service 10.30am · ☎ 020 7987 1502, ⓦ stanneslimehouse.org · Limehouse DLR

Limehouse's major landmark is Hawksmoor's **St Anne's Church**, rising up just north of the DLR viaduct. Begun in 1714, and dominated by a gargantuan west tower, topped by an octagonal lantern, it boasts the highest church clock in London. The interior was badly damaged by fire in 1850, though it does contain a superb organ built for the Great Exhibition the following year. In the graveyard Hawksmoor erected a pyramidal structure carved with masonic symbols, now hopelessly eroded; opposite is a war memorial with relief panels depicting the horrors of trench warfare.

Limekiln Dock

A pedestrian bridge carries the Thames Path over the entrance to Limehouse Basin and then the tidal inlet of **Limekiln Dock**, overlooked to the north by a picturesque gaggle of listed warehouses, and to the south by the gargantuan Dundee Wharf development, sporting a huge grey freestanding pylon of balconies. Beyond lies the mock-Egyptian development that houses the *Four Seasons Hotel* (see p.360). The Thames Path eventually ploughs its way right round the Isle of Dogs, but for now it's still a bit stop-start once you get past Canary Wharf Pier.

Isle of Dogs

A whole people toil at the unloading of the enormous ships, swarming on the barges, dark figures, dimly outlined, moving rhythmically, fill in and give life to the picture. In the far distance, behind the interminable lines of sheds and warehouses, masts bound the horizon, masts like a bare forest in winter, finely branched, exaggerated, aerial trees grown in all the climates of the globe. Gabriel Mourey (1865–1943)

The Thames begins a dramatic horseshoe bend at Limehouse, thus creating the **Isle of Dogs**. The origin of the peninsula's strange name has been much debated: a corruption of ducks, or of dykes, or, in fact, a reference to the royal kennels which once stood here. In 1802, London's first enclosed trade docks were built here to accommodate rum and sugar from the West Indies. The demise of the docks was slow in coming, but rapid in its conclusion: in 1975, there were still eight thousand jobs; five years later they were closed. Now at the heart of the new Docklands, the Isle of Dogs reaches its apotheosis in the skyscrapers of **Canary Wharf**. Yet while some ninety thousand workers trek to Canary Wharf each weekday, the rest of the "island" remains surreally lifeless, an

TRAINS, BOATS AND (SORT OF) PLANES – A TOUR OF DOCKLANDS

The best, all-weather way to get a sense of the scale and architecture of Docklands is to use the driverless, mostly elevated **Docklands Light Railway** or DLR. Arriving by DLR at Canary Wharf (from Bank or Tower Hill) is particularly spectacular, with the rail line cutting right through the middle of the office buildings, spanned by Cesar Pelli's parabolic steel-and-glass canopy. At this point, you could switch to Canary Wharf's **tube station**, which has its Norman Foster-designed, stingray-like entrance on West Plaza, amidst a forest of public clocks, and take the tube one stop to North Greenwich, home of the Dome (or O2).

From close to the Dome, you can leap aboard the most recent (and unusual) addition to London's transport system, the £60 million Emirates Air Line, a Swiss-built **cable car** (Mon–Fri 7am–9pm, Sat 8am–9pm, Sun 9am–9pm; £3.20 single with Oyster card), which will whisk you silently over the River Thames to the **Royal Docks**, the last remaining swathe of Docklands that has yet to be fully developed. Take the return trip to North Greenwich, and you can catch a **boat** into central London and enjoy a great river view of Docklands and Greenwich.

14

uneasy, socially divided community comprised of drab council housing, encompassed by a horseshoe of crass, super-rich, riverside developments.

Canary Wharf

The strip of land in the middle of the former West India Docks, **Canary Wharf** was originally a destination for rum and mahogany, and later tomatoes and bananas (from the Canary Islands, hence the name). It's the easiest bit of the Isle of Dogs to explore on foot, though the whole place feels a bit like a stage-set, a spotlessly clean business quarter policed by security guards, with make-believe streets like Wren Steps and Chancellor Passage. The most famous building is Cesar Pelli's 800ft-high stainless-steel **Canary Wharf Tower** (closed to the public) – the highest building in the country for two decades after it was completed in 1991. Officially known as One Canada Square, the tower is flanked by Norman Foster's HSBC and Pelli's Citigroup skyscrapers, both of which are 656ft high, glass-clad and rather dull.

West India Quay and around

North of Cabot Square, you can cross a floodlit floating bridge to **West India Quay**, probably the most pleasing development on the Isle of Dogs. Here, two Georgian warehouses (out of nine) have survived and now house flats, bars, restaurants and the Museum of London Docklands (see p.212). On the water, among other boats, is London's only floating church, **St Peter's Barge** (talks Wed & Thurs lunchtime & services on Sun), a Dutch freight barge that's run by St Anne's Church, Limehouse (see opposite).

Immediately to the west of the warehouses is the old entrance to the West India Docks, heralded by the **Ledger Building** (now a pub), which sports a dinky Doric portico and, round the corner, a splendidly pompous plaque commemorating the opening of the docks from 1800. Opposite, across Hertsmere Road, stands a small, circular, domed building, the lone survivor of two guardhouses that flanked the main entrance to the docks; behind it lies the former cooperage, now the **Cannon Workshops**.

To the northeast, behind the Ledger Building, are more little-known remnants of the old docks, among them the stately **Dockmaster's House**, built in 1809 as the Excise Office and now a restaurant, with a smart white balustrade. Behind here, on Garford Street, there's a prim row of **Dock Constables' Cottages**, built in pairs in 1802, with the one for the sergeant slightly detached. Before you reach them, you'll pass **Grieg House**, a lovely yellow-and-red-brick building, built in 1903 as part of the Scandinavian Seamen's Temperance Home, with a little cupola and lovely exterior mouldings.

> *Nothing will convey to the stranger a better idea of the vast activity and stupendous wealth of London than a visit to these warehouses, filled to overflowing with interminable stores of every kind of foreign and colonial products; to these enormous vaults, with their apparently inexhaustible quantities of wine; and to these extensive quays and landing-stages, cumbered with huge stacks of hides, heaps of bales, and long rows of casks…Those who wish to taste the wines must procure a tasting-order from a wine merchant. Ladies are not admitted after 1pm. Visitors should be on their guard against insidious effects of "tasting" in the heavy, vinous atmosphere.*   Baedeker's Handbook for London (1905)

Museum of London Docklands

West India Quay • Daily 10am–6pm • Free • ☎ 020 7001 9844, ⓦ museumoflondon.org.uk/docklands/ • West India Quay DLR

If you've any interest in the history of the docks or the Thames, then a visit to the **Museum of London Docklands** is well worth it. Housed in a warehouse built in 1803 for storing rum, sugar, molasses, coffee and cotton, the museum takes a chronological approach, beginning on the top floor, where you'll find a great model of old London Bridge, one side depicting it around 1450, the other around 1600. Also here is the Rhinebeck Panorama, an 8ft-long watercolour showing the "legal quays" in the 1790s, just before the enclosed docks were built. On the floor below are diverse sections on slavery, frost fairs and whaling, a reconstructed warren of late nineteenth-century shops and cobbled streets called "Sailortown", plus mock-ups of a cooperage, a bottling vault and a tobacco-weighing office. Look out, too, for the model of Brunel's *Leviathan*, the fascinating wartime film reel and the excellent even-handed coverage of the docks' postwar history. Those with kids should head for Mudlarks (daily 2–5.30pm; school holidays 10am–5.30pm), where children can learn a bit about pulleys and ballast, drive a DLR train or just romp around the soft play area.

Westferry Road

Points of interest elsewhere on the Isle of Dogs are few and far between, but one or two monuments are worth pointing out around Westferry Road. One of Docklands' more playful monuments is Pierre Vivant's **Traffic Light Tree**, west of Heron Quays, at the top of Westferry Road, which features a cluster of traffic signals all flashing madly – a strangely confusing sight for drivers after dark. Impossible to miss, to the southwest, is **Cascades**, a wedge of high-rise triangular apartments that's become something of a Docklands landmark. Equally unavoidable is **Millennium Harbour**, a gated development whose weatherboarded top-floor penthouses jut out like air-traffic-control towers.

Burrell's Wharf

At the southern end of Westferry Road, you come to **Burrell's Wharf**, a residential development based around the industrial relics of the old Millwall Ironworks, built in the 1830s. The boiler-house chimney survives, as does the Italianate Plate House, where the steel plates for Isambard Kingdom Brunel's 19,000-ton steamship, the *Great Eastern* (aka the *Leviathan*), were manufactured. Built at a cost of £1 million, the *Leviathan* was four times larger than any other ship in the world at the time, but enjoyed a working life of just sixteen years as a passenger liner and cable-layer. The timber piles of the ship's 1857 launching site can still be seen, a little further upstream.

Mudchute and Island Gardens

In the southeast corner of the Isle of Dogs is a hilly area called **Mudchute**, where the soil from digging out the nearby Millwall Docks was dumped in the 1860s. It's now home to **Mudchute City Farm** (see p.442), one of the largest in Europe, with a great café to boot (see p.379). From Mudchute, the DLR goes directly under the river to

Greenwich, but it's worth considering getting out at **Island Gardens**, in the far south of the Isle of Dogs. From the eponymous park here, Christopher Wren used to contemplate his masterpieces, the Royal Naval College and the Royal Observatory, and you, too, can do the same, before heading across the river via the 1902 **Greenwich Foot Tunnel**.

Trinity Buoy Wharf

64 Orchard Wharf • ☎ 020 7515 7153, ⓦ trinitybuoywharf.com • Longplayer Sat & Sun: April–Sept 11am–5pm; Oct–March closes 4pm; free • ⓦ longplayer.org • East India DLR or boat from the O2 QEII Pier (Mon–Fri 5am–8pm; £2)

14

Hidden to the east of East India Dock is the bizarre little enclave of **Trinity Buoy Wharf**. Built in 1803, it is home to London's only lighthouse, one of a pair built by Trinity House for experiments in optics and used by, among others, Michael Faraday. The wharf also houses offices, artist studios and flats, built out of old shipping containers, an original 1940s American mobile diner where you can get a bite to eat, and a whole array of boats. In the lighthouse itself, there's a musical installation called **Longplayer**, a twenty-minute recording of Tibetan singing bowls, manipulated to create a one thousand-year-long loop, and due to play until December 31, 2999. The wharf is a ten-minute walk from East India DLR station, at the end of Orchard Place, where the Bow Creek (part of the River Lee) winds its way into the Thames.

The South Bank

The South Bank has a lot going for it. As well as the massive waterside arts centre, it's home to a host of tourist attractions including the enormously popular London Eye, Europe's largest observation wheel, the London Aquarium and, further south, the Imperial War Museum, which harbours the country's only permanent exhibition devoted to the Holocaust. With most of London's major sights sitting on the north bank of the Thames, the views from here are the best on the river, and thanks to the wide, traffic-free riverside boulevard, the area can be happily explored on foot. Buskers congregate here to entertain the crowds, and for much of the year there's some kind of outdoor festival going on along the riverbank. You can continue your wanderings eastwards along the riverside towards Tate Modern and the regenerated districts of Bankside and Southwark (see p.223).

For centuries London stopped southwards at the Thames; the South Bank was a marshy, uninhabitable place, a popular place for duck-shooting, but otherwise seldom visited. Then, in the eighteenth century, wharves began to be built along the riverbank, joined later by factories, so that by 1905 the Baedeker guidebook characterized **Lambeth** and Southwark as "containing numerous potteries, glass-works, machine-factories, breweries and hop-warehouses". Slums and overhead railway lines added to the grime until 1951, when a slice of Lambeth's badly bombed riverside was used as a venue for the Festival of Britain, the site eventually evolving into the **Southbank Centre**, a vibrant arts complex, encased in an unlovely concrete shell. What helped kick-start the South Bank's more recent rejuvenation was the arrival of the spectacular **London Eye**, and the renovation of **Hungerford Bridge**, which is now flanked by a majestic symmetrical double-suspension footbridge, called the Golden Jubilee Bridges. To get the local view on the area and find out about the latest events on the South Bank (and in neighbouring Southwark), visit ⓦlondon-se1.co.uk.

Southbank Centre

15

ⓦ southbankcentre.co.uk

In 1951, the South Bank Exhibition, on derelict land south of the Thames, formed the centrepiece of the national **Festival of Britain**, an attempt to boost postwar morale by celebrating the centenary of the Great Exhibition (when Britain really did rule over half the world). The most striking features of the site were the Ferris wheel (now reincarnated as the London Eye), the saucer-shaped Dome of Discovery (inspiration for the Millennium Dome), the Royal Festival Hall (which still stands) and the cigar-shaped steel and aluminium Skylon tower.

The great success of the festival eventually provided the impetus for the creation of the **Southbank Centre** comprising the Royal Festival Hall, Queen Elizabeth Hall, the Purcell Room and the Hayward Gallery, all squeezed between Hungerford and Waterloo bridges. Unfortunately, however, it failed to capture the imagination of the public in the same way, and became London's much unloved culture bunker. The low point came in the 1980s when hundreds of homeless lived under the complex in a "Cardboard City". Since then, there have been considerable improvements, and the centre's unprepossessing appearance is softened, too, by its riverside location, its avenue of trees, fluttering banners, regular "pop up" festivals and food stalls, occasional buskers and skateboarders, and the weekend secondhand bookstalls outside nearby BFI Southbank. The nearest tube is Waterloo, but the most pleasant way to **approach** the Southbank Centre is via Hungerford Bridge from Embankment or Charing Cross tube.

Royal Festival Hall

Southbank Centre • Poetry Library Tues–Sun 11am–8pm • Free • ⓦ poetrylibrary.org.uk • ⊖ Waterloo

The only building left from the 1951 Festival of Britain is the **Royal Festival Hall** or RFH, one of London's main concert venues, whose auditorium is suspended above the open-plan foyer – its curved roof is clearly visible above the main body of the building. The interior furnishings remain fabulously period, and exhibitions and free events in the foyer – the **Clore Ballroom** – are generally excellent, making this one of the most pleasant South Bank buildings to visit. You can also kill time before a concert in the little-known **Poetry Library** on Level 5, where you can either browse or, by joining (membership is free), borrow from the library's vast collection of poetry accumulated since 1912.

Queen Elizabeth Hall and Hayward Gallery

Hayward Gallery Mon noon–6pm, Tues, Wed, Sat & Sun 10am–6pm, Thurs & Fri 10am–8pm • From £10 • ☎ 020 7960 4200 • ⊖ Waterloo

Architecturally, the most depressing parts of the Southbank Centre are the **Queen Elizabeth Hall** (QEH) and the more intimate **Purcell Room**, which share the same foyer

SOUTH BANK

● SHOPS		◆ CAFÉ		■ ACCOMMODATION		● PUBS AND BARS	
Gramex	3	Marsh Ruby	2	Captain Bligh House	4	Anchor & Hope	3
Konditor & Cook	2	● RESTAURANTS		Mad Hatter	1	The Cut Bar	4
South Bank Book Market	1	Laughing Gravy	1	Stamford Street		Kings Arms	2
What the Butler Wore	4	Masters Super Fish	3	Apartments	2	■ MUSIC VENUE	
				Tune Westminster	3	Southbank Centre	1

and are built in uncompromisingly brutalist 1960s style. Immediately above, and equally stark from the outside, is the **Hayward Gallery**, a large and flexible art gallery that puts on temporary art exhibitions, mostly (but not exclusively) modern or contemporary art. Not surprisingly then, there are currently £120-million plans afoot to transform this area into a new **Festival Wing**, with more cafés, a rooftop garden and clearer access from the rest of the centre.

Waterloo Bridge to Blackfriars Bridge

Waterloo Bridge, famous for being built mostly by women during World War II, marks the eastern limit of the Southbank Centre, but the next stretch of riverside to Blackfriars Bridge has cultural attractions of its own: from the city's leading arts cinema, **BFI Southbank**, to the retail-workshops of the renovated **Oxo Tower**. The bridge itself was the scene of the **assassination** of Georgi Markov, a Bulgarian dissident working at the BBC World Service, in 1978. He was shot in the leg with a ricin pellet fired from an umbrella by a member of the Bulgarian secret police and died three days later.

15

BFI Southbank

Belvedere Rd • Mediathèque Tues–Fri noon–8pm, Sat & Sun 12.30–8pm • Free • ☎ 020 7928 3232, ⓦ bfi.org.uk • ⊖ Waterloo

Tucked underneath Waterloo Bridge is **BFI Southbank**, which screens London's most esoteric films, hosts a variety of talks, lectures and mini-festivals and also runs **Mediathèque**, where you can settle into one of the viewing stations and choose from a selective archive of British films, TV programmes and documentaries. The BFI also runs the **BFI IMAX**, housed within the eye-catching glass drum, which rises up from the old "Bull Ring" beneath the roundabout at the southern end of Waterloo Bridge. Boasting the largest screen in the country, it's definitely worth experiencing a 3D film here at least once.

National Theatre

South Bank • Backstage tours Mon–Fri 6 daily, Sat 2 daily, Sun 1 daily; 1hr 15min • £8.50 • ☎ 020 7452 3400, ⓦ nationaltheatre.org.uk • ⊖ Waterloo

Just east of Waterloo Bridge, looking like a multistorey car park, is Denys Lasdun's **National Theatre** (officially the Royal National Theatre). An institution first mooted in 1848, it was only finally realized in 1976, and, like the Southbank Centre, its concrete brutalism tends to receive a lot of critical flak, with Prince Charles likening it to a nuclear power station. That said, the three auditoriums within are superb (see p.418), and the **backstage tours** here are excellent and popular, so book in advance if possible.

Gabriel's Wharf

East of the National Theatre, the riverside promenade brings you eventually to **Gabriel's Wharf**, an ad hoc collection of lock-up craft shops, brasseries and bars that has a small weekend craft market. It's a refreshing change from the franchises which have colonized much of the South Bank, and one for which **Coin Street Community Builders** (CSCB; ⓦ coinstreet.org) must be thanked. With the population in this bomb-damaged stretch of the South Bank down from fifty thousand at the beginning of the century to four thousand in the early 1970s, big commercial developers were keen to step in and build hotels and office blocks galore. They were successfully fought off, and instead the emphasis has been on projects that combine commercial and community interests.

OXO Tower

South Bank • **Exhibition Gallery** Daily 11am–6pm • Free • **Public viewing gallery** Daily 10am–10pm • Free • ⊖ Blackfriars

East of Gabriel's Wharf stands the landmark **OXO Tower**, an old power station that was converted into a meat-packing factory in the late 1920s by Liebig Extract of Meat Company, best known in Britain as the makers of OXO stock cubes. To get round the local council's ban on illuminated advertisements, the company cleverly incorporated the letters into the windows of the main tower, and then illuminated them from within. Now, thanks again to CSCB, the building contains an exhibition gallery on the ground floor, plus flats for local residents and a series of retail-workshops for designers on the first and second floors, and a swanky restaurant, bar and brasserie on the top floor. To enjoy the view, however, you don't need to eat or drink here: you can simply take the lift to the eighth-floor **public viewing gallery**.

Waterloo Station

Built in 1848, **Waterloo Station** is easily the capital's busiest train and tube station, serving the city's southwestern suburbs and the southern Home Counties. Its two finest features are easily missed: the station's ornate Edwardian-style facade is hidden behind the railway bridge on Mepham Street, while the snake-like, curving roof of the former Eurostar terminal, designed by Nicholas Grimshaw in 1993, is tucked away on the west side of the station.

Without doubt Waterloo's most bizarre train terminus was the former **London Necropolis Station**, whose early twentieth-century facade survives at 121 Westminster Bridge Rd, to the south of the station. Opened in 1854 following one of London's worst outbreaks of cholera, trains from this station took coffins and mourners to Brookwood Cemetery in Surrey (at the time, the world's largest cemetery). Brookwood Station even had separate platforms for Anglicans and Nonconformists and a licensed bar – "Spirits served here", the sign apparently read – but the whole operation was closed down after bomb damage in World War II.

Heading west from the main station concourse, an overhead walkway heads off to the South Bank, passing through the Stalinist-looking **Shell Centre**. Officially and poetically entitled the Downstream Building, it was built in the 1950s – and was the tallest building in London at the time – by oil giant Shell, which started life as a Jewish East End business importing painted seashells in 1833. Shell have recently sold the building on, and the main tower is set to be at the centre of a new high-rise housing development, partly Qatari-funded and due for completion in 2019.

London Eye

Daily April–June 10am–9pm; July & Aug 10am–9.30pm; Sept–March 10am–8.30pm • From £17 online • ☎ 0871 781 3000, Ⓦ londoneye.com • ➾ Waterloo or Westminster

Despite only gracing the skyline for a decade or so, the **London Eye** has secured its place as one of the city's most famous landmarks. Standing an impressive 443ft high, it's the tallest Ferris wheel in Europe, weighing over 2000 tons, yet as simple and delicate as a bicycle wheel. It's constantly in slow motion, which means a full-circle "flight" in one of its 32 pods (one for each of the city's boroughs) should take around thirty minutes – that may seem a long time, though in fact it passes incredibly quickly. Not surprisingly, you can see right out to the very edge of the city – bring some binoculars if you can – where the suburbs slip into the countryside, making the wheel one of the few places (apart from the Shard or a plane) from which London looks a manageable size. Book online (to save money) – on arrival, you'll still have to queue to be loaded on unless you've paid extra for fast track – or you'll have to buy your ticket from the box office at the eastern end of County Hall.

County Hall

Ⓦ londoncountyhall.com

The colonnaded crescent of **County Hall** is the only truly monumental building on the South Bank. Designed to house the London County Council, it was completed in 1933 and enjoyed its greatest moment of fame in the 1980s as the headquarters of the GLC (Greater London Council), under the Labour leadership of Ken Livingstone, or "Red Ken", as the right-wing press called him at the time. The Tories moved in swiftly, abolishing the GLC in 1986, and leaving London as the only European city without an elected authority. In 2000, Livingstone had the last laugh when he became London's first popularly elected mayor, and head of the new Greater London Authority (GLA), housed in City Hall, near Tower Bridge. The building's tenants are constantly changing, but it's currently home to, among other things, several hotels and restaurants, an aquarium and an amusement arcade. None of the attractions that have gravitated here is an absolute must, and several have fallen by the wayside, but they prosper (as do the numerous buskers round here) by feeding off the vast captive audience milling around the London Eye.

London Aquarium

County Hall • Mon–Thurs 10am–6pm, Fri–Sun 10am–7pm • From around £21 online • Snorkelling with Sharks daily 11.30am, 1.30 & 3.30pm; £125 • ☎ 0871 663 1678, ⓦ visitsealife.com/London • ⊖ Waterloo or Westminster

The most enduring County Hall tenant is the **Sea Life London Aquarium**, housed in the basement across three subterranean levels. With some super-large tanks, and everything from dog-face puffers and piranhas to robot fish (seriously) and crocodiles, this is an attraction that's pretty much guaranteed to please kids, albeit at a price (book online to save a few quid and avoid queuing, or save over a fiver by buying an after 3pm ticket). Impressive in scale, the aquarium boasts a thrilling Shark Walk, in which you have sharks swimming underneath you, as well as a replica blue whale skeleton encasing an underwater walkway. Ask at the main desk or check the website for details of the daily presentations and feeding times and if money's no object and fear's not in your vocabulary, enquire about the Snorkelling with Sharks Experience.

15

London Dungeon

County Hall • Mon–Wed & Fri 10am–5pm, Thurs 11am–5pm, Sat & Sun 10am–6pm; school holidays closes 7pm • From £22 online • ☎ 0871 423 2240, ⓦ thedungeons.com • ⊖ Waterloo or Westminster

The latest venture to join in the shenanigans at County Hall is the **London Dungeon**, a Gothic horror-fest that remains one of the city's major crowd-pleasers – to shorten the amount of time spent queuing (and save money), buy your ticket online. Young teenagers and the credulous probably get the most out of the various ludicrous live action scenarios, each one hyped up by the team of ham actors dressed in period garb. These are followed by a series of fairly lame horror rides such as "Henry's Wrath Boat Ride" and "Drop Dead Drop Ride", not to mention the latest "Jack the Ripper" experience.

London Film Museum

County Hall • Mon–Wed & Fri 10am–5pm, Thurs 11am–5pm, Sat 10am–6pm, Sun 11am–6pm • £13.50 • ☎ 020 7202 7040, ⓦ londonfilmmuseum.com • ⊖ Waterloo or Westminster

The **London Film Museum** occupies a labyrinth of rooms on the first floor of County Hall. It's not a particularly hi-tech exhibition, so the main draw is really the vast array of props and costumes from Hollywood franchises like *Alien*, *Star Wars* and *Batman*. And there's a firmly British bent to the place, with each exhibit chosen either because the studio, the designer, the writer or the director was a Brit. Appropriately enough, there's a whole section on Charlie Chaplin, a local Lambeth boy born in the borough in 1889, and naturally enough there's a room of Harry Potter props, from the Tri-Wizard Cup to Hogwarts school uniforms. The museum also regularly features special exhibitions on recent film releases with a British connection.

North Lambeth

South of Westminster Bridge, you leave the South Bank proper behind (and at the same time lose the crowds) and head upstream to what used to be the village of Lambeth (now a large borough stretching south to Brixton and beyond). Vestiges of village atmosphere are notably absent, although **Lower Marsh** with its weekday market and **The Cut** retain a local feel and have avoided the plague of the franchises that characterizes the South Bank. A few minor sights are worth considering, such as **Lambeth Palace** and the **Garden Museum**, and it's from this stretch of the riverbank that you get the best views of the Houses of Parliament. Inland lies London's most even-handed military museum, the **Imperial War Museum**, which has a moving permanent exhibition devoted to the Holocaust.

Florence Nightingale Museum

Lambeth Palace Rd · Daily 10am–5pm · £5.80 · ☎ 020 7620 0374, ⓦ florence-nightingale.co.uk · ⊖ Lambeth North, Waterloo or Westminster

On the south side of Westminster Bridge, a series of red-brick Victorian blocks and modern white accretions make up **St Thomas' Hospital**, founded in the twelfth century, but only established here after being ejected from its original location by London Bridge in 1862, when the railway came sweeping through Southwark. At the hospital's northeastern corner, off Lambeth Palace Road, is the **Florence Nightingale Museum**, celebrating the devout woman who single-mindedly revolutionized the nursing profession by establishing the first school of nursing at St Thomas' in 1860 and publishing her *Notes on Nursing*, emphasizing the importance of hygiene, decorum and discipline. The exhibition is imaginatively set out, aided by audioguides in the shape of a stethoscope. It hits just the right note by putting the two years she spent tending to the wounded of the Crimean War in the context of a lifetime of tireless social campaigning. Exhibits include the Turkish lantern she used in Scutari hospital, near Istanbul, that earned her the nickname "The Lady with the Lamp", and her pet owl, Athena (now stuffed), who used to perch on her shoulder.

Lambeth Palace

Lambeth Palace Rd · Certain Thurs & Fri 10.30am & 2pm · £10 · ☎ 0844 248 5134, ⓦ archbishopofcanterbury.org · ⊖ Westminster, Lambeth North or Vauxhall

A short walk south of St Thomas' stands the imposing red-brick Tudor Gate of **Lambeth Palace**, London residence of the Archbishop of Canterbury since 1197. The whole complex is well worth a visit, although guided tours are extremely popular, so you'll need to book in advance.

The most impressive room is, without doubt, the **Great Hall** (now the library), with its very late Gothic, oak hammerbeam roof, built after the Restoration by Archbishop Juxon, whose coat of arms, featuring African heads, can be seen on the bookshelves. Upstairs, the **Guard Room** boasts an even older, arch-braced timber roof from the fourteenth century, and is the room where Thomas More was brought for questioning before being sent to the Tower (and subsequently beheaded).

Among the numerous portraits of past archbishops, look out for works by Holbein, Van Dyck, Hogarth and Reynolds. The final point on the tour is the **palace chapel**, where the religious reformer and leader of the Lollards, John Wycliffe, was tried (for the second time) in 1378 for "propositions, clearly heretical and depraved". The door and window frames date back to Wycliffe's day, but the place is somewhat overwhelmed by the ceiling frescoes by Leonard Rosoman, added in the 1980s, telling the story of the Church of England. Best of all is the fact that you can see the choir screen and stalls put there in the 1630s by Archbishop Laud, and later used as evidence of his Catholic tendencies at his trial (and execution) in 1645.

Garden Museum

Lambeth Palace Rd · Mon–Fri & Sun 10.30am–5pm, Sat 10.30am–4pm; closed first Mon of month · £5· ☎ 020 7401 8865, ⓦ gardenmuseum.org.uk · ⊖ Westminster, Lambeth North or Vauxhall

Next door to Lambeth Palace stands the Kentish ragstone church of **St Mary-at-Lambeth**, largely rebuilt in Victorian times, but retaining its fourteenth-century tower. The church is now home to the **Garden Museum** which puts on excellent exhibitions on a horticultural theme in the ground-floor galleries, and has a small permanent exhibition in the "belvedere", reached by a new wooden staircase. There's a section on the two John Tradescants (father and son), gardeners to James I and Charles I, who are both buried in the churchyard. You can even view one of the Tradescants' curiosities – a "vegetable lamb" that's in fact a Russian fern – plus a few dibbers and grubbers, and some pony boots designed to prevent damage to your lawn.

You can visit the church's shop and café for free – what's more you can take your tea and cake out into the small graveyard, now laid out as a **seventeenth-century knot garden**, where two interesting sarcophagi lurk among the foliage. The first, topped by an ornamental breadfruit, is the resting place of **Captain Bligh** of *Mutiny on the Bounty* fame. More intriguing is the **Tradescant memorial** which features several very unusual reliefs: a seven-headed griffin contemplating a skull and a crocodile sifting through sundry ruins flanked by gnarled trees. The Tradescants were tireless travellers in their search for new plant species, and John the Elder set up a museum of curiosities known as "Tradescant's Ark" in Lambeth in 1629. Among the many exhibits were the "hand of a mermaid…a natural dragon, above two inches long…blood that rained on the Isle of Wight…and the Passion of Christ carved very daintily on a plumstone". The less fantastical pieces formed the nucleus of Oxford's Ashmolean Museum.

15

Imperial War Museum

Lambeth Rd · Daily 10am–6pm · Free · ☎ 020 7416 5000, ⓦ london.iwm.org.uk · ⊖ Lambeth North or Elephant & Castle

From 1815 until 1930, the domed building at the east end of Lambeth Road was the infamous lunatic asylum of Bethlem Royal Hospital, better known as **Bedlam**. (Charlie Chaplin's mother was among those confined here – the future comedian was born and spent a troubled childhood in nearby Kennington.) When the hospital was moved to Beckenham in southeast London, the wings of the 700ft-long facade were demolished, leaving just the central section, now home to the **Imperial War Museum**, by far the capital's best military museum. The IWM has recently been refurbishing its permanent galleries, while continuing to stage superb long-term temporary exhibitions – its busy schedule of talks and films are well worth checking out.

The main galleries

The treatment of the subject is impressively wide-ranging and fairly sober, once you've passed through the **Large Exhibits Gallery**, with its militaristic display of guns, tanks, fighter planes and a giant V-2 rocket. The galleries on the **lower ground floor** have been expensively refurbished, and catalogue the human damage of the last century of conflict, in particular the two World Wars. On the first floor, you'll find the permanent **Secret War** gallery, which follows the clandestine activities of MI5, MI6 and the SOE (the wartime equivalent of MI6) – expect exploding pencils, trip wires and spy cameras – though its finale is marred by an unrealistically glowing account of recent SAS operations in the Gulf.

The art galleries and Extraordinary Heroes

The museum's **art galleries**, on the second floor, put on superb exhibitions taken from their vast collection of works by war artists, official and unofficial, including the likes of David Bomberg, Wyndham Lewis, Stanley Spencer and John Nash. One painting that's on permanent display in its own room, alongside three other similarly grand canvases, is *Gassed*, by John Singer Sargent, a painter better known for his portraits of society beauties.

Crimes Against Humanity, also on the second floor, features a harrowing half-hour film on genocide and ethnic violence in the last century. You can also pay a visit to the nearby **Explore History Centre** and peruse the museum's reference books, archive film clips and its online collection. On the top floor, the **Extraordinary Heroes** exhibition displays the largest collection of Victoria Crosses in the world. However, this is much more than a medal gallery as touch-screen computers tell the moving stories behind the decorations.

The Holocaust Exhibition

Many people come to the Imperial War Museum specifically to see the **Holocaust Exhibition** (not recommended for under-14s), which you enter from the third floor. Taking a fairly conventional, sober approach to the subject, the museum has made a valiant attempt to avoid depicting the victims of the Holocaust as nameless masses, by focusing on individual cases, and interspersing the archive footage with eyewitness accounts from contemporary survivors.

The exhibition pulls few punches, bluntly stating that the pope failed to denounce the anti-Jewish **Nuremberg Laws**, that writers such as Eliot and Kipling expressed anti-Semitic views, and that at the 1938 Evian Conference, the European powers refused to accept any more Jewish refugees. Despite the restrictions of space, there are sections on the extermination of the gypsies, Nazi euthanasia, pre-Holocaust Yiddish culture and the persecution of the Slavs. The **genocide**, which began with the *Einsatzgruppen* and ended with the gas chambers, is catalogued in painstaking detail, while the problem of "proving" the Final Solution is also addressed, in a room that emphasizes the complexity of the Nazi bureaucracy, which, allied to an ideology of extermination, made the Holocaust not just possible but inevitable.

The centrepiece of the museum is a vast, all-white, scale model of (what is, in fact, only a very small slice of) **Auschwitz-Birkenau**, showing what happened to the two thousand Hungarian Jews who arrived at the camp from the town of Beregovo in May 1944. The significance of this transport is that, uniquely, photographs taken by the SS, of the selection process meted out on these particular arrivals managed to survive the war. In the alcoves overlooking the model, which has a pile of discarded possessions from the camps as its backdrop, survivors describe their first impressions of Auschwitz. This section is especially harrowing, and it's as well to leave yourself enough time to listen to the reflections of camp survivors at the end, as they attempt to come to terms with the past.

Southwark

In Tudor and Stuart London, the chief reason for crossing the Thames, to what is now Southwark, was to visit the disreputable Bankside entertainment district around the south end of London Bridge. Four hundred years on, Londoners have rediscovered the habit of heading for the area, thanks to the traffic-free riverside path and a wealth of top attractions, with the charge led by the mighty Tate Modern. Tourist spots now pepper the riverside from Blackfriars Bridge to Bermondsey from the remarkable reconstruction of Shakespeare's Globe Theatre to the sublime view from the Shard. East of Tower Bridge is the thriving little warehouse development of Butler's Wharf, and further east still, Rotherhithe clings onto its old seafaring identity despite the demise of its once extensive enclosed docks.

Bankside

Ⓦ visitbankside.com

Bankside is dominated by the awesome **Tate Modern**, while close by, the **Millennium Bridge** provides a wonderful pedestrian link from the City and St Paul's. To the east are two thoroughly researched reconstructions: **Shakespeare's Globe Theatre** and Drake's Tudor galleon, the **Golden Hinde**. At this point, the shops, cafés and stalls of nearby **Borough Market**, which has become a gourmet food haven (Thurs–Sat), provide a welcome refuelling stop, before you check out some of the city's best-preserved Gothic architecture in **Southwark Cathedral**.

The reconstruction of Shakespeare's Globe is pretty much all there is above ground today to remind you of Southwark's pre-industrial golden age of entertainment under the Tudors and Stuarts. For centuries, however, Bankside was best known for its **brothels**, which were already doing a thriving trade under the Romans. In 1161, the brothels were licensed by royal decree, but made to adhere to various rules and restrictions: prostitutes could now be fined three shillings for "grimacing to passers-by", but were given Sunday mornings off in order to attend church. The women wore red-and-white-striped caps and white aprons, and were known as "Winchester Geese", since the land was owned by the Bishop of Winchester. The Church made a small fortune out of the rent until Henry VIII closed the bawdy houses down.

In Elizabethan times, Bankside once more became the most nefarious area in London, known as "Stew's Bank" for its brothels or "stewhouses", and was studded with **bull- and bear-pits**. Pepys recalls seeing "some good sport of the bulls tossing of the dogs; one into the very boxes", but opinion was by then inclining towards Evelyn's description of the sport as a "rude and dirty pastime" and in 1682 the last bear-garden was closed down. Most famous of all, however, were Bankside's theatres (see p.228).

Tate Modern

Bankside • Daily 10am–6pm, Fri & Sat until 10pm • Free; special exhibitions from £10 • ☎ 020 7887 8888, ⓦ tate.org.uk • ⊖ Southwark or Blackfriars

Tate Modern is an absolute must for anyone visiting or living in London. Originally designed as an oil-fired power station by Giles Gilbert Scott, this austere, brick-built "cathedral of power" was closed down in 1981 and reopened as a modern art gallery in 2000. The masterful conversion, by the Swiss duo Herzog & de Meuron, has left plenty of the original industrial feel, while providing wonderfully light and spacious galleries to show off Tate's impressive collection of international twentieth-century artists, including the likes of Monet, Duchamp, Moore, Matisse, Mondrian, Picasso, Pollock, Rothko and Warhol.

Tate Modern receives over five million visitors a year, more than double what was envisaged. To alleviate this, the Tate has started to expand to the south of the power station. First came the **Tanks,** a new rough-edged space for live work, video installations and performance art, in the power station's subterranean oil tanks. To follow, in 2016, is the Tate's major **new extension**, also designed by Herzog & de Meuron, a distorted prism of latticed bricks rising to 215ft above the oil tanks.

Tate's **permanent collection** dates back to 1900, but the curators have eschewed a chronological approach, and gone instead for hanging works according to themes and -isms. So in among all the attention-grabbing conceptual stuff, you'll find some early

■ ACCOMMODATION		● SHOPS		● CAFÉS		■ PUBS	
Great Dover Street Apartments	2	Bermondsey Antique Market	2	Bar Tozino	4	The Mayflower	1
Thameside YHA	1	Maltby Street Market	1	El Vergel	1	Royal Oak	2
				José	2	The Woolpack	3
				● RESTAURANTS		■ CLUBS	
				40 Maltby Street	5	Coronet	5
				Village East	3	Corsica Studios	6
				Zucca	6	Ministry of Sound	4

twentieth-century paintings, looking terribly old-fashioned in their gilded frames. You'll need stamina to wade through more than one level in any one visit, so if there's something you really want to see, go there first before you run out of energy. And remember that one of the joys of Tate Modern is coming across artists or artistic movements about which you may know very little.

ARRIVAL, INFORMATION AND TOURS

Arrival For the best views of the Tate, approach from the Millennium Bridge. The nearest entrance to the bridge is the North Entrance underneath the chimney, which brings you out at Level 1. The best entrance, however, is via the ramp at the West Entrance, allowing you to fully appreciate the stupefying enormity of the main turbine hall, which sits on Level 0, below the Thames, rises to a height of 115ft and is used to display large-scale installations. There's also a Tate Boat, that plies between the two galleries (every 40min; 20min; £6.50; ⓦ thamesclippers.com).

Orientation Level 0 is also where you'll find the

information desk, and, on the opposite side, the museum's cloakroom and giant bookshop – escalators from this floor lead straight up to Level 2. Entering from the bridge or river brings you to Level 1, linked by stairs and elevators to the other floors, but not escalators.

Tours There are free guided tours (daily at 11am, noon, 2 & 3pm; 45min), multimedia guides (£4) and various apps available (Tate has free wi-fi).

Eating There's a pricey restaurant and bar on Level 7, with a great view over the river, and a more reasonably priced café on Level 2.

Level 2

On Level 2, **Poetry and Dream** concentrates, though by no means exclusively, on the interwar period. At the heart of the wing is a large room densely hung with works by the major Surrealists: **Miró**, **Magritte**, **Dalí** and the dreamlike **de Chirico**. Other rooms are given over to single artists like **Joseph Beuys**, whose bizarre choice of materials derives directly from his wartime experiences, when his plane crashed in the Crimea and he was saved by local Tartars, who cocooned him in felt and fat.

BANKSIDE AND BERMONDSEY

THE MILLENNIUM BRIDGE

The first bridge to be built across the Thames since Tower Bridge opened in 1894, the sleek, stainless-steel **Millennium Bridge** is London's sole pedestrian-only crossing. A suspension bridge of innovative design – the high-profile triumvirate responsible were sculptor Anthony Caro, architect Norman Foster and engineers Ove Arup – it famously bounced up and down when it first opened in 2000 and had to be closed for another two years for repairs. It still wobbles a bit, but most people are too busy enjoying the spectacular views across to St Paul's Cathedral and Tate Modern to notice.

The Tate owns works from every period of **Picasso**'s life, including *Weeping Woman*, which is both a portrait of his lover Dora Maar and a heartfelt response to the Spanish Civil War. Throughout Tate Modern, you'll also find quite a bit of overlap with Tate Britain, with works by British artists like **Stanley Spencer**, whose unique Biblical visions and domestic scenes are all set in and around his home village of Cookham.

Level 3

In **Transformed Visions**, the emphasis is on the postwar decades, so there's a fairly wide selection of abstract expressionist works, with the charge led by **Jackson Pollock**. It's here, too, that you can catch perennial Tate favourites like **Mark Rothko**'s abstract "Seagram Murals". Commissioned by the swanky *Four Seasons* restaurant in New York, they were withheld by Rothko, who decided he didn't wish his art to be a mere backdrop to the recreation of the wealthy. There's a wonderfully gloomy seascape by Emil Nolde and surprising new acquisitions such as Dia al-Azzawi's Guernica-like depiction of the Sabra and Shatila massacres. Like Rothko, **Gerhard Richter** gets an entire room in which to display his six, rather more upbeat, abstract "John Cage"

SHAKESPEARE & CO

London's first purpose-built theatres emerged in Shoreditch in the 1570s, but they flourished on Bankside, with no fewer than four during the reign of James I: the **Swan**, built in 1587, with Edward Alleyn (founder of Dulwich College) as the lead actor and Christopher Marlowe as its main playwright; the **Rose**, built in 1595, its foundations still extant on Park Street; the **Hope**, built in 1613, which doubled as a bear-garden and theatre; and the **Globe**, erected in 1599 on Park Street, where Shakespeare put on his greatest plays, now reconstructed on New Globe Walk. The theatres lasted barely half a century before being closed down by the Puritans, who considered them "chapels of Satan". With the Restoration, the focus of the theatre scene, and its accompanying vices, moved to Covent Garden, and Southwark faded from the limelight.

---

paintings from 2006. In the adjacent room hangs *Waterlilies*, one of **Monet**'s experiments with abstraction from nearly a century earlier.

Level 4

One of the central rooms in **Structure and Clarity**, on Level 4, has an impressive collection of interwar abstract art by the likes of Kandinsky, Naum Gabo, the De Stijl duo of Mondrian and van Doesburg, as well as the Brit duo of Ben Nicolson and Barbara Hepworth. Picasso and Braque's **Cubism** gets a room to itself, but the room that usually blows most visitors' minds is the one devoted to **Minimalism**. Here you have the epitome of modern art, *Monochrome White Painting* by Li Yuan-Chia, though to be fair there are four small white circles embossed on it, whereas Gerhard Richter's *Grey* does what it says on the tin.

Over in **Energy and Process**, there's a gallery devoted to the Italian art movement, *arte povera*, from the late 1960s, in which found objects played an important role. But this wing also has more recent acquisitions, such as Marisa Merz's giant floating aluminium sculpture, which used to hang in her house, and a whole room of Cy Twombly's late works: bronze casts and great Bacchic explosions of paint. Other highlights include Lucio Fontana's slashed canvases, and watching other visitors' embarrassment as they look at Art & Language's *Untitled Painting* (it's actually a mirror).

Shakespeare's Globe Theatre

21 New Globe Walk • Exhibition mid-April to mid-Sept Mon–Sat 9am–12.30pm & 1–5pm, Sun 9–11.30am & noon–5pm; mid-Oct to mid-April 9am–5.30pm • £11.50 • ☎ 020 7902 1500, ⓦ shakespearesglobe.com • ⊖ Southwark or London Bridge

Dwarfed by Tate Modern, but equally remarkable in its own way, **Shakespeare's Globe Theatre** is a more or less faithful reconstruction of the polygonal playhouse where most of the Bard's later works were first performed. The theatre, which boasts the first new thatched roof in central London since the Great Fire, puts on plays by Shakespeare and his contemporaries, using only natural light and the minimum of scenery. The season runs from May to September, and the performances are usually both fun, historically authentic and critically acclaimed (see p.419). Round the back of the Globe, **Sam Wanamaker's Playhouse** has recently been built, a faithful reconstruction of the sort of intimate, candlelit, indoor Jacobean theatre where Shakespeare's company would have performed during the winter months, and where plays will now be put on throughout the year.

To find out more about Shakespeare and the history of Bankside, the Globe's stylish **exhibition**, to the west of the theatre, is well worth a visit. It details the long campaign by the single-minded American actor Sam Wanamaker (1919–93) to have the Globe rebuilt, but it's the interactive exhibits that hit the spot. You can have a virtual play on period musical instruments such as the crumhorn or sackbut, prepare your own edition of Shakespeare and feel the thatch, hazelnut shell and daub used to build the theatre. There are even booths in which you can record and compare your own rendition of key

16

speeches with those of the stage greats, plus the odd live demo on the exhibition's stage. Visitors also get taken on an informative half-hour **guided tour** round the theatre itself; during the summer season, if you visit in the afternoon, you get to visit the nearby Rose Theatre instead for a reduced fee (see below).

Vinopolis

1 Bank End • Wed 6–9.30pm, Thurs & Fri 2–10pm, Sat noon–9.30pm, Sun noon–4pm • From £27 • ☎ 020 7940 8300, ⓦ vinopolis.co.uk • ⊖ London Bridge

Housed in the former wine vaults under the railway arches on Clink Street, **Vinopolis** is a strange fish: part wine bar-restaurant, part wine retailers (there's a branch of the excellent Majestic Wines round the back), part crash course in wine-tasting. If you've never really thought much about the plonk you're pouring down your throat, it's a good place to learn the basics, but tickets (which include at least seven wine tastings) are pricey. And following a revamp, drinks are now dispensed from a vending machine, which casts something of a pall over the whole experience. You can charge up your credit card ticket to include more tastings of wine and other alcoholic drinks if you don't want the party to stop.

Clink Prison Museum

1 Clink St • Mon–Fri 10am–6pm, Sat & Sun 10am–7.30pm; July–Sept closes 9pm • £7.50 • ☎ 020 7403 0900, ⓦ clink.co.uk • ⊖ London Bridge

Housed in the suitably dismal confines of an old cellar is the **Clink Prison Museum**, built near the site of the former Clink Prison, and the origin of the expression "in the clink". The prison began in the twelfth century as a dungeon for disobedient clerics under the Bishop of Winchester's Palace – the rose window of the palace's Great Hall has survived just east of the prison – and later it became a dumping ground for heretics, debtors, prostitutes and a motley assortment of Bankside lowlife, before being burnt to the ground during the 1780 Gordon Riots. The exhibition features a handful of prison-life tableaux and dwells on the torture and grim conditions within, but, given the rich history of the place, it's a disappointingly lacklustre display.

16

Golden Hinde

1 Pickfords Wharf, Clink St • Daily 10am–5.30pm, but phone ahead • £6 • ☎ 020 7403 0123, ⓦ goldenhinde.com • ⊖ London Bridge

At the east end of Clink Street, in St Mary Overie Dock, sits an exact replica of the **Golden Hinde**, the galleon in which Francis Drake sailed around the world from 1577 to 1580. This version was launched in 1973, and circumnavigated the world for the next twenty years, before eventually settling here in Southwark. The ship is surprisingly small and, with a crew of eighty-plus, must have been cramped, to say the least. There's a refreshing lack of interpretive panels, so it's worth trying to coincide with one of the tours, during which costumed guides show you the ropes, so to speak, and demonstrate activities such as firing a cannon or using the ship's toilet. Always phone ahead, though, to check that a group hasn't booked the place up.

THE ROSE THEATRE

The discovery of the remains of the **Rose Theatre** (☎ 020 7261 9565, ⓦ rosetheatre.org.uk), the Globe's great rival, beneath an office block on Park Street in 1989, helped enormously in the reconstruction of the Globe. The outline of the theatre can clearly be traced in the foundations, but most of the remains are currently flooded to preserve them while funds are gathered for a full excavation. Close by the Rose exhibition, there's a plaque showing where the Globe actually stood, before it was destroyed in a fire started by a spark from a cannon during a performance of Shakespeare's *Henry VIII*. The Rose can only be visited by tour, as part of the package offered by the Globe exhibition on summer afternoons (see opposite).

Southwark Cathedral

Mon–Fri 8am–6pm, Sat & Sun 8.30am–6pm · Free · ☎ 020 7367 6700, ⓦ cathedral.southwark.anglican.org · ➌ London Bridge

Built in the thirteenth century as the Augustinian priory church of St Mary Overie, it's a minor miracle that **Southwark Cathedral** survived the nineteenth century, which saw the east-end chapel demolished to make way for London Bridge, railways built within a few feet of the tower and some very heavy-handed Victorian restoration. As if in compensation, the church was given cathedral status in 1905, and has since gone from strength to strength; the cathedral refectory serves tasty food.

Of the original thirteenth-century **interior**, only the choir and retrochoir now remain, separated by a beautiful, high, stone Tudor screen; they are probably the oldest Gothic structures left in London and were used by the Bishop of Winchester as a court – those sentenced ended up in the nearby Clink. The cathedral contains numerous intriguing **monuments:** from a thirteenth-century oak effigy of a knight, to the brightly painted tomb of poet John Gower, Chaucer's contemporary, in the north aisle, his head resting on the three books he wrote – one in Latin, one in French and one in English. The quack doctor Lionel Lockyer has a humorous epitaph in the north transept, and, nearby, there's a chapel dedicated to John Harvard, who was baptized here in 1607 and whose deathbed bequest helped found Harvard College. In the south aisle, an early twentieth-century memorial to Shakespeare (he was a worshipper in the church and his actor brother is buried here) depicts the Bard in green alabaster lounging under a stone canopy. Above the memorial is a postwar stained-glass window featuring a whole cast of characters from the plays.

16

Borough Market

8 Southwark St · Mon–Wed 10am–3pm, Thurs 11am–5pm, Fri noon–6pm, Sat 8am–5pm · ☎ 020 7407 1002, ⓦ boroughmarket .org.uk · ➌ London Bridge

Medieval Southwark, also known as **The Borough**, was London's first suburb, clustered round the southern end of London Bridge, the only bridge over the tidal Thames until 1750, and thus the only route south. London Bridge was the most obvious place for the Kent farmers to sell their goods to the City grocers, and there's been a thriving market here since medieval times. The present **Borough Market** is squeezed beneath the railway arches between the High Street and the cathedral. The early morning wholesale fruit and vegetable market winds up around 8am and is one of the few still trading under its original Victorian wrought-iron shed. But the market is best known nowadays for its busy specialist food market (see p.433), with stalls selling top-quality produce from around the world, with permanent outlets such as Neal's Yard Dairy and Konditor & Cook in the shops close by.

Borough High Street

As the main road south out of the City, **Borough High Street** was for centuries famous for its **coaching inns**. Chaucer's Canterbury pilgrims set off from *The Tabard* (in Talbot Yard), but by Dickens' time "these great rambling queer old places", as he called them, were closing down. The only extant coaching inn is the **George Inn**, situated in a cobbled yard east off the High Street, dating from 1677 and now owned by the National Trust. Unfortunately, the Great Northern Railway demolished two of the three original galleried fronts, but the lone survivor is a remarkable sight nevertheless, and is still run as a pub (see p.392).

Opposite Borough tube station, at the southernmost end of Borough High Street, is **St George the Martyr**, built in the 1730s, with four clock faces: three white and illuminated at night; one black and pointing towards Bermondsey, whose parishioners refused to give money for the church. To the north of St George's, a wall survives from the **Marshalsea**, the city's main debtors' prison, where Dickens' father (and family) was incarcerated for six months in 1824.

Redcross Way

Running parallel with Borough High Street, one block to the west, is **Redcross Way**, a little-visited backstreet that hides a couple of remarkable sights. The first is **Red Cross Garden**, the row of cottage-style model dwellings established by the social reformer (and founder of the National Trust) Octavia Hill, to house the workers of a local rag factory. The row of houses faces onto a miniature village green, complete with village pond and even a maypole. Meanwhile, on the opposite side of the street, is the site of the **Cross Bones cemetery** (⦿crossbones.org.uk). It was on this unconsecrated land that the prostitutes who worked on Bankside were buried, and later, the local poor were interred. Local residents have turned the gates, leading to the plot of land, into an impromptu shrine of messages and tokens to those buried, and the plan is eventually to establish a Garden of Remembrance. A short vigil is held on the 23rd of every month around 7pm outside the gates.

Old Operating Theatre Museum and Herb Garret

St Thomas St • Daily 10.30am–5pm; closed mid-Dec to early Jan • £6.20 • ☎ 020 7188 2679, ⦿ thegarret.org.uk • ⊖ London Bridge

The most educative and the strangest of Southwark's museums is the **Old Operating Theatre Museum and Herb Garret**. Built in 1821 up a spiral staircase at the top of a church tower, where the hospital apothecary's herbs were stored, this women's operating theatre was once adjacent to the women's ward of St Thomas' Hospital (now in Lambeth). Despite being gore-free, the museum is as stomach-churning as the London Dungeon, for this theatre dates from the pre-anaesthetic era.

The surgeons who used this room would have concentrated on speed and accuracy (most amputations took less than a minute), but there was still a thirty percent mortality rate, with many patients simply dying of shock, and many more from bacterial infection (about which very little was known). This much is clear from the design of the theatre itself, which has no sink and is made almost entirely of mahogany and pine, a breeding ground for bacteria. Sawdust was sprinkled on the floor to soak up the blood and prevent it dripping onto the congregation in the church below. In the herbarium section, you can read up on the medicinal uses of the herbs stored and have a go at making your own pills.

Guy's Hospital

St Thomas St • ☎ 020 7188 7188, ⦿ guysandstthomas.nhs.uk • ⊖ London Bridge

Guy's Hospital was founded in 1726 by Thomas Guy, a governor of nearby St Thomas' Hospital, with the money he made in the City's South Sea Bubble fiasco. It was originally established to treat "incurables" discharged by neighbouring St Thomas' Hospital. With its 469ft-high concrete brutalist tower, Guy's is one of the tallest hospitals in the world, but it also retains several original eighteenth-century buildings: the courtyard on the south side of St Thomas Street, with a pretty little **Hospital Chapel**, on the west side of the courtyard. It's worth having a look at the interior with its cheerful light-blue paintwork, raked balconies on three sides and the giant marble and alabaster tomb of the founder, who's depicted welcoming a new patient to the hospital, though in fact Guy died a year before the first patients were admitted. To the south of the courtyard are the old cloisters, which now harbour one of the original alcoves from old London Bridge, with a statue of the poet **John Keats** (who trained as a surgeon at Guy's) seated within.

Bermondsey

Famous in the Middle Ages for its Cluniac abbey, **Bermondsey**, the area east of London Bridge, changed enormously in the nineteenth century. In 1836, the London and Greenwich Railway – the city's first – was built through the district, supported by 878 brick arches stretching for four miles. The area became famous for its wharves, its

16

tanneries and its factories. So much of the city's food – teas, wines, grain, butter, bacon and cheese – was stored here that it was nicknamed "London's Larder". Bermondsey also became infamous for some of the worst social conditions in Victorian London, as Charles Kingsley discovered: "O God! What I saw! People having no water to drink but the water of the common sewer which stagnates full of…dead fish, cats and dogs."

Badly bombed in the Blitz, the docks had closed down by the 1960s. They have since undergone a Docklands-style regeneration, and much of the original warehouse architecture has been preserved, particularly east of Tower Bridge, around Butler's Wharf. **HMS Belfast**, the cruiser moored near City Hall, is the only permanent maritime link. Nearby the curvaceous dock of Hay's Wharf, originally built to accommodate tea clippers like the *Cutty Sark*, has been filled and transformed into the **Hay's Galleria**, a shopping precinct whose (year-round) Christmas Shop is a must if you've got children. The area's most popular attraction today, however, is of course **The Shard**, London's latest priapic skyscraper.

The Shard

32 London Bridge • Daily 9am–10pm • £25 online • ☎ 0844 499 7111, ⍵ theviewfromtheshard.com • ⊖ London Bridge

London's – and the country's – tallest building, **The Shard** is squeezed in beside London Bridge Station. While there's a case to be argued for the City's skyscrapers, and for those at Canary Wharf, it's harder to justify such a hubristic (Qatari-funded) enterprise south of the river. Even less justifiable are the ticket prices to reach the viewing platforms on floors 68, 69 and 72 of Renzo Piano's 1016ft, tapered, glass-clad tower block. Still, once you're there, if you can ignore the New Age music, the views are sublime, making everything else in London look small, from the unicycle of the London Eye to the tiny little box of St Paul's Cathedral, while the model railway that is London Bridge is played out below you. Book online and make sure you go to the very top where you can feel the breeze blowing through the crowning shards.

London Bridge Experience

2–4 Tooley St • Mon–Fri & Sun 10am–5pm, Sat 10am–6pm • From £16 online • ☎ 0800 0434 666, ⍵ thelondonbridgeexperience.com • ⊖ London Bridge

Now the London Dungeon has fled to County Hall (see p.219), Gothic horror fans should head instead to the slightly more historically pertinent **London Bridge Experience**, in the railway vaults on the north side of Tooley Street. First off, you're led on a theatrical trot through the history of London Bridge, with guides in period garb hamming up the gory bits. Then, in case you're not scared enough yet, in the **London Tombs** section (no under-11s), more actors, dressed as zombies and murderers, leap out of the foggy gloom to frighten the wits out of you. Finally, in peace and quiet, you get to peruse some artefacts from (and a model of) old London Bridge.

HMS Belfast

The Queen's Walk • Daily: March–Oct 10am–6pm; Nov–Feb 10am–5pm • £13.15 • ☎ 020 7940 6300, ⍵ iwm.org.uk/visits/hms-belfast • ⊖ London Bridge

Permanently moored opposite Southwark Crown Court, the camouflage-painted **HMS Belfast** is an 11,550-ton Royal Navy cruiser. Launched in Belfast in 1938, the *Belfast* spent the first two years of the war in the Royal Naval shipyards, after being hit by a mine in the Firth of Forth. It later saw action in the 1943 Battle of North Cape and assisted in the D-Day landings before being decommissioned after the Korean War, and becoming an outpost of the Imperial War Museum.

The fun bit is exploring the maze of cabins and scrambling up and down the vertiginous ladders of the ship's seven confusing decks, which could accommodate a crew of over nine hundred. Be sure to check out the punishment cells, in the most

uncomfortable part of the ship, and to make it down to the airlocked Boiler Room, a spaghetti of pipes and valves, from which there was very little chance of escape in the event of the ship being hit. If you want to know more about the cruiser's history, head for the Exhibition Flat in Zone 5; next door, in the Life at Sea room, you can practise your Morse code and knots, and listen to accounts of naval life on board.

City Hall

The Queen's Walk • Mon–Thurs 8.30am–6pm, Fri 8.30am–5.30pm • Free • ☎ 020 7983 4000, ⓦ london.gov.uk • ⊖ London Bridge

East of the *Belfast*, overlooking the river, is Norman Foster's startling glass-encased **City Hall**, headquarters for the Greater London Authority and the Mayor of London, which looks like a giant car headlight or fencing mask. Visitors are welcome to stroll up the helical walkway, visit the café and watch proceedings from the second floor. For access to "London's Living Room" on the ninth floor, which boasts the best views over the Thames, contact City Hall. Before you leave the area, be sure to check out Fiona Banner's shiny black *Full Stops*, 3D renditions styled in different fonts and wrought in bronze.

Bermondsey Street

Once the area's high street, **Bermondsey Street** has been transformed over the last decade or so into a trendy strip of cafés, pubs, shops and art galleries. This was also once the heart of the tanning industry – hence Tanner Street, Morocco Street (where much of the leather came from) and Leathermarket Road, which leads to the former **Leather Hide and Wool Exchange** of 1878, decorated with roundels depicting the process of tanning. Next door is the former Leather Market, built in 1833 and now converted into workshops, including one where you can watch **glassblowing** demonstrations (Mon–Fri 10am–1pm & 2–5pm; free).

With Borough Market getting ever busier, an offshoot foodie market has begun to evolve on Saturdays around the Monmouth Coffee roastery under the railway arches on **Maltby Street**, at the end of Tanner Street. And finally, at the far end of Bermondsey Street, the venerable Bermondsey **antique market** takes place early on Friday mornings. The market is also known confusingly as the New Caledonian Market, after the prewar flea market that used to take place off Islington's Caledonian Road.

Fashion and Textile Museum

83 Bermondsey St • Tues–Sat 11am–6pm • £8 • ☎ 020 7407 8664, ⓦ ftmlondon.org • ⊖ London Bridge

The **Fashion and Textile Museum** is the lifelong dream of Zandra Rhodes, fashion *grande dame extraordinaire*. Designed by Mexican architect Ricardo Legorreta, and daubed in Rhodes' favourite colours of yellow, pink and orange, the FTM (a former cash-and-carry warehouse) is an arresting sight on an otherwise drab street architecturally. Rhodes opened her first boutique in the 1960s, and reached the peak of her popularity during the punk era. Her own sartorial taste hasn't changed much in the intervening years, but thankfully FTM's exhibitions are more wide-ranging – from designer tea cosies to 1970s fashion – and are often drawn from her own vast collection.

White Cube Bermondsey

144–152 Bermondsey St • Tues –Sat10am–6pm, Sun noon–6pm • Free • ☎ 020 7930 5373, ⓦ whitecube.com

The definitive sign that Bermondsey had come of age was the arrival of an absolutely enormous branch of the high-profile **White Cube** contemporary art gallery. Owned by Old Etonian Jay Jopling, White Cube started out in Mayfair in the 1990s, championing the art of the Young British Artists, such as Damien Hirst and Tracey Emin, opening a branch in Hoxton in 2000 (now closed), and moving south of the river in 2011. Inside, you'll find changing exhibits from an international roster of artists.

Butler's Wharf

East of Tower Bridge, **Butler's Wharf** is one of the densest networks of Victorian warehousing left in London and one of the most enjoyable parts of Docklands to explore. From Tower Bridge itself (see p.187), you can get a really good view of the old **Anchor Brewhouse**, which produced Courage ales from 1789 until 1982; a cheery, ad hoc sort of building, with a boiler-house chimney at one end and malt-mill tower and cupola at the other. Next door is the original eight-storey **Butler's Wharf**, the largest warehouse complex on the Thames when it was built in 1873. In the 1970s, it became London's largest artists' colony, home to everyone from Derek Jarman to Sid Vicious, but nowadays, its flats, shops and restaurants form part of Terence Conran's gastronomic empire, with a wide, public, riverside promenade.

   Shad Thames, the narrow street at the back of Butler's Wharf, has kept the wrought-iron overhead gangways by which the porters used to transport goods from the wharves to the warehouses further back from the river; it's one of the most atmospheric alleyways in the whole of Docklands. For a totally different ambience, head for **Horsleydown Square**, to the south of Shad Thames, where terracotta-rendered flats, with striking blue balconies, overlook a piazza centred on a fountain encrusted with naked women, whose belongings are sculpted around the edge. Also worth a look, two blocks south on Queen Elizabeth Street, is the **Circle**, a modern take on the Victorian "circus", its street facades smothered in shiny cobalt-blue tiles.

Design Museum

28 Shad Thames • Daily 10am–5.45pm • £8 • ☎ 020 7403 6933, ⓦ designmuseum.org • ⊖ Tower Hill

16

Just east of Butler's Wharf is the **Design Museum**, a stylish white Bauhaus-like conversion of an old 1950s banana warehouse designed by Terence Conran – the museum, which puts on exhibitions on designers, movements or single products from the era of mass production, is due to move to Kensington High Street in 2015 (see p.273).

St Saviour's Dock

East of Butler's Wharf, a stainless-steel footbridge takes you across **St Saviour's Dock**, a tidal inlet overlooked by swanky warehouse offices. Incredible though it may seem, it really is still possible to smell the spices – cinnamon, nutmeg and cloves, mostly – which were stored here until the 1970s, especially in the last section of Shad Thames after a shower of rain. The footbridge takes you over to **New Concordia Wharf** on Mill Street, one of the first warehouse conversions in the area, completed in 1984. Next door stands the photogenic **China Wharf**, with its stack of semicircular windows picked out in red.

   The area around St Saviour's Dock was dubbed by the Victorian press "the very capital of cholera". In 1849, the *Morning Chronicle* described it thus: "Jostling with unemployed labourers of the lowest class, ballast heavers, coal-whippers, brazen women, ragged children, and the very raff and refuse of the river, [the visitor] makes his way with difficulty along, assailed by offensive sights and smells from the narrow alleys which branch off." This was the location of Dickens' fictional **Jacob's Island**, a place with "every imaginable sign of desolation and neglect", where Bill Sikes met his end in *Oliver Twist*.

THE THAMES PATH

A leisurely way to reach Rotherhithe is to walk the mile along the **Thames Path** from Butler's Wharf, stopping en route at *The Angel*, a pub once frequented by Pepys and Captain Cook, which now stands all alone on Bermondsey Wall, with great views over to Wapping. Close by are the foundations of Edward III's moated manor house, begun in 1353, and the "Leaning Tower of Bermondsey", a precariously tilting riverside house just downstream from the pub.

Rotherhithe

Rotherhithe, the thumb of marshy land jutting out into the Thames east of Bermondsey, has always been slightly removed from the rest of London. It was a thriving shipbuilding centre even before the construction of the Surrey Commercial Docks in the nineteenth century. However, no other set of London dockyards took such a hammering in the Blitz, and the immediate postwar decades were years of inexorable decline. The docks have since been reclaimed for new housing estates and more upmarket Docklands developments. Despite its geographical isolation, you can reach Rotherhithe very easily via the tube and Overground network.

Around St Mary's Church

The bit of Rotherhithe worth visiting is the heart of the old eighteenth-century seafaring village around **St Mary's Church**, which stands in its own leafy square, northwest of the Overground station. The church itself is unremarkable, but it has rich maritime associations: several of the furnishings are made from the timber of the *Fighting Temeraire*, the veteran of Trafalgar which ended its days in a Rotherhithe breaker's yard (Turner's painting of its last voyage hangs in the National Gallery), and the master of the *Mayflower* was buried here. The **Mayflower** was Rotherhithe-owned and -crewed, and set off from outside the *Mayflower* pub in 1620 to transport the Pilgrim Fathers to the New World. (The ship only called in at Plymouth for repairs after being damaged in the English Channel.) The pub (see p.394), north of the church, is a rickety white weatherboarded building, badly damaged in the last war, and a minor pilgrimage site for Americans.

16

Brunel Museum

Railway Ave • Daily 10am–5pm, Tues until 9.30pm • £3 • ☎ 020 7231 3840, ⊛ brunel-museum.org.uk • ⊖ Rotherhithe

To the northeast of St Mary's, the **Brunel Museum** is a brick-built shed that marks the site of the Thames Tunnel, the world's first under-river tunnel. It was begun in 1825 by Marc Brunel and his more famous son, Isambard, and was originally designed for horse-drawn carriages to travel between Rotherhithe and Wapping. The technology used was invented by Brunel senior and its basic principles have been used for all subsequent tunnelling. However, plagued by periodic flooding, labour unrest, fatalities and lack of funds, the tunnel took eighteen years to construct and was nicknamed "The Great Bore" by the press.

Funds ran out before the spiral ramps, which would have allowed horse-drawn vehicles actually to use the tunnel, could be built. Instead, in 1843, the tunnel was opened to pedestrians as a tourist attraction, pulling in two million visitors in its first year. It was visited by Queen Victoria herself, who knighted Brunel junior, but the tunnel soon became the haunt of whores and "tunnel thieves". In 1869 it was taken over by the East London Railway (now the Overground) and remains the most watertight of all the rail tunnels under the Thames. As well as telling the tunnel's fascinating story, the museum displays some of the old souvenirs sold in Victorian times.

To the east of the engine house lies the circular working shaft, which now sports a lovely **garden** on its roof, and hosts the *Midnight Apothecary* cocktail bar (April–Sept Sat 5.30–10.30pm & Sun 12.30–5pm). Inside the shaft, the Grand Entrance Hall survives and is used to stage a wide variety of music and theatre events – you can also visit it as part of a guided tour of the area (see website for details).

Surrey Docks

The once marshy land of Rotherhithe peninsula, east of the old village, was chosen as the site for London's first wet dock, the Howland Great Dock, built in 1696 to take on any extra repair work and refitting emanating from the Royal Dockyards in nearby Deptford. Later renamed Greenland Dock, it became part of the network known as **Surrey Commercial Docks**. The main trade was timber, which was piled into stacks up

SCANDINAVIAN SEAMEN'S MISSIONS

One of the more unusual legacies of Rotherhithe's seafaring past is the trio of Scandinavian seamen's missions – a reminder of the former dominance of the timber trade in the nearby Surrey Docks – which survive to the south of the tube station, around Albion Street. The most prominent is the **Norwegian Seamen's Church**, by the approach road to the Rotherhithe Tunnel, which flies the Norwegian flag and features a longboat atop its weather vane. Albion Street itself still has a Scandinavian bent – even the nearby public toilets are bilingual – and further down you'll find the well-maintained **Finnish Seamen's Mission**, built in modernist style in 1958, with a freestanding belfry that looks more like a fire-station practice tower. The **Swedish Seamen's Church** (complete with hostel), further south at 120 Lower Rd, completes the trio but is architecturally undistinguished.

to 80ft high by porters nicknamed "Flying Blondins" (after the tightrope walker), who wore distinctive leather pads on their heads and shoulders to protect them from splinters. The docks took a pounding in the Blitz, and on one particular occasion, 350,000 tons of timber were set ablaze in one of the largest fires ever seen in Britain.

Rotherhithe Street

Rotherhithe Street, which hugs the riverbank, is the longest street in London at around a mile and a half. It's mainly residential, a mixture of new Docklands developments and council housing, but the **Thames Path**, which runs parallel to it for most of the way, is pleasant enough to walk or cycle along, with great views over to Limehouse and Canary Wharf.

Halfway along the street, you can learn more about the area's history at the **Pumphouse Museum** (Mon–Fri 10am–4pm; free; ☎020 7231 2976, ⓦthepumphouse.org.uk; bus #C10 from ⊖ Canada Water or Rotherhithe), housed in an old pumphouse on Lavender Road. Further along, you can catch a boat back into town or on to Greenwich, from the Nelson Dock Pier beside the *Hilton* hotel. If you've time to kill, check out the three-masted schooner (now a restaurant) built in the 1950s as a training ship for the French navy, and nearby **Nelson House**, a beautiful Georgian house built for one of the wealthy owners of Nelson Dock.

16

KENSINGTON PALACE

Hyde Park and Kensington Gardens

Most visitors are amazed at how green and pleasant so much of the city centre is, with three royal parks – St James's Park, Green Park and Hyde Park – forming a continuous grassy belt that stretches for nearly three miles. Hyde Park, together with its westerly extension, Kensington Gardens, is the largest of the trio, covering a distance of a mile and a half from Speakers' Corner in the northeast to Kensington Palace in the southwest. You can jog, swim, fish, sunbathe or mess about in boats on the Serpentine, cross the park on horseback or mountain bike, or view the latest in modern art at the Serpentine Gallery. At the end of your journey, you've made it to one of London's most exclusive districts, the Royal Borough of Kensington and Chelsea (see p.248).

Hyde Park

Daily 5am–midnight • ☎ 0300 061 2000, ⓦ royalparks.gov.uk • ⊖ Hyde Park Corner, Marble Arch, Knightsbridge or Lancaster Gate

17

Seized from the Church by Henry VIII to satisfy his desire for yet more hunting grounds, **Hyde Park** was first opened to the public by James I, when refreshments available included "milk from a red cow". Under Charles II, the park became a fashionable gathering place for the beau monde, who rode round the circular drive known as the Ring, pausing to gossip and admire each other's equipages. Its present appearance is mostly due to Queen Caroline, an enthusiast for landscape gardens, who spent a great deal of George II's money creating the park's main feature, the **Serpentine** lake.

Hangings, muggings and duels, the 1851 Great Exhibition and numerous public events have all taken place here – and it's still a popular gathering point for pop concerts in the summer, Christmas markets in the winter and political demonstrations all year round. For the most part, however, Hyde Park is simply a wonderful open space that allows you to lose all sight of the city beyond a few persistent tower blocks. The southeast corner of the park contains two conventional tourist attractions: **Apsley House**, housing a museum to the Duke of Wellington, and the triumphal **Wellington Arch**, which you can now climb.

Marble Arch

Marble Arch looks rather forlorn on a ferociously busy traffic island in the treeless northeastern corner of the park at the west end of Oxford Street. Designed in 1828 by John Nash as a triumphal entrance for Buckingham Palace, it has suffered over the years: the sculpted friezes intended to adorn it ended up on the palace, while the equestrian statue of George IV, intended to surmount it, was carted off to Trafalgar Square. When the palace was extended in the 1840s, the arch was moved to form an entrance to Hyde Park, its upper chambers used as a police observation post. During the 1855 riot (see below), a detachment of police emerged from the arch, like the Greeks from the Trojan Horse, much to the surprise of the demonstrators. The arch has been joined recently by a slightly surreal 33ft-high bronze sculpture of a horse's head by Nic Fiddian-Green.

Tyburn Convent

8 Hyde Park Place • Daily 6.30am–8.30pm • Guided tours 10.30am, 3.30 & 5.30pm • Free • ⓦ tyburnconvent.org.uk • ⊖ Marble Arch

Despite appearance, Marble Arch stands on the most historically charged spot in Hyde Park, as it marks the site of **Tyburn gallows**, the city's main public execution spot from at least 1196 until 1783 (when the action moved to Newgate). There's a plaque on the traffic island in the middle of Edgware Road where it joins Bayswater Road marking the approximate site of the gallows, where around fifty thousand lost their lives. Of these, some 105 were Catholics, martyred during the Reformation, in whose memory the **Tyburn Convent** was established in 1902. It's run by a group of cloistered French Benedictine nuns who are happy to show visitors round the basement shrine, which contains a mock-up of the Tyburn gibbet over the main altar, and various pictures and relics of the martyrs. The house next door to (and now part of) the convent, no. 10, is reputedly London's smallest, measuring just three and a half feet across.

Speakers' Corner

ⓦ speakerscorner.net • ⊖ Marble Arch

In 1855 an estimated 250,000 people gathered in the northeastern corner of the park to protest against the Sunday Trading Bill (Karl Marx was among the crowd and thought it was the beginning of the English Revolution), and ever since it has been one of London's most popular spots for political demos. In 1872 the government licensed free assembly at **Speakers' Corner**, a peculiarly English Sunday-morning tradition that continues to this day, featuring a motley assortment of ranters and hecklers. Despite the park authorities' best attempts, the largest demonstration in London's history took place in this section of the park in 2003 when over a million people turned up to try and stop the war against Iraq.

17

Hyde Park Corner

The park's southeast corner, **Hyde Park Corner** is a better place to enter the park than Marble Arch. You'll still have to battle with the traffic, but at least you can visit **Wellington Arch**, which stands at the centre of London's first roundabout. A statue of Wellington no longer graces the arch, but instead stands at ground level opposite his erstwhile residence, **Apsley House** (see p.242). Wellington is depicted seated astride his faithful steed, Copenhagen, who carried the field marshal for sixteen hours during the Battle of Waterloo; the horse eventually died in 1836 and was buried with full military honours at the duke's country pile in Hampshire.

Close by are two powerful war memorials unveiled in 1925: the first, the **Machine Gun Corps Memorial**, features the naked figure of David leaning on Goliath's sword and the chilling inscription, "Saul hath slain his thousands, but David his tens of thousands"; the larger of the two, the **Artillery Memorial**, includes a 9.2-inch howitzer rendered in Portland stone, realistic relief depictions of the brutality of war and the equally blunt, Shakespearean epitaph, "Here was a royal fellowship of death".

These two have since been joined by two much larger, very striking memorials: the **Australian War Memorial** is a gargantuan curved wall of grey granite slabs inscribed with the names of the towns in which the soldiers were born and the battles they fought; opposite stand the sixteen bronze spikes of the **New Zealand Memorial**, each of which is inscribed with text, patterns and sculptures commemorating the bonds between New Zealand and the UK.

Much more conventional in approach (and controversial in subject matter) is the gargantuan **RAF Bomber Command Memorial**, unveiled in 2012, just inside Green Park, on the eastern edge of Hyde Park Corner, as it joins Piccadilly. The tone is decidedly triumphant, with a Neoclassical portico sheltering a larger-than-life air crew amid defiant quotes from Churchill (and Pericles).

TYBURN GALLOWS

For nearly five hundred years, **Tyburn** was the capital's main **public execution** site, its three-legged gibbet known as the "Tyburn Tree" or the "Triple Tree", capable of dispatching over twenty people at one go. Dressed in their best clothes, the condemned were first processed through the streets in a cart (the nobility were allowed to travel in their own carriages) from Newgate Prison, often with the noose already in place. They received a nosegay at St Sepulchre, opposite the prison, and then a pint of ale at various taverns along the route, so that most were blind drunk by the time they arrived at Tyburn. The driver had to remain sober, however, hence the expression "on the wagon".

The condemned were allowed to make a speech to the crowd and were attended by a chaplain, though according to one eighteenth-century spectator he was "more the subject of ridicule than of serious attention". The same witness describes how the executioner, who drove the cart, then tied the rope to the tree: "This done he gives the horse a lash with his whip, away goes the cart and there swings my gentleman kicking in the air. The Hangman does not give himself the trouble to put them out of their pain but some of their friends or relations do it for them. They pull the dying person by the legs and beat his breast to dispatch him as soon as possible."

Not all relatives were so fatalistic, however, and some would attempt to support the condemned in the hope of a last-minute reprieve, or of reviving the victim when they were cut down. Fights frequently broke out when the body was cut down, between the relatives, the spectators (who believed the corpse had miraculous medicinal qualities), and the surgeons (who were allowed ten corpses a year for dissection). The executioner, known as "**Jack Ketch**" after the famous London hangman, was allowed to take home the victim's clothes, and made further profit by selling the hanging rope by the inch. Following the 1780 Gordon Riots, the powers-that-be took fright at unruly gatherings like Tyburn, and in 1783 the Tyburn Tree was demolished.

17 Wellington Arch

Hyde Park Corner • Wed–Sun: April–Oct 10am–5pm; Nov–March 10am–4pm • EH • £4 • ⊖ Hyde Park Corner

Designed by a youthful Decimus Burton in 1828 to commemorate Wellington's victories in the Napoleonic Wars, **Wellington Arch** originally served as the northern entrance to Buckingham Palace. Positioned opposite Burton's delicate Hyde Park Screen, the arch once formed part of a fine architectural ensemble with Apsley House, Wellington's London residence, and the former St George's Hospital, now *The Lanesborough Hotel* (see p.377). Unfortunately the symmetry was destroyed when the arch was repositioned in 1883 to line up with Constitution Hill – named after the "constitutional" walks that Charles II used to take here. The arch's original statue was an enormous equestrian portrayal of the "Iron Duke" erected in 1846 while he was still alive. The duke was taken down in 1883, and eventually replaced by Peace and her four-horse chariot, erected in 1912. Inside, you can view a permanent exhibition on the history of the arch, and special exhibitions on England's heritage, and take a lift to the top of the monument (once London's smallest postwar police station) where the exterior balconies offer a bird's-eye view of the swirling traffic of London's first-ever roundabout established in 1962.

Apsley House

149 Piccadilly • Wed–Sun: April–Oct 11am–5pm; Nov–March 11am–4pm • EH • £6.70 • ⊖ Hyde Park Corner

Known during the Iron Duke's lifetime as "Number One, London", **Apsley House** was once an immensely desirable residence, but nowadays, overlooking a very busy roundabout, it would be poor reward for any national hero. The interior isn't what it used to be either, but in this case it's Wellington who's to blame. Built and exquisitely decorated by Robert Adam in the 1770s for Baron Apsley, it was remodelled by Benjamin Wyatt

---

THE IRON DUKE

Perhaps if the **Duke of Wellington** had died, like Nelson, at his moment of greatest triumph, he too would enjoy an unsullied posthumous reputation. Instead, the famously blunt duke went on to become the epitome of the outmoded, reactionary conservative, earning his famous nickname, the "Iron Duke", not from his fearless military campaigning, but from the iron shutters he had to install at Apsley House after his windows were broken by demonstrators rioting in favour of the 1832 Reform Act, to which the duke was vehemently opposed.

Born **Arthur Wesley** in Dublin in 1769 – the same year as Napoleon – he never considered himself Irish: "just because you're born in a stable, doesn't make you a horse" he is alleged to have said. He was educated at (but hated) Eton and the French military academy at Angers, and campaigned out in India, helping to defeat Tipu Sultan, and becoming Governor of Mysore. After continued military success in his Napoleonic campaigns, he eventually became Duke of Wellington in 1814, shortly before achieving his most famous victory of all at Waterloo.

With great reluctance he became **prime minister** in 1828, "a station, to the duties of which I am unaccustomed, in which I was not wished, and for which I was not qualified…I should have been mad if I had thought of such a thing". Despite his own misgivings, his government passed the Catholic Relief Act – allowing Catholics to sit in Parliament – thus avoiding civil war in Ireland, but splitting the Tory ranks. Accused of popery by the Earl of Winchelsea, Wellington challenged him to a duel in Battersea Park; the duke fired and missed (he was a notoriously bad shot), while the earl shot into the air and apologized for the slur.

Wellington's opposition to the 1832 Reform Act brought down his government and allowed the Whigs (under Earl Grey, of tea fame) to form a majority government for the first time in sixty years. Despite retiring from public life in 1846, he was on hand to organize the defence of the capital against the Chartists in 1848, and strolled across to the Great Exhibition every day in 1851. Two million people lined the streets for his funeral in 1852 (more than for anyone before or since), and he has more outdoor statues (and pubs named after him) in London than any other historical figure. Despite this, his greatest legacy is, of course, the **Wellington boot**, originally made of leather, now rubber.

HYDE PARK STATUES AND MEMORIALS

Hyde Park is peppered with statues, none more colossal than the 18ft-high bronze of **Achilles**, in the southeastern corner of the park, designed in 1822 by Richard Westmacott to commemorate the Duke of Wellington, and cast from captured French cannon. As the country's first public nude statue it caused outrage, especially since many thought it a portrait of the duke himself, and the chief fundraisers were "the women of Great Britain". In actual fact, it represents neither the duke nor Achilles, but is a copy of one of the Horse Tamers from the Quirinal Hill in Rome. William Wilberforce led a campaign to have the statue removed for decency's sake; a fig leaf was placed in the appropriate place as a compromise.

Visible to the north is the **July 7 Memorial**, a simple, startling memorial to the 2005 London suicide bombings. The 52 stainless steel pillars stand nearly 12ft high, and each one is inscribed with the victim's time and place of death. Only a short distance to the west, in The Dell, a couple of boulders set in gravel within a copse of silver birch, form an even more understated **Holocaust Memorial**.

To the north of the nearby Serpentine stands the park's over-manicured bird sanctuary, overlooked by the **Hudson Memorial**, sculpted by Jacob Epstein and featuring a low relief of Rima, a naked, female, South American version of Tarzan, and several exotic birds. (Rima the Jungle Girl is the main protagonist in the 1904 adventure novel *Green Mansions*, written by the naturalist and writer W.H. Hudson.) It's difficult to believe now, but when the memorial was unveiled in 1925, there was a campaign of protest against the statue, led by the *Daily Mail*. Rima was considered too butch, the art too "Bolshevist" and the memorial later became the victim of several (anti-semitic) attacks.

after Wellington bought the place in 1817. Wyatt faced the red-brick exterior with Bath stone and more or less got rid of the Adam interiors. As a result, the house is very much as it would have been in Wellington's day, and the current duke still lives in the attic.

The art collection

The house is worth visiting for the **art collection** alone. Wellington acquired the paintings in 1813 after the Battle of Vittoria, when he seized the baggage train of Napoleon's brother, Joseph, who was fleeing for France with two hundred paintings belonging to the King of Spain. The best pieces, including works by de Hooch, Van Dyck, Goya, Rubens and Murillo, cover the red walls of the **Waterloo Gallery** on the first floor, where sliding mirrors cover the windows. The most prized works of all are a trio by Velázquez – *The Water-Seller of Seville, Portrait of a Gentleman* and *Two Young Men Eating at a Humble Table* – though Wellington preferred Correggio's *Agony in the Garden*, the key for which he used to carry round with him, so he could take the picture out of its frame and dust it fondly.

The rooms

Like several of the house's other rooms, the Waterloo Gallery was originally hung with yellow satin, which, as one of the duke's friends lamented, "is just the very worst colour he can have for the pictures and will kill the effect of the gilding". It was here that Wellington held his annual veterans' **Waterloo Banquet**, using the thousand-piece silver-gilt Portuguese service, now displayed in the rather lugubrious **Dining Room** at the other end of the house. Most of the Waterloo portraits are, in fact, hung in the adjacent **Striped Drawing Room**, which is decorated like a military tent in the manner of Napoleon's Loire chateau, Malmaison.

Canova's famous, more than twice life-sized, **nude statue of Napoleon** stands at the foot of the main staircase, having been bought by the government for the duke in 1816. It was disliked by the sitter, not least for the tiny figure of Victory in the emperor's hand, which appears to be trying to fly away. In the dimly lit **Plate and China Room**, also on the ground floor, you can view numerous gifts to the duke, including a four hundred-piece Prussian dinner service decorated with scenes of Wellington's life,

17

THE GREAT EXHIBITION AND THE CRYSTAL PALACE

South of the Serpentine was the site of the **Great Exhibition** of the Works and Industry of All Nations, held between May 1 and October 15, 1851. The idea originated with Henry Cole, a minor civil servant in the Record Office, and was taken up enthusiastically by Prince Albert despite opposition from snooty Kensington residents, who complained it would attract an "invasion of undesirables who would ravish their silver and their serving maids". A competition to design the exhibition building produced 245 rejected versions, until Joseph Paxton, head gardener to the Duke of Devonshire, offered to build his "**Crystal Palace**", a wrought-iron and glass structure some 1848ft long and 408ft wide. The acceptance of Paxton's radical proposal was an act of faith by the exhibition organizers, since such a structure had never been built, and their faith was amply rewarded – two hundred workers completed the building in just four months.

As well as showing off the achievements of the **British Empire**, it was also a unique opportunity for people to enjoy the products of other cultures. Thousands of exhibits were housed in the Crystal Palace, including the Koh-i-Noor diamond (displayed in a birdcage), an Indian ivory throne, a floating church from Philadelphia, a bed which awoke its occupant by ejecting him or her into a cold bath, false teeth designed not to be displaced when yawning, a fountain running with eau de Cologne and all manner of china, fabrics and glass.

To everyone's surprise, **six million visitors** came, and the exhibition made a profit, which was used to buy 87 acres of land south of Kensington Road, for the creation of a "Museumland" where "the arts and sciences could be promoted and taught in a way which would be of practical use to industry and make Britain the leading country of the industrialized world". The Crystal Palace itself was dismantled after the exhibition and rebuilt in southeast London in 1854, where it served as a concert hall, theatre, menagerie and exhibition space, only to be entirely destroyed by fire in 1936 (see p.313).

and the bizarre Egyptian service, which was originally a divorce present from Napoleon to Josephine; unsurprisingly, she rejected it and Louis XVIII ended up giving it to the duke. In the basement there's plenty of Wellingtonia, a goodly selection of cruel, contemporary caricatures and a pair of the famous boots.

Rotten Row

From behind the Hyde Park Screen, which stands beside Apsley House, two roads set off west to Kensington: South Carriage Road, which is open to cars, and **Rotten Row**, which remains a bridle path. The name is thought to be a corruption of *route du roi* (king's way), after William III who established it as a bridle path linking Westminster and Kensington. William had three hundred oil lamps hung from the trees to try to combat the increasing number of highwaymen active in the park, thus making Rotten Row the first road in the country to be lit at night. The measure was only partly successful – George II himself was later mugged here. To the south of Rotten Row, the **Hyde Park Barracks** are difficult to miss, thanks to Basil Spence's uncompromising 308ft-tall concrete residential tower block. Early in the morning, you might catch sight of the Household Cavalry exercising in the park, and at around 10.30am daily (Sun 9.30am) they set off for the Horse Guards building in Whitehall for Changing the Guard (see p.48).

The Serpentine

Rowing boats and pedalos Easter–Oct **Solarshuttle** June–Aug daily every 30min noon–dusk • One way £2.50

The Serpentine, Hyde Park's curvaceous lake, was created in 1730 by damming the Westbourne, a small tributary of the Thames, so that Queen Caroline might have a spot for the royal yachts to mess about on. A miniature re-enactment of the Battle of Trafalgar was staged here in 1814, and two years later Shelley's pregnant wife, Harriet Westbrook, drowned herself after the poet had eloped with the 16-year-old Mary Wollstonecraft Godwin. The popular **Lido** (see p.439) is on the south bank, alongside its lovely café, and rowing boats and pedalos can be rented from the **Boathouse** on the north bank. The solar-powered **Solarshuttle** boat ferries folk from one bank to the other in summer.

Diana Fountain

Daily: March & Oct 10am–5.45pm; April & Sept 10am–6.45pm; May–Aug 10am–7.45pm; Nov–Feb 10am–3.45pm • Free • ⊖ Knightsbridge or Lancaster Gate

17

Close to the Lido is the **Diana Fountain**, a memorial to the Princess of Wales, which opened in 2004. Less of a fountain, and more of a giant oval-shaped mini-moat, the intention was to allow children to play in the running water, but, after three people suffered minor injuries, the fountain has been fenced off and supplied with security guards, making it rather less fun for kids, who are now officially only allowed to dabble their feet. More fun is the **Diana Memorial Playground**, in the northwest corner of Kensington Gardens, featuring a ship stuck in sand, paving gongs and other groovy playthings.

Kensington Gardens

Daily 6am to dusk • ☎ 020 7298 2141, ⓦ royalparks.gov.uk • ⊖ Lancaster Gate, Queensway or High Street Kensington

The park's more tranquil half, west of the West Carriage Drive, is known as **Kensington Gardens**, and is, strictly speaking, separate from Hyde Park, though the only difference is that Kensington Gardens locks its gates at dusk. More exclusive because of the nearby royalty at Kensington Palace, the gardens were first opened to the public in George II's reign, but only on Sundays and only to those in formal dress, not including sailors, soldiers or liveried servants. Unrestricted access was only granted in Victoria's reign, by which time, according to the Russian ambassador's wife, the park had already been "annexed as a middle-class rendezvous. Good society no longer [went] there except to drown itself".

Long Water

The upper section of the Serpentine – beyond the bridge – is, officially, actually known as the **Long Water**, and is by far the prettiest section of the lake. It narrows until it reaches the lovely **Italian Gardens**, which boasts a group of five fountains, laid out symmetrically in the 1860s, in front of a pumphouse disguised as an Italianate loggia.

Pet Cemetery

To the east of the Italian Gardens, by Victoria Gate, lies the odd little **Pet Cemetery**, begun in the 1880s when Mr and Mrs J. Lewis Barnes buried their Maltese terrier, Cherry, here. When the Duke of Cambridge buried his wife's pet hound at the same spot after it had been run over on Bayswater Road, it became *the* place to bury your pooch; three hundred other cats and dogs followed, until the last burial in 1967. The cemetery – "perhaps the most horrible spectacle in Britain", according to George Orwell – is no longer open to the public, though you can peep over the wall.

Serpentine Gallery

Daily 10am–6pm; Teahouse mid-June to mid-Oct • Free • ☎ 020 7402 6075, ⓦ serpentinegallery.org • ⊖ Knightsbridge or South Kensington

In the southeast corner of the park stands the **Serpentine Gallery**, built as a tearoom in 1908 because the park authorities thought "poorer visitors" might otherwise cause trouble if left without refreshments. An art gallery since the 1960s, it has a reputation for lively, and often controversial, contemporary art exhibitions, and contains an

---

ROYAL GUN SALUTES

At noon in Hyde Park on February 6 (Accession Day), April 21 (Queen's Birthday) and November 14 (Prince of Wales's Birthday), the Royal Horse Artillery wheel out cannons and the park resounds to a 41-round **Royal Gun Salute**. If a date falls on a Sunday, then the salute takes place the next day. Further gun salutes take place in Green Park, on 2 June (Coronation Day), 10 June (Duke of Edinburgh's Birthday), at 11.08am for the State Opening of Parliament (in early May) and at 11am on the Queen's official birthday (a variable date in June), as well as for official State visits.

17

PETER PAN & CO

The best-known of all the park's outdoor monuments is **Peter Pan**, the fictional character who enters London along the Serpentine and whose statue stands by the west bank of the Long Water; fairies, squirrels, rabbits, birds and mice scamper round the pedestal. It was in Kensington Gardens that the author, J.M. Barrie, used to walk his dog, and it was here that he met the five pretty, upper-class Llewellyn Davies boys, who wore "blue blouses and bright red tam o'shanters", were the inspiration for the "Lost Boys", and whose guardian he eventually became. Barrie himself paid for the statue, which was erected in secret during the night in 1912.

The rough-hewn muscleman struggling with his horse, to the southwest of Peter Pan, is G.F. Watts' **Physical Energy**, a copy of the Rhodes memorial in Cape Town; to the north is a granite obelisk raised to **John Hanning Speke**, who was the first non-African to find the source of the Nile, and who died in 1864 after accidentally shooting himself rather than the partridge he was aiming at. Just outside the Diana Memorial Playground is the **Elfin Oak**, a gnarled stump from Richmond Park, carved with little animals and mystical creatures by children's-book illustrator Ivor Innes in the late 1920s.

excellent bookshop. Each year, the gallery also commissions a leading architect to design a funky temporary **pavilion** for its summer-only teahouse extension.

A second exhibition space, the **Serpentine Sackler Gallery**, is housed in the Magazine, a former munitions depot, built in 1805, on the north side of the Serpentine, so that the military could arm themselves in the event of a "foreign invasion or popular uprising". Designed in the style of a Palladian villa, it has been restored and extended by Zaha Hadid and features two annual commissions: a large-scale, indoor light installation and an outdoor "playscape" designed for children and adults.

Albert Memorial

45min guided tours March–Dec first Sun of month, 2 & 3pm • £6 • ☎ 020 7495 0916, ⓦ royalparks.org.uk • ⊖ South Kensington

Completed in 1876 by George Gilbert Scott, the **Albert Memorial**, on the south side of Kensington Gardens, is as much a hymn to the glorious achievements of Britain as to its subject, Queen Victoria's husband (who died of typhoid in 1861, aged 42), who sits under its central canopy, gilded from head to toe, clutching a catalogue for the 1851 Great Exhibition. The pomp of the monument is overwhelming: the spire, inlaid with semiprecious stones and marbles, rises to 180ft; a marble frieze around the pediment is cluttered with 169 life-sized figures (all men) in high relief, depicting poets, musicians, painters, architects and sculptors from ancient Egypt onwards; the pillars are topped with bronzes of Astronomy, Chemistry, Geology and Geometry; mosaics show Poetry, Painting, Architecture and Sculpture; four outlying marble groups represent the four continents; and other statuary pays homage to Agriculture, Commerce and other aspects of imperial economics. Albert would not have been amused: "I can say, with perfect absence of humbug, that I would rather not be made the prominent feature of such a monument…it would upset my equanimity to be permanently ridiculed and laughed at in effigy", he once claimed.

Kensington Palace

Daily: March–Oct 10am–6pm; Nov–Feb 10am–5pm • £15 • ☎ 020 3166 6000, ⓦ hrp.org.uk • ⊖ Queensway or High Street Kensington

On the western edge of Kensington Gardens stands **Kensington Palace**, a modestly proportioned, Jacobean brick mansion bought as an out-of-town residence by William and Mary in 1689 as the king's asthma and bronchitis were aggravated by Whitehall's damp and fumes. Wren, Hawksmoor and later William Kent were called in to embellish the place, though the palace was actually chief royal residence for barely fifty years.

Queen Victoria was born in Kensington Palace in 1819 and spent her dull, sad childhood cooped up here with her strict mother, the Duchess of Kent, who slept with her in the same room. According to her diary, her best friends were the palace's numerous "black beetles". Victoria's apartments have not been preserved, but you get to see the gloomy Red Saloon, where the 18-year-old queen held her first Privy Council meeting, just hours after William IV's death on June 20, 1837.

Nowadays, KP – as it's fondly known in royal circles – is the official London residence of Prince William and Kate Middleton (and the unofficial home of Prince Harry). It's also where William's mother, **Princess Diana**, lived until her death in 1997, although there's no access to her rooms, which were on the west side of the palace, where the dukes and duchesses of Kent and Gloucester all still live.

The palace is home to the **Royal Ceremonial Dress Collection**, which doesn't have a permanent display but there's always a selection exhibited. Usually you get to see a few of the Queen's dresses – from her haute 1950s wardrobe to her more suspect later penchant for peach-coloured frocks – and a selection of Diana's over-the-top 1980s dresses.

KP's most handsome facade faces south, behind a flamboyant statue of William III, given to Edward VII by the Kaiser. The public entrance is on the east side, and must be approached from the Round Pond, where George I used to keep his edible turtles, and the Broad Walk, a favourite rollerblading avenue; both are overlooked by a flattering statue of Queen Victoria sculpted by her daughter, Princess Louise.

INFORMATION

Tours Some of KP's themed tours change from year to year, others, like the King's and the Queen's State Apartments, are permanent. Unfortunately, instead of an audioguide, the palace offers relentlessly quirky multimedia installations.

Eating To the north of the palace there's a lovely café in Hawksmoor's Orangery, built for Queen Anne as a summer dining room, and decorated with carving and statues by Grinling Gibbons.

King's State Apartments

The palace's most impressive rooms are in the **King's State Apartments**, beginning with the grandiose **King's Staircase**, designed by William Kent, with its Irish black marble steps, its Tijou wrought-iron balustrade and trompe-l'oeil crowds of courtiers and yeomen. Another great Kent creation is the "grotesque"-style painting on the ceiling of the **Presence Chamber**, which also features a lovely pear-wood Gibbons overmantle with weeping putti. Further on, the **Cupola Room**, with its monstrously ugly clock occupying centre stage, features another wonderful trompe-l'oeil fresco, which gives the effect of a coffered dome. The palace's grandest room, the **Long Gallery**, has red damask walls hung with paintings by, among others, Tintoretto. Also of interest is the wind dial above the fireplace, connected to the palace weather vane, built for William III and still functioning.

Queen's State Apartments

The **Queen's State Apartments** begin with the **Queen's Gallery**, once magnificently decorated with 154 pieces of Oriental porcelain (a mere handful remain), and instead lined with royal portraits. At the far end is one by Peter Lely, of Anne Hyde, mistress and later first wife of the future James II; they officially married after she was already heavily pregnant, causing something of a royal scandal even in the libidinous Restoration period. The Queen's Apartments are much more modest than the King's, wood-panelled rooms hung with Dutch works reflecting the tastes of William and Mary, so to try and boost their appeal, the curators have stepped up the multimedia theatrics. There's an incessant whispering soundtrack to simulate gossip in the **Queen's Closet**, scene of a furious quarrel between Queen Anne and her lover, the Duchess of Marlborough, after which they never saw each other again. Eighteen little chairs are displayed to represent Queen Anne's children, all of whom pre-deceased her, including Prince William, who died after dancing too much on his 11th birthday. The best original decor is in the **Queen's Bedchamber**, which boasts a four-poster bed that belonged to Queen Mary of Modena, James II's second wife – it was here that the diminutive and corpulent Queen Anne died of gout.

ROYAL ALBERT HALL

South Kensington, Knightsbridge and Chelsea

The Royal Borough of Kensington and Chelsea, particularly the area around Knightsbridge, has been in vogue ever since royalty moved into Kensington Palace in the late seventeenth century. The popular tourist attractions lie in South Kensington, where three of London's top free museums – the Victoria and Albert, Natural History and Science museums – stand on land bought with the proceeds of the 1851 Great Exhibition. Chelsea, to the south, also has royal connections, though these date mostly from Tudor times and have left only a few scant remains. Since the nineteenth century, however, when artists and writers began to move here, Chelsea has been more bohemian than its neighbours – today, the Saatchi Gallery continues that tradition.

South Kensington

To everyone's surprise, the 1851 Great Exhibition was not only an enormous success, but also actually yielded a profit, with which Prince Albert and his committee bought 87 acres of land in **South Kensington**. Institutions and museums, whose purpose was to "extend the influence of Science and Art upon Productive Industry", were to be established here to form a kind of "**Museumland**". Albert died of typhoid in 1861 at the age of just 42, and never saw his dream fully realized, but "Albertopolis", with its remarkable cluster of **museums and colleges**, plus the vast Royal Albert Hall, now stands as one of London's most enlightened examples of urban planning.

With the founding of "Museumland", the surrounding area was transformed almost overnight into one of the most fashionable in town. Fields, farms and private estates were turned into street after street of ostentatious, whitewashed Italianate terraces, grandiose red-brick mansions and mews houses. Today, the borough includes some of the world's most expensive slices of real estate, and is the heartland of the privately educated, wealthy offspring of the English middle and upper classes and also the stamping ground of the international rich and famous.

Victoria and Albert Museum (V&A)

Cromwell Rd • Daily 10am–5.45pm, Fri until 10pm • Free • Various free tours set off regularly from the main information desk in the Grand Entrance • ☎ 020 7942 2000, ⓦ vam.ac.uk • ⊖ South Kensington

For variety and scale, the **Victoria and Albert Museum** is the greatest museum of applied arts in the world. The range of exhibits on display means that whatever your taste, there's bound to be something to grab your attention: the finest collection of Italian sculpture outside Italy, the world's largest collection of Indian art outside India, plus extensive Chinese, Islamic and Japanese galleries; a gallery of twentieth-century objets d'art; and more Constable paintings than Tate Britain. The V&A's temporary shows on art, photography and fashion – some of which you have to pay for – are among the best in Britain. As Baedeker noted in 1905, "it can hardly be claimed that the arrangements of the [museum] are specially perspicuous". Beautifully but haphazardly displayed across a seven-mile, four-storey maze of rooms, the V&A's treasures are impossible to survey in a single visit, so get hold of a **free floor plan** to help you decide which areas to focus on.

The V&A began life in 1852 as the Museum of Manufactures – it being Albert's intention to bolster Britain's industrial dominance by inspiring factory workers, students and craftspeople with examples of excellence in applied art and design. Later it was renamed the South Kensington Museum, with Queen Victoria laying the foundation stone in 1857. She was on hand again to give her blessing to the present, deeply colonial building in 1899 (her last major public engagement), after which it was known as the Victoria and Albert Museum; ten years later Aston Webb's imposing main entrance, with its octagonal cupola, flying buttresses and pinnacles, was finished. The side entrance on Exhibition Road, originally built in 1873 for the School of Naval Architects, is equally ornate, with terracotta arcading and Minton tiles.

Raphael Cartoons

The most famous of the V&A's many exhibits are the **Raphael Cartoons** (room 48a) – from the Italian *cartone* meaning a large piece of paper. They comprise seven vast, full-colour paintings in distemper, which are, in fact, designs for tapestries ordered in 1515 by Pope Leo X for the Sistine Chapel. The pictures – based on episodes from the New Testament – were bought by the future Charles I and subsequently reproduced in countless tapestries and engravings thereby becoming more familiar and influential than any of the artist's paintings. Alongside the paintings is an example of one of the tapestries woven at Mortlake.

At the far end of the room stands the **Retable of St George**, a huge fifteenth-century gilded altarpiece from Valencia, centred on a depiction of James I of Aragon defeating the Moors at the Battle of Puig in 1237. More alarming, though, are the bloodthirsty

18

side panels, which feature the gross tortures endured by St George, with him having nails driven through his body before being placed in a cauldron of molten lead, dragged naked through the streets and finally beheaded and sawn in half.

South Asia

Such are the constraints of space that a mere fraction of the world-class **South Asia** collection is displayed (room 41), much of it derived from London's former East India

ACCOMMODATION

Aster House	3
Barclay House	5
Earl's Court YHA	4
Nadler Kensington	1
Twenty Nevern Square	2

CAFÉS

Capote y Toros	4
The Troubadour	5

RESTAURANTS

Amaya	2
Chutney Mary	6
Dinner	1
No. 10	3

PUBS AND BARS

Grenadier	2
The Nag's Head	1
Star Tavern	3

MUSIC VENUES

606 Club	5
Hammersmith Apollo	4

SHOPS

Harrods	2
Harvey Nichols	1

Company Museum. The most popular exhibit is **Tipu's Tiger**, a life-sized wooden automaton of a tiger mauling an officer of the East India Company; the innards of the tiger feature a miniature keyboard which simulates the groans of the dying soldier. It was made for the amusement of Tipu Sultan, who was killed when the British took Seringapatam in 1799, and whose watch, telescope, brooch and sword are also displayed here. Close by is the **Golden Throne**, revered by the Sikh community as it belonged to **Ranjit Singh**, the first and last Sikh emperor, and was taken by the British

SOUTH KENSINGTON, KNIGHTSBRIDGE AND CHELSEA

when they annexed the Punjab in 1849. Next to it is a conical turban decorated with quoits, which can be taken off and hurled at your enemy. Elsewhere, there's a superb white nephrite-jade wine cup, carved in the shape of a shell, made for the Mogul emperor Shah Jahan.

Islam

The **Islamic Middle East** gallery (room 42), next door, has, as its centrepiece, the silk-and-wool **Ardabil Carpet**, the world's oldest dated Persian carpet from 1540: copies have variously adorned the floors of 10 Downing Street and Hitler's Berlin office. Unusually, on the west side of the gallery, there are several oil paintings of female acrobats, a harem's tea party and several full-length portraits from the Qajar dynasty in nineteenth-century Iran.

China and Japan

In the **China** gallery (room 44), the range of materials, from jade to rhino horn, lacquer to lapis lazuli, is more striking than any individual piece, though the pair of top-hatted gentlemen carved in marble stand out in the parade of Buddhas near the entrance – they are thought to represent Korean envoys. There's a surprising range, from a sixteenth-century Ming cupboard that's so minimalist, it could be modernist, to a great Art Deco clock from fashionable interwar Shanghai.

At the main entrance to the adjacent **Japan** gallery (room 45) is an incredible bronze incense burner, decorated with life-sized peacocks. Amid the wealth of silk, lacquer and samurai armour, look out for the tiny, elaborately carved, jade and marble *netsuke* (belt toggles) portraying such quirky subjects as "spider on aubergine", "starving dog on a bed of leaves" and "badger dressed in a lotus leaf".

Cast Courts

Two enormous **Cast Courts** (rooms 46a & 46b), filled with plaster casts of famous works of art and architecture, were created at the outset of the V&A so that ordinary Londoners could experience the glories of classical and ancient art. These newly refurbished, barrel-vaulted, glass-roofed rooms remain an astonishing sight. In room 46a, a copy of the colossal Trajan's Column, sliced in half to fit in the room, towers over the rest of the plaster casts, while over in room 46b, a life-sized replica of Michelangelo's *David* stands among the pulpits of Pisa cathedral and baptistry, and Ghiberti's celebrated bronze doors from the baptistry in Florence.

Sculpture

Along the south side of the central garden (rooms 21–24), in the V&A's showpiece **Sculpture** display, you'll find **Bernini**'s life-sized fountain sculpture, *Neptune and Triton*, amid a whole series of top-notch Italian pieces. Other highlights include Canova's depiction of Theseus astride the Minotaur, and his head of Helen of Troy about which Byron wrote an eight-line paean. **Auguste Rodin** donated several sculptures to the V&A in 1914, including his beautifully wrought *The Fallen Angel*, a swirling mass of rippling bronze, and his sensuous *Cupid and Psyche*, in which the lovers emerge half-hewn from the white marble. Look out, too, for a torso by Meštrovic, several strikingly simple works by Eric Gill and an Art Deco fireplace with a relief depicting society gossip.

Round the corner (rooms 17–20), the museum displays its impressive collection of **Buddhist sculpture**, from serene, gilded-copper seated figures from Tibet and Nepal to an entire Burmese shrine. There's also a corridor of **small-scale sculpture** on Level 3 in room 111, ranging from medieval religious ivories and English alabaster relief panels to German lime-wood masterpieces and a whole collection of works by Gilbert Bayes, who worked at Doulton, the ceramics company. (Bayes' Art Deco Doulton frieze from the company's headquarters in Lambeth is displayed in room 127.)

FUTURE PLANS

Like most big museums, the V&A is in a constant state of flux, with galleries opening and closing throughout the year. There will be new **Europe 1600–1800** galleries opening in winter 2014. And with Exhibition Road being made pedestrian-friendly, the V&A have commissioned a fancy new entrance which should be completed in 2016.

Medieval & Renaissance 300–1600

To visit the V&A's outstanding **Medieval & Renaissance** galleries chronologically, head for the lower level galleries (Level 0, room 8–10c), where the highlights include the **Gloucester Candlestick**, a mass of gilded foliage and figures commissioned for the city's Benedictine abbey around 1104, and the **Becket Casket**, a Romanesque reliquary in Limoges enamel designed to house the English saint's relics. Don't miss the German altarpiece, painted around 1400 and decorated with 45 vivid scenes from the Apocalypse.

18

The collection continues into the Renaissance upstairs (Level 2, rooms 62–64b), where you'll find the **Burghley Nef**, a slightly ludicrous sixteenth-century French gilded silver salt cellar in the shape of a ship. Even more incredible craftsmanship is on view in the Italian carved pearwood altarpiece, which features a complex crucifixion scene. Other highlights include a Tintoretto self-portrait, one of Leonardo's tiny notebooks and Donatello's *Chellini Madonna*, a bronze roundel given by the artist to his doctor in lieu of payment – the reverse was designed to cast replicas in glass, and a bronze of the good doctor stands close by.

The galleries to the right of the information desk (Level 1, rooms 50a–50d) display the large-scale **Renaissance sculptures** such as Giambologna's expressively brutal *Samson Slaying a Philistine*. Passing through the immense marble and alabaster choirscreen from 's-Hertogenbosch cathedral, you'll find a series of full-scale altarpieces and an entire Florentine chapel, plus a new ambulatory-cum-treasury of monstrances, fold-away croziers, crosses and chalices.

British Galleries 1500–1760

The superbly designed **British Galleries** are a joy to visit. The first series of rooms covers **Britain 1500–1760** (Level 2, rooms 52–58b), and begins in room 58 with Tudor times. Highlights include Torrigiani's bust of Henry VII, Holbein's miniature of Anne of Cleves, with its original ivory case, and the **Howard Grace Cup**, a medieval ivory cup associated with Thomas Becket, but given a Tudor silver-gilt makeover and crowned by a tiny St George and the dragon. Other specific items to look out for include the **Dark Jewel** given to Francis Drake by Queen Elizabeth I, the tapestries embroidered by **Mary, Queen of Scots** during her incarceration, James II's wonderfully camp wedding suit and the amazing high-relief lime-wood *Stoning of St Stephen* by Grinling Gibbons.

The galleries also contain a number of **period interiors** saved in their entirety from buildings that have since been demolished. These include a Jacobean panelled room from Bromley-by-Bow, a Georgian parlour from Henrietta Street in Covent Garden and a heavily gilded Rococo **Norfolk House Music Room** from St James's Square (where concerts are held on occasional Fridays at 6.30pm). Towards the end, you should pass Roubiliac's marble statue of **Handel**, carved in 1738 and the first statue in Europe of a living artist. It originally stood in the then-fashionable Vauxhall Gardens in south London, and caused a great stir in its day, with the composer depicted as Apollo slouching in inspired disarray, one shoe dangling from his foot.

British Galleries 1760–1900

Upstairs, **Britain 1760–1900** (Level 4, rooms 118–125) kicks off with a Chippendale four-poster made for the actor David Garrick, paintings by Gainsborough and Constable and Canova's *Three Graces*. Again, period interiors are a big feature of the collection: Adam's Venetian-red Glass Drawing Room from Northumberland House and the fan-vaulted Strawberry Room from Lee Priory in Kent, which was inspired by Walpole's Gothic Revival masterpiece in Twickenham, Strawberry Hill. You'll also find plenty of outpourings from the **Arts and Crafts movement**, starting with a cabinet painted with medieval scenes by William Morris, inspired by Walter Scott's novels. Other highlights to look out for include *La Belle Iseult*, Morris's only known painting (of his future wife), and a whole room on the Scottish School, including several tables and chairs from Glasgow tearooms designed by Charles Rennie Mackintosh.

THE WORLD'S FIRST MUSEUM CAFÉ

Whatever you do, make sure you pay a visit to the *V&A Café* in the museum's original refreshment rooms, the **Morris, Gamble & Poynter Rooms**, at the back of the main galleries.

Embellished by Edward Poynter with a wash of decorative blue tiling depicting the months and seasons of the year, the eastern **Poynter Room**, where the hoi polloi ate, was finished in 1881 and originally known as the Grill Room – the grill, also designed by Poynter, is still in place and was in use until 1939.

On the opposite side, the dark-green **Morris Room** (William Morris's first public commission), completed in 1868, accommodated a better class of diner. The decorative detail is really worth taking in – gilded Pre-Raphaelite panels and Burne-Jones stained glass, embossed olive-branch wallpaper and a running cornice frieze of dogs chasing hares.

The largest and grandest of the rooms lies between the two. The **Gamble Room**, completed in 1878 by the museum's own team of artists, boasts dazzling, almost edible decor, with mustard, gold and cream-coloured Minton tiles covering the walls and pillars from floor to ceiling. Fleshy Pre-Raphaelite nudes hold up the nineteenth-century chimneypiece from Dorchester House, while a ceramic frieze of frolicking cherubs accompanies a quote from Ecclesiastes, spelt out in decorative script around the cornice.

18

Silver, Gold, Mosaics and Ironwork

Like their centrepiece, the giant **Jerningham Wine Cooler**, smothered with images of Bacchic revelry, the vast **Silver** galleries (Level 3, rooms 65–70a) are almost overwhelming. More manageable is the wonderful nearby gallery of **Sacred Silver and Stained Glass** (rooms 83–84). The stained glass, all beautifully backlit, dates from around 1140 to the present day, while the silver includes reliquaries, crosses, crowns and medieval shrines from every era and from all over Europe.

The most remarkable exhibits in the **Gold, Silver & Mosaics** galleries (Level 3, rooms 70–73) are the **gold boxes**, used to hold snuff or sweets, which were the luxury item of choice in the eighteenth century. Equally mind-blowing are the nineteenth-century **micromosaics**, although the stupefying technique is more impressive than the end results: dull copies of the Old Masters. The Florentine *pietro dure* items, from the sixteenth century, represent another technically astounding artform – they're like stone collages – which verge on the kitsch.

Somewhat off the beaten path, it's worth persevering to find the V&A's **Ironwork** collection, a display of keys, locks, gates and grilles, ranged along a vast corridor (Level 3, rooms 113–114e). At the centre is George Gilbert Scott's Hereford Screen, an eight-ton neo-Gothic monster of copper and ironwork that was pulled out of the city's cathedral in 1967. Nearby, there are two great cabinets filled with every kind of tin, from a Huntley & Palmers biscuit-dispensing machine to a money box in the shape of a tea caddy.

Paintings

The V&A's collection of **Paintings** (Level 3, rooms 81, 82, 87–88a) includes minor works by Blake, Corot, Degas, Delacroix, Rembrandt, Tintoretto and Botticelli, a study for Ingres' *Odalisque*, a Tiepolo sketch, some Fantin-Latour flowers and several Pre-Raphaelite works, the best of which is Rossetti's verdant, emerald-green *The Day Dream*, one of his last great works. The V&A owns over four hundred works by John Constable, bequeathed by his daughter, including famous views of Salisbury Cathedral (in the British Galleries) and Dedham Mill, and full-sized preparatory oil paintings for *The Hay Wain* and *The Leaping Horse*, plus a whole host of his alfresco cloud studies and sketches. There are also several works by **Turner**, including a dreamy view of East Cowes Castle, painted for the castle's owner, John Nash, and **Gainsborough's Showbox**, in which he displayed the oil-on-glass landscapes he executed in the 1780s. Room 90 is used for temporary exhibitions of prints and drawings, and room 90a displays **portrait miniatures** by Holbein, Hilliard and others.

18

V&A'S HIDDEN GEMS

The V&A is so vast, it's very easy to miss one or two of its hidden gems. While you're on Level 3, make sure you see the spectacular Minton tiles of the **Ceramic Staircase**, designed by Frank Moody. Note the ceramic memorial to Henry Cole, the work of his niece, who has rendered her uncle in mosaic with "Albertopolis" in relief above. Make sure, too, that you get a close look at the grandiose **Leighton Frescoes** (Level 3, rooms 102 & 107), which used to look down onto the Cast Courts from on high.

The V&A's relatively small **20th Century** collection (Level 3, rooms 7 & 76) is easily overlooked, yet it's stuffed with high-quality artefacts: furniture by Otto Wagner, Charles Rennie Mackintosh, Bauhaus and the Wiener Werkstätte co-op; Constructivist fabrics and crockery; and a range of works by Finnish modernist supremo Alvar Aalto. Postwar design classics, from plywood chairs and melamine tableware to Olivetti typewriters and Dyson vacuum cleaners, are displayed in one half of the adjacent National Art Library.

Theatre

The display areas of the **Theatre & Performance** galleries (Level 3, rooms 103–106) are divided into themes – producing, rehearsing, promotion and so on – and cover every theatrical genre from music hall to straight theatre, plus a surprisingly large amount of pop memorabilia. You may not learn much about the history of London theatre, but you do get to see some great individual exhibits, from the rotating hook, tunic and shorts used by Pansy Chinery in her teeth-spinning act to Pink Floyd's Azimuth Co-ordinator, which could produce an early form of surround sound. Perhaps the best section is "costume and make-up" where you can examine General Tom Thumb's waistcoat, Adam Ant's self-made Prince Charming get-up, Elton John's lurex Bicycle John outfit from the height of glam rock and an exact replica of Kylie Minogue's dressing room c.2007.

Jewellery

The justifiably popular **Jewellery** galleries (Level 3, rooms 91–93) display everything from a Bronze Age gold collar from Ireland to contemporary jewellery made from recycled materials. Among the earlier pieces, there are some pretty impressive gold papal rings – giant knuckle-dusters made from rock crystal – and some lovely gilded pomanders used to ward off evil. Specific highlights to look out for, further on, include the emeralds and diamonds given by Napoleon to his adopted daughter in 1806 (cabinet 15), the emeralds and rubies captured from Seringapatam in 1799 and the rare Siberian amethysts given by Tsar Alexander I to the wife of the Third Marquess of Londonderry (all in cabinet 24). Elsewhere, there are Art Nouveau pieces by René Lalique (cabinet 26), Arts and Crafts works by May Morris (cabinet 29) and the ostentatious personal jewellery of the eccentric Edith Sitwell (cabinet 30). Check out cabinet 56, too, for the Fabergé cigarette cases, the spectacular Manchester Tiara from 1903 (cabinet 55a) and the whole series of semiprecious carved animals that belonged to Queen Alexandra (cabinet 56).

Architecture, Glass and Ceramics

The V&A's **Architecture** gallery (Level 4, rooms 127–128) puts on special exhibitions, but also has a permanent display of architectural models in room 128. It's an eclectic array of realized and unrealized projects – everything from a fifteenth-century mosque and a Le Corbusier villa, to Spiral (Daniel Libeskind's now-shelved extension for the V&A) and Bluewater, Britain's fourth largest mall. Beyond, lies the relatively small **Glass Gallery** (Level 4, room 131), with its spectacular modern glass staircase and balustrade. The beauty and variety of the glass on display is staggering, and ranges from the Greek and Roman world to objets d'art by contemporary artists.

For those with stamina, or who wish to lose the crowds, there's an exhaustively encyclopedic collection of **Ceramics** (Level 6, rooms 136–146) on the top floor.

The best stuff for non-specialists is in room 140, where you'll find work by the Wiener Werkstätte and the Omega Workshops, Clarice Cliff crockery, a Suffragette tea-set and Communist ceramics. The contemporary pieces in room 141 range from manga to mad, while room 142 features one-off modern pieces by everyone from Picasso to Grayson Perry. And for a global overview of ceramics through the ages, continue to room 145, which has everything from Greek black-figure vases to Victorian de Morgan tiles.

Finally, if you persevere, you'll make it to the museum's fabulous new **Furniture** galleries (Level 6, rooms 133–135), which tell the story of furniture over the past six hundred years. The most famous exhibit is the Great Bed of Ware, a king-sized Elizabethan oak four-poster designed to sleep twelve, and which gets a mention in Shakespeare's *Twelfth Night*. But there's plenty of modern stuff here, too, from an Isokon bookshelf and the UFO-like 1960s Garden Egg Chair to contemporary designers like Stephen Richards and the computer-aided designs of Jeroen Verhoeven.

18

Science Museum

Exhibition Rd · Daily 10am–6pm · Free · ☏ 020 7942 4000, ⓦ sciencemuseum.org.uk · ⊖ South Kensington

The **Science Museum**, which broke away from the V&A in 1914, is undeniably impressive, filling seven floors with items drawn from every conceivable area of science, with hands-on galleries that appeal to adults and kids. The spectacular **Wellcome Wing** dragged the museum into the twenty-first century, and by 2015 pretty much all the old galleries will have been swept away, replaced by new galleries on science, space, communications and climate change. The museum will also have a more arresting exterior, thanks to the planned Beacon – a glowing bulge in the museum's Neoclassical face on Exhibition Road.

INFORMATION AND TOURS

Tours and events Your first stop should be the information desk, in the Energy Hall, where you can pick up a museum plan and find out about the day's events and demonstrations; you can also sign up for a free guided tour on a specific subject. The museum's Dana Centre (165 Queen's Gate; ☏ 020 7942 4040, ⓦ danacentre.org.uk) puts on free talks, discussions and events aimed at adults.

Exhibitions The museum stages populist special exhibitions (for which you have to pay), often timed to coincide with the latest special-effects movie, and has flight simulators and a 3D IMAX cinema (£8).

Eating Refreshment pit-stops include the *Revolution Café* off the Energy Hall, and the funky *Deep Blue Café* in the Wellcome Wing, plus several picnic areas.

The ground floor

The largest exhibit in the **Energy Hall**, by the entrance, is the bright red Burnley mill engine, whose enormous wheel used to drive 1700 looms and worked *in situ* until as late as 1970. To the side is an exhibition on **James Watt** (1736–1819), the Scot who was instrumental in kick-starting the Industrial Revolution in Britain. As well as inspecting examples of his inventions, you can view the perfectly preserved garret room workshop that Watt used in his retirement.

Beyond lies the **Exploring Space** exhibition, which follows the history of rockets from tenth-century China and Congreve's early nineteenth-century efforts, through the V-1 and V-2 wartime bombs, right up to the Apollo landings. There's a great, full-size replica of the Apollo 11 landing craft which deposited US astronauts on the moon in 1969.

Beyond, **Making the Modern World** displays iconic inventions of modern science and technology. These include *Puffing Billy*, the world's oldest surviving steam locomotive, used for hauling coal in 1815, and Robert Stephenson's *Rocket* of 1829, which won the competition to haul the Manchester–Liverpool passenger service. Other ground-breaking inventions on display include a Ford Model T, the world's first mass-produced car, and a gleaming aluminium Lockheed 10A Electra airliner from 1935, which signalled the birth of modern air travel. Less glamorous discoveries, such as the brain scanner, occupy the sidelines, along with disasters such as the drug thalidomide.

Wellcome Wing

The darkened, ultra-violet **Wellcome Wing** beckons you on from Making the Modern World. The **Antenna** displays, on the ground floor, change regularly in order to cover contemporary science issues while they are topical. **Pattern Pod**, meanwhile, is for under-8s, and is basically a lot of interactive hi-tech fun. Kids can experiment with water ripples, footprints and the Penrose tessellation, and groove away in the multicoloured human shadow box.

On Floor 1, **Who am I?** is a guaranteed winner, as it concentrates on humans themselves. You can morph yourself into the opposite sex, watch a sperm race and test the gender of your brain. **Atmosphere**, on Floor 2, is a touch-screen exhibition exploring the causes and effects of climate change, and the possibilities for reducing carbon emissions. Floor 3 contains **In Future**, where you can play frivolous but fun multi-player educational games, and vote on contemporary socio-scientific questions, such as "Should you be able to choose the gender of your child?"

18

The basement

The basement houses two hands-on galleries perfect for children under 11. In the misleadingly entitled **Garden**, 3- to 6-year-olds don waterproofs to experiment with lock gates, and hard hats to play with pulleys. The imaginatively entitled **Things** is aimed at the natural curiosity of 7- to 11-year-olds about unidentifiable objects. A longer attention span and a fair bit of reading are involved, and there are the usual problems with crowds at the weekend and with the durability of the exhibits.

Floor 1

The **Challenge of Materials**, ranged around the balcony on the first floor, is an extremely stylish exhibition – the glass-floored suspension bridge is particularly cool – covering the use of materials ranging from aluminium to zerodur (used for making laser gyroscopes). As well as the excellent hands-on displays, there are aesthetically pleasing exhibits as diverse as a Bakelite coffin and an Axminster-carpet morning gown designed by Vivienne Westwood.

Further on, you'll find a very old-fashioned, little-visited section on **Agriculture**, perfect for those with a penchant for ploughs and tractors. Beyond lies **Cosmos & Culture**, which explores our relationship with the universe through astronomy, and features objects from the 7ft telescope used by William Herschel to discover Uranus in 1781, to DRIFT I, with which scientists attempted (and failed) to detect the invisible "dark matter" that's thought to make up around a quarter of the universe.

Floor 2

The most popular section on Floor 2 is **Energy**, with its "do not touch" electric-shock machine that absolutely fascinates kids. Much of it is thought-provoking stuff – you can play computer games to learn how to reduce your carbon emissions – and the rest comprises more conventional displays, everything from a bird oil lamp to a clay stove from contemporary Kenya.

Elsewhere on Floor 2, there are sections on **Computing** and **Mathematics** now renamed "histories", as they were designed some years ago. Taking up quite some space are Charles Babbage's gargantuan Difference Engine 1, the world's first computer built in 1832, and his unrealized second version, which the museum completed in 1991.

Floor 3

Floor 3 is now mobbed by kids having enormous fun at the **Launchpad**, the museum's chief interactive gallery where they can experiment with water, waves, light and sound and build a catenary arch (and knock it down again); "explainers" are on hand to try and impart some educational input.

If you're looking for peace and quiet, head next door for the exquisite scientific instruments, chiefly created by George Adams for George III, in **Science in the Eighteenth Century**. Close by, **Health Matters** dwells thoughtfully on modern medical history from the introduction of mass vaccination to the challenge of finding a cure for HIV.

Heading towards the Wellcome Wing, you eventually reach the giant hangar of **Flight**, festooned with aircraft of every description from a Spitfire to a modern executive jet. Look out for the scaled-down model of the Montgolfier balloon which recorded the first human flight in 1783, and the full-size model of the flimsy contraption in which the Wright brothers made their epoch-making power-assisted flight in 1903.

18

Floors 4 and 5

If old-fashioned displays are more your thing, head for **Glimpses of Medical History** on Floor 4. The exhibition features an attractive series of dioramas of medical operations, and larger mock-ups of surgeries and dentists' and chemists' premises through the ages, starting with Neolithic trepanning and finishing up with the gore-free spectacle of an open-heart operation c.1980.

Even more fascinating (but equally old-fashioned) is Wellcome's **Science and Art of Medicine** gallery on Floor 5. Using an anthropological approach, this is a visual and cerebral feast, galloping through ancient medicine, medieval and Renaissance pharmacy, alchemy, quack doctors, royal healers, astrology and military surgery. Offbeat artefacts include African fetish objects, an Egyptian mummy, numerous masks, an eighteenth-century Florentine model of a female torso giving birth and George Washington's dentures.

Natural History Museum

Cromwell Rd • Daily 10am–5.50pm • Free • ☎ 020 7942 5000, ⓦ nhm.ac.uk • ⊖ South Kensington

Alfred Waterhouse's purpose-built mock-Romanesque colossus, with its 675ft terracotta facade built in 1880, ensures the status of the **Natural History Museum** as London's most handsome museum. Its vast collections derive from a bequest by Hans Sloane to the British Museum, separated off in the 1860s after a huge power struggle. The founding director, Richard Owen, was an amazing figure, who arranged expeditions around the globe to provide everything from butterflies to dinosaurs for the museum's cabinets.

Nowadays, the museum copes manfully with the task of remaining an important resource for serious zoologists, and a major tourist attraction for the families with kids who flock here to check out the dinosaur collection. The **Central Hall** is dominated by "Dippy", a replica **Diplodocus** skeleton, 85ft from tip to tail, while the "side chapels" are filled with "wonders" of the natural world – a model of a sabre-toothed tiger, a stuffed Great Bustard, a dodo skeleton and so on. It's also worth pausing here to take in the architecture of this vast "nave", whose walls are decorated with moulded terracotta animals and plants.

INFORMATION AND TOURS

Arrival If the queues are long for the main entrance, you're better off heading for the Red Zone's side entrance on Exhibition Rd. The museum is divided into four colour-coded zones, but all you really need to know is that the Red Zone is the old Geology Museum linked to the rest of the museum by the Birds section, and the Orange Zone is the Darwin Centre.

Exhibitions and tours As well as large, very popular special exhibitions (for which there's a charge), the museum also puts on lots of free tours, talks, discussions, workshops and performances, and in the winter there's an ice rink in front of the building.

Eating There's a café behind the stairs in the Central Hall, and in the Red Zone and a picnic area in the basement, or you can head out to the Wildlife Garden (April–Oct), west of the entrance.

Blue Zone

In **Dinosaurs**, a raised walkway leads straight to the highlight for many kids, the grisly life-sized animatronic dinosaur tableau, currently a roaring *Tyrannosaurus rex*. The rest of the displays are less theatrical and more informative, with massive-jawed skeletons and more conventional models.

The old-fashioned **Mammals** section is filled with stuffed animals and plastic models and dominated by a full-sized model of a blue whale juxtaposed with its skeleton. It usually goes down well enough with younger children, but it's showing its age somewhat.

Green Zone

Investigate Mon–Fri 2.30–5pm, Sat & Sun 11am–5pm; during school holidays daily 11am–5pm

The other firm favourite with kids is the arthropod room, known as **Creepy Crawlies**. Filled with giant models of bugs, arachnids and crustaceans, plus displays on spiders, mites and other unlovely creatures, it's here that you'll find the museum's only live exhibits, a colony of leaf-cutter ants from Trinidad, which feed on a fungus that they grow on the leaves they've gathered.

Meanwhile down in the basement is the excellent futuristic **Investigate**, aimed at children aged 7 to 14 – in school term time, public visits are restricted to the afternoon and at busy times, you may need to obtain a timed ticket. Kids get to choose a tray of specimens and then play at being scientists, using microscopes, scales, a computer and various tools of the trade to examine and catalogue the items before them. There are one or two simpler hands-on exhibits too, as well as several plant species to look at.

Up on the first floor, **Minerals** features serried ranks of glass cabinets, culminating in a darkened chamber called **The Vault**. Here, the cream of the museum's rocks reside: a meteorite from Mars, a golden nugget weighing over 1000lb, one of the largest uncut emeralds in the world and the Star of South Africa, found in 1869, which triggered the South Africa diamond rush. Don't miss the 1300-year-old slice of **Giant Sequoia**, on the top floor, and while you're there, admire the view down onto the Central Hall, the moulded monkeys clinging to the arches and the ceiling panels depicting plant specimens.

Orange Zone

Little visited, compared to the rest of the museum, the **Orange Zone** is also known as the **Darwin Centre**, dominated by the giant concrete **Cocoon**, encased within the centre's glass-fronted atrium like a giant egg and home to over twenty million specimens. Visitors can take the lift to the seventh floor and enter the Cocoon to learn more about the history of the collection, about taxonomy and the research and field trips the museum funds.

In the nearby **Zoology spirit building**, you can view a small selection of bits and bobs pickled in glass jars, everything from silkworm larvae and a peculiar venomous snail that's killed more than one unwary collector, to a jar of parasitic worms from a sperm whale's stomach and a brown rat found during the building's construction. To join one of the **guided tours** that take you behind the scenes and allow you to talk to the museum's scientists, you need to book on the day at the information desk in Central Hall.

Red Zone

If you enter the museum from Exhibition Road, you enter the vast, darkened hall of the **Red Zone**, with the solar system and constellations writ large on the walls. Boarding the central escalator will take you through a partially formed globe to the top floor and **The Power Within**, an exhibition on volcanoes and earthquakes. The most popular section is the 1995 Kobe earthquake simulator, where you can enter a mock-up of a Japanese supermarket and see the soy sauce bottles wobble, while watching an in-store video of the real event. Despite the museum's protestations, the whole thing seems in very poor taste. On the same floor is **Restless Surface**, an interactive display on the earth's elements, soil and rock erosion and, of course, global warming.

Down one floor, **From the Beginning** covers the geological history of the planet from the Big Bang to the present day. The display ends with a crystal ball, which predicts the earth's future (bleak, but probably not within our lifetime). More alluring is **Earth's Treasury**, a dimly lit display of lustrous minerals and crystals, gemstones and jewels. Exhibits include rocks that shine in UV light, carved artefacts such as a lapis lazuli necklace, and even some recently discovered kryptonite (the mineral that weakens Superman).

Finally, **Earth Today and Tomorrow** (on the ground floor) is a look at how we are running down the earth's non-renewable natural resources, and polluting the planet in the process. Ironically, one of the chief sponsors is Rio Tinto, the distinctly environmentally unfriendly mining company.

Brompton Oratory

Brompton Rd • Mon–Fri 6.30am–8pm, Sat 6.30am–7.45pm, Sun 7.30am–8pm • Free • ☎ 020 7808 0900, ⓦ bromptonoratory.com • ⊖ South Kensington

London's most flamboyant and atmospheric Roman Catholic church, the **Brompton Oratory** stands just east of the V&A. The first large Catholic church to be built since the Reformation, it was begun by the young and unknown Herbert Gribble in 1880 and modelled on the Gesù church in Rome, "so that those who had no opportunity of going over to Italy to see an Italian church had only to come here to see a model of one". The ornate Italianate interior, financed by the Duke of Norfolk, is filled with gilded mosaics and stuffed with sculpture, much of it genuine Italian Baroque from the Gesù church and Siena cathedral, notably the seventeenth-century apostles in the nave and the main altar, and the reredos of the Lady Chapel. The pulpit is a superb piece of neo-Baroque from the 1930s, with a high cherub count on the tester. True to its architecture, the church practises a "rigid, ritualized, smells-and-bells Catholicism", as one journalist put it, with daily Mass in Latin, a top-notch choir on Sundays and some very high-society weddings throughout the year.

Royal Albert Hall

Kensington Gore • Guided tours depart from Door 12 • £11.50 • ☎ 0845 401 5045, ⓦ royalalberthall.com • ⊖ South Kensington or High Street Kensington

The funds raised on the death of the Prince Consort in 1861 were squandered on the nearby Albert Memorial (see p.246), and it took considerable effort by Henry Cole, his collaborator on the Great Exhibition, to get funding to complete the **Royal Albert Hall**. Plans for this splendid iron- and glass-domed auditorium had been drawn up during the prince's lifetime, with an exterior of red brick, terracotta and marble that was already the hallmark of South Ken architecture. Completed in 1871, the hall has hosted everything from Miss World to pop gigs, and is the main venue for London's most democratic classical music festival, the annual Henry Wood Promenade Concerts, better known as the **Proms** (see p.413).

FRENCH CONNECTIONS

Part of South Ken's cachet is thanks to its **French connections**, with a French school and creche, a couple of bookshops, a deli and several genuine patisseries and brasseries clustered around the **Institut Français** (ⓦ institut-francais.org.uk) on Queensberry Place, which itself maintains an interesting programme of theatre, cinema and exhibitions.

A further French sight worth checking out is the gorgeous Art Deco **Michelin House**, a short walk to the south down Brompton Road. Faced in white faïence and decorated with tyres and motoring murals by French artists in 1911, its ground floors now house the shop, café, oyster bar and restaurant of *Bibendum* (ⓦ bibendum.co.uk), all run by Terence Conran.

Several other educational institutions congregate around the Albert Hall, as was Albert's intention. The most striking architecturally is the former **Royal College of Organists** to the west of the Albert Hall, a strange neo-Jacobean confection, designed for free in 1875 by Henry Cole's eldest son and laced with cream, maroon and sky-blue sgraffito.

Also on the west side of the Albert Hall is the headquarters of the **Royal College of Art**, founded back in 1837 but now housed in a seven-storey concrete block, designed in the 1960s by RCA staff. A postgraduate art college, the RCA's past students range from Henry Moore and David Hockney to Adam Ant and Tracey Emin; student art exhibitions are held during term-time on the ground floor.

18

Royal College of Music

Prince Consort Rd • Term-time Tues–Fri 11.30am–4.30pm • Free • ☎ 020 7591 4842, ⓦ rcm.ac.uk • ⊖ South Kensington

Behind the Albert Hall, flanked by the monumental **South Steps**, is a memorial to the Great Exhibition, featuring the Prince Consort. Predating the Royal Albert Hall (which Albert turns his back on), it originally stood amid the gardens and pavilions of the Royal Horticultural Society, which were replaced in the 1880s by the colossal **Imperial Institute** building. Of this only the 287ft **Queen's Tower** (closed to the public) remains, stranded amid the modern departments of Imperial College.

Instead, Albert now stands facing the splendid, neo-Gothic **Royal College of Music**, whose students have included Ralph Vaughan Williams and Benjamin Britten. The college houses a **museum** containing a collection of over eight hundred instruments, dating from the fifteenth to the twentieth centuries, including the world's oldest surviving keyboard instrument.

Royal Geographical Society

1 Kensington Gore • Mon–Fri 10am–5pm • Free • ☎ 020 7591 3000, ⓦ rgs.org • ⊖ South Kensington

East of the Albert Hall is the **Royal Geographical Society**, a wonderful brick-built complex in the Queen Anne style, with statues of two of the society's early explorers, David Livingstone and Ernest Shackleton, occupying niches along the outer wall. The society gives regular talks, maintains a remarkable library and map room and puts on excellent special exhibitions in the Pavilion (entrance on Exhibition Rd).

Sikorski Museum

20 Prince's Gate • Tues–Fri 2–4pm, first Sat of month 10.30am–4pm • Free • ☎ 020 7589 9249, ⓦ pism.co.uk • ⊖ South Kensington

South Ken's Polish connections are exemplified by the **Sikorski Museum** and Polish Institute, east of the Royal Geographical Society. World War II militaria form the bedrock of the museum, along with the personal effects of General Wladyslaw Sikorski, the prewar prime minister who fled to London in 1939, only to die in a mysterious plane accident in 1943. The absence of a non-Communist leader of Sikorski's standing after the war was lamented by exiled Poles for the next forty years.

Czech Memorial Scrolls Museum

Kent House, Rutland Gardens • By appointment Tues & Thurs 10am–4pm • Free • ☎ 020 7584 3741, ⓦ czechmemorialscrollstrust.org • ⊖ Knightsbridge

One of South Kensington's East European connections is contained within the **Westminster Synagogue** in Kent House, a spacious Victorian mansion in Rutland Gardens, off Kensington Road. The synagogue occupies the first floor, while the third floor houses the **Czech Memorial Scrolls Museum**, which tells the miraculous story of the 1564 Torah scrolls which were gathered from all over Bohemia and Moravia by the Nazis, possibly for their planned "Museum of an Extinct Race", survived the Holocaust, and were purchased from the Communist government in 1964 and brought here. The shelves have been gradually emptying as the scrolls are restored and sent out to Jewish communities all over the world, but the remainder are displayed here.

Knightsbridge

Knightsbridge is irredeemably snobbish, revelling in its reputation as the swankiest shopping area in London, with designer stores all the way down **Sloane Street**, and its pretty little mews streets, built to house servants and stables, but now inhabited by the rich themselves. However, most people come to Knightsbridge for just one reason: to visit Harrods, London's most famous department store. **Belgravia**, over to the east and strategically close to Buckingham Palace, is London's chief embassy land, with at least 25 scattered among the grid-plan stuccoed streets. All in all, it's a pretty soulless place, although there are one or two lovely pubs hidden in the various mews.

18

Harrods

87–135 Brompton Rd · Mon–Sat 10am–8pm, Sun noon–6pm · ☎ 020 7730 1234, ⓦ harrods.com · ⊖ Knightsbridge

Housed in a grandiose 1905 terracotta building, which turns into a palace of fairy lights at night, **Harrods** has come a long way since it started out as a family-run grocer's in 1849. Nowadays, it is the UK's largest shop, spread over seven floors, five acres, with over 5000 staff, and over 15 million customers a year. If you are coming to visit, note that a "clean and presentable" **dress code** is enforced and backpacks either have to be carried in the hand or placed in the store's left luggage (£3). Once here, however, you can avail yourself of the first-floor "luxury washrooms" and splash on a range of perfumes for free.

Even if you don't want one of the distinctive olive-green Harrods carrier bags, the store has a few sections on the ground floor that are sights in their own right. Chief among these is the **Food Hall**, with its exquisite Arts and Crafts tiling. There's also an Egyptian Hall, with pseudo-hieroglyphs and sphinxes, and an Egyptian Escalator, with a **Di and Dodi fountain shrine**. Here, to the strains of Mahler (and the like), you can contemplate photos of the ill-fated couple, and, preserved in an acrylic pyramid, a used wine-glass from the couple's last evening and the engagement ring Dodi allegedly bought for Di the previous day. Another memorial has been erected at Door Three, a life-size bronze statue entitled *Innocent Victims*, depicting the couple dancing on a beach and clutching an albatross. Dodi's father, Mohamed Al-Fayed, sold Harrods to the Qatari royal family for £1.5 billion in 2010, but so far the memorials are still *in situ*.

Chelsea

Until the sixteenth century, **Chelsea** was nothing more than a tiny fishing village on the banks of the Thames, centred around Chelsea Old Church. It was Thomas More who started the upward trend by moving here in 1520, followed by members of the nobility, including Henry VIII himself. In the eighteenth century, Chelsea acquired its riverside houses along Cheyne Walk, which gradually attracted a posse of literary and intellectual types. However, it wasn't until the late nineteenth century that the area began to earn its reputation as London's very own Left Bank.

In the 1960s, Chelsea was at the forefront of "Swinging London", with the likes of David Bailey, Mick Jagger, George Best and the "Chelsea Set" hanging out in the boutiques and coffee bars. Later, the **King's Road** became a catwalk for hippies and in the late 1970s it was the unlikely epicentre of the punk explosion. Nothing so risqué goes on in Chelsea now, with franchise fashion rather than cutting edge couture the order of the day, though some of its residents like to think of themselves as a cut above the purely moneyed types of Kensington. The area's other aspect, oddly enough considering its reputation, is a **military** one, with the former Chelsea Barracks, the Royal Hospital and the National Army Museum.

Sloane Square

A leafy nexus on the very eastern edge of Chelsea, **Sloane Square** is centred on a modern Venus fountain, featuring a relief of Charles II and Nell Gwynne. On the east

side of the square, beside the tube station, stands the Victorian **Royal Court Theatre**, a bastion of new theatre writing since John Osborne's *Look Back in Anger* sent tremors through the establishment in 1956. On the opposite side is **Peter Jones**, a John Lewis department store housed in London's finest glass-curtain building, built in the 1930s, which curves its way seductively into the King's Road.

Holy Trinity, Sloane Square

Sloane St • Mon–Sat 8.30am–5.30pm, Sun 8.30am–1.30pm • ☎ 020 7730 7270, ⓦ holytrinitysloanesquare.co.uk • ⊖ Sloane Square

Just off Sloane Square is **Holy Trinity**, created in 1890, and probably the finest Arts and Crafts church in London. The east window is the most glorious of the furnishings, a vast 48-panel extravaganza designed by Edward Burne-Jones, and the largest ever made by Morris & Co. Despite the smell of incense, statues of the Virgin Mary, and even confession booths, Holy Trinity is simply High Church Anglican, not Roman Catholic.

King's Road

The **King's Road**, Chelsea's main artery, was designed as a royalty-only thoroughfare by Charles II, in order – so the story goes – to avoid carriage congestion en route to Nell Gwynne's house. Lesser mortals could travel down it on production of a special copper pass but it wasn't opened to the public until 1830. This prompted a flurry of speculative building that produced the series of elegant, open-ended squares – Wellington, Markham, Carlyle and Paultons – which still punctuate the road. If you don't fancy walking down the King's Road, hop on a bus: #11 and #22 run the length of it, and buses #19 and #319 run from Sloane Square partway down and then south across Battersea Bridge.

Saatchi Gallery

King's Rd • Daily 10am–6pm • Free • ☎ 020 7823 2363, ⓦ saatchi-gallery.co.uk • ⊖ Sloane Square

Set back from the King's Road, a short stroll from Sloane Square, is the former **Duke of York's HQ**, built in 1801 and fronted by a solid-looking Tuscan portico. The building is now the unlikely home of the **Saatchi Gallery**, which puts on changing exhibitions of contemporary art in its fifteen equally proportioned, whitewashed rooms. Charles Saatchi, the collector behind the gallery, was the man whose clever advertising campaigns kept Mrs Thatcher in power in the 1980s and who introduced Young British Artists (YBAs) like Damien Hirst, Sarah Lucas and Rachel Whiteread to the world in the 1990s. One of the most remarkable works Saatchi bought is Richard Wilson's *20:50*, the giant sump oil reservoir, first displayed in 1987 and now installed in the gallery's basement.

Royal Avenue

The first of the picturesque squares that open out onto the King's Road is **Royal Avenue**, on the south side. This particular one is rather like a Parisian *place*, with plane trees and gravel down the centre, and was originally laid out in the late seventeenth century as part of William III's ambitious (and unrealized) scheme to link Kensington Palace with the Royal Hospital to the south. The next square along is Wellington Square, suspected fictional London address of James Bond; Ian Fleming lived, on and off, in Chelsea and no. 30 is thought to have been the location of Bond's "comfortable ground-floor flat" (and was recently on the market for £6 million).

World's End

The stretch of the King's Road beyond Beaufort Street, known as **World's End**, was the fulcrum of Chelsea's Swinging Sixties scene, with boutiques like Granny Takes a Trip and hippie shops like Gandolf's Garden and the Sweet Shop. In 1971, Malcolm McLaren and his schoolteacher girlfriend, Vivienne Westwood, opened a Teddy Boy-revival store called Let It Rock, located, with a neat sense of irony, right next door to the Chelsea Conservative Club, at no. 430. In 1975 they changed tack and renamed the shop SEX, stocking it with proto-punk fetishist gear, with simulated burnt limbs in the window. It became a magnet for the likes of John Lydon and John Simon Ritchie, better known as Johnny Rotten and Sid Vicious, and was renamed Seditionaries – the rest, as they say, is history. Now known as World's End, the shop, with its landmark backward-running clock, continues to flog Westwood's eccentric designer clothes.

Royal Hospital Chelsea

Royal Hospital Rd · **Grounds** Daily: May–Sept 10am–8pm; Oct–April 10am-4.30pm · Free **Great Hall & Chapel** Mon–Sat 11am–noon & 2–4pm, Sun 2–4pm · Free **Museum** Mon–Fri 10am–noon & 2–4pm · Free **Guided tours** by appointment Mon–Fri 10am & 1.30pm · £8 · ☎ 020 7881 5516, ⓦ chelsea-pensioners.co.uk · ⊖ Sloane Square

18

Among the most nattily attired of all those parading down the King's Road are the scarlet- or navy-blue-clad Chelsea Pensioners, army veterans from the nearby **Royal Hospital** founded by Charles II in 1682. Designed by Wren, the hospital's plain, red-brick wings and grassy courtyards became a blueprint for institutional and collegiate architecture across the Empire. On Founder's Day (May 29), the Pensioners, wearing their traditional tricorn hats, festoon Grinling Gibbons' gilded statue of Charles with oak leaves to commemorate the day after the disastrous 1651 Battle of Worcester, when the future king hid in an oak tree to escape his pursuers.

The public are welcome to visit the hospital's austere **Chapel**, with its huge barrel vaulting and Sebastiano Ricci's colourful apse fresco *Resurrection*, in which Jesus patriotically bears the flag of St George. Opposite lies the equally grand, wood-panelled **Great Hall**, where the three hundred or so Pensioners still eat under portraits of the sovereigns and Antonio Verrio's vast allegorical mural of Charles II and his hospital. In the Secretary's Office, designed by John Soane, on the east side of the hospital, there's a small **Museum** (Mon–Fri only), displaying Pensioners' uniforms, medals and two German bombs. The playing fields to the south, from which you get the finest view of the hospital, are the venue for the annual **Chelsea Flower Show** (see p.25).

National Army Museum

Royal Hospital Rd · Daily 10am–5.30pm · Free · ☎ 020 7730 0717, ⓦ nam.ac.uk · ⊖ Sloane Square

The concrete bunker next door to the Royal Hospital houses the **National Army Museum.** There are plenty of interesting historical artefacts, plus an impressive array of uniforms and medals, but for a more balanced view of war, you're better off visiting the Imperial War Museum.

To follow the museum chronologically, start with **The Making of Britain** (1642–1783), which concentrates on the Civil War and the origins of the professional British Army,

---

LONDON'S PLEASURE GARDENS

"…the fragrancy of the walks and bowers, with the choirs of birds that sung upon the trees, and the loose tribe of people that walked under their shades, I could not but look upon the place as a kind of Mahometan paradise."
                                                                                    The Spectator, May 20, 1712

London's pleasure gardens were among the city's chief entertainments in the eighteenth century. **Vauxhall Gardens**, open from around 1660, on the south bank, provided the blueprint: formal, lantern-lit gardens, musical entertainments and "dark walks", perfect for secret assignations. Of Vauxhall, there is now no trace, but its nearest rival was **Ranelagh Gardens**, now a pleasant little landscaped park near the Royal Hospital. A couple of information panels in the gardens' Soane-designed shelter show what the place used to look like when Canaletto painted it in 1751. The main feature was a giant Rotunda, where the beau monde could promenade to musical accompaniment – the 8-year-old Mozart played here. Shortly after it opened in 1742, Walpole reported that "you can't set your foot without treading on a Prince or Duke". Fashion is fickle, though, and the rotunda was eventually demolished in 1805.

18

WILDE ABOUT CHELSEA

John Singer Sargent, Augustus John, James Whistler and Bertrand Russell all lived at one time or another in Tite Street, which runs alongside the National Army Museum, but the street's most famous resident was writer and wit **Oscar Fingal O'Flahertie Wills Wilde** (1856–1900), who moved into no. 1 in 1880 with an old Oxford chum, Frank Miles, only to be asked to leave the following year by the latter (under pressure from his father, Canon Miles), after the hostile reception given to Wilde's recently published poetry. Four years later, Wilde moved back into the street to no. 34, with his new bride Constance Lloyd. By all accounts he was never very good at "playing husband", though he was happy enough to play father to his two boys (when he was there). It was in Tite Street, in 1891, that Wilde first met **Lord Alfred Douglas**, son of the Marquis of Queensberry and known to his friends as "Bosie", who was to become his lover, and eventually to prove his downfall.

At the height of Wilde's fame, in 1895, just four days after the triumphant first night of *The Importance of Being Earnest*, the marquis left a visiting card for Wilde, on which he wrote "To Oscar Wilde, posing as a somdomite [sic]". Urged on by Bosie, Wilde unsuccessfully sued Queensberry, losing his case when the marquis produced incriminating evidence against Wilde himself. On returning to the *Cadogan Hotel* on Sloane Street, where Bosie had rooms, Wilde was arrested by the police, taken to Bow Street police station, charged with homosexual offences and eventually sentenced to **two years' hard labour**. Bankrupt, abandoned by Bosie and separated from his wife, he served his sentence in Pentonville, Wandsworth and later Reading jail. On his release he fled abroad, travelling under the pseudonym of Sebastian Melmoth, and died three years later from a syphilitic infection. He is buried in Paris's Père Lachaise cemetery.

before heading up to **Changing the World** (1784–1904), a none-too-critical look at the British Empire. Here you can see a vast spot-lit model of the Battle of Waterloo (at 7pm before the Prussians arrived to save the day). The skeleton of Marengo, Napoleon's charger at the battle, the saw used to amputate the Earl of Uxbridge's leg and Richard Caton-Woodville's famous painting of *The Charge of the Light Brigade* are among the highlights of this section.

World Wars has sections on just about every conflict zone of the two global conflicts from a slice of the Somme to the POW camps of the Far East. **Conflicts of Interest** (1969 to the present), on the top floor, with a good section on the Korean War, complete the story. Make sure you pop into the **Art Gallery**, where there are some excellent military portraits by the likes of Reynolds, Gainsborough, Romney and Lawrence, not to mention a suave self-portrait by a uniformed Rex Whistler, who died in action shortly after D-Day.

Chelsea Physic Garden

66 Royal Hospital Rd • April–Oct Tues–Fri & Sun 11am–6pm; July & Aug also Wed until 10pm; plus occasional winter weekend openings • £9 • ☎ 020 7352 5646, ⓦ chelseaphysicgarden.co.uk • ⊖ Sloane Square

Founded in 1673 by the Royal Society of Apothecaries, the **Chelsea Physic Garden** is the oldest botanical garden in the country after Oxford's: the first cedars grown in this country were planted here in 1683, cotton seed was sent from here to the American colonies in 1732, England's first rock garden was constructed here in 1773, and the walled garden contains Britain's oldest olive tree. Unfortunately, it's a rather small garden, and a little too close to Chelsea Embankment to be a peaceful oasis, but keen botanists will enjoy it nevertheless. A statue of Hans Sloane, who presented the Society with the freehold, stands at the centre of the garden; behind him there's a licensed café, serving afternoon tea and delicious home-made cakes.

Cheyne Walk

Chelsea Physic Garden marks the beginning of **Cheyne Walk** (pronounced "chainy"), whose quiet riverside locale and succession of Queen Anne and Georgian houses drew artists and writers here in great numbers during the nineteenth century. Since the building of the Embankment in the 1870s and the increase in traffic, however, the character of this peaceful haven has been lost. Novelist Henry James, who lived at no. 21, used to take "beguiling drives" in his wheelchair along the Embankment; today, he'd be hospitalized in the process. An older contemporary of James, Mary Ann Evans (better known under her pen name George Eliot), moved into no. 4 – the first blue plaque you come to – in December 1880, five months after marrying an American banker 21 years her junior. Three weeks later she died of a kidney disease. Composer Ralph Vaughan Williams lived at no. 13; thirty or so years later, composers Mick Jagger and Keith Richards followed suit, at no. 48 and no. 3 respectively.

18

Chelsea Old Church

64 Cheyne Walk • Tues–Thurs 2–4pm • ☎ 020 7795 1019, ⓦ chelseaoldchurch.org.uk • Bus #19 or #319 from ⊖ Sloane Square

At the end of Cheyne Walk's gardens, there's a garish, gilded statue of **Thomas More**, "Scholar, Statesman, Saint", a local who used to worship in nearby **Chelsea Old Church** where he built his own private chapel in the south aisle (the hinges for the big oak doors are still visible). More is best known for his martyrdom in 1535, though he himself showed little mercy to heretics – he even had some tied to a tree in his Chelsea back garden and flogged. Badly bombed in the last war, the church nevertheless contains an impressive number of monuments. Chief among them is Lady Cheyne's memorial (possibly by Bellini) and More's simple canopied memorial to his first wife, Jane, in which he himself hoped to be buried. In the event, his torso ended up in the Tower of London, while his head was stuck on a pike on London Bridge, but later saved and secretly buried in Canterbury by his adopted daughter, Margaret Roper. More's second wife, Alice, is also buried here.

Crosby Hall

You can get a flavour of Chelsea in Thomas More's day from **Crosby Hall**, part of a fifteenth-century wool merchant's house on Cheyne Walk once owned by More, transferred in 1910 bit by bit from Bishopsgate in the City to the corner of Danvers Street, west of Chelsea Old Church, on the site of More's gardens. Once occupied by the future Richard III (and used as a setting by Shakespeare), it's now a private residence, so you can admire its brick exterior, but not the great hall's fine hammerbeam roof.

Lindsey House and around

The continuation of **Cheyne Walk**, beyond Crosby Hall, is no less rich in cultural associations. Mrs Gaskell was born in 1810 at no. 93, while the painter James Whistler, who lived at ten different addresses in the 41 years he spent in Chelsea, lived for a time at no. 96, the house where the Provisional IRA and the British government met secretly in 1972, to discuss peace, some five months after Bloody Sunday. The Brunels, Marc and Isambard, both lived at no. 99, which form part of **Lindsey House**, built in 1674 on the site of Thomas More's farm – it's occasionally possible to visit the entrance hall, garden room and gardens (phone ☎ 020 7447 6605 for more details). Last but not least, the reclusive J.M.W. Turner lived at no. 119 for the last six years of his life under the pseudonym Booth, and painted many a sunset over the Thames.

Carlyle's House

24 Cheyne Row • April–Oct Wed–Sun 11am–5pm • NT • £5.10 • ☎ 020 7352 7087 • Bus #19 or #319 from ⊖ Sloane Square

Scottish historian **Thomas Carlyle** (1795–1881) set up home here with his wife, Jane, in 1834. Carlyle's full-blooded and colourful style of writing brought him great fame during his lifetime – a statue was erected to the "Sage of Chelsea" on Cheyne Walk less than a year after his death in 1881, and the house became a museum just fifteen years later. That said, the intellectuals and artists who visited Carlyle – among them Dickens, Tennyson, Chopin, Mazzini, Browning and Darwin – were attracted as much by the wit of his strong-willed wife, with whom Carlyle enjoyed a famously tempestuous relationship. The house itself is a typically dour Victorian abode, kept much as the

Carlyles would have had it – the historian's hat still hangs in the hall. Among the artefacts are a letter from Disraeli offering a baronetcy and Carlyle's reply, refusing it. The top floor contains the garret study where Carlyle tried in vain to escape the din of the street and the neighbours' noisy roosters, in order to complete his final magnum opus on Frederick the Great.

Brompton Cemetery

210 Old Brompton Rd • Daily: summer 8am–8pm; winter 8am–4pm • Free • Guided tours May–Aug Sun 2pm; Sept–April every other Sun • £5 donation requested • ☎ 020 7352 1201, ⓦ brompton-cemetery.org • ➌ West Brompton

Brompton Cemetery is the least overgrown of London's "Magnificent Seven" Victorian graveyards. Laid out on a grid plan in 1840 and now overlooked by the east stand of Chelsea Football Club, the cemetery's leafy central avenue leads south to an octagonal chapel. Here, you'll find the grave of Frederick Leyland, president of the National Telephone Company: designed by Edward Burne-Jones, it's a bizarre copper-green jewel box on stilts, smothered with swirling wrought-ironwork. Before you reach the chapel, eerie colonnaded catacombs, originally planned to extend the full length of the cemetery, open out into the Great Circle, a forest of tilted crosses.

Few really famous corpses grace Brompton, but enthusiasts might like to seek out Suffragette leader **Emmeline Pankhurst**; Henry Cole, the man behind the Great Exhibition and the V&A; Fanny Brawne, the love of Keats' life; and John Snow, Queen Victoria's anaesthetist, whose chloroform-fixes the monarch described as "soothing, quieting and delightful beyond measure". **Long Wolf**, a Sioux Indian chief, was a temporary resident here, after he died while on tour entertaining the Victorian masses with Colonel "Buffalo Bill" Cody. His body has since been returned to his descendants in America.

Fulham Palace

Bishop's Ave • **Palace** By guided tour only second and fourth Sun and third Tues at 2pm • £5 **Museum** Mon–Wed, Sat & Sun 1–4pm • Free • ☎ 020 7736 3233, ⓦ fulhampalace.org • ➌ Putney Bridge

It's worth venturing as far as the New King's Road by Putney Bridge in order to visit **Fulham Palace**, in Bishop's Park. Once the largest moated site in England, it was the residence of the Bishop of London from 704 to 1973. The oldest section of the present-day complex is the modestly scaled Tudor courtyard, patterned with black diamonds; the most recent is William Butterfield's neo-Gothic chapel, which, with the other period interiors, can only be seen on the **guided tours**. You can also visit the small **museum** which traces the building's complex history, and displays a few archeological finds, including a mummified rat. In the palace grounds there's a lovely walled herb garden, with a Tudor gateway and a maze of miniature box hedges, but sadly no sign of the moat, which was filled in in 1921.

Battersea

Folk who want, but can't afford, to live in Chelsea have colonized the terraces and mansions across the river in **Battersea**. For most of its history, however, Battersea was a staunchly working-class enclave. In 1913 it elected the country's first black mayor, John Richard Archer, and in the 1920s returned Shapurji Saklatvala as its MP – first for the Labour Party, then as a Communist. Saklatvala was always in the news: he was banned from entry into the US and even to his native India. He was also the first person to be arrested during the 1926 General Strike, after a speech in Hyde Park urging soldiers not to fire on striking workers, for which he received a two-month prison sentence.

Battersea Power Station

188 Kirtling St • Pop-Up Park open most weekends 10am–8pm • ⓦ batterseapowerstation.co.uk • Battersea Park train station

Physically, Battersea is dominated by the presence of **Battersea Power Station**, Giles

Gilbert Scott's awesome cathedral of power from 1933, which looks like an upturned table and featured (along with an inflatable flying pig) on the Pink Floyd album cover *Animals*. Closed down in 1983, it is finally being converted into flats, with Malaysian money, and may yet have a special branch of the Northern Line built to connect it to central London. Until the work is completed in 2017, there's a Pop-Up Park that you can visit most weekends – the entrance is through a gateway under the Grosvenor (railway) Bridge.

18

Battersea Dogs and Cats Home

4 Battersea Park Rd • Daily 10.30am–5pm • £2 • ☎ 0843 509 4444, ⓦ battersea.org.uk • ⊖ Vauxhall or Battersea Park train station

After the power station, most Londoners know Battersea for just one thing: its Dogs Home, now the **Battersea Dogs and Cats Home**, established here in 1871 as the "Home for Lost Dogs and Cats". Cats are still catered for, though it's better known for its dogs, with up to 180 dogs and 80 cats accommodated at any one time, and over sixteen thousand passing through their doors each year. Visitors are welcome, even if they're not thinking of adopting a pet.

Battersea Park

Park Daily 8am–dusk • Free • ☎ 020 8871 7530, ⓦ batterseapark.org **Children's Zoo** Daily 10am–5.30pm; closes 4.30pm or dusk in winter • £8.75 adult, £6.50 child • ☎ 0845 6016 679, ⓦ batterseaparkzoo.co.uk • Bus #19 or #319 from ⊖ Sloane Square or Battersea Park train station

Battersea being a place of great poverty, the Victorians decided, in the 1850s, to do something to help ameliorate the social conditions by establishing **Battersea Park**, connected to Chelsea by the Albert Bridge, one of the campest bridges to span the Thames, especially when lit up at night with fairy lights, like a seaside pier. Today, the park is probably best known for its two-tier **Peace Pagoda**, erected in 1985 by Japanese Buddhists. Made from a combination of reconstituted Portland stone and Canadian fir trees, the pagoda shelters four large gilded Buddhas. The park's **fountain lake**, to the southwest, is impressive in summer, and there's a small family-run **Children's Zoo**, established during the 1951 Festival of Britain, and home to monkeys, lemurs, mynah birds, otters and meerkats.

St Mary's Church

Battersea Church Rd • Mon–Fri 9am–1pm • Free • ☎ 020 7228 9648, ⓦ stmarysbattersea.org.uk • Bus #170 from ⊖ Victoria or Imperial Wharf Overground

The old village of Battersea was originally centred on St Mary's Church, half a mile upstream from Battersea Park. In 1775, when the current church was built, Battersea was a peaceful place with a population of less than two thousand, among them Catherine Boucher, who married the poet and visionary William Blake in the church in 1782. Another painter associated with St Mary's is Turner, who used to sit in the oriel vestry window and paint the clouds and sunsets (his favourite chair is now reverently preserved in the chancel) – both painters now have commemorative windows.

NOTTING HILL CARNIVAL

High Street Kensington to Notting Hill

Despite the smattering of aristocratic mansions and the presence of royalty in Kensington Palace, the village of Kensington remained surrounded by fields until well into the nineteenth century. The village has disappeared entirely now in the busy shopping district around Kensington High Street, and the chief attractions are the wooded Holland Park and the former artists' colony clustered around the exotically decorated Leighton House. Bayswater and Notting Hill, to the north, were for many years the bad boys of the borough, dens of vice and crime comparable to Soho. Gentrification has changed them beyond all recognition, though they remain more cosmopolitan districts, with a strong Arab presence and vestiges of the African-Caribbean community who initiated and still run the Notting Hill Carnival, one of Europe's largest street festivals.

High Street Kensington

The village of Kensington was centred on Kensington Church Street, but once the area was transformed into a residential suburb in the nineteenth century, the commercial centre shifted to **Kensington High Street** – better known as **High Street Ken**, after the tube. The street is dominated architecturally by the twin presences of George Gilbert Scott's neo-Gothic church of **St Mary Abbots** (whose 250ft spire makes it London's tallest parish church) and the Art Deco colossus of **Barkers** department store, remodelled in the 1930s. The rest of the street is nothing special, but in the quieter backstreets, you'll find one or two hidden gems like **Holland Park**, the former gardens of an old Jacobean mansion, and **Leighton House**, the perfect Victorian artist's pad.

Kensington Roof Gardens

99 Kensington High St • ☎ 020 7937 7994 for opening hours, ⓦ roofgardens.virgin.com • ⊖ High Street Kensington

A little-known feature of the High Street is Europe's largest **Roof Gardens**, which tops the former Derry & Toms department store, another monster 1930s building, next door to Barkers. Virgin, who now own the gardens, use them for events including a summer cinema (ⓦ rooftopfilmclub.com), so phone ahead to check they're open; to gain access, head for the side entrance on Derry Street and take the lift. The nightclub at the centre of the garden is pretty tacky, but the mock-Spanish convent, the formal gardens, the four pink flamingoes, sundry ducks and the views across the rooftops are surreal.

19

Kensington Square

On the south side of the High Street lies **Kensington Square**, an early piece of speculative building laid out in 1685. Luckily for the developers, royalty moved into Kensington Palace shortly after its construction, and the square soon became so fashionable that it was dubbed the "old court suburb". By the nineteenth century, the courtiers had moved out and the bohemians had moved in: Thackeray wrote *Vanity Fair* at no. 16; the Pre-Raphaelite painter Burne-Jones lived at no. 41; the actress Mrs Patrick Campbell, for whom George Bernard Shaw wrote *Pygmalion*, lived at no. 33; and composer Hubert Parry (of *Jerusalem* fame) gave music lessons to Vaughan Williams at no. 17. John Stuart Mill, philosopher and champion of women's suffrage, lived next door, and it was here that the first volume of Thomas Carlyle's sole manuscript of *The French Revolution* was accidentally used by a maid to light the fire.

Holland Park

Daily 7.30am to dusk • Free • ⓦ rbkc.gov.uk • ⊖ High Street Kensington

Hidden away in the backstreets north of High Street Kensington is the densely wooded **Holland Park**, popular with the neighbourhood's army of nannies and au pairs, who take their charges to the excellent adventure playground. To get there, take one of the paths along the east side of the former **Commonwealth Institute** – a bold 1960s building with a startling tent-shaped Zambian copper roof – which will house the **Design Museum** (see p.235) from 2015. The park is laid out in the former grounds of **Holland House** – only the east wing of the Jacobean mansion could be salvaged after World War II, but it gives an idea of what the place used to look like. A **youth hostel** is linked to the east wing (see p.363); the garden ballroom houses the spectacular *Belvedere* restaurant; and throughout the summer **outdoor performances** take place (ⓦ operahollandpark.com), continuing a tradition which stretches back to the first Lady Holland, who put on plays here in defiance of the puritanical laws of Cromwell's Commonwealth. Several formal **gardens** are laid out before the house, drifting down in terraces to the arcades, the orangery and the ice house, which have been converted into a café and an art gallery. The most unusual of the formal gardens, which are peppered

● SHOPS

Books for Cooks	6
Honest Jon's	2
Idler Academy	4
Kokon to Zai	1
Lutyens & Rubenstein	7
Paul Smith	9
Portobello Market	3
Rough Trade	5
Stumper and Fielding	10
Wolf and Badger	8

■ PUBS & BARS

Churchill Arms	9
Cock & Bottle	5
The Cow	3
The Elgin	4
Paradise by Way of Kensal Green	1
Victoria	6
The Westbourne	2
Windsor Castle	10

■ CLUB

Notting Hill Arts Club	7

■ MUSIC VENUES

Bush Hall	8
O2 Shepherd's Bush Empire	11

HIGH STREET KENSINGTON TO NOTTING HILL

Regent's Park

Maida Vale

Elgin Avenue

LITTLE VENICE

Warwick Avenue

Royal Oak

PORCHESTER RD

BAYSWATER

Whiteley's

Bayswater

Queensway

Baker Street

Marylebone Station

Marylebone

Edgware Road

MARYLEBONE ROAD

Rolling Bridge

Paddington Basin

Paddington Station

Paddington

Lancaster Gate

Marble Arch

OXFORD STREET

Marble Arch

BAYSWATER ROAD

Italian Garden

Hyde Park

Kensington Palace

Round Pond

Kensington Gardens

The Long Water

The Serpentine

Boathouse

Diana Fountain

Lido

Albert Memorial

ROTTEN ROW

SOUTH CARRIAGE ROAD

KENSINGTON GORE ROAD

Hyde Park Barracks

Royal Albert Hall

Knightsbridge

ACCOMMODATION

Caring Hotel	6
Garden Court Hotel	2
Holland House YHA	8
Main House	1
Portobello Gold	4
St David's Hotels	3
Vancouver Studios	5
Vicarage Hotel	7

CAFÉS

Books for Cooks	5
Lisboa Patisserie	1
Tom's Deli	6

RESTAURANTS

Le Café Anglais	8
Hereford Road	7
The Ledbury	4
Mandalay	2
Pearl Liang	3
Saf	9

with modern sculpture, is the **Kyoto Garden**, a Japanese-style sanctuary to the northwest of the house, complete with koi carp and peacocks.

Holland Park artists' colony

Several wealthy Victorian artists rather self-consciously founded an **artists' colony** around the fringes of Holland Park, and a number of their highly individual mansions are still standing. First and foremost is **Leighton House**, now a museum (see below). Leighton's neighbours included G.F. Watts and Holman Hunt, Marcus Stone, illustrator of Dickens, and, in the most outrageous house of all, architect William Burges, who designed his own medieval folly, the **Tower House**, at 29 Melbury Rd, now owned by Led Zeppelin guitarist, Jimmy Page. Slightly further afield, at 8 Addison Rd, is the Arts and Crafts **Debenham House**, designed by Halsey Ricardo in 1906 for the department-store Debenham family. The exterior is covered with peacock-blue and emerald-green tiles and bricks; the interior, which features a wonderful neo-Byzantine domed hall, is even more impressive. Sadly, both houses are closed to the public.

19

Leighton House Museum

12 Holland Park Rd • Daily except Tues 10am–5.30pm • £5 • ☎ 020 7602 3316, ⓦ rbkc.gov.uk • ⊖ High Street Kensington

Leighton House, the "House Beautiful", was built for Frederic Leighton, president of the Royal Academy and the only artist to be made a peer (albeit on his deathbed). "It will be opulence, it will be sincerity", the artist opined before starting work on the house in the 1860s.

The entrance hall, with its walls of peacock-blue de Morgan tiles, is wonderfully lugubrious, but the star attraction is the remarkable domed **Arab Hall**, built in 1877. Based on a Moorish palace in Palermo, it resounds to the trickle of a central black marble fountain, and is decorated with Saracen tiles, gilded mosaics and latticework drawn from all over the Islamic world. The other rooms are less spectacular in comparison, but are hung with excellent paintings by Lord Leighton and his Pre-Raphaelite friends, Burne-Jones, Alma-Tadema, Watts and Millais – there's even a Tintoretto. Skylights brighten the upper floor, which contains a lovely gilded boudoir looking down onto the Arab Hall and Leighton's vast studio, where he used to hold evening concerts.

18 Stafford Terrace

18 Stafford Terrace • Guided tours Wed 11.15am & 2.15pm, Sat & Sun 11.15am, 1, 2.15 & 3.30pm • £8 • ☎ 020 7602 3316, ⓦ rbkc.gov.uk • ⊖ High Street Kensington

18 Stafford Terrace is where the successful *Punch* cartoonist, Linley Sambourne, lived until his death in 1910. A grand, though fairly ordinary stuccoed terrace house by Kensington standards, it's less a tribute to the artist (though it does contain a huge selection of Sambourne's works) and more a showpiece for the Victorian Society, which helps maintain the house in all its cluttered, late-Victorian excess, complete with stained glass, heavy furnishings and richly decorative William Morris wallpaper. The ninety-minute guided tours are great fun, and, on weekend afternoons, are led by an actor in period garb; there are also occasional evening tours which re-create a night in with the Sambournes.

Bayswater and Paddington

It wasn't until the removal of the gallows at Tyburn (see p.241) that the area to the north of Hyde Park began to gain respectability. The arrival of the Great Western Railway at Paddington in 1838 further encouraged development, and the gentrification of **Bayswater**, the area immediately north of the park, began with the construction of an estate called Tyburnia. These days Bayswater is mainly residential, and a focus for London's widely dispersed Arab community, who are catered for by some excellent restaurants and cafés along the busy **Edgware Road**.

Paddington Station

Paddington Station, on Praed Street, is one of the world's great early train stations: the 1850s facade of the station hotel has been mucked about with over the years and lost its charm, but cathedral-scale wrought-iron sheds, designed by Isambard Kingdom Brunel, are looking better than ever. An earlier wooden structure was the destination of Victoria and Albert's first railway journey in 1842. The train, pulled by the engine *Phlegethon*, travelled at an average speed of 44mph, which the prince consort considered excessive – "Not so fast next time, Mr Conductor", he is alleged to have remarked. To the north and east of Paddington is **Paddington Basin**, built as the terminus of the Grand Union Canal in 1801. Now regenerated, it's worth exploring if only to admire the trio of unusual footbridges which span the water. Funkiest of the lot is Thomas Heatherwick's **Rolling Bridge**, a hydraulic gangway that coils up into an octagon rather like a curled-up woodlouse – it curls up every Friday at noon. If you follow the basin to the northwest, you'll reach Little Venice in about five minutes (see p.281).

Fleming Museum

Praed St • Mon–Thurs 10am–1pm • £4 • ☎ 020 3312 6528, Ⓦ imperial.nhs.uk • ⊖ Paddington

19

One block east of Paddington up Praed Street is St Mary's Hospital, home of the **Fleming Museum**, on the corner of Norfolk Place, where the young Scottish bacteriologist Alexander Fleming accidentally discovered penicillin in 1928. A short video, a small exhibition and a reconstruction of Fleming's untidy lab tell the story of the medical discovery that saved more lives than any other during the last century. Oddly enough, it aroused little interest at the time, until a group of chemists in Oxford succeeded in purifying penicillin in 1942. Desperate for good news in wartime, the media made Fleming a celebrity, and he was eventually awarded the Nobel Prize, along with several of the Oxford team.

Queensway

Bayswater's main drag is **Queensway**, a cosmopolitan street peppered with Middle Eastern cafés. Queensway is best known, however, for **Whiteley's**, opened in 1885 as the city's first real department store or "Universal Provider" with the boast that it could supply "anything from a pin to an elephant". The present building opened in 1907, and in the same year was the scene of the murder of the store's founder, William Whiteley, by a man claiming to be his illegitimate son. Whiteley's also had the dubious distinction of being Hitler's favourite London building – he planned to make it his HQ once the invasion was over. The store closed in 1981, and now houses shops, restaurants and a multiscreen cinema, but the original wrought-iron staircase, centaurs' fountain and glass-domed atrium all survive.

St Sophia's Cathedral

Moscow Rd • Tues–Fri 11am–2pm • Free • ☎ 020 7229 7260, Ⓦ stsophia.org.uk • ⊖ Queensway or Bayswater

Hidden away up Moscow Road, off Queensway itself, is the Greek Orthodox **Cathedral of St Sophia**, built in 1882 by John Oldrid Scott (son of George Gilbert Scott of St Pancras fame). From the red-brick exterior, you only get the merest hint of the richly decorated atmospheric, candlelit interior, where every surface is covered in polychrome marble and gilded mosaics by, among others, Boris Anrep. Services are well worth attending as the cathedral has a polyphonic choir and afterwards, on the last Sunday of the month, you can visit the treasury in the crypt where there's a small museum.

Notting Hill

Notting Hill is home to one of London's most popular markets, **Portobello Road**, and its most famous annual street festival, the **Notting Hill Carnival**. It's also one of the city's most affluent neighbourhoods, characterized by leafy avenues, private garden squares,

19

NOTTING HILL CARNIVAL

When it emerged in the 1960s, **Notting Hill Carnival** was little more than a few church-hall events and a carnival parade by Trinidadians. Today Carnival, held over the August Bank Holiday weekend, still belongs to West Indians (from all parts of the city), but there are participants too from London's Latin American and Asian communities, and Londoners of all descriptions turn out to watch the bands and parades, drink Red Stripe, eat curry goat and generally hang out.

The main sights of Carnival are the **costume parades**, which take place on the Sunday (for kids) and Monday (for adults) from around 9am until 7pm. The parade makes its way around a three-mile route, and consists of big trucks which carry the soundsystems and *mas* (masquerade) bands, behind which the masqueraders dance in outrageous costumes. Most of the *mas* bands play a variety of soca or calypso featuring steel bands – the "pans" of the **steel bands** are one of the chief sounds of Carnival and have their own contest on the Saturday at Horniman's Pleasance, off Kensal Road by the canal. As well as the parade, there are several stages for live music and numerous soundsystems where you can catch reggae, ragga, drum'n'bass, jungle, garage, house and much more.

Over the last decade or so, the Carnival has generally been fairly relaxed, considering the huge numbers of people it attracts. However, this is not an event for you if you're at all bothered by very loud music or crowds – around a million people attend the festival each year and you can be wedged stationary during the parades. It's also worth taking more than usual care with yourself and your belongings. The static soundsystems are switched off at 7pm each day – if there's going to be any trouble it tends to come after that point or, if you feel at all uneasy, head home early.

Getting to and from the Carnival is quite an event in itself. Ladbroke Grove tube station is closed for the duration, while other stations have restricted hours or are open only for incoming visitors. The event's website ✪ thenottinghillcarnival.com provides helpful advice on how to plan your journey to and from the carnival.

trendy shops and white stuccoed mansions. Back in the 1950s, however, it was described as "a massive slum, full of multi-occupied houses, crawling with rats and rubbish". Along with Brixton in south London, it was one of the main neighbourhoods settled by Afro-Caribbean immigrants, invited over to work in the public services. Tensions between the black families who'd moved into the area and the young white working-class "Teddy Boys" were exploited by far-right groups. And for four days in August 1958, Pembridge Road became the focal point of the UK's first **race riots**.

The following year, the **Notting Hill Carnival** (see above) was begun as a response to the riots; in 1965 it took to the streets and has since grown into one of Europe's biggest street festivals. In the 1970s and early 1980s, tensions between the black community and the police came to a head at carnival time, but strenuous efforts on both sides have meant that such conflict has generally been avoided in the last two decades.

Portobello Road

Portobello Road is a meandering, beguiling street that starts just up Chepstow Road from the tube and is famed for its market (see p.434), at its busiest on Saturdays. A short distance up the road stands the **Electric Cinema** (see p.421), London's oldest movie house, which opened in 1910 on the corner of Blenheim Crescent. Portobello Road is the chief location in the movie *Notting Hill*: Hugh Grant's travel bookshop is at 142 Portobello Rd (now a shoe shop), though the real Travel Bookshop is actually round the corner at 13–15 Blenheim Crescent, his house is nearby at 280 Westbourne Park Rd and the private gardens he and Julia Roberts break into are on Rosmead Road.

Trellick Tower

Passing under the **Westway** flyover and east into Golborne Road, you come face-to-face with the awesome **Trellick Tower**, a 31-floor high-rise block of flats designed by Ernö Goldfinger in 1973. The separate service tower has arrow slits and an overhanging boiler tower, yet despite its uncompromising concrete brutalist appearance, it remains popular with its residents. Golborne Road itself is known for its Portuguese and Moroccan cafés, giving the road some of the bohemian feel of old Notting Hill, and making it the perfect place to wind up a visit to the market.

Museum of Brands, Packaging and Advertising

2 Colville Mews • Tues–Sat 10am–6pm, Sun 11am–5pm • £6.50 • ☎ 020 7908 0880, Ⓦ museumofbrands.com • ⊖ Notting Hill Gate

Despite its rather unwieldy title, it's definitely worth popping into the **Museum of Brands, Packaging and Advertising**, hidden away off Lonsdale Road, one block east of Portobello Road. The museum houses an awesome array of old British shop displays through the decades, based on the private collection of Robert Opie, a Scot whose compulsive collecting disorder has left him with ten thousand yoghurt pots alone. From Victorian ceramic pots of anchovy paste to the alcopops of the 1990s, the displays provide a fascinating social commentary on the times. Look out for the militarization of marketing during the two world wars, with their bile beans "for radiant health and a lovely figure" and V for Victory mugs, and clock the irony of the glamorous early cigarette adverts or the posters for Blackpool "for happy, healthy holidays".

Kensal Green Cemetery

April–Sept Mon–Sat 9am–6pm, Sun 10am–6pm; Oct–March closes 5pm • Free • Guided tours March–Oct Sun 2pm; Nov–Feb first & third Sun 2pm • £7 donation suggested • ☎ 020 8969 0152, Ⓦ kensalgreen.co.uk • ⊖ Kensal Green

Beside the gasworks, the Great Western Railway and the Grand Union Canal, lies **Kensal Green Cemetery**, the first of the city's commercial graveyards, opened in 1833 to relieve the pressure on overcrowded inner-city churchyards. Highgate may be the most famous of the "Magnificent Seven" Victorian cemeteries, but Kensal Green has by far the best funerary monuments. It's still owned by the founding company and remains a functioning cemetery, with services conducted daily in the central Greek Revival Anglican chapel. The excellent **guided tours** of the cemetery also include a visit to the **catacombs** (bring a torch).

The graves of the more famous incumbents – Thackeray, Trollope and the Brunels – are less interesting architecturally than those arranged on either side of the Centre Avenue, which leads from the easternmost entrance on Harrow Road. Vandals have left numerous headless angels and irreparably damaged the beautiful Cooke family monument, but still worth looking out for are Major-General Casement's bier, held up by four grim-looking turbaned Indians, circus manager Andrew Ducrow's conglomeration of beehive, sphinx and angels, and artist William Mulready's neo-Renaissance extravaganza. Other interesting characters buried here include Walter Clopton Wingfield, who invented lawn tennis; Marcus Garvey, the black nationalist (until exhumed and taken to Jamaica in 1964); Charles Blondin, the famous tightrope walker; Carl Wilhelm Siemens, the German scientist who brought electric lighting to London; and "James" Barry, Inspector-General of the Army Medical Department, who, it was discovered during the embalming of the corpse, was in fact a woman. Playwright Harold Pinter was buried here and Queen singer Freddie Mercury was cremated here, but his ashes were scattered in Mumbai. Mary Seacole, the "black Florence Nightingale", is buried in the adjacent Roman Catholic cemetery.

KENWOOD, HAMPSTEAD HEATH

North London

Everything north of the Marylebone and Euston roads was, for the most part, open countryside until the mid-nineteenth century, and is now largely built up, right the way up to the "green belt" created in the immediate postwar period to try and limit the continuing urban sprawl. North London begins at the Regent's Canal, which traced the limit of the city's northern outskirts when it was completed in 1820 and now passes through the heart of Camden Town, with its famous market. Further north are a handful of former satellite villages, now subsumed into the general mass of north London, that run the gamut from wealthy Hampstead to gritty Hackney. Most of north London is easily accessible by tube; in fact, it was the expansion of the tube that encouraged the forward march of bricks and mortar in the outer suburbs.

On its completion in 1820, the **Regent's Canal** delineated the city's northern periphery, passing along the north side of one of London's finest parks, **Regent's Park**, framed by Nash-designed architecture and home to London Zoo. The canal forces its way into most Londoners' consciousness only at **Camden**, a rakish place even today, whose market is one of the city's big attractions – a warren of stalls selling funky wares, street fashion, books and music.

Few visitors to the capital head out to neighbouring **Islington**, which has its own flourishing antiques trade, and **Dalston** and **Hackney**, further east, with their ethnically diverse population, thus missing out on some of north London's defining areas. The real highlights, though, for visitors and residents alike, are **Hampstead** and **Highgate**, elegant, largely eighteenth-century developments, which still reflect their village origins. They have the added advantage of proximity to one of London's wildest patches of greenery, **Hampstead Heath**, where you can enjoy stupendous views, kite flying and outdoor bathing, as well as high art at the Neoclassical mansion of **Kenwood House**.

A few sights in more far-flung suburbs are also worth seeking out: the nineteenth-century utopia of **Hampstead Garden Suburb**; the Orthodox Jewish suburb of **Golders Green**; the **RAF Museum** at Hendon; and the spectacular **Hindu temple** in Neasden.

Little Venice

⊖ Warwick Avenue

The Regent's Canal starts out from the west in the triangular leafy basin known as **Little Venice**, a nickname coined by one-time resident and poet Robert Browning. The title may be far-fetched, but the willow-tree Browning's Island is one of the prettiest spots on the canal, and the houseboats and barges moored hereabouts are brightly painted and strewn with tubs of flowers. While you're here, try and catch a marionette performance on the **Puppet Theatre Barge** (see p.441), moored on the Blomfield Road side of the basin, a unique and unforgettable experience; performances take place every weekend at 3pm, and daily throughout the school holidays (except Aug & Sept). You can also catch a **canal boat** to Camden (see p.287), or walk south to the Paddington Basin (see p.277).

20

REGENT'S CANAL

The **Regent's Canal**, completed in 1820, was constructed as part of a direct link from Birmingham to the newly built London Docks in the East End. After an initial period of heavy usage it was overtaken by the railway, and never really paid its way as its investors had hoped. By some miracle, however, it survived, and its nine miles, 42 bridges, twelve locks and two tunnels stand as a reminder of another age. The lock-less stretch of the canal **between Little Venice and Camden Town** is the busiest, most attractive section, tunnelling through to Lisson Grove, skirting Regent's Park, offering views of London Zoo and passing straight through the heart of Camden Market. You can walk, jog or cycle along the towpath, but this section of the canal is also served by scheduled narrowboats.

Three companies run daily **boat services** between Camden and Little Venice, passing through the Maida Hill tunnel. Whichever you choose, you can board at either end; **tickets** cost around £10 return, and journey time is fifty minutes one-way.

Jenny Wren ☏ 020 7485 4433, **🖥** walkersquay .com. The narrowboat *Jenny Wren* starts off at Camden, goes through a canal lock (the only company to do so) and heads for Little Venice (with a live commentary). March Sat & Sun only; April–Oct daily.

Jason's Trip ☏ 020 7286 3428, **🖥** jasons.co.uk. This one hundred-year-old traditional narrow boat has been running trips since 1951; services set off three or four times a day from Little Venice to Camden. Cash only, no commentary. April–early Nov daily.

London Waterbus Company ☏ 020 7482 2550, **🖥** londonwaterbus.com. Services leave from both Camden and Little Venice, and call in at London Zoo en route. April–Sept daily; Oct Thurs–Sun only; Nov–March Sat & Sun only, weather permitting.

St John's Wood

The residential district of **St John's Wood** was built over in the nineteenth century by developers hoping to attract a wealthy clientele with a mixture of semi-detached Italianate villas, multi-occupancy Gothic mansions and white stucco terraces. Edwin Landseer (of Trafalgar Square lions fame), novelist George Eliot and Mrs Fitzherbert, the uncrowned wife of George IV, all lived here, while current residents include knights Richard Branson and Paul McCartney and supermodel Kate Moss.

Lord's Cricket Ground

St John's Wood Rd • Museum Non-match days daily 9.30am-4.30pm • £7.50 Guided tours all year round daily • £15 • ☎ 020 7616 8500, ⓦ lords.org • ⊖ St John's Wood

The Regent's Canal was bad news for Thomas Lord, who had only recently been forced to shift his cricket ground due to the construction of Marylebone Road. In 1813, with the canal coming, he once more upped his stumps and relocated, this time to St John's Wood Road, where **Lord's**, as the ground is now known, remains to this day. Lord's is, of course, home of the **MCC** (Marylebone Cricket Club), founded in 1787, and the most hallowed institution in the game, boasting a very long members waiting list (unless you're exceptionally famous or rich). Its politics were neatly summed up by Viscount Monckton of Brenchley, who said, "I have been a member of the Committee of the MCC and of a Conservative cabinet, and by comparison with the cricketers, the Tories seem like a bunch of Commies."

Lord's is home to the **MCC Museum**, the world's oldest sports museum, which houses the minuscule pottery urn containing the Ashes (along with the complex tale of this odd trophy), numerous historic balls, bats and bails, and a sparrow which was "bowled out" by Jehangir Khan at Lord's in 1936. The museum can also be visited as part of a **guided tour**, which sets off from the Grace Gates at the southwest corner of the ground. On the tour, you get to see the famous Long Room (from which the players walk onto the pitch), Lord's Real Tennis Court, the various stands and the futuristic aluminium Media Centre.

20

Regent's Park

Daily 5am to dusk • ☎ 0300 061 2300, ⓦ royalparks.org.uk • ⊖ Regent's Park, Baker Street, Great Portland Street, St John's Wood or Camden Town

Regent's Park is one of London's smartest parks, with a boating lake, ornamental ponds and waterfalls and wonderful gardens all enclosed in a ring of magnificent nineteenth-century mansions. As with almost all of London's royal parks, we have Henry VIII to thank for Regent's Park which he confiscated from the Church for yet more hunting grounds. However, it wasn't until the reign of the Prince Regent (later George IV) that the park began to take its current form – hence its official title, "The Regent's Park" – and the public weren't allowed in until 1845 (and even then for just two days of the week). According to John Nash's 1811 master plan, the park was to be girded by a continuous belt of terraces, and sprinkled with a total of 56 villas, including a magnificent pleasure palace for the prince himself, linked by Regent Street to Carlton House, George's palace in St James's. Inevitably, the plan was never fully realized, but enough was built to create something of the idealized garden city that Nash and the Prince Regent envisaged.

The eastern terraces

Nash's terraces form a near-unbroken horseshoe of cream-coloured stucco around the Outer Circle. By far the most impressive are the eastern terraces, especially **Cumberland Terrace**, completed in 1826, and intended as a foil for George IV's planned pleasure palace and tea pavilion. Its 800ft-long facade, hidden away on the eastern edge of the park, is punctuated by Ionic triumphal arches, peppered with classical alabaster statues and centred on a Corinthian portico with a pediment of sculptures set against a vivid sky-blue background. In 1936 an angry crowd threw bricks through the windows of no. 16, which belonged to American divorcée Mrs Wallis Simpson, whose relationship with Edward VIII was seen as a national calamity, and eventually led to his abdication.

Fifty-two more statues depicting British worthies were planned for the even longer facade of **Chester Terrace**, to the south, but Nash decided the ridicule they provoked was "painful to the ears of a professional man" and ditched them. Nevertheless, Chester Terrace is worth walking down if only to take in the splendid triumphal arches at each end, which announce the name of the terrace in bold lettering; the northern one features a bust of Nash.

To the north of Cumberland Terrace, the neo-Gothic **St Katharine's Precinct** provides a respite from the Grecian surroundings, though not one Nash was at all happy with. The central church serves the Danish community, who have erected a copy of the imposing tenth-century **Jelling Stone** in an alcove to the right.

The Inner Circle

Of the numerous villas planned for the park itself in Nash's master plan, only eight were actually built, and of those just two originals have survived around the **Inner**

● SHOPS		● CAFÉS		● RESTAURANTS		■ PUBS & BARS			
Annie's Vintage		Afghan Kitchen	8	Gem	6	69 Colebrooke Row	29	Duke of Cambridge	3
Costume & Textiles	4	Issy's Milky Way	10	Manna	1	The Albert	11	Edinboro Castle	1
Camden Market	1	M. Manze/Seagrass	9	Namaaste Kitchen	3	Brewdog	17	The Enterprise	
Rokit	2	My Village	2	Ottolenghi	7	Bridge House	25	The Hops & Glory	2
Sounds that Swing	3			El Parador	5	The Charles Lamb	36	Island Queen	3
				Trullo	4	The Crown	27	King's Head	2

REGENT'S CANAL: LITTLE VENICE TO ISLINGTON

Circle: St John's Lodge, built in 1812 and now owned by the Sultan of Brunei, and **The Holme**, Decimus Burton's first-ever work (he was just 18 at the time), picturesquely sited by the Y-shaped **Boating Lake** (open March–Oct), and now owned by a Saudi prince. Within the Inner Circle is the Open Air Theatre (see p.419), and **Queen Mary's Gardens**, which is by far the prettiest section of the whole park. A large slice of the gardens is taken up with a glorious rose garden, featuring some four hundred varieties, surrounded by a ring of ramblers.

London Central Mosque

146 Park Rd • Daily 9am–10pm • Free • ☎ 020 7724 3363, Ⓦ iccuk.org • ⊖ Marylebone or St John's Wood

The skyline of Regent's Park is punctuated by the shiny copper dome and minaret of the **London Central Mosque** (also known as the Islamic Cultural Centre), built in 1977, and an entirely appropriate addition given the Prince Regent's taste for the Orient (as expressed in the Brighton Pavilion). Non-Muslim visitors are welcome to visit the information centre, the exhibition on Islam, and the café, and to glance inside the hall of worship, which can hold five thousand or more worshippers and which is dominated by an enormous, sparkling, central chandelier.

		■ CLUBS		■ MUSIC VENUES		Hope & Anchor	24	■ GAY & LESBIAN VENUE	
e Lansdowne	7	Big Chill House	30	Academy Islington	31	Jazz Cafe	14	The Black Cap	16
ck Tavern	9	Egg	15	Barfly	6	KOKO	23	■ ACCOMMODATION	
nce Alfred	21	Electric Ballroom	12	Buffalo Bar	20	Lexington	32	New Inn	1
Richard Steele	1	Proud Camden	8	Bull and Gate	3	Roundhouse	5		
e Warrington	18	Slimelight at Electrowerkz	33	Dingwalls	10	Underworld	13		
				Forum	2	Union Chapel	22		

THE BEATLES IN LONDON

Since the Fab Four lived in London for much of the 1960s, it's hardly surprising that the capital is riddled with Beatle associations. The prime Beatles landmark is, of course, the **Abbey Road zebra crossing** featured on the album cover, located near the EMI studios where the group recorded most of their albums. The nearest tube is St John's Wood – remember to bring three friends plus another to take the photos. Incidentally, Paul McCartney still owns the house at 7 Cavendish Ave, which he bought in 1966, two blocks east of the zebra crossing.

One (short-lived) nearby curiosity was the **Apple Boutique**, opened by The Beatles at 94 Baker St (⊖ Baker Street), in December 1967, as a "beautiful place where you could buy beautiful things". The psychedelic murals that covered the entire building were whitewashed over after a lawsuit by the neighbours, and eight months later The Beatles caused even more pandemonium when they gave the shop's entire stock away free in the closing-down sale – a blue plaque commemorates the shenanigans.

Other Beatles locations include the old Apple headquarters in Savile Row, Mayfair, where the 1969 rooftop concert took place, while Macca has his current office on Soho Square (see p.101). Real devotees of the group should sign up for a Beatles tour, run by The Original London Walks (☎020 7624 3978, ⓦwalks.com).

Winfield House

On the opposite side of the road from the London Central Mosque is **Winfield House**, a dull 1930s replacement for Decimus Burton's Hertford House, built by the heiress to the Woolworth chain, Countess Haugwitz-Reventlow (better known as Barbara Hutton), who gifted Winfield House to the US government during World War II and went on to marry Cary Grant; it's now the American ambassador's residence, and tends to be where the US President stays when he visits London.

London Zoo

The lion sits within his cage,
Weeping tears of ruby rage,
He licks his snout, the tears fall down
And water dusty London town.

The Zoo, Stevie Smith

Regent's Park • Daily March–Oct 10am–5.30pm; Nov–Feb 10am–4pm • £23 peak season online • Zoo Lates for adults only June & July Fri 6–10pm • ☎020 7722 3333, ⓦzsl.org/zsl-london-zoo • ⊖ Camden Town

The northeastern corner of Regent's Park is occupied by **London Zoo**. Founded in 1826 with the remnants of the royal menagerie (see p.184), the enclosures here are as humane as any inner-city zoo could make them, and kids usually enjoy themselves. In particular they love Animal Adventure, the new children's zoo (and playground) where they can actually handle the animals, and the regular live shows. The invertebrate house (BUGS), Gorilla Kingdom, Butterfly Paradise and the walk-through Rainforest Life and Meet the Monkeys enclosures are also guaranteed winners – book online to avoid queuing.

The zoo boasts some striking architectural features, too, such as the 1930s modernist, spiral-ramped, concrete former penguin pool (where Penguin Books' original colophon was sketched), designed by the Tecton partnership, led by Berthold Lubetkin, who also made the zoo's Round House. The Giraffe House, by contrast, was designed in Neoclassical style by Decimus Burton, who was also responsible for the mock-Tudor Clock Tower. Other landmark features are the mountainous Mappin Terraces and the colossal tetrahedral aluminium-framed tent of Lord Snowdon's modern aviary.

Primrose Hill

The small northern extension of Regent's Park, known as **Primrose Hill**, commands a great view of central London from its modest summit. And it lends its name to the much sought-after residential area, to the northeast, which has attracted numerous successful literati and artists over the years: H.G. Wells, W.B. Yeats, Friedrich Engels, Kingsley Amis and Morrissey have all lived here. You might catch the present denizens such as Jamie Oliver, Ewan McGregor, Alan Bennett or Martin Amis browsing the bookshops and galleries on **Regent's Park Road**, which skirts Primrose Hill to the east. Ted Hughes and Sylvia Plath lived in a flat at 3 Chalcot Square, just east of Regent's Park Road, and it was nearby at 23 Fitzroy Rd, the house that Yeats once lived in, that Plath committed suicide in 1963.

Camden Town

Until the canal arrived, **Camden Town** wasn't even a village, but by Victorian times it had become a notorious slum area, an image it took most of the past century to shed. In the meantime, it attracted its fair share of artists, most famously the Camden Town Group formed in 1911 by Walter Sickert, later joined by the likes of Lucian Freud, Frank Auerbach and Leon Kossoff. These days, you're more likely to bump into young foreign tourists heading for the market, and as-yet-unknown bands on the lookout for members of the local music industry.

For all the gentrification of the last thirty years, Camden retains a gritty aspect, compounded by the various railway lines that plough through the area, the canal and the large shelter for the homeless on Arlington Road. Its proximity to three mainline stations also made it an obvious point of immigration over the years, particularly for the Irish, but also for Greek Cypriots during the 1950s. Nowadays, the **market** overwhelms the area, especially at weekends, and is now the district's best-known attribute.

20

Camden Lock

If you've seen enough market stalls for one day, stand on the bowed iron footbridge by **Camden Lock** itself, and admire the castellated former lock-keeper's house, to the west. You can catch a boat to Little Venice (see p.281); the flight of three locks to the east begins the canal's descent to Limehouse and the Thames. The first lock pound is overlooked by Terry Farrell's former **TV-AM Building**, now occupied (and revamped) by MTV, but still retaining its giant blue-and-white egg cups from breakfast television days. To the south are the covered basins of the Interchange Warehouse, linked by a disused railway line to the **Camden Catacombs**, built in the nineteenth century as stables for the pit ponies that used to shunt the railway wagons.

Roundhouse

Chalk Farm Road · ☎ 0844 482 8008, ⓦ roundhouse.org.uk · ⊖ Chalk Farm

Camden's brick-built **Roundhouse**, on Chalk Farm Road, is now a performing arts venue, but was originally built in 1846 as an engine repair shed for 23 goods engines, arranged around a central turntable. Within fifteen years the engines had outgrown the building, and for the next century it was used for storing booze. In 1964, Arnold Wesker established

---

CAMDEN MARKET

Camden Market was confined to Inverness Street until the 1970s, when the focus shifted to the disused warehouses around Camden Lock. The tiny crafts market which began in the cobbled courtyard by the lock has since mushroomed out of all proportion, with stalls on both sides of Camden High Street and Chalk Farm Road. More than one hundred thousand shoppers turn up here each weekend and **Camden Lock** and the vast labyrinth of the **Stables Market** now stay open all week long (see p.434). For all its tourist popularity, Camden remains a genuinely offbeat place. To avoid the crowds, which can be overpowering in the summer, aim to come either early (before noon) or late (after 4pm), or on a Friday. The nearest tube is Camden Town, though this is exit-only at peak times; Chalk Farm tube is only ten minutes' walk up Chalk Farm Road from Camden Lock.

the place as a political theatre venue, and two years later, the Roundhouse began to stage rock gigs – everyone from Hendrix and The Doors to The Ramones and Kraftwerk – and other nonconformist happenings. In 1966, it held a launch party for the underground paper, *International Times*, at which Pink Floyd and Soft Machine both performed, later hosting a Dialectics of Liberation conference organized by R.D. Laing, not to mention performances by the anarchist Living Theatre of New York, featuring a naked cast.

Jewish Museum

129 Albert St • Mon–Thurs & Sun 10am–5pm, Fri 10am–2pm • £7.50 • First Thurs of month 5–9pm • £3.50 • ☎ 020 7284 7384, ⓦ jewishmuseum.org.uk • ⊖ Camden Town

Despite having no significant Jewish associations, Camden is home to London's purpose-built **Jewish Museum**. The Welcome Gallery, on the ground floor, features ten extremely varied accounts of what it's like to be Jewish in contemporary London, from a teenager at the JFS to an Orthodox rabbi – you also get to see a thirteenth-century ritual bath (mikveh) from the City. On the first floor, there's an engaging exhibition explaining Jewish practices and illustrated by cabinets of Judaica from all over Europe, including a seventeenth-century Venetian Ark of the Covenant and treasures from London's Great Synagogue in the City, burnt down by Nazi bombers in 1941. On the second floor, there's an interactive display on the history of British Jews from 1066 onwards, with good sections on Yiddish theatre, boxing, tailoring plus a special Holocaust gallery which focuses on Leon Greenman (1920–2008), one of only two British Jews who suffered and survived Auschwitz. The museum also puts on a lively programme of special exhibitions on the top floor, as well as various talks, films, discussions and concerts, and has a café on the ground floor.

Islington

⊖ Angel

Since the 1960s, **Islington**'s picturesque but dilapidated Regency and early Victorian squares and terraces have been snapped up by professionals and City types and comprehensively renovated. The impact of this gentrification, however, has been relatively minor on the borough as a whole, which stretches as far north as Highgate Hill, and remains one of the city's poorest. **Chapel Market** (Tues–Sun), to the west of Upper Street, selling cheap clothes, fruit and veg and Arsenal football memorabilia, is a salutary reminder of Islington's working-class roots. For more on the history of Islington, visit the borough's museum (see p.151).

There's little evidence of those roots on the main drag, **Upper Street**: the arrival of its antique market – confusingly known as **Camden Passage** – coincided with the new influx of cash-happy customers, and its pubs and **restaurants** reflect the wealth of its new residents. For entertainment, Islington boasts the long-established *King's Head* **pub theatre** (see p.419), the Little Angel **puppet theatre** and the ever-popular Almeida plus several live-music venues (see p.400). All of which make Islington one of the liveliest areas of north London in the evening – a kind of off-West End.

> ### THE NEW RIVER
>
> In 1613, **Hugh Myddelton** (1560–1631), Royal Jeweller to James I, revolutionized London's water supply by drawing fresh water direct from the River Lee, 38 miles away in Hertfordshire, via an aqueduct known as the **New River**. A weathered statue of Myddelton, unveiled by Gladstone in 1862, stands at the apex of Islington Green. Right up until the late 1980s the New River continued to supply most of north London with its water – the original termination point was at **New River Head**, near Sadler's Wells theatre (see p.416); the succession of ponds to the northeast of Canonbury Road is a surviving fragment of the scheme; north of Stoke Newington, much of the river remains *in situ*.

Upper Street

Looking at the traffic fighting its way along **Upper Street**, it's hard to believe that "merry Islington", as it was known, was once a spa resort to which people would come to drink the pure water and breathe the clean air. And walking along Upper Street (and several of the surrounding streets), it's impossible not to be struck by one of the area's quirky architectural features – the raised pavements which protected pedestrians from splattered mud. Such precautions were especially necessary since Islington was used as a convenient grazing halt for livestock en route to the local Royal Agricultural Hall or nearby Smithfield.

Royal Agricultural Hall

The ugly modern glass frontage of the Business Design Centre hides the former **Royal Agricultural Hall**, Islington's finest Victorian building, completed in 1862, and known locally as the "Aggie". As well as hosting agricultural and livestock exhibitions, it used to host the World's Fair, the Grand Military Tournament, Cruft's Dog Show and such marvels as Urbini's performing fleas. During World War II, however, it was requisitioned by the government for use by the Post Office, who remained in residence until 1971. The interior is still magnificent – even if the exhibitions now held there are more prosaic (think packaging conferences and careers fairs) – with the best exterior view from Liverpool Road, where two large brick towers rise up either side of the roof, like a Victorian train station.

Islington Green to Cross Street

Today, Islington has fewer green spaces than any other London borough – one of the few being the minuscule **Islington Green**, just up from Angel tube. Twice a week (Wed & Sat), the pavements to the east of the green are occupied by the antique stalls of the **Camden Passage market**, although the antique shops in the market's narrow namesake and the surrounding streets stay open all week.

20

Just north of the green stands **St Mary's Church**, originally built in the 1750s. Only the steeple survived the Blitz, though the light, spacious 1950s interior is an interesting period piece, with six fluted Egyptian-style columns framing the sanctuary. The churchyard opens out into Dagmar Passage, where in 1961 a former temperance hall was converted into the **Little Angel Puppet Theatre** (see p.441). The archway at the end of Dagmar Terrace brings you out onto **Cross Street**, Islington's loveliest street, with eighteenth-century houses sloping down to Essex Road and raised pavements on both sides.

Union Chapel

North of **Islington Town Hall**, a handsome 1920s Neoclassical Portland-stone building, set back from Upper Street, is the fancifully extravagant **Union Chapel**. Built in 1888, at the height of the Congregationalists' popularity, it remains a church, but is now also an innovative independent concert venue (see p.400). Its lugubrious, spacious, octagonal interior is designed like a giant Gothic auditorium, with raked seating and galleries capable of holding 1650 rapt worshippers (or concert goers) with the pulpit centre stage.

Highbury Fields

At the top of Upper Street lies the largest open space in the entire borough, the modestly sized park of **Highbury Fields**, where over two hundred thousand people gathered in 1666 to escape (and watch) the Great Fire. Now overlooked on two sides by splendid Georgian and Victorian terraces, and fringed with plane trees, it's one of Islington's more elegant green spaces. A plaque on the park's public toilets commemorates the country's first-ever gay rights demonstration (against police harassment) which took place here in 1970. Of course Highbury is also world famous as the former home of **Arsenal** football club, who now play at a modern sixty thousand-seat stadium, ten minutes' walk away (see p.436).

ORTON IN ISLINGTON

Playwright **Joe Orton** and his lover **Kenneth Halliwell** lived together for sixteen years, spending the last eight years of their lives in a top-floor bedsit at 25 Noel Rd, to the east of Upper Street, where the Regent's Canal emerges from the Islington tunnel. It's ironic that the borough council has seen fit to erect a plaque on the house commemorating the couple, when it was instrumental in pressing for harsh prison sentences after both men were found guilty of stealing and defacing local library books in 1962. A few of the wittily doctored books are now on display at the **Islington Museum** (see p.151).

Six months in prison worked wonders for Orton's writing, as he himself said: "Being in the nick brought detachment to my writing". It also brought him success, with irreverent comedies like *Loot*, *Entertaining Mr Sloane* and *What the Butler Saw* playing to sell-out audiences in the West End and on Broadway. Orton's meteoric fame and his sexual profligacy drove Halliwell to despair, however, and on August 9, 1967, Halliwell finally cracked – beating Orton to death with a hammer and then killing himself with a drug overdose. Their ashes were mixed together and scattered over the grass at **Golders Green Crematorium** (see p.307). Apart from the local public toilets, Orton's favourite hangout was the appropriately entitled *Island Queen* pub (see p.396), at the end of Noel Road.

Canonbury Square

Islington's most perfect Regency set piece, **Canonbury Square** is centred on a smartly maintained flower garden, but blighted by traffic ploughing up Canonbury Road. In 1928, **Evelyn Waugh** moved into the first floor of no. 17 with his wife Evelyn Gardiner (they called themselves "He-Evelyn" and "She-Evelyn"). In those days, the square was nothing like as salubrious as it is now. In fact, it was precisely the square's squalor that appealed to **George Orwell**, who moved into the top floor of no. 27 in 1944, with his wife and son, having been bombed out of his digs in St John's Wood; he later used it as the prototype for Winston Smith's home in *1984*.

Canonbury Tower

Guided tours contact ☎ 020 7359 6888, ⓦ canonburytower.org.uk

Immediately to the northeast of the square stands the last remaining relic of Islington's bygone days as a rural retreat, the red-brick **Canonbury Tower**, originally part of a Tudor mansion built for the prior of St Bartholomew in the City. The very top floor boasts three Elizabethan interiors, with carved oak panelling and fireplaces carved with Freemasonic and Rosicrucian symbols from when the rooms were used by Renaissance man Francis Bacon. The tower is currently looked after by the Canonbury Tower Charitable Trust, who can organize guided tours.

Estorick Collection of Modern Italian Art

Canonbury Rd • Wed–Sat 11am–6pm, Sun noon–5pm, first Thurs of month until 9pm • £5 • ☎ 020 7704 9522, ⓦ estorickcollection .com • ⊖ Highbury & Islington

Islington's most intriguing attraction is the **Estorick Collection of Modern Italian Art**, which occupies a Georgian mansion on Canonbury Square, with the entrance on Canonbury Road. The most exciting works in the gallery are those of the early Italian Futurists, although their founding manifesto of 1909 urged followers to "divert the canals to flood the museums"! Futurism's mouthpiece was the fascist Filippo Marinetti, a rich boy with a penchant for crashing fast cars, and, as evidenced by the photos, an eye for natty waistcoats, complete with appliqué hands patting the pockets.

The permanent collection, spread out over the two upper floors, ranges from the rainbow colours of *Music* by Luigi Russolo (inventor of the *intonarumori* – a sort of avant-garde hurdy-gurdy), which is firmly Futurist, to a few portraits by Modigliani, and a typically melancholic canvas by Symbolist painter, Giorgio de Chirico. One of the strangest works is Medardo Rosso's wax sculpture *Woman with a Veil*, from 1893, which had a profound influence on the Futurists. Other highlights include Giacomo Balla's *Hand of the Violinist*, a classic Futurist study of movement, speed and dexterity, and Gino Severini's Cubist *Dancer*. The gallery also features paintings by lesser-known Italian artists such as Giorgio Morandi, Massimo Campigli, Mario Sironi and Zoran Music, as well as by Italy's two leading postwar sculptors, Emilio Greco and Marino Marini. Excellent special exhibitions are held on the lower floors, and there's a pleasant Italian café that spills out into the back courtyard in good weather.

Hackney

The borough of **Hackney** stretches from Shoreditch (see p.196), on the East End edge of the City, to the predominantly Jewish north London suburb of **Stamford Hill**. One of the most ethnically diverse of all London boroughs, it comes as no surprise that the country's longest-serving black woman MP, Diane Abbott, has her constituency in Hackney. The fact that the borough has tourist signposts comes as a surprise to many visitors, yet Hackney repays selective visits: **Dalston** is now at the heart of London's alternative nightlife (see p.403); **Stoke Newington** is a haven of inexpensive restaurants and laidback cafés; and **Hackney Central** boasts the former music hall of the Hackney Empire, with the red-brick Tudor mansion of **Sutton House** a short stroll away.

Dalston

Dalston has undergone a seismic transformation, and has now overtaken Shoreditch as London's hippest, grittiest new *quartier*. Among the early pioneers was the excellent *Vortex Jazz Club*, on the frankly quite sleazy Gillett Square, followed by the Arcola Theatre, one of the city's most dynamic fringe venues, which now occupies a former paint factory on Ashwin Street, next door to the avant-garde music venue *Café Oto*. This trio has been accompanied by bars and clubs dotted up and down the high street

---

THE ANGRY BRIGADE

On August 20, 1971, six alleged members of the **Angry Brigade** – at the time Britain's only home-grown urban terrorist group – were arrested at 359 Amhurst Rd, off Stoke Newington High Street, along with (according to the police) a small arsenal of weapons and explosives. The police attempted to link the Angries with the explosives (despite the lack of forensic evidence) and a total of 25 bomb attacks on the homes of Tory politicians and other members of the Establishment, during which one person had been slightly injured. After one of the longest criminal trials in English history, at which two other alleged members were also charged, four of the accused were sent to prison for conspiracy to cause explosions and four were acquitted.

---

from Dalston Junction. With two Overground stations, and trains capable of whizzing you in all directions, Dalston's transport has vastly improved, too.

Kingsland High Street

Kingsland High Street had a history of entertainment long before the current crop of clubs and bars came along, with four or five cinemas in close proximity. The lone survivor is the Art Deco **Rio Cinema**, at no. 107, opened in 1937 as the Dalston Classic, replacing the 1915 Kingsland Empire, and still going strong. Dalston's other heritage sight is the *Shanghai* restaurant, which preserves the 1910 decor of tiles, marble and glass from its days as an eel and pie shop, founded in 1862 by the ubiquitous Cooke family.

Ridley Road Market

Mon–Thurs 6am–6pm, Fri & Sat 6am–7pm • Dalston Kingsland or Dalston Junction Overground

In the immediate postwar period, Dalston was a predominantly Jewish area, and **Ridley Road Market** (Mon–Sat) was the scene of battles between Mosley's fascists and Jewish ex-servicemen. The market is still in good health, and an accurate reflection of Dalston's ethnic diversity, with Cockney fruit and veg stalls, halal butchers, a 24-hour bagel bakery, West Indian grocers and African and Asian fabric shops. A Turkish/Kurdish supermarket marks the eastern end of the market, its railings still displaying the Star of David from its original Jewish occupants.

Stoke Newington

Bus #73 or #476 from ⊖ Angel or Stoke Newington train station from Liverpool St

Stoke Newington (or "Stokey") is probably the most immediately appealing area of Hackney, though like much of the borough, it's off the tube map. Stokey's best attribute is **Church Street**, a more or less franchise-free, former village high street of little independent shops and restaurants.

The whole area was, for several centuries, a haven for Nonconformists (Christians who were not members of the Anglican church), who were denied the right to live in the City. The most famous Dissenter to live in Stokey was **Daniel Defoe**, who wrote *Robinson Crusoe* on the corner of what is now Defoe Road and Church Street; his gravestone is displayed in the Hackney Museum – stolen from Bunhill Fields in the 1870s, it was discovered in Southampton in 1940.

Abney Park Cemetery

Stoke Newington High St • **Cemetery** 8am to dusk **Visitor Centre** Mon–Fri 10am–4pm • Free • ☎ 020 7275 7557, ⓦ abney-park.org.uk • Stoke Newington train station

When Bunhill Fields (see p.198) became overcrowded, **Abney Park Cemetery** became the "Campo Santo of English non-Conformists", in the words of the 1903 brochure. The most famous grave is that of **William Booth**, founder of the Salvation Army (see p.201), by the Church Street entrance, but the romantically overrun cemetery was originally planted as an A–Z arboretum, and is now an inner-city wildlife reserve (not

to mention a gay cruising area). A **visitors' centre** is housed in one of the Egyptian-style lodges at the main entrance, on busy Stoke Newington High Street.

Clissold Park

Stoke Newington Church St • Daily 7.30am–dusk • Free • ☎ 020 7923 3660, ⓦ hackney.gov.uk • Stoke Newington train station

Stoke Newington's two main churches, both dedicated to **St Mary**, stand either side of Church Street and reflect the changes wrought on the area in the last couple of centuries: the sixteenth-century village church firmly in the shadow of the more urbane structure built by George Gilbert Scott in the 1850s, with a spire that outreached all others in London in its day. This pair marks the entrance to **Clissold Park**, founded in 1889 and centred on a porticoed mansion built in the 1790s as a country house for the Quaker Hoare banking family, now beautifully restored and housing the park café. The duck and terrapin pond in front was once part of the New River; elsewhere are goats, deer, a small aviary and a butterfly tunnel.

Stamford Hill

In the northern tip of Hackney, **Stamford Hill** is home to a tight-knit, mostly Yiddish-speaking, community of Hasidic Jews, one of the borough's oldest immigrant populations. The most visually striking aspect of this ultra-Orthodox community is the men's attire – frock coats, white stockings and elaborate headgear – which derives from that worn by the Polish nobility of the period. The shops on Stamford Hill and Dunsmure Road, running west, are where the Hasidim buy their kosher goods.

20

Springfield Park

Springfield • Daily 7.30am–dusk • Free • ☎ 020 8356 8428, ⓦ hackney.gov.uk • Stamford Hill train station

On Sundays, large numbers of Hasidic families take the air at **Springfield Park**, opened in 1905 "to change the habits of the people and to keep them out of the public houses". The park boasts an awesome view east across the Lee Valley to the adjacent **Walthamstow Marshes**, a valuable stretch of wetland that's alive with butterflies and warblers in the summer. The park also has a decent **café** (ⓦspringfieldparkcafe.co.uk) in the White Lodge Mansion by the pond.

To reach Springfield Park from Stamford Hill, walk across Clapton Common, and down Spring Hill. En route, check out the four winged beasts (characters from the Book of Revelation) at the base of the spire of the **Cathedral Church of the Good Shepherd** on the corner of Rookwood Road, built for the sect of Spiritual Free Lovers, the Agapemonites, in 1892. Six thousand gathered outside here in 1902 to throw rotten tomatoes at the womanizing vicar, who had declared himself the Second Messiah, and drive him into Clapton Pond to see if he could walk on water.

Middlesex Filter Beds

Sat & Sun: Easter–Sept 10am–6pm; Oct–Easter 10am–4pm; summer holidays also Mon–Fri 10am–5pm • Free • Clapton train station

If you follow the River Lee south of Walthamstow Marshes, you will eventually reach the **Middlesex Filter Beds**, originally built in 1852 on the south side of Lea Bridge Road. Closed in 1969 and mostly drained, the filter beds now serve as a nature reserve – in the spring check out the noisy frogs in the pond by the main culvert. To the south of the filter beds lie the **Hackney Marshes**, best known as the venue for Sunday League football matches, beyond which is the 2012 Olympic Park (see p.202).

Hackney Central

The old parish of Hackney was originally centred around the dumpy fifteenth-century tower of the former parish church of **St Augustine**, and next to it, the Old Town Hall, built in 1802 (now a betting shop). At this point, Mare Street is still discernably a village high street, and is known, for obvious reasons, as the **Narroway**. The modern borough has its headquarters further south on Mare Street around **Hackney Town Hall**, built in a very restrained 1930s Art Deco style and set back from the high street. Close by is the ornate terracotta **Hackney Empire**, one of the last surviving music halls in London, built in typically extravagant style by Frank Matcham in 1899.

Hackney Museum

1 Reading Lane • Tues, Wed & Fri 9.30am–5.30pm, Thurs 9.30am–8pm, Sat 10am–5pm • Free • ☎ 020 8356 3500, ⓦ hackney.gov.uk • Hackney Central Overground

Beside the town hall stands the borough's new library and the **Hackney Museum**. As well as excellent temporary exhibitions, the museum has an interesting permanent display with lots of personal accounts from local residents. Specific exhibits to look out for include the "upside-down" map of the borough and the Saxon log boat found in Springfield Park, thought to have been a ferry for taking folk across the River Lee.

Sutton House

2–4 Homerton High St • Feb to mid-Dec Thurs & Fri 10.30am–5pm, Sat & Sun noon–5pm; daily during school Easter & summer holidays • NT • £3.50 • ☎ 020 8986 2264, ⓦ nationaltrust.org.uk • Hackney Central Overground

Hidden away, at the east end of the Georgian terrace of Sutton Place, stands **Sutton House**. Built in 1535 for Ralph Sadleir, a rising star at the court of Henry VIII, the house takes its name from Thomas Sutton, founder of Charterhouse, who lived in an adjacent building (he is buried at Charterhouse, minus his entrails, which you've probably just walked over in the graveyard by Mare Street). The National Trust have done their best to adapt to unfamiliar surroundings and have preserved not just the exquisite Elizabethan "linenfold" wooden panelling, but also a mural left by squatters in 1986. In addition to showing its rambling complex of period rooms, the house puts on classical concerts, hosts contemporary art exhibitions and even runs a tearoom.

20

Walthamstow

East of the River Lee and the marshes, the chief reason to head out to **Walthamstow** is to visit the William Morris Gallery, but there are one or two other points of interest in the district. **Walthamstow Market** (Mon–Sat) stretches for almost a mile along the old High Street, north of the tube station, and claims to be the country's longest street market. For a traditional East End snack, head for *Manzes*, at no. 76, one of London's finest pie-and-mash shops, with its traditional tiled walls and ceiling.

Vestry House Museum

2 Vestry Rd • Wed–Sun 10am–5pm • Free • ☎ 020 8496 4391, ⓦ walthamforest.gov.uk • ⊖ Walthamstow Central

At the peaceful heart of the old village of Walthamstow is the **Vestry House Museum**, built in 1730 and at one time the village workhouse. Later on, it became the police station, and a reconstructed police cell from 1861 is one of the museum's chief exhibits. Pride of place, however, goes to the tiny Bremer car, Britain's first-ever petrol-driven automobile, designed in 1892 by local engineer Fred Bremer, 20-year-old son of German immigrants. Victorian times are comprehensively covered, while the temporary exhibitions tend to focus on contemporary topics. The other point of interest nearby is the fifteenth-century half-timbered **Ancient House**, a short walk up Church Lane.

Civic Centre

Walthamstow's **Civic Centre** is an arresting sight, set back from Forest Road around a huge open courtyard. Designed in an unusual 1930s Scandinavian style, it is, without doubt, London's grandest town-hall complex. Indeed, there's a touch of Stalinism about the severe Neoclassical central portico and in the William Morris-inspired exhortation above the adjacent Assembly Hall: "Fellowship is life and the lack of fellowship is death." Sadly, construction of the law courts that would have completed the ensemble was interrupted by the war, but this remains one of the most startling public buildings in London.

WILLIAM MORRIS

Poet, artist, designer and socialist, **William Morris** (1834–96) was one of the most fascinating characters of Victorian London. Closely associated with both the Pre-Raphaelite and Arts and Crafts movements, he set up Morris & Co, whose work covered all areas of applied art: glasswork, tiles, metalwork, furniture, calligraphy, carpets, book illumination and (perhaps most famously) wallpaper. As well as being a successful capitalist – the company's flagship store was on Mayfair's Hanover Square – Morris also became one of the leading political figures of his day, active in the Socialist League with Eleanor Marx, and publishing several utopian tracts, most famously *News from Nowhere*, in which he suggested that the Houses of Parliament be used as "a storage place for manure" (you can buy a copy in the William Morris Gallery bookshop). If you like your WM, you can see more of his work elsewhere in London: at the V&A, Holy Trinity Church and the Red House.

William Morris Gallery

Forest Rd • Wed–Sun 10am–5pm • Free • ☎ 020 8496 4390, ⓦ wmgallery.org.uk• ⊖ Walthamstow Central

The **William Morris Gallery** is housed in a lovely Georgian mansion with two big bay windows. This was the Morris family home from 1848, following the death of Morris's father, a wealthy businessman in the City, the previous year. The gallery has benefitted from a total refurb, and is now a very attractive museum (and café) to visit.

Ground floor displays tell the story of Morris's early life and business projects, accompanied by examples of his first wallpaper design (a rose trellis), a lovely oak settle and some glorious De Morgan animal tiles for a nursery. Upstairs, there are "Brownies" (fairies) in stained glass, and beautiful first editions from the Kelmscott Press, souvenirs from Iceland and the modest leather satchel he took everywhere with him. The contradiction between his rich clients and his socialist ideals is touched upon, and there's a copy of the anti-war song he wrote in 1878. There's also a whole room devoted to Frank Brangwyn, who trained at Morris & Co and was something of a jack-of-all-trades like Morris.

Hampstead

Perched on a hill to the west of Hampstead Heath, **Hampstead** village developed into a fashionable spa in the eighteenth century, and was not much altered thereafter. Its sloping site, which deterred Victorian property speculators and put off the railway companies, saved much of the Georgian village from destruction. Later, it became one of the city's most celebrated literary *quartiers* and even now it retains its reputation as a bolt hole of the high-profile intelligentsia and discerning pop stars. You can get some idea of its tone from the fact that the local Labour MP for many years was the actress Glenda Jackson.

The steeply inclined **High Street**, lined with trendy shops and arty cafés, flaunts the area's ever-increasing wealth without completely losing its charm, though the most appealing area is the extensive, picturesque and precipitous network of alleyways, steps and streets east and west of Heath Street. Proximity to **Hampstead Heath** is, of course, the real joy of the area, for this mixture of woodland, smooth pasture and landscaped garden is quite simply the most exhilarating patch of greenery in London.

Holly Bush Hill

If you wander into the backstreets north of Hampstead tube, you will probably end up at the small triangular green on **Holly Bush Hill**, where the white weatherboarded **Romney House** stands (closed to the public). In 1797, painter George Romney converted the house and stables into London's first purpose-built artist's studio house, though he spent only two years here before returning to the Lake District and the wife he had abandoned thirty years earlier. Later, it served as Hampstead's Assembly Rooms, where Constable used to lecture on landscape painting. Several houses are set grandly behind wrought-iron gates, on the north side of the green, including the late seventeenth-century **Fenton House**.

Fenton House

Hampstead Grove • March–Oct Wed–Sun 11am–5pm • NT • House £6.50; garden only £2 • ☎ 020 7435 3471, ⓦ nationaltrust.org.uk • ⊖ Hampstead

All three floors of **Fenton House** are decorated in the eighteenth-century taste and currently house a collection of **European and Oriental ceramics** bequeathed by the house's last private owner, Lady Binning. The house also contains a smattering of British twentieth-century paintings by the likes of Walter Sickert, Duncan Grant and Spencer Gore, plus a superb collection of **early musical instruments** – all displayed on the top floor, from which you can see right across London. Among the many spinets, virginals and clavichords is an early Broadwood grand piano and an Unverdorben lute from 1580 (one of only three in the world). Experienced keyboard players are occasionally let loose on some of the instruments during the day; **concerts** also take place (book in advance); alternatively, look out for one of the regular **demonstration tours**. Tickets for the house also allow you to take a stroll in the beautiful terraced **garden**, with an orchard, a kitchen garden and a formal garden, featuring some top-class topiary and herbaceous borders.

Admiral's House

Up Hampstead Grove, beyond Fenton House, is Admiral's Walk, so-called after its most famous building, **Admiral's House**, a whitewashed Georgian mansion with nautical excrescences. Once painted by Constable, it was later lived in by Victorian architect George Gilbert Scott, of Albert Memorial fame. Until his death in 1933 John Galsworthy lived in the adjacent cottage, **Grove Lodge** – "[it] wasn't cheap, I can tell you", he wrote to a friend on arrival – where he completed *The Forsyte Saga* and received the 1932 Nobel Prize, which was presented to him here since he was too ill to travel abroad. Opposite is **The Mount**, a gently sloping street descending to Heath Street, which has changed little since it was depicted in *Work* by Pre-Raphaelite artist (and local resident) Ford Madox Brown.

20

St John-at-Hampstead

Church Row • Daily 9am–5pm • Free • ☎ 020 7794 5808, ⓦ hampsteadparishchurch.org.uk • ⊖ Hampstead

The Georgian terraces of tree-centred **Church Row**, at the south end of Heath Street, are where City gents would stay for the week when Hampstead was a thriving spa. The street forms a grand approach to **St John-at-Hampstead**, which has an attractive period-piece Georgian interior and a romantically overgrown cemetery. The chest-tomb of the clockmaker John Harrison lies in the churchyard; **John Constable** is buried in the southeastern corner; Hugh Gaitskill, Labour Party leader from 1955 to 1963, lies in the Churchyard Extension to the northeast. If you continue up Holly Walk, you'll come to **St Mary's Church**, whose Italianate facade is squeezed into the middle of a row of three-storey cottages. This was one of the first Catholic churches built in London after the Reformation, and the original facade from 1816 was much less conspicuous.

Hampstead Cemetery

Fortune Green Rd • Mon–Fri 7.30am–dusk, Sat 9am–dusk, Sun 10am–dusk • Free • ⊖ Hampstead or Finchley Road & Frognal Overground

A good selection of Hampstead luminaries are buried in the neatly maintained **Hampstead Cemetery**, half a mile west of central Hampstead, on the west side of Finchley Road, and founded in 1876 when St John's Churchyard Extension was full. The pioneer of antiseptic surgery Joseph Lister, music-hall star Marie Lloyd and children's book illustrator Kate Greenaway are among those buried here. The full-size stone organ monument to the obscure Charles Barritt is the most unusual piece of funerary art, while the most unlikely occupant is Grand Duke Mikhail Mikhailovitch, uncle to the last Russian tsar, Nicholas II.

Hampstead Garden Suburb

⊖ Golders Green

Hampstead Garden Suburb

NORTH END ROAD

FINCHLEY ROAD

Heath Extension

HAMPSTEAD WAY

WILDWOOD ROAD

INGRAM AVENUE

WELLGARTH ROAD

WINNINGTON ROAD

THE BISHOP'S AVENUE

HAMPSTEAD LANE

Golders Hill Park

Café

Old Bull & Bush

NORTH END

Sandy Heath

1

Kenwood House

Leg of Mutton Pond

NORTH END AVE

NORTH END WAY

SPANIARDS ROAD

Kenwood

Hill Garden

Pergola

Inverforth House

West Heath

WEST HEATH ROAD

Hampstead Heath

TEMPLEWOOD AVENUE

WEST HEATH ROAD

Whitestone Pond

Vale of Health

Viaduct Pond

REDINGTON ROAD

BRANCH HILL

JUDGES' WALK

LOWER TERRACE

HAMPSTEAD GROVE

HOLLY HILL

Admiral's House

OAK HILL WAY

ADMIRAL'S WALK

THE MOUNT

FROGNAL RISE

Fenton House

CANNON PLACE

EAST HEATH ROAD

Boudicca's Mound

Hampstead Cemetery

FROGNAL

MT. VERNON

HOLLY BUSH HILL

3

HEATH STREET

NEW END

CANNON LANE

CHRISTCHURCH HILL

WELL ROAD

Mixed Bathing Pond

CHESTERFORD GARDENS

ST Mary's Church

HOLLY WALK

St John-at-Hampstead

FROGNAL

CHURCH ROW

BLACK WALK

FLASK WALK

Burgh House

WELL WALK

FROGNAL LANE

LANGLAND GARDENS

HEATH STREET

⊖ Hampstead

4

GAYTON ROAD

WILLOW ROAD

Parliament Hill (319ft)

Camden Arts Centre

FROGNAL WAY

PERRIN'S LA.

GREENHILL

PRINCE ARTHUR ROAD

WILLOUGHBY ROAD

DENNING ROAD

CARLINGFORD RD

KEMPLAY RD

PILGRIM'S LANE

HAMPSTEAD

SOUTH END ROAD

SOUTH HILL PARK

2 Willow Road

NARRINGTON ROAD

⊖ Finchley Road & Frognal

ELLERDALE ROAD

ARKWRIGHT ROAD

THURLOW ROAD

DOWNSHIRE HILL

KEATS GROVE

Keats' House

ROSSLYN HILL

PARLIAMENT HILL

Hampstead Heath

FINCHLEY ROAD

NETHERHALL GARDENS

MARESFIELD GARDENS

FITZJOHN'S AVENUE

KIDDERPORE GARDENS

LYNDHURST ROAD

LYNDHURST GARDENS

WEDDERBURN ROAD

HAVERSTOCK HILL

POND STREET

CONSTANTINE ROAD

FLEET ROAD

AGINCOURT ROAD

⊖ Finchley Road

NUTLEY TERRACE

Freud Museum

ORNAN ROAD

BELSIZE AVENUE

Belsize Park

Isokon building

4

LAWN ROAD

PUBS & BARS
The Holly Bush	3
Red Lion and Sun	2
Southampton Arms	5
The Spaniard's Inn	1
The Stag	4

ACCOMMODATION
Hampstead Residence	1
Hampstead Village Guesthouse	2

CAFÉS
Brew House	1
Lauderdale House	2
Louis Patisserie	4

RESTAURANTS
Czechoslovak Restaurant	5
Jin Kichi	3

Alexandra Palace

Highgate Wood

Queen's Wood

Highgate

Highpoint 182

HIGHGATE

Highgate School

Highgate Society

St Michael's Church

West Cemetery

Lauderdale House

The Archway

St Joseph

Ladies' Pond

Men's Pond

Waterlow Park

East Cemetery

Whittington Stone

Archway

Upper Holloway

Lido

Gospel Oak

MANSFIELD ROAD

Tufnell Park

N

0   400
yards

HAMPSTEAD & HIGHGATE

HAMPSTEAD WHO'S WHO

Over the years, countless writers, artists and politicos have been drawn to Hampstead, which has more blue plaques commemorating its residents than any other London borough. **John Constable** lived here in the 1820s, trying to make ends meet for his wife and seven children and painting cloud formations on the Heath, several of which hang in the V&A. **John Keats** moved into Well Walk in 1817, to nurse his dying brother, then moved to a semi-detached villa, fell in love with the girl next door, bumped into Coleridge on the Heath and in 1821 went to Rome to die; the villa is now a museum (see opposite). In 1856, **Karl Marx** finally achieved bourgeois respectability when he moved into Grafton Terrace, a new house on the south side of the Heath. **Robert Louis Stevenson** stayed here when he was 23 suffering from tuberculosis, and thought it "the most delightful place for air and scenery".

Author **H.G. Wells** lived on Church Row for three years just before World War I. In the same period, the photographer **Cecil Beaton** was attending a local infants' school, and was bullied there by author **Evelyn Waugh** – the start of a lifelong feud. The composer **Edward Elgar**, who lived locally, became a special constable during the war, joining the Hampstead Volunteer Reserve. **D.H. Lawrence**, and his German wife Frieda, watched the first major Zeppelin raid on London from the Heath in 1915 and decided to leave. Following the war, Lawrence's friend and fellow writer, **Katherine Mansfield**, lived for a couple of years in a big grey house overlooking the Heath, which she nicknamed "The Elephant". Actor **Dirk Bogarde** was born in a taxi in Hampstead in 1921. **Stephen Spender** spent his childhood in "an ugly house" on Frognal, and went to school locally. **Elizabeth Taylor** was born in Hampstead in 1932, and came back to live here in the 1950s during her first marriage to Richard Burton.

In the 1930s, Hampstead's modernist Isokon Flats, on Lawn Road, became something of an artistic hangout, particularly its drinking den, the *Isobar*: architect **Walter Gropius**, and artists **Henry Moore**, **Ben Nicholson** and his wife **Barbara Hepworth** all lived here (Moore moved out in 1940, when his studio was bombed, and retired to Herefordshire); another tenant, **Agatha Christie**, compared the exterior to a giant ocean liner. Architect **Ernö Goldfinger** built his modernist family home at 2 Willow Rd, now a museum, (see opposite) and local resident **Ian Fleming** named James Bond's adversary after him. **Mohammed Ali Jinnah** abandoned India for Hampstead in 1932, living a quiet life with his daughter and sister, and working as a lawyer. **George Orwell** lived rent-free above Booklovers' Corner, a bookshop on South End Road, in 1934, in return for services in the shop in the afternoon; *Keep the Aspidistra Flying* has many echoes of Hampstead and its characters. **Sigmund Freud** spent the last year of his life in Hampstead, having reluctantly left Austria, following the Nazi Anschluss; his house is now a museum (see below). Artist **Piet Mondrian** also escaped to Hampstead from Nazi-occupied Paris, only to be bombed out a year later, after which he fled to New York. Nobel Prize-winning writer **Elias Canetti** was another refugee from Nazi-occupied Europe, as was **Oskar Kokoschka** who, along with photomontage artist John Heartfield, was given assistance by the Hampstead-based Artists Refugee Committee, set up by local Surrealist artist, Roland Penrose. **General de Gaulle** lived on Frognal with his wife and two daughters and got some first-hand experience of Nazi air raids.

Ruth Ellis, the last woman to be hanged in Britain in 1955, shot her lover outside the *Magdala Tavern* by Hampstead Heath train station. **Sid Vicious** and **Johnny Rotten** lived in a squat on Hampstead High Street in 1976. **John le Carré** lived here in the 1980s and 1990s and set a murder in *Smiley's People* on Hampstead Heath. **Michael Foot**, the former Labour leader, lived in a house he bought in 1945 with his redundancy cheque from *The Evening Standard* until the age of 96. Actors Hugh Grant and Stephen Fry, writer Doris Lessing and pop stars Robbie Williams and George Michael have homes here.

Freud Museum

20 Maresfield Gardens • Wed–Sun noon–5pm • £6 • ☎ 020 7435 2002, ⓦ freud.org.uk • ➔ Finchley Road

One of the most poignant of London's house museums is the **Freud Museum** in the leafy suburban streets of south Hampstead. Having fled Vienna after the Anschluss, **Sigmund Freud** arrived in London in the summer of 1938, and was immediately Britain's most famous Nazi exile. He had been diagnosed as having cancer way back in 1923 (he was an inveterate cigar-smoker) and given just five years to live. He lasted sixteen, but was a semi-invalid when he arrived in London, and rarely left the house except to visit his pet dog, Chun, who was held in quarantine for nearly a year. On September 21, 1939, Freud's doctor fulfilled their secret pact and gave his patient a lethal dose of morphine.

The ground-floor study and library look exactly as they did when Freud lived here (they are modelled on his flat in Vienna); the large collection of antiquities and the psychiatrist's couch, sumptuously draped in opulent Persian carpets, were all brought here from Vienna in 1938. Upstairs, where the Freud archive now resides, there's some old footage of the family, while another room is dedicated to his favourite daughter, Anna, herself an influential child analyst, who lived in the house until her death in 1982. Sigmund's architect son, Ernst, designed a loggia at the back of the house so that Freud could sit out and enjoy the garden; it has since been enclosed and serves as the museum shop, which flogs Freudian merchandise such as a "Brainy Beanie" – Freud himself as a cuddly toy – and stocks a superb range of books.

Burgh House

New End Square • Wed–Fri & Sun noon–5pm; Sat café only • Free • ☎ 020 7431 0144, ⓦ burghhouse.org.uk • ⊖ Hampstead

The Queen Anne mansion of **Burgh House** dates from Hampstead's halcyon days as a spa, known briefly as Hampstead Wells, and was at one time occupied by Dr Gibbons, the physician who discovered the spring's medicinal qualities. The house hosts art exhibitions and its attractive wood-panelled Music Room is a popular wedding venue. Upstairs, there's a modest museum, telling the history of Hampstead. The museum's most prized possessions are the modernist Isokon plywood stacking tables and a long chair by Marcel Breuer, found in a Hampstead skip by a local councillor. The *Buttery* café in the basement has outdoor seating in the summer on a lovely terrace.

2 Willow Road

March–Oct Wed–Sun 11am–5pm; note that before 3pm, visits are by hourly guided tour • NT • £6 • ☎ 020 7435 6166, ⓦ nationaltrust .org.uk • ⊖ Hampstead

Hampstead's most unusual sight is **2 Willow Road**, the central house in a modernist red-brick terrace, built in the 1930s by the Budapest-born architect **Ernö Goldfinger**, best known for his concrete brutalist high-rises, such as Trellick Tower (see p.278). Completed in 1939, this was a state-of-the-art house at the time, its open-plan rooms flooded with natural light and much of the furniture designed by Goldfinger himself. The family home for fifty years, the Goldfingers changed very little in the house, so what you see is a 1930s avant-garde dwelling preserved in aspic, a house at once both modern and old-fashioned. An added bonus is that the rooms are packed with the Goldfingers' extensive art collection: Surrealist *objets trouvés* and works of art by the likes of Léger, Duchamp, Max Ernst, Henry Moore and Man Ray.

Keats' House

Keats Grove • March–Oct Tues–Sun 1–5pm; Nov–Feb Fri–Sun 1–5pm • £5 • ☎ 020 7332 3868, ⓦ cityoflondon.gov.uk • ⊖ Hampstead

Hampstead's most lustrous figure is celebrated at **Keats' House**, an elegant, whitewashed Regency double villa. The consumptive poet lodged here with his friend Charles Brown, in 1818, after his brother Tom had died of the same illness. Inspired by the peacefulness of Hampstead, and by his passion for girl-next-door Fanny Brawne (whose house is also part of the museum), Keats wrote some of his most famous works here before leaving for Rome, where he died in 1821 at the age of just 25.

In the pretty front garden, as you approach the house, a diminutive plum tree stands on the site of the much larger specimen in whose shade Keats is said to have sat for two or three hours before composing *Ode to a Nightingale*. The simple interior contains books and letters, an anatomical notebook from Keats' days as a medical student at Guy's Hospital, Fanny's engagement ring and the four-poster bed in which the poet first coughed up blood, and proclaimed "that drop of blood is my death warrant". There are regular events – poetry readings, performances and talks – so check the website.

20

Hampstead Heath

🌐 cityoflondon.gov.uk • 🚇 Hampstead or Hampstead Heath and Gospel Oak Overground

Hampstead Heath, north London's "green lung", is the city's most enjoyable public park. Little of the original heathland survives, but the Heath nevertheless packs in a wonderful variety of bucolic scenery, from the formal **Hill Garden** and rolling green pastures of **Parliament Hill** to the dense woodland of **West Heath** and the landscaped grounds of **Kenwood**. As it is, the Heath was lucky to survive the nineteenth century intact, for it endured more than forty years of campaigning by the Lord of the Manor, Thomas Maryon Wilson, who introduced no fewer than fifteen parliamentary bills in an attempt to build over it. It wasn't until after Wilson's death in 1871 that 220 acres of the Heath passed into public ownership. The Heath now covers over eight hundred acres, and is run by the Corporation of London (see p.155).

Parliament Hill

Parliament Hill, the Heath's southernmost ridge, is perhaps better known as Kite Hill, since this is north London's premier spot for **kite flying**, especially busy at weekends when some serious equipment takes to the air. The parliamentary connection is much disputed by historians, so take your pick: a Saxon parliament met here; Guy Fawkes' cronies gathered here (in vain) to watch the Houses of Parliament burn; the Parliamentarians placed cannon here during the Civil War to defend London against the Royalists; and the Middlesex parliamentary elections took place here in the seventeenth century. Whatever the reason for the name, the view over London is unrivalled.

20

Boudicca's Mound to Viaduct Pond

To the northwest of Parliament Hill is a fenced-off tumulus, known as **Boudicca's Mound**, where, according to tradition, Queen Boudicca was buried after she and ten thousand other Brits had been massacred at Battle Bridge; another legend says she's buried under Platform 10 in King's Cross Station. Due west lies the picturesque **Viaduct Pond**, named after its red-brick bridge, which is also known as Wilson's Folly. It was built as part of Thomas Maryon Wilson's abortive plans to drive an access road through the middle of the Heath to his projected estate of 28 villas.

Vale of Health

To the west of Viaduct Pond, an isolated network of streets nestles in the **Vale of Health**, an area that was, in fact, a malarial swamp until the late eighteenth century. Literary lion Leigh Hunt moved to this quiet backwater in 1816, after serving a two-year prison sentence for calling the Prince Regent "a fat Adonis of fifty", among other things; Hunt was instrumental in persuading Keats to give up medicine for poetry. Other artistic residents have included Nobel Prize-winner Rabindranath Tagore, who lived here in 1912, and painter Stanley Spencer, who stayed here with the Carline family and married their daughter Hilda in the 1920s. Author D.H. Lawrence spent a brief, unhappy period here in 1915: in September of that year his novel *The Rainbow* was banned for obscenity, and by December, Lawrence and his wife, Frieda von Richthofen, whose German origins were causing the couple immense problems with the authorities, had resolved to leave the country.

POND DIPPING

The Heath is the source of several of London's lost rivers – the Tyburn, the Westbourne and the Fleet – and home to some 28 natural ponds, three of which are used as **Bathing Ponds**, all of which are very popular in good weather: the single-sex men's and ladies' ponds, on the Highgate side are open all year; mixed bathing on the Hampstead side in the summer only (see p.439).

West Heath

Northwest of the Vale of Health is the busy road junction around **Whitestone Pond**, which marks the highest point in this part of north London (440ft), overlooked by the faux-ancient *Jack Straw's Castle* pub. To the west lies **West Heath**, a densely wooded, boggy area with a thick canopy of deciduous trees sloping down towards Childs Hill; it's a very peaceful place for a stroll and a popular gay cruising area. A track leads northwest from *Jack Straw's Castle*, across West Heath, over to **Hill Garden** (daily 8.30am to dusk), the Heath's most secretive and romantic little gem. Originally an extension to the grounds of nearby Hill House, built by Lord Leverhulme in 1906 (and now converted into flats), the garden's most startling feature is the 800ft-long zigzag **Pergola**, whose Doric columns support a host of climbers including a wonderfully gnarled wisteria. The pergola is elevated some 15ft above the ground in order to traverse a public footpath that Lord Leverhulme tried in vain to have removed.

Golders Hill Park

West Heath Ave • Daily 7.30am–dusk • Free • ⊖ Golders Green

Adjacent to the West Heath are the landscaped gardens of **Golders Hill Park**. Near the main entrance is the park café, serving delicious Italian ice cream, courtesy of *Arte Gelato*, and close by, a beautifully kept walled garden and pond. The central section of the park is taken up by a **zoo** containing alpacas, red-legged seriemas, ring-tailed lemurs, and a series of impeccably maintained aviaries, home to white-naped cranes and other exotic birds.

Kenwood

Gardens Daily summer 8am–8pm; winter 8am–4pm • Free **House** Daily 10am–5pm • Free • ☎ 020 8348 1286, ⓦ english-heritage.org .uk • Bus #210 from ⊖ Archway or Golders Green

20

Hampstead Heath's most celebrated sight is **Kenwood**, the former private estate whose beautiful off-white Neoclassical mansion faces south to catch the sun. The house dates from the seventeenth century, but was later remodelled by Robert Adam for the Earl of Mansfield, the most powerful jurist in the country. Mansfield, who sent 102 people to the gallows and sentenced another 448 to transportation, was a deeply unpopular character and one of the prime targets of the 1780 Gordon Riots. Having ransacked his Bloomsbury house, a mob headed for Kenwood, but were waylaid by the canny landlord of the nearby *Spaniards Inn* (an ex-butler of Mansfield's), who plied them with free drink until soldiers arrived to disperse them.

Nowadays, with its free art collection and magnificently landscaped grounds, Kenwood is a deservedly popular spot. The gardens, to the west of the house, boast splendid azaleas and rhododendrons; to the south, a huge grassy amphitheatre slopes down to a lake. The whole area is something of a suntrap and a favourite picnic spot, while the provision-less can head for the excellent *Brew House Café* in the old coachhouse.

Kenwood House

The house is now home to a superb seventeenth- and eighteenth-century **art collection** from the English, Dutch and French schools. First off, head for the Dining Room, where a superb late self-portrait by **Rembrandt** shares space with marvellous portraits by Franz Hals, Van Dyck and Ferdinand Bols, and **Vermeer**'s delicate *Guitar Player*. Of the house's many wonderful period interiors, the most spectacular is Adam's sky-blue and gold **Library**, its book-filled apses separated from the central area by paired columns. The *pièce de résistance* is the tunnel-vaulted ceiling, decorated by Antonio Zucchi, who fell in love with and married Kenwood's other ceiling painter, Angelica Kauffmann.

Upstairs, you'll find more paintings, including William Larkin's full-length portraits, possibly of a Jacobean wedding party, the arrogant Richard Sackville, a dissolute aristocrat resplendent in pompom shoes, and his much nicer brother, Edward, sporting earrings festooned with ribbons. Don't miss the room of shoe buckles, jewellery and portrait miniatures donated by local collectors. Back downstairs in the Music Room, are more masterful portraits by **Gainsborough**, most strikingly the diaphanous *Countess Howe*, caught up in a bold, almost abstract landscape, plus several by **Reynolds**, including his whimsical *Venus Chiding Cupid for Learning to Cast Accounts*.

Highgate

Northeast of Hampstead Heath, and fractionally lower than Hampstead (appearances notwithstanding), **Highgate** lacks the literary cachet of Hampstead, but makes up for it with London's most famous **cemetery**, resting place of, among others, Karl Marx. It also retains more of its village origins, especially around **The Grove**, Highgate's finest row of houses, set back from the road in pairs overlooking the village green, and dating back to 1685. Their most famous one-time resident, the poet **Samuel Taylor Coleridge**, lived at no. 3 from 1816, with a certain Dr Gillman and his wife. With Gillman's help, Coleridge got his opium addiction under control and enjoyed the healthiest, if not necessarily the happiest, period of his life, until his death here in 1834.

Coleridge was initially buried in the local college chapel, but in 1961 his remains were reburied in **St Michael's Church**, in South Grove. Its spire is a landmark, but St Michael's is much less interesting architecturally than the grandiose, late seventeenth-century Old Hall next door, or the two tiny ramshackle cottages opposite, built for the servants of one of the luxurious mansions that once characterized Highgate. Arundel House, which stood on the site of the Old Hall, was where **Francis Bacon**, the Renaissance philosopher and statesman, is thought to have died, having caught a chill while trying to stuff a chicken full of ice for an early experiment in refrigeration.

Highgate High Street

Highgate gets its name from the tollgate – the highest in London and the oldest in the country – that stood where the *Gatehouse* pub now stands on **Highgate High Street**. The High Street itself, though architecturally pleasing, is packed out with franchises and estate agents, and marred by heavy traffic, as is its northern extension, North Road. If you persevere with North Road, however, you'll pass **Highgate School**, founded in 1565 for the local poor but long since established as an exclusive fee-paying public school, housed in suitably impressive Victorian buildings. T.S. Eliot was a master here for a while, and famous poetical alumni, known as Cholmeleians after the founder Sir Roger Cholmeley, include Gerard Manley Hopkins and John Betjeman.

Highpoint 1 and 2

At the top end of North Road, on the left, are the whitewashed high-rises of **Highpoint 1** and **2**, seminal early essays in modernist architecture designed by Berthold Lubetkin and his Tecton partnership from the late 1930s. Highpoint 1, the northernmost of the two blocks, was conceived as workers' housing, with communal roof terraces and a tearoom. The locals were outraged so Highpoint 2 ended up being luxury apartments, the caryatids at the entrance a joke at the expense of his anti-modernist critics. Lubetkin also designed himself a penthouse apartment on the roof in the style of a Georgian dacha, with views right across London, where he lived until 1955.

Waterlow Park and Lauderdale House

Park Daily dawn to dusk • Free • ⓦ waterlowpark.org.uk **Lauderdale House** Wed–Fri 11am–4pm, Sat 1.30–5pm, Sun 10am–5pm • Free **Café** Tues–Sun 9am–5pm • ☎ 020 8348 8716, ⓦ lauderdalehouse.org.uk • ⊖ Archway

To the west of Highgate Hill lies **Waterlow Park**, named after Sydney Waterlow, who donated it in 1889 as "a garden for the gardenless". Waterlow also bequeathed **Lauderdale House**, a much-altered sixteenth-century building, on the eastern edge of the park, which is thought to have been occupied at one time by Nell Gwynne and her infant son. The house stages live performances, puts on art exhibitions and is also home to a decent **café** that spills out into the terraced gardens. The park itself, occupying a dramatic sloping site, to the west, is an amalgamation of several house gardens, and is one of London's finest landscaped parks, providing a through route to Highgate Cemetery. Not far from the park, down Highgate Hill, you'll find the **Whittington Stone**, with cat, marking the spot where Dick Whittington miraculously heard the Bow Bells chime (see p.164).

Highgate Cemetery

Swain's Lane **East Cemetery** April–Oct Mon–Fri 10am–5pm, Sat & Sun 11am–5pm; Nov–March closes 4pm • £4 • Guided tour Sat 2pm; £8 **West Cemetery** Guided tours March–Nov Mon–Fri 1.45pm, Sat & Sun hourly 11am–4pm; Dec–Feb Sat & Sun hourly 11am–3pm; £12; No under-8s • ☎ 020 8340 1834, ⓦ highgatecemetery.org • ⊖ Archway

Ranged on both sides of Swain's Lane and receiving far more visitors than Highgate itself, **Highgate Cemetery** is London's most famous graveyard. Opened in 1839, it quickly became the preferred resting place of wealthy Victorian families, who could rub shoulders with numerous intellectuals and artists. As long as prime plots were available, business was good and as many as 28 gardeners were employed to beautify the place.

But as the plots filled, funds dried up and the place fell prey to **vandalism**. The cemetery, which had provided inspiration for Bram Stoker's *Dracula*, found itself at the centre of a series of bizarre incidents in the early 1970s. Graves were smashed open, cadavers strewn about, and the High Priest of the British Occult Society, Allan Farrant, was arrested, armed with a stake and crucifix with which he hoped to destroy "the Highgate Vampire". He was eventually sentenced to four years' imprisonment, after being found guilty of damaging graves, interfering with corpses and sending death-spell dolls to two policemen.

In 1975, the old (west) cemetery was closed completely and was taken under the wing of the Friends of Highgate Cemetery. Nowadays, you have to take a guided tour to visit the West Cemetery, though you can still wander freely in the less dramatic east cemetery – both sections have entrance charges.

20

West Cemetery

The old, overgrown **West Cemetery** is the ultimate Hammer-horror graveyard, and one of London's most impressive sights. It may not have a celebrity corpse to compete with Karl Marx (in the East Cemetery), but wins hands down when it comes to atmosphere, with its huge vaults and eerie statuary. The most famous names here are Chubb (of the locks), Cruft (of the Dog Show) and scientist Michael Faraday, who, as a member of the Sandemanian sect, is buried along the unconsecrated north wall.

All tours are different, but you're quite likely to be shown the lion that snoozes above the tomb of menagerist George Wombwell, and the faithful dog (confusingly called Lion) that lies on bare-knuckle fighter Thomas Sayers' grave. Another popular sight is the **Rossetti family tomb**, resting place of Elizabeth Siddall, Pre-Raphaelite model and wife of Dante Gabriel Rossetti, who buried the only copy of his love poems along with her. Seven years later he changed his mind and had the poems exhumed and published. The poet Christina Rossetti, Dante's sister, is also buried in the vault.

The cemetery's spookiest section is around **Egyptian Avenue**, entered through an archway flanked by Egyptian half-pillars, known as the "Gateway to the City of the Dead". The avenue slopes gently upwards to the Circle of Lebanon, at the centre of which rises a giant cedar. The circular Egyptian-style sunken catacombs here include the tomb of the lesbian novelist Radclyffe Hall (her lover, Mabel Batten, is also buried here). Above are the **Terrace Catacombs**, and the cemetery's most ostentatious mausoleums, some of which hold up to fifteen coffins; the largest – based on the tomb of Mausolus at Halicarnassus – is that of Julius Beer, one-time owner of the *Observer* newspaper.

East Cemetery

What the **East Cemetery** lacks in atmosphere, it makes up for by the fact that you can wander at will through its maze of circuitous paths. The most publicized occupant is

Karl Marx who spent more than half his life in London, much of it in bourgeois Hampstead. Marx asked for a simple grave topped by a headstone, but by 1954 the Communist movement decided to move his tomb to a more prominent position and erect the vulgar bronze bust that now surmounts a granite plinth bearing the words "Workers of all lands, unite", from *The Communist Manifesto*. He has been visited here by Khrushchev, Brezhnev and just about every postwar Communist leader in the world.

Buried along with Marx are his grandson, wife and housekeeper, Helene Delmuth, whom he got pregnant. Engels accepted paternity to avoid a bourgeois scandal and only told Marx's daughter, Eleanor, on his deathbed in 1895. Eleanor committed suicide a few years later after discovering her common-law husband had secretly married someone else. Her ashes were finally placed in the family vault in 1954, having been seized from the Communist Party headquarters in London by the police in 1921. Lesser-known Communists such as Yusef Mohamed Dadoo, chairman of the South African Communist Party until his death in 1983, cluster around Marx. Not far away is **George Eliot**'s grave and, behind it, that of her lover, George Henry Lewes.

Alexandra Palace

Alexandra Palace Way · ☎ 020 8365 2121, ⓦ alexandrapalace.com · Bus #W3 from Alexandra Palace train station or walk from ⊖ Wood Green

Built in 1873 on North London's commanding heights of Muswell Hill, **Alexandra Palace** is London's only surviving example of a Victorian "People's Palace", since its more famous rival, Crystal Palace, burnt down in 1936 (see p.313). However, the history of "Ally Pally" is almost as tragic as that of Crystal Palace. Sixteen days after the official opening, the place burnt down and, despite being rebuilt within two years and boasting a theatre, a reading room, an exhibition hall and a concert room with one of the world's largest organs, it was a commercial failure. During World War I more than seventeen thousand German POWs passed through its gates, and in 1936 the world's first television transmission took place here. It was the venue for the *International Times*' "14 Hour Technicolour Dream" in 1967, which featured performances by, among others, Pink Floyd and Soft Machine. The palace was rebuilt again after another devastating fire in 1980, and there are plans afoot to restore the Victorian theatre and BBC studios for visitors. Meanwhile, the annual round of shows and gigs continues, and there's a pub – appropriately named *Phoenix Bar* – with great views, an indoor ice rink, a boating lake, a pitch and putt course and a garden centre, as well as regular funfairs.

Golders Green

If the East End is the spiritual home of working-class Jews, **Golders Green** and the suburbs to the northwest of Hampstead, are its middle-class equivalent. A hundred years ago this whole area was open countryside but, like much of suburbia, it was transformed overnight by the arrival of the tube in 1907. Before and after World War II, the area was heavily colonized by Jews moving out of the old East End ghetto around Spitalfields or fleeing as refugees from the Nazis. Nowadays, Golders Green, along with Stamford Hill, is one of the most distinctively Jewish areas in London. The Orthodox community has a particularly strong presence here and there's a profusion of kosher shops beyond the railway bridge on Golders Green Road, at their busiest on Sundays.

Hampstead Garden Suburb

ⓦ hgs.org.uk · ⊖ Golders Green

Much of Golders Green is architecturally bland, the one exception being **Hampstead Garden Suburb**, begun in 1907. This model housing development was the Utopian dream of **Henrietta Barnett**, who believed the key to social reform was to create a mixed social environment where "the poor shall teach the rich, and the rich, let us hope, shall help the poor to help themselves". Yet from the start the suburb was socially segregated, with artisan dwellings to the north, middle-class houses to the west and the wealthiest villas overlooking the Heath to the south. As a social engineering experiment it was a failure – the area has remained a thoroughly middle-class ghetto – but as a blueprint for suburban estates it has been enormously influential.

The suburb's formal entrance is the striking Arts and Crafts gateway of shops and flats on Finchley Road. From here, ivy-strewn houses, each with its own garden encased in privet, yew and beech hedges, fan out eastwards along tree-lined avenues towards **Central Square**, laid out by Edwin Lutyens in a neo-Georgian style he dubbed "Wren-aissance". (Pubs, shops, cinemas and all commercial buildings were, and still are, excluded from the suburb.) Lutyens also designed the square's twin churches: the Nonconformist **Free Church**, with an octagonal dome, and the Anglican **St Jude's-on-the-Hill** with its steeply pitched roof and spire, and unusual 1920s murals. East of Central Square is the Lutyens-designed **Institute**, with its clock tower, now occupied by an education centre and school.

Golders Green Crematorium

Hoop Lane • Daily: summer 9am–6pm; winter 4pm • ☎ 020 8455 2374 • ⊖ Golders Green

The **Golders Green Crematorium** is where over three hundred thousand Londoners have been cremated since 1902. More famous names have been scattered over the unromantically named Dispersal Area than have been buried at any single London graveyard: Boris Anrep, Enid Blyton, Seán O'Casey, Charles Rennie Mackintosh, H.G. Wells, Kathleen Ferrier, Joe Orton, Don Revie, Peter Sellers, Peggy Ashcroft, Joyce Grenfell, Sid James, Marc Bolan, Keith Moon, Bram Stoker and Prajadhipok, the former King of Thailand; Neville Chamberlain, Rudyard Kipling, Henry James and T.S. Eliot were cremated here, but their ashes lie elsewhere. Finding a particular memorial plaque among the serene red-brick chapels and arcades is no easy task, so it's best to enquire at the office in the main courtyard. The Ernst George Columbarium is where you'll find the ashes of Anna Pavlova; Freud and his wife Martha are contained within one of Freud's favourite Greek red-figure vases in an adjacent room, with their daughter Anna in her own urn close by.

Golders Green Jewish Cemetery

Hoop Lane • Daily except Sat 8.30am–5pm or dusk • ⊖ Golders Green

The **Jewish Cemetery** was founded in 1895 before the area was built up. The eastern section, to your right, is for Orthodox Sephardic Jews, whose tombs are traditionally laid flat with the deceased's feet pointing towards Jerusalem. To the left are the upright headstones of Reform Jews, including the great cellist Jacqueline du Pré, and Lord Hore-Belisha, Minister of Transport in the 1930s, who gave his name to "Belisha beacons" (the yellow flashing globes at zebra crossings for pedestrians).

Hendon: the RAF Museum

Grahame Park Way • Daily 10am–6pm; Grahame-White Factory closed noon–1.30pm • Free • ☎ 020 8205 2266, ⓦ rafmuseum.org.uk • ⊖ Colindale

One of the world's most impressive collections of historic military aircraft is lodged at the **RAF Museum**, in the former Hendon Aerodrome. The most obvious place to start is in the **Historic Hangars**, dominated by a vast 1920s Southampton reconnaissance flying boat. Be sure to check out the Hoverfly, the first really effective helicopter, and, of course, the most famous British plane of all time, the Spitfire. By the exit is a Harrier jump jet, the world's first vertical takeoff and landing aircraft, labelled with a text extolling its role in the Falklands War. Those with children should head for the hands-on **Aeronauts** gallery, which teaches the basic principles of flight and airplane construction.

The most chilling section is the adjacent **Bomber Hall**, where you're greeted by a colossal Lancaster bomber, similar to those used in Operation Chastise, the mission carried out by Squadron 617 (and immortalized in the film *The Dambusters*), about which there's a short documentary. To the museum's credit, the assessment of Bomber Command's wartime policy of blanket-bombing gives both sides of the argument. The video of the "precision bombing" conducted during the 1991 Gulf War is given rather less even-handed treatment. Two other exhibits deserve special mention: the crumbling carcass of a Halifax bomber, recovered from the bottom of a Norwegian fjord, and the clinically white Valiant, the first British aircraft to carry thermonuclear bombs.

The outbuildings

If you've still got time and energy, there are several more hangars across the courtyard. Closest to hand is **Milestones of Flight**, where there's a century's worth of aircraft from an early airship gondola to the state-of-the-art Eurofighter Typhoon. The **Grahame-White Factory** is the UK's first aircraft factory, purpose-built in Hendon in 1917, and now used to display the oldest aircraft including a Sopwith Triplane and a flimsy Hanriot fighter, both from World War I. Finally, there's the **Battle of Britain Hall**, which contains a huge Sunderland flying boat, a V-1 flying bomb and a V-2 rocket. The main event though, is *Our Finest Hour*, an unashamedly jingoistic fifteen-minute audiovisual on the aerial battle between the RAF and the Luftwaffe during the autumn of 1940.

Neasden: the Swaminarayan temple

The lotus blooms in splendour, but its roots lie in the dirt.   Hindu proverb

20

105-119 Brentfield Rd • Daily 9am–6pm • Temple, public tours and audioguides free; Understanding Hinduism £2 • ☎ 020 8965 2651, ⓦ mandir.org • ⊖ Neasden

One of the most remarkable buildings in London lies just off the busy North Circular, in the glum suburb of Neasden. Rising majestically above the dismal interwar housing like a mirage, the **Shri Swaminarayan mandir** is a traditional Hindu temple topped with domes and *shikharas*, erected in 1995 in a style and scale unseen outside of India for over a millennium. The building's vital statistics are incredible: 3000 tons of Bulgarian limestone and 2000 tons of Carrara marble were shipped out to India, carved by over 1500 sculptors, and then shipped back to London and assembled in a matter of weeks. Even more surprising is the fact that **Lord Swaminarayan** (1781–1830), to whom the temple is dedicated, is a relatively obscure and very recent Hindu deity. There are no more than ten thousand followers in Britain, mostly from Gujarat, and no more than a million worldwide.

The Mandir (temple)

To reach the temple, you must enter through the adjacent **Haveli**, or cultural complex, with its carved wooden portico and balcony, and twin covered, carpeted courtyards. Shoes are the only thing that are sexually segregated inside the temple, so, having placed yours in the appropriate alcove, you can then proceed to the **Mandir**. The temple is carved entirely out of Carrara marble, with every possible surface transformed into a honeycomb of arabesques, flowers and seated gods. Intricate pillars are decorated with figures of gods and goddesses, while on three sides are alcoves sheltering serene life-sized **Murti** (idols), garish figures in resplendent clothes representing Rama, Sita, Ganesh the elephant god, Hanuman the monkey god and Shri Swaminarayan himself. The Murti are only periodically on display (9–11am, 11.45am–12.15pm & 4–6pm).

Understanding Hinduism

Beneath the mandir, an **exhibition** explains Hinduism's basic tenets through dioramas, extols the virtues of vegetarianism and details the life of Lord Swaminarayan, who became a yogi at the age of 11, and stood naked on one leg for three months amid snowstorms and "torturing weather". There's also a short video about the building's history.

BRIXTON VILLAGE ARCADE

South London

Real and imagined, there's a big divide between north and south London, certainly as far the residents are concerned. Put simply, north Londoners generally don't go south, unless they can help it, and yet south London has a lot of (albeit quite scattered) points of interest. One area stands head and shoulders above the rest: Greenwich, with its riverside setting, nautical associations, Baroque architecture and Royal Observatory. Other highlights include Dulwich, whose public art gallery is older than the National Gallery, and, on the edge of London, the Arts and Crafts Red House, William Morris's former home, and Down House, home of Charles Darwin. But south London is so much more than a hotchpotch of suburban sights, incorporating such diverse neighbourhoods as Brixton, with its African-Caribbean roots, and Woolwich, with its military past.

21 Brixton

Brixton is a classic Victorian suburb, transformed from open fields into bricks and mortar in a couple of decades following the arrival of the railways in the 1860s. The viaducts still dominate the landscape of central Brixton, with shops and arcades hidden under their arches, but it's the West Indian community, who arrived here in the 1950s and 1960s, who still define the character of the place – Notting Hill may have Carnival, but it's Brixton that has the most upfront African-Caribbean consciousness. Brixton also suffered from a reputation for violence and gun crime, earned during the 1981, 1985 and 1995 riots when tensions between the police and the local youth came to a head.

Brixton's main axis is the junction of Brixton Road, Acre Lane and Coldharbour Lane, south of the tube station and overlooked by the slender clock tower of the immense Edwardian **Lambeth Town Hall**; the dinky neo-Renaissance Tate Library built in 1892; the Ritzy cinema, which opened in 1911 as the Electric Pavilion; and, on the triangular traffic island, the Neoclassical church of **St Matthew**, from 1824, with its grandiose Doric portico, its crypt now used as a bar. A short walk up Effra Road brings you to Brixton's main green space, hilly **Brockwell Park**, beloved for its lido (see p.439), and venue for the Lambeth Country Show, a celebration of *rus in urbe* held every July (see p.25).

21

Brixton Market

Street stalls Mon–Sat 8am–6pm, Wed closes 3pm; Arcades Mon 8am–6pm, Tues–Sun 8am–11.30pm (shops shut earlier, check individual café and restaurant times); farmers' market Sun 10am–2pm • ⓦ brixtonmarket.net • ⊖ Brixton

The commercial lifeblood of Brixton pulses most strongly through **Brixton Market**, whose stalls spread out through the warren of streets and covered arcades east of Brixton Road. **Electric Avenue** – made famous by Eddy Grant's 1983 hit single – runs behind the tube station, and is so-called as it was one of the first London shopping streets to be lit by electricity in the 1880s. A network of interwar arcades, known as **Market Row**, runs parallel with the avenue, with another set called **Brixton Village** (originally the Granville Arcade), on the other side of Atlantic Road with its main entrance past the bridge on Coldharbour Lane. These covered streets still harbour a vibrant mixture of well-established stalls selling Caribbean fruit and veg, bold African fabrics, religious artefacts, pigs' trotters, Latino street food and much more besides. But the market is also peppered with a dozen or more trendy new cafés, serving everything from gluten-free cakes and freshly baked bread to Thai and Mexican food, all following in the wake of the famous *Franco Manca* (see p.385) in Market Row. On the north side of the railway tracks, the market continues along Brixton Station Road, with stalls

PUBS & BARS		CLUBS	
Bread & Roses	13	The Lambeth	20
Crown & Greyhound	24	Bussey Building	11
Effra	22	Plan B	17
Hare & Billet	12	**GAY VENUES**	
Kaff Bar	21	Area	3
Trinity Arms	19	BarCode Vauxhall	1
MUSIC VENUES		Bridge	15
Academy Brixton	14	The Eagle	5
Amersham Arms	9	Fire	7
Jamm	10	The Hoist	6
New Cross Inn	8	Kazbar	16
Windmill	23	Royal Vauxhall Tavern	4
		Two Brewers	18
		Union	2

● CAFÉS	
Elephant	1
Franco Manca	3
Kao Sarn	2

■ ACCOMMODATION	
The Lilac Door	1

● SHOP	
Brixton Market	1

21

selling everything from cheap clothes to reggae soundtracks: weekday lunchtimes, there are also food stalls for the workers; on Saturdays, the market usually has a theme (from kids' market to flea market), and on Sundays the farmers' market takes place here.

Brixton Windmill

Blenheim Gardens • April–Oct check website for open days • ☎ 020 7926 2559, ⓦ brixtonwindmill.org • ⊖ Brixton

Brixton is about the last place in London you'd expect to find a fully functioning **windmill**, but if you duck down Blenheim Gardens, off Brixton Hill, past the venue of the same name (see p.401), you'll see a tower mill nearly 40ft high, built in 1816, with its blades intact (but no sails) and a fetching weatherboarded "hood". Wind power drove the mill until 1862 when the area became too built-up, then steam and gas followed until the mill fell into disuse in the 1930s. Now restored, it's only open sporadically and you need to book in advance. In the 1820s, the mill gained another source of power for its corn-grinding: the country's first **treadmill**, designed by William Cubitt and worked by inmates of Brixton Prison.

Dulwich and around

Dulwich is just two stops from Brixton on the railway, but light years away in every other respect. This affluent, middle-class enclave is one of southeast London's prettier patches – its leafy streets boast handsome Georgian houses and even a couple of weatherboarded cottages, while the Soane-designed **Dulwich Picture Gallery** is one of London's finest small museums. If Dulwich has a fault, it's the somewhat cloying self-consciousness about its "village" status, with its rather twee little shops, rural signposts and fully functioning tollgate (£1) from 1789 – the only one remaining in London.

A day out in Dulwich can be combined with a visit to the nearby **Horniman Museum**, an enjoyable ethnographic collection, and, for the very curious, the remnants of the old **Crystal Palace**, further south. The green spaces between these sights are also worth exploring. **Dulwich Park**, opposite the Picture Gallery, is a pleasant enough public park, but for something a bit wilder, **Sydenham Hill Wood**, a nature reserve south of Dulwich Common, is the one to head for.

Dulwich College

Dulwich came to prominence in 1619 when its lord of the manor, actor-manager Edward Alleyn, founded the **College of God's Gift** as a school for twelve poor boys on the profits of his whorehouses and bear-baiting pits on Bankside. Dulwich College has long since outgrown its original buildings, which still stand to the north of the Picture Gallery, and is now housed in a fanciful Italianate complex designed by Charles Barry (son of the architect of the Houses of Parliament), south of Dulwich Common. The college is now a large, fee-paying, independent boys' school, with an impressive roll call of old boys, including Raymond Chandler, P.G. Wodehouse and Ernest Shackleton, although they tend to keep quiet about World War II traitor Lord Haw-Haw.

Dulwich Picture Gallery

Gallery Rd • Tues–Fri 10am–5pm, Sat & Sun 11am–5pm • Permanent collection £6; exhibitions £10 • Guided tours Sat & Sun 3pm; free •
☎ 020 8693 5254, ⓦ dulwichpicturegallery.org.uk • West Dulwich (from Victoria) or North Dulwich (from London Bridge) train stations;
buses #3 or #P4 from Brixton

Dulwich Picture Gallery, the nation's oldest public art gallery, was designed by John Soane in 1814, and houses, among other bequests, the collection assembled in the 1790s by the French dealer Noel Desenfans on behalf of King Stanislas of Poland, who planned to open a national gallery in Warsaw. In 1795, Poland disappeared from the map of Europe, Stanislas abdicated and Desenfans was left with the paintings. Neither the British nor Russians would buy the collection, so Desenfans proposed founding a national gallery. In the end it was left to his business partner, the landscape painter Francis Bourgeois, and

21

Desenfans' widow, to complete the task and open the gallery in 1817. Soane, who worked for no fee, created a beautifully spacious building, awash with natural light, and added a tiny **mausoleum** at the centre for the sarcophagi of the Desenfans family and of Francis Bourgeois. Based on an Alexandrian catacomb, it's suffused with golden-yellow light from the mausoleum's coloured glass – a characteristic Soane touch.

The paintings

The gallery itself is crammed with superb paintings – elegiac landscapes by **Cuyp**, one of the world's finest **Poussin** series and splendid works by Hogarth, Murillo and Rubens. There's an unusually cloudy **Canaletto** of Walton Bridge on the Thames, **Rembrandt**'s tiny *Portrait of a Young Man*, a top-class portrait of poet, playwright and Royalist, the future Earl of Bristol, by **Van Dyck**, and a moving one of his much lamented kinswoman by marriage, Venetia Stanley, on her deathbed. Among the gallery's fine array of **Gainsborough** portraits are his famous *Linley Sisters*, sittings for which were interrupted by the elopement of one of them with the playwright Sheridan, and a likeness of Samuel Linley that's said to have been painted in less than an hour. There are regular special exhibitions, for which there is an extra charge.

Horniman Museum

100 London Rd • Daily 10.30am–5.30pm • Museum free; aquarium £3, free on the first Tues of the month 4–5.30pm • Gardens daily 7.15am to dusk • Free • ☏ 020 8699 1872, ⟨W⟩ horniman.ac.uk • Forest Hill Overground and train station; bus #P4 from Brixton and Dulwich

The wonderful **Horniman Museum** was purpose-built in 1901 by Frederick Horniman, a tea trader with a passion for collecting. The building itself is a striking edifice designed by Charles Harrison Townsend, architect of the Whitechapel Gallery. Its most arresting features are the massive clock tower, with its smoothly rounded bastions and circular cornice, and the polychrome mosaic of allegorical figures in classical dress on the facade.

Entry to the museum is from the **gardens** to the west, where you'll find turkeys, goats and hens, a sunken water garden and a graceful Victorian conservatory, brought here from the Horniman mansion in Croydon. Entry to the museum is free, except for special exhibitions and the state-of-the-art **Aquarium** in the basement, featuring everything from British pond life to tropical jellyfish, sea horses and monkey frogs.

The collections

A ramp leads down from the foyer to the **Natural History** collection of stuffed animals and birds – everything from a half-dissected pigeon to an ostrich – and their skeletons, with pride of place going to the Horniman Walrus, lying flat out on a mocked-up iceberg. On the lower ground floor, head first for the dimly lit **Centenary Gallery**, which contains an eclectic ethnographic collection, much of it gathered by Horniman himself, from the precious butterflies that started his obsession at the age of 8 to a papier-mâché figure of Kali dancing on Siva. Equally arresting are the more recent acquisitions like the Nigerian puppets of Charles, Di and a British bobby, or the "ugly masks" used to chase the winter away in the Alps.

The **African Worlds** gallery contains a wide-ranging anthropological collection from African masks and voodoo altars to Egyptian sarcophagi and Sudanese dung bowls. In the **Music Gallery** you can see and hear more than 1500 instruments including Chinese gongs and electric guitars, or have a go at some of the instruments yourself in the hands-on room. Look out for the special sessions at the **Hands On Base**, which allow you to handle and learn more about a whole range of the museum's artefacts.

Crystal Palace

Anerley Hill • Museum Sat & Sun 11am–4pm; park daily 7.30am–dusk • Free • ☏ 020 8676 0700, ⟨W⟩ crystalpalacemuseum.org.uk • Crystal Palace train station and Overground

After the 1851 Great Exhibition (see p.244), the **Crystal Palace** was enlarged and re-erected on the commanding heights of Sydenham Hill, to the south of Dulwich,

21

affording spectacular views over London, Kent and Surrey. A fantastic pleasure garden was laid out around this giant glasshouse, with a complex system of fountains, some of which reached a height of 250ft. Exhibitions, funfairs, a pneumatic railway and a whole range of events were staged here. Despite its initial success, though, the palace soon became a financial liability – then, in 1936, the structure burnt to the ground overnight.

All that remains now are the stone terraces, the triumphal staircase, a few sphinxes and a small **museum** on nearby Anerley Hill that tells the history of the place. Nowadays, the **park** is dominated by a TV transmitter, visible from all over London, and the **National Sports Centre**, whose tartan athletics track (Europe's first) was opened in the 1960s and where some 21 world records were set in the following two decades. The stadium stands on the site of the old Crystal Palace football ground, where the FA Cup Final was held from 1895 to 1914. There are further reminders of the park's Victorian heyday in and around **Lower Lake**, in the southeast corner of the park, whose islands feature around thirty life-sized **dinosaurs** lurking in the undergrowth, built out of brick and iron. Look out, too, for the circular hornbeam **Maze**, London's largest, originally established in 1872 and replanted in 1988.

Greenwich

Greenwich is the one area in southeast London that draws tourists out from the centre in considerable numbers. At its heart is the outstanding architectural set piece of the **Old Royal Naval College** and the **Queen's House**, courtesy of Christopher Wren and Inigo Jones respectively. Most visitors, however, come to see the restored **Cutty Sark**, the **National Maritime Museum** and the **Royal Observatory** in Greenwich Park. With the added attractions of its riverside pubs and walks – plus startling views across to Canary Wharf and Docklands – it makes for one of the best weekend trips in the capital.

ARRIVAL AND INFORMATION

By DLR and train Greenwich can be reached by train from Charing Cross, Waterloo East or London Bridge (every 15–30min), or by DLR from Bank or Tower Gateway to Cutty Sark DLR station. For the best view of the Wren buildings across the river, get out at Island Gardens, and then take the Greenwich Foot Tunnel under the Thames.

By boat The most scenic and leisurely way to reach Greenwich is to take a boat from one of the piers in central London (every 20–30min).

Information Greenwich tourist information centre (daily 10am–5pm; ☎ 0870 608 2000) is located in Pepys House in the Discover Greenwich centre.

Greenwich Market

Greenwich Church St • Tues–Sun 10am–5.30pm • ⓦ greenwich-market.co.uk • Cutty Sark DLR

Greenwich town centre was laid out in the 1820s, hence the Nash-style terraces of Nelson Road, College Approach and King William Walk, and is now a one-way system plagued with heavy traffic. However, at the centre of these busy streets, filled with nautical knick-knack shops and bookshops, stands **Greenwich Market**, an old covered market where you can still see the wonderfully Victorian inscription on one of the archways: "A false balance is abomination to the Lord, but a just weight is his delight." Stalls differ on each day: food and homewares (Wed), antiques and crafts (Thurs & Fri) and food and crafts (Sat & Sun).

St Alfege's Church

Greenwich Church St • Mon–Wed 11am–4pm, Thurs & Fri 11am–2pm, Sat 10am–4pm, Sun noon–4pm • ☎ 020 8858 6828, ⓦ st-alfege.org • Cutty Sark DLR

Rising above the town centre is the Doric portico and broken pediment of Nicholas Hawksmoor's **St Alfege's Church**, built in 1712–18 to replace a twelfth-century structure in which Henry VIII was baptized and Thomas Tallis, the "father of English church music", was buried. The church was flattened in the Blitz, but its lovely wooden galleries and its trompe-l'oeil coffered apse, originally by Thornhill, have since been magnificently restored.

21

> ## GREENWICH RIVERSIDE
>
> A fine vantage point for viewing the Old Royal Naval College is the **Five-Foot Walk**, which squeezes between the college railings and the riverbank. It was here that George I, Elector of Hannover (and a Protestant), landed to take the throne on September 18, 1714, though it was estimated that over fifty other (Catholic) cousins had a better claim. If you're in need of riverside refreshment, drop into the Regency-style **Trafalgar Tavern** (see p.398), at the east end of the walk. Just beyond the pub, down Crane Street, is the **Trinity Hospital**, founded in 1613 by the Earl of Northampton for 21 pensioners; the entry requirements declared the hospital would admit "no common beggar, drunkard, whore-hunter, nor unclean person…nor any that is blind…nor any idiot". The cream-coloured mock-Gothic facade and chapel (which contains the earl's tomb) date from the nineteenth century, but the courtyard of almshouses remains much as it was at its foundation. Beyond the Trinity Hospital, the Thames Path continues along the river, past a few more pubs, and eventually all the way to the Dome.

Cutty Sark

Greenwich Church St · Daily 10am–5pm · £12 · ☎ 020 8312 6608, ⓦ rmg.co.uk · Cutty Sark DLR

Launched from the Clydeside shipyards in 1869, the majestic **Cutty Sark** is the world's last surviving tea clipper, which would race to get the tea harvest to Britain in the shortest possible time, with a dividend being paid to the ship that won. In actual fact, the Cutty Sark spent more time as a wool clipper, returning from Australia in just 72 days.

The ship suffered a devastating fire in 2007, whilst mid-restoration, but has since risen from the ashes, fully restored and with interactive displays to engage children and adults alike. First off, you get to inspect below decks, where every single bit of space would have been taken up with cargo, leaving most of the thirty-strong crew to sleep in specially constructed bunkhouses on deck – only the officers' quarters provide any privacy and creature comforts. The stunning brass-clad hull has been lifted up off the ground to allow space underneath for a café, and an impressive display of multi-coloured figureheads beneath the ship's prow, itself adorned with Nannie, the angry witch from Robbie Burns' poem *Tam O'Shanter*.

Old Royal Naval College

Cutty Sark Gardens · Daily: grounds 8am–6pm; buildings 10am–5pm · Free · ☎ 020 8269 4747, ⓦ ornc.org · Cutty Sark DLR

It's entirely appropriate that the one London building that makes the most of its riverbank location should be the **Old Royal Naval College**, a majestic Baroque ensemble which opens out onto the Thames. Despite the symmetry and grace of the four buildings, which perfectly frame the Queen's House beyond, the whole complex has a strange and piecemeal history.

The first of the four blocks was built in the 1660s as a **royal palace** for Charles II, but the money ran out. William and Mary preferred Hampton Court and turned Greenwich into a **Royal Hospital for Seamen**, along the lines of the Royal Hospital in Chelsea. Wren, working for nothing, had his original designs vetoed by the queen, who insisted the new development must not obscure the view of the river from the Queen's House – what you see now is Wren's revised plan, augmented by, among others, Hawksmoor and Vanbrugh. The naval hospital moved out in 1869, replaced by the **Royal Naval College**, which, in turn, was supplanted by the current incumbents, the **University of Greenwich** and **Trinity College of Music**. The two grandest rooms, situated underneath Wren's twin domes, are open to the public and well worth visiting, and there's an excellent exhibition on the history of the area called **Discover Greenwich.**

Painted Hall

The magnificent **Painted Hall**, in the west wing, is dominated by James Thornhill's gargantuan allegorical ceiling painting, which depicts William and Mary enthroned, with a vanquished Louis XIV clutching a broken sword. Equally remarkable are Thornhill's trompe-l'oeil fluted pilasters and decorative detailing, while on the far wall, behind the high table, Thornhill himself appears (bottom right) beside George I and family, with St Paul's in the background. Designed as the sailors' dining hall, it was later used for Nelson's lying-in-state in 1806 and then as a naval art gallery.

Chapel

The **Chapel** (service Sun 11am), in the east wing, was designed by James Stuart after a fire in 1779 destroyed its predecessor. However, it is Stuart's assistant, William Newton, whom we have to thank for the chapel's exquisite pastel and sky-blue plasterwork and spectacular decorative detailing, among the finest in London. The altarpiece, by Benjamin West, depicts St Paul wrestling with the viper that leapt out of the fire after he was shipwrecked off Malta.

Discover Greenwich

If you're interested in Greenwich's rich history, you can get a good overview at **Discover Greenwich**, in the Pepys Building, which has a permanent exhibition on the area. Among the museum's prize possessions are *Beer* and *Gin*, two oak sculptures from the buttery screen of old Greenwich Palace. Adults can learn about scagliola and Coade stone, while junior Christopher Wrens can build their own version of Greenwich with building blocks. The building also contains a tourist information office and the Royal Hospital's old brewhouse, which used to supply a ration of three pints to each seaman, and has now been revived and turned into a micro-brewery.

National Maritime Museum

Romney Rd • Daily 10am–5pm, Thurs until 8pm • Free • ☎ 020 8858 4422, ⓦ rmg.co.uk • Cutty Sark DLR

The main building of the **National Maritime Museum** occupies the west wing of the former Naval Asylum, and has two separate entrances: from Romney Road you enter a glass-covered courtyard, while from the park, you enter the new Sammy Ofer Wing, where the special exhibitions are staged. The museum's permanent galleries are ranged over three floors, and imaginatively designed to appeal to visitors of all ages, with plenty of hands-on stuff to keep children amused.

The museum also runs two other sights: the **Queen's House**, a beautiful Palladian villa used to display the cream of the museum's vast maritime art collection, located close by the main building (see p.318), and the **Royal Observatory**, perched on the hill in the adjacent park (see p.320).

Ground floor: Royal Barge, Explorers and Voyagers

The main covered courtyard has several "streets" along the sides, which house some of the museum's largest artefacts, among them the splendid 63ft-long **Royal Barge**, a gilded Rococo confection designed by William Kent for Prince Frederick, the much-unloved eldest son of George II. In the centre are a couple of galleries: **Maritime London from 1700** and a temporary exhibition space.

To the side, **Explorers** takes you from the Vikings to Franklin's attempt to discover the Northwest Passage; on display are the relics recovered from the Arctic by John Rae in 1854, many of which had to be bought from the local Inuit.

ROYAL MUSEUMS GREENWICH

The **Royal Museums Greenwich** (RMG) is an umbrella name for the Cutty Sark, the National Maritime Museum (NMM), the Queen's House and the Royal Observatory. As a national museum, the permanent collection of the NMM remains free, and so too does the Queen's House. For the other fee-paying venues, and for special exhibitions, you can buy a combined ticket (£16), valid for thirty days.

21

ROYAL GREENWICH

The history of Greenwich is replete with **royal connections**. Edward I appears to have been the first of the English kings to have stayed here, though there was nothing resembling a palace until Henry V's brother, the Duke of Gloucester, built **Bella Court** (later known as the Palace of Placentia) in 1447. Henry VI honeymooned here with his new wife, Margaret of Anjou, and eventually took over the place and rebuilt it in her honour. However, it was under the Tudors that the riverside palace enjoyed its royal heyday. **Henry VIII** was born there and made it his main base, pouring even more money into it than into Hampton Court. He added armouries, a banqueting hall and a huge tiltyard, hunted in the extensive grounds and kept a watchful eye over proceedings at the nearby **Royal Dockyards** in Deptford. His daughters, Mary and Elizabeth, were both born here.

Edward VI came to Greenwich in 1553 to try to restore his frail health, but died shortly afterwards. Mary came here rarely as queen, and on one of her few visits had the wall of her personal apartment blasted away by a cannonball fired in salute. For Elizabeth, Greenwich was the **chief summer residence**, and it was here in 1573 that she revived the Maundy Ceremony, washing the feet of 39 poor women (though only after three others had washed them first). The royal palace fell into disrepair during the 1650s Commonwealth, when it was turned into a biscuit factory, and was finally torn down by Charles II to make way for a new edifice, which eventually became the Royal Naval College.

If you come in via the Sammy Ofer Wing, you'll find **Voyagers** straight ahead, focusing on the emotions evoked by travels on the oceans. As well as moving personal stories about the sea, there are some remarkable objects such as Captain Cook's sextant, John Franklin's snow goggles, a musical pig that survived the *Titanic* and the horn beaker Captain Bligh used to measure out water rations on his epic 41-day voyage to Timor.

Floor one: The Great Map, the Atlantic and Traders

The museum's **Great Map** is displayed on the Upper Deck – kids get to sail their own personal boats (and hopefully learn a bit of maritime geography, while their parents relax in the adjacent museum café). The nearby **Traders** gallery tells the story of the all-important East India Company, which was given a monopoly on British trade with the East, and ended up taking over and more or less running India until the 1857 Rebellion.

The Atlantic focuses on the history of the trade links with the New World, from slavery to whaling. While you're here, don't miss the **stained glass** from the **Baltic Exchange**, a colourful 1920s memorial salvaged from the Baltic Exchange in the City, after it was blown up by the IRA in 1992.

Floor two: Children's Gallery, Ship of War and Nelson

This is the place to head if you've got kids, as it boasts the **Children's Gallery** which gives kids a taste of life on the seas, loading miniature cargo, firing a cannon, learning to use Morse code and so forth. Next door, older children and adults alike will enjoy the **Ship Simulator** in which you have to demonstrate your boat handling skills. The **Ship of War** gallery displays the museum's collection of model sailing warships (1650–1815), most made by the Navy Board at the same time as the ships they represent. Floor two is also where the long-awaited **Nelson** gallery will be.

Queen's House

Daily 10am–5pm • Free • ☎ 020 8858 4422, ⓦ rmg.co.uk • Cutty Sark DLR

Inigo Jones's **Queen's House**, originally built on a cramped site amid the Tudor royal palace, is now the focal point of the Greenwich ensemble. As royal residences go, it's an unassuming little Palladian country house, "solid…masculine and unaffected" in Jones's own words. Its significance in terms of British architecture, however, is immense. Commissioned in 1616, it was the first Neoclassical building in the country, signifying a clear break with all that preceded it. The interior, exterior and setting of the

Queen's House have all changed radically since Jones's day, making it difficult to imagine the impact the building must have had when it was built. The house is now linked to its neighbouring buildings by open colonnades, added in the early part of the nineteenth century along the course of the muddy road which the H-shaped block originally straddled.

Inside, very few features survive from Stuart times. The **Great Hall**, a perfect cube, remains, but Orazio Gentileschi's ceiling paintings were removed to Marlborough House by the Duchess of Marlborough during the reign of Queen Anne. The southeastern corner of the hall leads to the beautiful **Tulip Staircase**, Britain's earliest cantilevered spiral staircase, whose name derives from the floral patterning in the wrought-iron balustrade. The only other significant interior decoration is upstairs, in the room intended as the bedchamber of Charles I and Henrietta Maria, which retains its ceiling decoration from the 1630s.

The art collection

The rooms of the Queen's House now provide a permanent home for the museum's vast **art collection**. Downstairs, there are paintings, portraits and models illustrating the history of royal Greenwich. Upstairs, in among the naval battles and portraits of admirals, there are works by the likes of Reynolds, Hogarth, Gainsborough, Lely, Kneller and Myrtens, as well as twentieth-century works by official war artists, plus one by Lowry and even an Alfred Wallis. Look out, too, for the oil paintings by the official artists on board Cook's last two voyages to the Pacific, Thornhill's portrait of a naval pensioner – the sort who would have inhabited the Royal Hospital for Seamen – and Zoffany's unfinished, nightmarish *Death of Captain Cook*. There's a typically infatuated portrait of Lady Hamilton as Ariadne by Romney, a Canaletto of Greenwich, painted from Island Gardens, and the only major British portrait of (a wistful and dreamy) Napoleon, painted while he was a prisoner on board the *Bellerophon*. Downstairs, one room is set aside for Turner's *Battle of Trafalgar, 21st October, 1805*, his largest work and only royal commission, which was intended for St James's Palace.

Greenwich Park

Daily 6am to dusk • ⓦ royalparks.org.uk • Cutty Sark or Greenwich DLR

Greenwich Park is one of the city's oldest royal parks, having been enclosed in the fifteenth century by the Duke of Gloucester, who fancied it as a hunting ground. Henry VIII was particularly fond of the place, introducing deer in 1515, as well as archery and jousting tournaments, and sword-fighting contests. The park was opened to the public in the eighteenth century, but it was only after the arrival of the railway in 1838 that it began to attract Londoners in great numbers. In 1894, a young **French anarchist** called Martial Bourdin was killed in the park, outside the Royal Observatory, when the bomb he was carrying in a brown-paper bag exploded. Joseph Conrad used the unexplained incident as the inspiration for his novel *The Secret Agent*.

The descendants of Henry's deer are now safely enclosed within **The Wilderness**, a fenced area in the southeast corner where they laze around "tame as children", in Henry James's words. Don't miss **Vanbrugh Castle**, halfway down Maze Hill, on the east side of the park, England's first mock-medieval castle, designed by the architect John Vanbrugh as his private residence in 1726. Note, too, **Queen Caroline's Bath**, by the park's southern wall, which is all that remains of the house where the queen used to hold her famous orgies – the rest of the house was destroyed by her estranged husband George IV after she left the country in 1804. If you're heading for the Ranger's House, the best approach is via the semicircular **Rose Garden**, laid out in front of it, which is worth a visit itself from June to August.

One of the park's chief delights is the view over to the Isle of Dogs from the steep hill crowned by a statue of **General James Wolfe** (1727–59), who spent part of his childhood in Greenwich, lived near the park and is buried in St Alfege. Wolfe is famed

21

THE PRIME MERIDIAN AND GREENWICH MEAN TIME

Greenwich's greatest claim to fame is as the home of the **Prime Meridian** – a meridian being any north–south line used as a basis for astronomical observations, and therefore also for the calculation of longitude and time. In 1884, the International Meridian Conference in Washington DC agreed to make Greenwich the Prime Meridian of the World – in other words, **zero longitude**. As a result, the longitude of the entire world is fixed as either east or west of Greenwich. Unfortunately for Greenwich, more and more people use **Global Positioning System (GPS)**, which makes its calculations from the centre of the earth, not the surface, and places the meridian approximately 336ft to the east of the observatory's red strip.

The world also used to set its clocks according to **Greenwich Mean Time (GMT)**. However, in many spheres of life and countries across the globe, GMT has been usurped by **Coordinated Universal Time (UTC)**, which is basically the same as GMT, except that it is more accurately calculated using atomic clocks and therefore better for sub-second precision.

for the audacious, successful campaign to capture Quebec from the French in 1759, a battle in which he and his opposite number, General Montcalm, were both mortally wounded. Victory celebrations took place throughout England, but were forbidden in Greenwich out of respect for Wolfe's mother, who had also lost her husband only a few months previously.

Royal Observatory

Blackheath Ave · **Astronomy Centre** Daily 10am–5pm · Free **Flamsteed House** Daily 10am–5pm · £7 **Planetarium** shows every 45min · £6.50 · ☏ 020 8858 4422, ⓦ nmm.ac.uk · Greenwich DLR/train station

Established by Charles II in 1675, the **Royal Observatory** is the longest-established scientific institution in Britain. The chief task of John Flamsteed, the first Astronomer Royal, was to study the night sky in order to discover an astronomical method of finding the longitude of a ship at sea, the lack of which was causing enormous problems for the emerging British Empire. Astronomers continued to work here at Greenwich until the postwar smog and light pollution forced them to decamp to Herstmonceux Castle in Sussex; the observatory, meanwhile, is now a very popular museum.

Flamsteed House

The oldest part of the observatory is **Flamsteed House**, designed by Wren (himself an astronomer) "for the observator's habitation and a little for pompe". The northeastern turret sports a bright-red **Time Ball** that climbs the mast at 12.58pm and drops at 1pm GMT precisely; it was added in 1833 to allow ships on the Thames to set their clocks. The red strip in the observatory's main courtyard is the **Meridian Line**, and at night a green laser beam shines northwards along the meridian. On the house's balcony overlooking the Thames, you can take a look at a **Camera Obscura**, of the kind which Flamsteed used to make safe observations of the sun.

Inside, beyond the **Astronomers' apartments** in which the cantankerous Flamsteed lived, you eventually reach the impressive **Octagon Room**, built so that the king could show off his astronomical toys to guests. The ceiling plasterwork is all that remains of the original decor, but there are replicas of the precision clocks installed behind the original walnut panelling in 1676.

Time galleries

The **Time and Longitude** gallery focus on the search for longitude and display the first four marine chronometers built by **John Harrison**. Harrison eventually went on to win the £20,000 **Longitude Prize** in 1763 with his giant pocket watch, H4 – the only one that no longer functions – after much skulduggery against his claims, most notably by the Astronomer Royal at the time, Nevil Maskelyne (a story wonderfully told by Dava

Sobel in her book *Longitude*). Downstairs, in **Time and Greenwich**, you can learn about the story of GMT, UTC and even GPS, view the electrical contacts that used to provide the hourly six pips for the BBC and listen to three generations of the speaking clock.

Meridian Building

Flamsteed carried out more than thirty thousand observations – "nothing can exceed the tediousness and ennui of the life" was his dispirited description of the job – in the Quadrant House, which now forms part of the **Meridian Building**. Edmond Halley, who succeeded Flamsteed as Astronomer Royal, bought more sophisticated quadrants, sextants, spyglasses and telescopes, which are among those displayed in the **Quadrant Room**. With the aid of his 8ft iron quadrant, he applied historical astronomy methods to predict the next appearance of the eponymous comet – though he never lived to see it. Next door, you'll find **Bradley's Meridian**, used for Ordnance Survey maps since 1801. Finally, you reach a room that's sliced in two by the present-day Greenwich Meridian, fixed by the cross hairs in "Airy's Transit Circle", the astronomical instrument that dominates the room.

Astronomy Centre and Planetarium

Housed in the fanciful, domed terracotta South Building, built in the 1890s, the **Astronomy Centre** houses hi-tech galleries giving a brief rundown of the Big Bang theory of the universe. You can conduct some hands-on experiments to explore concepts such as gravity and spectroscopy, and you're then invited to consider the big questions of astronomy today. You can also choose to watch one of the thirty-minute presentations in the state-of-the-art **Planetarium**, introduced by a Royal Observatory astronomer.

Ranger's House

Guided tour only April–Sept Mon–Wed & Sun 11am & 2pm (1hr 30min) • EH • £6.70 • ☎ 020 8294 2548 • Greenwich DLR or Blackheath train station

In the southern corner of Greenwich Park stands the **Ranger's House**, a red-brick Georgian villa looking out over Blackheath. Built as a private residence, it became the official residence of the park ranger (hence its name), a sort of top-notch grace-and-favour home. The house currently displays the private collection of **Julius Wernher** (1850–1912), an Edwardian German-born millionaire who made his money by exploiting the diamond deposits of South Africa, and at his death was one of the world's richest men. His taste in art is eclectic, ranging from medieval ivory miniatures to Iznik pottery, though he was definitely a man who placed technical virtuosity above artistic merit, and who, despite his Lutheran upbringing, amassed a vast array of Catholic bric-a-brac. Highlights on the top floor include Memlinc's *Virgin and Child*, the jewellery cabinet and the pair of sixteenth-century majolica dishes decorated with mythological scenes for Isabella d'Este, wife of the Marchese of Mantua and a great patron of the arts.

Downstairs, there's a sparkling Reynolds portrait of Lady Caroline Price, a top-notch de Hooch interior, and, in the splendid main gallery with its three bow windows and duck-egg-green coffered ceiling, a whole series of seventeenth-century French tapestries depicting life in the court of the Emperor of China. Finally, at the far end of the main gallery is Bergonzoli's striking *Love of Angels*, a highly charged sculpture that, despite weighing two tons, succeeds in appearing light and ethereal.

Fan Museum

12 Crooms Hill • Tues–Sat 11am–5pm, Sun noon–5pm • £4 • ☎ 020 8305 1441, ⓦ thefanmuseum.org.uk • Greenwich DLR

At the bottom of Crooms Hill, you'll find the **Fan Museum**. It's a fascinating little place (and an extremely beautiful house), revealing the importance of the fan as a social and political document. The permanent exhibition on the ground floor traces the history of the fan and the materials employed, from peacock feathers to straw, while temporary

THE DOME

21

[A] yellow-spiked Teflon tent… a genetically modified mollusc… The Dome is a blob of correction fluid, a flick of Tipp-Ex to revise the mistakes of nineteenth-century industrialists… a poached egg designed by a committee of vegans.

Iain Sinclair, *Sorry Meniscus*

Clearly visible from Greenwich's riverside and park is the marquee-like former **Millennium Dome**: over half a mile in circumference and 160ft in height, it's the world's largest dome, held up by a dozen, 300ft, yellow steel masts. Built in 2000 at a cost of £800 million, it housed the Millennium Experience exhibition, which was panned by critics and dismantled after one year.

Since then entertainment giants AEG spent another £600 million turning it into **The O2** (🆆 theo2.co.uk), a mall of restaurants and bars, a museum space (currently occupied by the British Music Experience; 🆆 britishmusicexperience.com), a nightclub, a multiplex cinema, and, occupying forty percent of the Dome, the 23,000-seat **O2 Arena**, venue for sports events and big name gigs. For a hefty fee (from £25), you can even climb up onto the roof of the Dome, though the astronaut suits and the carabiners are more memorable than the view. Meanwhile, the land to the southeast is being transformed into the Millennium Village, a conglomeration of riverside flats, plus the mini-wetlands of the **Greenwich Peninsula Ecology Park** (Wed–Sun 10am–5pm; free).

The easiest way to get to the Dome is to take the tube to **North Greenwich**, as the Dome has its very own Will Alsop-designed tube station (with a bus station by Norman Foster). It's also possible to walk or cycle the mile and a half along the riverside pathway from Greenwich. The most enjoyable ways to reach the Dome, though, are by boat to the **QEII Pier**, or by **cable car** across the Thames from Royal Victoria DLR (see p.211). The Dome itself is fenced off, but you can walk around the outside and admire the odd work of art: Antony Gormley's very busy *Quantum Cloud* and Richard Wilson's *Slice of Reality*, the bridge of a boat cut away from its mother ship.

---

exhibitions on the first floor explore conditions of production, the fan's link with the Empire and changing fashion. Outside, there's a tearoom, housed in the kitsch, hand-painted orangery, with afternoon tea served (Wed & Sun 3pm).

Blackheath

South of Greenwich lies the well-to-do former village of **Blackheath** (so-called because of the colour of the soil), whose bleak, windswept heath, crisscrossed with busy roads, couldn't be more different from the adjacent royal park. Nonetheless, with its pair of century-old pubs, the *Princess of Wales* and *Hare and Billet*, each set beside a pond, it can be pleasant on a summer afternoon. The odd fair takes place here on public holidays, and it's south London's chief kite-flying spot.

Lying on the main road to Dover, Blackheath was a convenient spot on which to pitch camp, as the Danes did in 1011, having kidnapped St Alfege. During the **1381 Peasants' Revolt**, Wat Tyler's rebels were treated to a rousing revolutionary sermon by John Bull, which included the famous lines "When Adam delved and Eve span, who was then the gentleman?" **Henry V** was welcomed back from the Battle of Agincourt here in 1415, while Henry VII fought the Cornish rebels here in 1497. It was at Blackheath, also, that Henry VIII suffered disappointment on meeting his fourth wife, **Anne of Cleves**, in 1540; he famously referred to her as "the Flanders mare" and filed for divorce after just six months.

The heath's chief landmark is the rugged Kentish ragstone **All Saints' Church**, a Victorian church which nestles in a slight depression in the south corner. The most striking building on the heath, though, is **The Paragon**, to the east, a crescent of four-storey Georgian mansions linked by Doric colonnades. An even earlier ensemble, set in its own grounds further east, is **Morden College**, the aristocrat of almshouses, built in 1695 for "decayed Turkey merchants" who'd lost their fortunes. The quadrangular red-brick building, built by Wren's master mason, was designed to reflect the (lost) status of its original inhabitants.

21

DOWN IN DEPTFORD

Deptford, just west of Greenwich, is not high up on most people's list of places to visit in London. However, it does have a rich history thanks to the **Royal Dockyards**, which existed here (and at Woolwich) from 1513 until 1869. It was at Deptford in 1581 that Francis Drake moored the *Golden Hinde* (see p.229) after circumnavigating the globe, had Elizabeth I on board for dinner, and was knighted for his efforts. And it was in Deptford that the playwright **Christopher Marlowe** was murdered (possibly) in the company of three men who had links with the criminal underworld and the Elizabethan intelligence service.

All that remains of the old dockyards today are a few officers' quarters hidden in the Pepys housing estate, and the **Master Shipwright's House** of 1708, at the bottom of Watergate Street – a little downstream, there's even a waterfront statue of Peter the Great (flanked by a dwarf and an empty chair), who came to Deptford in 1798 to learn about shipbuilding. You can get an idea of how prosperous the area once was just off the High Street at **St Paul's Church**, the local architectural gem, designed by Thomas Archer in 1720, whose interior Pevsner described as "closer to Borromini and the Roman Baroque than any other English church".

Reminiscence Centre

11 Blackheath Village • Mon–Fri 8am–6pm, Sat 9am–5pm • Free • ☎ 020 8318 9105, ⓦ age-exchange.org.uk • Blackheath train station from London Bridge

It's worth venturing down the charmingly named Tranquil Vale into the village-like centre of Blackheath, if only to visit the **Reminiscence Centre**, situated opposite the train station. A favourite with the older folks of Blackheath, the centre is packed full of memorabilia from photos to two-pin plugs, chalk powder and a whole host of everyday objects now rarely seen. The centre also acts as the local library and out the back, you can get a cuppa from the café which features a rapid-wire cash system, via which banknotes could be whizzed from cashier to till worker.

Woolwich

In 1847, a visitor to **Woolwich** commented that it was the "dirtiest, filthiest and most thoroughly mismanaged town of its size in the kingdom". With its docks and factories defunct, Woolwich remains one of the poorest parts of the old Docklands. However, if you have a fascination for military history, it's worth exploring the old dockyards and arsenal, for their architecture and the **Firepower** artillery museum. The other reason to come to Woolwich is to visit the **Thames Barrier**, an awesome piece of modern engineering and the largest movable flood barrier in the world.

ARRIVAL AND DEPARTURE

By DLR and train The easiest way to reach Woolwich is by DLR from Canning Town; you can also take a train from London Bridge to Woolwich Dockyard (for the Royal Artillery Barracks) or Woolwich Arsenal (for the Arsenal).

By boat During the week, there's a limited commuter boat service to and from Woolwich Arsenal, and at the weekend a more regular service; there are also boat trips that cruise round the barrier (ⓦ tfl.gov.uk for details).

Royal Arsenal

Close to Woolwich Arsenal DLR station, on the market square is **Beresford Gateway**, built in 1828 as the Arsenal's main entrance, but now separated from the rest of the complex to the north by busy Beresford Street/Plumstead Road.

Across the road, you enter **Dial Square**, overlooked by some of the Arsenal's most historic buildings, built by the likes of Vanbrugh, Wren and Hawksmoor: the Main Guard House, with its eighteenth-century Doric portico; Verbruggen's House, opposite, begun in 1772, and former residence of the Master Founder; and the Royal Brass Foundry, made of wood, but encased in brick, from 1717. To the north, the **Dial Arch Block** is distinguished by its central archway, sporting a sundial, pillars and a pile of cannonballs. A football on a plinth commemorates the fact that it was here in 1886 that a group of machinists formed Dial Square Football Club, later Woolwich Arsenal FC, and then just **Arsenal FC**, eventually moving to Highbury in north London. The team used to get changed in the toilets of the *Royal Oak* (now the Woolwich Arsenal DLR station).

21

Greenwich Heritage Centre

Artillery Square • Tues–Sat 9am–5pm • Free • ☎ 020 8854 2452, ⓦ greenwichheritage.org • Woolwich Arsenal DLR

If you head down Number One Street, towards the river, you'll come to the **Greenwich Heritage Centre**, on the left, which houses a small informative permanent exhibition on the history of the Arsenal. Next door is the distinctive eighteenth-century, brown-brick building that served as the Royal Military Academy, from 1741 until 1806, when new barracks were built.

Firepower: Royal Artillery Museum

Tues–Sun 10am–5pm • £5.30 • ☎ 020 8855 7755, ⓦ firepower.org.uk • Woolwich Arsenal DLR

Firepower, the Royal Artillery Museum, is housed, appropriately enough, in a former bomb factory. To enjoy the museum, you do have to be seriously into **guns** – lots of them. Inevitably, there's a propaganda video on today's Royal Artillery, along with a twenty-minute multimedia show, *Field of Fire*, concentrating on the chief conflicts of the twentieth century. The main **Gunnery Hall** features ancient World War I field guns, old and new howitzers, anti-tank guns, Thunderbird guided-missile launchers and Rapier surface-to-air missiles used in the Gulf War, and allows you to play various war games, fire simulator guns and watch lots of wartime film clips. Upstairs, the **History Gallery** takes you through the history of artillery and rocket science, features the gun carriage used in the funeral cortège for Georges V and VI, and includes the Medals Gallery. Finally, at the **Camo Zone**, you can have a go at the bungee run, test your marksmanship on the firing range and take part in a virtual tank battle (£1.50 each).

Royal Artillery Barracks

The **Royal Artillery Barracks**, half a mile to the south of the Royal Arsenal, are still seen as the spiritual home of the Royal Artillery, even though the last artillery regiment moved out in 2007. Completed in 1802 by James Wyatt, the barracks' three-storey Georgian facade, interrupted by stucco pavilions and a central triumphal arch, runs for an amazing 1080ft, making it one of the longest in Europe. Appropriately enough, the barracks hosted the shooting competition during the 2012 Olympics.

The barracks face south onto the grassy parade ground, to the east of which lies the abandoned **Garrison Church of St George**, built in neo-Romanesque style in 1863. Gutted in the last war, it's now an attractive husk, with fragments of its colourful interior decor still surviving. To the west of the Royal Artillery Barracks, off Repository Road, stands John Nash's bizarre Chinese-style **Rotunda** (closed to the public). Originally used as a marquee in the gardens of Carlton House during the celebrations

---

MILITARY WOOLWICH

Woolwich, like Deptford, owes its existence to its **Royal Dockyards**, founded here in 1513 by Henry VIII. The men-of-war that established England as a world naval power were built in these dockyards: the *Great Harry*, the largest ship in the world, was launched from here in 1514; Walter Raleigh and Captain Cook set out from Woolwich on their voyages of discovery. The docks closed in 1869, and the area is better known for the **Royal Arsenal**, which reached its heyday during World War I, when it stretched for three miles along the Thames, employed nearly one hundred thousand workers (half of whom were women) and had its own internal railway system. The ordnance factories were closed altogether in 1967, and council housing built over much of the site. However, a fine collection of mostly eighteenth-century buildings survives and has been converted into flats, plus a couple of museums.

at the end of the Napoleonic Wars, it was damaged by a gas explosion, repaired and re-erected on its present site.

Royal Military Academy

On the south side of Woolwich Common stands James Wyatt's former **Royal Military Academy**, completed in 1806 in an imposing mock-Tudor style as a foil to his Royal Artillery Barracks (see p.325). The 720ft facade faces north onto a parade ground, with an imitation of the Tower of London's White Tower as its centrepiece. The academy, known as "The Shop" in the British Army – because its first building was a converted workshop in the Arsenal – closed in 1939, and merged with Sandhurst after the war.

Thames Barrier

Unity Way • Thurs–Sun 10.30am–5pm • £3.75 • ☎ 020 8305 4188, ⓦ environment-agency.gov.uk • Charlton or Woolwich Dockyard train station

London has been subject to flooding from surge tides since before 1236, when it was reported that in "the great Palace of Westminster men did row with wherries in the midst of the Hall". A flood barrier was advocated as far back as the 1850s, but it was only after the 1953 flood that serious consideration was given to defences. Opened in 1982, the **Thames Barrier** is a mind-blowing feat of engineering, with its gleaming fins and movable steel gates weighing 3300 tons. If you want to find out more, head for the **information centre**, on Unity Way, where glossy models and macho videos help explain the basic mechanism of the barrier (by no means obvious from above the water). If you want to see the barrier in action, phone ahead to find out the date of the monthly test.

Eltham Palace

Court Yard • Mon–Wed & Sun: April–Oct 10am–5pm; Nov–March 10am–4pm • EH • £9.90, gardens only £5.80 • ☎ 020 8294 2548, ⓦ elthampalace.org.uk • Eltham train station from Victoria, London Bridge or Charing Cross

Eltham Palace was one of the country's foremost medieval royal residences and even a venue for Parliament for some two hundred years from the reign of Edward II. All that remains now is the fifteenth-century bridge across what used to be the moat, and the **Great Hall**, built by Edward IV in 1479, with a fine hammerbeam roof hung with pendants, and two fan-vaulted stone oriels at the far end.

Somewhat incredibly, in the 1930s, millionaire **Stephen Courtauld** (of art-collecting fame) got permission to build his own "Wrenaissance"-style house onto the Great Hall, and convert the moat into landscaped gardens. He lavished a fortune on the place, creating a movie star's party palace for his glamorous half-Italian, half-Hungarian wife, Virginia (who sported a risqué tattoo of a snake above one ankle). The house was designed by **Seely and Paget**, furnished by the best Swedish and Italian designers, and kitted with the latest mod cons: underfloor heating, a centralized vacuum cleaner, a tannoy system and ten en-suite bedrooms. Then, shortly before the end of the war, the family left for Rhodesia, taking most of the furniture with them.

Inside, there are acres of exotic veneer, an onyx and gold-plated bathroom, and lots of quirky little **Art Deco** touches – check out the Alice in Wonderland relief above the door in the circular entrance hall, which is flooded with light from a spectacular glazed dome. The audiotours fill visitors in on the family's various eccentricities, which included keeping a **pet ring-tailed lemur** called Mah-Jongg, which had its own centrally heated bedroom approached by a bamboo ladder and was notorious for biting disliked male visitors.

Bexleyheath

Bexleyheath, three miles east of Eltham, is a pretty nondescript 1930s suburb, but it has three significant architectural attractions from the days when it was still mostly heath, peppered with houses of the wealthy.

21

Danson House

April–Oct Mon–Thurs & Sun noon–5pm • £7 • ☎ 020 8303 6699, ⓦ bexleyheritagetrust.org.uk • Bexleyheath train station from Victoria, Charing Cross or London Bridge

Danson House is a modest little Palladian villa, built in the 1760s as a country retreat for John Boyd, who'd made a fortune from the slave trade, and had a new 19-year-old bride to impress. The highlights of the *piano nobile* are the paintings telling the love story of Vertumnus and Pomona in the Dining Room, the Chinoiserie wallpaper in the octagonal Salon, and the built-in organ in the library, which is still used for recitals. It's also worth climbing up to inspect the trompe-l'oeil paintings of Jupiter's thunderbolts in the oval dome. There's a **tearoom** on the ground floor and a **pub-restaurant** in the old stables at the eastern edge of the park.

Red House

Red House Lane • March–Oct Wed–Sun 11am–5pm; Nov & Dec Fri–Sun 11am–5pm; pre-booked tours before 1.30pm • NT • £7.20; garden £2 • ☎ 020 8304 9878, ⓦ nationaltrust.org.uk • Bexleyheath train station from Victoria, Charing Cross or London Bridge

Hidden among the surrounding suburbia lies **Red House**, a wonderful red-brick country house designed by Philip Webb in 1859 for his friend **William Morris**, following Morris's marriage to Pre-Raphaelite heart-throb Jane Burden. The mock-medieval exterior features pointed brick arches, steep gables, an oriel window and even a turreted well in the garden, and the whole enterprise stands as the embodiment of the Arts and Crafts movement. Sadly, after just five years, with "Janey" conducting an affair with Dante Gabriel Rossetti, the couple were forced to leave their dream home due to financial difficulties and move to Kelmscott in Oxfordshire. It has to be said the interior is a bit gloomy, half-finished even in Morris's time, still in need of restoration and not at all cosy, with only a few of the larger interior furnishings still in place. The tours are excellent at bringing the place to life, though, thanks to the various anecdotes about Morris and his entourage, about how they used to eat in the hallway, indulge in apple fights and wear medieval clothes at the weekend.

Hall Place

Bourne Rd • **House** Mon–Sat 10am–4.30pm, Sun 11am–4.30pm; Nov–March closes 4pm • £3 • **Gardens** daily 9am–dusk • Free • ☎ 01322 526574, ⓦ bexleyheritagetrust.org.uk • Bexley train station from Charing Cross or London Bridge

Hall Place is a mishmash of a place, but its Tudor half sports a wonderful chequerboard flintwork exterior and gardens full of top-class topiary, including an entire set of the Queen's Beasts wrought in yew. The house itself has a municipal feel (it's used by the local council), but there's an introductory gallery on the ground floor which gives you the background to the place. Downstairs, the wood-panelled Great Hall survives with its coved ceiling and carved bosses; upstairs, head for the principal bedroom which boasts an ornate Jacobean plasterwork ceiling featuring grotesques.

Down House

Luxted Rd, Downe • March–June, Sept & Oct Wed–Sun 10am–5pm; July & Aug daily 10am–5pm; Nov–Feb Sat & Sun 10am–4pm • EH • £10 • ☎ 01689 859119, ⓦ english-heriage.org.uk • Bus #146 from Bromley South train station or #R8 from Orpington

Down House was the home of the scientist **Charles Darwin** (1809–82). Born in Shrewsbury, Darwin showed little academic promise at Cambridge. It was only after returning from his five-year tour of South America aboard HMS *Beagle* – when he visited the Galapagos Islands – that he began work on the theory he would publish in 1859 as *On the Origin of Species*. Darwin moved to Down House in 1842, shortly after marrying his cousin Emma Wedgwood, who nursed the valetudinarian scientist here until his death. The house itself is set in lovely grounds, and is stuffed with Darwin memorabilia, though there's no sign (or smell) of the barnacles which he spent eight years dissecting – he later moved on to the study of orchids (to the relief, no doubt, of his wife and children), several examples of which you can find in the glasshouse.

West London: Hammersmith to Hampton Court

Hammersmith to Hampton Court – a distance of some seven miles overland (more by the river) – takes you from the traffic-clogged western suburbs of London to the royal outpost of Hampton Court. In between, London seems to continue unabated, with only fleeting glimpses of the countryside, in particular the fabulous Kew Gardens and the two old royal hunting parks, Richmond and Bushy Park – though, as one nineteenth-century visitor observed, they are "no more like the real untrimmed genuine country than a garden is like a field". Running through this stretch of west London is the River Thames, once known as the "Great Highway of London" and still the most pleasant way to travel in these parts during the summer.

Aside from the river and the parks, the chief attractions of West London are the royal palaces and lordly mansions that pepper the riverbanks: textbook Palladian style at **Chiswick House**, unspoilt Jacobean splendour at **Ham House** and Tudor and Baroque excess (and the famous maze) at **Hampton Court**. For riverside walks and pubs, you can't beat the stretch of the river from **Hammersmith** – London's gateway to the west, by road or tube – and neighbouring **Chiswick**, to **Kew**, **Richmond** and **Twickenham** beyond.

22

Hammersmith

The transport and traffic interchange hellhole of **Hammersmith** is worth visiting for one simple reason: the tube station gives easy access to the Wetland Centre (see p.330) and to the riverside walk to Chiswick. The riverside walk begins a short way southwest of the tube, down Queen Caroline Street. First off, you pass underneath **Hammersmith Bridge**, a graceful green-and-gold suspension bridge from the 1880s that the IRA have tried to blow up three times: first in 1939, as part of their attempt to disrupt the British war effort, secondly by the Provisional IRA in 1996, and finally four years later by the Real IRA. From the bridge, you can walk all the way to Chiswick along one of the most picturesque stretches of riverbank in the whole of London, much of it closed to traffic.

The riverside

The first section of the riverside, just west of the bridge, known as **Lower Mall**, is a mixture of Victorian pubs, boathouses, Regency verandas and modern flats. An interesting array of boats huddles around the marina outside the *Dove*, an atmospheric seventeenth-century riverside pub (see p.398). This started out as a coffee house and has the smallest back bar in the country, copious literary associations – regulars have included Graham Greene, Ernest Hemingway and William Morris – and a canopied balcony overlooking the Thames.

Kelmscott House

26 Upper Mall • Thurs & Sat 2–5pm • Free • ☎ 020 8741 3735, ⓦ williammorrissociety.org • ➐ Ravenscourt Park

It's strange to think that this genteel part of the Thames was once a hotbed of radicals, who used to congregate at **Kelmscott House**, where **William Morris** lived and worked from 1878 until his death in 1896. (Morris used to berate the locals from a soapbox on Hammersmith Bridge.) From 1885 onwards, the local socialists used to meet here on a Sunday evening, with Labour leader Keir Hardie, anarchist Prince Kropotkin, writer George Bernard Shaw and Fabian founders the Webbs among the speakers – their photos now line the walls.

7 Hammersmith Terrace

7 Hammersmith Terrace • April to mid-Sept pre-booked guided tours only Sat 11am, 12.30 & 2.30pm • £10 • ☎ 020 8741 4104, ⓦ emerywalker.org.uk • ➐ Stamford Brook

A socialist mate of Morris, the printer Emery Walker lived just down the riverbank at **7 Hammersmith Terrace**, one of a line of tall Georgian houses built facing the river

---

THE THAMES BY BOAT

From **Westminster**, from April to October, Westminster Passenger Services (☎ 020 7930 2062, ⓦ wpsa.co.uk) run a scheduled service from Westminster Pier to Kew, Richmond and Hampton Court. The full trip takes three hours one-way, and costs £15 single, £22.50 return. In addition, Turks (☎ 020 8546 2434, ⓦ turks.co.uk) runs a regular service from **Richmond** to **Hampton Court** (April to mid-Sept Tues–Sun; Aug daily; journey time 1hr 45min) which costs £7 single or £9.50 return. For the latest on **boat services** on the Thames, see ⓦ tfl.gov.uk.

sometime before 1755. The house has a well-preserved Arts and Crafts interior and contains lots of Morris memorabilia as well as de Morgan ceramics and furniture by Philip Webb, architect of Morris's Red House in Bexleyheath (see p.327) – tours are very popular so book ahead online.

London Wetland Centre

22

Queen Elizabeth's Walk • Daily: April–Oct 9.30am–6pm; Nov–March 9.30am–5pm • £10.59 • Guided tours daily 11.30am & 2.30pm • Free • Duck feeding daily, 3pm • ☎ 020 8409 4400, ⓦ wwt.org.uk • Bus #283 from ⊖ Hammersmith

For anyone even remotely interested in wildlife, the **London Wetland Centre**, in well-to-do Barnes, is an absolute must. Lying on the site of four disused reservoirs, the Wildfowl & Wetlands Trust (WWT) has created a mosaic of wetland habitats. On arrival – unless it's raining – skip the introductory audiovisual, and head straight out to the ponds. If the weather's bad, head for the **Discovery Centre**, where kids can take part in a swan identification parade, or take a duck's-eye view of the world. You can also look out over the wetlands from the glass-walled **Observatory** next door, or from the tables of the *Water's Edge Café*. Visitors with children should make their way to **Explore**, a nature-themed adventure playground, while the **Pond Zone** gives younger children a chance to do some pond-dipping.

The centre basically serves a dual function: to attract native species of bird to its watery lagoons, and to assist in the WWT's programme of breeding rare wildfowl in captivity. The **World Wetlands** area harbours a variety of extremely rare wildfowl – from White-faced Whistling Ducks to the highly endangered Blue Duck – whose wetland habitats have been re-created in miniature (3pm is feeding time). In the **Wildside** are the reedbeds and pools that attract native species, such as lapwing, sand martins, water rail and, if you're lucky, even the odd wintering bittern, all of which you can view from a moss-roofed hide. At the far end is the **Peacock Tower**, the mother of all hides: a triple-decker octagonal one with a lift, allowing views over the whole of the reserve.

Chiswick

The old riverside village of **Chiswick** was centred on the Church of St Nicholas from medieval times until the Victorian period, when the action moved north to **Chiswick High Street**, near the tube. The most picturesque approach is to walk along the river from Hammersmith. If you do so, you'll soon come to **Chiswick Mall**, which continues for a mile or so along the river to the church. A riotous ensemble of seventeenth- and eighteenth-century mansions lines the north side of the Mall, which cuts them off from their modest riverside gardens. Halfway along, a particularly fine trio ends with **Walpole House**, once the home of Barbara Villiers, Duchess of Cleveland, Countess of Castlemaine and one of Charles II's many mistresses.

Church of St Nicholas

Church St • ☎ 020 8995 7876, ⓦ stnicholaschiswick.org • ⊖ Turnham Green

At the very western end of Chiswick Mall stands the church of **St Nicholas**, rebuilt in the 1880s, but still retaining its original fifteenth-century ragstone tower. Lord Burlington and his architect friends William Kent and Colen Campbell are all buried in the graveyard, as is the aforementioned Barbara Villiers, though only the painters William Hogarth and James Whistler are commemorated by gravestones, the former enclosed by wrought-iron railings.

Fuller's Griffin Brewery

Chiswick Lane South • Mon–Fri guided tours hourly 11am–3pm • £10 online • ☎ 020 8996 2063, ⓦ fullers.co.uk • ⊖ Turnham Green

Church Lane was the medieval village high street, and its oldest building today is the Old Burlington, originally a sixteenth-century inn, and now a private residence.

Beyond, lies **Fuller's Griffin Brewery**, dating back to the seventeenth century and still going strong. You can book yourself onto one of the ninety-minute **guided tours**, which include the inevitable tasting session, and also give visitors the chance to see the country's oldest wisteria, which has clung to the brickwork for over 180 years.

RESTAURANTS
| Azou | 1 |
| The Gate | 2 |

PUBS & BARS
Blue Anchor	2
Dove	1
Fox & Grapes	4
The Greyhound	3

**WEST LONDON:
HAMMERSMITH TO HAMPTON COURT**

22

Chiswick House

Great Chertsey Rd · **House** April–Oct Mon–Wed & Sun 10am–5pm · EH · £5.90 **Gardens** Daily 7am–dusk · Free · ☎ 020 8995 0508, ⓦ chgt.org.uk · Chiswick train station from Waterloo or ⊖ Turnham Green

Chiswick House is a perfectly proportioned classical villa, designed by Richard Boyle, third Earl of Burlington, in the 1720s, and set in a beautifully landscaped garden. Like its prototype, Palladio's Villa Capra near Vicenza, the house was purpose-built as a "Temple to the Arts" – an extension to Burlington's adjacent Jacobean mansion (which was torn down in 1788). Here, amid his fine art collection, Burlington used to entertain such friends as Swift, Handel and Pope, who lived in nearby Twickenham.

Guests and visitors (who could view the property on payment of an admission fee even in Lord Burlington's day) would originally have ascended the quadruple staircase and entered the *piano nobile* through the magnificent Corinthian portico. The public entrance today is via the **lower floor**, where the earl had his own private rooms and kept his extensive library. Here, you can pick up an audioguide, watch a short video and peruse an exhibition on the history of the house and grounds.

Entertaining took place on the **upper floor**, a series of cleverly interconnecting rooms, each enjoying a wonderful view out onto the gardens – all, that is, except the **Tribunal**, the domed octagonal hall at the centre of the villa, where the house's finest paintings and sculptures are displayed, just as they would have been in Burlington's day. The other rooms retain much of their rich decor, in particular the ceilings, designed by William Kent. The most sumptuous is the **Blue Velvet Room**, decorated in a deep Prussian blue, with eight pairs of heavy gilded brackets holding up the ceiling.

The gardens

Like the villa, the house's extensive **gardens** were influenced by descriptions of the gardens of classical Rome and, in their turn, became the inspiration for the **English landscape garden**. You can admire the northwest side of the house from the stone benches of the exedra, a set of yew-hedge niches harbouring lions and copies of **Roman statuary**, and overlooking a smooth carpet of grass, punctuated by urns and sphinxes, that sit under the shadow of two giant cedars of Lebanon. Other highlights include England's first **mock ruin** – the Kent-designed cascade – and the network of narrow yew-hedge avenues, each one ending at some diminutive building or statue. One of the most remarkable focal points is the grassy **amphitheatre**, by the side of the lake, centred on an obelisk in a pond and overlooked by an Ionic temple. To the north of the villa, beside a section of the gardens' old **ha-ha**, stands a grand stone gateway designed by Inigo Jones, and close by a **café**. Beyond lies a large **conservatory**, built to grow peaches, grapes and pineapples and now stuffed with camellias. It looks out onto the formal **Italian Garden**, laid out in the early nineteenth century by the sixth Duke of Devonshire, who also established a zoo (now gone) featuring an elephant, giraffe, elks and emus.

Hogarth's House

Hogarth's Lane, Great West Rd · Tues–Sun noon–5pm · Free · ☎ 020 8994 6757, ⓦ hounslow.info · Free · Chiswick train station from Waterloo or ⊖ Turnham Green

Hogarth's House, where the artist spent each summer with his wife, sister and mother-in-law from 1749 until his death in 1764, sits by the thunderous A4 road. Nowadays it's difficult to believe Hogarth came here, from Leicester Square, for "peace and quiet", but in the eighteenth century the house was almost entirely surrounded by countryside. Compared to nearby Chiswick House, whose pretentious Palladianism and excess epitomized everything Hogarth loathed the most, the domesticity here is something of a relief. Among the scores of Hogarth's engravings, you can see copies of his satirical series – *An Election, Marriage à la Mode, A Rake's Progress* and *A Harlot's Progress* – and compare the modern view from the parlour with the more idyllic scene in *Mr Ranby's House*.

Brentford

Named after the River Brent, which empties into the Thames, just west of Chiswick, **Brentford** was the first point at which you could ford the tidal river in ancient times, and (very possibly) the place where Julius Caesar crossed in 54 BC. Nowadays, it's worth visiting, not for its humdrum high street, but for its various scattered historic landmarks, from the conspicuous campanile of **Kew Bridge Steam Museum** to the discreet charm of the aristocratic estate of **Syon**.

Gunnersbury Park

Daily: park 8am–dusk; museum April–Oct 11am–5pm; Nov–March closes 4pm • Free • ☎ 020 8992 1612, ⓦ hounslow.info • ⊖ Acton Town

Like Chiswick Park, **Gunnersbury Park** used to have a Palladian villa at its centre, in this case designed by Inigo Jones' son-in-law, John Webb, for George II's favourite daughter, Princess Amelia. Amelia used the place as a summer retreat and also erected the Neoclassical temple that overlooks the boating lake to this day. At one time, the temple was used as a private synagogue by the Rothschilds, the last owners of the estate, who sold it to the local council in the 1920s. The park has plenty of history – but it could do with some love and attention, too. Nevertheless, it's still worth popping into the **Gunnersbury Park Museum**, housed in the Rothschilds former double mansion. The highlights of the museum are a fully restored set of Victorian kitchens, and a permanent collection of historical vehicles, including a tandem tricycle and the Rothschilds' own Victorian "chariot".

Kensington Cemetery

143 Gunnersbury Ave • Daily 9am–dusk • Free • ☎ 020 8992 2924, ⓦ rbkc.gov.uk • ⊖ Gunnersbury

When the local council bought neighbouring Gunnersbury Park in the 1920s, they put aside the southeast corner for a new cemetery, known as Gunnersbury or **Kensington Cemetery**. The nearby borough of Ealing has a large Polish community, and the cemetery contains a black marble obelisk erected in 1976 to the 14,500 **Polish POWs** who went missing in 1940, when the Nazi–Soviet Pact carved up Poland. A mass grave containing 4500 bodies was later discovered by the advancing Nazis at Katyn, near Smolensk, but responsibility for the massacre was denied by the Russians until fifty years later, as a plaque bitterly records. Fifty yards to the south is the grave of **General Komorowski**, leader of the Polish Home Army during the ill-fated 1944 Warsaw Uprising, who lived in exile in Britain until his death in 1966. Also buried here is the film director **Carol Reed**, best known for *The Third Man*. There's no direct access to the graveyard from the park, only from Gunnersbury Avenue.

Kew Bridge Steam Museum

Green Dragon Lane • Tues–Sun 11am–4pm • £10 • ☎ 020 8568 4757, ⓦ kbsm.org • Bus #237 or #267 from ⊖ Gunnersbury or Kew Bridge train station from Waterloo

Difficult to miss thanks to its stylish, tapered, Italianate standpipe tower, **Kew Bridge Steam Museum** occupies an old pumping station, 100yd west of Kew Bridge. At the heart of the museum is the **Steam Hall**, which contains a green triple-expansion steam engine, similar to the one used by the *Titanic*, and four gigantic nineteenth-century Cornish beam engines, while two adjoining rooms house the pumping station's original beam engines, including the world's largest.

The steam engines may be things of great beauty, but they are primarily of interest to enthusiasts. Not so the museum's wonderfully imaginative and educational **Water for Life** gallery, situated in the basement and overlooked by a vast bank of ancient boilers, baths, sinks, taps and kettles. The exhibition tells the history of the capital's water supply: the section on rats and cockroaches goes down particularly well with kids, while the tales of the Victorian "toshers", who had to work the sewers in gangs of three to protect themselves from rat attacks, will make adults' stomachs turn. The best time to visit is at weekends, when the museum's industrial dinosaurs are put through their paces, and on Sundays in summer a narrow-gauge **steam railway** runs back and forth round the yard.

Musical Museum

399 Brentford High St • Tues–Sun 11am–5.30pm • £8 • ☎ 020 8560 8108, Ⓦ musicalmuseum.co.uk • Bus #237 or #267 from ⊖ Gunnersbury or Kew Bridge train station from Waterloo

The **Musical Museum** is stuffed with the world's largest collection of self-playing instruments. The best time to come is for the noisy hour-long live demonstrations (phone ahead for times) when the enthusiastic staff put all the mechanical music-making machines through their paces, from cleverly crafted music boxes, through badly tuned barrel organs, to the huge orchestrions that were once a feature of London cafés. The museum also boasts one of the world's finest collections of player-pianos, which can reproduce live performances of the great pianists. In addition, regular concerts, tea dances and silent films are put on to the accompaniment of the museum's enormous Art Deco Wurlitzer, which once graced the Regal cinema in Kingston upon Thames.

Boston Manor

Boston Manor Rd • Park daily 8am–dusk; house April–Oct Sat & Sun noon–5pm • Free • ☎ 0845 456 2800, Ⓦ hounslow.info • ⊖ Boston Manor

Built by a wealthy widow who married into the Spencer family, the Jacobean **Boston Manor House** was bought by James Clitherow, a City merchant, in 1670 and remained in the family until taken over by the local council in the 1920s. With magnificent cedar trees and ornamental flowerbeds, the grounds are well worth a visit, despite the nearby presence of the M4. The highlight of the house is the Drawing Room on the first floor, which retains a sumptuous mantelpiece and an extraordinarily elaborate, original Jacobean plaster ceiling. In an unusual break with protocol, William IV and Queen Adelaide paid a visit to the Clitherows (mere commoners), and dined in the Dining Room, which also boasts a fine plaster ceiling, in 1834.

Syon Park

House Mid-March to Oct Wed, Thurs & Sun 11am–5pm • £11 (including gardens) Gardens Mid-March to Oct daily 10.30am–5pm; Nov–Feb Sat & Sun 10.30am–4pm • £6 • ☎ 020 8569 7497, Ⓦ syonpark.co.uk • Bus #237 or #267 to Brent Lea bus stop from ⊖ Gunnersbury or Kew Bridge train station, or 15min walk from Syon Lane train station

Syon Park sits directly across the Thames from Kew Gardens, and is one of the few aristocratic estates left intact in London, with a fantastically lavish stately home, Syon House, at its heart. It has been in the hands of the Percy family since Elizabethan times, although these days it's more of a working commercial concern than a family retreat, with a garden centre, an indoor adventure playground and various other attractions on offer. The main reason to come here, though, is to view the magnificent house and its accompanying gardens. Syon started out as one of the richest monasteries in the country, established by Henry V after the Battle of Agincourt. Dissolved by Henry VIII, who incarcerated his fifth wife, Catherine Howard, here shortly before her execution in 1542, it was eventually granted to the Percys, earls (and later dukes) of Northumberland.

Syon House

From its rather plain castellated exterior, you'd never guess that **Syon House** contains the most opulent eighteenth-century interiors in London. The splendour of Robert Adam's refurbishment is immediately revealed, however, in the pristine **Great Hall**, where you can pick up the excellent audioguide. An apsed double cube with a screen of Doric columns at one end and classical statuary dotted around the edges, the hall has a chequered marble floor that cleverly mirrors the pattern of the coffered ceiling. It was in the hall's Tudor predecessor that Henry VIII's body lay in state en route to Windsor, and was discovered the next morning surrounded by a pack of hounds happily lapping the blood seeping from the coffin.

The state apartments

From the austerity of the Great Hall you enter the lavishly decorated **Ante Room**, with its florid scagliola floor and its green-grey Ionic columns topped by brightly gilded classical statues. Here, guests could mingle before entering the **State Dining Room**, a compromise between the two preceding rooms, richly gilded with a double apse but otherwise calm in its overall effect. The remaining rooms are warmer and softer in tone, betraying their Elizabethan origins much more than the preceding ones. The **Red Drawing Room** retains its original red-silk wall hangings from Spitalfields, upon which are hung portraits of the Stuarts by Lely, Van Dyck and others, and features a splendid ceiling studded with over two hundred roundels set within gilded hexagons. Looking out to the Thames, the **Long Gallery** – 136ft by just 14ft – stretches the entire width of the house, decorated by Adam's busy pink and gold plasterwork and lined with 62 individually painted pilasters. It was in the Long Gallery that Lady Jane Grey was formally offered the crown by her father-in-law, John Dudley, the owner of Syon at the time; nine days later they were arrested and eventually beheaded.

The private apartments

The private apartments pale in comparison with the first five rooms. However, there are still one or two highlights to look out for: more works by Lely and Van Dyck, as well as Gainsborough and Reynolds in the **Print Room**; a superb Adam fireplace and ornate fan-patterned ceiling, plus portraits by Holbein and Reynolds, in the **Green Drawing Room** – still used by the family; and a monster golden Sèvres vase at the foot of the modest principal **staircase**. Upstairs, past the delicate thousand-piece Sèvres dinner service, there are several plush bedrooms, including two refurbished in 1832 for the future Queen Victoria and her mother, the Duchess of Kent, with magnificent canopied beds, blue silk outside and yellow within.

The gardens

While Adam beautified Syon House, Capability Brown laid out its **gardens** around an artificial lake, surrounding it with oaks, beeches, limes and cedars. Since then, the gardens have been further enhanced by still more exotic trees, ranging from an Indian bean tree to a pagoda tree. Beside the lake, there's a stretch of lawn overlooked by a Doric column topped by a fibreglass statue of Flora, but the gardens' real highlight is the crescent-shaped **Great Conservatory**, an early nineteenth-century addition which is said to have inspired Joseph Paxton, architect of the Crystal Palace.

Osterley Park

Jersey Rd • **Park** Daily 8am–6pm • Free **House** April –Sept Wed–Sun 11am–5pm; Oct Wed–Sun noon–4pm; Nov–March Sat & Sun noon–4pm • NT • £9 • ☎ 020 8232 5050, ⓦ nationaltrust.org.uk • ➌ Osterley

Robert Adam redesigned another colossal Elizabethan mansion three miles northwest of Syon at **Osterley Park** – one of London's largest surviving estate parks, which still gives the impression of being in the middle of the countryside, despite the M4 motorway to the north of the house. The main approach is along a splendid avenue of sweet chestnuts to the south, past the National Trust-sponsored **farmhouse** (whose produce you can buy all year round). The driveway curves past the southernmost of the park's three lakes, with a Chinese pagoda at one end. Cedars planted in the 1820s and oaks planted in Victorian times stand between the lake and the house, and to the north are the grandiose Tudor stables of first owner Thomas Gresham, now converted into a **café**.

Osterley House

Unlike Syon, **Osterley House** was built with mercantile rather than aristocratic wealth: it was erected in 1576 by Thomas Gresham, the brains behind the City's Royal Exchange. Later it was bought by another City gent, the goldsmith and banker Francis Child, who used it merely as a kind of giant safe-deposit box – it was his grandsons who employed Robert Adam to create the house as it is today. From the outside, Osterley bears some similarity to Syon, the big difference being the grand entrance portico, with a broad flight of steps rising to a tall, Ionic colonnade, which gives access to the central courtyard.

22

The interior

From the central courtyard, you enter Adam's characteristically cool **Entrance Hall**, a double-apsed space decorated with grisaille paintings and classical statuary. The finest rooms are the State Rooms of the south wing, where the nouveaux riches Childs hoped, in vain, to entertain royalty as Gresham had once done. The **Drawing Room** is splendid, with Reynolds portraits on the damask walls and a coffered ceiling centred on a giant marigold, a theme continued in the lush carpet and elsewhere in the house. The **Tapestry Room** is hung with Boucher-designed Gobelins tapestries, while the silk-lined **State Bedchamber** features an outrageous domed bed designed by Adam. Lastly, there's the **Etruscan Dressing Room**, in which every surface is covered in delicate painted trelliswork, sphinxes and urns, dubbed "Etruscan" by Adam (and Wedgwood), though it is in fact derived from Greek vases found at Pompeii.

The **Long Gallery** is much broader, taller and plainer than the one at Syon and, like much of the house, features Adam-designed furniture, as well as some fine Chinoiserie. Sadly, the Childs' Rubens, Van Dyck and Claude pictures no longer hang here, having been transported to the family's home in the Channel Islands (where they were destroyed by fire), and replaced instead by B-list works from the V&A. In the north wing, the whitewashed Library is worth a quick peek as is the Neoclassical **Great Staircase**, with its replica Rubens ceiling painting.

PM Gallery & House

Mattock Lane • Tues–Fri & Sun 1–5pm, Sat 11am–5pm • Free • ☎ 020 8567 1227, ⓦ ealing.gov.uk • ⊖ Ealing Broadway

Now known as the **PM Gallery & House**, Pitzhanger Manor is the solitary jewel in the borough of Ealing, and is well worth a visit. Designed in 1770 by George Dance, but later bought and extensively remodelled by John Soane, the balustraded main facade, though small, is magnificent, its bays divided by Ionic pillars topped by terracotta statues. As soon as you enter the narrow vestibule, Soane stops you short with some spatial gymnastics by taking a section of the ceiling up through the first floor. To the right is the now book-less Library, which features a cross-vaulted ceiling, decorated with an unusual trelliswork pattern. Soane's masterpiece, though, is the **Breakfast Room**, with caryatids in the four corners and lush red porphyry and grey marbling on the walls.

An unexpected bonus is the **Martinware Gallery**, a display of the idiosyncratic stoneware pottery produced around 1900 by the four Martin brothers from the nearby Southall Pottery. Its centrepiece is their Moorish ceramic fireplace; the rest of the ware, including face mugs and bird jars, is more of an acquired taste. The manor's south wing is all that survives from Dance's original house (Soane's architectural teacher), the rest of which Soane demolished. The rooms here are on a much larger scale, providing an interesting contrast to Soane's intimate and highly wrought style, while the Monk's Dining Room in the basement is the precursor of Soane's Monk's Parlour (see p.145).

Kew

Kew is famous for its **Royal Botanic Gardens**, which manage the extremely difficult task of being both a world leader in botanic research and an extraordinarily beautiful and popular public park at the same time. Kew began life in the eighteenth century as the pleasure gardens of two royal estates, but it was Princess Augusta, the widow of Prince Frederick, eldest son of George II, who turned the estate into the first botanic gardens in the 1750s, with the help of her paramour, the Earl of Bute. Some of the earliest specimens were brought back from the voyages of Captain Cook, instantly establishing Kew as a leading botanical research centre. From its original eight acres the gardens have grown into a 300-acre site in which more than 33,000 species are grown in plantations and glasshouses, a display that attracts nearly two million visitors annually, most of them with no specialist interest at all. The only drawbacks with Kew are the hefty entry fee, and the fact that it's on the main flight path to Heathrow. That said, it's a wonderful place with something to see whatever the season. Outside of the gardens, there's not much reason to linger in Kew, although Kew Green, to the north of the gardens, is quite pretty, and the National Archives lurk in the backstreets.

22

Royal Botanic Gardens

There are four entrances, Victoria Gate is a short walk from the tube down Lichfield Rd • Daily 9.30am–6.30pm or dusk; April–Aug closes 7.30pm at weekend; at weekends arrive early to avoid the queues • £14.50 • ☎ 020 8332 5000, ⓦ kew.org • ⊖ Kew Gardens

Most folk arrive at **Kew Gardens** by tube and enter via the **Victoria Gate**, where you'll find the main shop and visitor centre, and the distinctive **campanile**, which originally served as the chimney for the furnaces below the glasshouses. Beyond lies the **Pond**, home to two ten-ton Ming lions, and the best vantage point from which to appreciate Kew's magnificent **Palm House**, which is a great place to start any visit to Kew.

The glasshouses

A curvaceous mound of glass and wrought iron, designed by Decimus Burton in the 1840s, the **Palm House** is the most distinctive of Kew's glasshouses. It nurtures most of the known palm species in its drippingly humid atmosphere, while in the basement there's a small, but excellent, tropical aquarium. From the Palm House, head north to the diminutive **Waterlily House**, where a canopy of plants and creepers overhangs a circular pond boasting spectacular, giant water lilies.

Further north still, is the rather less graceful **Princess of Wales Conservatory**, opened in 1987. However, the cacti collection here is awesome, as are the giant koi fish that swim stealthily beneath the pathways – look out, too, for the bizarre plants in the insectivorous section. Immediately east, set amid Kew's gargantuan Rock Garden, is the extraordinary **Alpine House**, a glasshouse shaped like the sail on the back of a dimetrodon. Twice the size (and to the south) of the Palm House, and almost forty years in the making, Decimus Burton's **Temperate House** is the largest glasshouse in the world and is currently under restoration until at least 2018.

The eighteenth-century gardens

His mosque, waxworks, observatory and House of Confucius may be gone, but several of the buildings William Chambers created in the 1760s for the amusement of Princess Augusta remain dotted about the gardens. The most famous is his ten-storey, 163ft-high **Pagoda**, Kew's most distinctive landmark, albeit minus the eighty enamelled dragons that used to adorn it. Standing nearby in a sort of miniature tea garden is the ornate **Japanese Gateway**, a scaled-down version of

---

KEW FOR KIDS

If you've kids with you, the good news is that they get in **free**. If it's raining, the **aquarium** beneath the Palm House usually goes down well, while under-10s will enjoy the indoor interactive play area, **Climbers & Creepers**. If the weather's good, there's the **Treetop Walkway**, **Treehouse Towers** – an outdoor play area full of ropes and ladders – a giant **Badger Sett** and the **Stag Beetle Loggery**, home to stag beetles and the like.

the one in Kyoto and a legacy of the 1910 Japan–British Exhibition, built in cedar wood and topped by a copper roof.

North of the pagoda, you can walk through Chambers' **Ruined Arch**, purpose-built with sundry pieces of Roman masonry strewn about as if tossed there by barbarian hordes. Chambers is also responsible for the classical temples, the most picturesque being the **Temple of Aeolus**, situated on one of Kew's few hillocks near Cumberland Gate, surrounded in spring by a carpet of bluebells and daffodils.

Capability Brown's horticultural work has proved more durable than Chambers': his lake remains a focal point of the Syon vista from the Palm House, and the hidden **Rhododendron Dell** he devised survives to the south of it. More recent nearby additions include the **Bamboo Garden**, laid out in 1891, and the **Minka House**, a thatched wooden farmhouse built in the suburbs of Okazaki in Japan, and transferred here in 2001. Even more recent is the **Treetop Walkway**, in the centre of the gardens – not a thing of beauty in itself, but the views are good and it's quite novel to be 60ft in the air among the tree canopy.

Queen Charlotte's Cottage

April–Sept Sat & Sun 10am–4pm • Free

The thickly wooded, southwestern section of Kew Gardens is the bit to head for if you want to lose the crowds, few of whom ever make it to **Queen Charlotte's Cottage**, a fairly substantial thatched summerhouse built in brick and timber in the 1770s as a royal picnic spot for George III's wife. The cottage was adjacent to a mini royal menagerie, which featured England's first kangaroos and the now extinct, zebra-like, quagga. Today, there's very little to see inside, beyond a room of Hogarth prints and a trompe-l'oeil pergola (possibly painted by one of the Queen's daughters), but the surrounding native woodland is very peaceful and carpeted with bluebells in spring.

The museum and art galleries

Kew's **Museum No. 1**, designed by Decimus Burton across the Pond from the Palm House (and now called **Plants and People**), provides an excellent wet-weather retreat. Inside, an exhibition shows the myriad uses to which humans have put plants, from food and medicines to clothes and tools. Along with the usual static glass-case displays, there are also touch-screen computers to hand, a scent station and various hands-on exhibits which should keep younger visitors happy. There's also a great 1886 model of an Indian indigo factory, with over one hundred clay figures and one colonial overseer in a pith helmet.

Kew also boasts three art galleries. To the south of Victoria Gate is the **Shirley Sherwood Gallery of Botanical Art**, a modern space that displays the most exquisitely executed botanical art from the last three centuries. Next door stands the resolutely old-fashioned **Marianne North Gallery**, purpose-built in 1882 to house the prolific output of the self-trained artist Marianne North. Over eight hundred paintings, completed in fourteen years of hectic world travel, are displayed end to end, filling every single space in the gallery. Finally, **Kew Gardens Gallery**, the largest of the lot, in Cambridge Cottage, in the northeastern corner of the gardens, puts on temporary exhibitions often on more general botanical themes.

Kew Palace

April–Sept daily 9.30am–5.30pm • Free • ☏ 020 8332 5655, ⓦ hrp.org.uk

In the north of the gardens stands the country's smallest royal residence, **Kew Palace**, a three-storey red-brick mansion measuring a mere 70ft by 50ft, and commonly known as the "Dutch House", after its fancy Flemish-bond brickwork and its curly Dutch gables. It's the smallest (and sole survivor) of Kew's three former royal residences and was bought from a City merchant by George II as a nursery and schoolhouse for his umpteen children.

The only king to live here was **George III**, confined to the palace from 1801 onwards and subjected to the dubious attentions of doctors who attempted to find a cure for his "madness" by straitjacketing him and applying poultices of mustard and Spanish fly – only his strong constitution helped him to pull through.

Inside the palace, there are one or two bits and bobs belonging to the royals, like the much-loved doll's house, on the ground floor, which belonged to George III's daughters. Upstairs, you can view the chair in which Queen Charlotte passed away in 1818, while the top floor has been left pretty much untouched since those days. You also get to visit the **Royal Kitchens** for a glimpse into Georgian life below stairs. Take time, too, to explore the secluded **Queen's Garden**, behind the palace, set out in a formal late seventeenth-century style, with a pleached hornbeam avenue and a lovely sunken nosegay garden.

Kew Green

Kew's majestic **Main Gates**, designed by Decimus Burton, fulfilled their stated function until the arrival of the railway at Kew. Nowadays, you only get to see them if you're walking from Kew Bridge or exploring **Kew Green**, one of London's prettiest village greens. Lined with Georgian houses, the green is centred on the delightful church of **St Anne** (for opening times, visit ⓦsaintanne-kew.org.uk), an unusual building sporting a Victorian polygonal clock turret at one end and a peculiar Georgian octagonal cupola at the other; the painters Gainsborough and Zoffany lie in the churchyard. Inside, there's a royal Georgian gallery, held up by Tuscan columns, while at the east end is a rather fine late-Victorian chancel with scagliola columns and a top-lit dome. There are music recitals, tea and cakes on summer Sunday afternoons.

National Archives

Off Mortlake Rd, down Ruskin Ave • Tues & Thurs 9am–7pm, Wed, Fri & Sat 9am–5pm • Free • ☏ 020 8876 3444, ⓦ nationalarchives.gov .uk • ⊖ Kew Gardens

Hidden in the residential backstreets of Kew is the Public Records Office, a rather nasty-looking beige and green premises housing the **National Archives**. Its research library is full of historians consulting primary source materials, while its exhibition gallery displays a changing rota of fascinating artefacts ranging from the likes of the Domesday Book and the trial record of Charles I, to Queen Victoria's 1851 census return and Elton John's Deed Poll certificate changing his name (wisely) from Reginald Kenneth Dwight.

Richmond

Richmond, upstream from Kew, basked for centuries in the glow of royal patronage, with Plantagenet kings and Tudor monarchs frequenting the riverside Palace of Shene, as Richmond Palace was then called. In the eighteenth century Richmond enjoyed a brief life as a spa, and its agreeable locale began to attract City merchants, as well as successful artists, actors and writers: Pope, Gainsborough, Garrick and Reynolds are just some of the plaque-worthy names associated with the place. Although most of the courtiers and aristocrats have gone, as has the Tudor palace on the green, Richmond is still a wealthy district, with two theatres and highbrow pretensions. To appreciate its attractions fully, you need to visit the old village green, take in the glorious view from **Richmond Hill** and pay a visit to the vast acreage of **Richmond Park**, the old royal hunting grounds, still wild and replete with deer, and walk along the riverside to the nearby Jacobean mansion of **Ham House**.

Richmond Green

George Street, Richmond's main street, is traffic-clogged and dominated by chain stores, but take one of the narrow pedestrianized alleyways, lined with arty shops and tearooms, and you'll emerge onto the wonderful open space of **Richmond Green**, one of London's finest village greens, and one of the most peaceful, except for the planes overhead on the main flight path into Heathrow. Handsome seventeenth- and eighteenth-century houses line the southwest and southeast sides of the green, with the most striking building of all, the flamboyant **Richmond Theatre**, designed by the great Frank Matcham in terracotta and brick in 1899, in the northeast corner.

Richmond Museum

Whittaker Ave • Tues–Sat 11am–5pm • Free • ☎ 020 8332 1141, ⓦ museumofrichmond.com • ⊖ Richmond

The old town hall, set slightly back from the riverside now houses the library and, on the top floor, the **Richmond Museum**. The museum contains a small permanent exhibition on the history of the town, plus the lowdown on (and a model of) the old royal palace; special exhibitions tend to focus on Richmond's past luminaries.

Richmond Riverside

To the untrained eye, the buildings that form the backdrop to the pedestrianized terraces of **Richmond Riverside** look Georgian, but closer inspection reveals the majority to be a sham: the cupolas conceal air vents, the chimneys are decorative and the facades hide offices and flats. Still, Quinlan Terry's pastiche from the late 1980s has proved very popular. One of the few originals is **Heron House**, a narrow three-storey building where Lady Hamilton and her daughter Horatia came to live shortly after Trafalgar, the battle in which the girl's father died.

22

To the south of the modern riverside development lies **Richmond Bridge**, an elegant span of five arches made from Purbeck stone in 1777, and cleverly widened in the 1930s, thus preserving London's oldest extant bridge. From April to September you can rent bikes or rowing boats from the nearby jetties, or take a boat trip to Hampton Court or Westminster (see p.329). If you continue along the towpath beyond Richmond Bridge, you will pass the cows grazing on **Petersham Meadows**, and leave the rest of London far behind, before eventually coming to Ham House.

Ham House

Ham St • **House** Mid-March to Oct daily except Fri noon–4pm; mid-July to early Sept daily noon–5pm • NT • £10 **Gardens** mid-March to Oct daily except Fri 11am–5pm; mid-July to early Sept daily 11am–6pm; Jan–mid-Feb & Nov Sat & Sun 11am–4pm; Dec daily except Fri 11am–4pm • NT • £4 • ☎ 020 8940 1950, ⓦ nationaltrust.org.uk • Bus #371 or #65 from ⊖ Richmond

Hidden in the woods that line the south bank of the Thames lies the red-brick Jacobean mansion of **Ham House**, home to the Earl of Dysart for nearly three hundred years. The first Earl of Dysart was Charles I's childhood whipping boy (he literally received the punishment on behalf of the prince when the latter misbehaved), but it's his ambitious daughter, **Elizabeth**, the second Countess – a Royalist spy and at one time Oliver Cromwell's lover – who's most closely associated with the place. With the help of her second husband, the First Duke of Lauderdale, one of Charles II's Cabal Ministry, she added numerous extra rooms, "furnished like a great Prince's" according to diarist John Evelyn, and succeeded in shocking even **Restoration** society with her extravagance.

Elizabeth's profligacy, and a ruinous legal battle over her husband's inheritance, meant she died penniless in 1698, having not ventured out of the house for eight years. She also left the family heavily in debt, so they could afford to make few alterations to one of the finest **Stuart interiors** in the country, prompting Horace Walpole (who lived across the river at Strawberry Hill) to describe Ham as a "Sleeping Beauty". The Great Staircase, off the Central Hall, is stupendously ornate, featuring huge bowls of fruit at the newel posts and trophies of war carved into the balustrade. The rest of the house is equally sumptuous, with lavish plasterwork, silverwork and parquet flooring, **Verrio ceiling paintings** and rich hangings, tapestries, silk damasks and cut velvets. The Long

---

RICHMOND'S LOST PALACE

Richmond Palace was acquired by Henry I in 1125, when it was still known as **Shene Palace**. The first king to frequent the place was Edward III, who lay dying here in 1377 while his mistress urged the servants to prise the rings from his fingers. Seventeen years later a grief-stricken Richard II razed the place to the ground after his wife, Anne of Bohemia, died here of the plague. Henry V had it restored and Edward IV held jousting tournaments on the green, but it was Henry VII who, in an atypical burst of extravagance, constructed the largest complex of all, renaming it **Richmond Palace** after his Yorkshire earldom. Henry VIII granted the palace to his fourth wife, Anne of Cleves, as part of their divorce settlement. Queen Mary and Philip of Spain spent part of their honeymoon here and Elizabeth I came here to die in 1603. A lot of history is attached to the place, but very little of Richmond Palace survived the Commonwealth and even less is visible now. The most obvious relic is the unspectacular red-brick **Tudor Gateway**, in the southwest corner of Richmond Green.

Gallery, in the west wing, features a Van Dyck self-portrait, a portrait of Elizabeth Dysart and six "Court Beauties" by **Peter Lely**.

The gardens

Ham House's formal seventeenth-century **gardens** have been beautifully restored to something like their former glory. To the east of the house lies the Cherry Garden, laid out with a pungent lavender parterre, and surrounded by yew hedges and pleached hornbeam arbours. On the south terrace, the Lauderdales would display their citrus trees, considered the height of luxury at the time, while across the lawn lies the "Wildernesse" of hornbeam hedges and maple trees. Finally, to the west, you'll find the partially resurrected kitchen garden, overlooked by the Orangery – the oldest in Britain – which serves as a tearoom.

Richmond Hill

If you're still wondering what's so special about Richmond, take a hike up **Richmond Hill**. To get there, head up Hill Rise from the top of Bridge Street, passing between the eighteenth-century antique shops and tearooms on your left, and the small sloping green on your right. Eventually you come to the **Terrace Gardens**, celebrated for the view up the thickly wooded Thames valley. Turner, Reynolds, Kokoschka and countless other artists have painted this view, which remains relatively unchanged and takes in six counties from Windsor to the North Downs. Richmond's wealthiest inhabitants have flocked to the hill's commanding heights over the centuries. The future George IV is alleged to have spent his secret honeymoon at **3 The Terrace**, after marrying Mrs Fitzherbert; twice divorced and a Catholic to boot, she was never likely to be Queen, though she bore the prince ten children.

Further along, on the opposite side of the street, William Chambers built **Wick House** in 1772 as a summer residence for the enormously successful Joshua Reynolds. The building currently houses the nurses who work at the nearby **Royal Star & Garter Home**, a rest home for war veterans built shortly after World War I, and now the dominant feature of the hillside. Disabled war veterans are also among the workforce at Richmond's **Poppy Factory** (Ⓦ poppyfactory.org), who produce the thousands of poppies, petals and wreaths used during the build-up to Remembrance Day in November; the factory welcomes visitors and conducts regular ninety-minute guided tours.

Richmond Park

Daily March–Sept 7am–dusk; Oct–Feb 7.30am–dusk • Free • ☎ 0300 061 2200, Ⓦ royalparks.org.uk • Bus #371 from ⊖ Richmond to Richmond Gate or #65 from ⊖ Richmond to Petersham Gate

Richmond's greatest attraction is the enormous **Richmond Park**, at the top of Richmond Hill – 2500 acres of undulating grassland and bracken, dotted with coppiced woodland and as wild as anything in London. Royal hunting ground since the thirteenth century (when it was known as Shene Chase), this is Europe's largest city park – eight miles across at its widest point. It's famous for its red and fallow deer, which roam freely – and breed so successfully, they have to be culled twice a year – and for its ancient oaks. Though for the most part untamed, there are a couple of deliberately landscaped plantations which feature splendid springtime azaleas and rhododendrons.

From Richmond Gate, at the top of Richmond Hill, it's a short walk south along the crest of the hill to **Pembroke Lodge** (originally known as The Molecatcher's), the childhood home of the philosopher Bertrand Russell. Set in its own lovely garden, the house is now a tearoom with outdoor seating and more spectacular views up the Thames valley. Close by, to the north, is the highest point in the park, known as **King Henry VIII's Mount**, where tradition has it the king waited for the flare launched from the Tower of London, which signalled the execution of his second wife, Anne Boleyn, though historians believe he was in Wiltshire at the time.

22

Exploring the Park

For a longer stroll through the park, head east from Pembroke Lodge into **Sidmouth Wood**, whose sweet chestnuts, oaks and beeches were planted during the nineteenth century. Originally established as pheasant cover, the wood is now a bird sanctuary, and walkers must keep to the central path, known as the Driftway. A little further east lie the **Pen Ponds**, the largest stretches of water in the park and a good spot for birdwatching. To the south is the park's extremely popular **Isabella Plantation**, a carefully landscaped woodland park, with a little rivulet running through it, two small artificial ponds, and spectacular rhododendrons and azaleas in the spring. The round trip from Richmond Gate is about four miles.

The two most important historic buildings in the park are both closed to the public. Of the two, the **White Lodge**, to the east of the Pen Ponds, is the more attractive, a Palladian villa commissioned by George II, and frequented by his wife, Queen Caroline, and their daughter, Princess Amelia. Much altered over the years, it was also the birthplace of the ill-fated Edward VIII, and it was home to the Duke and Duchess of York (later George VI and the Queen Mother); it currently houses the Royal Ballet School. The **Thatched House Lodge**, in the southernmost corner of the park, was built in the 1670s for the park's rangers, and gets its name from the thatched gazebo that can be found in the garden. General Eisenhower hung out in the lodge during World War II, and it's now home to Princess Alexandra.

Twickenham

Twickenham, on the opposite side of the river from Richmond, is best known as the home of English rugby – there's a museum if you're really keen (see opposite) – but it also conceals a cluster of lesser-known sights close to the river, all of which repay a brief visit. Most sights are by the river, and, if you want to learn a bit more about the local area, pop into the **Twickenham Museum** (Tues & Sat 11am–3pm, Sun 2–4pm; free; ☎020 8408 0070, ⊛twickenham-museum.org.uk), 25 The Embankment, which puts on changing historical exhibitions.

ARRIVAL AND DEPARTURE

By ferry The most picturesque approach to Twickenham is to walk along the towpath from Richmond Riverside to Hammerton's Ferry, which takes people (and bicycles) over to the Twickenham side (March–Oct Mon–Fri 10am–6pm, Sat & Sun 10am–6.30pm; Oct–Feb Sat & Sun 10am–6.30pm; £1; ☎020 8892 9620, ⊛hammertonsferry.com).

Marble Hill House

Richmond Rd · Guided tours April–Oct Sat 10.30am & noon, Sun 10.30am, noon, 2.15 & 3.30pm · EH · £5.70 · ☎020 8892 5115, ⊛english-heritage.org.uk · St Margarets train station from Waterloo

A stuccoed Palladian villa set in rolling green parkland, **Marble Hill House** was completed in 1729 for Henrietta Howard, Countess of Suffolk, mistress of George II for some twenty years and, conveniently, also a lady-in-waiting to his wife, Queen Caroline (apparently "they hated one another very civilly"). She was renowned not just for her "long chestnut tresses", but also for her wit and intelligence and she entertained the Twickenham Club of Alexander Pope, John Gay and Horace Walpole.

The few original furnishings in the house are enhanced with reproductions giving the place something of the feel of a fashionable Georgian villa. The Great Room, on the *piano nobile*, is a perfect cube whose coved ceiling carries on up into the top-floor apartments. Copies of Van Dycks decorate the walls as they did in Lady Suffolk's day, but the highlight is Lady Suffolk's Bedchamber, with its Ionic columned recess – a classic Palladian device – where she died in 1767 at the age of 79. There's a **café** in the coach house open daily and open-air concerts in the surrounding park on occasional summer evenings.

Orleans House Gallery

Riverside • April–Sept Tues–Sat 1–5.30pm, Sun 2–5.30pm; Oct–March closes 4.30pm • Free • ☎ 020 8831 6000 • St Margarets train station from Waterloo

Set in a small wood to the west of Marble Hill Park is the **Orleans House Gallery**, in what began life as a retirement villa built in 1710 for James Johnston, who had been Secretary of State for Scotland under William III. It was most famously occupied in 1815–17 by Louis-Philippe, the exiled Duke of Orléans (and future King of the French), who referred to it as "dear quiet Twick". In 1926, it was all but entirely demolished – all, that is, except for the **Octagon**, designed for Johnston by James Gibbs in 1720 in honour of a visit by Queen Caroline. The café and the exhibitions staged in the old stables and the modern extension are appealing enough, but it's the Octagon that steals the limelight, an unusually exuberant Baroque confection celebrated for its masterly Italian stucco decoration.

22

York House

Sion Rd • Mon–Sat 7.30am to dusk, Sun 9am to dusk • Free • St Margarets train station from Waterloo

The early seventeenth-century, Twickenham riverside residence **York House** has had a series of illustrious residents including Prince Philippe, Count of Paris and grandson of Louis-Philippe. The house itself is now owned by the local council and is used for weddings, but the **gardens**, laid out by the last private owner, the Indian businessman Ratan Tata, are open to the public. The bit to head for is the riverside section – a great picnic spot – that lies beyond the sunken garden, on the other side of the delicate arched bridge spanning the road. Here, in among the yew hedges, you'll find the gardens' celebrated "**naked ladies**", seven larger-than-life marble nymphs frolicking in the water lilies of an Italian fountain, above which Venus rises up at the head of two winged horses.

World Rugby Museum

200 Whitton Rd • Tues–Sat 10am–5pm, Sun 11am–5pm • £7; Stadium tours £15 • ☎ 020 8892 8877, ⓦ rfu.com • Twickenham train station from Waterloo

The English Rugby Union fan's number-one pilgrimage site is the national stadium at Twickenham, and the pompously entitled **World Rugby Museum** in the East Stand. The exhibition is full of video footage and lots of memorabilia from the sport, which was famously invented in 1823, when W.W. Ellis picked up and ran with the ball during a game of football at Rugby School. There's not much here for the nonspecialist, however, save for the Calcutta Cup, an object of supreme beauty, having been made from 270 silver rupees, with great cobra handles and an elephant lid. You can also sign up for a **stadium tour**, which allows you to see the dressing rooms and walk onto the pitch itself, and includes a visit to the museum. Note that on match days the museum is only open to match ticket-holders.

ISLANDS IN THE THAMES

If you take the boat upriver (see p.329), or walk along the towpath, you'll pass a number of islands in the middle of the Thames. Several were used in the past to grow grass and willows for basketry, but most now act as formal or informal nature reserves, like **Brentford Ait** – "ait" or "eyot" is the word used on the Thames to denote an island – which supports a large heronry. There's even a makeshift raft floating mid-river, near Marble Hill House, where a local eccentric has lived for over 25 years. The only inhabited island on the tidal Thames is **Eel Pie Island**, connected to the bank near York House by a pedestrian bridge. Tea dances began at the island's *Eel Pie Hotel* back in the 1920s; bawdy jazz nights were the staple diet in the 1950s; Pink Floyd, the Rolling Stones and the Who all played there in the 1960s. The hotel burned down in 1971 (ⓦ eelpie.org), and the island is now better known for its eccentric community of independent-spirited artists and artisans (ⓦ eelpieislandartists.co.uk), among them Trevor Baylis, inventor of the clockwork radio.

Strawberry Hill

268 Waldegrave Rd **House** March–Oct Mon–Wed 2–5.30pm, Sat & Sun noon–5.30pm (last admission 4.20pm) • £8.40 **Guided tour** Sat 10.30am • £13 **Garden** Daily 10am–6pm • Free • ☎ 020 8744 1241, ⓦ strawberryhillhouse.org.uk • Strawberry Hill train station from Waterloo

One last oddity well worth making the effort to visit is **Strawberry Hill**. In 1747 writer, wit and fashion queen Horace Walpole, youngest son of former prime minister Robert Walpole, bought this "little play-thing house…the prettiest bauble you ever saw…set in enamelled meadows, with filigree hedges", renamed it Strawberry Hill and set about inventing the most influential building in the Gothic Revival. Walpole appointed a "Committee of Taste" to embellish his project with details from other Gothic buildings: screens from Old St Paul's and Rouen cathedrals, and fan vaulting from Henry VII's Chapel in Westminster Abbey.

The house quickly became the talk of London, a place of pilgrimage for royalty and foreign dignitaries alike. Walpole was forced to issue tickets in advance (never more than four and no children) to cut down the number of visitors. Those he wished to meet he greeted dressed in a lavender suit and silver-embroidered waistcoat, sporting a cravat carved in wood by Grinling Gibbons and an enormous pair of gloves that once belonged to James I. When he died in 1797, he left the house to his friend, the sculptor Anne Damer, who continued to entertain in the same spirit, giving lavish garden parties dressed in a man's coat, hat and shoes. Walpole wanted visits of Strawberry Hill to be a theatrical experience, and, with its eccentric Gothic decor, it remains so to this day. There's a Committtee of Taste **café** in the Great Cloister, open slightly earlier hours than the house.

Wimbledon

Wimbledon is a dreary, high, bleak, windy suburb, on the edge of a threadbare heath. Virginia Woolf

Nowadays, of course, **Wimbledon** is best known for its tennis tournament, the Wimbledon Championships, held every year in the last week of June and the first week of July, on the grass courts of the All England Lawn Tennis and Croquet Club – to give the ground its grand title. For the rest of the year, Wimbledon's vast **common** is its most popular attraction, worth a visit for its **windmill**, and for the remarkable **Southside House**.

Wimbledon Lawn Tennis Museum

Gate 4, Church Rd **Museum** daily 10am–5pm • £12 **Guided tours** book online • £22 • ☎ 020 8946 2244, ⓦ wimbledon.com • Bus #493 from ⊖ Southfields

If you've missed the tournament itself (see p.437), the next best thing for tennis fans is a quick spin around the state-of-the-art **Wimbledon Lawn Tennis Museum**. It traces the history of the game, which is descended from the *jeu de paume* played by the French clergy from the twelfth century onwards. The modern version, though, is considered to have been invented by a Victorian major, who called it "Sphairstike", a name that, not surprisingly, failed to stick. The new sport was initially seen as a genteel pastime, suitable for both gentlemen and ladies, and its early enthusiasts hailed almost exclusively from the aristocracy and the clergy – the museum's Edwardian dressing room is the epitome of upper-class masculinity. As well as the historical and fashion angles and the tennis-star memorabilia, there's also plenty of opportunity for watching vintage game footage.

Wimbledon Windmill

Wimbledon Rd • April–Oct Sat 2–5pm, Sun 11am–5pm • £2 • ☎ 020 8947 2825, ⓦ wimbledonwindmill.org.uk • Bus #93 from ⊖ Wimbledon

With none of the views of Richmond, **Wimbledon Common** can appear rather bleak: mostly rough grass and bracken punctuated by playing fields and golf courses, and cut through by the busy A3. The chief reason to come here is the **Wimbledon Windmill**, situated at the end of Windmill Road in the northern half of the common, with conveniently placed tearooms nearby. Built in 1817, the mill was closed down in 1864, and converted into cottages, one of which was home to Baden-Powell when he began writing his *Scouting for Boys* in 1908. Subsequently restored and turned into a museum, the windmill is the last remaining hollow-post flour mill in the country; you can also climb into the first section of the wooden cap and see the giant chain wheel.

Putney Vale Cemetery

Stag Lane • Mon–Sat 8am–dusk, Sun 10am–dusk • Free • ☎ 020 8871 7820, ⓦ wandsworth.gov.uk • Bus #85 or #265 from ⊖ Putney Bridge

Sandwiched between Wimbledon Common and Richmond Park, by the busy A3, is **Putney Vale Cemetery**, worth a visit for its wonderful array of Victorian angels and its peaceful Gardens of Remembrance, at their best in early summer. Once you enter, turn right, and head to the end of Richards Way, where you'll find the nautical grave of Bruce Ismay, *Titanic* survivor and chairman of the ill-fated White Star Line; close by lies Sandy Denny, lead singer of Fairport Convention. The cemetery's most illustrious incumbent is Alexander Kerensky, along Alexander Way, who died in New York, but was refused burial there by the Russian Orthodox Church. Kerensky was the leader of the Russian Revolution of February 1917, which overthrew the tsar, but was himself ousted by the Bolshevik Revolution of October 1917.

Cannizaro Park

West Side Common • Mon–Fri 8am–dusk, Sat & Sun 9am–dusk • Free • ☎ 020 8946 7349, ⓦ cannizaropark.com • Bus #93 from ⊖ Wimbledon

Cannizaro Park is a small, sheltered, wooded public park, made up of the grounds of Cannizaro House (now a hotel frequented by the tennis glitterati), and entered from Wimbledon Common. Within its walls are a grotesque teapot fountain, a lovely stretch of lawn for picnicking, a maze of paths, an aviary, an Italian garden and a wonderful array of rhododendrons, azaleas and magnolias. The park also stages occasional student art shows and has an open-air music and theatre festival every July.

Wat Buddhapadipa

14 Calonne Rd • Daily 9am–5pm • Free • ☎ 020 8946 1357, ⓦ buddhapadipa.org • Bus #93 from ⊖ Wimbledon

Probably the most unusual and intriguing sight in Wimbledon is the **Wat Buddhapadipa**, a startling, white-washed and gabled Thai Buddhist temple, with a richly decorated red and gold roof, completed in 1982. You can visit the temple grounds any day of the week, and there are classes, courses and ceremonies throughout the year, but the temple itself is only accessible at the weekend.

Southside House

3–4 Woodhayes Rd • Guided tours Easter–Sept Wed 2 & 4pm, Sat & Sun 2, 3 & 4pm • £9 • ☎ 020 8946 7643, ⓦ southsidehouse.com • Bus #93 from ⊖ Wimbledon

Hidden from the road behind high walls is the Dutch-Baroque mansion of **Southside House**, built in the late seventeenth century, and now hemmed in by Wimbledon's King's College School. Visiting the house is an unforgettable experience, not least because you may be guided round, and fed with anecdotes, by the eccentric descendants of the Pennington-Mellor-Munthe family who first built the house – several of whom still live here in a kind of time warp, using only candles for light and open fires for warmth, surrounded by the house's rich and slowly disintegrating decor, and the family's ancestral hangings, many of which are extremely valuable.

Inside, the place has a ramshackle feel, partly because at heart it's still an old Tudor farmhouse, onto which a Dutch facade has been added. Nevertheless, virtually every room is stuffed to the rafters with artworks and other sundry heirlooms. In the Dining Room alone, there are no fewer than 34, mostly full-length, portraits, including three by Van Dyck, one each by Hogarth and Goya, and a depiction of St George by Burne-Jones. Other treasures on show include the sapphire worn by the last king of

Serbia on the day of his assassination, and, in a cabinet of curiosities in the royal bedroom upstairs, you can see the pearl necklace worn by Marie Antoinette on the day of her execution. Finally, in the Music Room, there's a portrait of Angelica Kauffmann, a Reynolds self-portrait, a Fragonard and one of George Romney's famous portraits of Emma, Lady Hamilton, who used to strike her "attitudes" in that very room.

Hampton Court Palace

April–Oct daily 10am–6pm • Nov–March closes 4.30pm • £15 • ☎ 020 3166 6000, Ⓦ hrp.org.uk • Hampton Court train station from Waterloo

Hampton Court Palace, a sprawling red-brick ensemble on the banks of the Thames, thirteen miles southwest of London, is the finest of England's royal abodes. And it's up there with the Tower of London when it comes to the variety of attractions on offer: not only does it boast Tudor halls and kitchens, it's got some fabulous Baroque interiors in the wings designed by Wren, superb works of art, a beautiful riverside setting, a yew hedge maze, a Real Tennis court, impressive formal gardens and a vast royal park. If your time is limited, the most rewarding sections are Henry VIII's Apartments, William III's Apartments and Henry VIII's Kitchens – and be sure to leave time for the Maze.

Brief history

The present building was begun in 1516 by the upwardly mobile **Cardinal Wolsey**, Henry VIII's high-powered, fast-living Lord Chancellor. Wolsey fell from favour when he failed to secure a papal annulment for Henry's marriage to Catherine of Aragon, and Hampton Court (and his palace in Whitehall) fell to the king in 1528.

Like Wolsey, **Henry VIII** spent enormous sums of money on the palace, enlarging the kitchens, rebuilding the chapel and altering the rooms to suit the tastes of the last five of his six wives. Under Elizabeth I and James I, Hampton Court became renowned for its masques, plays and balls; during the Civil War, it was a refuge and then a prison for Charles I. The palace was put up for sale during the Commonwealth, but, with no buyers forthcoming, Cromwell decided to move in and lived here on and off until his death in 1658. Charles II laid out the gardens, inspired by what he had seen at Versailles, but it was **William and Mary** who instigated the most radical alterations, hiring Christopher Wren to remodel the buildings. Wren was told to tear down the whole palace and build a new Versailles, but, in the end, had to content himself with rebuilding the east and south wings, adding the Banqueting House on the river and completing the chapel for Queen Anne.

George III eschewed the place, apparently because he associated it with the beatings he received here from his grandfather. Instead, he established grace-and-favour residences for indigent members of the royal household, which still exist today. The palace was opened to the public in 1838, and, along with the vast expanse of **Bushy Park**, it's now a major tourist attraction.

INFORMATION AND TOURS

Admission Tickets to the Royal Apartments cover entry to everything in the palace and grounds – to save money and avoid queuing, buy your tickets online. If you don't want to visit the apartments, you can buy a separate ticket for the gardens (April–Sept; £5.20) and the Maze (£4).

Tours The State Apartments are divided into six thematic walking tours, which are numbered and colour-coded. There's not a lot of information in the rooms, but guided tours, lasting half an hour or so, are available at no extra charge; all are led by period-costumed historians, who do a

fine job of bringing the place to life. In addition, audioguides are available from the information centre on the east side of Clock Court.

Events The Hampton Court Palace Flower Show takes place in early July, rivals Chelsea for sheer snob factor, and is likewise organized by the Royal Horticultural Society (⊕ rhs.org.uk). The Hampton Court Palace Festival (⊕ hamptoncourtpalacefestival.com) features stars from the classical and pop music worlds, and takes place each year in June.

The Palace

The Tudor west front may no longer be moated but it positively prickles with turrets, castellations, chimneypots and pinnacles. The **Great Gatehouse** looks suitably imposing, but was in fact five storeys high until George III's reign. The first and largest courtyard, **Base Court**, is reminiscent of an Oxbridge college and features another Tudor gateway known as Anne Boleyn's Gateway, though it too dates from the time of Wolsey. Beyond lies **Clock Court**, which has none of the uniformity of the other two quadrangles: to the north rises the Tudor Great Hall, to the south Wren's colonnade, announcing the new State Apartments, and to the east a fairly convincing mock-Tudor gateway by William Kent. Originally centred on a large fountain which was equipped by Elizabeth I with a nozzle that soaked innocent passers-by, the courtyard gets its

THE GHOST OF CATHERINE HOWARD

Henry VIII married his fifth wife, **Catherine Howard**, in July 1540, just weeks after having annulled his six-month marriage to Anne of Cleves. Unfortunately, despite being less than 20, Catherine had already had sexual relations with her music tutor, **Henry Mannox**, was pre-contracted to marry her lover, another courtier named **Francis Dereham**, and began an affair with another courtier named **Thomas Culpeper**. Her ambitious family – who were out of favour since the execution of Anne Boleyn, Catherine's cousin – somewhat optimistically hoped to conceal these inconvenient truths from Henry, and to restore their influence at court.

It took until November 1541 for Henry to find out he'd been duped. Seated in the Royal Pew at Hampton Court, he was passed the note from Thomas Cranmer, the Archbishop of Canterbury, alleging that Catherine was not in fact a virgin when he married her. Catherine was arrested a few days later, but is alleged to have given her guards the slip and run down the **Haunted Gallery** in an attempt to make a final plea for mercy to the king, who was praying in the chapel. Henry refused to see her, and she was dragged kicking and screaming back to her chambers. To this day, a ghost can be heard re-enacting the scene – or so the story goes.

22

current name from the **astronomical clock** on the inside of the Anne Boleyn Gateway, made in 1540 for Henry VIII, which was used to calculate the high tide at London Bridge (and thus the estimated time of arrival of palace guests travelling by boat). The last and smallest of the three courtyards is Wren's **Fountain Court**, which crams in more windows than seems possible.

Henry VIII's Apartments

Henry VIII lavished more money on Hampton Court than on any other palace except Greenwich (which no longer exists). The only major survival from Tudor times, however, is his **Great Hall**, completed with remarkable speed in 1534, with Henry having made the builders work day and night – a highly dangerous exercise in candlelight. The ornate double hammerbeam roof would originally have been painted blue, red and gold and featured a louvre to allow the smoke to escape from the central hearth. Later, the hall served as the palace theatre, where theatrical troupes, among them Shakespeare's, entertained royalty. Even Cromwell had an organ installed here so he and his family could enjoy recitals by John Milton, an accomplished musician as well as a poet.

Passing through the Horn Room, you enter the **Great Watching Chamber**. The gilded oak-ribbed ceiling is studded with leather-mâché Tudor insignia, and hung with tapestries that were part of Wolsey's vast collection. Up to eighty yeomen would have been stationed here, guarding the principal entrance to the king's private chambers, which William and Mary found "old-fashioned and uncomfortable" and consequently demolished.

From here you reach the **Haunted Gallery**, built by Wolsey to connect his apartments to the chapel, and home to the ghost of Catherine Howard (see box above). The gallery gives access to the Royal Pew, where you can see a replica of **Henry VIII's Crown of State**, a magnificent piece of imperial Tudor pomp used for all royal coronations until the Commonwealth. From the Royal Pew you can look down on the **Chapel Royal**, and admire the colourful false-timber Tudor vaulting wrought in plaster, heavy with pendants of gilded music-making cherubs – one of the most memorable sights in the whole palace. It was here that Henry married the sixth of his wives (and the only one to outlive him), Catherine Parr.

Mary II's Apartments

The Queen's apartments remained unfinished at Queen Mary's death in 1694, and weren't fully furnished and decorated until the time of Queen Caroline, George II's wife. The main approach is via the grandiose **Queen's Staircase**, splendidly decorated with trompe-l'oeil reliefs and a coffered dome by William Kent.

One of the finest rooms here is the **Queen's Drawing Room**, decorated top to bottom with trompe-l'oeil paintings depicting Queen Anne's husband, George of Denmark – in heroic naval guise, and also, on the south wall, riding naked and wigless on the back of a "dolphin". Queen Anne takes centre stage on the ceiling as Justice, somewhat inappropriately given her habit of not paying her craftsmen, including Verrio, the painter of this room. After Anne's death in 1714, the Prince and Princess of Wales (later George II and Queen Caroline) took over the Queen's Apartments, though they hated the trompe-l'oeil paintings and hung Mantegna's works over the top of them. In 1717, the couple fell out with the king and moved to Kew; the ceiling painting in the **Queen's Bedroom** by James Thornhill predates the quarrel, with four portraits of a seemingly happy Hanoverian family staring at one another from the coving.

22

The **Queen's Gallery** features one of the most ornate marble fireplaces in the palace – originally intended for the King's Bedchamber – with putti, doves and Venus frolicking above the mantelpiece; the walls, meanwhile, are hung with Gobelin tapestries depicting Alexander the Great's exploits and lined with Chinese vases and Delftware.

Georgian Private Apartments

The **Georgian Private Apartments** begin with the rooms of the **Cumberland Suite**, lived in by George II before his accession, then by his eldest son, Prince Frederick, and redesigned for William, Duke of Cumberland, Frederick's brother and better known as "Butcher Cumberland" for his ruthless suppression of the Jacobites in Scotland. The rooms were decorated by Kent, who added Gothic touches to the first two rooms and a grandiose Neoclassical alcove in the bedchamber.

Beyond here you'll find the tiny **Wolsey Closet**, which, although a Victorian invention, gives a tantalizing impression of the splendour of Wolsey's original palace. It's a jewel of a room – though at 12ft square it's easily missed – with brightly coloured early sixteenth-century paintings set above exquisite linenfold panelling and a fantastic gilded ceiling of interlaced octagons.

Next is the **Communication Gallery**, constructed to link the King's and Queen's apartments, now lined with Lely's "Windsor Beauties", flattering portraits of the best-looking women in the court of Charles II. The **Cartoon Gallery** was purpose-built by Wren to display the Raphael Cartoons – the originals are in the V&A, and what you see are late seventeenth-century oil painting copies. Tapestries made from the cartoons are scattered throughout William and Mary's apartments.

The next sequence of rooms is of minor interest, though they do include an excellent Gibbons overmantle in the Queen's Private Bedchamber (which, unusually, could be locked from the inside). Last of all, you enter the **Queen's Private Oratory**, used by Queen Caroline for private worship – it's one of the few windowless rooms, hence the octagonal dome and skylight.

William III's Apartments

William III's Apartments are approached via the **King's Staircase**, the grandest of the lot thanks chiefly to Verrio's busy, militaristic trompe-l'oeil paintings glorifying the king, depicted here as Alexander the Great. The **King's Guard Chamber** is notable chiefly for its three thousand-piece display of arms, arranged as they were laid out in the time of William III. William's rather modest throne still stands in the **King's Presence Chamber**, under a canopy of crimson damask. The sixteenth-century Brussels tapestries in the room were originally commissioned by Henry VIII for Whitehall Palace.

Further on, in the **King's Privy Chamber**, there's a much grander throne used by William, with a silk and gold lace canopy that still retains its original ostrich feathers. The most impressive room here is the **Great Bed Chamber**, which boasts a superb vertical Gibbons frieze and ceiling paintings by Verrio – just as you're leaving this floor, you'll catch a glimpse of a splendidly throne-like velvet toilet. Ground-floor highlights include a semi-nude portrait by Van Dyck of his mistress Margaret Lemon, in the East

Closet, the **Lower Orangery**, built to house the queen's orange trees during the winter. Past here is the **King's Private Dining Room**, its table laden with pyramids of meringues and fruit and its walls hung with eight full-length portraits of Queen Mary's favourite ladies-in-waiting (known as the "Hampton Court Beauties"), for which the German-born painter Godfrey Kneller received a knighthood.

Young Henry VIII's Story

Several early Tudor rooms, with striking linenfold panelling and gilded strapwork ceilings, are now used to display **Young Henry VIII's Story**. This is a worthy attempt by the palace to portray Henry in his virile youth, during his happy, twenty-year marriage to his first wife, Catherine of Aragon. Interactive screens help tell the story of the Battle of the Spurs at Guinegate in 1613, when Henry led his troops from the front, and of the Field of the Cloth of Gold, Henry's famous meeting with the French king, François I, in 1620.

Henry VIII's Kitchens

After a surfeit of opulent interiors, the workaday **Tudor Kitchens** come as something of a relief. Henry VIII quadrupled the size of the kitchens, large sections of which have survived to this day and have been restored and embellished with historical reconstructions. Past the Boiling Room and Flesh Larder (not for squeamish vegetarians) you come to the **Great Kitchen**, where a fire is still lit in the main hearth every day. This kitchen is only one of three Henry built to cope with the prodigious consumption of the royal court – six oxen, forty sheep and a thousand or more larks, pheasants, pigeons and peacocks were an average daily total. The tour ends in Henry's vast **Wine Cellar**, where the palace's Rhineland wine was stored. At each main meal, the king and his special guests would be supplied with eight pints of wine; courtiers had to make do with three gallons of beer.

The Gardens

The gardens' magnificent **Broad Walk** runs for half a mile from the Thames past Wren's austere East Front to the putti-encrusted Flower Pot Gate, and is lined with some of the country's finest Victorian herbaceous borders. Halfway along lies the indoor **Royal Tennis Court**, established here by Wolsey (a keen player of Real Tennis himself), but extensively restored by Charles II. If you're lucky, you might even catch a game of this arcane precursor of modern tennis, though the rules are incredibly tricky.

Fanning out from the Broad Walk is William's **Fountain Garden**, a grand, semicircular parterre, which in William's day featured box hedges, thirteen fountains and dwarf yew trees pruned to look like obelisks. A fair number of these "black pyramids", as Virginia Woolf called them, have been reduced to chubby cone shapes, while a solitary pool stands in place of the fountains, and the box hedges have become plain lawns. A semicircular canal separates the Fountain Garden from the Home Park beyond, its waters feeding Charles II's **Long Water**, Hampton Court's most Versaillean feature, which slices the Home Park in two.

Privy Garden

Overlooked by Wren's magnificent South Front is the formal **Privy Garden**, laid out as it would have been under William III; the twelve magnificent wrought-iron panels at the river end of the garden are the work of Jean Tijou. To the west, you can peek into the **Pond Gardens**, which were originally constructed as ornamental fish ponds stocked with freshwater fish for the kitchens, and feature some of the gardens' most spectacularly colourful flowerbeds. Further along, protected by glass, is the palace's celebrated **Great Vine**, grown from a cutting in 1768 by Capability Brown and averaging about seven hundred pounds of Black Hamburg grapes per year (sold at the palace in September).

Close by stands the **Lower Orangery**, designed by Wren and used as a dimly lit gallery for *The Triumphs of Caesar*, a series of heroic canvases by **Andrea Mantegna**, bought by Charles I in 1629 and kept here ever since. Painted around 1486 for the Ducal Palace in Mantua, Mantegna's home town, these nine richly coloured paintings, depicting the general's victory parade, are among his best works, characterized by his obsessive interest in archeological and historical accuracy. Beyond the South Gardens, beside the river, is William III's dinky little red-brick **Banqueting House**, built for intimate riverside soirees, with castellations and mouldings by Gibbons and exuberant paintings by Verrio.

The Maze

To the north of the palace, Henry VIII laid out a **Tiltyard** with five towers for watching jousting tournaments, one of which survives near the garden restaurant. William III transformed the tiltyard into a **Wilderness** – an informal park of evergreens – which now contains the most famous feature of the palace gardens, the deceptively tricky trapezoidal **Maze**, laid out in 1714. Mazes, or labyrinths as they were called at the time, were used by pilgrims, who used to crawl along on hands and knees reciting prayers, as penance for not making a pilgrimage to the Holy Land. They were all the rage among the eighteenth-century nobility, who used them primarily for amusement, secret conversations and flirtation. The maze was originally planted with hornbeam, but, with the onset of the tourist boom in the 1960s, the hornbeam had to be replaced with yew.

Bushy Park

Beyond the Lion Gates, to the north of the Maze, across Hampton Court Road, lies **Bushy Park**, the palace's semi-wild enclosure of over a thousand acres, which sustains copious herds of fallow and red deer. Wren's mile-long royal road, Chestnut Avenue, cuts through the park, and is at its best in May when the trees are in blossom. The main architectural feature of the park is the **Diana Fountain**, situated a third of the way along the avenue to help break the monotony. The statue – which, in fact, depicts Arethusa – was commissioned by Charles II from Francesco Fanelli and originally graced the Privy Garden; stranded in the centre of this vast pond, she looks ill-proportioned and a bit forlorn.

Off to the west, a little further up the avenue, you'll come upon the **Waterhouse Woodland Gardens**, created in 1949, and at their most colourful each spring when the rhododendrons, azaleas and camellias are in bloom. The crowds are fairly thin even here, compared with the crush around the palace, but if you really want to seek out some of the park's abundant wildlife head for its wilder western section, where few visitors venture.

Accommodation

Accommodation in London is expensive. Compared with most European cities, you pay top dollar in every category from the cheapest hostel to the swankiest five-star. Add to that the fact that most B&Bs and many hotels are housed in historic, formerly residential properties – so rooms tend to be small, bathrooms are tiny and lifts are rare – and it's understandable that some unprepared visitors come away feeling shortchanged. With a little savvy, however, you can get some great deals – just don't expect a mansion for the price of a garret. Remember that rooms with shared facilities may be larger than en-suites, where showers and loos are often shoehorned into tiny corners. In some of the newer breed of boutique guesthouses, small needn't mean inconvenient anyhow – bijou can be great fun when delivered with wit and style in a buzzy location.

Talking of **location**, bear in mind that travelling around London is not that difficult with an Oyster card and a tube map. While the central London hotels are the hippest and the most exciting, the prices reflect this, and it may suit you better to head out of zone 1, especially if you're not short of time.

Demand for beds is so great that the city doesn't really have a **low season**, though things do slacken off a little in the months just after Christmas.

ESSENTIALS

Costs London's hostels are among the costliest in the world, while an astonishing number of hotels charge guests the very top international prices – from £300 per luxurious night. Even the most basic B&Bs struggle to bring their tariffs below £90 for a double with shared facilities, which is why so many people head for the budget chain hotels (see p.356) for a cheap sleep. For a decent hotel room, you shouldn't expect much change out of £100 a night. That said, even the basic places tend to have TVs, tea- and coffee-making facilities and telephones, and breakfast is very often included in the price. Many of the more upmarket hotels quote expensive walk-in or rack rates, but there are usually deals to be had online and there may be additional low-season discounts. You'll get the best prices by booking online well in advance.

Useful websites You can book accommodation for free online at ⓦlondontown.com; payment is made directly to the hotel and they offer very good discounts. Other useful websites for last-minute offers include ⓦlaterooms.com and ⓦlastminute.com.

Alternative accommodation If you want to live like a local, try the network of rooms and flats, often in interesting locations, offered via ⓦairbnb.co.uk. ⓦcouchsurfing.com puts travellers in touch with people to stay or hang out with for free, while going upmarket, ⓦonefinestay.com offers luxurious "unhotels" – posh private residences with all manner of guest services thrown in.

British Hotel Reservation Centre (BHRC) If you arrive without having made plans (which is *not* a good idea), head for the BHRC (24hr helpline ☎020 7592 3055, ⓦbhrc.co.uk) desks at Heathrow airport, Victoria bus station and St Pancras and Victoria train stations. BHRC offices are open daily from early till late, and there's no booking fee – they can also get big discounts at the more upmarket hotels.

23

HOTELS AND B&BS

The bulk of the recommendations here cost between £110 and £170 a double, though there are some good basic options for under £100. Prices listed are the quoted rack rates for the **cheapest double room** in mid-summer; even these should be taken as a rule of thumb, however – you may be able to get rooms more cheaply at the last minute, or if booked well in advance, depending on the day of the week and availability.

WHITEHALL AND WESTMINSTER

B&B Belgravia 64–66 Ebury St, SW1 ☎020 7259 8570, ⓦbb-belgravia.com; ⊖ Victoria; map p.36. A rarity in this neck of the woods – a light and well-designed B&B with flair, very close to the train and coach stations. The seventeen simple rooms have original features and modern styling; those on the ground floor can be noisy, however. They also offer nearby studios from £135. Comfy guest lounge with tea and coffee, garden, free wi-fi and bike loan; unusually, dogs are allowed. **£130**

Cherry Court Hotel 23 Hugh St, SW1 ☎020 7828 2840, ⓦcherrycourthotel.co.uk; ⊖ Victoria; map p.36. Very inexpensive, mid-terrace Victorian B&B on a quiet street, with amiable staff, clean rooms and a small garden. The rooms are tiny, but all are en suite and there are triples (£105) and a family room sleeping five (£130). The in-room breakfast is minimal – a fresh fruit basket – but there are tea and coffee facilities, plus free wi-fi. **£68**

★ **Luna & Simone Hotel** 47–49 Belgrave Rd, SW1 ☎020 7834 5897, ⓦlunasimonehotel.com; ⊖ Victoria; map p.36. Family-run guesthouse with a bright foyer, friendly staff, colourful touches and spruce, well-maintained if unexciting en-suite rooms, including triples (£180) and quads (£200). The full English breakfasts are substantial, and there's free wi-fi. **£130**

★ **Morgan Guesthouse** 120 Ebury St, SW1 ☎020 7730 2384, ⓦmorganhouse.co.uk; ⊖ Victoria; map p.36. Brilliantly located a short hop from Chelsea, this is a lovely B&B in a peaceful Georgian building. The sizeable, spotless rooms all have character and most are en suite; the family room crams in a double and a bunk bed. Full breakfasts are served in a pretty room; free wi-fi in the lobby. **£135**

St Ermin's Hotel 2 Caxton St, SW1 ☎020 7222 7888, ⓦsterminshotel.co.uk; ⊖ St James's Park; map p.36. Set in a sturdy Victorian mansion block, this large, peaceful hotel (part of the *Marriott* group) manages to maintain both a sense of place and a sense of history – check out the tiled floors and the MPs' bell in the stunning white plaster-encrusted lobby, which was traditionally rung to call MP guests back to parliament. The modern rooms are tasteful and comfortable. Wi-fi costs extra. **£220**

Sanctuary House Hotel 33 Tothill St, SW1 ☎020 7799 4044, ⓦsanctuaryhousehotel.co.uk; ⊖ St James's Park; map p.36. Fuller's pubs run a number of hotels in London; this one has a terrific location by St James's Park. The 34 rooms, despite being above the drinking action, are quiet enough, decked out in uncontroversial modern boutique styling. Breakfast is extra, and served in the pub. Free wi-fi. **£135**

ST JAMES'S

41 Hotel 41 Buckingham Palace Rd, SW1 ☎020 7300 0041, ⓦ41hotel.com; ⊖ Victoria; map p.66. Intimate boutique chic with thirty individually decorated rooms opposite the Royal Mews. Some rooms are tiny, some have open fires, but they're all decorated in black and white. Service is highly attentive – it's not a place for anyone who values anonymity. **£350**

MARYLEBONE

Lincoln House 33 Gloucester Place, W1 ☎020 7486 7630, ⓦlincoln-house-hotel.com; ⊖ Marble Arch or Baker Street; map p.89. Warm-hearted guesthouse in one of Marylebone's lovely Georgian terraces: beyond the eccentric, vaguely nautical, public spaces, the well-equipped en-suite rooms all have a dash of style, though walls can be thin. Rates vary from day to day; there are some excellent online discounts. Breakfast costs extra; you can have it served in your room or in the little budget dining room downstairs (also serving dinner). Free wi-fi. **£110**

Sumner Hotel 54 Upper Berkeley St, W1 ☎020 7723 2244, ⓦthesumner.com; ⊖ Marble Arch; map p.89. A spruce, friendly guesthouse – with boutique hotel aspirations – in an elegant townhouse. The twenty rooms vary in size and style – the best are light and modern, some are very small, some have tiny balconies, those at the back are quieter – but all are tasteful and comfortable, and there's a tranquil, well-equipped sitting room for guests. A hot buffet breakfast is included. Free wi-fi. **£170**

SOHO AND FITZROVIA

Charlotte Street Hotel 15–17 Charlotte St, W1 ☎020 7806 2000, ⓦfirmdale.com; ⊖ Goodge Street or Tottenham Court Road; map p.97. Swanky Georgian townhouse hotel in a restaurant-filled street just north of Oxford St. It's from the designer boutique hotel stable *Firmdale*, which also has gorgeous properties in Soho and Covent Garden (see p.358), which are pricier, and in South Ken, Knightsbridge, Piccadilly and St John's Wood, which are around the same price. Public spaces are lined with Bloomsbury-set originals, while the quiet, English eccentric and decidedly un-minimal rooms have sumptuous fittings, Tivoli radios, DVD players and the like. There's a gym, a restaurant (popular for afternoon tea) and a cinema that hosts a popular Sunday movie club. Free wi-fi. **£265**

★ **Dean Street Townhouse** 69–71 Dean St, W1 ☎020 7434 1775, ⓦdeanstreettownhouse.com; ⊖ Tottenham Court Road or Leicester Square; map p.100. One of a chic set of hotels owned by the trendy Soho House members' club, this relaxed 1730s beauty sits next to its starry, stylishly bohemian dining room. There's a split-level "broom cupboard" and a few "tiny" rooms (from £160) – manageable if you're just staying one night – but the "small" (from £180) rooms are ample, and once you get to "medium" and "bigger" you have plenty of space. Each is different and all are luxurious, with gorgeous details

BUDGET CHAINS

Chain hotels have pretty much got the **budget hotel** market sewn up. B&Bs may be able to offer a more personal touch and more character, but the franchises are often – though not always – cheaper, in unbeatable central locations, and guarantee clean, no-surprises rooms.

Bumping along at the bottom is *easyHotel* (ⓦeasyhotel.com), whose prices start at just £29 for a tiny en-suite double with no window – the earlier you book the less you pay, and if you want a window, wi-fi, TV use or room cleaning, it's extra; there are branches in South Ken, Paddington, Victoria, Earl's Court and Barbican. Operating under similar terms, offering a base rate with add-ons, the Asian *Tune* chain offers stylish minimalism in Westminster (see p.360), Liverpool Street, Paddington and King's Cross, with prices starting at around £50.

It's worth checking rates at *Travelodge* (ⓦtravelodge.co.uk), which can be found all over town, with handy locations in Covent Garden, King's Cross, Euston, Waterloo, Marylebone and Southwark; rooms are utilitarian, but if you book online well in advance, en-suite doubles can cost less than £60. *Premier Inn* (ⓦpremierinn.com) is generally considered a cut above *Travelodge*, and also has good online bargains; locations are good, too, with branches in Leicester Square (quite expensive), by County Hall, near Tate Modern, by the Tower of London, in Hampstead and King's Cross, among many others. If you want a quick nap at the airport – either Heathrow or Gatwick – *Yotel* (ⓦyotel.com) cabin rooms are handy. You pay for as long as you stay, which can work out as little as £60 per night – for this you get a bed (or a bunk) in a capsule, complete with tiny toilet and monsoon shower, foldout desk and TV (and free wi-fi). The rest of the chain gang aren't worth considering – you can get better value elsewhere.

including handpainted wallpaper, posh toiletries, fresh milk and cookies, and clawfoot tubs, some of them in the bedrooms themselves. Free wi-fi. **£110**

Grange Langham Court Hotel 31–35 Langham St, W1 ☎ 020 7436 6622, ⓦ grangehotels.com; ⊖ Oxford Circus; map p.97. Rooms may be tiny at this fifty-room hotel in a quiet location near Regent St, but they're clean, modern and comfortable, and the price, for this location, is reasonable. **£130**

★ **Hazlitt's** 6 Frith St, W1 ☎ 020 7434 1771, ⓦ hazlittshotel.com; ⊖ Tottenham Court Road; map p.100. Off the south side of Soho Square, this early eighteenth-century building hides away a hotel of extraordinary character and charm. Creaky, crooked old stairs lead up to romantic en-suite rooms, exquisitely and quirkily decorated with period furniture and old books. A continental breakfast (not included) is served in your room. **£250**

Nadler Soho 10 Carlisle St, W1 ☎ 020 3697 3697, ☎ thenadler.com; ⊖ Tottenham Court Road; map p.100. Glossy new hotel offering reasonable prices for this premium location. Rooms are modern, if unexciting (the cheapest are pretty small), but each has a microwave, fridge and kettle – along with coffee machine – so you could effectively self-cater. A bagged breakfast is provided from the superb *Fernandez & Wells* (see p.369). Free wi-fi. **£160**

One Leicester Street 1 Leicester St, WC2 ☎ 020 3301 8020, ⓦ oneleicesterstreet.com; ⊖ Leicester Square; map p.100. Rooms in the heart of Chinatown, providing diners at the restaurant downstairs – helmed by Tom Harris of the *St John* stable (see p.370) – an opportunity to sleep off their snail and sweetbread feasts. The fifteen rooms are fresh, contemporary, minimal and stylish. Free wi-fi. **£180**

BLOOMSBURY

Arosfa Hotel 83 Gower St, WC1 ☎ 020 7636 2115, ⓦ arosfalondon.com; ⊖ Goodge Street or Euston Square; map p.120. Though the public spaces are relatively swish, the fifteen en-suite rooms in this popular, friendly B&B are basic and some are very small. But it's clean, comfortable and homely, with TVs, tea and coffee facilities, and a little garden out back. Free wi-fi in the guest lounge. **£107**

Jesmond Hotel 63 Gower St, WC1 ☎ 020 7636 3199, ⓦ jesmondhotel.org.uk; ⊖ Goodge Street; map p.120. Very good-value Bloomsbury hotel with a peaceful little garden. Rooms are clean but can be on the small side; staff are unfailingly friendly and they'll do your laundry for £7.50. Six of the fifteen rooms (from singles to rooms sleeping five) have shared facilities. Full breakfast; free wi-fi in the lounge. **£85**

Morgan Hotel 24 Bloomsbury St, WC1 ☎ 020 7636 3735, ⓦ morganhotel.co.uk; ⊖ Tottenham Court Road; map p.120. A reliable guesthouse, right by the British Museum, with functional, clean and comfortable

rooms – including a few apartment suites, sleeping from one to four people. **£135**

★ **Ridgemount Hotel** 65–67 Gower St, WC1 ☎ 020 7636 1141, ⓦ ridgemounthotel.co.uk; ⊖ Goodge Street; map p.120. Old-fashioned, friendly and popular family-owned B&B, faded but clean, with a variety of rooms (around half of the 33 have shared facilities – which are spotless, and sizeable). The smallest rooms (very small!) are cosy; family rooms available. Full breakfast and free wi-fi. **£78**

KING'S CROSS

Great Northern Hotel Pancras Rd, N1C ☎ 020 3388 0800, ⓦ gnhlondon.com; ⊖ King's Cross St Pancras; map p.120. With King's Cross/St Pancras continuing to blossom as a railway hub, and following in the wake of the *St Pancras Renaissance* (see below), the *Great Northern*, another lovely old Victorian railway hotel, re-opened in 2013. It offers a fresher, hipper vibe than its stately neighbour, with a vaguely Deco feel, and unusually for a luxury hotel, extras – including wi-fi, plus coffee, pastries, books and mags in the "pantries" on each floor – are free. All the ninety or so boutiquey rooms have huge windows; the smallest, "couchettes", turn their diminutive size into a positive by evoking the romance of a railway sleeper. The huge bar is modelled on a buzzing French railway station brasserie, and the Modern European restaurant, *Plum + Spilt Milk*, is excellent. **£150**

Rough Luxe 1 Birkenhead St, WC1 ☎ 020 7837 5338, ⓦ roughluxe.co.uk; ⊖ King's Cross St Pancras; map p.120. In an unlikely setting on the gentrifying streets of King's Cross, this high-concept nine-room hotel offers warmth, comfort and über shabby chic. Each room is different, and some are minuscule, but the arty, nostalgic aesthetic – ripped wallpaper and peeling plaster, the odd vintage TV, original artworks, creaky old floorboards – runs throughout. A posh continental breakfast is served. Free wi-fi. **£170**

St Pancras Renaissance Euston Rd, NW1 ☎ 020 7841 3540, ⓦ marriott.co.uk/hotels/travel/lonpr-st-pancras; ⊖ King's Cross St Pancras; map p.120. George Gilbert Scott's Gothic Revival masterpiece (see p.129), now a five-star *Marriott* hotel, is certainly a thrilling spectacle – the lofty public spaces and colossal lobby evoke the golden era of railway travel, and old-style glamour seeps from every surface. It's only worth staying in the main building, though – which has fewer than fifty of the 250 or so rooms – these, with their arched windows and high ceilings, and slight rumblings from the station below, might justify the stratospheric prices. The others are in an annexe behind, and better value can be found elsewhere. The atmospheric, expensive, bar is a destination in itself. Online deals and *Marriott* promotions can halve the rack rates. Wi-fi costs extra. **£275**

23

COVENT GARDEN AND THE STRAND

Covent Garden Hotel 10 Monmouth St, WC2 ☎ 020 7806 1000, ⓦ firmdale.com; ⊖ Covent Garden or Leicester Square; map p.132. Another gorgeous and luxurious boutique hotel from the *Firmdale* group (see p.356), housed in an old French hospital in a characterful location. This one feels clubbier and cosier than the others, without losing the designer details; there's a cool in-house cinema and an upmarket brasserie. Unusually, they offer free wi-fi. **£396**

The Fielding 4 Broad Court, Bow St, WC2 ☎ 020 7836 8305, ⓦ www.thefieldinghotel.co.uk; ⊖ Covent Garden; map p.132. On a pedestrianized court opposite the Royal Opera House, this hotel is delightfully quiet for central London. Its en-suite rooms are simple, but clean – the refurbished ones are more stylish than others – and a firm favourite with visiting performers. No lift and no breakfast (tea and coffee in room). Free wi-fi. **£140**

The Savoy Strand, WC2 ☎ 020 7836 4343, ⓦ fairmont .com/savoy-london/; ⊖ Covent Garden or Charing Cross; map p.132. This iconic Art Deco hotel, dripping with history, is glamorous and a little flashy, with classic bars and gorgeously comfortable rooms. Even if you can't afford to stay, you might splash out on a classic afternoon tea (a cool £48). **£350**

Seven Dials Hotel 7 Monmouth St, WC2 ☎ 020 7681 0791, ⓦ sevendialshotellondon.com; ⊖ Covent Garden; map p.132. A friendly, family-run B&B brilliantly located on one of Covent Garden's nicest streets. It's in no way fancy: the staircase is narrow and steep (no lift) and the en-suite rooms (from singles to quads) are small, but all are clean, well equipped and comfy, and you're made to feel at home. Free wi-fi. **£105**

CLERKENWELL

★ **The Rookery** 12 Peter's Lane, Cowcross St, EC1 ☎ 020 7336 0931, ⓦ rookeryhotel.com; ⊖ Farringdon; map p.150. This rambling Georgian townhouse, all panelled walls, flagstoned floors and creaky timeworn floorboards, makes a charming bolthole in trendy Clerkenwell. Rooms, some of which are a little dark, offer faded Baroque glam, with antique fittings and super bathrooms. Breakfast, not included in the price, is served in your room, though there's a comfy lounge with honesty bar. There's even a hotel cat. **£210**

TOP 5 HIDEAWAYS

40 Winks East London. See p.360
The Fielding Covent Garden. See above
Hazlitt's Soho. See p.357
The King's Wardrobe The City. See opposite
The Rookery Clerkenwell. See above

The Zetter Hotel & Townhouse 86–88 Clerkenwell Rd, EC1 ☎ 020 7324 4444, ⓦ thezetter.com; ⊖ Farringdon; map p.150. The sixty-room hotel, in a warehouse converted with style and a dash of 1960s glamour, is a fixture on Clerkenwell's hipster scene. Rooms are simple, modern and bold, with colourful panache and lots of eco touches; because of its popular bar and bistro, some rooms suffer from noise at night. The Georgian *Townhouse*, across the square, is if anything even more whimsical, with thirteen colourful, boudoirish rooms and a fabulous, cosy bar. Free wi-fi, and free continental breakfast if you book online. Hotel **£160**, Townhouse **£180**

THE CITY

Andaz 40 Liverpool St, EC2 ☎ 020 7961 1234, ⓦ london.liverpoolstreet.andaz.hyatt.com; ⊖ Liverpool Street; map pp.156–157. The venerable 1884 *Great Eastern Hotel* by Liverpool Street Station had a complete makeover in 2000 to become the first in *Hyatt's* stylish worldwide *Andaz* hotel group. Rooms are unfussy and minimal, with a complimentary (non-alcoholic) minibar and free wi-fi, and service is so fashion-forward that there's not even a reception desk – you relax on a plush sofa while check-in staff, brandishing iPads, come to you. The six restaurants and bars keep the place buzzing, and service is excellent. **£240**

Apex City of London Hotel 1 Seething Lane, EC3 ☎ 020 7977 9593, ⓦ apexhotels.co.uk; ⊖ Tower Hill; map pp.156–157. A swish, comfortable and nicely appointed modern hotel on a secluded City street near the Tower of London. It's geared towards a corporate clientele, but has a good variety of rooms – the priciest have great views – and service is superb. Rates vary according to availability so book early. Free wi-fi. There are two other branches nearby – *Apex London Wall* (7–9 Copthall Ave, EC2; ⊖ Moorgate) and *Apex Temple Court*, near Fleet St (1 Serjeants' Inn, EC4; ⊖ Temple) – whose prices tend to be a little higher. **£130**

Doubletree by Hilton London – Tower of London 7 Pepys St, EC3 ☎ 020 7709 1000, ⓦ doubletree3 .hilton.com; ⊖ Tower Hill; map pp.156–157. Though it's geared towards business travellers, this large, modern and bright hotel is a good option for all. Rooms – nearly 600 of them – are clean, airy and comfortable, all with iMacs. The rooftop bar, *Skylounge*, offers amazing views. Online promotions bring good discounts. Free wi-fi. **£220**

The King's Wardrobe 6 Wardrobe Place, Carter Lane, EC4 ☎ 020 7792 2222, ⓦ bridgestreet.com; ⊖ St Paul's; map pp.156–157. In a quiet courtyard just behind St Paul's Cathedral, these serviced studios and apartments prove exceptionally good value. It's a favourite with business visitors – fully equipped kitchens, workstations, concierge service and housekeeping are standard, and

23

some have fabulous views. Though housed in a fourteenth-century building that once contained Edward III's royal regalia, the interior is modern. **£150**

EAST LONDON

Boundary Hotel 2–4 Boundary St, E2 ☎020 7729 1051, ⓦtheboundary.co.uk; Shoreditch High Street Overground; map pp.192–193. A Terence Conran creation, this slick Shoreditch hotel offers seventeen funky rooms, each themed on different design styles from Eames to Shaker, and most of them offering ample space. There are two good, lively restaurants on site – the *Albion* (British), and the *Boundary* (French) and a stunning all-weather rooftop bar (see p.391). Free wi-fi. **£170**

40 Winks 109 Mile End Rd, E1 ☎020 7790 0259, ⓦ40winks.org; ⊖ Stepney Green; map p.190. To stay here – in the early eighteenth-century home of interior designer David Carter – is to enter a fairytale world. Witty, theatrical and achingly beautiful, it offers all the wow factor of a magazine lifestyle shoot, but with real creature comforts. The only problems may be snagging a room – there are just two, a single (£110) and a large double, sharing a jaw-droppingly glamorous bathroom – and living up to the stunning surroundings (it's a shoe-free house, so make sure your socks are clean). Free wi-fi in the common areas. **£185**

Hoxton Hotel 81 Great Eastern St, EC2 ☎020 7550 1000, ⓦhoxtonhotels.com; ⊖ Old Street; map pp.192–193. "The Hox" is an established, youthful hotel in this nightlife neighbourhood, with modern but warm public spaces – all exposed brick and burnished metal – and comfy boutique rooms. Downstairs, the *Hoxton Grill* and the DJ bar are popular hangouts – there's a party vibe down here and it can be noisy, so ask for a quiet room if you value your sleep. A light breakfast is delivered to your room, wi-fi is free, you get an hour's free local calls a day and they also lend out bikes. Rates depend entirely on availability; you might pay as little as £79 or as much as £199. **£120**

Shoreditch Rooms Shoreditch House, Ebor St, E1 ☎020 7739 5040, ⓦshoreditchhouse.com/bedrooms; Shoreditch High Street Overground; map pp.192–193. Linked to the Shoreditch House members' club, and from the same stable as the *Dean Street Townhouse* (see p.356) this hip little place has the same no-nonsense room-naming policy, with 26 options from "Tiny" up to "Small-plus", which have minuscule balconies. Rooms may be small but they're comfy and beautifully designed, with lots of tongue-and-groove, fresh, sunbleached colours and vintage tiled bathrooms; there's a Cowshed spa, rooftop pool and restaurants at the members' club next door, where you can hang out with the beautiful media types and where, refreshingly, no mobile phones (and no suits!) are allowed. **£125**

DOCKLANDS

Four Seasons Hotel Canary Wharf 46 Westferry Circus, E14 ☎020 7510 1999, ⓦfourseasons.com/canarywharf; Westferry DLR or ⊖ Canary Wharf; map pp.206–207. A spectacular riverfront setting, sleek modern interiors and good links to the City (including the option of taking a boat into town) make this hotel popular with business folk, while good-value weekend rates make it a feasible base for sightseeing. Service is impeccable, and there's access to a good pool, gym, spa and tennis courts. Several rooms have Thames views. **£160**

THE SOUTH BANK

★ **Captain Bligh House** 100 Lambeth Rd, SE1 (no phone), ⓦcaptainblighhouse.co.uk; ⊖ Lambeth North; map p.216. Captain Bligh's former house can now be your home from home – a charming, cosy Georgian building, opposite the Imperial War Museum and a short walk from the South Bank, run by a friendly, though wonderfully unobtrusive, couple. The four rooms are all very different, varying in size, but each is comfortable and stylish, and they all have kitchenettes. Rates are low, but there's a four-night minimum. No cards. **£90**

Mad Hatter 3–7 Stamford St, SE1 ☎020 7401 9222, ⓦmadhatterhotel.co.uk; ⊖ Southwark or Blackfriars; map p.216. Good-value Fuller's hotel with thirty clean and comfy en-suite rooms, above a Fuller's pub, in an old hat factory. This is a great location, a short walk from Tate Modern and the South Bank, and staff are friendly. Free wi-fi. **£120**

Tune Westminster 118–120 Westminster Bridge Rd, SE1 ☎020 7633 9317, ⓦtunehotels.com; ⊖ Lambeth North or Waterloo; map p.216. The first London branch of the Malaysian chain ("five-star beds at one-star prices"), whose minimal modern rooms and down-to-earth pricing policy have made it a firm favourite. It's a clever idea: by doing away with niceties like tables, chairs and closets, prices stay low and you simply opt to pay for extras, including towels, TV, hairdryers and wi-fi, on the easy-to-use booking site. Rooms are capsule-style, but well designed and bright, with comfy beds and spotless showers; the very cheapest are windowless and rather small. The other three branches (see p.356) are slightly cheaper. **£65**

SOUTHWARK

★ **Citizen M Bankside** 20 Lavington St, SE1 ☎020 3519 1680, ⓦcitizenm.com/london-bankside; ⊖ Southwark; map pp.226–227. Though the high-design concept may jar a bit – guests are "citizens" and staff are "ambassadors", check-in is super-cool airport-style – this is a good option, part of a growing European chain, with 200 compact rooms with a modern, pod-like design, hi-tech touch tablet room controls and smart storage solutions. The public spaces tick all the lifestyle mag choices – Eames chairs, block colours, coffee table books – while managing to be comfy and welcoming, and staff are great. The buzzing restaurant/bar is handy, too. More London branches are planned. Free wi-fi and movies. **£160**

Ibis Styles London Southwark Rose 43–47 Southwark Bridge Rd, SE1 ☎ 020 7015 1480, �🖳 ibis.com; ⊖ London Bridge; map pp.226–227. The *Southwark Rose* has funky design touches that raise the rooms a little above the bland chain hotels in the area, and rooms are comfortable and generally spacious. Don't expect much more, though a buffet breakfast is included in rates, which vary widely depending on availability. Free wi-fi. **£110**

London Bridge Hotel 8–18 London Bridge St, SE1 ☎ 020 7855 2200, �🖳 londonbridgehotel.com; ⊖ London Bridge; map pp.226–227. Perfectly placed for Southwark and Bankside or the City, this is a plush, contemporary, independent hotel in a Victorian building in the heart of things right by the station and the Shard. Free wi-fi. **£200**

HYDE PARK AND KENSINGTON GARDENS

Columbia Hotel 95–99 Lancaster Gate, W2 ☎ 020 7402 0021, ⚇ columbiahotel.co.uk; ⊖ Lancaster Gate; map p.240. This large, old-fashioned hotel, once five Victorian houses, offers en-suite singles, doubles, triples and quads, some with views over Hyde Park. It's all a bit dated, but comfortable and good value; the bar, and the public lounge, have a certain faded charm. Free wi-fi in lobby and bar. **£105**

Kensington House Hotel 15–16 Prince of Wales Terrace, W8 ☎ 020 7937 2345, ⚇ kenhouse.com; ⊖ High Street Kensington; map p.240. Little details help give this independent hotel, brilliantly located in a nineteenth-century townhouse near Kensington Gardens, a personal touch. The en-suite rooms are smallish, and worn in places, but light, clean and contemporary; some have tiny balconies. A good continental breakfast is included. Free wi-fi. **£156**

SOUTH KENSINGTON AND CHELSEA

Aster House 3 Sumner Place, SW7 ☎ 020 7581 5888, ⚇ asterhouse.com; ⊖ South Kensington; map pp.250–251. Friendly, upmarket B&B, wonderfully located in a luxurious South Ken white-stuccoed street; one of the thirteen rooms opens out onto the back garden (complete with little pond), and there's a conservatory, where the hot buffet breakfast is served. Note there's no lift to get to the top-floor rooms. Free wi-fi, though service is patchy. **£190**

Myhotel Chelsea 35 Ixworth Place, SW3 ☎ 020 7225 7500, ⚇ myhotels.com; ⊖ South Kensington; map p.265. Though the slightly cheap-looking decor isn't to everyone's taste, rooms (which vary wildly in size) are well equipped and comfortable, staff are friendly and the

atmosphere is generally peaceful. Above all, though, the prices are not to be sniffed at in this area, and online deals are excellent. Free wi-fi. **£120**

EARL'S COURT AND FULHAM

★ **Barclay House** 21 Barclay Rd, SW6 ☎ 07767 420943, ⚇ barclayhouselondon.com; ⊖ Fulham Broadway; map pp.250–251. Small Fulham B&B – just three rooms, one of them a single – in a quiet street near the tube. Though quite luxurious – the spotless rooms have oak flooring and fancy Philippe Starck-designed bathrooms – it's comfortable and relaxed, run by friendly hosts; there's a small shared kitchen area, filled with home-made pastries, bread, tea and coffee, so you can have breakfast when you like, perhaps on the roof terrace if the weather is good. Usually a four- or five-night minimum stay. Free wi-fi. **£110**

Nadler Kensington 25 Courtfield Gardens, SW5 ☎ 020 7244 2255, ⚇ thenadler.com/kensington.shtml; ⊖ Earl's Court; map pp.250–251. Excellent-value accommodation, with no fussy extras. Rooms range from "bijou singles" via "luxury bunks" to "deluxe"; all are comfortable, clean and quiet, modern and attractive, with mini-kitchens and free wi-fi. A good choice for groups and families. **£150**

Twenty Nevern Square 20 Nevern Square, SW5 ☎ 020 7565 9555, ⚇ 20nevernsquare.co.uk; ⊖ Earl's Court; map pp.250–251. In an area of bog-standard B&Bs, this is a welcome and inexpensive alternative, a boutique hotel decked out in bold, warm colours and strewn with Oriental and European antiques. Rooms are en suite, comfortable and with good facilities; some, however, are teensy. Continental buffet breakfast included. Free wi-fi. **£85**

HIGH STREET KENSINGTON

Vicarage Hotel 10 Vicarage Gate, W8 ☎ 020 7229 4030, ⚇ londonvicaragehotel.com; ⊖ Notting Hill Gate or High Street Kensington; map pp.274–275. Laidback, quiet B&B on a residential street a step away from Kensington Gardens. The seventeen clean rooms are traditionally decorated and a little old-fashioned; some have shared facilities, and quads are available. A full English breakfast is included. Free wi-fi (in the lounge). **£110**

> ### TOP 5 UNDER £100
>
> **Avo** North London. See p.362
> **Captain Bligh House** The South Bank. See opposite
> **Caring Hotel** Paddington. See p.362
> **Ridgemount Hotel** Bloomsbury. See p.357
> **Tune Westminster** The South Bank. See opposite

23

23

PADDINGTON

★ **Caring Hotel** 24 Craven Hill Gardens, W2 ☎020 7262 8708, ⓦcaringhotel.com; ⊖ Paddington, Bayswater or Lancaster Gate; map pp.274–275. This large, handsome building, in a quiet, leafy residential street, is a popular, reliable guesthouse. Rooms are clean and functional, if unexciting: some have shared facilities, some showers only and others are full en suites. Free wi-fi in public areas, and a free continental breakfast. **£85**

St David's Hotels 14–20 Norfolk Square, W2 ☎020 7723 3856, ⓦstdavidshotels.com; ⊖ Paddington; map pp.274–275. Pleasantly located on a hotel-fringed square, this no-frills budget guesthouse offers a full English breakfast (included in the room rate). Rooms range from singles to good-value family options; all are pretty small and some have shared facilities. Free wi-fi in reception. **£85**

BAYSWATER, WESTBOURNE GROVE AND NOTTING HILL

Garden Court Hotel 30–31 Kensington Gardens Square, W2 ☎020 7229 2553, ⓦgardencourthotel .co.uk; ⊖ Bayswater or Queensway; map pp.274–275. Unfussy, friendly B&B on a nice street close to Portobello Market; some rooms (from singles to triples) are a little tired, but they're clean and comfy, and there's a lift. The cheaper ones have shared facilities. Buffet breakfast included. **£125**

★ **Main House** 6 Colville Rd, W11 ☎020 7221 9691, ⓦthemainhouse.co.uk; ⊖ Ladbroke Grove or Notting Hill Gate; map pp.274–275. You get total privacy in this quirky guesthouse, which manages to be both homely – thanks to some lovely period furniture – and a little bohemian. The suites (two of them have two bedrooms) are huge, covering a whole floor each. Breakfast is not included, but there's a fridge for guests' use and you can have tea/coffee brought to your room; a couple of good local cafés offer special prices for guests. Free wi-fi. Three-night minimum. **£130**

Portobello Gold 95–97 Portobello Rd, W11 ☎020 7460 4910, ⓦportobellogold.com; ⊖ Notting Hill Gate or Holland Park; pp.274–275. Location, in the heart of Portobello Rd, is key at this boho, hostel-style place above a lively pub/restaurant. The rooms are worn but clean and some are tiny, with miniature en-suite bathrooms; those at the back are quieter. There's also an apartment (sleeps six – at a pinch) with a roof terrace, for £150. Continental breakfast included. Free wi-fi. **£75**

Vancouver Studios 30 Prince's Square, W2 ☎020 7243 1270, ⓦvancouverstudios.co.uk; ⊖ Bayswater; map pp.274–275. Comfortable, quiet self-catering suites (from singles to triples, some with balconies) in a grand old Victorian townhouse with maid service, a 24hr reception and a pretty walled garden. Decor is to a high standard, though the public spaces are a bit tired. Free wi-fi. **£120**

NORTH LONDON

★ **Avo** 82 Dalston Lane, E8 ☎020 3490 5061, ⓦavohotel.com; Dalston Junction Overground; map p.291. Offering friendly boutique luxury in the heart of urban Dalston, this family-owned B&B has just six glamorous modern rooms, with lovely bathrooms, and a sweet little bar downstairs. It's all very sociable and cosy, with a DVD lending library, and makes a welcoming base. **£89**

Hampstead Village Guesthouse 2 Kemplay Rd, NW3 ☎020 7435 8679, ⓦhampsteadguesthouse.com; ⊖ Hampstead; map pp.298–299. Prettily located on a quiet backstreet between Hampstead village and the Heath, this is an unconventional guesthouse in a large Victorian home. Rooms (most en suite) are full of character, crammed with books, pictures and handmade and antique furniture – one has a freestanding antique steel bathtub. This is very much a family home, with all the warmth and charm that implies. Breakfast costs £9. The little garage apartment, sleeping five and starting at £115 for one person (£200 for five), is a bargain. **£95**

New Inn 2 Allitsen Rd, NW8 ☎020 7722 0726, ⓦnewinnlondon.co.uk; ⊖ St John's Wood; map p.284. Nothing too fancy here, just a comfortable, clean B&B above a gastropub, just a few minutes' walk from the north edge of Regent's Park. Two of the five en-suite rooms (#2 and #3) are surprisingly large for the price, and bathrooms are sizeable. Breakfast £7.50–11.50. Excellent value. **£85**

Rose and Crown Guesthouse 199 Stoke Newington Church St, N16 ☎020 7923 3337, ⓦroseandcrownn16 .co.uk; ⊖ Manor House or Arsenal; map p.291. Boutique accommodation on lively Church St with its quirky shops, restaurants and bars. Superbly placed above a splendid local pub and opposite Clissold Park, the six rooms are chic, large and luxurious, and although prices seem steep, the quality – including healthy breakfasts, and a roof terrace to chill out on in the evenings – make it worth it. **£120**

SOUTH LONDON

The Lilac Door 140 Rosendale Rd, West Dulwich, SE21 ☎020 8761 8218, ⓦlilacdoor.co.uk; West Dulwich train station; map pp.310–311. Behind the pretty exterior of this elegant Edwardian house – flowers tangled around the eponymous lilac door – are three sleek, modern and light B&B rooms. It's all rather luxurious, with robes, glamorous toiletries and the like, and a leafy garden to enjoy in good weather. Rates include a fabulous continental breakfast. No children under 12. **£100**

Number 16 16 St Alfeges Passage, SE10 ☎020 8853 4337, ⓦst-alfeges.co.uk; Cutty Sark DLR; map p.315. Tucked behind Hawksmoor's St Alfeges church, this welcoming Greenwich B&B – owned by a flamboyant ex-antique dealer/actor – offers a warm welcome, offbeat designer touches and the feel of being in a slightly eccentric home from home. One small single/double and two larger doubles. **£90**

WEST LONDON

The Old Stables 1 Bridle Lane, Twickenham ☏ 020 8892 4507, ⓦ oldestables.com; St Margarets train station from Waterloo; map p.341. Three bedrooms and one studio apartment (sleeping three) in a pretty house in a quiet street right by the train station, walking distance to Richmond and the Thames. No on-site staff, which means you get a lot of privacy, but the friendly, efficient manager is a phone call away, and they provide a complimentary continental breakfast in a small servery with a fridge, kettle and toaster. Rates drop the longer you stay. Doubles **£85**, apartment **£135**

HOSTELS

Hostels run the gamut from the efficient and safe YHA establishments to funkier and more relaxed independent hostels, some of which have a serious party vibe. Virtually all have internet/wi-fi access, and most include breakfast in the price. ⓦ hostellondon.com is a good website for booking online.

YHA HOSTELS

London's Youth Hostel Association (YHA; ⓦ yha.org.uk) hostels are guaranteed to be clean and efficiently run. Their rates depend on availability, special events and the like: dorm prices start at around £19, doubles/twins at £50; wi-fi is available for a fee. Advance booking is recommended. You don't have to be a member of the YHA or an affiliated hostel association to stay (membership costs £16/year), but nonmembers are charged a £3 surcharge per night.

★ **Central** 104 Bolsover St, W1 ☏ 0845 371 9154, ⓔ londoncentral@yha.org.uk; ⊖ Great Portland Street; map p.97. Excellent, secure and clean 300-bed hostel, in a surprisingly quiet West End location, with a kitchen and a late-opening café-bar/lounge area. No groups; families welcome. Most dorms (4–8 beds) are en suite; others have showers next door. Dorms **£23**

Earl's Court 38 Bolton Gardens, SW5 ☏ 0845 371 9114, ⓔ earlscourt@yha.org.uk; ⊖ Earl's Court; map p.250. Buzzy, busy 186-bed hostel with small kitchen, café and patio garden. Dorms **£24**, doubles **£70**

Holland House Holland Walk, W8 ☏ 0845 371 9122, ⓔ hollandhouse@yha.org.uk; ⊖ Holland Park or High Street Kensington; map pp.274–275. Idyllically situated in a Jacobean mansion in Holland Park and fairly convenient for the centre, this 200-bed hostel has a kitchen and café. Popular with groups. Dorms (12–20 beds) only. Dorms **£19**

Lee Valley Windmill Lane, Cheshunt, EN8 ☏ 0845 371 9057, ⓔ leevalley@yha.org.uk; Cheshunt train station. In the 10,000-acre Lee Valley Country Park in deepest North London, this place offers a rural experience in the city, with six waterside log cabins and lots of water-based activities available on the reservoir. Good cycling and birdwatching nearby, too. There's a café-bar, and no self-catering. Rooms are clean and quiet. Dorms **£25**

Oxford Street 14 Noel St, W1 ☏ 0845 371 9133, ⓔ oxfordst@yha.org.uk; ⊖ Oxford Circus or Tottenham Court Road; map p.97. The Soho location and modest size (just 93 beds) mean this hostel tends to be full year-round, and the atmosphere is more party central than family-friendly. No groups, no café, but a large kitchen, and everything is clean. Dorms **£30**, doubles **£80**

St Pancras 79–81 Euston Rd, NW1 ☏ 0845 371 9344, ⓔ stpancras@yha.org.uk; ⊖ King's Cross St Pancras; map p.120. This hostel, on the busy Euston Rd has nearly 200 rooms and is popular with families. Rooms are clean, bright, double-glazed and have en-suite facilities. No kitchen, but there's a nice café. No groups. Dorms **£28**, doubles **£72**

St Paul's 36 Carter Lane, EC4 ☏ 0845 371 9012, ⓔ stpauls@yha.org.uk; ⊖ St Paul's; map pp.156–157. A 210-bed hostel in a superb location opposite St Paul's Cathedral. Breakfast included, in the café, and there's a restaurant for dinner, but no kitchen. No groups. Popular with families. Dorms **£25**, doubles **£75**

Thameside 20 Salter Rd, SE16 ☏ 0845 371 9756, ⓔ thameside@yha.org.uk; ⊖ Rotherhithe; map pp.224–225. London's largest purpose-built hostel, with 320 beds, is in a quiet spot near the river, 15min from the nearest tube. It can feel a bit of a trek, but has space when more central places are full. Self-catering available, and a restaurant serving breakfast and dinner. Dorms (4–10 beds) and doubles. Dorms **£28**, doubles **£50**

INDEPENDENT HOSTELS

Astor hostels Astor Quest, 45 Queensborough Terrace, W2, map p.240; Astor Hyde Park, 191 Queen's Gate, SW7, map p.252; Astor Victoria, 71 Belgrave Rd, SW1, map p.36; Astor Museum Inn, 27 Montague St, WC1, map p.120; ⓦ astorhostels.co.uk. They only take guests aged between 18 and 35, so there's quite a party atmosphere at these four central hostels. All except the *Museum Inn* have en-suite dorms, and all except the *Hyde Park* have female dorms available. There are private rooms at all four; only those at the *Hyde Park* are en suite. Free continental breakfast included, plus use of kitchens and free wi-fi. Dorms (4–12 beds) **£20**, twins/doubles **£80**

Clink 261 Hostel 261–265 Gray's Inn Rd, WC1 ☏ 020 7833 9400, ⓦ clinkhostels.com; ⊖ King's Cross;

23

23

map p.120. Small, quiet hostel in a converted office block near King's Cross/St Pancras, with laundry, kitchen facilities and a very stylish, if tiny, lounge. Dorms – including two female-only dorms (4-bed & 10-bed) – have 4–18 beds and there are private rooms, sleeping up to three, with shared facilities. Breakfast included. Dorms £19, doubles £66

Clink 78 Hostel 78 King's Cross Rd, WC1 ☎020 7183 9400, ⊚clinkhostels.com; ⊖ King's Cross; map p.120. Occupying an old magistrates' court – Dickens once worked here; a century later the Clash were put on trial here for bothering pigeons – this funky, friendly (and huge) party hostel, run by the same folk as *Clink 261* around the corner, has plenty of jazzed-up period features (you can even stay in one of the tiny old prison cells). It can get crowded and noisy, but it's fun if you're feeling sociable and there's a lively bar. Dorms (4–16 beds, some pod beds; some en suite) include special "girls-only" options (hairdryers, hangers, mirrors), and there are doubles/twins/triples (some en suite). Breakfast included. Kitchen facilities. Dorms £19, doubles £66

Generator 37 Tavistock Place, WC1 ☎020 7388 7666, ⊚generatorhotels.com; ⊖ Russell Square or Euston; map p.120. One of a small European chain, this huge party hostel is tucked away in a converted police barracks on a cobbled street. The decor may not be to everyone's taste, but it is friendly, and good value. Dorms (some women-only) have 4–12 beds, and there are singles, twins, triples and quads – none en suite, though there are plans in the pipeline to upgrade. There's a young, lively atmosphere with themed nights in the late-night bar. Laundry, but no kitchen; a continental breakfast buffet is served in their

café for £4.50. Free wi-fi. Groups, including school groups, welcome. Dorms £25, doubles £78

★ **Meininger** 65–67 Queen's Gate, SW7 ☎020 3318 1407, ⊚meininger-hotels.com; ⊖ Gloucester Road or South Kensington; map p.252. Cheery, secure and high-quality modern hostel near the South Ken museums, run by a German chain. Dorms (4–12 beds), some women-only, plus singles and doubles. Groups welcome. No kitchen; breakfast costs £6. There's a laundry. Dorms £27, doubles £112

Palmers Lodge Swiss Cottage 40 College Crescent, NW3 ☎020 7483 8470, ⊚palmerslodges.com; ⊖ Swiss Cottage. A decent, clean and safe backpackers' lodge in a vast Victorian mansion in south Hampstead with period features galore in the public rooms. Many of the dorms (mixed or female-only; 6–28 beds) have beds with curtains and reading lights for added privacy; there are also twins, some of them en suite. Breakfast is included, and you can get cheap meals and a drink at the bar. Free wi-fi. There's another branch, *Hillspring Lodge*, in Willesden Green. Dorms £17, doubles £75

St Christopher's Inns ☎020 8600 7500, ⊚st -christophers.co.uk; map pp.226–227. *St Christopher's* run seven party hostels across London, with three near London Bridge, and branches in Camden, Greenwich, Shepherd's Bush and Hammersmith. The vibe is upbeat and cheerful, with most people out to socialize and hang out at the hostel bars. The *London Bridge Village* hostel also has a nightclub and comedy club, while the nearby *London Bridge Oasis* branch is women-only. Free breakfast and laundry facilities but no kitchens. Free wi-fi. Dorms £16, doubles £79

STUDENT HALLS

Outside term-time, it's possible to stay in **student halls of residence**, which provide safe, respectable lodgings often in very good, central locations. The quality of the rooms varies enormously, but they tend to be small, neat and basic and get booked up quickly. Some have shared kitchen facilities, some offer B&B – student and senior discounts are often available.

International Students House 229 Great Portland St, W1 ☎020 7631 8300, ⊚ish.org.uk; ⊖ Great Portland Street; map p.89. Hundreds of hostel-style beds in a vast student complex, with two sites near Regent's Park. Rooms are light, spacious and clean. Rates include continental breakfast and free wi-fi, but there is no kitchen. Open all year, though with variable availability. Dorms (4–10 beds), plus singles, twins, triples and quads, some en suite. Dorms £21, twins £66

KING'S COLLEGE

Great Dover Street Apartments 165 Great Dover St, SE1 ☎020 7848 1700, ⊚kingsvenues.com; ⊖ Borough; map pp.224–225. Huge Victorian building not far from Bankside, with modern en-suite rooms and kitchen facilities. July & Aug only. Singles £55, twins £78

Hampstead Residence Kidderpore Ave, NW3 ☎020 7848 1700, ⊚kingsvenues.com; ⊖ Hampstead; map pp.298–299. A nice Victorian building on a tree-lined avenue, off Finchley Rd, within walking distance of the West Heath. B&B rooms, with shared facilities (and no kitchen). July & Aug only. Singles £35, twins £45

King's College Hall Champion Hill, SE5 ☎020 7848 1700, ⊚kingsvenues.com. Refurbished rooms in leafy Denmark Hill in suburban south London. Singles only, en suite and shared. Singles £35

Stamford Street Apartments 127 Stamford St, SE1 ☎020 7848 1700, ⊚kingsvenues.com; ⊖ Waterloo; map p.216. Modern, conveniently located purpose-built block close to the South Bank, with en-suite single rooms and kitchen facilities. July & Aug only. Singles £55

LSE

LSE (London School of Economics) has a host of halls scattered across central London, all of which offer rooms in the vacations and sometimes beyond. Most are available from July to September, with some at Christmas, too. For details of self-catering apartments (year-round; from around £100) at all the sites below except Rosebery Ave – and at the Anchorage and George IV Apartments, on the main LSE campus – see ⓦlsetopfloor.co.uk. Wi-fi is not free unless otherwise stated.

Bankside House 24 Sumner St, SE1 ☎020 7107 5750, ⓦwww.lsevacations.co.uk ⊖ Southwark; map pp.226–227. En-suite B&B rooms, next to Tate Modern; singles to quads. July–Sept. Twins **£81**

Carr-Saunders Hall 18–24 Fitzroy St, W1 ☎020 7107 5888, ⓦwww.lsevacations.co.uk ⊖ Warren Street; map p.97. In an office block north of Oxford Street, the B&B rooms here have shared facilities. There's a kitchen. July–Sept & Christmas. Doubles **£63**

Grosvenor House Studios 141–143 Drury Lane, WC2 ☎020 7107 5950, ⓦwww.lsevacations.co.uk ⊖ Covent Garden; map p.132. Well situated in Covent Garden, offering self-catering en-suite studios and B&B. Mid-Aug to Sept. Doubles **£90**

High Holborn Residence 178 High Holborn, WC1 ☎020 7107 5737, ⓦlsevacations.co.uk; ⊖ Tottenham Court Road; map p.132. A modern block on a busy street near Covent Garden. B&B singles to quads, and self-contained flats with three singles and a double. Mid-Aug to end Sept. Doubles **£86**

Northumberland House 8a Northumberland Ave, WC2 ☎020 7107 5603, ⓦwww.lsevacations.co.uk; ⊖ Charing Cross; map p.46. Self-catering en-suite rooms, some with free wi-fi, in a grandiose building just off Trafalgar Square. Aug & Sept. Twins **£96**

Passfield Hall 1–7 Endsleigh Place, WC1 ☎020 7107 5925, ⓦwww.lsevacations.co.uk; ⊖ Euston; map p.120. These attractive, late Georgian buildings in Bloomsbury hold a variety of B&B rooms, from singles to triples, some en suite. July to end Sept & mid-Dec to mid-Jan. Twins **£72**

Rosebery Hall 90 Rosebery Ave, EC1 ☎020 7107 5850, ⓦwww.lsevacations.co.uk; ⊖ Angel; map p.150. B&B singles, twins and triples, some en suite, near Sadlers Wells and Clerkenwell. Mid-Aug to end Sept & mid-Dec to mid-Jan. Twins **£72**

23

CAMPSITES

London has a couple of campsites on the perimeter of the city. Rates shown here are for high season; you'll pay considerably less during the winter months.

Abbey Wood Federation Rd, Abbey Wood, SE2 ☎020 8311 7708, ⓦcaravanclub.co.uk; Abbey Wood train station from Charing Cross or London Bridge. Spacious, woody, well-equipped Caravan Club site, ten miles southeast of central London, with space for 100 tents. Open all year. Per pitch **£9.90** plus per adult **£8**

Crystal Palace Crystal Palace Parade, SE19 ☎020 8778 7155, ⓦcaravanclub.co.uk; Crystal Palace train station from Victoria or London Bridge. A decent Caravan Club site on south London's most famous woody hill, best suited for caravans and campervans. The station is a 5min walk away. Open all year. Per pitch **£10** plus per adult **£8**

Lee Valley Camping & Caravan Park Meridian Way, Edmonton N9 ☎020 8803 6900, ⓦleevalleypark.org.uk; Ponders End train station from Liverpool Street. Well-equipped site at Pickett's Lock on the River Lee, backing onto a vast reservoir. Multiplex cinema and eighteen-hole golf course, in addition to some bracing inner-city countryside, on your doorstep. Also pods sleeping two and cabins sleeping four. Open all year. Per pitch **£19.20** plus per adult **£9.50**, pods **£35**, cabins **£50**

STEIN'S, RICHMOND

Cafés and restaurants

London is an exciting place in which to eat out, and, compared to many cities in Europe, offers gratifyingly good value. As it's home to people from all over the globe, you can sample pretty much any kind of cuisine here, and standards are increasing year on year. The city boasts some of the best Cantonese restaurants in the whole of Europe, and has plenty of places to eat Indian and Bangladeshi food. As well as some excellent Spanish, Italian, Japanese, French and Middle Eastern restaurants, the capital also offers less fashionable, but also interesting, culinary options, from Polish and Moroccan to Korean and Brazilian. And there are of course, examples of wonderful British cooking all over town, from retro eel-and-pie-caffs to Michelin-starred Modern British affairs.

We cover the full range of eating options from cheap-and-cheerful pitstops via a few fashionable favourites to London's smartest destination restaurants. Among the **cafés**, you'll find bakeries, brasseries, chippies, sandwich bars, coffee shops and several ethnic eating places where speedy service and low prices are the priority, whether you're grabbing a quick lunch or a late-night snack. In any of these, you should be able to fill up for under £10. Our **restaurant** listings, meanwhile, concentrate on places where you can get a sit-down meal, with full service and all the trimmings, usually in the evening but at lunchtime too. We've also provided a list of the top **gastropubs**, where you can eat great, modern food in relaxed surroundings (see box, p.383), and a list of **specialist food stores** for top-notch picnic supplies (see p.431).

ESSENTIALS

Costs It is possible to pay an awful lot for a meal in London, but, compared with many European cities, you can get considerable value in the mid-range places. Even in the most expensive restaurants, set menus (most often served at lunch) can be a great deal, and, as small "sharing plates" are all the rage, you can eat for a very reasonable price in some very smart venues.

Tipping Tipping 12.5 to 15 percent for service is usually discretionary, but considered normal practice. Some restaurants will add a service charge automatically to the bill, so it's always worth checking.

WHITEHALL, WESTMINSTER AND ST JAMES'S

CAFÉS

Café in the Crypt St Martin-in-the-Fields, Duncannon St, WC2 ☎020 7766 1158, ⓦstmartin-in-the-fields.org; ⊖ Charing Cross; map p.46. This handy location – below the church in the eighteenth-century crypt – is a nice spot to fill up cheaply before hitting the West End. The daily changing selection consists of standard, if tasty, British comfort food, with lots of veggie dishes. Jazz nights Wed 8pm. Mon & Tues 8am–8pm, Wed 8am–10.30pm (jazz ticket holders only after 6.30pm), Thurs–Sat 8am–9pm, Sun 11am–6pm.

RESTAURANTS

Inn the Park St James's Park, SW1 ☎020 7451 9999, ⓦwww.innthepark.com; ⊖ St James's Park; map p.66. Park restaurant in a stylish curving wooden building with panoramic windows, and decking, overlooking the lake. It can get chaotic, but the Modern British food – including afternoon teas (£7.50–25.50) and breakfasts – is tasty, if pricey, from the Peyton & Byrne restaurant group. The café section is cheaper. Daily 8–11am (from 9am Sat & Sun), noon–4.30pm & 5–11pm.

The Vincent Rooms 76 Vincent Square, SW1 ☎020 7802 8391, ⓦwww.westking.ac.uk/The_vincent_rooms/brasserie.html; ⊖ Victoria or St James's Park; map p.36. A daily changing menu of modern French food – open lasagne of duck livers, pan-fried sea bream with crab and chilli risotto – is cooked and served by the young student chefs of Westminster Kingsway College (where Jamie Oliver and Antony Worall Thompson, among others, learned their craft) in this excellent-value dining room. Mains £8–12. Mon–Fri noon–2pm, plus some eves 6–9pm; closed Easter, summer & Christmas holidays.

MAYFAIR

CAFÉS

MoCafé 25 Heddon St, W1 ☎020 7434 4040, ⓦmomoresto.com; ⊖ Piccadilly Circus; map p.78. This is the café of the more expensive *Momo* restaurant, serving reasonably priced, tasty meze, honey-soaked pastries and aromatic mint tea in a wonderful Arabic tearoom that spills out onto a terrace. Everything, from the lanterns to the crockery, can be bought to take home. The main restaurant, meanwhile, serves pricey couscous, tagines and North African/Mediterranean fusion in a dining room that transports you straight to the Kasbah. Daily noon–1am.

Tibits 12–14 Heddon St, W1 ☎020 7758 4110, ⓦtibits .co.uk; ⊖ Piccadilly Circus; map p.78. Modern Swiss-German veggie café offering seasonal self-service salads, sandwiches and hot dishes from across the globe. You pay by weight, so prices can mount if you're feeling greedy. Mon–Wed 9am–10.30pm, Thurs–Sat 9am–midnight, Sun 11.30am–10.30pm.

★ **The Wolseley** 160 Piccadilly, W1 ☎020 7499 6996, ⓦthewolseley.com; ⊖ Green Park; map p.78. The lofty and stylish 1920s interior (built as the showroom for Wolseley cars) is the big draw in this opulent old café-restaurant. The Viennese-inspired comfort/bistro food is good, though pricey – come for a big breakfast (haggis with fried duck egg, perhaps?) or afternoon tea (£9.75–32.50). Mon–Fri 7am–midnight, Sat 8am–midnight, Sun 8am–11pm.

RESTAURANTS

Kiku 17 Half Moon St, W1 ☎020 7499 4208, ⓦkikurestaurant.co.uk; ⊖ Green Park; map p.78. An elegant, simple Japanese place serving up top-quality sushi and sashimi (£2.20–45), along with hot dishes,

24

zousui (porridge; £10–15), a set lunch for £22 and dinner menus starting at £55. Mon–Sat noon–2.30pm & 6–10.15pm, Sun 5.30–9.45pm.

★ **Little Social** 5 Pollen St, W1 ☎020 7870 3730, ⓦlittlesocial.co.uk; ⊖ Oxford Circus; map p.78. Opposite its sister restaurant, the excellent *Pollen Street Social*, the trendy *Little Social* offers classy British/French food, for lower prices, in a bistro-style space done up with banquettes, booths and retro stylings. The gutsy food – roast halibut BLT, perhaps, or slow-cooked egg with parmesan and squash soup – is exquisitely presented, using top-notch seasonal ingredients. Starters from £8.50, mains from £17; two-/three-course lunch £21/£25. Mon–Sat noon–2.30pm & 6–10.30pm.

Rasa W1 6 Dering St, W1 ☎020 7629 1346, ⓦrasarestaurants.com; ⊖ Oxford Circus or Bond Street; map p.78. This Indian restaurant, one of the excellent *Rasa* family (see p.384), doles out delicious, sophisticated South Indian veggie dishes from £6 – try the beet *cheera pachadi*. The northern Indian specialities keep the carnivores happy,

too. Mon–Sat noon–3pm & 6–11pm.

Truc Vert 42 North Audley St, W1 ☎020 7491 9988, ⓦtrucvert.co.uk; ⊖ Bond Street; map p.78. An upmarket but friendly restaurant, offering sunny food with a southern French accent – artichoke soup, pan-fried smoked haddock – in a comfortable, somewhat rustic setting. The daily changing menu begins with breakfast (£4–11); there's also a deli for takeaway. Mains from £16; quiche and salads are far cheaper. Mon–Fri 7am–10pm, Sat 9am–10pm, Sun 9am–6pm.

Wild Honey 12 St George St, W1 ☎020 7758 9160, ⓦwildhoneyrestaurant.co.uk; ⊖ Oxford Street or Bond Street; map p.78. Regularly changing menus offer splendid haute cuisine in this mellow oak-panelled dining room. Everything, from ravioli of wild Italian greens with lemon peel via slow-cooked beef cheek to their signature wild honey ice cream, is delicious. Mains from £23, but fixed-price menus, from £28 at weekday lunch, are a great deal. Mon–Thurs noon–2.30pm & 6–11pm, Fri & Sat noon–2.30pm & 6–11.30pm, Sun noon–3pm & 6–10pm.

MARYLEBONE

CAFÉS

Comptoir Libanais 65 Wigmore St, W1 ☎020 7935 1110, ⓦlecomptoir.co.uk; ⊖ Marble Arch; map p.89. With Lebanese kitsch splashed across everything from the cutlery cans to the ads on the wall, this is a cheap and cheerful Middle Eastern deli and diner; food is simple, from crunchy falafels to tagines and succulent rose-infused baklava. Mains from £7. Branches in Soho and South Kensington. Mon–Sat 8am–11.30pm, Sun 9am–10.30pm.

Golden Hind 73 Marylebone Lane, W1 ☎020 7486 3644; ⊖ Bond Street; map p.89. Marylebone's heritage fish-and-chip restaurant, founded in 1914, serves classic cod and chips from around £7, as well as slightly fancier

---

VEGGIE LONDON

Vegetarians will be able to eat well in most places in London. Below is a list of exclusively veggie cafés and restaurants.

Beatroot Soho. See opposite
Diwana Bhel Poori House Bloomsbury. See p.373
Food for Thought Covent Garden. See p.373
The Gate Hammersmith. See p.385
Manna Camden. See p.382
Mildred's Soho. See p.370
My Village Camden Town. See p.382
Poetry Café Covent Garden. See p.374
Rasa Stoke Newington. See p.384
Saf South Kensington. See p.382
Tibits Mayfair. See p.367

---

food like steamed skate and a deep-fried feta starter. Mon–Fri noon–3pm & 6–10pm, Sat 6–10pm.

Patisserie Valerie 105 Marylebone High St, W1 ☎020 7935 6240, ⓦpatisserie-valerie.co.uk; ⊖ Bond Street; map p.89. Founded as Swiss-run *Maison Sagne* in the 1920s, and preserving its glorious decor from those days, the café is now run by Soho's fab patissiers (see opposite). The light lunches and brunch dishes (from £5) are great, but the plump, creamy cakes are the big draw. Mon–Fri 7.30am–7pm, Sat 8am–7pm, Sun 8.30am–6pm.

★ **Paul Rothe & Son** 35 Marylebone Lane, W1 ☎020 7935 6783, ⓦpaulrotheandsondelicatessen .co.uk; ⊖ Bond Street; map p.89. Wonderfully old-fashioned deli/corner shop established in 1900, selling "English & Foreign Provisions" and serving inexpensive soups, toasties and sandwiches at formica tables. Mon–Fri 8am–6pm, Sat 11am–5pm.

RESTAURANTS

★ **The Providores and Tapa Room** 109 Marylebone High St, W1 ☎020 7935 6175, ⓦtheprovidores.co.uk; ⊖ Baker Street or Bond Street; map p.89. Outstanding fusion restaurant, run by the genius New Zealand chef Peter Gordon, with the more casual *Tapa Room* downstairs. The Pacific Rim-influenced food is original and satisfying. Upstairs sees mains at £17–21, with set menus from £20 (lunch) and £33 (dinner); the *Tapa Room* (no reservations) offers lots of small plates at £5–17. Providores: Mon–Fri noon–2.45pm & 6–10.30pm, Sat 11am–3pm & 6–10.15pm, Sun 11am–3pm & 6–10pm. Tapa Room: Mon–Fri 9am–10.30pm, Sat 10am–3pm & 4–10.30pm, Sun 10am–3pm & 4–10pm.

24

STREET LIFE

London's dynamic and recession-friendly **street food** scene, in which trucks, carts and temporary stalls dish up artisan food, from jerk chicken to Vietnamese buns, to hungry foodie crowds, shows no sign of slowing down. You'll find excellent street food at the city's markets (see p.434), and in particular, of course, at the food markets – **Borough**, **Broadway** and **Maltby Street** are the biggies, along with **Brixton Village**, but you can also check out the **Real Food Market** on the South Bank (Fri–Sun; ⓦrealfoodfestival.co.uk) and **Berwick Street** in Soho (ⓦberwickstreetlondon.co.uk). To be sure of keeping up with this dizzying scene, check out the activity on ⓦkerbfood.com, a loose collective of traders and trucks who pop up at various locations – including a residency at **King's Cross** (Tues–Fri) – and foodie events.

SOHO

CAFÉS

★ **Bar Italia** 22 Frith St, W1 ☎020 7437 4520, ⓦbaritaliasoho.co.uk; ⊖ Leicester Square; map p.100. Tiny, family-owned coffee bar that's been a Soho institution since the 1950s, keeping many of its original features (including the Gaggia coffee machine) and its iconic neon sign. A happy crowd of clubbers, Italian soccer fans, celebs, tourists and locals fill the place more or less around the clock for espressos, croissants, beers and sandwiches. A real slice of old Soho life. Nearly 24hr; closed Mon–Fri 4–6am.

Beatroot 92 Berwick St, W1 ☎020 7437 8591, ⓦbeatroot.org.uk; ⊖ Piccadilly Circus, Oxford Circus or Tottenham Court Road; map p.100. Bustling little veggie/vegan café by the market, heaping savoury bakes, stews and salads into cardboard boxes priced from £4.70 to £7.20. Great cakes and smoothies, too. Takeaway available. Mon–Sat 9am–9pm.

Breakfast Club 33 D'Arblay St, W1 ☎020 7434 2571, ⓦthebreakfastclubcafes.com; ⊖ Oxford Circus; map p.100. With its comfy, battered furnishings and cheery, slightly tatty retro decor, this laidback place is a fun (and popular) spot to linger over big all-day breakfasts and brunches and to pop in for wraps, burgers, burritos and the like as the day progresses. Branches in Islington, Hoxton, London Bridge, Battersea and Spitalfields. Mon–Wed 8am–9pm, Thurs & Fri 8am–10pm, Sat 9am–9pm, Sun 9am–7pm.

★ **Fernandez & Wells** 73 Beak St, W1 ☎020 287 8124, ⓦfernandezandwells.com; ⊖ Piccadilly Circus or Oxford Circus; map p. 97. Fabulous, freshly prepared sandwiches for around £5, great coffee and amazing cakes – most people take away, but there are one or two tables. There are two more Soho branches – a wine bar-deli around the corner at 43 Lexington St, which does small plates, too, and an espresso-wine bar (closed Sun) on St Anne's Court, off Dean St (see map p.100) – plus another on Exhibition Rd near the V&A, and one in Somerset House on the Strand. Mon–Fri 7.30am–6pm, Sat & Sun 9am–6pm.

Gaby's 30 Charing Cross Rd, WC2 ☎020 7836 4233; ⊖ Leicester Square; map p.97. This simple, no-nonsense deli has long been beloved of Londoners for its home-cooked (non-kosher) Jewish/Middle Eastern specialities and its late hours. The takeaway falafel is a bargain for these parts at £4.90. Mon–Sat 10am–midnight, Sun noon–10pm.

★ **Maison Bertaux** 28 Greek St, W1 ☎020 7437 6007, ⓦmaisonbertaux.com; ⊖ Leicester Square; map p.100. Established in 1871, this charmingly old-fashioned and terribly French patisserie, with two floors and some outdoor seating, is an unmissable Soho experience. The decor is simple but pretty and a little bohemian, with art on the walls and fresh flowers on every table, and the cakes are to die for. Some French-accented savoury treats are on offer, too. Mon–Sat 9am–9pm, Sun 9am–8pm.

Nordic Bakery 14a Golden Square, W1 ☎020 3230 1077, ⓦnordicbakery.com; ⊖ Piccadilly Circus; map p.97. Fill up on colossal cinnamon buns, delicate rye-bread sandwiches and strong coffee at this super-sharp minimalist Scandinavian café. There are two more branches in Marylebone. Takeaway available. Mon–Fri 8am–8pm, Sat 9am–7pm, Sun 10am–7pm.

Patisserie Valerie 44 Old Compton St, W1 ☎020 7437 3466, ⓦpatisserie-valerie.co.uk; ⊖ Leicester Square; map p.100. This beloved old Soho patisserie, dating back to the 1920s, is the nicest of the ever-expanding chain. Come here to enjoy croissants, mousses and gooey cakes to die for, as well as great brunches and sandwiches, in a wonderful old dining room. Takeaway available. Many other branches, including in Marylebone (see opposite). Mon–Fri 8am–11pm, Sat 9am–11pm, Sun 10am–11pm.

RESTAURANTS

Bar-shu 28 Frith St, W1 ☎020 7287 8822, ⓦbar-shu.co.uk; ⊖ Leicester Square or Tottenham Court Road; map p.100. *Bar-shu* was one of the first places to introduce fiery Szechuan cuisine to a city far more familiar with Cantonese food, offering zingy dishes – pepper-fragrant pigs' kidney on enoki mushrooms, for example, or fried sea bass in a mustard greens soup – in a vibrant space decorated with wooden screens, masks and lanterns. Mains £8–30. Daily noon–11pm.

Bocca di Lupo 12 Archer St, W1 ☎020 7734 2223, ⓦboccadilupo.com; ⊖ Piccadilly Circus; map p.100.

24

Rustic specialities from all over Italy are served in this lively modern trattoria, where it's the done thing to share, tapas-style. It's small, but there are seats at the bar, where you can see everything being prepared. The menu changes almost daily, but typical dishes might include clams with breadcrumbs, chilli and lemon zest, or broad bean purée with nettle and dandelion. With small dishes at £2–16 costs can creep up. Mon–Sat 12.30–3pm & 5.30–11pm, Sun 12.30–3.15pm & 5–9pm.

★ **Dehesa** 25 Ganton St, W1 ☎020 7494 4170, ⓦdehesa.co.uk; ⊖ Oxford Circus or Piccadilly Circus; map p.97. Very classy Spanish-Italian charcuterie and tapas bar from the always excellent *Salt Yard* stable (see p.373). The room is modern but warm, and the rustic, robust tapas out of this world – try deep-fried courgette flowers with goat's cheese and honey, or salt cod croquettes, or just enjoy a plate of *jamón Iberico* and a glass of Albariño. Tapas £5–10; cheese or charcuterie platters £11/£12. Mon–Fri noon–3pm & 5–11pm, Sat noon–11pm, Sun noon–5pm.

Koya 49 Frith St, W1 ⓦkoya.co.uk; ⊖ Leicester Square; map p.100. This low-key *udon-ya* dishes up some of the finest *Sanuki udon* noodles this side of Japan, freshly made each day and served three ways – hot in hot broth, cold in hot broth or cold with a pouring/dipping sauce – with extra toppings, *donburi* rice dishes and small plates. It's very moreish and hugely popular, so expect a wait before you get slurping (they don't take reservations). Bowls from £7; small plates £2–12. Mon–Sat noon–3pm & 5.30–10.30pm, Sun noon–3pm & 5.30–10pm.

Mildred's 45 Lexington St, W1 ☎020 7494 1634, ⓦmildreds.co.uk; ⊖ Oxford Circus or Piccadilly Circus; map p.97. *Mildred's* veggie restaurant, serving home-made global cuisine, is an old Soho standby, as popular with carnivores as vegetarians. It's small, and can get busy, but takes no bookings. Mains £8–11. Mon–Sat noon–11pm.

One Leicester Street 1 Leicester St, WC2 ☎020 3301 8069, ⓦoneleicesterstreet.com; ⊖ Leicester Square; map p.100. This minimalist restaurant, helmed by a *St John* (see p.376) alumni, offers the same superb, creative British food as its Spitalfields forerunner – snails, duck heart and lovage, for example, or smoked cod roe with devilled pigs' skin. There's a hotel upstairs if you're too full to drag yourself home (see p.357), and they do breakfast. Small mains from £7; two-/three-course lunch menus £16/£19. Mon–Fri 8–11am, noon–3pm & 5.30–11pm, Sat & Sun 8–11am, 1–3.30pm & 5.30–11pm.

Polpo 41 Beak St, W1 ☎020 7734 4479, ⓦpolpo.co.uk; ⊖ Piccadilly Circus; map p.97. *Polpo*'s dining room, reminiscent of a cosy Venetian wine bar, or *bacaro*, is welcoming and warm. Food is tapas-style, with *cicheti* (bar snacks) and small plates from £3 to £9.50 – try grilled fennel with white anchovy, *pizzette* or any of the *polpette*

(meatballs). Reservations are taken for lunch only, which adds to the sense of triumph when you score an evening table. There are two more *Polpo*s in Covent Garden and Smithfield. Mon–Sat noon–11pm, Sun noon–4pm.

★ **Quo Vadis** 26–29 Dean St, W1 ☎020 7437 9585, ⓦquovadissoho.co.uk; ⊖ Tottenham Court Road; map p.100. Treat yourself in this classic 1920s restaurant, in a building where Karl Marx wrote much of *Das Kapital*; the desirable British food is simple, gutsy and unbelievably moreish, full of good seasonal ingredients. Typical offerings include roast duck with potato cake and asparagus or a mackerel, seaweed and cucumber sandwich, with more than a nod to the current craze for sweetbreads and traditional pies. Mains from £17; pre-theatre dinner £17.50/£20 for two/three courses. Mon–Fri 8–11am, noon–3pm & 5.30–11pm, Sat noon–3pm & 5.30–11pm.

★ **Spuntino** 61 Rupert St, W1 ⓦspuntino.co.uk; ⊖ Piccadilly Circus; map p.100. From the same team as *Polpo, Spuntino* presents a hip, and fun, take on American regional food – sliders (mini burgers, or meatballs, in a brioche), cheesy grits – in an artfully distressed space that evokes a decaying Lower East Side warehouse. Some dishes are seriously classy, with a Mediterranean accent – truffled egg on toast, fabulously inky calamari – and all are served on tin sharing plates. No reservations, and it only seats around thirty at a counter and a couple of booths, so be prepared to queue. Dishes from £5. Mon–Sat 11am–midnight, Sun noon–11pm.

Stockpot 18 Old Compton St, W1 ☎020 7287 1066; ⊖ Leicester Square; map p.100. You get (very) cheap and cheerful comfort food at this old Soho institution. It's in no way gourmet, but the large platters of pasta, liver and onions, omelettes and crumble with custard keep hungry punters happy. Mains from £5, set menus from £7.60. No cards. Mon & Tues 11.30am–11.30pm, Wed–Sat 11.30am–midnight, Sun noon–11.30pm.

Tonkotsu 63 Dean St, W1 ☎020 7437 0071, ⓦtonkotsu.co.uk; ⊖ Tottenham Court Road; map p.100. If you're craving ramen, forget the chains and head here to slurp silky home-made noodles and rich, savoury stocks. Ramen – the two pork options are best, but there's one with smoked haddock and a veggie variety – from £9, plus gyoza and sides. No reservations. Mon–Fri noon–3pm & 5–10.30pm, Sat noon–10.30pm, Sun noon–10pm.

Yalla Yalla 1 Green's Court, W1 ☎020 70287 7663, ⓦyalla-yalla.co.uk; ⊖ Piccadilly Circus; map p.100. The name is Lebanese for "hurry, hurry!", and the ambience in this hole-in-the-wall is buzzy and fast. The Beirut street food includes good-value veggie meze and plenty of nicely spiced skewered meats. Meze from £3. Branches in Shoreditch and Fitzrovia. Mon–Fri 10am–11.30pm, Sat 11am–11pm.

CLOCKWISE FROM TOP LEFT BAR ITALIA (P.369); TRUC VERT (P.368); PATISSERIE VALERIE SOHO (P.369); LEONG'S LEGEND (P.372)>

Yauatcha 15 Broadwick St, W1 ☎020 7494 8888; ⓦyauatcha.com; ⊖ Piccadilly Circus; map p.100. Popular, minimalist Chinese teahouse-restaurant serving up really good, contemporary dim sum (from £4) and nice cakes. Come outside peak times to ensure a table and avoid the rush. Mon–Sat noon–11.30pm, Sun noon–10.30pm.

CHINATOWN

RESTAURANTS

Four Seasons 12 Gerrard St, W1 ☎020 7494 0870, ⓦfs-restaurants.co.uk; ⊖ Leicester Square; map p.100. There's just one dish you need to order here – the roast duck, which even has the likes of Heston Blumenthal raving. All the barbecued and roast meats are good, as are the hotpots, but they're merely supporting players. The original *Four Seasons* is in Bayswater, and there's another on Wardour St, but this place has the edge. Dishes from £4, duck from £8. Mon–Sat noon–1am, Sun 11am–1am.

Leong's Legend 4 Macclesfield St, W1 ☎020 7287 0288; ⊖ Leicester Square; map p.100. Attractive multistorey teahouse-style restaurant serving Taiwanese cuisine – try the spicy noodle and dumpling soups – along with Cantonese, Szechuan and good daytime dim sum. Dishes £3–11. Sun–Thurs noon–11pm, Fri & Sat noon–11.30pm.

Misato 11 Wardour St, W1 ☎020 7734 0808; ⊖ Leicester Square; map p.100. Basic, canteen-style Japanese place serving filling rice and noodle dishes, plus hearty bento boxes and sushi, at rock-bottom prices. Mains £4–8. Daily noon–midnight.

★ **Mr Kong** 21 Lisle St, WC2 ☎020 7437 7341, ⓦmrkongrestaurant.com; ⊖ Leicester Square; map p.100. Late-opening Chinatown stalwart, with a long menu of Cantonese food – don't miss the mussels in black bean sauce – and a good range of veggie dishes. Dishes £3–25. Mon–Sat noon–2.45am, Sun noon–1.45am.

New World 1 Gerrard Place, W1 ☎020 7434 2508; ⊖ Leicester Square; map p.100. Fantastic dim sum (served till 6pm, from £4) is the main attraction in this large old dining hall, with steaming, laden trolleys rumbling by at a rapid rate. Mon–Fri noon–11.45pm, Sat 11am–midnight, Sun 11am–11pm.

FITZROVIA

24

CAFÉS

★ **Honey and Co** 25a Warren St, W1 ☎020 7388 6175, ⓦhoneyandco.co.uk; ⊖ Warren Street; map p.97. They'll charm the socks off you at this sweet, simple café run by a husband-and-wife team, both of them *Ottolenghi* (see p.383) alumni. It's a nice spot to enjoy fantastic, flavour-packed Middle Eastern food, created from the very best ingredients – the menu changes, but you'll find delicately spiced meze, rainbow-coloured salads, comforting couscous and delicious lemonade made with foraged elderflower and rose petals. Dishes from £5; lunchtime gets busy. Mon 8am–6pm, Tues–Fri 8am–10.30pm, Sat 9.30am–10.30pm.

Indian YMCA 41 Fitzroy Square, W1 ☎020 7387 0411; ⊖ Warren Street; map p.97. Ignore the signs saying the canteen is only for students – this basic place, which has a cultish following, is open to all; just press the bell and pile in. The food (non-veg and veg) is filling, and prices unbelievably low; simply collect what you want from the counter and pay at the till. Dishes from £3. Mon–Fri noon–2pm & 7–8pm, Sat & Sun 7–8pm.

Riding House Café 43–51 Great Titchfield St, W1 ☎020 7927 0840, ⓦridinghousecafe.co.uk; ⊖ Oxford Circus; map p.97. Funky brasserie (look out for the light sconces) offering comforting, interesting food. Whatever your appetite – whether you fancy an eggy brunch, a simple dish of goat's curd with pear and honey, a half-dozen oysters or a plate of Moorish lamb with smoked aubergine – something will fit the bill. Small plates from £5, mains from £11. Mon–Fri 7.30am–11pm, Sat 9am–11pm, Sun 9am–10.30pm.

RESTAURANTS

Barrica 62 Goodge St, W1 ☎020 7436 9448, ⓦbarrica.co.uk; ⊖ Goodge Street or Tottenham Court Road; map p.97. Be transported to Spain in this cosy tapas restaurant complete with hanging hams, dark wood furnishings, terracotta dishes and sunny yellow walls. Food is hearty and honest, with nuanced flavours, and drinks range through all the Iberian favourites from Asturian cider and sherries to oaky Riojas. Tapas £4–15 (for the finest *lomo iberico* ham). Mon–Fri noon–11.30pm, Sat 1–11.30pm.

Dabbous 39 Whitfield St, W1 ☎020 7323 1544, ⓦdabbous.co.uk; ⊖ Goodge Street; map p.97. One of London's hottest restaurants, serving light modern cuisine in a warmly distressed space. Every dish, while practically bite-sized, is exquisitely presented, scattered with sprigs and tiny blossoms or presented with wit (coddled egg with mushrooms comes in a fragile eggshell, balanced on a nest, for example), but it's the fresh, clean flavours that really amaze. It's pricey, for sure, but a four-course lunch menu for £28 will allow you to taste the best creations. Just don't turn up with a rumbling tum – that's missing the point entirely. Tues–Fri noon–3pm & 5.30–11.30pm, Sat noon–3pm & 6.30–11.30pm.

Hakkasan 8 Hanway Place, W1 ☎020 7927 7000, ⓦhakkasan.com; ⊖ Tottenham Court Road; map p.97. Very swanky, atmospheric designer restaurant with a long, fashionably crammed cocktail bar attached. The exquisite and novel Chinese dishes are expensive, but you can cut costs by sticking with the dim sum. Mains from £14.

Mon–Wed noon–3.15pm & 6–11.15pm, Thurs & Fri noon–3.15pm & 6pm–12.15am, Sat noon–4.15pm & 6pm–12.15am, Sun noon–4.15pm & 6–11.15pm.
Salt Yard 54 Goodge St, W1 ☎020 7637 0657, ⓦsaltyard.co.uk; ⊖ Goodge Street; map p.97. This sleek, stylish charcuterie/tapas bar brings a dash of Italy to the proceedings, too. Dishes use the finest ingredients – the rarest hams, truffles – on seasonally changing menus. Try the signature courgette flowers stuffed with goat's cheese and drizzled with honey (£7.95). Tapas/small plates £4–9. Mon–Fri noon–11pm (bar snacks only 3–5.30pm), Sat noon–11pm.

BLOOMSBURY

CAFÉS
Abeno 47 Museum St, WC1 ☎020 7405 3211, ⓦwww .abeno.co.uk; ⊖ Tottenham Court Road or Holborn; map p.120. Small Japanese place that specializes in hearty *okonomiyaki* (£9.50–25), a cabbage, egg and ginger pancake filled with pork, bacon, seafood, cheese, tofu – the sky's the limit – prepared before your eyes. Noodles and interesting side dishes, too. There's another branch, *Abeno Too*, on Great Newport St near Leicester Square. Daily noon–10pm.
Bloomsbury Coffee House 20 Tavistock Place, WC1 ☎020 7837 2877, ⓦbloomsburycoffeehouse.co.uk; ⊖ Russell Square; map p.120. This basement coffee bar, a popular place for local students to chill out, study and chat, is a cosy little hideaway. Savoury dishes are healthy and comforting, and the coffee and home-made cakes, are great. Free wi-fi. Mon–Fri 8am–4.30pm, Sun 8am–12.30pm.
★ **Hummus Bros** Victoria House, 37–63 Southampton Row, WC1 ☎020 7404 7079, ⓦhbros.co.uk; ⊖ Holborn; map p.120. Fabulous fresh hummus and a choice of toppings – chicken, fava beans, mushroom, guacamole – with pitta bread, feta, tabbouleh and the like on the side (plates from £5). Don't miss their refreshing mint and ginger lemonade. Also takeaway. Branches on Cheapside in the City, on Wardour St in Soho and on Exmouth Market in Clerkenwell; the latter two are open at the weekends. Mon–Fri 11am–9pm.

RESTAURANTS
Caravan 1 Granary Square, N1 ☎020 7101 7661, ⓦcaravankingscross.co.uk; ⊖ King's Cross; map p.120. Occupying an old granary building in the rapidly redeveloping area behind King's Cross/St Pancras station – now home to St Martin's School of Art – this trendy, busy fusion restaurant is popular for breakfast (coconut bread with lemon cream cheese and poached rhubarb?) or brunch (parmesan grits, girolles and boar sausage?), with an all-day menu of small plates, pizza and heartier dishes. The priciest mains are around £16, but you can spend as little as £4 for a snack. Takeaway coffee, cakes and pizza, too. Mon & Tues 8am–10.30pm, Wed & Thurs 8am–11pm, Fri 8am–midnight, Sat 10am–midnight, Sun 10am–4pm.
★ **Diwana Bhel Poori House** 121–123 Drummond St, NW1 ☎020 7387 5556; ⊖ Euston; map p.120. On a street lined with good, cheap Indian restaurants, this South Indian veg diner wins out for its scrumptious all-you-can-eat lunchtime buffet (£7) and huge thalis brimming with fresh, flavoursome dishes. Dishes from £4. BYOB. Daily noon–11pm.
GAIL's Kitchen 11 Bayley St, WC1 ☎020 7323 9694; map p.120. The setting, linked to a hotel, isn't inspiring, but you get good wholesome and creative comfort food, from Taleggio and truffle toasties to clam and bean stew, in this restaurant offshoot of the *GAIL's* artisan bakery chain; sharing plates from £7. The bakery, on the other side of the hotel, serves bread, scones and cakes, along with good salads and savouries to eat in or take away. Mon–Thurs noon–3pm & 5.30–10.30pm, Fri & Sat noon–3pm & 5.30–11pm, Sun noon–4pm.

COVENT GARDEN AND THE STRAND

CAFÉS
Canela 33 Earlham St, WC2 ☎020 7240 6926, ⓦcanelacafe.com; ⊖ Covent Garden or Leicester Square; map p.132. A casual little Brazilian/Portuguese café-bar that serves up strong coffee, cakes and a few hot dishes including warm cheese bread and *feijoada*, the pork and bean stew. The high-ceilinged, chandeliered interior is a nice place for a coffee and a *pasteis de nata*, or sit outside with a Caipirinha and watch the action on Seven Dials. Mon–Wed 9.30am–10.30pm, Thurs & Fri 9.30am–11.30pm, Sat 10.30am–11.30pm, Sun 10.30am–8pm.
★ **Food for Thought** 31 Neal St, WC2 ☎020 7836 0239, ⓦfoodforthought-london.co.uk; ⊖ Covent Garden; map p.132. This minuscule veggie restaurant and takeaway is a very old friend in Covent Garden – dishing out its hearty veggie/vegan soups, salads, hot dishes and desserts for nearly forty years. The menu changes daily, but always features favourites like strawberry and banana "scrunch". Expect to queue and to get cosy with your neighbour at peak times. Hot dish with salads around £7. Mon–Sat noon–8pm, Sun noon–5pm.
Homeslice Pizza 13 Neal's Yard, WC2 ☎020 7836 4604, ⓦhomeslicepizza.co.uk; ⊖ Covent Garden; map p.132. *Homeslice*, a popular street food fixture, now has a permanent home in this lively Covent Garden courtyard. Wood-fired and thin-crust, the pizzas are piled high with delicious toppings, from smoked trout, baby beets and goat's curd to courgette and artichoke; it's de rigueur to wash them down with Prosecco (which is on tap). £4 per slice or £20 for a 20" pizza. Mon–Sat noon–11pm, Sun noon–6pm.

24

★ **Kastner & Ovens** 52 Floral St, WC2 ☎020 7836 2700; ⊖ Covent Garden; map p.132. Minimalist takeaway where the emphasis is on top-quality fresh salads and heart-warming savoury dishes, plus an amazing selection of cakes, all made on the premises. You'll pay around £4 for three salads. Mon–Fri 8am–4pm.

Monmouth Coffee Company 27 Monmouth St, WC2 ⓦmonmouthcoffee.co.uk; ⊖ Covent Garden or Leicester Square; map p.132. The marvellous aroma is the first thing that greets you when you walk in to this tiny old coffee shop run by the quality Monmouth Coffee roasters. Pick and mix your coffee from a fine selection (or buy the beans to take home) and grab a pastry to go with. Branches in Borough Market and Bermondsey. Mon–Sat 8am–6.30pm.

Poetry Café 22 Betterton St, WC2 ☎020 7420 9888, ⓦpoetrysociety.org.uk; ⊖ Covent Garden or Holborn; map p.132. This simple veggie café, which has been around for years, is a pleasant place to relax, with salads, soups, light meals and cakes on offer; mains £5–7. Evenings see regular, high-standard poetry readings. Mon–Fri noon–11pm, Sat 7–11pm.

Rock & Sole Plaice 47 Endell St, WC2 ☎020 7836 3785; ⊖ Covent Garden; map p.132. No-nonsense fish-and-chip shop where they do all the staples just right; eat in or at one of the pavement benches, or takeaway. It's not that cheap; fish and chips costs around £12. Mon–Sat 11.30am–10.30pm, Sat & Sun noon–9.30pm.

Spud 26 New Row, WC2 ☎020 7240 2215, ⓦilovespud .com; ⊖ Covent Garden; map p.132. A groovier version of *Spud-U-Like*, this hole in the wall gussies up the humble baked potato (or sweet potato) with rich, tasty toppings – more toppings than tater, in fact, whether you go for Sicilian aubergine stew or *merguez* sausage and beans, or keep it old school with tuna, sweetcorn and mayo. From around £4.50. Take away or eat downstairs. Mon–Fri 10am–7.30pm, Sat 11am–7.30pm.

RESTAURANTS

Dishoom 12 Upper St Martin's Lane, WC2 ☎020 7420 9320, ⓦdishoom.com; ⊖ Leicester Square or Covent Garden; map p.132. Re-creating the atmosphere of the Persian cafés of Old Bombay, complete with arcane "rules of the house" signs and faded movie posters, *Dishoom* is buzzy and fun but, most importantly, serves good food – don't miss the *pau bhaji*, a toasted bun filled with veggie curry, and the really good, filling black dhal. Their breakfasts, with fruit-packed lassis and spicy scrambled eggs, are a hit too. Mains from £6.50, small dishes for less. There's another branch in Shoreditch. Mon–Thurs 8am–11pm, Friday 8am–midnight, Sat 9am–midnight, Sun 9am–10pm.

Green Man and French Horn 54 St Martin's Lane, WC2 ☎0207 836 2645, ⓦgreenmanfrenchhorn.co; ⊖ Leicester Square; map p.132. Victorian pub refashioned as a trendily rustic French restaurant, specializing in food from the Loire region. The daily changing menu might feature such dishes as squid and black pudding or lamb chops, chard and anchovies, along with a number of simple fish dishes, and the wine list features lots of organic and biodynamic varieties. Mains around £12–21; *plat* plus wine £10. Mon–Sat noon–11pm.

★ **Hawksmoor** 11 Langley St, WC2 ☎020 420 9390, ⓦthehawksmoor.com; ⊖ Covent Garden; map p.132. Covent Garden branch, in an atmospheric old brewery, of this bijou group of contemporary steak restaurants – the original is in Spitalfields (see p.378). You could spend well over £50 per head on the best British beef and flavoursome extras, including roast bone marrow, roast mushrooms and mac 'n' cheese, but there's a two-/three-course express menu (£23/£26; not served 6.30–10pm), which includes rib-eye steak, and you can eat burgers (including their trademark *kimchi* burger) for £15 in the bar. Mon–Thurs noon–3pm & 5–10.30pm, Fri & Sat noon–3pm & 5–11pm, Sun noon–9.30pm.

J. Sheekey 28–35 St Martin's Court, WC2 ☎020 7240 2565, ⓦj-sheekey.co.uk; ⊖ Leicester Square; map p.132. A *grande dame* of the London dining scene – established in 1896 in the heart of theatreland – this lovely old seafood restaurant is a glittering, special occasion kind of place. Price-wise, the weekend lunch three-course menu, at £26.50, is your best bet, along with the oyster bar. Mains from £16. Mon–Sat noon–3pm & 5.30pm–midnight, Sun noon–3.30pm & 6–11pm.

Kopapa 32–34 Monmouth St, WC2 ☎020 7240 6076, ⓦkopapa.co.uk; ⊖ Covent Garden; map p.132.

COFFEE AND LUNCH CHAINS

Although London's old-fashioned caffs of the 1950s and 60s have all but died out, the city today has a number of reliable **chains** where you can grab a coffee and a sandwich. Three are particularly worthy of mention, offering healthy and well-priced food to grab and go.

Home-grown **sandwich** chains **Pret à Manger** (ⓦpret.com) and **EAT** (ⓦeat.co.uk) produce reliable lunchtime food, with good sandwiches, salads and cakes. ★ **Leon** (ⓦleonrestaurants .co.uk), meanwhile, is a smaller, but gently expanding, family-owned chain that does delicious coffee, juices, breakfasts, wraps, soups and salads in cheery premises whose artfully colourful decor evoke the sunny holidays of youth. Food is healthy and locally sourced, and there are lots of amazing wheat- and gluten-free cakes.

Friendly fusion restaurant from the Kiwi chef behind Providores (see p.368). Dishes like tempura spicy dahl-stuffed *inari* pocket on caramelized coconut with pickled green papaya offer fresh, complex flavours; many are designed to share. Breakfasts and weekend brunches are great. Large plates from £13; small plates from £6; two-/three-course express menu for £17.95/£20.95 (early evening most nights, Mon 5–10.30pm). Mon–Fri 8.30–11.30am & noon–10.45pm, Sat 9.30am–4pm & 4.30–10.45pm, Sun 9.30am–4pm & 4.30–9.45pm.

Masala Zone 48 Floral St, W1 ☎020 7379 0101, ⓦmasalazone.com; ⊖ Covent Garden; map p.132. Attractive, reliable restaurant, decorated with Rajasthani puppets, serving modern Indian food, including lots of veggie options. Start with little dishes of "street food", then move on to the well-balanced, richly flavoured curries or thalis. Branches in Soho, Camden, Islington, Earl's Court and Bayswater. Dishes from £4.50. Mon–Sat noon–11pm, Sun 12.30–10.30pm.

Opera Tavern 23 Catherine St, WC2 ☎020 7836 3680, ⓦoperatavern.co.uk; ⊖ Covent Garden; map p.132.

Another classy Spanish-Italian restaurant from the *Salt Yard* team (see p.373), with sharing plates and fine wines by the glass. Star turns include a mini foie gras and Iberico burger – or indeed anything featuring the Iberico ham or prepared on the charcoal grill. Sit in the buzzy downstairs bar rather than in the more formal upstairs dining room. Charcuterie and tapas from £5. Mon–Fri noon–3pm & 5–11.30pm (bar snacks, charcuterie and cheese 3–5pm), Sat noon–11.30pm, Sun noon–5pm.

★ **Terroirs** 5 William IV St, WC2 ☎0207 036 0660, ⓦterroirswinebar.com; ⊖ Charing Cross; map p.132. Great wines – including "natural", additive-free wines – and excellent Mediterranean/Modern British food at this convivial wine bar-restaurant. The ground floor serves small plates (from £6.50) – dishes like smoked eel with soft boiled egg, horseradish and pea shoots (£9.50) – along with French-accented *plats du jour* (from £12), home-made charcuterie, cheese and bar snacks, while the basement offers more formal dining, with mains, the like of confit duck with hazelnuts, from £16. Mon–Sat noon–11pm (charcuterie and cheese 3–5.30pm).

CLERKENWELL

CAFÉS

Clerkenwell Kitchen 27–31 Clerkenwell Close, EC1 ☎020 7101 9959, ⓦtheclerkenwellkitchen.co.uk; ⊖ Farringdon or Angel; map p.150. Bright, airy place serving good food from a River Cottage alumni. The short, seasonal menu uses sustainably sourced ingredients in dishes like wild garlic, red onion and potato frittata or simple fish pie, and the open-plan kitchen serves everything from breakfast through to tea and cakes, with deli sandwiches, soups and savoury tarts to take away. There's a courtyard for outdoor dining. Mains £8–14. Mon–Fri 8am–5pm; till 10.30pm on Thurs.

Kurz & Lang 1 St John St, EC1 ☎020 7993 2923, ⓦkurzandlang.com; ⊖ Farringdon; map p.150. An *echt* German Bratwurst in a prominent corner site off Smithfield. Choose from a variety of fresh, authentic sausages accompanied with bread, mustard and sauerkraut (from £6), and finish off with a sticky German pastry. Mon–Wed 11am–11.30pm, Thurs 11am–1am, Fri 11am–6.30am, Sat noon–6am, Sun noon–5pm.

Morito 32 Exmouth Market, EC1 ☎020 7278 7007, ⓦmorito.co.uk; ⊖ Angel or Farringdon; map p.150. As an offshoot of *Moro* and right next door, this long, skinny tapas bar allows you to enjoy the same fabulous flavours and fine wines in more casual, bare-bones surrounds. Don't think of it as a cheap option, however – though the most expensive dishes (fried baby squid; lamb chops grilled *a la plancha*) are just £8.50, everything is tiny and wickedly moreish, and what with all the great wines costs can really mount. Tapas from £4. Daily noon–4pm & 5–11pm, Sun noon–4pm.

★ **Pho** 86 St John St, EC1 ☎020 7253 7624, ⓦphocafe.co.uk; ⊖ Farringdon or Barbican; map p.150. Small café serving freshly made Vietnamese noodle soups, washed down with strong weasel coffee (don't ask). They have five more London branches – in Oxford Circus, Soho, Shepherd's Bush, Stratford and Spitalfields – but this is the original. Phô from £7.75. Takeaway available. Mon–Thurs noon–3pm & 6–10pm, Fri noon–3pm & 6–10.30pm, Sat 6–10.30pm.

Prufrock Coffee 23–25 Leather Lane, EC1 ☎020 7242 0467, ⓦprufrockcoffee.com; ⊖ Chancery Lane or Farringdon; map p.150. A spacious and tranquil shrine to the coffee bean, brainchild of world barista champion Gwilym Davies. The coffee, of course, is superb – what with this and the *Department of Coffee & Social Affairs* opposite, Leather Lane has become quite the caffeine-fiend's haven. Mon–Fri 8am–6pm, Sat & Sun 10am–5pm.

RESTAURANTS

Caravan 11–13 Exmouth Market, EC1 ☎020 7833 8115, ⓦcaravanonexmouth.co.uk; ⊖ Farringdon; map p.150. True to its Kiwi roots, this funky Exmouth Market favourite is great for creative brunches (Sat & Sun 10am–4pm) – try the baked eggs with tomato, pepper and Greek yoghurt or the avocado with chilli flakes on sourdough toast. At other times the modern fusion menu might feature anything from almond couscous via pickled mackerel with corn, avocado and jalapeno to Arabica oxtail with polenta. Their coffee (takeaway available) is roasted on site. Small and large plates £5–18. Mon–Fri 8–11.30am, noon–10.30pm, Sat 10am–4pm & 5–10.30pm, Sun 10am–4pm.

24

Fish Central 149–155 Central St, EC1 ☎ 020 7253 4970, Ⓦ fishcentral.co.uk; ⊖ Old Street; map p.150. Straddling the Barbican/City and Clerkenwell's council estates, this friendly chippie/fish restaurant attracts hungry diners from both. The cod or haddock with chips are pretty good, but it's the likes of chargrilled squid, fresh scallops and oysters that give this place the edge. Mains £8–20, express two-course lunch £6.95. Mon–Sat 11am–2.30pm & 5–10.30pm.

Medcalf 40 Exmouth Market, EC1 ☎ 020 7833 3533, Ⓦ medcalfbar.co.uk; ⊖ Farringdon or Angel; map p.150. A turn-of-the-twentieth-century butcher's shop converted into an effortlessly stylish, appealing Modern British restaurant. The atmosphere is relaxed, and the daily changing menus offer deliciously simple dishes, such as dressed Dorset crab with Jersey Royals or goat's curd and St George mushroom tart, using the best ingredients. Mains £13–20. Mon–Thurs & Sat noon–3pm & 6–9.45pm, Fri noon–3pm & 6–10.20pm, Sun noon–4pm.

The Modern Pantry 47–48 St John's Square, EC1 ☎ 020 7553 9210, Ⓦ themodernpantry.co.uk; ⊖ Farringdon; map p.150. A brace of elegant Georgian townhouses make a nice setting for this contemporary café with a smart dining room upstairs. Chef Anna Hansen, a Kiwi alumni of *Providores* (see p.368), brings Pacific Rim and fusion flavours to dishes from liquorice and tamari-marinated venison haunch to wild garlic, roast celeriac and pecorino fritters with pear tonka puree (...us neither). The simpler café offers good value (breakfasts won't hit £20, and there's a weekday two-course lunch menu for £21.50). Takeaway deli foods, too. Mains £15–22. Café: Mon 8am–11am & noon–10pm, Tues–Fri 8am–11am & noon–10.30pm, Sat 9am–4pm & 6–10.30pm, Sun 10am–4pm & 6–10pm; restaurant: Mon noon–3pm,

Tues–Fri noon–3pm & 6–10.30pm, Sat 11am–4pm & 6–10.30pm, Sun 11am–4pm.

★ **Moro** 34–36 Exmouth Market, EC1 ☎ 020 7833 8336, Ⓦ moro.co.uk; ⊖ Farringdon or Angel; map p.150. Lovely, warmly decorated restaurant that's a place of pilgrimage for disciples of Sam and Sam Clark's Moorish/Iberian/Middle Eastern cuisine. The daily changing menus are outstanding, especially the lamb dishes and their speciality lemon yoghurt cake, and service is friendly; it's best to book well in advance. Tapas (around £4) are served all day Mon–Sat. Mains £16.50–19.50. Mon–Sat noon–2.30pm & 6–10.30pm (tapas available 2.30–6pm), Sun 12.30–2.45pm.

St John 26 St John St, EC1 ☎ 020 7251 0848, Ⓦ stjohnrestaurant.com; ⊖ Farringdon; map p.150. Former smokehouse close to Smithfield meat market that's famous for Fergus Henderson's perfect, utterly simple, execution of traditional British dishes – often involving unfashionable animal parts – on a menu that's as pared down as the dining room itself. There's a less expensive sister restaurant in Spitalfields (see p.378). Mains £17–24. Mon–Fri noon–3pm & 6–11pm, Sat 6–11pm, Sun 1–3pm.

Sushi Tetsu 12 Jerusalem Passage, EC1 ☎ 020 3217 0090, Ⓦ sushitetsu.co.uk; ⊖ Farringdon; map p.150. A really good, very fashionable, sushi bar that specializes in super-fresh *nigiri* sushi, sashimi and hand rolls. It's hugely popular, and as it seats fewer than ten it's difficult to get in, but for once the hype is justified. Sushi from £3; there's a £20/person minimum for lunch, £30 at dinner. Reservations advised, as much as a month in advance; they can't accommodate groups larger than four. Tues–Fri 12.30–3pm (last seating 1pm) & 6–10.30pm (last seating 8.30pm), Sat 6–10.30pm (last seating 8.30pm).

THE CITY

CAFÉS

Café Below Church of St Mary-le-Bow, Cheapside, EC2 ☎ 020 7329 0789, Ⓦ cafebelow.co.uk; ⊖ St Paul's or Bank; map p.170. A rare City gem: a cosy, good-value café-restaurant, in a wonderful Norman church crypt, serving home-cooked modern Mediterranean food, with lots of veggie choices, on daily changing menus. Simple, tasty hot breakfasts, too. Lunch mains from £6.50; takeout is cheaper. Mon–Fri 7.30am–2.30pm.

De Gustibus 53–55 Carter Lane, EC4 ☎ 020 7236 0056, Ⓦ degustibus.co.uk; ⊖ St Paul's or Blackfriars; map pp.156–157. Award-winning artisan bakery in the heart of the City, offering sandwiches, bruschette, croques-monsieurs and quiche to eat in or take away, along with espresso and herbal teas. There's another branch in Borough Market. Mon–Fri 7am–5pm.

RESTAURANTS

Duck and Waffle Heron Tower, 110 Bishopsgate, EC2

☎ 020 3640 7310, Ⓦ duckandwaffle.com; ⊖ Aldgate; map pp.156–157. The improbable juxtaposition of swanky City location – the view, from forty floors up, is amazing – and funky, hipster comfort food (the signature dish features waffles, duck confit, fried duck egg and mustard maple syrup; £17) somehow works. Many menu items, from the spicy ox cheek doughnuts to crispy pig's ears and an all-day foie gras breakfast are adventurous, but there are simpler options too. Prices (small plates from £9), for the location, aren't too bad, and the hours make it a useful late-night, or breakfast, destination. Daily 6am–5am.

L'Anima 1 Snowden St, EC2 ☎ 020 7422 7000, Ⓦ lanima.co.uk; ⊖ Liverpool Street; map pp.156–157. Amazingly good southern Italian and Sardinian food in a highly designed, icy-cool dining room. You can't go wrong here, whether you choose fresh pasta (nettle *stracci* with veal ragout and pistachios, maybe, or spaghetti *chitarra* with lobster, herbs and black anise seeds), or a

TOP 5 AFTERNOON TEAS

The classic English **afternoon tea** – sandwiches, scones and cream, cakes and tarts, and, of course, pots of tea – is available all over London. The most popular venues are the capital's top hotels and most fashionable department stores; a selection of the best is given below. To avoid disappointment, book well in advance – in the case of the *Ritz*, as far as twelve weeks ahead for the weekends – and leave your jeans and trainers at home, as most hotels will expect at least "smart casual attire". Prices quoted here are for the standard teas; most places offer champagne teas, or more substantial high teas, for a higher price.

Claridge's Brook St, W1 ☎020 7107 8886, ⓦ claridges.co.uk; ⊖ Bond Street; map p.78. Fabulous menu with around forty teas and exquisite cakes in stunning Art Deco surrounds. £45. Daily 3pm, 3.30pm, 5pm & 5.30pm.

Fortnum & Mason 181 Piccadilly, W1 ☎0845 602 5694, ⓦ fortnumandmason.com; ⊖ Green Park; map p.78. Take tea in this wonderful old store's *Diamond Jubilee Tea Salon*; menus change to reflect the seasons or cultural events, and they have savoury, vegetarian, vegan, dairy-free, gluten-free and diabetic-friendly options for the same price. £40. Mon–Sat noon–9pm, Sun noon–8pm.

Lanesborough Hyde Park Corner, SW1 ☎020 7259 5599, ⓦ lanesborough.com; ⊖ Hyde Park Corner; map p.240. This one is so grand that a tea sommelier will discuss suitable tea and cake pairings with you. Gluten- and dairy-free choices available. £38. Daily 4pm, 4.30pm & 5pm.

The Ritz Piccadilly, W1 ☎020 7493 8181, ⓦ theritzlondon.com; ⊖ Green Park; map p.78. Seriously posh teas in the hotel's Palm Court – gents must wear a jacket and tie. £45. Daily 11.30am, 1.30pm, 3.30pm, 5.30pm & 7.30pm.

The Wolseley 160 Piccadilly, W1 ☎020 7499 6996, ⓦ thewolseley.com; ⊖ Green Park; map p.78. The atmosphere is grand without being intimidating at this Viennese-style café (see p.367), where the sumptuous European pastries are the speciality. £22.50. Mon–Fri & Sun 3–6.30pm, Sat 3.30–5.30pm.

24

main like black Scotch beef with marrowbone or octopus a la plancha – prices (mains £15–33) reflect the quality and the wallets of the clientele. The two-/three-course menu (all day Mon–Fri; £22.50/£24.50) is well worth considering. Mon–Fri 11.45am–3pm & 5.30–11.30pm, Sat 5.30–11.30pm.

SHOREDITCH AND HOXTON

CAFÉS

The Bridge 15 Kingsland Rd, E2 ☎020 3489 2216; ⊖ Old Street; map pp.192–193. Designers get paid a mint to re-create the kind of Miss Havisham mish-mash that comes naturally to this eccentric little Shoreditch coffee house; the warm, friendly atmosphere, however, can't be faked. The pub-like room downstairs, every inch crammed with bric-a-brac, is delightful, and you could lose hours nursing a coffee and a baklava in the kitsch Baroque boudoir/granny's living room upstairs. Sun & Mon 11am–10pm, Tues & Wed 11am–1am, Thurs–Sat 11am–2am.

Fabrique Arch 385, Geffrye St, E2 ☎020 7033 0268, ⓦ fabrique.co.uk; Hoxton Overground; map pp.192–193. This Scandinavian-style bakery – the Hoxton outpost of a Stockholm chain – keeps it simple but oh so on trend, serving spicy cinnamon buns, croissants, stone-oven-baked sourdough breads and Johan & Nyström coffee. The white-tile and unvarnished wood space, tucked into a railway arch by Hoxton station, is lovely. Tues–Fri 8am–6pm, Sat & Sun 10am–6pm.

★ **Leila's Shop** 17 Calvert Ave, E2 ☎020 7729 9789; Shoreditch High Street Overground; map pp.192–193. Relaxed neighbourhood café, linked to an artlessly nostalgic and appealing little deli, serving creative, Mediterranean-tinged breakfasts, brunches, light meals and lusciously rich hot chocolate to a devoted Shoreditch crowd. Wed–Sat 10am–6pm, Sun 10am–5pm.

Sông Quê 134 Kingsland Rd, E2 ☎020 7613 3222, ⓦ songque.co.uk; Hoxton Overground; map pp.192–193. In a Hoxton street heaving with budget Vietnamese restaurants, this basic, busy place has the edge, with good *phở* (from £7.80) and lip-tinglingly spicy seafood dishes. Mon–Fri noon–3pm & 5.30–11pm, Sat noon–11pm, Sun noon–10.30pm.

RESTAURANTS

Clove Club Shoreditch Town Hall, 380 Old St, EC1 ☎020 7729 6496, ⓦ thecloveclub.com; ⊖ Old Street; map pp.192–193. You'll eat what you're given at this hugely hyped Shoreditch restaurant; dinner consists solely of a five-course tasting menu (£47; vegetarian also £47). The Modern food – radishes with sesame and *gochuchang* mayo, buttermilk-fried chicken with pine salt, blood orange with sheep's milk mousse and wild fennel – is delicious, packed with impeccably sourced, mainly British ingredients. Some sharing plates are available at lunchtime (mains £13) and at the bar in the evenings (£4–14). Restaurant: Mon 6–10pm, Tues–Sat noon–2.30pm & 6–10pm; bar: Mon–Sat 6–11pm.

Eyre Brothers 70 Leonard St, EC2 ☎020 7613 5346, ⓦeyrebrothers.co.uk; ⊖ Old Street; map pp.192–193. Large, swish restaurant offering unusual Iberian dishes to a

City-ish crowd. The menu ranges from rustic, punchy Portuguese and Spanish specialities to favourites from Mozambique – piri piri tiger prawns, for example. Mains £12–25; tapas and *petiscos* £3–7.50; two-course *menu del día* £18. Mon–Fri noon–3pm & 6.30–10.45pm, Sat 7–10.45pm.

SPITALFIELDS, BRICK LANE AND WHITECHAPEL

CAFÉS

Brick Lane Beigel Bake 159 Brick Lane, E1 ☎020 7729 0616; Shoreditch High Street Overground; map pp.192–193. Bagels baked on the spot in the heart of the East End – very cheap, even for your top-end filling, smoked salmon and cream cheese, and a particular hit late at night and in the early mornings. The salt beef sandwiches are good, too. Daily 24hr.

Café 1001 The Old Truman Brewery, 91 Brick Lane, E1 ☎020 7247 9679, ⓦcafe1001.co.uk; ⊖ Shoreditch High Street Overground; map pp.192–193. Quintessential Brick Lane hip, with a beaten-up look, lots of outdoor seating, sofas to crash on, used books to read and freshly made burgers, soups, salads and cakes to sample. It's also a bar/club, with DJ sets and live music. Daily 6am–midnight.

Verde and Co 40 Brushfield St, E1 ☎020 7247 1924, ⓦverdeandco.co.uk; ⊖ Liverpool Street; map pp.192–193. Author Jeanette Winterson, who owns this Spitalfields deli/grocer's/café, has preserved the original eighteenth-century shopfront and bareboard interior; an adorable setting for classy and quirky deli goods, with some seating for coffee, gourmet salads, sandwiches, soups and quiche (£4–6). Mon–Fri 9am–6pm, Sat & Sun 11am–5pm.

RESTAURANTS

Chez Elles 45 Brick Lane, E1 ☎020 7247 9699, ⓦchezellesbistroquet.co.uk; ⊖ Aldgate East; map pp.192–193. Opened in 2012, this pretty bistro, incongruous on curry-house-lined Brick Lane, has quickly become a firm neighbourhood favourite; it's French-owned, and attracts lots of French customers. The interior, all shabby Gallic chic, may be a tad twee, but the food is the real thing – deliciously rustic French classics such as onion soup, moules, duck confit, chocolate mousse – and the atmosphere is relaxed and warm. Mains £11.50–16.50. Tues–Sat noon–3pm & 6.30–10.30pm, Sun 11am–5pm.

Hawksmoor 157 Commercial St, E1 ☎020 7426 4850, ⓦthehawksmoor.co.uk; ⊖ Liverpool Street or Shoreditch High Street Overground; map pp.192–193. Carnivores drool at the very mention of this steakhouse,

where the charcoal-grilled cuts of meat, impeccably sourced, are huge and succulent. The Sunday roasts are fantastic, naturally; a full meal could set you back well over £40, but the two-/three-course menu (Mon–Fri noon–3pm & 5–6pm, Sat noon–3pm) cuts costs at £23/£26. Branches in Covent Garden (see p.374), Mayfair and the City. Mon–Fri noon–2.30pm & 5–10.30pm, Sat noon–2.30pm & 6–10.30pm, Sun noon–4.30pm.

Lahore Kebab House 2–10 Umberston St, E1 ☎020 7481 9737, ⓦlahore-kebabhouse.com; ⊖ Aldgate East; map pp.192–193. A legendary Pakistani kebab house, just off Commercial Rd. Go for the lamb cutlets and roti, and turn up hungry. BYOB. Mains £7–11. Daily noon–1am.

Needoo Grill 87 New Rd, E1 ☎020 7247 0648, ⓦneedoogrill.co.uk; ⊖ Whitechapel; map pp.192–193. Run by a *Tayyabs* alumni (see below), this excellent, lively Pakistani restaurant maintains its forerunner's standards – the grills are excellent – offers many of the same dishes, and has added some veggie specialities to boot. Mains from £6. BYOB. Daily noon–11pm.

★ **St John Bread and Wine** 94–96 Commercial St, E1 ☎020 7251 0848, ⓦstjohnbreadandwine.com; ⊖ Liverpool Street; map p.192. A simpler offshoot of *St John* (see p.376) with the same superlative British food on a regularly changing menu – featuring offal, pig's cheek and the like, but with wonderful veg and fish dishes, too. It's also great for breakfasts (try the Old Spot bacon sandwich), puds and buns. Dishes £4–18. Mon–Fri 9–11am & noon–11pm, Sat 9–11am, noon–4pm & 6–11pm, Sun 9–11am, noon–4pm & 6–9pm.

★ **Tayyabs** 83–89 Fieldgate St, E1 ☎020 7247 9543, ⓦtayyabs.co.uk; ⊖ Whitechapel; map pp.192–193. Opened in 1974, *Tayyabs* has smartened itself up over the years but still offers the same straightforward Pakistani food: meat-heavy dishes, freshly cooked and without pretension, served with flavoursome breads. The grilled lamb chops are divine. Prices are still low, booking is essential and service is speedy. BYOB. Mains from £6. Daily noon–11.30pm.

BETHNAL GREEN

CAFÉS

★ **E. Pellicci** 332 Bethnal Green Rd, E2 ☎020 7739 4873; ⊖ Bethnal Green; map pp.192–193. London's old Italian-owned caffs are dropping like flies, and *Pellicci's*

(open since 1900) is a rare jewel: an iconic East End institution with its – stunning –1940s decor intact, serving great fry-ups and good Anglo-Italian grub at low prices. Mon–Sat 7am–4pm.

★ **Frizzante at City Farm** 1a Goldsmith's Row, E2 📞020 7739 2266, 🌐frizzanteltd.co.uk; 🚇 Bethnal Green; map p.190. Hackney City Farm's rustic, and very family-friendly, café serves great home-made breakfasts, Italian-style lunches and Sunday roasts, all for less than a tenner. Tues–Sun 10am–4.30pm.

G. Kelly 414 Bethnal Green Rd, E2 📞020 7739 3603; 🚇 Bethnal Green; map pp.192–193. This old-school, no-frills (at all!) caff, lined with photos of local boxing heroes, is one of London's few remaining pie shops and a Cockney vanguard. Order meat pies with "liquor" (parsley sauce) and mash, and you'll pay less than a fiver. If you fancy a side of jellied eels, head to the other *G. Kelly* eel and pie shop (no relation), further into Bow at 526 Roman Rd, E3 (📞020 8980 3165; 🚇 Mile End; map p.190). Mon–Fri 10am–3pm, Sat 9.30am–4pm.

Jones Dairy 23 Ezra St, E2 📞020 7739 5372, 🌐jonesdairy.co.uk; 🚇 Bethnal Green; map pp.192–193. Take a quick detour from Sunday's Columbia Rd Market (see p.434) to this gorgeous, old-fashioned little place, which sells great breads, bagels and fine cheeses, along with all-day breakfasts and salads, fresh oysters and home-made cakes. Fri 9am–3pm, Sat 9am–4.30pm, Sun 8am–3pm.

Story Deli 123 Bethnal Green Rd, E2 📞07918 197352, 🌐storydeli.com; Shoreditch High Street Overground; map pp.192–193. Funky little ex-scout hut serving very good, quite expensive, all-organic pizza with flatbread-like bases. Topped with interesting herbs, pestos, cheeses and hams, they all cost £16, from the *fico*, made with goat's cheese, figs, capers, thyme and Parma

TOP 5 BRUNCH SPOTS
Breakfast Club Soho. See p.369
Caravan King's Cross. See p.373
Leila's Shop Shoreditch. See p.377
Riding House Café Fitzrovia. See p.372
Towpath Café Hoxton/Dalston. See p.384

ham, to the chilli-hot Charlie Jones with spicy sausage. No cards. Daily noon–10.30pm.

RESTAURANTS
Bistrotheque 23–27 Wadeson St, E2 📞020 8983 7900, 🌐bistrotheque.com; Cambridge Heath station; map p.190. Listing Modern British food and bistro staples – fish and chips or *onglet* with frites? Oysters with Cava and mushroom and celeriac Dauphinoise? – and adding a dash of Manhattan sass, this huge monochrome brasserie is also a hit for its cocktails and buzzy brunches. Mains from £13, brunch dishes from £4; three-course menu (except 7.15–9.45pm) £17.50. Mon–Thurs 6–10.30pm, Fri 6–11pm, Sat 11am–4pm & 6–11pm, Sun 11am–4pm.

Viajante Patriot Square, E2 📞020 7871 0461, 🌐viajante.co.uk; 🚇 Bethnal Green; map p.190. Cult chef Nuno Mendes – *El Bulli* alumni and star of London's supper club scene – offers surprise tasting menus featuring Modern molecular cuisine without too much pretension. Tiny plates offer amazing flavours; choose a number of courses and see what turns up. Lunch £35 for 3 courses/£65 for 6/£80 for 9; dinner £70 for 6/£85 for 9/£95 for 12. Wed & Thurs 6–9.30pm, Fri–Sun noon–2pm & 6–9.30pm.

DOCKLANDS

CAFÉS
Frizzante at Mudchute Mudchute City Farm, Pier St, E14 📞020 3069 9290, 🌐mudchute.org; Mudchute DLR; map pp.206–207. Run by the same team as *Frizzante* at the Hackney City Farm (see above), and serving the same satisfying, home-made food to a kiddie-focused crowd. Tues–Fri 9.30am–3.30pm, Sat & Sun 9.30am–4.30pm.

Hubbub 269 Westferry Rd, E14 📞020 7515 5577, 🌐hubbubcafebar.com; Mudchute DLR; map pp.206–207. An oasis in the Docklands desert, this casual café-bar is housed in a former Victorian church, now an arts centre, and does decent fry-ups, sandwiches and tapas.

Mon–Wed noon–11pm, Thurs & Fri noon–midnight, Sat 10am–midnight, Sun 10am–10.30pm.

RESTAURANTS
Mem Saheb on Thames 65–67 Amsterdam Rd, E14 📞020 7538 3008, 🌐memsaheb.net; Crossharbour DLR; map pp.206–207. Very decent riverside Indian restaurant (Delia Smith is a fan!) in an area not known for great places to eat, with a superb view over the river to the O2 Dome. Mains £8–18. Mon–Fri noon–3pm & 6–11pm, Sat 6–11pm, Sun noon–4pm & 6–10pm.

SOUTH BANK

CAFÉS
★ **Marsh Ruby** 30 Lower Marsh, SE1 📞020 7620 0593, 🌐marshruby.com; 🚇 Waterloo; map p.216. Basic, cheery place offering terrific filling lunchtime curries for around a fiver: the food, on seasonally changing menus, uses a lot of organic/free-range ingredients. Mon–Fri 11.30am–3pm.

RESTAURANTS
★ **Laughing Gravy** 154 Blackfriars Rd, SE1 📞020 7998 1707, 🌐thelaughinggravy.co.uk; 🚇 Southwark; map p.216. There's a cosy, neighbourhood vibe at this welcoming brasserie, which serves hearty English and Mediterranean bistro food in a brick-walled dining room. Mains £9–20. Mon–Thurs noon–3pm & 5–10pm, Fri

24

noon–3pm & 5–10.30pm, Sat 11am–4pm & 5–10.30pm, Sun 11am–4.30pm.

Masters Super Fish 191 Waterloo Rd, SE1 ☎020 7928 6924; ⊖ Waterloo; map p.216. This unreconstructed fish-and-chip restaurant serves a good-value lunch deal for £7 – huge portions with all the trimmings (gherkins, pickled onions, coleslaw and even a few complimentary prawns) – along with some fancier options. Mains £7.50–13. Mon 5.30–10.30pm, Tues–Thurs & Sat noon–3pm & 4.30–10.30pm, Fri noon–3pm & 4.30–11pm.

SOUTHWARK

CAFÉS

★ **Bar Tozino** Ropewalk, Maltby St, SE1 ⓦbartozino .com; ⊖ London Bridge; map pp.224–225. Glorious Spanish wines and acorn-fed ham, along with a couple of cheeses and tapas (£3–10), are all you'll get at this wildly popular *jamón bodega* in the up-and-coming Maltby St food market (see p.434). Dark, friendly and redolent with the aroma of sweet ham, it's a welcome slice of Spain in southeast London. Wed–Fri 5–10pm, Sat 10am–10pm, Sun noon–5pm.

El Vergel 132 Webber St, SE1 ☎020 7401 2308, ⓦelvergel.co.uk; ⊖ Borough; map pp.224–225. Small, busy Latin American/Mediterranean café that does authentic breakfast tacos, salads and gourmet sandwiches, along with Latin American specialities including empanadas filled with meat and spices, cheese, seafood or spinach and feta, from £3.50. Takeaway available. Mon–Fri 8am–3pm, Sat 10am–4pm.

José 104 Bermondsey St, SE1 ⓦjosepizarro.com; ⊖ London Bridge; map pp.224–225. This sherry and tapas bar, run by José Pizarro, one of London's finest Spanish chefs – his more formal restaurant, *Pizarro*, nearby at no.194, is also terrific – is at the heart of Bermondsey's burgeoning foodie scene. Unfussy but beautifully executed tapas, on a regularly changing list, cost just £2–7, and the Spanish wines and sherries come by the reasonably priced glass. No reservations. Mon–Sat noon–10.30pm, Sun noon–5.30pm.

RESTAURANTS

★ **40 Maltby Street** 40 Maltby St, SE1 ☎020 7237 9247; ⊖ Bermondsey; map pp.224–225. A Maltby St favourite, this unpretentious wine bar, selling natural wines to drink in or take away, has the feel of a European market bar, serving simple plates of rustic, creative and extremely delicious French-influenced food to go with the wine. Dishes around £7. Wed & Thurs 5.30–10pm, Fri 12.30–2pm & 5.30–10pm, Sat 11am–5pm.

The Table 83 Southwark St, SE1 ☎020 7401 2760, ⓦthetablecafe.com; ⊖ Southwark or London Bridge; map pp.226–227. A modern restaurant, handy for the Tate, serving creative, seasonal food, largely Italian, at chunky canteen tables. Good breakfasts, too. Mains from £10 at dinner. Mon 7.30am–4.30pm, Tues–Fri 7.30am–4.30pm & 6–10.30pm, Sat 8.30am–4pm & 6–10.30pm, Sun 8.30am–4pm.

Village East 171–173 Bermondsey St, SE1 ☎020 7357 6082, ⓦvillageeast.co.uk; ⊖ London Bridge; map pp.224–225. Another Bermondsey St star, serving fresh and wild food – brunches, artisan burgers, gourmet salads, simple Modern European mains – and creative cocktails. Dishes £5–20. Mon–Fri noon–3pm & 6–10pm, Sat 9am–4pm & 6–10pm, Sun 9am–5pm & 6–9.30pm.

Zucca 184 Bermondsey St, SE1 ☎020 7378 6809, ⓦzuccalondon.com; ⊖ London Bridge; map pp.224–225. Prices for the modern Italian food in this restaurant, which sat here long before Bermondsey got trendy, are far lower than you'd expect. Fresh pasta, risottos, grilled razor clams, lamb chop with potato and anchovy – all of it is seasonal, made with the freshest, simplest ingredients, and served in huge portions. Mains £10–16. Tues–Fri noon–3pm & 6–10pm, Sat noon–3.30pm & 6–10pm, Sun 12–3.30pm.

SOUTH KENSINGTON & KNIGHTSBRIDGE

CAFÉS

Capote y Toros 157 Old Brompton Rd, SW5 ☎020 7373 0567, ⓦcambiodetercio.co.uk; ⊖ Gloucester Road or South Kensington; map pp.250–251. The emphasis at this classy bar is on Spain's wonderful sherries, with more than forty available by the glass, along with interesting modern tapas made with the stuff (£4–12). The same people run another tapas bar, *Tendido Cero*, at 174 Old Brompton Rd, and a more formal restaurant, *Cambio de Tercio*, at 163, which are also great. Tues–Sat 6–11.30pm.

The Troubadour 263–267 Old Brompton Rd, SW5 ☎020 7370 1434, ⓦtroubadour.co.uk; ⊖ Earl's Court; map pp.250–251. A classic 1950s folk bar, this cluttered boho café-club once played host to Hendrix, Bob Dylan and Joni Mitchell. It still runs terrific folk and blues nights, and dishes up omelettes, steaks and burgers and breakfasts. Daily 9am–midnight.

RESTAURANTS

Amaya Halkin Arcade, Motcomb St, SW1 ☎020 7823 1166, ⓦwww.amaya.biz; ⊖ Knightsbridge; map pp.250–251. The creative contemporary Indian food served in this smart dining room – delicate, finely flavoured grills, prepared in front of you in the open kitchen – well deserves its Michelin star. Dishes, served as sharing

24

plates, change regularly and cost from £11. Mon–Sat 12.30–2.15pm & 6.30–11.30pm, Sun 12.45–2.45pm & 6.30–10.30pm.

Dinner Mandarin Oriental Hotel, 66 Knightsbridge, SW1 ☎020 7201 3833, ⓦdinnerbyheston.com; ⊖ Knightsbridge; map pp.250–251. You know what to expect from Heston – imaginative, witty food that tastes amazing and gives you a once in a lifetime experience. Blumenthal doesn't actually cook here – the head chef worked with him at the *Fat Duck* – and there is less emphasis on flash and dazzle and molecular cuisine. Dishes are taken from British culinary history right through from medieval times, and some are marvellously odd – powdered duck, "meat fruit", taffety tart, frumenty. The sky's the limit as far as costs go, of course, though there's a three-course weekday lunch menu for £36, and the atmosphere is gratifyingly unintimidating. Mains from £25.

Daily noon–2.30pm & 6.30–10.30pm.

No.10 10 Hogarth Place, SW5 ☎020 7373 7000, ⓦno10-earlscourt.co.uk ⊖ Earl's Court; map pp.250–251. Stick to the Szechuan food and you're onto a winner in this small, low-key restaurant. Many dishes offer the peppery kick you'd expect, but they also have a number of less fiery treats. Mains around £7; you won't spend more than £18 a head for a big meal. Mon–Fri 12.30–2.15pm & 5.30–10.50pm, Sat & Sun 12.30–2.15pm & 5.30–10.20pm.

Racine 239 Brompton Rd, SW3 ☎020 7584 4477, ⓦracine-restaurant.com; ⊖ Knightsbridge or South Kensington; map p.252. The food here is French – rich, nostalgic dishes from the glory days of Gallic cuisine, perfectly executed. Mains from £16.50; two- or three-course menus £15.50/£17.75 Mon–Sat, £18/£20 Sun. Daily noon–3pm & 6–10.30pm.

CHELSEA

CAFÉS

Mona Lisa 417 King's Rd, SW10 ☎020 7376 5447; ⊖ Fulham Broadway; map p.265. This genuine old caff – very unusual in chichi Chelsea – dishes up cheap, good, old-fashioned food in plain, convivial surroundings. The mixed local crowd – from Sloanes to regulars from the adjoining council estate – enjoy anything from big fry-ups to great Italian comfort food – including good fish dishes. Mon–Sat 8am–6pm, Sun 9am–4pm.

RESTAURANTS

Chutney Mary 535 King's Rd, SW10 ☎020 7351 3113, ⓦwww.chutneymary.com; ⊖ Fulham Broadway; map pp.250–251. *Chutney Mary* turns out gourmet Indian food – complicated, subtle dishes with modern twists – and rather wonderful Anglo-Indian puds on changing menus. Mains £17–25; Sunday lunch buffet £26. Mon–Fri 6.30–11.30pm, Sat 12.30–2.45pm & 6.30–11.30pm, Sun 12.30–2.30pm & 6.30–10.30pm.

Hunan 51 Pimlico Rd, SW1 ☎020 7730 5712, ⓦhunanlondon.com; ⊖ Sloane Square; map p.265. Don't go too much by its name – rather than Hunanese cuisine, this acclaimed restaurant serves delicious Taiwanese/Chinese fusion food. There's no menu: tell them how spicy you like things, and any other preferences, and they'll bring you an array of small dishes to your table for a "leave-it-to-us feast". Reservations essential. Feasts from £45 per head, drinks included. Mon–Sat 12.30–2pm & 6.30–11pm.

★ **Medlar** 438 Kings Rd, SW10 ☎020 7349 1900, ⓦmedlarrestaurant.co.uk; ⊖ Fulham Broadway; map p.265. Really good, Michelin-starred French-influenced Modern British food with deceptively simple dishes, the like of duck egg tart with red wine sauce or wild turbot with ginger, mushroom and soy broth, served in a relaxed, welcoming dining room. It's *prix fixe*, and excellent value: three-course lunch £26 Mon–Fri, £30 Sat & Sun, three-course dinner £42. Daily noon–3pm & 6.30–10.30pm.

HIGH STREET KENSINGTON TO NOTTING HILL

CAFÉS

Books for Cooks 4 Blenheim Crescent, W11 ☎020 7221 1992, ⓦwww.booksforcooks.com; ⊖ Ladbroke Grove or Notting Hill Gate; map pp.274–275. Cute dining area within London's top cookery bookshop (see p.429). Conditions are cosy, to say the least, but it's a great little find. Wander in and have a coffee and cake while browsing, or get there in time to grab a seat for the set-menu lunch, using recipes from one of the books in the store (noon–1.30pm). Tues–Sat 10am–6pm.

Lisboa Patisserie 57 Golborne Rd, W10 ☎020 8968 5242; ⊖ Westbourne Park; map pp.274–275. Authentic Portuguese *pastelaria*, a perfect Portobello Rd pitstop, with the best coffee and *pasteis de nata* (custard tarts) this side

of Lisbon. *Café O'porto* at 62a Golborne Rd is a good fall-back if this is full. Daily 8am–6pm.

Tom's Deli 226 Westbourne Grove, W11 ☎020 7221 8818, ⓦtomsdeli.co.uk; ⊖ Westbourne Park; map pp.274–275. It's all very Notting Hill – relaxed, cluttered, boho-posh – at this charming, bustling deli-café, which

---

TOP 5 BUDGET-BLOWERS

Dabbous The City. See p.372
Dinner Knightsbridge. See above
The Ledbury Notting Hill. See p.382
St John Clerkenwell. See p.376
Viajante Bethnal Green. See p.379

serves tasty all-day breakfasts, soups, casseroles and gooey puds. Prices, starting at £6 for eggs on toast or a fresh fruit salad, can mount up. Mon–Sat 8am–6.30pm, Sun 9am–5pm.

RESTAURANTS

Le Café Anglais 8 Porchester Gardens, W2 ☎ 020 7221 1415, ⊛ lecafeanglais.co.uk; ⊖ Bayswater; map p.274. Modern British/European brasserie in an airy, vaguely Art Deco space within the Whiteley's shopping mall. Food is tempting, from the pike *boudin* with *beurre blanc* to the signature parmesan custard with anchovy toast, and there's an oyster bar for smaller dishes. Mains £13–35; set lunch menus (two/three courses) £19.50–27.50/£24.50–32.50. Mon–Thurs noon–3.30pm & 6.30–10.30pm, Fri & Sat noon–3.30pm & 6.30–11pm, Sun noon–3.30pm & 6.30–10pm; oyster bar Mon–Sat noon–10.30 pm, Sun noon–5pm.

Hereford Road 3 Hereford Rd, W2 ☎ 020 7727 1144, ⊛ herefordroad.org; ⊖ Queensway or Notting Hill Gate; map pp.274–275. The contemporary dining room, with bustling open kitchen, is a smart setting for the accomplished English cooking from St John alumni Tom Pemberton. You'll find the same emphasis on simple, old-fashioned excellence – ham hock and pea shoots, stuffed lamb heart with nettles, and the like, with a good list of Old World wines by glass, carafe or bottle. The set meals are an astonishing bargain. Mains £10–23. Two- or three-course weekday lunch menu £13/£15.50, or an "express lunch" for £9.50. Mon–Sat noon–3pm & 6–10.30pm, Sun noon–4pm & 6–10pm.

★ **The Ledbury** 127 Ledbury Rd, W11 ☎ 020 7792 9090, ⊛ www.theledbury.com; ⊖ Westbourne Park; map pp.274–275. Australian wünderkind Brett Graham has scooped two Michelin stars for his fabulous French-inspired food – elegant, confident, a bit nouvelle and packed with flavour. Typical dishes include Berkshire Muntjac with celeriac baked in juniper bone marrow and wild garlic. The atmosphere, for such a raved about restaurant, is gratifyingly warm and welcoming. Mains from £28; set lunch menus at £30 for two courses or £35 for three. Mon 6.30–10.15pm, Tues–Sat noon–2pm & 6.30–10.15pm, Sun noon–2.30pm & 7–10pm.

★ **Mandalay** 444 Edgware Rd, W2 ☎ 020 7258 3696, ⊛ mandalayway.com; ⊖ Edgware Road; map pp.274–275. Authentic Burmese cuisine – a melange of Thai, Malaysian, a bit of Chinese and a lot of Indian. The portions are huge, the service friendly and the prices low. Booking recommended in the evening. Mains £5–8.50. Mon–Sat noon–2.30pm & 6–10.30pm.

Pearl Liang 8 Sheldon Square, W2 ☎ 020 7289 7000, ⊛ www.pearlliang.co.uk; ⊖ Paddington; map pp.274–275. The setting, in a modern development near Paddington station, is unpromising, but it's well worth the trek to this classy spot for superb dim sum (try the wasabi prawn dumplings). Dim sum around £3 at lunch, £4.50 in the evening, takeaway weekday lunch boxes from £5.50. Daily noon–11pm.

Saf Whole Foods Market, Barkers, W8 ☎ 020 7368 4555, ⊛ safrestaurant.co.uk; ⊖ High Street Kensington; map pp.274–275. *Saf* stands for "simply authentic food" – this modern, vegan restaurant, set in a kind of open food court, specializes in vibrant (mostly raw) fruit and veg dishes from around the world. Many ingredients (including the dairy-free cheeses) are created on site. Natural wines and cocktails, too. Mains £9–13, with wraps, burgers and salads for less. Mon–Sat noon–10pm, Sun noon–6pm.

CAMDEN TOWN

CAFÉS

★ **My Village** 37 Chalk Farm Rd, NW1 ☎ 020 3489 2293, ⊛ myvillagecafebar.co.uk; ⊖ Chalk Farm; map pp.284–285. There aren't many places like this left in London nowadays: a funky, friendly, ramshackle café whose bare-brick walls, handpainted glass, battered furniture, well-thumbed mags and fairy lights welcome you in to hang out for hours. Stop by for a coffee or a glass of wine, or tuck into the cheap and tasty organic, veggie and vegan Middle Eastern food – you'll get a heaped plate for a fiver. Takeaway available. Mon–Thurs 9am–7.30pm, Fri 9am–8.30pm, Sat & Sun 10.30am–8.30pm.

RESTAURANTS

★ **El Parador** 245 Eversholt St, NW1 ☎ 020 7387 2789, ⊛ elparadorlondon.com; ⊖ Mornington Crescent; map pp.284–285. Though there's little fuss here, the tapas (£4.20–8.50), served in a small, simple dining room with a friendly neighbourhood buzz, are some of London's best. There's a splendid, creative veggie selection (try the rosemary- and garlic-roasted beet salad or the fennel hearts roasted with tarragon). Mon–Thurs noon–3pm & 6–11pm, Fri & Sat noon–3pm & 6–11.30pm, Sun 6.30–9.30pm.

Manna 4 Erskine Rd, NW3 ☎ 020 7722 8028, ⊛ mannav.com; ⊖ Chalk Farm; map pp.284–285. Longstanding, upscale veggie restaurant, full of Primrose Hill yoga types, serving large portions of mostly organic, food, much of it vegan, from around the world. Mains £11–14, less at lunch. Tues–Fri 6.30–10.30pm, Sat noon–3pm & 6.30–10.30pm, Sun noon–3pm & 6.30–10pm.

Namaaste Kitchen 64 Parkway, NW1 ☎ 020 7485 5977, ⊛ namaastekitchen.co.uk; ⊖ Camden Town; map pp.284–285. The modern Pakistani and Indian food in this contemporary restaurant – prepared with top-quality ingredients and cooked with flair in an open kitchen – well deserves its many accolades. Some dishes, like tandoori Portobello mushroom filled with

24

figs, cashew and raisins, are unusual, and even the more familiar options, like pistachio chicken korma, are given a fresh twist. Mains £8–19; six-course tasting menu

£24.95. Takeaway available. Mon–Thurs noon–2.30pm & 5.30–11.30pm, Fri & Sat noon–11.30pm, Sun noon–11pm.

ISLINGTON

CAFÉS

Afghan Kitchen 35 Islington Green, N1 ☎020 7359 8019; ⊖ Angel; map pp.284–285. Austere, two-floor café with bare bench seating, featuring a short menu of spiced stews dished up with rice and hot, fresh bread. Tues–Sat noon–3.30pm & 5.30–10.30pm.

Issy's Milky Way 28 Camden Passage, N1 ⓦfacebook .com/issys.milkyway; ⊖ Angel; map pp.284–285. The kitschy vintage decor at this tiny soda fountain is as much a draw as the fab fifties-style food (shakes and sundaes, toasties, hotdogs, bagels, sponge cakes). Perch at a tiny formica table, order an Elvis cupcake and a root beer shake, check out the juke box and feel your mood lift. Daily.

M. Manze/Seagrass 74 Chapel Market, N1 ☎020 7837 5270 (M.Manze), ☎07902 015 200 (Seagrass), ⓦtheseagrassrestaurant.com; ⊖ Angel; map pp.284–285. With its gleaming tiled walls, marble tables, wooden booths and unchanging menu, this traditional eel, pie and mash shop offers a uniquely nostalgic experience (not least in the prices – pie and mash costs around £5). In the evenings, it's taken over by a Modern European restaurant, where £30 gets you a simple but good three-course meal, focusing on game and fish (BYOB). M.Manze: Mon 11am–3pm, Tues–Sat 11am–5pm, Sun 10.30am–4pm; Seagrass: Wed–Sat 7–11.30pm

RESTAURANTS

Gem 265 Upper St, N1 ☎020 7359 0405,

ⓦgemrestaurant.org.uk; ⊖ Highbury & Islington; map pp.284–285. This high-ceilinged, simple Turkish and Kurdish restaurant specializes in charcoal-grilled dishes, but ordering a selection of hot and cold starters (meze, from £3) will get you a delicious, inexpensive meal. Mop them all up with the smoky Turkish bread that's freshly prepared at the front of the restaurant. Mon–Thurs noon–11pm, Fri & Sat noon–midnight, Sun noon–10.30pm.

Ottolenghi 287 Upper St, N1 ☎020 7288 1454, ⓦottolenghi.co.uk; ⊖ Angel; map pp.284–285. Yotam Ottolenghi's vibrant cuisine raised the bar for Mediterranean food in Britain, and this modern café-restaurant, with long communal tables, is a buzzy spot to enjoy his trademark imaginative salads and fantastic desserts (check out those meringues!). They do breakfast, too, with table-top toasters and piles of newspapers. It's not, in any way, cheap. Takeaway available. Branches in Notting Hill, Kensington and Belgravia. Mains from £11. Mon–Sat 8am–11pm, Sun 9am–7pm.

★ **Trullo** 300–302 St Paul's Rd, N1 ☎020 7226 2733, ⓦtrullorestaurant.com; ⊖ Highbury & Islington; map pp.284–285. Relaxed, warm elegance and stunningly simple seasonal Italian food at this lovely little local restaurant, a tranquil hideaway on traffic-choked Highbury Corner. Mains from £14 at dinner, £10 at lunch. Two-course weekday lunch £12. Mon–Sat 12.30–2.45pm & 6–10.15pm, Sun 12.30–2.45pm.

STOKE NEWINGTON AND DALSTON

CAFÉS

Blue Legume 101 Stoke Newington Church St, N16 ☎020 7923 1303, ⓦthebluelegume.co.uk; Stoke

Newington train station; map p.291. The chatty atmosphere, arty-hippie decor and big, wholesome portions of mainly veggie food – colourful salads, pies,

24

GREAT GASTROPUBS

Gone are the days when eating in a pub meant settling for a Ploughman's and a packet of pork scratchings – the following places, reviewed in our Pubs and bars chapter, offer gourmet food to rival some of the city's best restaurants, in laidback, friendly surroundings.

Anchor & Hope South Bank. See p.392
The Cow Notting Hill. See p.395
The Dove Hackney. See p.397
The Duke of Cambridge Islington. See p.396
The Eagle Clerkenwell. See p.390
The Elgin Notting Hill. See p.395
The Empress Hackney. See p.397
Fox & Anchor Clerkenwell. See p.390
Greenwich Union Greenwich. See p.398
The Greyhound Kew. See p.398

The Gun Docklands. See p.392
Island Queen Islington. See p.396
The Lansdowne Camden/Primrose Hill. See p.396
Paradise by Way of Kensal Green Notting Hill. See p.395
The Peasant Clerkenwell. See p.390
The Pig's Ear Chelsea. See p.395
The Stag Hampstead. See p.397
The Westbourne Notting Hill. See p.395

24

bakes – make this longstanding café a cheery stalwart on Stoke Newington's liveliest street. Good all-day breakfasts too – eggs Benedict, wild mushrooms on toast and the like, from £5–7 – and great cakes, coffee and fresh juices. Branches in Islington and Crouch End. Mon–Sat 9.30am–11pm, Sun 9.30am–6.30pm.

F.Cooke 9 Broadway Market, E8 ☎020 7254 6458; London Fields train station; map p.291. "Eat more eels!" announces an old sign at this friendly, traditional eel and pie shop that's been in the family for generations and on this spot since 1900. Order pie, mash, liquor (parsley gravy) and a side of jellied eels and enjoy a nostalgic taste of old East End history on foodie Broadway Market, where funky indie cafés rule the roost. They host pop up restaurants in the evenings, too. Mon–Thurs 10am–7pm, Fri & Sat 10am–8pm.

★ **Towpath Café** Whitmore Bridge, 42 de Beauvoir Crescent, N1 ☎020 7254 7606, Ⓦtowpathcafe .wordpress.com; Haggerston Overground; map p.291. With outdoor benches by the Regent's canal near Dalston, Hoxton and Broadway Market, this is a lovely, sunny find on the towpath; food is creative and seasonal, using unusual and impeccably sourced ingredients – great for brunch, with the likes of truffle and parmesan buns, organic sausages and toasted cheese on sourdough, or something a bit more complex, like a paella, later on. Good soups, coffees and fresh home-made juices, too. Dishes from £3; no credit cards. March–Nov Tues–Fri 8am–dusk, Sat & Sun 10am–dusk.

Voodoo Ray's 95 Kingsland High St, E8 ☎020 7249 7865, Ⓦvoodoorays.co.uk; Dalston Junction

Overground; map p.291. Grungy late-night drinking dens come and go in Dalston like a rash, but *Voodoo Ray's* seems set to stay – a late-night pizza/Margarita joint where the American-style pizzas (from £3.50/slice) are huge and flavourful, and the Margaritas – usually being necked by a crowd who've had quite enough already – are cold and strong. Craft beers, too, and a DJ bar downstairs. Mon–Thurs & Sun 6pm–1am, Fri & Sat 4pm–3am.

RESTAURANTS

Mangal Ocakbasi 10 Arcola St, E8 ☎020 7275 8981, Ⓦmangal1.com; Dalston Junction Overground; map p.291. Generally agreed to be the best of the excellent Turkish diners in a neighbourhood that's spilling over with them, *Mangal* is renowned for its grills and skewered meats, many of them served with yoghurt sauce; the veggie mezes and fresh breads are good, too. At its sister restaurant, *Mangal II*, around the corner on Stoke Newington High St, you will join artists Gilbert and George, who eat here nightly, for similarly simple food and friendly service. Dishes from £5. Daily noon–midnight.

★ **Rasa** 55 Stoke Newington Church St, N16 ☎020 7249 0344, Ⓦrasarestaurants.com; Stoke Newington train station; map p.291. Cosy Keralan restaurant, the first in London's *Rasa* family, with amazingly good, unusual and very inexpensive South Indian vegetarian specialities. The equally fine *Rasa Travancore* across the road specializes in Syrian Christian cooking, serving some meat and fish. Mains £4–6. Mon–Thurs 6–10.45pm, Fri 6–11.30pm, Sat noon–3pm & 6–11.30pm, Sun noon–3pm & 6–10.45pm.

HAMPSTEAD AND HIGHGATE

CAFÉS

Brew House Kenwood House, Hampstead Lane, NW3 ☎020 8341 5384, Ⓦcompanyofcooks.com; ⊖ Highgate; map pp.298–299. Appealing park café, in the servants' wing of the Robert Adam mansion, serving everything from home-made sausage and mash to gourmet sandwiches, cakes and teas. Lots of seating in the huge, sunny garden courtyard. Daily: spring & summer 9am–6pm; autumn & winter 9am–4pm.

Lauderdale House Waterlow Park, Highgate Hill, N6 ☎020 8341 4807, Ⓦlauderdalehouse.org.uk; ⊖ Archway; map pp.298–299. Fill up on home-made comfort food in this casual arts centre café, or simply enjoy a cuppa and a slab of cake. On sunny days the terrace, overlooking the park, is a great spot. Tues–Sun 9am–5pm (6pm in summer).

Louis Patisserie 32 Heath St, NW3 ☎020 7435 9908; ⊖ Hampstead; map pp.298–299. Coffee house trends may come and go, but for more than fifty years now this tiny, understated and gloriously old-fashioned Hungarian tearoom/patisserie has been serving sticky

cakes, tea and coffee to a mixed local crowd. Daily 9am–6pm.

RESTAURANTS

Czechoslovak Restaurant 74 West End Lane, NW6 ☎020 7372 1193, Ⓦczechoslovak-restaurant.co.uk; ⊖ West Hampstead; map pp.298–299. Classic, unreconstructed Czech and Slovak meat and dumplings washed down with Czech beer. Set in a tatty residential house with a back garden, it's a blast from the past, quite unique and very popular with Czech expats. Mains £8–13. Tues–Fri 5–10pm, Sat & Sun noon–10pm.

★ **Jin Kichi** 73 Heath St, NW3 ☎020 7794 6158, Ⓦjinkichi.com; ⊖ Hampstead; map pp.298–299. Book ahead for this tiny, homely and very busy neighbourhood Japanese diner, which specializes in charcoal-grilled *yakitori* (skewers): lots of chicken, of course, but also quails' eggs or ox tongue, among others. The sushi, black cod and other Japanese staples are great, too. Mains £7–15. Tues–Sat 12.30–2pm & 6–10.45pm, Sun 12.30–2pm & 6–10pm.

BRIXTON

CAFÉS

Elephant 55 Granville Arcade, Brixton Village, Coldharbour Lane, SW9 ☎07715 439857, Ⓦelephantcafeonline.blogspot.co.uk; map pp.310–311. An unpretentious star among Brixton Market's foodie Brixton Village, dishing up huge plates of perfectly spiced home-cooked Pakistani street food, from lamb samosas to thalis and veg curries. Most dishes around £5. Tues noon–5.30pm, Wed noon–4pm, Thurs–Sat noon–4pm & 6–10pm, Sun noon–5pm.

★ **Franco Manca** 4 Market Row, SW9 ☎020 7738 3021, Ⓦfrancomanca.co.uk; ⊖ Brixton; map pp.310–311. Fabulous, tiny gourmet pizza joint in Brixton Market that offers amazingly inexpensive sourdough pizzas (£4.50–7) – there are just six options, all wood-fired and made with the finest ingredients – washed down with organic wine or lemonade. Mon noon–5pm, Tues–Sat noon–11pm, Sun noon –10.30pm.

★ **KaoSarn** Brixton Village, Coldharbour Lane, SW9 ☎020 7095 8922; ⊖ Brixton; map pp.310–311. This little family-run Thai place may not be as trendy as some of the Brixton Village hot spots, but it serves consistently excellent, flavoursome and authentic food – curries, noodle salads and seafood are all superb – from around £6. BYOB. Tues–Sat noon–10pm, Sun noon–9pm.

GREENWICH

CAFÉS

Red Door 10 Turnpin Lane, SE10 ☎020 8858 2131, Ⓦreddoorgallery.co.uk; Cutty Sark DLR; map p.315. An arty little café/shop/gallery, handy for the market – where you will also find plenty of good street food – serving gourmet sandwiches and snacks, with lots of gluten-free options, along with Monmouth coffee and home-made cakes. Mon–Wed 10am–6pm, Thurs–Sun 9am–6pm.

RESTAURANTS

Old Brewery Pepys Building, The Old Royal Naval College, SE10 ☎020 3327 1280, Ⓦwww.oldbrewerygreenwich.com; Cutty Sark DLR; map p.315. During the day, this warm, historic dining room, home to the Meantime microbrewery, serves bar snacks and Modern British gastropub lunches, before transforming with aplomb into a relaxed neighbourhood brasserie at night. Mains from £7 at lunch, £11 at dinner. Daily 10am–11pm (10.30pm on Sun).

24

HAMMERSMITH AND CHISWICK

RESTAURANTS

Azou 375 King St, W6 ☎020 8563 7266, Ⓦazou.co.uk; ⊖ Stamford Brook; map p.331. Small, informal North African restaurant where you can enter into the spirit and sit on a cushion on the floor. A friendly welcome is assured and the classics – tagines and couscous – are presented with panache. Mains £11–23. Mon–Sat 6–11pm, Sun 6–10pm.

The Gate 51 Queen Caroline St, W6 ☎020 8748 6932, Ⓦthegate.tv; ⊖ Hammersmith; map p.331. In a converted church with a courtyard, *The Gate* serves excellent and original vegetarian and vegan dishes – Arabic/Jewish with Mediterranean influences – with intense and satisfying tastes. The weekend brunch is popular. Mains around £13; three meze for £10. Branch in Islington. Mon–Fri noon–2.30pm & 6–10.30pm, Sat 6–11pm.

KEW AND RICHMOND

CAFÉS

Greenhouse 1 Station Parade, Richmond, TW9 ☎020 8940 0183; ⊖ Kew Gardens; map p.341. A pretty, simple stop off near Kew Gardens, with light lunches, traditional pies, cream teas and home-made tarts. Daily 8am–dusk.

Pembroke Lodge Richmond Park, Richmond, TW10 ☎020 8940 8207; ⊖ Richmond; map p.341. This park café, in a gorgeous Georgian mansion in Richmond Park, has one of the best views in London, looking west over the Thames valley, and nice outdoor seating – there are some hot dishes, plus sandwiches and cakes. Daily 9am–5.30pm or dusk.

★ **Stein's** Richmond Towpath, Richmond, TW10 ☎020 8948 8189, Ⓦstein-s.com; ⊖ Richmond; map p.341. A Bavarian-style riverside beer garden, serving up wurst and sauerkraut washed down with *echt* beers and finished off with strudel. Outdoor seating only; it's likely to be closed in bad weather. Summer Mon–Fri noon–10pm, Sat & Sun 10.30am–10pm; rest of year Sat & Sun noon–dusk.

RESTAURANTS

Chez Lindsay 11 Hill Rise, Richmond, TW10 ☎020 8948 7473, Ⓦchezlindsay.co.uk; ⊖ Richmond; map p.341. Small, bright, riverside Breton restaurant, with a loyal local following. There's a wide choice of galettes, crêpes and more formal French main courses, including lots of fresh fish and shellfish. Galettes from £5, mains £10–20. Mon–Sat noon–11pm, Sun noon–10pm.

ROYAL OAK, BOROUGH

Pubs and bars

London is a great drinking city. The range and quality of the pubs and bars in the capital is extraordinary. Whether you're looking for a handsome Victorian gin palace or a down-and-dirty hipster dive, the problem isn't finding it but making a choice. The pub remains one of the country's most enduring social institutions, and is still the place where folk of all ages choose to meet up of an evening. Charming, historic pubs can be found all over the city, often in the backstreets, while many of the capital's best bars – serving everything from fine wine and craft beers to cutting-edge cocktails – are clustered around buzzy nightlife zones like Soho and Shoreditch. Wherever you drink, the choice available in most places has improved in recent years and decent pub food is now the rule rather than the exception.

Most good pubs serve at least two or three **real ales** (see p.389), as well as the usual array of drinks. The rise of **gastropubs**, where the food is as important as the booze, if not more so, has had a knock-on effect on all pubs, improving the overall standard of cooking as well as increasing the amount pubs can charge for food. We've also reviewed some of the capital's bars, which go in and out of fashion with incredible speed. London also boasts numerous pubs that are primarily live music venues (see p.400), and gay and lesbian pubs and bars (see p.405). **Prices** can be steep, with the £4 pint common, and bottled beers almost as much. A good cocktail, meanwhile, could set you back more than £8. However, prices drop a little out of the centre, while many bars run weekday happy hours, usually 5–7pm, when drinks are either half-price or discounted.

WHITEHALL, WESTMINSTER AND ST JAMES'S

The Chandos 29 St Martin's Lane, WC2 ☎020 7836 1401; ⊖ Charing Cross; map, p.46. If you can get one of the booths downstairs, or the leather sofas upstairs in the more relaxed Opera Room Bar, then you'll find it difficult to leave this Sam Smith's pub. Mon–Sat 11am–11pm, Sun noon–10.30pm.

ICA Bar The Mall, SW1 ☎020 7930 3647, ⓦica.org.uk; ⊖ Piccadilly Circus or Charing Cross; map p.66. Cool, minimal drinking venue in this excellent gallery/arts centre/cinema. Tues–Sun 11am–11pm.

Red Lion 23 Crown Passage, SW1 ☎020 7930 4141; ⊖ Green Park; map p.66. Hidden away in a passageway off Pall Mall, this is a warm and cosy local, with super friendly bar staff, well-kept beer and good sandwiches. Mon–Sat 11.30am–11pm.

St Stephen's Tavern 10 Bridge St, SW1 ☎020 7925 2286, ⓦststephenstavern.co.uk; ⊖ Westminster; map p.46. Opulent Victorian pub opposite the Houses of Parliament and wall to wall with civil servants and MPs. Good real ales, plus fish and chips and pies. Mon–Thurs & Sat 10am–11.30pm, Fri 10am–midnight, Sun noon–10.30pm.

MAYFAIR

Audley 41 Mount St, W1 ☎020 7499 1843; ⊖ Hyde Park Corner or Bond Street; map p.78. A grand Mayfair pub, with original Victorian lincrusta ceiling, beautiful wood-panelled walls, chandeliers and clocks. Mon–Sat 11am–11pm, Sun noon–10.30pm.

The Windmill 6–8 Mill St, W1 ☎020 7491 8050, ⓦwindmillmayfair.co.uk; ⊖ Oxford Circus; map p.78. Convivial pub just off Regent St, and a perfect retreat for exhausted shoppers. The Young's beers are top-notch, as are the traditional pies, which have won numerous awards. Its sister pub, *The Guinea*, nearby on Bruton Place is also good. Mon–Fri 11am–11pm, Sat noon–4.30pm.

Ye Grapes 16 Shepherd Market, W1 ☎020 7493 4216; ⊖ Green Park or Hyde Park Corner; map p.78. Very popular pub in Shepherd Market, a charming corner of Mayfair hidden away to the north of Piccadilly. If the *Grapes* is too busy, try the *King's Arms*, also in Shepherd Market. Mon–Sat noon–11pm, Sun noon–10pm.

MARYLEBONE

Golden Eagle 59 Marylebone Lane, W1 ☎020 7935 3228; ⊖ Bond Street; map p.89. Proper old one-room, neighbourhood pub – a delight in this swanky area – with a good range of real ales, and regular singalongs on the old Joanna. Mon–Sat 11am–11pm, Sun noon–7pm.

Gunmakers 33 Aybrook St, W1 ☎020 7487 4937; ⊖ Bond Street; map p.89. Tucked away to the west of Marylebone's high street, this is a characterful joint, all wood panelling and Churchill memorabilia. Good pub grub, too. Can get very busy on Saturdays, and avoid if you're bothered by sport on the TV. Mon–Sat 11am–midnight, Sun 11am–10.30pm.

SOHO

Blue Posts 28 Rupert St, W1 ☎020 7437 1415; ⊖ Leicester Square; map p.100. Soho boasts no less than six *Blue Posts*; this is our favourite, a raffish, shabby and convivial bolthole on the area's less trendy fringes. This is definitively not a gastropub; you can soak up the real ales with their trademark salt beef sandwiches and enjoy live jazz on Sundays. Mon–Thurs 11am–11.30pm, Fri & Sat 11am–midnight, Sun noon–10.30pm.

Dog & Duck 18 Bateman St, W1 ☎020 7494 0697; ⊖ Tottenham Court Road; map p.100. Tiny Nicholson's pub that retains much of its old character, beautiful Victorian tiling and mosaics, a good range of real ales and a loyal clientele. If it gets too busy downstairs, head upstairs to the George Orwell Bar (he used to drink here). Daily 10am–11pm.

★ **French House** 49 Dean St, W1 ☎020 7437 2799, ⓦfrenchhousesoho.com; ⊖ Leicester Square; map p.100. This cosy French pub has been a boho Soho institution since Belgian Victor Berlemont bought the place shortly before World War I. Free French and literary

DRINKING IN LONDON: NEIGHBOURHOOD BY NEIGHBOURHOOD

Clerkenwell A good mix of traditional pubs and cool bars in a small area. The newest places are concentrated on Exmouth Market and around Smithfield Market. It's also a foodie hotspot – *The Eagle* on Farringdon Road was a pioneer of the gastropub scene (see p.390).

Notting Hill The pick of West London's neighbourhoods, with a mix of comfy old favourites and newbies. The area around Portobello Road and Westbourne Grove is a good hunting ground.

The riverside A drink by the river is a great London experience, but the centre is notoriously thin on riverside pubs. Travel out a little – to Hammersmith to the west and Wapping and Bermondsey to the east – to find the best places (see box, p.394).

Shoreditch/Hoxton Although East London isn't quite as cool as it was in the 1990s, nowhere else has quite such an eclectic mix of historic pubs, rough-and-ready dives and hip new arrivals.

Soho Renowned for its bohemian old boozers, Soho also has more than its fair share of cool, contemporary spots. It's always crowded, boasting an unrivalled range of watering holes within a small area. Drink here, and you'll feel at the very heart of the action.

Southwark The area around Borough Market has many enjoyable places to drink, from historic gems to the newer bars around the market itself. There's a great concentration of top-notch places in a small area here, but it can be extremely busy.

associations galore, and half-pints, bottled beers, wine and champagne only at the bar (no real ale). No mobile phones. Mon–Sat noon–11pm, Sun noon–10.30pm.

Phoenix Artist Club 1 Phoenix St, WC2 ☎020 7836 1077, ⓦphoenixartistclub.com; ⊖ Leicester Square; map p.100. This members' bar, tucked away beneath a theatre, has been hosting high-spirited ne'er-do-wells since way before London's Prohibition/members' club scene became trendy. And trendy this place is not – it's a high-spirited dive, with theatrical types of all stripes making merry. Nonmembers need to arrive before 8pm. Mon–Sat 5pm–2.30am, Sun 5pm–1am (roughly).

FITZROVIA

Bourne and Hollingsworth 28 Rathbone Place, W1 ☎020 7636 8228, ⓦbourneandhollingsworth.com; ⊖ Goodge Street; map p.97. One of the first, and still one of the best, of London's Prohibiton-style vintage cocktail bars, offering creative gin cocktails and punches served in jars, tin mugs and tea cups, in a delicately shabby subterranean granny's parlour. Mon–Wed 5pm–1am, Thurs–Sat 5pm–1.30am.

Bradley's Spanish Bar 42–44 Hanway St, W1 ☎020 7636 0359, ⓦbradleysspanishbar.co.uk; ⊖ Tottenham Court Road; map p.97. Appealingly unpretentious backstreet bar with a mixed, merry clientele, a variety of Spanish beers and an excellent vinyl jukebox. When the doors close the diehards tumble out into *Mia Sevilla*, another tiny, shabby and good fun Spanish bar a couple of doors down (opens late; closed Sun). Mon–Thurs noon–11.30pm, Fri & Sat noon–midnight, Sun 3–10.30pm.

The Green Man 36 Riding House St, W1 ☎020 7580 9087, ⓦthegreenmanw1.co.uk; ⊖ Oxford Circus; map p.97. Slightly more offbeat than most pubs this close to Oxford and Regent streets, the *Green Man* is a real find, with an excellent range of craft beers, ciders and cask ales. Mon–Sat noon–11pm, Sun noon–10.30pm.

★ **Newman Arms** 23 Rathbone St, W1 ☎020 7636 1127, ⓦnewmanarms.co.uk; ⊖ Tottenham Court Road or Goodge Street; map p.97. Intimate, friendly, family-run free house, popular with a mixed and loyal crowd. Try one of their fabulous pies, from lamb-and-rosemary to roast vegetable. Mon–Fri noon–11.30pm.

The Yorkshire Grey 46 Langham St, W1 ☎020 7636 4788; ⊖ Oxford Circus; map p.97. This cosy and appealing place has good-value Sam Smith's beer and a snug corner beside the fire (something you'll need to compete for). Mon–Sat noon–11pm, Sun 6pm–10.30pm.

BLOOMSBURY

Bar Pepito 3 Varnishers Yard, The Regent Quarter, N1 ☎020 7841 7331, ⓦbarpepito.co.uk; ⊖ King's Cross; map p.120. A welcoming sherry bodega, an offshoot of the Spanish restaurant *Camino* opposite, offering simple cold tapas to go with your manzanilla or your fino. Mon–Fri 5pm–midnight, Sat 6pm–midnight.

★ **The Duke** 7 Roger St, WC1 ☎020 7242 7230, ⓦdukepub.co.uk; ⊖ Russell Square; map p.120. Lovely little neighbourhood pub with an unusual, unforced Art Deco flavour and lots of interwar design details. Its discreet location keeps the crowd in the small bar manageable; simple, good food, too. Mon–Sat noon–11pm.

Euston Tap 190 Euston Rd, NW1 ☎020 3137, ⓦeustontap.com; ⊖ Euston; map p.120. Crammed into a tiny Victorian gatehouse outside the railway station, this is a sociable and high-spirited micropub for serious ale lovers. Regularly changing cask, keg and bottle beers and ciders and perries on tap. Daily noon–11.30pm.

The Lamb 94 Lamb's Conduit St, WC1 ☎020 7405 0713; ⊖ Russell Square; map p.120. Well-preserved Victorian pub with mirrors, polished wood, leather banquettes and etched glass "snob" screens. Rather peaceful, as there's no music or TV. Mon–Wed noon–11pm, Thurs–Sat noon–midnight, Sun noon–10.30pm.

Museum Tavern 49 Great Russell St, WC1 ☎020 7242 8987; ⊖ Tottenham Court Road or Russell Square; map p.120. The erstwhile drinking hole of Karl Marx is a handsome, quite touristy, old pub opposite the main entrance to the British Museum. A range of ales and British spirits available. Mon–Thurs 11am–11.30pm, Fri & Sat 11am–midnight, Sun 10am–1pm.

Parcel Yard King's Cross station, N1C ☎020 7713 7258, ⓦparcelyard.co.uk; ⊖ King's Cross; map p.120. A train-lover's delight – and handy if you're between connections – this spacious Fuller's pub is handily located in the station concourse. Occupying the old station's 1850 parcel yard, with lots of original features and a huge, glass-ceilinged atrium, it's a nice spot for cask ales, guest beers and classy pub grub. Mon–Sat 8am–11pm, Sun 9am–10.30pm.

Queen's Head 66 Acton St, WC1 ☎020 7713 5772, ⓦqueensheadlondon.com ⊖ King's Cross; map p.120. Attractive and laidback Victorian local, modernized but not to within an inch of its life, offering cheese, chunky pies and charcuterie alongside craft beers and ciders. Events include comedy, quizzes and occasional live folk and blues. Mon 4–11pm, Tues–Sat noon–midnight, Sun noon–11pm.

COVENT GARDEN AND THE STRAND

Cross Keys 31 Endell St, WC2 ☎020 7836 5185, ⓦcrosskeyscoventgarden.com; ⊖ Covent Garden; map p.132. Stuffed with copper pots, brass instruments, paintings and memorabilia, and fronted with a profusion of flowers and shrubs, this most welcoming of West End pubs attracts an appealing blend of older Covent Garden residents, young workers and tourists – you'll do well to find a seat. Mon–Sat 11am–11pm, Sun noon–10.30pm.

Gordon's 47 Villiers St, WC2 ☎020 7930 1408, ⓦgordonswinebar.com; ⊖ Charing Cross or Embankment; map p.132. Cavernous, shabby, atmospheric old wine bar, open since 1890 and specializing in ports, sherries and Madeiras. It's a favourite with local office workers, who spill outdoors in the summer. Good, if pricey, food, too. Mon–Sat 11am–11pm, Sun noon–1pm.

★ **Harp** 47 Chandos Place, WC2 ☎020 7836 0291, ⓦharpcoventgarden.com; ⊖ Leicester Square; map p.132. You'll get excellent and unusual real ales and ciders at this brilliant little free house. The tiny bar is invariably packed; there's more room in the comfortably battered upstairs. Mon–Sat 10am–11pm, Sun noon–10.30pm.

Lamb & Flag 33 Rose St, WC2 ☎020 7497 9504, ⓦlambandflagcoventgarden.co.uk; ⊖ Leicester Square; map p.132. More than three hundred years old, this agreeably tatty Fuller's pub, tucked down an alley between Garrick and Floral streets – where John Dryden was attacked in 1679 (see p.134) – is perennially popular. Mon–Sat 11am–11pm, Sun noon–10.30pm.

★ **Princess Louise** 208 High Holborn, WC1 ☎020 7405 8816; ⊖ Holborn; map p.132. One of London's most glorious Victorian pubs, with six rooms of gold-trimmed mirrors, gorgeous mosaics and fine moulded ceilings – even the toilets are listed. The Sam Smith's beer is inexpensive. Mon–Fri 11.30am–11pm, Sat noon–11pm, Sun noon–10pm.

The Salisbury 90 St Martin's Lane, WC2 ☎020 7836 5863; ⊖ Leicester Square; map p.132. This Taylor Walker's pub is one of the capital's most beautifully preserved Victorian taverns, with etched and engraved windows, bronze figures and Art Nouveau light fittings. Mon–Thurs 11am–11pm, Fri 11am–midnight, Sat noon–midnight, Sun noon–10.30pm.

HOLBORN AND THE INNS OF COURT

Bounce 121 Holborn, EC1 ☎020 3657 6525, ⓦbouncepingpong.com; ⊖ Chancery Lane; map p.144. Fashionable combination of gin palace and ping pong bar, with cocktails, pizza and posh bar snacks, on the site where table tennis was invented in 1891. Ping pong reservations are only available for groups of six or more, so you should be prepared to wait on weekend evenings; (tables Mon–Sat before 6pm & Sun £10/30min, £18/hr; all other times £13/30min, £26/hr). Mon–Wed 4pm–midnight, Thurs 4pm–1am, Fri & Sat noon–1am, Sun noon–10pm.

REAL ALE

Gone are the days when lager reigned supreme: nowadays, when real drinkers talk about a pint they're talking about real ale. With the rise in interest in local, artisan and micro producers, real ale – CAMRA (Campaign for Real Ale; ⓦcamra.org.uk) first coined the term, to differentiate traditional ale from processed keg beer – is increasingly fashionable, and any pub worth its stripe has a few on offer. Most real ales, uncarbonated and dark, matured in barrels or casks and pumped by hand fresh from the cellar, are also referred to as **bitter**; terms like Mild, Best and Special merely refer to the strength, and the acronym IPA (India Pale Ale) refers to bitter's colonial precursor.

25

Old Bank of England 194 Fleet St, EC4 ☎020 7430 2255, ⓦoldbankofengland.co.uk; ⊖ Temple or Chancery Lane; map p.144. Not the actual Bank of England, but in the Law Courts' branch, this imposing High Victorian banking hall is now an opulent Fuller's ale-and-pie pub. Unusually for this area, there's courtyard seating, too. Mon–Fri 11am–11pm.

★ **Seven Stars** 53–54 Carey St, WC1 ☎020 7242 8521; ⊖ Holborn; map p.144. This diminutive boozer dates from 1602 and oozes quirky charm – there's even a sleepy pub cat. It's a friendly spot, attracting a surprisingly mixed clientele. Real ales and home-made food. Mon–Fri 11am–11pm, Sat noon–11pm, Sun noon–10.30pm.

Ye Olde Mitre 1 Ely Court, EC1 ☎020 7405 4751, ⓦyeoldemitreholburn.co.uk; ⊖ Farringdon; map p.144. Hidden down a tiny alleyway between Ely Place and Hatton Garden, this Fuller's pub dates back to 1546, although it was rebuilt in the eighteenth century. The low-ceilinged, wood-panelled rooms are packed with history and the real ales are excellent. Mon–Fri 11am–11pm.

CLERKENWELL

Café Kick 43 Exmouth Market, EC1 ☎020 7837 8077, ⓦcafekick.co.uk; ⊖ Farringdon or Angel; map p.150. This chaotic, shabbily cool French-style café-bar is a great spot for a beer, usually accompanied by high-spirited table-football games. There's another ranch (*Bar Kick*) at 127 Shoreditch High St, E1. Mon–Thurs 11am–11pm, Fri & Sat 11am–midnight, Sun noon–10.30pm.

Dovetail 9 Jerusalem Passage, EC1 ☎020 7490 7321, ⓦdovepubs.com; ⊖ Farringdon; map p.150. Marvellous, understated Belgian bar, from the same people behind the *Dove* in Broadway Market (see p.397) offering around one hundred Belgian beers, including a dozen or so on tap. First-rate food, too, much of it Belgian. Mon–Sat noon–11pm.

★ **The Eagle** 159 Farringdon Rd, EC1 ☎020 7837 1353; ⊖ Farringdon; map p.150. The first (and still one of the best) of London's gastropubs, serving excellent Mediterranean food. This place is often heaving for lunch and dinner, but you should be able to find a seat at other times. Mon–Sat noon–11pm, Sun noon–5pm.

Fox & Anchor 115 Charterhouse St, EC1 ☎020 7250 1300, ⓦfoxandanchor.com; ⊖ Barbican; map p.150. The cosy snugs in this gloriously restored Victorian Smithfield pub are perfect for hunkering down to drink cask ales – in a pewter tankard if you want to go the whole hog. Good British gastro food, too, and guest rooms upstairs. Mon–Fri 7am–11pm, Sun 8.30am–11pm, Sun 8.30am–10pm.

★ **Jerusalem Tavern** 55 Britton St, EC1 ☎020 7490 4281; ⊖ Farringdon; map p.150. Tiny, converted Georgian coffee house – the frontage dates from 1810 – that has a raffish, sociable character. The excellent draught beers are from St Peter's Brewery in Suffolk. Mon–Fri 11am–11pm.

The Peasant 240 St John St, EC1 ☎020 7336 7726, ⓦthepeasant.co.uk; ⊖ Farringdon or Angel; map p.150. Handsome, spacious gastropub – smart but relaxed – serving good food upstairs or at the bar. It can get busy, but it's large enough never to be oppressive. Mon–Sat noon–11pm, Sun noon–10.30pm.

Slaughtered Lamb 34–35 Great Sutton St, EC1 ☎020 7253 1516, ⓦtheslaughteredlambpub.co.uk; ⊖ Barbican or Farringdon; map p.150. Lots of live music and events downstairs, with funky pub grub served in the spacious upstairs room. Mon–Thurs 11.30am–midnight, Fri 11.30am–1am, Sat noon–1am, Sun 12.30–10.30pm.

★ **The Three Kings** 7 Clerkenwell Close, EC1 ☎020 7253 0483; ⊖ Farringdon; map p.150. Unimprovable Clerkenwell favourite tucked away just north of Clerkenwell Green, with an eclectic interior, big windows and two small rooms upstairs perfect for lingering. Interesting craft beers and food, too. It's next to *The Crown*, which is also worth a trip. Mon–Fri noon–11pm, Sat 5.30–11pm.

THE CITY

The Black Friar 174 Queen Victoria St, EC4 ☎020 7236 5474; ⊖ Blackfriars; map pp.156–157. Quirky, relaxing place to drink, now a Nicholson's pub, with Art Nouveau marble friezes of boozy monks and a highly decorated alcove – all original, dating from 1905. Mon–Thurs 10am–11.30pm, Fri & Sat 10am–midnight, Sun 10am–11pm.

Jamaica Wine House St Michael's Alley, EC3 ☎020 7929 6972, ⓦshepherdneame.co.uk; ⊖ Bank; map pp.156–157. The "Jam Pot", in a narrow alleyway on the site of London's first coffee house (1652), is an old City institution, now owned by Shepherd Neame. It's divided into four large "snugs" by original, high wood-panelled partitions. Mon–Fri 11am–11pm.

The Lamb Tavern/Old Tom's Bar 10–12 Leadenhall Market, EC3 ☎020 7626 2454, ⓦlambtavernleadenhall.com; ⊖ Monument; map pp.156–157. In the middle of Leadenhall Market, this historic Young's pub offers almost exclusively standing room only (both inside and out) for a suited local crowd. The basement bar, *Old Tom's*, is a little more on-trend, serving London beers and artisan cheese and meat platters. Mon–Fri 11am–11pm.

The Old Bell 95 Fleet St, EC4 ☎020 7583 0216; ⊖ Blackfriars or St Paul's; map pp.156–157. Excellent Nicholson's pub – worth going out of your way for in this corner of town. The hassle-free atmosphere combines the bustle of Fleet St with the quiet calm of St Bride's, which the pub opens out to at its rear. Mon–Fri 11am–11pm, Sat noon–8pm, Sun noon–5pm.

Viaduct Tavern 126 Newgate St, EC1 ☎020 7600 1863, ⓦviaducttavern.co.uk; ⊖ St Paul's; map pp.156–157. Fuller's pub, on the site of an old jail across from the Old Bailey, with a glorious Victorian interior from 1869. Check out the amazing ceiling, the faded oils of comely women representing Commerce, Agriculture and the Arts, and the old cells in the basement. Mon–Fri 8.30am–11pm.

★ **Ye Olde Cheshire Cheese** 145 Fleet St, EC4 ☎020 7353 6170; ⊖ Temple or Blackfriars; map pp.156–157. A famous – chiefly because of its historic literary associations, with patrons including Dickens and Dr Johnson – seventeenth-century watering hole. Its dark-panelled

TOP 5 HISTORIC PUBS

25

Ye Olde Cheshire Cheese Fleet Street. See p.391

George Inn Southwark. See p.392

The Jerusalem Tavern Clerkenwell. See p.390

The Mayflower Rotherhithe. See p.394

Princess Louise Holborn. See p.389

bars and real fires make it a cosy maze, popular with tourists and locals alike. Mon–Fri 11am–11pm, Sat noon–11pm.

SPITALFIELDS AND WHITECHAPEL

★ **The Carpenter's Arms** 73 Cheshire St, E2 ☎020 7739 6342; Shoreditch High Street Overground; map pp.192–193. Iconic East End pub – it once belonged to the Kray twins – with an excellent range of craft lagers and ales, good home-made food and a tiny courtyard for warm evenings. A friendly, relaxed place that avoids the hectic, sometimes forced feel of some of the other pubs and bars nearby. Mon–Wed 4–11.30pm, Thurs & Sun noon–11.30pm, Fri & Sat noon–12.30am.

★ **The George Tavern** 373 Commercial Rd, E1 ☎020 7790 7335, ⓦthegeorgetavern.co.uk; Whitechapel; map p.190. Arty, shabby, dilapidated pub, packed with history and all sorts of lovely period detail. There's a bohemian theatre space, and regular, very cool, live music. Mon–Thurs 4pm–midnight, Fri & Sat 4pm–3am, Sun 4pm–midnight.

Indo 133 Whitechapel Rd, E1 ☎020 7247 4926; ⊖ Aldgate East or Whitechapel; map pp.192–193.

Tiny, dark, grungy bar, with lots of funky art, good pizzas, interesting music and a decent range of beers, all enjoyed by a laidback and generally non-hipster crowd. Mon–Thurs & Sun noon–1am, Fri & Sat noon–3am.

Ten Bells 84 Commercial St, E1 ☎020 7366 1721; ⊖ Shoreditch High Street Overground; map, pp.192–193. Stripped-down pub (with Jack the Ripper associations), with some great Victorian tiling. The hip, young, local crowd is joined nowadays by foodies here for the superb restaurant, the brainchild of alumni from destination restaurants *St John*, *The Ledbury* and *Clove Club*. Mon–Wed & Sun noon–midnight, Thurs–Sat noon–1am.

Vibe Bar Old Truman Brewery, 91–95 Brick Lane, E1 ☎020 7247 3479, ⓦvibe-bar.co.uk; ⊖ Shoreditch High Street Overground; map, pp.192–193. Shabby, art-strewn stalwart at the heart of the Brick Lane scene, with sofas, a big beer garden and DJs and live bands in the evenings. Mon–Thurs & Sun 11am–11.30pm, Fri & Sat 11am–1am.

SHOREDITCH AND HOXTON

Boundary 2–4 Boundary St, E2 ☎020 7729 1051, ⓦtheboundary.co.uk; Shoreditch High Street Overground; map pp.192–193. The rooftop bar at this snazzy hotel (see p.360) is a gorgeous spot, complete with its own olive tree and grapevines, a covered area for when the weather's bad and blankets to snuggle under when it's chilly. You pay for the setting – cocktails start at £9.50 – but the views are unbeatable. Daily 10am–11pm.

Happiness Forgets 8–9 Hoxton Square, N1 ☎020 7613 0325, ⓦhappinessforgets.com; Old Street; map pp.192–193. Candlelit, bare-brick Hoxton bar with a Hoxton-via-New York vibe, serving fashionably obscure, serious cocktails to a cool crowd. Mon–Sat 5.30–11pm.

The Owl & Pussycat 34 Redchurch St, E2 ☎020 3487 0088, ⓦowlandpussycatshoreditch.com; Shoreditch

High Street Overground; map pp.192–193. One of many old boozers in the area to have been gussied up and hipsterfied, this friendly backstreet pub has managed to keep a generally mellow vibe. It can get more hectic at the weekends, but that comes with the territory. Decent range of beers, good food and a courtyard out back. Sun & Mon noon–11pm, Tues–Sat noon–midnight.

Worship Street Whistling Shop 63 Worship St, EC2 ☎020 7247 0015, ⓦwhistlingshop.com; Old Street; map pp.192–193. This theatrical, shabbily opulent cocktail bar looks set to outlive London's current gin palace craze, chiefly because the drinks, composed with unusual and creative ingredients are works of art, made in their Gothic in-house lab. Mon & Tues 5pm–midnight, Wed & Thurs 5pm–1am, Fri & Sat 5pm–2am.

MILE END AND BETHNAL GREEN

The Approach 47 Approach Rd, E2 ☎020 8980 2321; ⊖ Bethnal Green; map p.190. One of the best pubs in an area becoming increasingly well stocked, with a local,

unaffected feel. Cosy and spacious, it offers food and a fine range of beers, and there's an art gallery attached. Mon–Sat noon–11pm, Sun noon–10.30pm.

25

★**Camel** 277 Globe Rd, E2 ☎020 8983 9888, ⓦthecamele2.co.uk; ⊖ Bethnal Green; map p.190. Beer and pies – the great British combination. This neighbourhood favourite serves pies that are a cut above – from steak with chorizo, olives and beans to goat's cheese, sweet potato and spinach – along with real ales. Mon–Thurs 4–11pm, Fri & Sat noon–11pm, Sun noon–10.30pm.

The Palm Tree Haverfield Rd, E3 ☎020 8980 2918; ⊖ Bow Road; map p.190. It's hard to believe that pubs like this, standing alone in Mile End Park, still exist. The traditional pleasures – well-worn wooden benches, bunches of dried hops – are the real thing, enjoyed by a laidback local crowd. Good live jazz at the weekend. Mon–Thurs noon–midnight, Fri & Sat noon–2am, Sun noon–1am.

STRATFORD: AROUND THE OLYMPIC PARK

Edward VII 47 Broadway, E15 ☎020 8534 2313, ⓦkingeddie.co.uk; ⊖ Stratford; map p.190. The only notable pub in Stratford itself, the listed *Edward VII* has an old-fashioned, low-ceilinged front bar, spacious rooms behind, good British ales and wines and decent food. Live music on Thurs. Mon–Wed noon–11pm, Thurs–Sat noon–midnight, Sun noon–11.30pm.

DOCKLANDS

The Grapes 76 Narrow St, E14 ☎020 7987 4396, ⓦthegrapes.co.uk; Westferry DLR; map pp.206–207. A lovely, narrow little pub on a quiet Limehouse street, dating from around 1583 and featuring in Dickens's *Our Mutual Friend*. There's lots of seafaring paraphernalia and a great riverside balcony. Mon–Wed noon–3.30pm & 5.30–11pm, Thurs–Sat noon–11pm, Sun noon–10.30pm.

The Gun 27 Coldharbour, E14 ☎020 7515 5222, ⓦthegundocklands.com; ⊖ Canary Wharf, South Quay or Blackwall DLR; map pp.206–207. Legendary dockers' pub, once the haunt of Lord Nelson, *The Gun* is now a classy gastropub, with a cosy back bar and a deck offering unrivalled views. It's on the eastern side of the Isle of Dogs – directly opposite the O2 – but worth the excursion.

Mon–Sat 11am–midnight, Sun 11am–11pm.

★**Prospect of Whitby** 57 Wapping Wall, E1 ☎020 7481 1095; ⊖ Wapping; map pp.206–207. Steeped in history, this is London's most famous riverside pub, with a pewter bar, flagstone floor, ancient timber beams and stacks of maritime memorabilia. Decent beers and terrific views out across the Thames. Mon–Thurs noon–11pm, Fri & Sat noon–midnight, Sun noon–10.30pm.

Town of Ramsgate 62 Wapping High St, E1 ☎020 7264 0001; ⊖ Wapping; map pp.206–207. Dark, narrow, medieval pub located by Wapping Old Stairs, which once led down to Execution Dock. Captain Blood was discovered here with the Crown Jewels under his cloak. Mon–Sat noon–midnight, Sun noon–10.30pm.

SOUTH BANK

Anchor & Hope 36 The Cut, SE1 ☎020 7928 9898; ⊖ Southwark; map p.216. *The Anchor* gastropub dishes up excellent, simple British grub – slow-cooked pork with *choucroute*, rabbits' livers, asparagus soup – and mouthwatering puds. You can't book, so the bar is basically the waiting room. Mon 5–11pm, Tues–Sat 11am–11pm, Sun 12.30–5pm.

The Cut Bar The Young Vic, 66 The Cut, SE1 ☎020 7928 4400, ⓦthecutbar.com; ⊖ Waterloo or Southwark; map p.216. Very lively theatre bar-café spread over two floors of the Young Vic with an outside terrace – it's big enough to find a corner even when it's packed with theatregoers. Mon–Fri 9am–late, Sat 10am–late.

★**Kings Arms** 25 Roupell St, SE1 ☎020 7207 0784; ⊖ Waterloo; map p.216. On a quiet terraced street, this terrific local is divided into two parts: in the front, a traditional drinking area, in the rear a tastefully cluttered, conservatory-style space with a large open fire and long wooden table. Real ales and good Thai food. Mon–Fri 11am–11pm, Sat noon–11pm, Sun noon–10.30pm.

SOUTHWARK

The Anchor 34 Park St, SE1 ☎020 7407 1577; ⊖ London Bridge; map pp.226–227. First built in 1615, this sprawling pub retains few vestiges of the past, but it does have one of the few riverside terraces hereabouts – it's often crowded. Mon–Wed 11am–11pm, Thurs–Sat 11am–midnight, Sun noon–11pm.

George Inn 77 Borough High St, SE1 ☎020 7407 2056, ⓦnationaltrust.org.uk/george-inn; ⊖ Borough; map pp.226–227. London's only surviving galleried coaching inn (see p.230), dating from the seventeenth century and owned by the National Trust; it serves a good range of real ales, and is very popular with tourists. Daily 11am–11pm.

Market Porter 9 Stoney St, SE1 ☎020 7407 2495; ⊖ London Bridge; map pp.226–227. Handsome semicircular pub by Borough Market, with an interesting range of real ales and decent food. It's outrageously popular, with crowds spilling out onto the surrounding pavements. Mon–Fri 6–8.30am & 11am–11pm, Sat noon–11pm, Sun noon–10.30pm.

CLOCKWISE FROM TOP THE DOVE (P.397); THE LAMB (P.389); THE PROSPECT OF WHITBY (ABOVE) >

25

TOP 5 RIVERSIDE DRINKS

Dove Hammersmith. See p.398
The Gun Docklands. See p.392
The Mayflower Rotherhithe. See p.394
Prospect of Whitby Docklands. See p.392
Trafalgar Tavern Greenwich. See p.398

The Rake 14 Winchester Walk, SE1 ☎ 020 7407 0557, ⓦ utobeer.co.uk; ⊖ London Bridge; map pp.226–227. Bright little real ale bar – an offshoot of Borough Market's Utobeer crafts beer stall – with regularly changing draught beers from Germany, America, Belgium and Holland, as well as more than a hundred bottled beers from around the globe. There's an outdoor deck, too. Mon–Fri noon–

ROTHERHITHE AND BERMONDSEY

The Mayflower 117 Rotherhithe St, SE16 ☎ 020 7237 4088, ⓦ themayflowerrotherhithe.com; ⊖ Rotherhithe; map pp.224–225. This eighteenth-century pub, in a very quiet and attractive spot in the heart of old Rotherhithe, is steeped in history. The blackened brick walls, wonky timber frames and creaky floorboards give it character, while the terrace offers splendid Thames views. Decent real ales from the Mayflower microbrewery, and occasional barbecues. Mon–Sat 11am–11pm, Sun noon–10.30pm.

SOUTH KENSINGTON

Anglesea Arms 15 Selwood Terrace, SW7 ☎ 020 7373 7960; ⊖ South Kensington; map p.265. Charming little local, with hanging baskets on the outside and dark wooden tables and green leather benches inside. There's an elegant dining area, too, and a pleasant courtyard. There are half a dozen first-class ales on offer. Mon–Sat 11am–11pm, Sun noon–10.30pm.

KNIGHTSBRIDGE

Grenadier 18 Wilton Row, SW1 ☎ 020 7235 3074; ⊖ Hyde Park Corner or Knightsbridge; map pp.250–251. Hidden away in a private mews, this charming little pub was Wellington's local and his officers' mess; the original pewter bar survives, and there's plenty of military paraphernalia on display. Daily noon–11pm.
★ **The Nag's Head** 53 Kinnerton St, SW1 ☎ 020 7235 1135; ⊖ Hyde Park Corner or Knightsbridge; map pp.250–251. A convivial, quirky and down-to-earth pub in a posh cobbled mews, with dark wood panelling, china handpumps and walls crammed with vintage prints – the

CHELSEA

Cooper's Arms 87 Flood St, SW3 ☎ 020 7376 3120, ⓦ coopersarms.co.uk; ⊖ Sloane Square; map p.265. Decent, spacious neighbourhood pub, which may not be quite the sum of its parts – reasonable food, a good range

11pm, Sat 10am–11pm, Sun noon–10pm.
★ **Royal Oak** 44 Tabard St, SE1 ☎ 020 7357 7173; ⊖ Borough; map pp.224–225. Lovingly restored Victorian pub that eschews jukeboxes and one-armed bandits and opts simply for serving well-kept real ales from Harvey's brewery in Sussex. Good pub grub, too. Mon–Fri 11am–11pm, Sat noon–11pm, Sun noon–6pm.

The Southwark Tavern 22 Southwark St, SE1 ☎ 020 7403 0257, ⓦ thesouthwarktavern.co.uk; ⊖ London Bridge; map pp.226–227. All the pubs and bars in this area can get extremely busy, but this one is big enough to soak up the crowds and remain pleasant. There are some cosy booths downstairs and a good range of beers. Mon–Wed 11am–midnight, Thurs & Fri 11am–1am, Sat 10am–1am, Sun noon–midnight.

The Woolpack 98 Bermondsey St, SE1 ☎ 020 7357 9269, ⓦ woolpackbar.com; ⊖ London Bridge; map pp.224–225. A pleasant stop-off on this foodie street, the spacious *Woolly* serves real ales and a good range of other drinks in a tiled ground-floor space, a quiet upstairs room and a sunny garden. You can eat seasonal British pub food, or head across the road to the swanky *Garrison* gastropub – all scrubbed wood, mismatched chandeliers and artisan suppliers. Mon–Sat 11am–11pm, Sun 11am–10.30pm.

Queen's Arms 30 Queens Gate Mews, SW7 ☎ 020 7823 9293, ⓦ thequeensarmskensington.co.uk ⊖ Gloucester Road; map p.252. Brilliantly located in a quiet mews around a 10min walk from the Royal Albert Hall, and serving real ales, speciality beers and interesting food, this great spot is popular with musicians from the nearby Royal College of Music. Mon–Sat noon–11pm, Sun noon–10.30pm.

unusual sunken back room has a flagstone floor and fires in winter. Mobile phones are banned; this is a place to relax with your fellow drinkers. Mon–Sat 11am–11pm, Sun noon–10.30pm.

Star Tavern 6 Belgrave Mews West, SW1 ☎ 020 7235 3019, ⓦ star-tavern-belgravia.co.uk; ⊖ Knightsbridge; map pp.250–251. Quiet and traditional two-storey mews pub with a large open sitting room and a murky past: allegedly, it was from here that the Great Train Robbery was planned. Fuller's beer and traditional pub grub. Mon–Sat 11am–11pm, Sun noon–10.30pm.

of beers, plenty of spots to choose from – but is still a good local find so close to the King's Rd. Daily noon–10pm.
Fox and Hounds 29 Passmore St, SW1 ☎ 020 7730 6367; ⊖ Sloane Square; map p.265. With its open fire,

faux books, oil paintings and flagstone floor, not to mention its hunting memorabilia, this cosy Young's pub feels more like a country tavern than a London boozer. No music or TVs, and a friendly buzz. Daily noon–11pm.
The Pig's Ear 35 Old Church St, SW3 ☎020 7352 2908, ⓦthepigsear.info; ⊖ Sloane Square; map

p.265. Genuinely charming despite its moneyed milieu, this gastropub has a busy and beguiling interior, interesting French-influenced food and drink, and the ambience of somewhere treasured by those fortunate enough to call it their local. Mon–Sat noon–11pm, Sun noon–10.30pm.

PADDINGTON

★ **Victoria** 10a Strathearn Place, W2 ☎020 7724 1191, ⓦvictoriapaddington.co.uk; ⊖ Lancaster Gate or Paddington; map pp.274–275. Beautiful, unspoiled Victorian Fuller's pub, with green-and-gold wallpapered walls enclosing a long bar with fine mirrors and elaborate carvings. There's a little outdoor space, too. An especially valuable find so near Paddington station. Mon–Sat 11am–11pm, Sun noon–10.30pm.

NOTTING HILL

Churchill Arms 119 Kensington Church St, W8 ☎020 7227 4242, ⓦchurchillarmskensington.co.uk; ⊖ Notting Hill Gate; map pp.274–275. Justifiably popular, flower-festooned local serving Fuller's beers, Guinness and good Thai food in a quirky, eclectic space. Mon–Wed 11am–11pm, Thurs–Sat 11am–midnight, Sun noon–10.30pm.
Cock & Bottle 17 Needham Rd, W11 ☎020 7229 1550; ⊖ Westbourne Park or Notting Hill Gate; map pp.274–275. Remarkably unpretentious two-room corner pub with smart Victorian fittings and good ales. No children. Mon–Sat noon–11pm, Sun noon–10.30pm.
★ **The Cow** 89 Westbourne Park Rd, W2 ☎020 7221 0021, ⓦthecowlondon.co.uk; ⊖ Westbourne Park or Royal Oak; map pp.274–275. This good-looking Tom Conran gastropub pulls in a cool, slightly raffish crowd. Tasty British food, including oysters, is served in the bar area and in a more formal dining room. Mon–Thurs noon–11pm, Fri & Sat noon–midnight, Sun noon–10.30pm.
The Elgin 96 Ladbroke Grove, W11 ☎020 7229 5663; ⊖ Ladbroke Grove; map pp.274–275. Enormous pub with a riot of original features as well as modish decorative touches and a stylish gastropub menu. Buzzy, with regular live music. Mon–Wed 11am–11pm, Thurs–Sat 11am–midnight, Sun noon–10.30pm.
Paradise by Way of Kensal Green 19 Kilburn Lane, W10 ☎020 8969 0098, ⓦtheparadise.co.uk; ⊖ Kensal Green; map pp.274–275. Big gastropub near the Kensal Green Cemetery, with a theatrically dishevelled interior and a hip, young West London crowd. Mon–Wed 4pm–midnight, Thurs 4pm–1am, Fri 4pm–2am, Sat noon –2am, Sun noon–11.30pm.
The Westbourne 101 Westbourne Park Villas, W2 ☎020 7221 1332, ⓦthewestbourne.com; ⊖ Westbourne Park or Royal Oak; map pp.274–275. This popular gastropub has an elegantly ramshackle interior and lots of space outside at the front. There's a tapas menu and bar snacks available. Mon 4.30–11pm, Tues–Sat 11am–11pm, Sun noon–10.30pm.
★ **Windsor Castle** 114 Campden Hill Rd, W8 ☎020 7243 8797; ⊖ Notting Hill; map pp.274–275. More like something you'd find in the country than tucked away in the backstreets of one of London's poshest neighbourhoods, this is a pretty, popular, early Victorian wood-panelled pub with a great courtyard. Craft beers, and nice food, too. Mon–Sat noon–11pm, Sun noon–10.30pm.

ST JOHN'S WOOD

Bridge House 13 Westbourne Terrace Rd, W2 ☎020 7266 4326, ⓦthebridgehouselittlevenice.co.uk; ⊖ Warwick Avenue; map p.284. Theatre pub right by the canal in Little Venice, a positively bohemian hangout for the area. Excellent real ales and good food. Mon–Thurs noon–11pm, Fri & Sat noon–11.30pm, Sun noon–10.30pm.
★ **Prince Alfred** 5a Formosa St, W9 ☎020 7286 3287, ⓦtheprincealfred.com; ⊖ Warwick Avenue; map p.284. A period-piece Victorian pub with all its original 1862 fittings intact, right down to the glazed "snob" screens that divide the bar into a series of snugs. There's a pricey Modern European restaurant, Formosa, and classy bar snacks. Mon–Thurs noon–11pm, Fri & Sat noon–midnight, Sun noon– 10.30pm.
The Warrington 93 Warrington Crescent, W9 ☎020 7286 8282; ⊖ Maida Vale; map p.284. Grand Victorian pub with a flamboyant Art Nouveau interior. Worth a visit for the architecture and decor alone, but probably best to avoid the restaurant. Mon–Thurs 11am–11pm, Fri & Sat 11am–midnight, Sun 11am–10.30pm.

PRIMROSE HILL, CAMDEN TOWN AND AROUND

The Albert 11 Princess Rd, NW1 ☎020 7722 1886; ⊖ Camden Town; map pp.284–285. This unpretentious, relaxed Primrose Hill watering hole offers a safe retreat if the area's other pubs are very crowded. Mon–Sat 11am–11pm, Sun noon–10.30pm.
Brewdog 113 Bayham St, NW1 ☎020 7284 4626,

25

ⓦ brewdog.com; ⊖ Camden Town; map pp.284–285. Spacious and comfy bar owned by the Scottish microbrewery, with pizza, too, perfect to pick at as you chill out on the squidgy sofas. There's a second *Brewdog* in Shoreditch. Mon–Thurs noon–11.30pm, Fri & Sat noon–midnight, Sun noon–10.30pm.

Edinboro Castle 57 Mornington Terrace, NW1 ☎020 7255 9651, ⓦ edinborocastlepub.co.uk; ⊖ Camden Town; map pp.284–285. The main draw at this large, high-ceilinged pub, despite its glammed-up interior, is the leafy beer garden which hosts summer weekend barbecues and hog roasts. Good selection of draught continental lagers and a couple of real ales. Mon–Fri noon–11pm, Sat 11am–11pm, Sun noon–10.30pm.

The Enterprise 2 Haverstock Hill, NW3 ☎020 7485 2659, ⓦ camdenenterprise.com; ⊖ Chalk Farm; map pp.284–285. Chalk Farm institution, almost opposite the tube, with an unmatched atmosphere – there are live gigs/ DJs at night – in an area that can sometimes be very quiet. Sun–Thurs 11am–11pm, Fri & Sat 11am–1am.

★ **The Lansdowne** 90 Gloucester Ave, NW1 ☎020 7483 0409, ⓦ thelansdownepub.co.uk; ⊖ Chalk Farm; map pp.284–285. Primrose Hill's liveliest and coolest pub, with a diverse crowd, a reliable buzz and classy Mediterranean gastropub grub. Mon–Fri noon–11pm, Sat 10am–11pm, Sun 10am–10.30pm.

Lock Tavern 35 Chalk Farm Rd, NW1 ☎020 7482 7163, ⓦ lock-tavern.co.uk; ⊖ Chalk Farm; map pp.284–285. Archetypal Camden cool at this rambling music and DJ pub, with large, battered wooden tables, comfy sofas, a leafy upstairs terrace and beer garden down below. Music can be anything from punk funk and electro to rock; the pub grub is mainly dude food. Mon–Thurs noon–midnight, Fri & Sat noon–1am, Sun noon–11pm.

Sir Richard Steele 97 Haverstock Hill, NW3 ☎020 7483 1261; ⊖ Chalk Farm; map pp.284–285. The cluttered and oddball decor and friendly crowd here make for a fun, laidback atmosphere; plus there's modish pub food and a small beer garden. Mon–Sat 11am–midnight, Sun noon–midnight.

ISLINGTON

69 Colebrooke Row 69 Colebrooke Row, N1 ☎07540 528593, ⓦ 69colebrookerow.com; ⊖ Angel or Highbury & Islington; map pp.284–285. This supercool cocktail bar – all old-school Hollywood glamour – was at the vanguard of London's craft cocktail scene and, with delicious concoctions such as apple and hay bellinis or rhubarb gimlets, looks set to stay the course. It's tiny; reservations recommended at weekends. Sun–Wed 5pm–midnight, Thurs 5pm–1am, Fri & Sat 5pm–2am.

The Charles Lamb 16 Elia St, N1 ☎020 7837 5040, ⓦ thecharleslambpub.com; ⊖ Angel; map pp.284–285. Popular local on a tranquil street, with good food and a pleasant, well-worn interior. Lots of community events. Mon & Tues 4–11pm, Wed–Sat noon–11pm, Sun noon–10.30pm.

The Crown 116 Cloudesley Rd, N1 ☎020 7837 7107; ⊖ Angel; map pp.284–285. Refined Fuller's pub, with lots of Victorian fixtures and fittings. on beautiful Cloudesley Rd. Generally calmer than the pubs and bars closer to Upper St, and serves upmarket food. Mon–Sat noon–11pm, Sun noon–10.30pm.

Duke of Cambridge 30 St Peter's St, N1 ☎020 7359 3066, ⓦ dukeorganic.co.uk; ⊖ Angel; map pp.284–285. The focus at this gastropub is most definitely organic, with a daily changing menu of award-winning organic food, as well as organic beers (including real ales), wines

and soft drinks. Unsurprisingly, none of it comes cheap. Mon–Sat noon–11pm, Sun noon–10.30pm.

The Hops & Glory 382 Essex Rd, N1 ☎0207 226 2277, ⓦ hopsandglory.co.uk; ⊖ Highbury & Islington; map pp.284–285. A bit on the outskirts, but this fresh and no-fuss contemporary pub pulls in the CAMRA crew and laidback drinkers with its regularly changing selection of craft beers and ciders. Posh bar snacks, too. Mon–Wed 4–11pm, Thurs 4pm–midnight, Fri & Sat noon–2am, Sun noon–10.30pm.

★ **Island Queen** 87 Noel Rd, N1 ☎020 7354 8741, ⓦ theislandqueenislington.co.uk; ⊖ Angel or Highbury & Islington; map pp.284–285. Beautiful, weathered, wood-panelled Victorian pub in the backstreets, with lovely etched glass, high ceilings and eccentric bits and bobs all over the place. Good range of beers and decent pub food. A real gem. Sun–Thurs noon–11.30pm, Fri noon–midnight, Sat 11am–midnight.

★ **King's Head** 115 Upper St, N1 ☎020 7226 4443, ⓦ kingsheadtheatrepub.co.uk; ⊖ Angel; map pp.284–285. Lively, very appealing old pub theatre in the heart of Islington. The grand Victorian boozer is a corker, with real fires, vintage decor, fresh flowers and lots of theatrical memorabilia; the little theatre (see p.419) is at the back. Mon–Wed noon–1am, Thurs–Sat noon–2am, Sun noon–12.30am.

STOKE NEWINGTON AND HACKNEY

Auld Shillelagh 105 Stoke Newington Church St, N16 ⓦ theauldshillelagh.com; Stoke Newington station; map p.291 Nights don't get much better than at this genuine Irish pub, a long narrow corridor of a place with fantastic live Irish

and bluegrass music – there's no stage, as such – slow-pulled Guinness, occasional offbeat themed nights and a friendly, very mixed crowd. Mon–Wed 11am–11pm, Thurs–Sat 11am–1am, Sun noon–midnight.

★ Dove 24–28 Broadway Market, E8 ☎020 7275 7617, ⊛dovepubs.com; London Fields or Cambridge Heath stations from Liverpool Street; map p.291. Cosy, low-lit and plant-filled, this characterful pub, a friendly stalwart on trendy Broadway Market, offers a stupendous selection of draught and bottled Belgian beers, plus a few real ales, and specializes in excellent home-made food. Mon–Thurs noon–11pm, Fri & Sat noon–midnight, Sun noon–10.30pm.

The Empress 130 Lauriston Rd, E9 ☎020 8533 5123, ⊛theempressofindia.com; ⊖ Bethnal Green; map p.291. Smart Victoria Park gastropub at the heart of the South Hackney boom. Tues–Sat noon–10.30pm, Sun noon–10pm.

The Fox 372 Kingsland Rd, E8 ☎07807 217734, ⊛thefoxe8.com; ⊖ Haggerston; map p.291. An excellent choice of craft beers, real ales and ciders along with good

British food are the big appeal at this bare-bones, on-trend pub, along with the flower-bedecked roof terrace, which is a fabulous spot for a summer tipple. Mon–Fri 4pm–midnight, Sat noon–midnight, Sun noon–11.30pm.

Off Broadway 63–65 Broadway Market, E8 ☎020 7241 2786, ⊛offbroadway.org.uk; ⊖ Bethnal Green; map p.291. Relaxed, friendly, popular and family-owned bar, styled after a New York drinking hole, with cocktails, American beers on tap and Mexican street food to soak it all up. Mon–Fri 4pm–midnight, Sat 10am–midnight, Sun noon–midnight.

The Prince George 40 Parkholme Rd, E8 ☎020 7254 6060; Hackney Central Overground; map p.291. One of a cluster of good pubs just west of Hackney Central, *The Prince George* is the pick for its reliably buzzy atmosphere and air of faded grandeur. Mon–Thurs 5pm–midnight, Fri 5pm–1am, Sat 2pm–1am, Sun 2–10.30pm.

HAMPSTEAD AND HIGHGATE

The Holly Bush 22 Holly Mount, off Holly Hill, NW3 ☎020 7435 2892, ⊛hollybushhampstead.co.uk; ⊖ Hampstead; map pp.298–299. A lovely, creaking old pub, with a real fire in winter, tucked away in the steep backstreets of Hampstead village. Some fine real ales on offer, as well as excellent food; it can get mobbed at weekends. Mon–Sat noon–11pm, Sun noon–10.30pm.

Red Lion and Sun 25 North Rd, N6 ☎020 8340 1780, ⊛theredlionandsun.com; ⊖ Highgate; map pp.298–299. Prettily set in chichi Highgate Village, this place is popular with locals for its ales and its whiskies, its Modern British food with a French accent and, unusually, its good take out food. There's loads of space, with two gardens. Mon–Sat noon–midnight, Sun noon–11pm.

★ Southampton Arms 139 Highgate Rd, NW5 ⊛thesouthamptonarms.co.uk; ⊖ Kentish Town; map pp.298–299. They keep things simple but spot-on in this big old place, with a fabulous, rotating range of real ales and ciders, all British, along with scotch eggs, pork baps

and the like to snack on, music on vinyl or the old Joanna and a real fire in winter. No cards. Daily noon–11pm/midnight.

The Spaniards Inn Spaniards Rd, NW3 ☎020 8731 8406, ⊛thespaniardshampstead.co.uk; ⊖ Hampstead; map pp.298–299. Rambling sixteenth-century coaching inn near Kenwood and the Heath, frequented by everyone from Dick Turpin to John Keats. With a huge garden and good food, it gets extremely busy on Sun afternoons. Sun–Tues noon–11pm, Wed–Fri noon–midnight, Sat 11am–midnight.

The Stag 67 Fleet Rd, NW3 ☎020 7722 2646, ⊛thestaghampstead.com; ⊖ Belsize Park; map pp.298–299. Welcoming gastropub with a varied and unusual beer selection, good British food, a big garden with weekly live music and summer barbecues, and a merry mix of locals and pre- or post-Heath ramblers. Mon–Thurs noon–11pm, Fri & Sat noon–midnight, Sun noon–10.30pm.

BRIXTON AND CLAPHAM

Bread & Roses 68 Clapham Manor St, SW4 ☎020 7498 1779, ⊛breadandrosespub.com; ⊖ Clapham North or Clapham Common; map pp.310–311. This Workers' Beer Company pub serves fine ales, and puts on comedy and cabaret, charity events and live music. Mon–Thurs 4.30–11.30pm, Fri 4.30pm–12.30am, Sat noon–12.30am, Sun noon–10.30pm.

Effra 38A Kellet Rd, SW2 ☎020 7274 4180; ⊖ Brixton; map pp.310–311. An unreconstructed slice of old Brixton, with a friendly crowd of old and new regulars enjoying Red Stripe and Caribbean food, along with frequent live jazz. Mon–Thurs noon–11pm, Fri noon–midnight, Sat 10am–midnight, Sun 10am–10.30pm.

Kaff Bar 64 Atlantic Rd ☎020 7274 5373, ⊛kaff-bar .co.uk; ⊖ Brixton; map pp.310–311. Cool but unintimidating Brixton bar with art-lined walls and great cocktails – try the Brixton Mule, made with the locally produced Ossie's ginger beer, for just £3 – along with all manner of high-spirited live events. Mon–Thurs 11am–midnight, Fri & Sat 11am–2am.

Trinity Arms 45 Trinity Gardens, SW9 ☎020 7274 4544, ⊛trinityarms.co.uk; ⊖ Brixton; map pp.310–311. Charming old local in a quiet square just off Acre Lane, with a very traditional interior – complete with pub cats – and an eclectic crowd. Mon–Thurs 11am–11pm, Fri & Sat 11am–midnight, Sun noon–11pm.

25

25

DULWICH

Crown & Greyhound 73 Dulwich Village, SE21 ☎ 020 8299 4976, ⓦ thecrownandgreyhound.co.uk; North Dulwich station from London Bridge; map pp.310–311. Large Victorian pub, convenient for the Picture Gallery, with a big beer garden to boot. Mon–Wed 11am–11pm, Thurs–Sat 11am–midnight, Sun noon–10.30pm.

GREENWICH

Cutty Sark Ballast Quay, off Lassell St, SE10 ☎ 020 8858 3146, ⓦ cuttysarkse10.co.uk; Cutty Sark DLR or Maze Hill station from Charing Cross; map p.315. This three-storey Georgian pub, much less touristy than the *Trafalgar Tavern* (see p.398), is another good place for a riverside pint. Mon–Sat 11am–11pm, Sun noon–10.30pm.

Greenwich Union 56 Royal Hill, SE10 ☎ 020 8692 6258, ⓦ greenwichunion.com; Greenwich DLR & station; map p.315. A modern, laidback pub, owned by the local Meantime brewery but also featuring guest ales, with a youthful feel, gastro grub and a garden. Mon–Fri noon–11pm, Sat 11am–11pm, Sun 11.30am–10.30pm.

Richard I 52–54 Royal Hill, SE10 ☎ 020 8692 2996; Greenwich DLR & station; map p.315. Right next door to the *Union*, but a world away, this nice old-fashioned local offers Young's beers and a spacious garden. Mon–Sat noon–11pm, Sun noon–10.30pm.

Trafalgar Tavern 5 Park Row, SE10 ☎ 020 8858 2909, ⓦ trafalgartavern.co.uk; Cutty Sark DLR or Maze Hill station from Charing Cross; map p.315. A commanding riverside location and a mention in Dickens' *Our Mutual Friend* have made this large Regency-style inn a firm tourist favourite. Mon–Thurs noon–11pm, Fri & Sat noon–midnight, Sun noon–10.30pm.

BLACKHEATH

Hare & Billet 1a Eliot Cottages, SE3 ☎ 020 8852 2352, ⓦ capitalpubcompany.com; Blackheath station from Charing Cross; map pp.310–311. A 10min walk from the village up on the heath, this pleasantly refurbished, comfortable pub is the place to visit for a quiet drink – the real ale selection is exemplary and there's good seasonal pub grub, too. Mon–Wed 11am–11pm, Thurs–Sat 11am–midnight, Sun noon–10.30pm.

Zerodegrees 29–31 Montpelier Vale, SE3 ☎ 020 8852 5619, ⓦ zerodegrees.co.uk; Blackheath train station from Charing Cross. The somewhat hollow atmosphere at this microbrewery is compensated for by the beer – Black, Pale, Pilsner and Wheat are the four main varieties, in addition to some speciality offerings. Wood-fired pizza, pasta and the like are also on offer. Mon–Sat noon–midnight, Sun noon–11pm.

BEXLEYHEATH

Robin Hood & Little John 78 Lion Rd, DA6 ☎ 020 8303 1128, ⓦ robinhoodbexleyheath.co.uk; Bexleyheath station. This small local, in a residential street, has an impressive range of well-kept ales, and is a good place for a post-Red House pint. Mon–Fri 11am–3pm & 5.30–11pm, Sat 11am–3pm & 7–11pm, Sun noon–4pm & 7–10.30pm.

HAMMERSMITH AND CHISWICK

Blue Anchor 13 Lower Mall, W6 ☎ 020 8748 5774, ⓦ blueanchorlondon.com; ⊖ Hammersmith; map p.331. A good riverside pub, with a boaty theme and a beautiful pewter bar; the upstairs room offers good views of Hammersmith Bridge, or sit outside to enjoy the river. Mon–Sat 11am–11pm, Sun noon–10.30pm.

★ **Dove** 19 Upper Mall, W6 ☎ 020 8748 9474, ⓦ dovehammersmith.co.uk; ⊖ Ravenscourt Park; map p.331. Very old, low-beamed, riverside pub with literary associations – Ernest Hemingway and Graham Greene used to drink here – the smallest bar in the UK (4ft by 7ft), popular Sunday roasts, and riverside terrace. Continue along Upper Mall for other riverside pubs. Mon–Sat 11am–11pm, Sun noon–10.30pm.

KEW, RICHMOND AND WIMBLEDON

Fox & Grapes 9 Camp Rd, SW19 ☎ 020 8619 1300, ⓦ foxandgrapeswimbledon.co.uk; ⊖ Wimbledon; map p.331. Right on the edge of Wimbledon Common, with good real ales and upmarket food, this place is great in the summer, when you can sit outside on the grass. Mon–Sat 11am–11pm, Sun 11am–10.30pm.

The Greyhound 82 Kew Green, Richmond, TW9 ☎ 020 8332 9666, ⓦ thegreyhoundkew.co.uk; ⊖ Kew Gardens; map p.331. One of a handful of good options on Kew Green – the *Botanist* and *Coach and Horses* are also worth a try – this gastropub offers tasty food and real ales. The patio at the back has cosy heated bamboo "pods". Daily 9am–11.30pm.

White Cross Hotel Water Lane, Richmond, TW9 ☎ 020 8940 6844, ⓦ thewhitecrossrichmond.com; ⊖ Richmond; map p.341. With a longer pedigree and more character than its rivals, the *White Cross* has a very popular, large garden overlooking the river. In winter, you can decamp to the lounge with its bay windows and open fire. Mon–Sat 10am–11pm, Sun 10am–10.30pm.

FABRIC

Live music and clubs

Genres, venues, fashions and intoxicants come and go, but London's nightlife – sprawling, chaotic and impossibly varied – carries on regardless. Clubs play everything from pop to house, techno to punk and drum'n'bass to r'n'b on virtually any night of the week. Gigs are equally wide ranging, encompassing rock, roots, jazz, hip-hop and world music. Dividing these scenes into categories makes them easier to navigate, but shouldn't obscure the ever-deepening crossover: club nights take over music venues, DJ sets are lifted by live percussion, gay venues (see p.405) host mixed nights and jazz acts play at rock venues. Virtually all venues listed have events' calendars on their websites – keep your eyes peeled and your dancing shoes ready.

Clubs and venues tend to cluster together, but despite its hedonistic reputation, Soho is surprisingly sparse for live music and straight clubs, so it's best to venture out of zone 1 to find decent gigs. Camden is still the place to rock; the once-cool Shoreditch still has its moments but is generally going mainstream, chasing the best club nights up the road to Dalston; or you can head to Brixton, Peckham and New Cross for something edgier.

LIVE MUSIC

26

From grimy pub back rooms, through O2's franchise and on to the mega-stadiums, talent can play out their entire careers in London's venues. If you are after those that have already made it, check the listings for Wembley (ⓦ wembley.co.uk) and the O2 Dome (ⓦ theo2.co.uk). The Royal Albert Hall (ⓦ royalalberthall.com) – traditionally a classical music venue – and summer concerts in the beautiful courtyard at Somerset House (ⓦ somerset-house.org.uk) are more atmospheric alternatives. Pricewise, you might get in free to see an unknown band or pay £80 for a visiting legend. Most acts will set you back £10–30. **Booking tickets** online for anything but the smallest gigs is standard – the biggest websites are ⓦ seetickets.com, ⓦ ticketweb.co.uk, ⓦ ticketmaster.co.uk and ⓦ wegottickets.com.

GENERAL VENUES

★ **Academy Brixton** 211 Stockwell Rd, SW9 ☎020 7771 3000, ⓦ o2academybrixton.co.uk; ⊖ Brixton; map pp.310–311. Balancing its size with some classy curation, the *Academy* has seen them all, from mods and rockers to Chase and Status. The 4900-capacity Victorian hall's sound quality isn't immaculate, but it makes up for it with great atmosphere and good local bars for before and after the gig.

Academy Islington N1 Centre, N1 ☎020 7288 4400, ⓦ o2academyislington.co.uk; ⊖ Angel; map pp.284–285. One of the better O2 venues, despite being wedged in a shopping centre, with two rooms showcasing a guitar-led programme of good up-and-coming bands. Also home to Saturday night cheesy club triumph, Club De Fromage.

Cargo 83 Rivington St, EC2 ☎020 7739 3440, ⓦ cargo-london.com; ⊖ Old Street or Shoreditch High Street Overground; map pp.192–193. Mixed line-up of live acts, including jazz, hip-hop, indie and folk.

Forum 9–17 Highgate Rd, NW5 ☎020 7428 4099, ⓦ mamacolive.com/theforum; ⊖ Kentish Town; map pp.284–285. Mid-sized venue. The programming has moved towards a reliance on nostalgia acts, but it still occasionally surprises with special events.

Hammersmith Apollo 45 Queen Caroline St, W6 ☎0844 249 1000, ⓦ hammersmithapollo.com; ⊖ Hammersmith; map pp.250–251. The former Hammersmith Odeon is a cavernous space (downstairs can be seating or standing), with the nostalgia circuit sharing the bill with the arts.

O2 Shepherd's Bush Empire Shepherd's Bush Green, W12 ☎020 8354 3300, ⓦ o2shepherdsbushempire.co.uk; ⊖ Shepherd's Bush; map pp.274–275. Great mid-league bands play here. Good news if you want to watch from seating in the vertigo-inducing balconies, but downstairs lacks atmosphere if you're not right down the front.

Roundhouse Chalk Farm Rd, NW1 ☎0844 482 8008, ⓦ roundhouse.org.uk; ⊖ Chalk Farm; map pp.284–285. Magnificent Victorian-era steam engine shed turned performing arts centre. It pulls in huge names like the Flaming Lips with more eclectic choices, but whatever the act, they always make a hell of a show.

★ **Union Chapel** Compton Terrace, N1 ☎020 7226 1686, ⓦ unionchapel.org.uk; ⊖ Highbury & Islington; map pp.284–285. Intimate venue that doubles as a church, hence the pew-style seating; the array of artists ranges from contemporary stars to world-music legends, and there are regular free Saturday-lunchtime sessions.

ROCK, BLUES AND INDIE

12 Bar Club Denmark St, WC2 ☎020 7240 2622, ⓦ 12barclub.com; ⊖ Tottenham Court Road; map p.100. Central London has haemorrhaged good venues but *12 Bar* remains firmly in Tin Pan Alley: expect cheap, intimate indie/blues/rock gigs aplenty.

★ **Amersham Arms** 388 New Cross Rd, SE14 ☎020 8469 1499, ⓦ theamershamarms.com; ⊖ New Cross; map pp.310–311. The backroom line-up covers everything from guitary album launches to cabaret and club nights, catering for whatever takes the whims of the local art student crowd.

Barfly 49 Chalk Farm Rd, NW1 ☎020 7688 8994, ⓦ barflyclub.com; ⊖ Chalk Farm; map pp.284–285. *Barfly* offers a relentless roster of gigs (three nightly), typically indie, rock, punk and metal, in its simple upstairs space.

The Book Club 100–106 Leonard St, EC2 ☎020 7684 8618, ⓦ wearetbc.com; ⊖ Old Street; map pp.192–193. Artfully selected line-up in the cute and popular basement, covering DJs, bands and more.

Borderline Orange Yard, Manette St, W1 ☎020 7734 5547, ⓦ mamacolive.com/theborderline; ⊖ Tottenham Court Road; map p.100. Small and slightly ramshackle basement joint with awkward pillars but good sound and diverse music policy.

★ **Buffalo Bar** 259 Upper St, N1 ☎020 7359 6191, ⓦ buffalobar.co.uk; ⊖ Highbury & Islington; map pp.284–285. Friendly basement bar with great soundsystem and excellent scheduling, focused on guitar music. Look out for the rocking Wrongpop nights as well.

Bull & Gate 389 Kentish Town Rd, NW5 ☎020 7704 0187, ⓦbullandgate.co.uk; ⊖ Kentish Town; map pp.284–285. If you want to chance your hand at finding an unsigned indie-rock band, the *Bull and Gate*'s back room should be your first stop. Gigs nightly for about £5.

Dingwalls Middle Yard, Camden Lock, NW1 ☎020 7428 5829, ⓦdingwalls.com; ⊖ Camden Town; map pp.284–285. This split-level music/club venue is a good place to catch new indie and rock, though views aren't always great.

Hope & Anchor 207 Upper St, N1 ☎020 7354 1312, ⓦbugbearbookings.com; ⊖ Angel; map pp.284–285. This cramped venue is popular with punkish indie acts, many playing their first gigs here.

Hoxton Square Bar & Kitchen 2–4 Hoxton Square, N1 ☎020 7613 0709, ⓦmamacolive.com/thehoxtonplaza; ⊖ Old Street; map pp.192–193. The bar is self-conscious and unexceptional, but it gets some fine rock and electronic talent through its doors, and the occasional secret gig.

KOKO 1a Camden High St, NW1 ☎0870 432 5527, ⓦkoko.uk.com; ⊖ Mornington Crescent; map pp.284–285. A Camden institution, hosting clubs (Fri & Sat) and gigs (the rest of the time), with a cracking assortment of indie-pop types dominating proceedings.

Lexington 96–98 Pentonville Rd, N2 ☎020 7837 5371, ⓦthelexington.co.uk; ⊖ Angel; map pp.284–285. Above the bourbon-packed downstairs lounge bar is a two hundred-capacity venue with good sound, a hip but relaxed vibe and a solid, indie-dominated roster.

★ **The Macbeth** 70 Hoxton St, N1 ☎020 7749 0600, ⓦthemacbeth.co.uk; ⊖ Old Street; map pp.192–193. Beautiful venue, good soundsystem and great nights programmed by those in the know, running across rock and dance. Need a breather? Try their awesome roof terrace.

New Cross Inn 323A New Cross Rd, SE14 ☎020 8691 7222, ⓦnewcrossinn.com; New Cross Gate Overground; map pp.310–311. Relaxed boozer that's the best place to see unsigned guitar bands in south London.

Sebright Arms 31–35 Coate St, E2 ☎020 7729 0937, ⓦsebrightarms.co.uk; ⊖ Bethnal Green; map p.190. Basement venue to an east London boozer that hosted everyone from The XX to Laura Marling before they made it.

Shacklewell Arms 71 Shacklewell Lane, E8 ☎020 7249 0810, ⓦshacklewellarms.com; Dalston Kingsland Overground; map p.291. Cooler-than-thou genre-bending venue that's worth a visit for the free gigs early in the week.

Underworld 174 Camden High St, NW1 ☎020 7482 1932, ⓦtheunderworldcamden.co.uk; ⊖ Camden Town; map pp.284–285. Shouty, scruffy, tattoo-packed warren under the *World's End* pub that's a great place to check out metal, hardcore and heavy rock bands.

★ **Village Underground** 54 Holywell Lane, EC2 ☎020 7422 7505, ⓦvillageunderground.co.uk; ⊖ Old Street; map pp.192–193. A more tasteful artsy line-up than most places in this part of town, playing host in a truly beautiful site – there are even abandoned tube carriages.

Windmill 22 Blenheim Gardens, SW2 ☎020 8671 0700, ⓦwindmillbrixton.co.uk; ⊖ Brixton; map pp.310–311. A fine, left-field mix of bands play at this pokey pub halfway up Brixton Hill. Entry for everything from swirly electronica to throbbing post-rock is rarely much over £5.

JAZZ

100 Club 100 Oxford St, W1 ☎020 7636 0933, ⓦthe100club.co.uk; ⊖ Tottenham Court Road; map p.97. Dinky club with a schedule evenly split between jazz and rock; reasonable prices.

Jazz Cafe 5 Parkway, NW1 ☎020 7485 6834, ⓦmamacolive.com/thejazzcafe; ⊖ Camden Town; map pp.284–285. There's the odd cheesy pop night here, but a combination of big names (at big prices) and clubbier jazz acts keep the dancefloor and balcony buzzing.

Jazz@ Pizza Express 10 Dean St, W1 ☎0845 602 7017, ⓦpizzaexpresslive.com; ⊖ Tottenham Court Road; map p.100. Small basement of this branch of the pizza chain hosts consistent quality, with established and new jazz artists.

26

LONDON'S MUSIC FESTIVALS

Want to experience the Great British music festival without trudging to the countryside? Then head to London's parks. Several new festivals have come and gone in the last few years with some notable disasters, so the following represent the tried, tested and trustworthy names.

Field Day May ⓦfielddayfestivals.com. Victoria Park's hipster day out, where people are there as much to be seen as to see Savages or TNGHT.

Hard Rock Calling June ⓦhardrockcalling.co.uk. The first festival to relocate to post-Olympic Stratford, with big-name acts such as Bruce Springsteen headlining.

Wireless July ⓦwirelessfestival.co.uk. For the biggest names in international R&B, try Hyde Park's Wireless, recently featuring Justin Timberlake and Snoop Lion.

Lovebox July ⓦlovebox.net. Groove Armada are the big name behind the long-running Lovebox bringing dance and urban music to East London's Victoria Park.

South West Four Aug ⓦsouthwestfour.com. Head down south for DJs like Armin Van Buuren and Eric Prydz making the most of the sunshine on Clapham Common.

26

★ **King's Place** 90 York Way, N1 ☎020 7520 1490, ⓦkingsplace.co.uk; ➔ King's Cross; map p.120. Two halls host classical and jazz gigs at this rather swish development – the acoustics are excellent and the acts class.

Ronnie Scott's 47 Frith St, W1 ☎020 7439 0747, ⓦronniescotts.co.uk; ➔ Leicester Square; map p.100. The most famous jazz club in London has smartened up in recent years. The sell-out Sunday Jazz lunches are worth trying.

The Vortex 11 Gillett Square, N16 ☎020 7254 4097, ⓦvortexjazz.co.uk; Dalston Kingsland Overground; map p.291. The small venue is a serious player on the live jazz scene, managing to combine a touch of urban style with a cosy, friendly atmosphere.

URBAN

Indig02 The O2, SE10 ☎0844 844 0002, ⓦtheo2 .co.uk; ➔ North Greenwich. Mixed in among the old pop acts you'll find big-name r'n'b stars at The O2's smaller (well, 2500 capacity) sister venue. Also look out for commercial urban/BME club nights.

Jamm 261 Brixton Rd, SW9 ☎020 7274 5537, ⓦbrixtonjamm.org; ➔ Brixton; map pp.310–311. Two big rooms and a great courtyard (expect a barbecue) with reggae, drum'n'bass and jungle all featuring.

WORLD MUSIC, FOLK AND ROOTS

Barbican Silk St, EC2 ☎020 7638 8891, ⓦbarbican.org .uk; ➔ Barbican; map p.156. It's easy to lose yourself in the Barbican, the largest arts centre in Europe and a focal point for the best world-music bands and orchestras. It also hosts contemporary music events, and free music in the foyer.

Bush Hall 310 Uxbridge Rd, W12 ☎020 8222 6955, ⓦbushhallmusic.co.uk; ➔ Shepherd's Bush; map pp.274–275. Acoustic performers, folk and blues artists play beneath the cool chandeliers of this elegant former dancehall – it gets the odd rock band too.

★ **Cafe OTO** 18–22 Ashwin St, E8 ⓦcafeoto.co.uk; Dalston Kingsland; map p.291. London's most innovative folk, classical and electronica is on offer here – along with a café vibe and intelligent crowd.

Passing Clouds 1 Richmond Rd, E8 ☎020 7241 4889, ⓦpassingclouds.org; ➔ Haggerston; map p.291. Charismatic world music and beats is the focus here, alongside an awareness of global social and political issues.

Southbank Centre South Bank, SE1 ☎0844 875 0073, ⓦsouthbankcentre.co.uk; ➔ Waterloo; map p.216. The all-seater auditoriums of the Royal Festival Hall, Queen Elizabeth Hall and Purcell Room host imaginative programmes of world music, classical, jazz and folk.

CLUBS

Disco tunnels, sticky-floored indie clubs and epic house nights: London has it all. While the capital has lost most of its superclubs, the current spread of mid-sized venues gives more choice than ever. **Opening time** for most is between 10pm and midnight – check online before you go and treat our listed timings as a rough guide. Some keep irregular days, others open only at the weekend and often times are determined by the club night. **Admission prices** vary enormously: the handful of midweek nights charge a few quid or less while big all-nighters cost as much as £30; £10–15 is average at the weekend although east and south London can be cheaper – also bear in mind that prices at the bar can be outrageous. Some things are common to all London clubs: security can be enthusiastic and deserve treating with respect if you want to get in; make sure you have **ID**; and if you're heading to an up-and-coming area, work out a route home beforehand. London's scene is fairly **dressed down** – West End clubs may want you to wear smart shoes, but trainers are often fine, although in east London you may feel underdressed if you haven't made at least some effort to wear a vintage frock or grow a bad moustache.

VICTORIA

Pacha London Terminus Place, SW1 ☎0845 371 4489, ⓦpachalondon.com; ➔ Victoria; map p.36. Sister to the iconic Ibiza venue, with nights from brands like Cafe Mambo and Space bringing house-led music to a classy crowd – just expect to dress and pay accordingly. Around 10pm–5am.

SOHO AND AROUND

Café de Paris 3–4 Coventry St, W1 ☎020 7734 7700, ⓦcafedeparis.com; ➔ Piccadilly Circus; map p.100. Crushed velvet drapes and blood-red beds would be gaudy if the whole shebang wasn't carried off with Moulin Rouge-esque (pricey) gusto. Regular weekend cabaret, but often closed for private events. Check for times but typically Fri & Sat 7pm–3am.

Madame JoJo's 8–10 Brewer St, W1 ☎020 7734 3040, ⓦmadamejojos.com; ➔ Piccadilly Circus; map p.100.

Louche, enjoyable and ever-so-slightly battered institution. Alongside cabaret, you'll find electronica, disco, rock and funk – the big nights here include funky groovefest The Good Foot (Fri), and indie White Heat (Tues). Usually Tues–Sun 10pm–3am, with shows earlier in the eve.

Moonlighting 17 Greek St, W1 ☎020 7437 5782, ⓦmoonlightingnightclub.co.uk; ➔ Tottenham Court Road; map p.100. So cheap and cheerful they named a night after it (Cheap$kates, Wed & Thurs, drinks from £1.50). It kicks over to a more urban feel at weekends. Mon 10pm–3.30am, Wed & Thurs 9pm–3.30am, Fri & Sat 10pm–5am.

★ **The Phoenix** 37 Cavendish Square, W1 ☎020 7493 8003, ⓦphoenixcavendishsquare.co.uk; ➔ Oxford Street; map p.89. You can find a few great club nights in this pub basement: monthly Feeling Gloomy is dedicated to sad music, Four Weddings has the cheesiest music in town and monthly How does it feel to be loved? is a top night of

GETTING THE LOWDOWN

Check these **websites** for upcoming club nights, with Resident Advisor the best for dance, and The Fly for guitar music.

Drowned In Sound ⓦdrownedinsound.com

Fact Mag ⓦfactmag.com
The Fly ⓦmamacolive.com/thefly
London Gigs ⓦlondongigs.net
NME ⓦnme.com
Resident Advisor ⓦresidentadvisor.net
Time Out ⓦtimeout.com/london/

indie pop and Sixties soul. Club nights from around 10pm.
The Roxy 3–5 Rathbone Place, W1 ☎020 255 1098, ⓦtheroxy.co.uk; ⊖ Tottenham Court Road; map p.97. One of very few surviving student nights in town, this is a broadly indie/pop club that's a decent enough West End bet. Not many places still do student discount – here does, plus there's a lengthy (very) happy hour. Mon–Thurs 5pm–3am, Fri 5pm–3.30am, Sat 9.30pm–3.30am.

CLERKENWELL

Fabric 77a Charterhouse St, EC1 ☎020 7336 8898, ⓦfabriclondon.com; ⊖ Farringdon; map p.150. Despite big queues (you're best buying tickets online) and a confusing layout, this 1600-capacity club gets in the big names. Genres booming from the devastating soundsystem include drum'n'bass (most Fri) and techno and house (most Sat). Fri & Sun 10pm–6am, Sat 11pm–8am, Sun 11pm–5.30am.

SHOREDITCH, WHITECHAPEL AND BETHNAL GREEN

★ **Bethnal Green Working Men's Club** 44–46 Pollard Row, E2 ☎020 7739 7170, ⓦworkersplaytime.net; ⊖ Bethnal Green; map pp.192–193. Old school decor and postwar kitsch set the backdrop for some serious playtime: fifties dress-up, burlesque, disco, rock'n'roll, cheese and a whole lot more. Thurs–Sat 9pm–2am, check listings for other days.

Cargo 83 Rivington St, EC2 ☎020 7739 3440, ⓦcargo-london.com; ⊖ Old Street; map pp.192–193. Shoreditch has haemorrhaged cool in recent years, and *Cargo* has suffered more than most. While the crowd can be pretty hard work, you can have a decent night in the sunny terrace, at a gig or its mixed (often house) club nights. Mon–Thurs 6pm–1am, Fri–Sat 6pm–3am, Sun 6pm–midnight.

East Village 89 Great Eastern St, EC2A ☎020 7739 5173, ⓦeastvillageclub.co.uk; ⊖ Old Street; map pp.192–193. House and hip-hop nights at this big, fun, bolshy basement and lounge. Bar daily, club Fri & Sat 9pm–3.30am.

The Old Blue Last 38 Great Eastern St, EC2 ☎020 7739 7033, ⓦtheoldbluelast.com; ⊖ Old Street; map pp.192–193. Definitive Shoreditch pub and venue, with hip gigs and semi-ironic dancefloor cheese upstairs, a decent bar downstairs and energetic hipsters everywhere, many complaining that it isn't as cool as it was last year. Occasional charges for bands, otherwise free. Daily noon–midnight, Fri–Sat till 2am.

Plastic People 147–149 Curtain Rd, EC2 ☎020 7739 6471, ⓦplasticpeople.co.uk; ⊖ Old Street; map pp.192–193. Thumping basement club whose cheeringly broad booking policy stretches through techno, rock'n'roll and Afro-pop. Try hit new night Deep Shit, set up by Foals and Friendly Fires. Usually Fri & Sat 11pm–4am.

Rhythm Factory 16–18 Whitechapel Rd, E1 ☎020 7375 3774, ⓦrhythmfactory.co.uk; ⊖ Aldgate East or Whitechapel; map pp.192–193. Plays heavy dance, with techno and house leading the field. Fine if you're in the area but don't go out of your way. Bar all day, club usually Wed & Thurs 6pm–midnight, Fri & Sat 10pm–6am.

★ **XOYO** 42–37 Cowper St, EC2 ☎020 7354 9993, ⓦxoyo.co.uk; ⊖ Old Street; map pp.192–193. This big (it can hold nine hundred) venue and club has an annoying layout (the main corridors get packed) but its well-connected team bring in some tasty rock and hip-hop talent. Club nights until 3am.

DALSTON AND HACKNEY

The Alibi 91 Kingsland High St, E8 ☎020 7249 2733, ⓦthealibilondon.co.uk; Dalston Kingsland Overground; map p. 291. The outside doesn't look like much, but there's fun, hip DJ nights in the basement. Best of all, it's free entry every night. Mon–Wed & Sun 5pm–2am, Thurs–Sat 5pm–3am.

★ **Dalston Superstore** 177 Kingsland High St, E8 ☎020 7254 2273, ⓦdalstonsuperstore.com; Dalston Kingsland Overground; map p.291. The *Superstore* has maintained its role as Dalston's capital with picky door staff, fashionable straight/gay clientele and a hedonistic mix of disco, house and party tunes. Bar daily, club usually Wed–Sun 9pm–2am.

★ **Dance Tunnel** 95 Kingsland High St, E8 ☎020 7249 7865, ⓦfacebook.com/dancetunnel; Dalston Kingsland Overground; map p.291. *Superstore's* sister venue – it would be just a dingy basement if the music wasn't so impeccably designed to get people moving. Home to dubstep night FWD>>. Usually Thurs–Sat 9pm–5am.

The Nest 36 Stoke Newington Rd, N16 ☎020 7354 9993, ⓦilovethenest.com; Dalston Kingsland Overground; map p.291. Electro-house and disco for the arty hipster crowd. Long sets from decent names and cheap drinks and entry on Thursday. Usually Thurs–Sat 9pm–4am.

NOTTING HILL

Notting Hill Arts Club 21 Notting Hill Gate, W11 ☎020 7460 4459, ⓦnottinghillartsclub.com; ⊖ Notting Hill

26

Gate; map pp.274–275. Groovy dressed-down basement club-bar playing everything from funk, jazz and hip-hop through to soul and indie. Usually Tues–Sun 7pm–2am.

CAMDEN, KING'S CROSS AND ISLINGTON

Big Chill House 257–259 Pentonville Rd, N1 ☎020 7427 2540; ⊖ King's Cross; map pp.284–285. Friendly bar-cum-club that rarely has a door charge for its drum'n'bass, house, funk and boogie vibes. Mon–Wed 9am–midnight, Thurs 9am–1am, Fri 9am–3am, Sat 11am–3am, Sun 11am–midnight.

EGG 200 York Way, N7 ☎020 7871 7111, ⓦegglondon .net; ⊖ King's Cross; map pp.284–285. Three floors and a decent outdoor space host a mixed crowd there for the house and rave, including lots of new tunes but often kicking it old school. Usually Fri–Sun 10pm–6am.

Electric Ballroom 184 Camden High St, NW1 ☎020 7485 9006, ⓦelectricballroom.co.uk; ⊖ Camden Town; map pp.284–285. Historic club and rock venue, hosting rock and metal (Fri) and indie and pop nights (Sat), plus mid-tier gigs earlier in the evening. Fri & Sat 10.30pm–3am.

Proud Camden Stables Market, NW1 ☎020 7482 3867, ⓦproudcamden.com; ⊖ Camden Town; map pp.284–285. Crossing the dance/rock spectrum with live celebrity acts, costume parties and more, *Proud Camden* is as mixed up as you'd expect a former horse hospital to be, with acoustic music during the days at weekends and an outdoor terrace in summer. Hours vary, club usually till 2.30am.

Scala 275 Pentonville Rd, N1 ☎020 7833 2022, ⓦscala -london.co.uk; ⊖ King's Cross map p.120. This cavernous former cinema is just the right side of labyrinthine. Stages fine gigs and weekend club nights covering rock and soca to dub and cheese. Club usually Fri–Sun 10pm–6am.

Slimelight at Electrowerkz 7 Torrens St, EC1 ☎020 7837 6419, ⓦfacebook.com/slimelightofficial; ⊖ Angel; map pp.284–285. If you're into goth, aggrotech and other dark scene genres best displayed by the colour black, here should be your first port of call. Sat 10pm–7.30am.

SOUTH LONDON

★ **Bussey Building** 133 Rye Lane, SE1 ☎020 7732 5275, ⓦclfartcafe.org; Peckham Rye Overground; map pp.310–311. The heart of Peckham's cool, *Bussey* delivers three floors of mixed bills with loads of space to dance, a friendly crowd and lots of afrobeat and disco vibes. Usually Thurs 8pm–2am, Fri & Sat 10pm–4am.

Coronet 28 New Kent Rd, SE1 ☎020 7701 1500, ⓦcoronettheatre.co.uk; ⊖ Elephant and Castle; map pp.224–225. Theatre-turned-cinema-turned-music venue, with a gorgeous Art Deco interior, regular club nights and gigs, catering for a vaguely more knowing crowd than nearby *Ministry*. Until 6am on club nights.

★ **Corsica Studios** 5 Elephant Rd, SE17 ☎020 7703 4760, ⓦcorsicastudios.com; ⊖ Elephant & Castle; map pp.224–225. Faintly scuzzy and very cool mid-sized venue that worships the bass, with breaks, dubstep, electro and techno dominating the speakers, frequent live sessions and artistic/community projects. Look out for signature night Troublevision. Usually Fri–Sun 10pm–6am.

The Lambeth 467 Brixton Rd, SW9 ☎☎020 7383 7788, ⓦfacebook.com/thelambeth; ⊖ Brixton; map pp.310–311. Formerly the *Brixton Clubhouse*, the *Lambeth* has rooftop partying high above the hubbub of Brixton. Lots of urban and house nights, but look out for house/cheese fun with Gym & Tonic. Times vary, check site for nights.

Ministry of Sound 103 Gaunt St, SE1 ☎0870 060 0010, ⓦministryofsound.com/club; ⊖ Elephant & Castle; map pp.224–225. The vast headquarters of this clubbing brand may sometimes seem peopled by corporate clubbers and gawping visitors, but the soundsystem is exceptional and it gets the pick of visiting house and trance DJs. Usually Fri 10.30pm–6am, Sat 11pm–7am.

Plan B 418 Brixton Rd, SW9 ☎020 7733 0926, ⓦplan -brixton.co.uk; ⊖ Brixton; map pp.310–311. Small, laidback Brixton club with a good soundsystem, friendly staff, a great bar and a house- and hip-hop-oriented music policy that gets in good acts. Usually Fri–Sun 10pm–4am.

SECRET NIGHTS AND SPECIAL EVENT SPACES

The last few years have seen a revival in nights where you only discover the venue at the last minute, especially for big warehouse parties. The good news is that the most likely spaces are great sites, with several venues around that just host others' special events. The best bet for finding out what's on is Resident Advisor (ⓦresidentadvisor.net).

Ewer Street Car Park (ⓦbit.ly/18wBM3I) near Southwark Tube is a series of cavernous arches that provide great atmosphere for events, although it's fairly infrequently used. **Netil House** has hosted all sorts of great after-parties and events (ⓦwww.netilhouse.com) near London Fields train station, while **Autumn Street Studios** (ⓦfacebook.com/autumnstreet studios) is a fun one-room studio behind the Olympic site run by major UK promoters Bloc. While the term "pop-up" has been tarnished by overuse, there are many genuinely spontaneous venues. Homerton's **The Dentist** (ⓦfacebook.com/33ChatsworthRd) is a squatted shop front with atmospheric gigs, friendly parties and an artsy crowd. You may also see the name **Loft Studios** (ⓦhttp://bit.ly/18i7GVf) listed for dance music events, bringing house music to parties in northwest London near Willesden Junction.

KITSCH CABARET, MADAME JOJO'S

Lesbian and gay London

London's lesbian and gay scene today is so huge, diverse and well established that it's easy to forget just how fast it has grown and been accepted into the mainstream over the last couple of decades. Political progress has been accompanied by a depoliticized scene, as pink power has given way to the pink pound and gay liberation to gay lifestyle. As a result, straight Londoners tend to be a fairly homo-savvy bunch and are happy to embrace and even dip into the city's queer offerings. The gay community currently clusters in three main areas: though Soho remains gay London's spiritual heart, Vauxhall is home to the big clubs, while Dalston and around is fast becoming something of a third leg to the gay scene in London.

In central London, Soho's **Old Compton Street** (see p.99) is, so to speak, its main drag; traditional gay pubs rub alongside cafés and bars selling expensive designer beers and lattes, while hairdressers, letting agencies, sex boutiques and spiritual health centres offer a vast range of gay-run services. Lesbian bars complete the diverse mix in Soho.

The biggest and best **clubs** are now found just south of the river in **Vauxhall**, catering for every musical, sartorial and sexual taste, but there are well-established venues all over the city. **Clapham** also hosts a smaller gay contingent for the south.

In **east and northeast London**, the clubs and bars of Shoreditch and particularly Dalston cater for a younger, cooler and substantially more mixed crowd, to the point you can struggle to tell the gay and straight nights – and clienteles – apart from each other. Head further north again for London's main lesbian contingent in Stoke Newington and Hackney.

Despite some recent homophobic attacks, you may see some gay couples holding hands around town. Still, it's probably wise not to follow suit until you have a feel for any given area.

27

ESSENTIALS

LESBIAN AND GAY MEDIA
PRINT
While glossy print titles have to appeal to a broader UK audience, the free magazines have excellent London listings. Pick them up in gay bars around town.

Paid-for titles include **Attitude** (ⓦ attitude.co.uk) and rival **Gay Times** (ⓦ gaytimes.co.uk) with **Diva** (ⓦ divamag.co.uk) and **G3** (ⓦ g3mag.co.uk) aimed squarely at the lesbian market. As for the freebies, check out **Boyz** (ⓦ boyz.co.uk) and **qx** (ⓦ qxmagazine.com), which are also available in full on their websites.

ONLINE
Where print media has wilted, online sources have filled the void

ⓦ **pinknews.co.uk** An LGBT slant on news from the UK and abroad.

ⓦ **gaytoz.com** Directory of LGBT-friendly organizations and businesses.

ⓦ **gingerbeer.co.uk** Regularly updated website for London lesbians, offering listings and reviews of bars, clubs and events.

ⓦ **twatboutique.com** The best grrl listings for the east London crowd.

HELPLINES
London Lesbian & Gay Switchboard ☎ 0300 330 0630, ⓦ llgs.org.uk. Whether you need to talk through coming out or other personal problems, find legal advice and counselling, or just get some information on their massive database, this should be your first port of call. Lines are open 365 days a year, 10am to 11pm: keep trying if you can't get through, or try contacting through the website.

THT Direct ☎ 0808 802 1221, ⓦ tht.org.uk. Helpline for anyone worried about HIV, as well as other STIs and problems.

TOURS
A good introduction to Soho's lesbian and gay history is offered by the walking tour (2–4pm) organized by Centred most Sundays (☎ 020 7437 6063, ⓦ centred.org.uk to check it is running; £5) – meet outside the *Admiral Duncan* pub (see opposite).

HOTELS

Homophobia in mainstream services has dropped massively in recent years, but these hotels are specifically gay run. London's best-known gay accommodation options cater mostly for men, though all are lesbian friendly. Self-catering **apartments** are available through the gay-run Outlet Gay Accommodation, 32 Old Compton St, W1 (☎ 020 7287 4244; ⓦ outlet4holidays.com). *Number 16*, a charming, tiny gay-run B&B in Greenwich is also a good choice (see p.362).

Fitzbb 15 Colville Place, W1 ☎ 07834 372866; ⓦ fitzbb .me.uk; ⊖ Goodge St; map p.97. This eighteenth-century townhouse only has two rooms so book ahead, but it's a great price in stumbling distance from Soho. There's a minimum booking of three nights. Or try its younger sibling via ⓦ sohobb.me.uk. Fitzbb £70, Sohobb £55

Griffin House Holiday Apartments 22 Stockwell Green, SW9 ☎ 020 7096 3332, ⓦ griffinhouse .info; ⊖ Stockwell. Highly rated self-catering accommodation with an emphasis on providing a home from home. A 10min walk from the Vauxhall scene. Apartments from £115

CAFÉS, BARS AND PUBS

There are loads of lesbian and gay eating and watering holes in London, many of them operating as cafés by day and transforming into drinking dens by night. Lots have cabaret or disco nights and are open until the early hours, making them an affordable alternative to clubs. Most have free admission, though a few levy a charge after 10.30pm (expect to pay about £5) if there's music, cabaret or a disco. The places below represent a selective list of the best and most accessible, from self-consciously minimalist bars to shabby old pubs. We use "mixed" to mean places for both gays and lesbians, though many are mostly frequented by men.

MIXED CAFÉS, BARS AND PUBS
SOHO

The Admiral Duncan 54 Old Compton St, W1 ☎020 7437 5300; ⊖ Leicester Square; map p.100. Unpretentious, traditional-style gay bar in the heart of Soho, popular and busy with the post-work crowd. Expect cocktails and camp classics on the jukebox. Mon–Thurs noon–11pm, Fri & Sat noon–midnight, Sun noon–10.30pm.

Balans 34 Old Compton St, W1 ☎020 7439 3309; 60 Old Compton St, W1 ☎020 7439 2183; ⓦbalans.co.uk; ⊖ Leicester Square; map p.100. *Balans* has spawned several branches across the city but these two remain a Soho institution, serving a menu that includes a lengthy hangover-busting breakfast and brunch section. No. 34 24hr; no. 60 Mon–Thurs 8am–5am, Fri & Sat 7.30am–6am, Sun 7.30am–2am.

Circa 62 Frith St, W1 ☎020 7734 6826, ⓦcircasoho .com; ⊖ Tottenham Court Road; map p.100. An unpretentious new entrant to the Soho scene. There's little to differentiate it from more established boy bars, but when the drinks are this cheap, who cares? Daily 4pm–1am.

City of Quebec 12 Old Quebec St, W1 ☎020 7629 6159; ⊖ Marble Arch; map p.89. Aimed at an older gay audience, but given the number of weary shoppers drinking pints, you might not even notice it's a gay bar. Mon–Thurs noon–2am, Fri & Sat noon–3am, Sun noon–1am.

★ **Duke of Wellington** 77 Wardour St, W1 ☎020 7439 1274; ⊖ Piccadilly Circus; map p.100. Traditional pub on two floors in the heart of Soho, with cheap lager and real ale on pump and a down-to-earth, male-dominated crowd, keen on chatting and socializing. Mon–Wed noon–11pm, Thurs–Sat noon–midnight, Sun noon–10.30pm.

The Edge 11 Soho Square, W1 ☎020 7439 1313, ⓦedgesoho.co.uk; ⊖ Tottenham Court Road; map p.100. Sister to *The Yard*, it may be a regular Soho bar by night, but by day it's a useful stop-off point with decent food. Mon–Wed 4pm–1am, Thurs 3pm–1am, Fri & Sat 3pm–3am, Sun 3–11.30pm.

Escape 10a Brewer St, W1 ☎020 7734 3040, ⓦescapesoho.com; ⊖ Piccadilly Circus; map, p.100. If you're heading to *Madame Jojo's*, then head to *Escape* first, the club's trendy sister DJ bar. Tues Queerly Out prides itself

on being Soho's cheapest gay night out. Sun & Mon 9pm–3am, Tues–Sat 5pm–3am.

Freedom 66 Wardour St, W1 ☎020 7734 0071, ⓦfreedombarsoho.com; ⊖ Piccadilly Circus; map p.100. Hip, metrosexual place, popular with a straight/gay Soho crowd. The basement becomes an intimate club at night that plays home to cabaret and comedy. Mon–Thurs 4pm–3am, Fri & Sat 2pm–3am, Sun 2–10.30pm.

G-A-Y Bar 30 Old Compton St, W1 ☎020 7494 2756, ⓦg-a-y.co.uk; ⊖ Leicester Square; map p.100. Vast, pinky-purple video bar that attracts a young, fashionable, pre-G-A-Y crowd. There is a basement bar for women and guests only in the evening. Daily noon–midnight.

Green Carnation 4 Greek St, W1 ☎020 8123 4267, ⓦgreencarnationlondon.com; ⊖ Tottenham Court Road; map p.100. The classiest cocktail joint in gay Soho, it's still affordable if you hit happy hour. Mon–Sat 4pm–2am, Sun 4pm–12.30am.

★ **Ku Bar** 30 Lisle St, WC2 ☎020 7437 4303; 25 Frith St, W1 ☎020 7437 4303, ⓦku-bar.co.uk; ⊖ Leicester Square; map p.100. The Lisle St original, with a downstairs club open till 3am, is one of Soho's largest and best-loved gay bars, serving a scene-conscious yet low-on-attitude clientele. It's now joined by a stylish sibling bar on Frith St; the basement holds Ruby Tuesdays for lesbians only. Lisle St: Mon–Sat noon–3am, Sun noon–midnight; Frith St: Mon–Thurs noon–11pm, Fri & Sat noon–midnight, Sun noon–10.30pm.

Rupert Street 50 Rupert St, W1 ⓦrupert-street.com; ⊖ Piccadilly Circus; map p.100. Smart, mainstream bar attracting a mixed after-work crowd, but with a more pre-club vibe at weekends. Ideal central location to start a Soho night out. Mon–Fri noon–11pm, Sat noon–midnight, Sun noon–10.30pm.

Village Soho 81 Wardour St, W1 ☎020 7478 0530, ⓦvillage-soho.co.uk; ⊖ Piccadilly Circus; map p.100. Elegant three-floor café-bar attracting pretty boyz: clean and modern on the ground floor, with a stylish basement and a plush, comfortable upstairs boudoir. Mon–Sat 4pm–1am, Sun 4–11.30pm.

The Yard 57 Rupert St, W1 ☎020 7437 2652, ⓦyardbar.co.uk; ⊖ Piccadilly Circus; map p.100. The only central al fresco gay bar, it has a laidback, sociable atmosphere. Expect a packed-out varied post-work crowd when the sun is out. Mon–Wed 4–11.30pm, Thurs 3–11.30pm, Fri & Sat noon–midnight, Sun 2–10.30pm.

27

COVENT GARDEN

Retro Bar 2 George Court (off Strand), WC2 ☎ 020 7839 8760, ⓦ retrobarlondon.co.uk; ⊖ Charing Cross; map p.132. Friendly bar tucked down a quiet alleyway off the Strand, playing classic indie, rock and pop. Mon–Fri noon–11pm, Sat 2–11pm, Sun 2–10.30pm.

KING'S CROSS AND BLOOMSBURY

Central Station 37 Wharfdale Rd, N1 ☎ 020 7278 3294, ⓦ centralstation.co.uk; ⊖ King's Cross; map p.120. Late-opening pub offering cabaret, cruisey club nights and the UK's only gay sports bar. Sun–Wed noon–1am, Thurs noon–2am, Fri & Sat noon–4am.

New Bloomsbury Set 76 Marchmont St, WC1 ☎ 020 7383 3084, ⓦ newbloomsburyset.co.uk; ⊖ Russell Square; map p.120. Hit happy hour at the right time and get cheap and cheerful cocktails in this basement bar. Best enjoyed by securing one of their cute and cosy snugs. Mon–Sat 4–11.30pm, Sun 4–10.30pm.

SHOREDITCH

George & Dragon 2–4 Hackney Rd, E2 ☎ 020 7012 1100; ⊖ Old Street; map pp.192–193. Dandies, fashionistas and locals meet in this lively, often rammed east London hangout. The interior set-up is traditional, but the attitudes are not. A perfect place to start a night in the east – it's only stumbling distance from the *Joiners Arms*. Daily 6pm–midnight.

★ **Joiners Arms** 116–118 Hackney Rd, E2 ☎ 07916 868839, ⓦ joinershoreditch.com; ⊖ Old Street; map pp.192–193. Atmospheric bar with regular DJs and funky dancefloor. Open late at weekends, it attracts a diverse crowd with a trendy-cum-eurotrash sweaty vibe. Mon–Wed 5pm–2am, Thurs 5pm–3am, Fri & Sat 5pm–4am, Sun 2pm–2am.

CAMDEN

The Black Cap 171 Camden High St, NW1 ☎ 020 7485 0538, ⓦ theblackcap.com; ⊖ Camden Town; map pp.284–285. Venerable north London establishment offering cabaret and dancing almost every night. The upstairs *Shufflewick* bar is in a quieter pub style with an attached terrace. Sun–Tues noon–1am, Wed & Thurs noon–2am, Fri & Sat noon–3am.

DALSTON

★ **Dalston Superstore** 117 Kingsland High St, E8 ☎ 020 7254 2273, ⓦ dalstonsuperstore.com; Dalston Junction Overground; map p.291. The hottest late-night destination in east London, catering for a fashionably mixed but often gay crowd, with some nights gayer than others; try out Handsome for the boys, or Club Lesley and Sister Pantychrist for the girls. Daytimes bring music, art and food. Check site for closing times; open Mon from noon, Tues–Sun 10am.

SOUTH LONDON

Bridge 8 Voltaire Rd, SW4 ☎ 020 3632 6426. Clapham North; map pp.310–311. New, brash venue in a train arch, mixing cocktails and tunes for a buff Clapham crowd. Sun–Thurs 4pm–midnight, Fri & Sat 4pm–3am.

Kazbar 50 Clapham High St, SW4 ☎ 020 7622 0070, ⓦ kazbarclapham.com; ⊖ Clapham North; map pp.310–311. Modern, mostly buff boyz, split-level bar; upstairs is a lounge area, while there is popular alfresco eating out front on the street. A touch of Soho in south London. Mon & Tues 5–11pm, Wed & Thurs 5pm–midnight, Fri 5pm–1am, Sat 4pm–1am, Sun 1–11pm.

The Royal Vauxhall Tavern 372 Kennington Lane, SE11 ☎ 020 7820 1222, ⓦ rvt.org.uk; ⊖ Vauxhall; map pp.310–311. This huge, disreputable, divey drag and cabaret pub is home to legendary alternative night Duckie on Saturdays. The rest of the week brings a changing calendar of performance that attracts a varied but often older crowd. Mon–Thurs 7pm–midnight, Fri 7pm–2am, Sat 9pm–2am, Sun 2pm–midnight.

EVENTS AND FESTIVALS

London's biggest gay events – Pride and the Lesbian and Gay Film Festival – have both had cash woes the last few years, but remain centrepieces of the calendar. London's **Pride** lands in late June or early July, taking over central London and featuring a massive rally in Trafalgar Square, a colourful, whistle-blowing march through the city streets, live cabaret in Leicester Square and a women's stage in Soho. Full details on the website ⓦ pridelondon.org.

Gay festivals provide a new way to enjoy the summer: As One In The Park (May, ⓦ asoneinthepark.co.uk) brings a pop-led programme to east London's Victoria Park, while weekender Lovebox (July, ⓦ lovebox.net) is at its gayest on Sundays.

In March and April, the British Film Institute hosts the annual **Lesbian and Gay Film Festival** (ⓦ llgff.org.uk), which celebrates new cinema from around the world. For more arts check out the local gay press, try Tuesday's Bar Wotever at the *Royal Vauxhall Tavern*, or check radical gay arts group LeftFrontArt (ⓦ facebook.com/leftfrontart) for more pointers.

Two Brewers 114 Clapham High St, SW4 ☎020 7819 9539, ⓦthe2brewers.com; ⊖ Clapham Common; map pp.310–311. Big, long-established and popular south London pub, with nightly cabaret in the front bar and a more cruisey dancefloor in the back that stays open late. Sun–Thurs 4pm–2am, Fri & Sat 4pm–4am.

LESBIAN CAFÉS, BARS AND PUBS
SOHO

Candy Bar 4 Carlisle St, WC2 ☎020 7287 5041, ⓦcandybarsoho.com; ⊖ Tottenham Court Road; map p.100. This Sapphic magnet has been in operation since 1996 and still has the same crucial, cruisey vibe that makes it the hottest girl bar in central London – they even made a TV show about it. Mon–Fri 3pm–3am, Sat 1pm–3am, Sun 1pm–12.30am.

Star at Night 22 Great Chapel St, W1 ☎020 7494 2488, ⓦthestaratnight.com; ⊖ Tottenham Court Road; map p.100. Comfortable mixed but female-led venue, popular with a slightly older crowd who want somewhere to sit, a decent glass of wine and good conversation. Tues–Sat 6–11.30pm.

NORTH LONDON

★ **Blush** 8 Cazenove Rd, Stoke Newington, N16 ☎020 7923 9202; bus #73 from ⊖ King's Cross or Angel; map p.291. Two floors of fun with quizzes, games nights and lazy Sundays with roast dinners and the newspapers make this local popular among lesbians. Tues–Sat 5pm–midnight, Sun 1pm–midnight.

GAY MEN'S CAFÉS, BARS AND PUBS
SOHO

Comptons of Soho 51–53 Old Compton St, W1 ☎ 020 3238 0163, ⓦfaucetinn.com/comptons; ⊖ Leicester Square; map p.100. This large, traditional-style pub attracts a butch, cruising yet relaxed 25-plus crowd. Upstairs is more chilled and draws younger folks. Mon–Thurs noon–11.30pm, Fri & Sat noon–midnight, Sun noon–10.30pm.

The King's Arms 23 Poland St, W1 ☎020 7734 5907; ⊖ Oxford Circus; map p.97. London's best-known and perennially popular bear bar, with a traditional London pub atmosphere. Head down on Sundays for the raucous karaoke night. Mon–Thurs noon–11pm, Fri & Sat noon–midnight, Sun noon–10.30pm.

COVENT GARDEN

Halfway 2 Heaven 7 Duncannon St, WC2 ☎020 7484 0736, ⓦhalfway2heaven.net; ⊖ Charing Cross; map p.132. Friendly, traditional pub off Trafalgar Square, featuring pub quizzes, karaoke and occasional cabaret. Attracts a largely male crowd older than that in Soho. Mon–Sat noon–midnight, Sun noon–11pm.

SOUTH LONDON

★ **BarCode Vauxhall** Arch 69, Albert Embankment, SE11 ☎020 7582 4180, ⓦbar-code.co.uk; ⊖ Vauxhall; map pp.310–311. Cruisey gay men's bar in the heart of Vauxhall's clubbing quarter, convenient for *Area* and *Fire*. Look out for nu-disco night Tin Tin. Mon–Wed 4pm–1am, Thurs 4pm–2am, Fri 4pm–5am, Sat 4pm–7am, Sun 5pm–1am.

27

CLUBS

London's club nights tend to open up and shut down with surreal frequency, so do check location, times and prices online before heading out. Places are listed by club name if this is well known and long lived, and by venue where there's a variety of changing theme nights. Entry **prices** start at around £3–5, but are more often between £10 and £16 for all-nighters, rising to around £35 or even £50 for special events like New Year's Eve extravaganzas. A shrinking number of places offer student concessions; picking up a flyer may help you save a few quid instead, especially for venues with attached bars. Most clubs **open** at around 11pm (although some don't get going until the small hours) and close between 3am and 6am, while after-hours clubs provide somewhere to dance the next morning.

MIXED CLUBS

Popstarz Moves venue every week ⓦpopstarz.org. The original Friday-night indie club's still-winning formula of alternative tunes, 1970s and 80s trash, cheap beer and no attitude attracts a mixed, studenty crowd till late. Be sure to print the web flyer.

SOHO

G-A-Y Late 5 Goslett Yard, WC2 ☎020 7494 2756, ⓦg-a-y.co.uk; ⊖ Tottenham Court Road; map p.100. No-frills cheese and pop princesses at the late night sister bar to *G-A-Y*, where you should grab a flyer for free entry. Members only Sundays. Daily 11pm–3am.

Madame Jojo's 8–10 Brewer St, W1 ☎020 7734 3040, ⓦmadamejojos.com; ⊖ Piccadilly Circus; map p.100. Lush, louche club offering cabaret and drag shows for office girls, gay boys and those in between, plus a variety of dance nights. Surrender your gender at Trannyshack on Wednesdays. Opening hours vary so check the website, but it is typically open until 3am.

COVENT GARDEN

Heaven Villiers St, WC2 ☎020 7930 2020, ⓦheavennightclub-london.com; ⊖ Charing Cross; map p.132. Said to be the UK's most popular gay club, this two thousand-capacity venue is now home to G-A-Y from

27

SAUNAS AND GYMS

The following saunas are large sites, although there are more intimate venues around town. There have been some high-profile incidents in London saunas so be safety-minded. They all charge around £10–15.

SAUNAS

Chariots 1 Fairchild St, EC2, ⊖ Liverpool Street; 63–64 Albert Embankment, SE1, ⊖ Vauxhall; 101 Lower Marsh, SE1, ⊖ Waterloo; 574 Commercial Rd, E14, ⊖ Limehouse; 292 Streatham High Rd, SW16; ☎ 020 7247 5333, ⓦ gaysauna.co.uk. London's Roman sauna chain has five locations: the Waterloo branch never closes, while the other four are open daily. Expect steam, sweat and saucy videos, plus private rest rooms to retire to with your man of choice. The Shoreditch branch is the largest and has a heated pool.

Pleasuredrome Sauna Arch 124, Alaska St, SE1 ☎ 020 7633 9194, ⓦ pleasuredrome.com; ⊖ Waterloo. Facilities here include two saunas, two steam rooms, dark areas and private rooms, plus café-bar and spa. Mixed ages, fast turnover, highly rated. Open 24hr.

The Sauna Bar 29 Endell St, WC2 ☎ 020 7836 2236, ⓦ thesaunabar.co.uk; ⊖ Covent Garden. Very central, this friendly place offers the usual facilities, along with masseurs, a bar and video entertainment. Mon–Thurs 11am–11.30pm, Fri 11am–7am, Sat noon–2am, Sun noon–11pm.

GYM

Sweatbox Ramillies House, 1–2 Ramillies St, Soho ⓦ sweatboxsoho.com. There's a line of argument that says lots of gyms in central London are gay gyms. Well, it's a little more explicit at gym/sauna Sweatbox. If you want to get pumped before a big night out, you can pick up a one-day pass for £16 – it's valid for 24 hours so you can make the most of it.

Thursdays to Saturdays, the queen of London's scene nights, with big-name DJs and PAs. Popcorn Monday brings the weekday pop fun till 5.30am, while Thursday is amateur strip night Porn Idol.

THE CITY

WayOut Club Check online for location ☎ 07778 157 290, ⓦ thewayoutclub.com. Long-established Saturday night for the transgendered crowd and friends, offering a warm welcome, changing rooms, video screen and cabaret until 4am.

SHOREDITCH AND THE EAST END

East Bloc 217 City Road, EC1 ☎ 020 7253 0367, ⓦ eastbloc.co.uk; ⊖ Old Street; map pp.192–193. Retaining its cool as most of Shoreditch goes mainstream, *East Bloc* brings electro beats to its cute basement site. Look out for Thursdays men-only cruise night Butch.

Sink the Pink Bethnal Green Working Men's Club (see p.403), 42–46 Pollard Row, E2 ⓦ sinkthepinklondon .com; ⊖ Bethnal Green. Silly, young and stupidly fun, attracting a handsome, mixed and inclusive crowd on the first Saturdays of the month. The guys run extra nights around town too.

Unskinny Bop Bethnal Green Working Men's Club (see p.403), 42–46 Pollard Row, E2 ⓦ unskinnybop.co.uk; ⊖ Bethnal Green. Monthly alternative night that strays out of standard indie to bring the best of everything from pop to hip-hop. Born out of female festival Ladyfest, it's particularly welcoming for girls. The team also DJ all over town.

NORTH LONDON

Bionic Changes venues ⊕ bionicclubinfo@gmail .com. Relative newcomer bringing house beats from excellent DJs to a cool Dalston crowd. Check the gay press for details.

Club Kali The Dome, 178 Junction Park, N19 ⓦ clubkali .com; ⊖ Tufnell Park. Held on the third Friday of every month, Kali is the world's biggest Asian music LGBT night, offering bhangra, Bollywood, Arabic, r'n'b and dance flavours for an attitude-free crowd.

★ **Vogue Fabrics** 66 Stoke Newington Rd N16, ⓦ voguefabricsdalston.com; map p.291. When they say they're Dalston's favourite disco basement, they're not kidding. Incredible array of nights attracting an artsy/fashion crowd. Highlights including the does-what-it-says-on-the-tin Naked Boys Reading and gay hip-hop party Gully.

SOUTH LONDON

Bootylicious Club Colosseum, 1 Nine Elms Lane, SW8 ⓦ bootylicious-club.co.uk; ⊖ Vauxhall. Despite London's large black community, this is the capital's only dedicated gay and lesbian urban music/BME night, held every third Saturday of the month and featuring r'n'b, hip-hop, dancehall, house and classic vibes.

★ **Duckie** Royal Vauxhall Tavern (see p.408), 372 Kennington Lane, SE11 ☎ 020 7737 4043, ⓦ duckie .co.uk; ⊖ Vauxhall. Duckie's mix of regular live art performances and theme nights, as well as cult DJs The Readers Wifes playing everything from Kim Wilde to the Velvet Underground, has kept the night going strong for fifteen years.

Exilio Latino Guy's Bar, St Thomas St, SE1 ☎07956 983230, ⓦexilio.co.uk; ⊖ London Bridge. Every other Sat night, *Exilio* erupts in a lesbian and gay Latin frenzy.

LESBIAN CLUBS
THE CITY

Rumours 64–73 Minories, EC3 ☎07949 477 804, ⓦgirl-rumours.co.uk; ⊖ Tower Hill or Aldgate. There's room for five hundred grrrls at this monthly, women-only Saturday-nighter. The popular and cheap club night offers two bars, quiet lounges and a dancefloor until 3am.

NORTH LONDON

Blue Monday Boogaloo, 312 Archway Rd, N6, ⓦgroups.to/bluemonday; ⊖ Highgate. Live indie music night for lesbians and bisexuals on the second Mon of every month. Events are streamed live on the internet.

Saturday Night Fish Fry Birthdays, 33–35 Stoke Newington Rd, N16, ⓦfacebook.com/satnightfishfry; ⊖ Dalston Kingsland. While *Dalston Superstore* does the heavy lifting for east London lesbian nights, this newcomer provides a sharply dressed alternative. Bring your cool and dance the night away.

Waltzing with Hilda Jacksons Lane Arts Centre, 269a Archway Rd, N6 ☎07939 072958, ⓦhildas.org.uk; ⊖ Highgate. Women-only Latin and ballroom dancing club with classes for beginners and the more experienced. Held on the second Sat of every month (7.30–11.30pm) but closed in Aug.

GAY MEN'S CLUBS
SOHO

Room Service At Miabella, 12–13 Greek St, W1; ⊖ Tottenham Court Road. Created by legendary party maker Jodie Harsh in late 2010, this weekly Thursday night event is the latest attempt to re-create 1970s New York in old London town. Probably only worth it if you're feeling confident in your abs...and you can get on the guest list.

Manbar 79 Charing Cross Rd, WC2 ☎020 7434 2567, ⓦmanbarsoho.com; ⊖ Leicester Square; map p.100. Big, busy, cruisey older men den on two floors, with a late licence and a no-messing atmosphere. Rejuvenated since replacing the grubbier 79CXR.

Shadow Lounge 5–7 Brewer St, W1 ☎020 7317 9270, ⓦtheshadowlounge.co.uk; ⊖ Piccadilly Circus; map p.100. Classier than the general Soho vibe, expect bubbles with your boys. Look out for porno disco beats with midweek night Gigolo.

SOUTH LONDON

Area 67–68 Albert Embankment, SE1 ☎020 3242 0040, ⓦarealondon.net; ⊖ Vauxhall; map pp.310–311. With two dancefloors, chic decor and impressive laser and light displays, it offers a London venue for big-name international DJs, as well as hosting the after-hours club *Beyond* on Sunday mornings.

★ **The Eagle** 349 Kennington Lane, SE11 ☎020 7793 0903, ⓦeaglelondon.com; ⊖ Vauxhall; map pp.310–311. Home to the excellent disco Sunday-nighter Horse Meat Disco, the vibe here is a loose, friendly re-creation of late 1970s New York, complete with facial hair, checked shirts and a pool table. Also check out beary night Tonker on Fridays.

★ **Fire** South Lambeth Rd, SW8 ☎020 73252 0040, ⓦfirelondon.net; ⊖ Vauxhall; map pp.310–311. *Fire* is London's superclub of choice for a mixed though mostly male crowd of disco bunnies and hardboyz. The party runs from Saturday night to Sunday morning, then on Sunday afternoon, and from Sunday night to Monday morning.

The Hoist Railway Arches, 47b–47c South Lambeth Rd, SW8 ☎020 7735 9972, ⓦthehoist.co.uk; ⊖ Vauxhall; map pp.310–311. London's biggest and best-known leather/dress code bar for men with few inhibitions. *The Hoist* also hosts regular nights for rubber and other fetishes, as well as NBN and SBN: Nearly/Stark Bollock Naked.

Union 66 Albert Embankment, SE1 ☎07970 193236, ⓦfacebook.com/unionvauxhall; ⊖ Vauxhall; map pp.310–311. With semi-clothed, arousing nights, this venue appeals to the unabashedly cruisey. Also offers after-hours Wrong! on Sunday mornings, and Suzie Krueger's celebrated raunchy fetish/dance club night Hard-On, which has a very strict dress code.

XXL The Arches, 51/53 Southwark St, SE1, ⓦxxl-london.com; ⊖ London Bridge. Massively popular Saturday dance club for big, burly men and their fans, attracting a diverse crowd with its two dancefloors, two bars and a chillout area.

KING'S CROSS AND AROUND

Underground Club 37 Wharfdale Rd, N1 ☎020 7278 3294, ⓦtheundergroundclub.net; ⊖ King's Cross. Situated underneath *Central Station* (see p.408), you can expect a much darker vibe at this fetish bar: check the site to find nights for feet, adult babies and more.

The Vault 139–143 Whitfield St, W1 ☎020 7388 5500, ⓦvault-london.com; ⊖ Warren Street; map p.97. The cruisiest club around, with about half its schedule handed over to fully stripped nights.

27

ENGLISH NATIONAL BALLET'S SWAN LAKE AT THE COLISEUM

Classical music, opera and dance

With established venues like the Southbank Centre, the Barbican and Wigmore Hall offering year-round appearances by first-rate musicians, and numerous smaller venues providing a stage for less-established or more specialized performers, the capital should satisfy most devotees of classical music. What's more, in the annual Proms (see opposite), London has one of the world's greatest, most democratic music festivals. Opera has an enthusiastic following, too, with live screenings and an excellent pub theatre venue making it increasingly accessible to those who can't afford full-price tickets at the grand opera houses. You'll also find a broad spectrum of ambitious dance performances in a range of excellent venues to suit all pockets.

London is spoilt for choice when it comes to **orchestras**. On most days you should be able to catch a concert by one of the many superb major orchestras, or more specialized ensembles, based here, and prices aren't too high. While the **Royal Opera House** (ROH) can attract top international stars, the downside is the prohibitive price (and availability) of most of the tickets. The nearby **English National Opera** (ENO) tends to be better value, and can be more adventurous in its repertoire and productions. Staged in an Islington pub, small-scale and intimate **OperaUpClose** productions have brought opera to the masses, while many of the off-West End theatres (see p.419) extend the boundaries of contemporary classical music and physical theatre in lively ways. As for dance, your first stop should be **Sadler's Wells**, where some of the world's outstanding companies regularly appear. Fans of classicism can revel in the **Royal Ballet**, a company with some of the most accomplished dancers in Europe.

CLASSICAL MUSIC

Unless a glamorous guest conductor is wielding the baton, or one of the world's high-profile orchestras is giving a performance, you should be able to attend a **classical concert** for around £15 (the usual range is about £12–50), and a good few concerts are **free**; check ⍵ cityevents.co.uk for a guide to free concerts in the City's many churches. In addition to the venues listed below, check schedules at the Victorian Wilton's music hall (see p.420), which occasionally stages classical concerts with an avant-garde edge.

CONCERT VENUES

Barbican Centre Silk St, EC2 ☎ 020 7638 8891, ⍵ barbican.org.uk; ⊖ Barbican or Moorgate. With the outstanding resident London Symphony Orchestra (⍵ lso .co.uk), the BBC Symphony Orchestra (⍵ bbc.co.uk/orchestras)

as associate orchestra, and top foreign orchestras, ensembles and big-name soloists in regular attendance, the Barbican is an outstanding arena for classical music.
Cadogan Hall Sloane Terrace, SW1 ☎ 020 7730 4500, ⍵ cadoganhall.com; ⊖ Sloane Square. This handsome

28

THE PROMS AND OTHER CLASSICAL MUSIC FESTIVALS

THE PROMS

The **BBC Henry Wood Promenade Concerts** (Royal Albert Hall ☎ 0845 401 5040, ⍵ bbc .co.uk/proms; ⊖ South Kensington), or the Proms, tend to be associated with the raucous "Last Night", when the flag-waving audience sings its patriotic heart out to *Land of Hope and Glory*. In fact, this jingoistic knees-up is untypical of the season (mid-July to mid-Sept), which features around seventy concerts with an exhilarating mix of favourites and new or recondite works. The unique aspect of the Proms is that seats in the stalls, and the upper gallery, are removed to create up to 1400 **standing places** – these cost £5, even on the last night, and must be bought on the door, on the day. Seated **tickets** cost £7.50–95; those for the last night are allocated by ballot, and start at £57. Weekly passes range from £32.50–42.50. The acoustics aren't the world's best – OK for orchestral blockbusters, less so for small-scale works – but the performers are usually outstanding, the atmosphere is great and the hall is so vast that the likelihood of being turned away if you turn up on the night is slim. A handful of chamber music concerts are also held in Cadogan Hall, usually at lunchtime, just off Sloane Square.

OTHER FESTIVALS

London has several more classical music festivals that provide a feast of music throughout the year in some of the city's most appealing venues. The most prestigious is probably the **City of London Festival** (⍵ colf.org), which takes place in the City's churches, music venues and livery halls for a month from late June. St Leonard's Church, Spitalfields, is at the centre of several music events. The largest of them, **Spitalfields' summer festival** in June (⍵ spitalfieldsfestival.org.uk), stages music in a variety of intriguing venues in east London; the same organizers also put on a shorter music festival in December. Other annual musicfests to look out for include the **Festival of Baroque Music** (tickets from £10; ⍵ lufthansafestival.org .uk), held in May, and with some concerts in Westminster Abbey, and the **Early Music Festival and Exhibition** (⍵ earlymusicfestival.com), held in November in Greenwich's beautiful Old Royal Naval College.

neo-Byzantine building, built in 1901 as a Christian Science church, now serves as a nine hundred-seat concert hall with outstanding acoustics. The Royal Philharmonic (Ⓦrpo .co.uk) is its resident orchestra and it hosts Proms chamber concerts (see p.413).

Kings Place 90 York Way, N1 ☎020 7520 1490, Ⓦkingsplace.co.uk; ⊖ King's Cross. Headquarters of the London Sinfonietta (Ⓦlondonsinfonietta.org.uk), one of the world's finest contemporary classical music groups, the innovative Aurora Orchestra (Ⓦauroraorchestra.com) and the Orchestra of the Age of Enlightenment (Ⓦoae.co.uk), who play on period instruments, this modern, purpose-built venue, by the canal behind King's Cross, has two performance spaces. The London Chamber Music Society (Ⓦlondonchambermusic.org.uk) holds excellent Sunday evening concerts.

LSO St Luke's 161 Old St, EC1 ☎020 7638 8891, Ⓦlso .co.uk/lsostlukes; ⊖ Old Street. This Hawksmoor church has been beautifully converted into a 450-seat performance/rehearsal space for the London Symphony Orchestra and its splendid young associate Aurora Orchestra (Ⓦauroraorchestra.com). It's also used for a wide variety of concerts from world music to experimental jazz. Thursday lunchtimes see popular chamber recitals (£10), recorded for BBC Radio 3, and there's a summer series of free lunchtime concerts in the garden.

St John's Smith Square, SW1 ☎020 7222 1061, Ⓦsjss .org.uk; ⊖ Westminster. Built in 1728 and firebombed in 1941, this striking Baroque church is home to an exceptional concert hall, with fine acoustics and a great organ. Its varied musical season includes orchestral and choral concerts, chamber music and solo recitals, mostly in the evenings but also on some Thursday lunchtimes (£10). There's a good restaurant in the crypt.

Southbank Centre Belvedere Rd, South Bank, SE1 ☎08448750073, Ⓦsouthbankcentre.co.uk; ⊖ Waterloo or Embankment. The South Bank has three concert venues, none of which is exclusively used for classical music. The 2500-seat Royal Festival Hall (RFH) is tailor-made for large-scale choral and orchestral works, and home to the Philharmonia (Ⓦphilharmonia.co.uk) and the London Philharmonic (Ⓦlpo.co.uk). The Queen Elizabeth Hall (QEH) is the prime location for chamber concerts, solo recitals, opera and choirs; while the intimate Purcell Room, in the QEH building, sees excellent chamber music and recitals by up-and-coming instrumentalists and singers. Other resident orchestras at the Southbank include the experimental Orchestra of the Age of Enlightenment (Ⓦoae.co.uk) and the superb London Sinfonietta (Ⓦlondonsinfonietta.org.uk).

Wigmore Hall 36 Wigmore St, W1 ☎020 7935 2141, Ⓦwigmore-hall.org.uk; ⊖ Bond Street or Oxford Circus. With its near-perfect acoustics, the intimate Wigmore Hall – built in 1901 as a hall for the adjacent Bechstein piano

showroom – is a favourite with artists and audiences alike, so book well in advance. It's brilliant for piano recitals and chamber music, but best known for its song recitals by some of the world's greatest singers. Some Monday lunchtime and mid-morning Sunday performances.

CHURCHES AND FREE CONCERTS

BBC SO Studio Concerts Delaware Rd, W9 Ⓦbbc .co.uk/orchestras; ⊖ Warwick Avenue or Maida Vale. The BBC Symphony Orchestra and Singers stage a number of free concerts, performed by various BBC ensembles and artists.

Royal Academy of Music Marylebone Rd, NW1 ☎020 7873 7326, Ⓦram.ac.uk; ⊖ Baker Street. The academy's excellent "Free on Fridays" lunchtime concerts, featuring a variety of performers and music styles, are a firm fixture on its concert schedule (book in advance), along with free chamber concerts on Tuesday (no booking required).

Royal College of Music ☎020 7591 4300, Ⓦrcm .ac.uk. The RCM hosts regular concerts of an amazingly high standard, many of them free, in a variety of venues around the capital from concert halls to churches and parks.

St Anne's Lutheran Church Gresham St, EC2 ☎020 7606 4986, Ⓦstanneslutheranchurch.org.uk; ⊖ St Paul's. As well as free lunchtime recitals (Mon & Fri), this Wren-designed church has guest musicians for various services, and an annual Bach festival.

St Giles-in-the-Fields 60 St Giles High St, WC2 ☎020 7240 2532, Ⓦstgilesonline.org; ⊖ Tottenham Court Road. Free lunchtime organ recitals or chamber music (Fri) in the spring and autumn, plus evening concerts, some of which are also free.

St James Piccadilly 197 Piccadilly, W1 ☎020 7734 4511, Ⓦsjp.org; ⊖ Piccadilly Circus. Wren church with superb free lunchtime piano and chamber recitals (Mon, Wed & Fri), plus fee-paying evening concerts.

St Lawrence Jewry Guildhall Yard, EC2 ☎020 7600 9478, Ⓦstlawrencejewry.org.uk; ⊖ Bank or St Paul's. A full schedule of free concerts in this Wren church includes piano concerts (Mon), organ recitals (Tues) and a special summer season.

St Martin-in-the-Fields Trafalgar Square, WC2 ☎020 7839 8362, Ⓦstmartin-in-the-fields.org; ⊖ Charing Cross or Leicester Square. St Martin's has a fine musical pedigree (guest musicians have included Handel and Mozart). Free lunchtime recitals (Mon, Tues & Fri) are superb, while fee-charging evening concerts feature acclaimed musicians, including the top-notch orchestra or chamber ensemble of the Academy of St Martin-in-the-Fields (Ⓦasmf.org).

St Olave 8 Hart St, EC3 ☎020 7488 4318, Ⓦsanctuaryinthecity.net; ⊖ Tower Hill. St Olave's is an atmospheric medieval setting – Samuel Pepys is buried here, too – for chamber pieces or solo recitals (Wed & Thurs lunchtimes).

28

St Sepulchre-without-Newgate Holborn Viaduct, EC1 ☎020 7236 1145, ⓦst-sepulchre.org.uk; ⊖ St Paul's. The "National Musicians' Church" holds free piano recitals, chamber and organ concerts (Wed lunchtimes) and fee-paying evening performances.

St Stephen Walbrook 39 Walbrook, EC4 ☎020 7626 9000, ⓦststephenwalbrook.net; ⊖ Bank. Free lunchtime concerts (recitals Tues; sung Eucharist from the professional choir Thurs; organ concerts Fri) in one of the finest of all Wren's churches.

OPERA

Of the two main companies, the **Royal Opera House** is the place to go to see the top international stars, while **English National Opera** continues to show what can be achieved with largely home-grown talent and lively, radical productions. Other, smaller venues provide more intimate and less expensive alternatives. In addition to the listings below it's worth checking listings at the Battersea Arts Centre (see p.419), which occasionally stages experimental opera shows.

OPERA COMPANIES AND VENUES

Barbican Centre Silk St, EC2 ☎020 7638 8891, ⓦbarbican.org.uk; ⊖ Barbican or Moorgate. The Barbican's regular operatic events include superb baroque operas from the Academy of Ancient Music and innovative works from the ENO.

English National Opera London Coliseum, St Martin's Lane, WC2 ☎0207 845 9300, ⓦeno.org; ⊖ Leicester Square or Charing Cross. The ENO is committed to keeping opera accessible, with operas sung in English, an adventurous repertoire, dazzling modern productions and non-prohibitive pricing (£20–99). Standbys for students, senior citizens, under-16s and the unemployed (£15–35) go on sale 3hr before the performance; under-30s can also join, for free, the "Access all Arias" scheme, which gives excellent discounts.

King's Head Theatre 115 Upper St, N1 ☎020 7478 0160, ⓦkingsheadtheatre.com; ⊖ Angel or Highbury and Islington. The acclaimed *King's Head* pub theatre, home to resident company OperaUpClose, hosts an exciting rep programme of new opera, experimental pieces and old favourites re-imagined, all accompanied by piano, along with classical music concerts with a twist. The intimate space – just one hundred bench seats – means the performers are within touching distance. Tickets around £20.

Opera Holland Park Holland Park, Kensington High St, W8 ☎0300 999 1000, ⓦrbkc.gov.uk; ⊖ High Street Kensington or Holland Park. Opera takes to the great outdoors (albeit covered by a canopy) in leafy Holland Park (June–Aug). Standard repertoire is the order of the day, and productions range unpredictably from the inspired to the workaday. Tickets £12–67.50.

Royal Opera House Bow St, WC2 ☎020 7304 4000, ⓦroh.org.uk; ⊖ Covent Garden. The ROH, one of the world's leading opera houses, puts on wonderfully lavish operas, with slightly more experimental productions staged in the Linbury Studio Theatre. All are performed in the original language with surtitles. Most tickets are expensive (reaching as high as £900), though there is some restricted-view seating (or standing room), which aren't at all bad, from around £15, and various special offers. Just 67 day seats (at various prices) go on sale from 10am on the day of a performance (not from visiting companies); these are restricted to one per person, and you need to get there before 9am for popular shows. Student standby tickets (subject to availability) can be bought for £10 online.

28

DANCE

The current craze for **street dance** and sexed-up ballroom dancing has seen high-energy, populist dance shows take to the stage at a number of **West End theatres** (see p.418). For classical ballet, the esteemed **Royal Ballet**, with a number of outstanding ballet soloists, is based at the Royal Opera House, while the **English National Ballet** (ⓦeno.org) regularly performs at the Coliseum (see above). The intimate **The Place** and **Laban** and the larger **Sadler's Wells** stage the best contemporary work. The biggest of London's annual dance festivals, **Dance Umbrella** (ⓦdanceumbrella.co.uk), stages a season (Oct/Nov) of fresh new work at various venues around town. For an excellent **round-up** of the city's dance events, check ⓦlondondance.com.

COMING SOON TO A SCREEN NEAR YOU...

If you are hungry for high culture, have very low funds, and don't mind being one step removed from the live experience, simply head to the pictures. Many **cinemas** in the capital screen live performances of the finest ballets, operas and theatrical performances – beamed from gilded London venues including the Royal Opera House, or from esteemed stages around the world – for little more than the price of a movie ticket. It's an odd feeling, giving a rousing round of applause to performers who can't see or hear you, but the acoustics and HD visuals tend to be superb, and the cost can't be argued with.

VENUES

Barbican Centre Silk St, EC2 ☎020 7638 8891, ⓦbarbican.org.uk; ⊖ Barbican or Moorgate. As part of its mixed programming the Barbican regularly stages contemporary dance by top international companies.

Laban Creekside, SE8 ☎020 8305 9300, ⓦlaban.org; Cutty Sark DLR or Deptford or Greenwich train stations. This funky Herzog & de Meuron building in deepest Deptford includes a three hundred-seat theatre. The venue showcases many leading names in contemporary dance as well as staging work by students at the Trinity Laban Conservatoire of Music and Dance.

The Place 17 Duke's Rd, WC1 ☎020 7121 1100, ⓦtheplace.org.uk; ⊖ Euston. The Place has a small theatre that presents the work of contemporary choreographers and student performers.

Rich Mix 35–47 Bethnal Green Rd, E1 ☎020 7613 7498, ⓦrichmix.org.uk; Shoreditch High Street Overground. Excellent physical theatre and dance, with an emphasis on black companies and choreographers, from this cutting-edge cultural centre in the East End.

Royal Opera House Bow St, WC2 ☎020 7304 4000, ⓦroh.org.uk; ⊖ Covent Garden. Based at the Opera House, the Royal Ballet is a world-renowned classical company. Tickets for the main house may be cheaper than for opera (£3–100); more experimental work can be seen in the smaller Linbury Studio Theatre. It's best to book early.

Sadler's Wells Theatre Rosebery Ave, EC1 ☎0844 412 4300, ⓦsadlerswells.com; ⊖ Angel. With a number of resident contemporary dance companies, Sadler's Wells also hosts many of the finest international companies and celebrates everything from street dance to flamenco. The Lillian Baylis Theatre, tucked around the back, stages smaller productions, while the Peacock Theatre near Covent Garden adds some populist shows to the mix.

Southbank Centre Belvedere Rd, South Bank, SE1 ☎0844 875 0073, ⓦsouthbankcentre.co.uk; ⊖ Waterloo or Embankment. The Southbank Centre's three venues (see p.215) see an impressive roster of dance performances, from Bollywood to the Ballet Rambert.

28

OPEN-AIR THEATRE, REGENT'S PARK

Theatre, comedy and cinema

London has enjoyed a reputation for quality theatre since the time of Shakespeare and still provides platforms for innovation and new writing. The West End is the heart of London's "Theatreland", with Shaftesbury Avenue its main drag; the less mainstream, "off-West End" theatres, and the smaller, edgier places on the fringe are often more interesting. The capital's comedy scene remains lively, too, whether you want to keep things low-key in an intimate neighbourhood pub or pay top dollar for high-profile shows with huge audiences. As for film, the city abounds in offbeat little clubs screening obscure, classic and cult movies, along of course, with scores of multiplexes and trendy chains where you can sip wine and snuggle up on velvet sofas in front of the silver screen.

29

THEATRE

London's love affair with musical theatre shows no sign of abating, despite the fact that only half the shows actually make money. *Les Misérables* is the longest-running musical, on the go since 1985, closely followed by *The Phantom of the Opera*, which opened in 1986; both are mere babies, though, compared with *The Mousetrap* by Agatha Christie, which began its West End run in 1952, and is the longest-running play in the world. The **Royal Shakespeare Company** (ⓦ rsc.org.uk), who tour in London each year, and the **National Theatre** (ⓦ nationaltheatre.org.uk) stage challenging performances of mainstream masterpieces, and there is original, exciting work found in what have become known as the **Off-West End** theatres. At the **fringe** theatres, more often than not pub venues, quality is more variable (and ticket prices are lower). The listings below by no means represent the full tally of London's stages – there are plenty more West End theatres showing long-running musicals and family-friendly mainstream entertainment, plus scores of fringe places that present work intermittently.

Information For details and news about the West End shows, along with tickets and promotions, see ⓦ officiallondontheatre.co.uk. Also check *Time Out* (ⓦ timeout.com/london/theatre) for listings.

Prices Full-price tickets for £15 are restricted to the fringe; the box-office average is around £35–40, with £50–110 the usual top price. If you want to buy from the theatre direct it's best to go to the box office in person; booking over the phone or online, you'll probably be charged a booking fee. Cheap Monday tickets or standbys are often very good value, and some major theatres do keep some to sell on the door on the day; check the website of the venue, and be prepared to put up with a restricted view. Students, senior citizens and the unemployed can get concessionary rates on tickets, including standbys, for most shows. Ticket agencies such as Ticketmaster (ⓦ ticketmaster.co.uk) can get seats for West End shows well in advance, but can add hefty booking fees.

Discount tickets Whatever you do, avoid the touts and the ticket agencies that abound in the West End – there's no guarantee that they are genuine. The Society of London Theatre (ⓦ officiallondontheatre.co.uk) offers online discounts and special offers on West End shows and run a very useful booth in Leicester Square called "tkts" (Mon–Sat 9am–7pm, Sun 10.30am–4.30pm; ⓦ tkts.co.uk), which sells on-the-day tickets for the West End shows at discounts of up to fifty percent. These tend to be in the top end of the price range and are limited to four per person, and prices include a service charge of £3 per ticket. Tkts also sells some tickets up to a week in advance, some of them discounted. Another option is the Encore London theatre passport, which costs £21.90 and can be redeemed for the best available seat at a weekday or matinee performance at some of the West End's most popular shows. Buy the pass from the Visit Britain website (ⓦ visitbritain.com), and redeem it on the day of the show you want to see at the Encore booth opposite the Garrick Theatre on Charing Cross Rd (Mon–Sat 9.30am–6pm, Sun 10am–2.30pm; avoid school holidays and busy periods).

Live screenings Check out the capital's cinema screenings (see p.415), when you can watch performances from the NT (ⓦ ntlive.nationaltheatre.org.uk) and other prestigious companies as they happen, or see recorded past productions from the likes of Shakespeare's Globe (ⓦ onscreen.shakespearesglobe.com), for a fraction of the cost of the real thing.

Festivals London's two main theatre festivals are Mimefest (ⓦ mimefest.co.uk), a feast of puppetry, mime and physical theatre which takes place over a fortnight in January, and LIFT (ⓦ liftfestival.com), a summer jamboree of innovative international productions.

WEST END THEATRES

Barbican Silk St, EC2 ☎ 020 7638 8891, ⓦ barbican .org.uk; ⊖ Barbican or Moorgate. The Barbican's two venues – the excellently designed Barbican Theatre and the much smaller Pit – put on a wide variety of shows from puppetry and musicals to new drama and twists on old classics. Box office Mon–Sat 10am–9pm, Sun noon–9pm; phone bookings Mon–Sat 10am–8pm, Sun 11am–8pm.

★ **National Theatre** Southbank Centre, South Bank, SE1 ☎ 020 7452 3000, ⓦ nationaltheatre.org.uk; ⊖ Waterloo. The NT consists of three separate theatres: the raked, 1150-seat Olivier, the proscenium Lyttelton and the experimental Cottesloe, to be re-opened as the expanded Dorfman Theatre in 2014. Standards set by the late Laurence Olivier, founding artistic director, are maintained by the country's top actors and directors in a programme ranging from Greek tragedies to Broadway musicals. Tickets needn't break the bank – and on special "Travelex" performances, half the seats go for £12. Some productions sell out months in advance, but £12 day tickets, available for the lowest-priced seats available, go on sale on the morning of each performance – get to the box office at least an hour in advance for the popular shows (two tickets per person only). In addition, standbys, available 90min before the performance, can lop £15 off the top prices. Box office Mon–Sat 9.30am–8pm, Sun noon–6pm.

Old Vic The Cut, SE1 ☎ 0844 871 7628, ⓦ oldvictheatre .com; ⊖ Waterloo. The venerable Old Vic, established in 1818, is a producing house under the stewardship of Oscar-winning American actor Kevin Spacey, who occasionally treads the boards himself. Shows include classics and new works, usually with big-name stars. Box office Mon–Sat 10am–7pm (6pm when there are no performances); phone bookings Mon–Fri 9am–7.30pm, Sat 9am–4pm, Sun 9.30am–4pm.

29

Royal Court Sloane Square, SW1 ☎020 7565 5000, ⓦroyalcourttheatre.com; ⊖ Sloane Square. The Royal Court is one of the best places in London to catch radical new writing, either in the proscenium arch Jerwood Theatre Downstairs, or the smaller studio space Jerwood Theatre Upstairs (unreserved seating). No standbys; returns re-sold 1hr before performance. All tickets £10 on Monday. Box office and phone bookings Mon–Sat 10am–6pm.

★ **Shakespeare's Globe** 21 New Globe Walk, SE1 ☎020 7401 9919, ⓦshakespearesglobe.com; ⊖ London Bridge, Blackfriars or Southwark. This open-roofed replica Elizabethan theatre uses only natural light and the minimum of scenery, and puts on superb Shakespearean shows – some from exciting international companies, and including midsummer midnight matinees – along with works from the Bard's contemporaries and occasional new works on Tudor or otherwise historical themes. Seats aound £15–40, with "Yard" tickets (standing-room only, at the front) for around a fiver. The season runs from spring to autumn, but a new, indoor Jacobean-style theatre, due to open in 2014 – its performances to be lit by candles – will stage performances year-round.

OFF-WEST END

★ **Almeida** Almeida St, N1 ☎020 7359 4404, ⓦalmeida.co.uk; ⊖ Angel or Highbury & Islington. Popular little Islington venue that premieres excellent new plays and excitingly reworked classics from around the world, and has attracted some big Hollywood names.

Battersea Arts Centre 176 Lavender Hill, SW11 ☎020 7223 2223, ⓦbac.org.uk; Clapham Junction train station from Victoria or Waterloo. The BAC is a multistage building, housed in an old Victorian town hall in south London, and is known for excellent cutting-edge contemporary productions, from radical drama and physical theatre to comedy and cabaret.

Bush 7 Uxbridge Rd, W12 ☎020 8743 5050, ⓦbushtheatre.co.uk; ⊖ Shepherd's Bush Market. This lively local theatre, housed in an old library, is London's most reliable venue for new writing after the Royal Court.

Donmar Warehouse 41 Earlham St, WC2 ☎0844 871 7624, ⓦdonmarwarehouse.com; ⊖ Covent Garden. A small, non-profit space in the heart of Covent Garden, noted for new writing, top-quality reappraisals of the classics and big-name performers.

The Gate The Prince Albert, 11 Pembridge Rd, W11 ☎020 7229 0706, ⓦgatetheatre.co.uk; ⊖ Notting Hill Gate. Seating around seventy, this small producing pub-theatre has a huge reputation for its excellent new writing and innovative revivals of neglected international classics.

Hampstead Theatre Eton Ave, NW3 ☎020 7722 9301, ⓦhampsteadtheatre.com; ⊖ Swiss Cottage. A prestigious, modern theatre with two stages in Swiss Cottage (not Hampstead proper) whose productions often

move on to the West End. Their Shakespearean productions are always worth a look.

Menier Chocolate Factory 53 Southwark St, SE1 ☎020 7378 1713, ⓦmenierchocolatefactory.com; ⊖ London Bridge. Great name, great venue in a former Victorian factory, with a decent bar and restaurant attached. It's a producing house and the shows – musical revivals, old classics, new writing – are consistently good.

Open Air Theatre Regent's Park, Inner Circle, NW1 ☎0844 826 4242, ⓦopenairtheatre.org; ⊖ Baker Street. If the weather's good, there's nothing like a dose of alfresco theatre at this beautiful space in Regent's Park. The tourist- and family-friendly summer programme features Shakespeare, musicals, some film screenings and concerts.

Riverside Studios 1 Crisp Rd, W6 ☎020 8237 1111, ⓦriversidestudios.co.uk; ⊖ Hammersmith. Edgy performance and physical theatre in a converted film studio in West London.

Soho Theatre 21 Dean St, W1 ☎020 7478 0100, ⓦsohotheatre.com; ⊖ Tottenham Court Road. Great, very central theatre with three spaces featuring new writing from around the globe, as well as alternative comedy and cabaret, at affordable prices.

Theatre Royal Stratford East Gerry Raffles Square, E15 ☎020 8534 0310, ⓦstratfordeast.com; ⊖ Stratford. Beautiful Victorian theatre in the East End, where the community-pleasing shows include excellent Christmas panto, comedy and new writing.

Tricycle Theatre 269 Kilburn High Rd, NW6 ☎020 7328 1000, ⓦtricycle.co.uk; ⊖ Kilburn. One of London's most dynamic venues, showcasing a mixed bag of new plays, often aimed at the theatre's multicultural neighbourhood, and often with a sharp political focus.

Young Vic 66 The Cut, SE1 ☎020 7922 2922, ⓦyoungvic.org; ⊖ Waterloo. The Young Vic opened in 1970 as a temporary structure with a five-year lifespan – more than forty years later, it has been rebuilt from scratch and has a vibrant contemporary programme, concentrating on the work of young directors.

FRINGE AND OCCASIONAL VENUES

★ **Arcola Theatre** 24 Ashwin St, E8 ☎020 7503 1646, ⓦarcolatheatre.com; Dalston Kingsland or Dalston Junction Overground. Exciting fringe theatre housed in an old Dalston factory and a pop-up tent space. They have a strong reputation for their challenging plays – classics and modern works – with shows from young, international companies, and cabaret, burlesque and music in the tent. Some "pay what you can" tickets on Tuesday nights.

King's Head Theatre 115 Upper St, N1 ☎020 7478 0160, ⓦkingsheadtheatre.com; ⊖ Angel or Highbury & Islington. Fabulous, intimate pub theatre staging exciting contemporary productions and brand new works from emerging writers.

29

Rich Mix 35–47 Bethnal Green Rd, E1 ☎020 7613 7498, ⓦrichmix.org.uk; Shoreditch High Street Overground. This charity-funded arts center offers a stimulating mix of new theatre, spoken word, comedy and dance, with a strong emphasis on black and minority works from the local area and around the world.

Roundhouse Chalk Farm Rd, NW1 ☎0844 482 8008, ⓦroundhouse.org.uk; ⊖ Chalk Farm. Camden's exciting cultural venue in an old – round – engine repairs shed, puts on cutting-edge theatre, performance art, contemporary circus and spoken word performances.

Southwark Playhouse 77–85 Newington Causeway, SE1 ☎020 7407 0234, ⓦsouthwarkplayhouse.co.uk;

⊖ Elephant and Castle. With two theatre spaces, this energetic theatre concentrates on new and young writers, reinterpreting old classics and contemporary plays.

★ **Wilton's Music Hall** Grace's Alley, off Cable St, E1 ☎020 7702 2789, ⓦwiltons.org.uk; ⊖ Aldgate East or Tower Gateway DLR. The world's oldest surviving music hall, built in 1858, is a crumbling, hugely atmospheric space, with barley-sugar wrought-iron columns holding up the gallery, peeling walls and a stunning, decaying old bar. It's a wonderful venue for innovative theatre, comedy, poetry and variety as well as magic shows, cinema and a variety of hipster events. Unmissable.

COMEDY

From the big-name, big-theatre, big-ticket shows, to old favourites like the Comedy Store – at the heart of the alternative comedy movement of the 1980s – or even shabby neighbourhood pubs hosting shambolic open-mic nights, you're never too far away from a chuckle in London. Note that many venues only have gigs on Friday and Saturday nights, and that August can be a lean month, as much of London's talent heads north for Edinburgh. See also Rich Mix (see above), the Soho Theatre (see p.419), Union Chapel (see p.289) and Wilton's Music Hall (see above), all of which host excellent comedy nights. Full listings appear in *Time Out*.

Amused Moose Soho 17 Greek St, W1 ☎020 7287 3727, ⓦamusedmoose.com; ⊖ Tottenham Court Road. Top-notch stand-up in Soho, and comedy courses too. Every Saturday, plus other occasional nights, and Edinburgh previews in July. Branches in Marylebone, Camden, Islington and off Shaftesbury.

Boat Show Comedy Club Tattershall Castle, Victoria Embankment, SW1 ☎07932 658895, ⓦboatshow comedy.co.uk; ⊖ Embankment. It's certainly a novel venue – on a paddlesteamer, bobbing on the Thames opposite the London Eye – and the comedy nights (Fri & Sat, and 1st Mon of the month) frequently feature big names trying out their TV material.

Camden Head 100 Camden High St, NW1 ☎020 7485 4019, ⓦcamdenhead.com; ⊖ Camden Town. Consistently good, and very inexpensive open mic, sketches and stand-up, every weeknight, in this friendly Camden boozer.

Canal Café Theatre The Bridge House, Delamere Terrace, W2 ☎020 7289 6054, ⓦcanalcafetheatre .com; ⊖ Warwick Avenue. Set above a nice waterside pub in Little Venice, this venue is home to the fast-paced

NewsRevue team of topical gagsters (Thurs–Sun).

Comedy Store 1a Oxendon St, SW1 ☎0844 871 7699, ⓦthecomedystore.co.uk; ⊖ Piccadilly Circus. Widely regarded as the birthplace of alternative comedy, the Comedy Store has catapulted many a stand-up onto primetime TV. Improvisation by in-house comics and top-notch stand-up bills; Friday and Saturday are the busiest nights, with two shows, at 7.30pm and 11pm – book ahead.

★ **Downstairs at the King's Head** 2 Crouch End Hill, N8 ☎020 8340 1028, ⓦdownstairsathekingshead .com; bus #W7 from ⊖ Finsbury Park. Friendly, very long-running north London comedy night where stand-up, cabaret and new material from top comedians is played out in a cosy basement. Thurs, Sat & Sun, plus regular other nights.

Leicester Square Theatre 6 Leicester Place, WC2 ☎0844 873 3433, ⓦleicestersquaretheatre.com; ⊖ Leicester Square. A kind of off-West End comedy space that sees new performers, comedy theatre and some of the edgier big names in current comedy – Stewart Lee, Doug Stanhope, Bill Bailey and the like – performing new material and warm-up gigs.

CINEMA

There are an awful lot of cinemas in London, especially the **West End**. The biggest are on and around Leicester Square, including the **Empire Leicester Square** (ⓦempirecinemas.co.uk), a former Victorian variety theatre whose 1330-seat main auditorium has a state-of-the-art soundsystem, and the 1700-seat **Odeon Leicester Square** (ⓦodeon.co.uk), a favourite for celeb-packed premieres. These concentrate on Hollywood crowdpleasers and new releases, but there are a few classy chains that show more offbeat screenings – check out the **Picturehouse** (ⓦpicturehouses.co.uk), **Curzon** (ⓦcurzoncinemas.com) and **Everyman** (ⓦeverymancinema.com) websites for locations – and a number of one-off independent cinemas. You can also watch films in lush surroundings at the hip **boutique hotels** *Charlotte Street Hotel* (see p.356), and *Covent Garden Hotel* (see p.358), all of which offer packages linking classic movies in their bespoke

MOVIES ALFRESCO

A new wave of moviewatching has swept the capital in recent years, taking the cinema-going experience out of dark, popcorn-scattered screening rooms and into the fresh air. Whether it's at a hip Hoxton bar or a leafy royal park, if you're willing to brave the elements (and you can always take a blanket) there's nothing like watching a movie classic with hundreds of other wide-eyed fans beneath the stars. Each year sees different events and pop-up screenings – and summer is, naturally, the most popular time; the following is a list of the more established events.

Film4 Summer Screen Somerset House, Strand, WC2 ⓦsomersethouse.org.uk/film; ⊖ Covent Garden, Charing Cross or Holborn. This is the big one: for ten days or so in late July and early August, this magnificent setting (see p.139), home to the Courtauld gallery and an ice rink in winter, is a venue for classic, indie and new movies, with DJs and "behind the screen" talks and events; bring your own cushion. Tickets sell out fast.

More London Free Film Festival Near Tower Bridge, SE1 ⓦwww.morelondon.com; ⊖ London Bridge or Tower Hill. The location – a modern mixed-use development that includes City Hall – may sound unpromising, but More London's vibrant annual festival in mid-September screens free, family-friendly films – box-office hits, guilty pleasures and a few golden oldies – in the "Scoop", an eight hundred-seat, riverside amphitheatre.

Nomad Cinema ⓦwhereisthenomad.com. Showing classics, arthouse movies and fond old favourites, this peripatetic screen might turn up anywhere – a circus tent in Mile End, under the trees in a royal park, in the elevated surrounds of the Old Royal Naval College – always offering intriguing movie "happenings" and superb food and drink from London's best restaurateurs and street food sellers. Profits go to The Sustainability Institute, a sustainable living charity based in South Africa.

Rooftop Film Club Queen of Hoxton 1 Curtain Rd, EC2 ⓦrooftopfilmclub.com; ⊖ Liverpool Street or Old Street or Shoreditch High Street Overground. Settle down in a comfy seat, grab a cocktail and hook up to your own wireless headphones at these trendy summertime screenings – cultish blockbusters and kitsch 80s classics, mostly – in the rooftop garden of a hip bar/club/gallery. Around five nights a week May–Sept. Plus one-off screenings at Kensington Roof Gardens. Advance booking recommended.

---

screening rooms with afternoon tea, lunch or a fancy dinner (ⓦfirmdalehotels.com). Many of London's more cultish **arthouse** cinemas – showing obscure and B-movies to a keen crowd of cinephiles – may have gone, but the gap has been filled somewhat in recent years by a rash of **indie film clubs**, which colonize pub basements, back rooms and pop-up spaces all over the city. Organized by enthusiasts and often free, these offer a splendid night out with their witty double bills and themed nights, often adding music, quizzes and all sorts of extras to the mix.

Tickets West End screens and multiplexes will charge at least £12 for a standard adult ticket; independent cinemas may be a little cheaper and arthouse shows can be a lot less. Concessionary rates are offered for some shows at virtually all cinemas, usually at off-peak times on weekdays, and anyone with an Orange phone can make use of the two for one "Orange Wednesday" tickets.

ARTHOUSE CINEMAS

★ **Barbican** Silk St/Beech St, EC2 ☎020 7638 8891, ⓦbarbican.org.uk; ⊖ Barbican or Moorgate. Comfy seats, three screens and a terrific rota of obscure classics and world cinema plus silent movies with live music accompaniment and excellent festivals, talks and seasons.

BFI Southbank Belvedere Rd, South Bank, SE1 ☎020 7928 3232, ⓦbfi.org.uk; ⊖ Waterloo. Exhaustive, eclectic programmes based around themed seasons, showing between seven and fourteen films daily on four screens. The BFI, in association with Odeon, also runs the IMAX (☎0330 333 7878, ⓦbfi.org.uk/imax), a huge glazed drum in the middle of Waterloo roundabout where the colossal screen (20m high by 26m wide) is not recommended for anyone with vertigo.

Cinema Museum 2 Dugard Way, SE11 ☎020 7840 2200, ⓦcinemamuseum.org.uk; ⊖ Elephant & Castle or Kennington. There's always something interesting going on here, with cult movies, silent films, kooky double bills (*Star Trek V* with Blaxploitation, for example) and themed nights, all presented by knowledgeable industry experts, and staged either in their bijou vintage screening room or larger hall. It's a great opportunity to look around the lovingly assembled movie memorabilia collection, which is otherwise open for tours by appointment.

Electric 191 Portobello Rd, W11 ☎020 7908 9696, ⓦthe-electric.co.uk; ⊖ Notting Hill Gate or Ladbroke Grove. One of the oldest cinemas in the country (opened 1911), the Electric keeps much of its lovely old interior, but has added trendy leather armchairs, footstools, two-seater sofas and even a few double beds in the front row. The in-house fresh donuts are the icing on the cake, while the hip

FILM FESTIVALS

Birds Eye View Film Festival ⓦbirds-eye-view
.co.uk. Splendid week-long festival, held at various
venues in March, with a creative programme
celebrating the work of women directors – and
pioneers in all areas of moviemaking – from around
the world and during all historic periods.

East End Film Festival ⓦeastendfilmfestival
.com. High-profile event in late June/early July,
bursting with international premieres, workshops, free
screenings and live happenings. Its day-long "fringe
event", Cine East, uses a host of quirky East End venues
for exciting, immersive screenings.

London Film Festival ⓦbfi.org.uk/lff. One of the
major players on the world movie festival circuit, the
LFF is held over a fortnight in late October, with movies
shown across ten or so West End cinemas. Many sell out
soon after publication of the programme in early Sept.

London International Animation Festival
ⓦliaf.org.uk. Hundreds of animated shorts, features,
documentaries and retrospectives from all over the
world are shown during this dynamic ten-day festival,
held at various venues in Oct/Nov.

Portobello Film Festival ⓦportobellofilmfestival
.com. Fortnight-long free film festival, in September,
showing innovative independent works by British
filmmakers in cinemas, clubs and bars in West London.

Raindance Festival ⓦraindance.co.uk. Major
independent film festival, held over two weeks in late
September/early October, showing new work by indie
directors from across the globe.

---

retro diner next door is a great place to hang out before or
after the show. The programme concentrates on mainstream
hits, with more offbeat offerings on Sundays.

ICA Cinema Nash House, The Mall, SW1 ☎020 7930
3647, ⓦica.org.uk; ⊖ Piccadilly Circus or Charing Cross.
One of the capital's most cutting-edge programmes – offering
avant-garde, world, documentary and underground movies
on two screens (one of them with just 45 seats) in the seriously
hip HQ of the Institute of Contemporary Arts. Tues–Sun.

Lexi 194b Chamberlayne Rd, NW10 ☎0871 704 2069,
ⓦthelexicinema.co.uk; ⊖ Kensal Green. Calling itself
the "UK's first social enterprise independent boutique
digital cinema", this friendly little volunteer-run place has a
film club feel, screening the best contemporary and indie
films and donating all profits to charity.

Phoenix 52 East Finchley High Rd, N2 ☎020 8444
6789, ⓦphoenixcinema.co.uk; ⊖ East Finchley. Run by
a charitable trust, this beautiful Art Deco cinema, open
since 1910, is a neighbourhood favourite that pulls
audiences from all over London for its intelligent mix of
indies and classics, themed seasons and events.

★ **Prince Charles** 7 Leicester Place, WC2 ☎020 7494
3654, ⓦprincecharlescinema.com; ⊖ Leicester Square.
Two screens in the heart of the West End, with good prices
(rep tickets start at just £6.50, new releases at £8) and a
daily changing, lively programme of newish movies, classics
and cult favourites, plus marathons and all-nighters and
participatory "singalong" and "quotealong" romps.

★ **Rio** 107 Kingsland High St, E8 ☎020 7241 9410,
ⓦriocinema.ndirect.co.uk; Dalston Kingsland
Overground. This Deco beauty, with a cosy screening
room, offers a good mix of the most interesting current US
releases, world cinema, arthouse classics and
documentaries. Frequent Q&As and special themed events
and festivals, with excellent Sunday matinees.

Riverside Studios Crisp Rd, W6 ☎020 8237 1111,
ⓦriversidestudios.co.uk; ⊖ Hammersmith. In addition
to its splendid fringe theatre (see p.419), this space is
worth checking out for its mini film festivals and innovative
programming, including themed double bills and seasons.

FILM CLUBS

Duke Mitchell Film Club ⓦfacebook.com
/thedukemitchell. After a long residency in King's Cross, this
popular cult movie club was looking for a new permanent
base at the time of writing; check the Facebook page for
news. They offer free monthly screenings of quirky and trash
movies, often based on obscure themes – heist night, lost
films night and Canadian exploitation night, for example.

The Flicker Club Stoke Newington Town Hall, Stoke
Newington Church St, N16 ⓦtheflickerclub.com; Stoke
Newington train station. Classic movies, usually based,
however loosely, on a literary text. The revamped Art Deco
environs of Stoke Newington town hall, along with
cocktails and themed treats, keep the mood merry, and all
profits go to charity. Monthly; Thurs evenings.

Hidden Cinema The Organ Factory, St Ann's Rd, N8
ⓦtheorganfactory.co.uk; ⊖ Manor House. Tucked away
in a ghostly old organ factory, this monthly gathering screens
cult and underground movies to a crowd of thirty. A laidback
way to spend a Sunday afternoon; email for tickets.

Sands Films Cinema Club 82 St Marychurch St, SE16
☎020 7231 2209, ⓦsandsfilms.co.uk; Rotherhithe
Overground. There couldn't be a more atmospheric venue
than this old movie studio – weave your way through
costumes and set designs to the bashed-up opulence of the
back room, and settle down to enjoy anything from war-time
musicals to world cinema classics. Tickets are free, allocated
first-come, first-served; you need to sign up for weekly
emails and reserve by email in advance. Tues 8.30pm.

Shops and markets

From the *folie de grandeur* that is Harrods to the hip street markets of the
East End, London is a shopper's playground – whether you want to spend
enormous amounts of money, loading yourself up with posh bags of
designer gear, or to rifle around scruffy markets seeking out quirky treasures
for a few quid. As befits a city of villages, London's shopping districts all
have their own flavour, and many of them are known for their specialities
– Oxford Street's the place to head for chains and department stores;
Jermyn Street for upmarket gentlemen's outfitters; Charing Cross Road for
used books; Brick Lane for vintage, for example. In the sections that follow,
we've listed shops according to what they sell, rather than by area, and have
erred away from chain stores unless they display some distinctive – and
distinctively British – style.

ESSENTIALS

30

Sales The cheapest time to shop in London is during one of the two big annual sale seasons, centred on January and July, when prices are routinely slashed by anything between twenty and seventy percent. An increasing number of mid-season sales mean that you may be lucky whenever you visit. The best place to find details of other discount events is in *Time Out* (🖥 timeout.com).

Cash, cards and exchange Some stores, notably Selfridges and Harrods, will take payment in euros and US dollars, too, although this is still quite rare. Market stalls tend to take cash only. Always keep receipts: whatever the shop may tell you, the law allows a full refund or replacement on purchases which turn out to be faulty. There's no such legal protection if you just decide you don't like something, but some retailers are happy to exchange and most retailers will at least offer a credit note.

VAT Overseas (non-EU) visitors can sometimes claim back the value-added tax (VAT) that applies to most goods sold in British shops, although you will need to spend well over £100 for this to be worthwhile. Check 🖥 hmrc.gov.uk/vat/sectors /consumers/overseas-visitors.htm for the latest details.

Opening hours We've given the days and hours for each shop reviewed below, but as a rule of thumb central London shops open from Monday to Saturday from 10am to 6pm and many also open on Sunday, from around noon to 5pm or 6pm. Some of the bigger stores stay open later, and extend their hours on Thursdays and in the weeks leading up to Christmas.

WHERE TO GO

In the centre of town, **Oxford Street** is the city's hectic chain-store heartland and, together with **Regent Street**, offers pretty much every mainstream clothing label you could wish for. Just off Oxford Street expensive designer outlets clutter **St Christopher's Place** and **South Molton Street**, with even pricier designers and jewellers lining chic **Bond Street**. To the north, **Marylebone High Street** offers a pretty (and upmarket) village oasis in the middle of town – a laidback place to get all your labels, treats and gifts away from the bustle.

Tottenham Court Road is the place for electrical goods, sportswear and, in its northern section, furniture and design shops, while **New Oxford Street** has a few new and used camera equipment shops. **Charing Cross Road** is the centre of London's book trade, both new and secondhand. At its northern end, particularly on **Denmark Street** (once the heart of Britain's music industry), music shops sell everything from instruments to sound equipment and sheet music. On the other side of Charing Cross Road, stretching down to Piccadilly, **Soho** offers an increasingly mainstream mix of funky gift shops, specialist record stores, delis and the odd old-fashioned fabric retailers, while the streets surrounding **Covent Garden** yield art and design, fashion, designer wear and camping gear; the streets around **Seven Dials** are best for indie designers and offbeat stores.

Just off Piccadilly, **St James's** is the domain of the quintessential English gentleman, with the shops of **Jermyn Street** in particular dedicated to his grooming. Swanky **Knightsbridge**, further west, is home to Harrods and the big-name fashion stores of **Sloane Street** and **Brompton Road,** while the **King's Road**, having all but lost any raffish edge it once had, is now lined with upmarket indie fashion stores, expensive designer shops and high-street chains. You can still find some offbeat shops in Notting Hill and Kensington Church Street; this rather smart part of town is enlivened by Portobello Road, which has been a hotspot for antique and vintage for decades, and its offshoot, Golborne Road. On the South Bank, just a stone's throw from Waterloo, **Lower Marsh** is also burgeoning, harbouring one-off shops and studios and a local street market.

Hampstead, in a luxurious and leafy world of its own north of the centre, is a great place to browse upmarket fashion stores, posh delis and patisseries, antiquarian booksellers and tasteful arts and crafts shops. **Greenwich**, south of the river, has an eclectic range of shops and markets, while **Richmond**, out to the west, has the mainstream staples and one-off boutiques in a moneyed riverside setting. For an edgier experience, head east, where independent stores and markets in and around **Brick Lane**, **Shoreditch, Dalston** and **Spitalfields** specialize in quirky one-offs and vintage gear for hip young things; this is by far the coolest neighbourhood to shop in London. Other popular market areas (see p.433) are also good hunting grounds for small independent stores and vintage outlets.

CLOTHES AND SHOES

We concentrate on the home-grown and local rather than the ubiquitous international names, but if it's global **designer wear** you're after, bear in mind that nearly all the department stores stock lines from major and up-and-coming names. For designer-style fashion at lower prices, try the more upmarket high-street **chains** such as Jigsaw and Whistles. Mango, Zara, Monsoon, H&M and Warehouse are good bets for cheaper versions of the same. For street and clubwear, also try London's **markets** (see p.433), the hippest of which have become breeding grounds for indie shops and one-offs. They're also good places to hunt down **vintage** clothes, an area in which London excels.

DESIGNER FASHION

Alexander McQueen 4–5 Old Bond St, W1 ☎ 020 7355 0088, ⓦ alexandermcqueen.co.uk; ⊖ Bond Street; map p.78. Fabulous fashionista temple to the haute concept McQueen brand, which, since the maverick designer's suicide in 2011, has been headed by Sarah Burton. Mon–Sat 10am–6pm (Thurs 7pm).

Browns 24–27 South Molton St, W1 ☎ 020 7514 0016, ⓦ brownsfashion.com; ⊖ Bond Street; map p.78. A reliable choice for a huge range of designer wear, handpicked with impeccable taste from all the major labels from international names to hip young things. This is the flagship store, but they spread out all along South Molton Street: Browns Focus (no. 38–39; ☎ 020 7514 0063) has a slightly more avant garde bent, while Browns Menswear, for the gents, is at nos. 23 (☎ 020 7514 0038). All Mon & Tues 10.30am–6.30pm, Wed–Sat 10.30am–7.30pm.

★ **Dover Street Market** 17–18 Dover St, W1 ☎ 020 7518 0680, ⓦ london.doverstreetmarket.com; ⊖ Green Park; map p.78. Your go-to store for uber-fierce style: a six-floor designer megastore showcasing directional names such as Comme des Garçons, Chalayan and Alaïa, along with young Turks and perennials from Prada to Saint Laurent. Mon–Wed 11am–6.30pm, Thurs–Sat 11am–7pm, Sun noon–5pm.

Kokon to Zai 86 Golborne Rd, W10 ☎ 020 8960 3736; ⊖ Ladbroke Grove or Westbourne Park, map pp.274–275; 57 Greek St, W1 ☎ 020 7434 1316, map p.100; ⓦ kokontozai.co.uk. Wild, fashion-forward pieces from the KTZ line, beloved by the funkiest celebs and musos, plus work from Saint Martin's School of Art graduates. Golborne Rd: Mon–Sat 10am–6pm; Greek St: Mon–Sat 11am–7.30pm, Sun noon–7pm.

Paul Smith Westbourne House, 122 Kensington Park Rd, W11 ☎ 020 7727 3553; ⊖ Notting Hill Gate or Ladbroke Grove, map pp.274–275; 40–44 Floral St ☎ 020 7379 7133; ⊖ Covent Garden, map p.132; ⓦ paulsmith.co.uk. Though there are branches throughout London, including Borough Market and Marylebone High St, Paul Smith's Notting Hill shop-in-a-house, and his cosily contemporary Covent Garden store are particularly worth a visit: they're ever so English in Smith's quirky way, and sell the range of his well-tailored and whimsical clothes and accessories for men, women and children. Notting Hill: Mon–Fri 10am–6pm, Sat 10am–6.30pm, Sun noon–5pm; Floral St: Mon–Wed

10.30am–6.30pm, Thurs & Fri 10.30am–7pm, Sat 10am–7pm, Sun 12.30–5.30pm.

Vivienne Westwood 44 Conduit St, W1 ☎ 020 7439 1109, ⓦ viviennewestwood.co.uk; ⊖ Oxford Circus, map p.78; 430 King's Rd, SW10 ☎ 020 7352 6551, ⓦ worldsendshop.co.uk; ⊖ Sloane Square, map p.265. Revered by the international fashion pack, this quintessentially English rebel is going strong. Punks-at-heart with money to burn should make for the historic World's End shop on the King's Road imbued with her personal stamp since she took it over with boyfriend Malcolm McLaren in the 1970s Conduit St: Mon–Wed, Fri & Sat 10am–6pm, Thurs 10am–7pm, Sun noon–5pm; World's End: Mon–Sat 10am–6pm.

Wolf and Badger 46 Ledbury Rd, W11 ☎ 020 7229 5698; ⊖ Notting Hill Gate, map pp.274–275; 32 Dover St, W1 ☎ 020 3627 3191; ⊖ Green Park, map p.78; ⓦ wolfandbadger.com. Super-cool little Notting Hill shop selling cutting-edge pieces – clothes, jewellery, accessories, homeware – from young independent designers; a good place to come to sniff out the Next Big Thing. There's another branch in Dover St, Mayfair. Ledbury Rd: Mon–Sat 10am–6.30pm, Sun 11am–5pm; Dover St: Mon–Wed 11am–6.30pm, Thurs–Sat 11am–7pm, Sun noon–5pm.

BUDGET AND MID-RANGE FASHION

& Other Stories 256–258 Regent St, W1 ☎ 020 7479 7070, ⓦ stories.com; ⊖ Oxford Circus; map p.78. High-street budget favourite H&M's cooler younger sister, selling high-end pieces and directional looks at affordable prices. Mon–Fri 10am–9pm, Sat 10am–8pm, Sun noon–6pm.

The Laden Showroom 103 Brick Lane, E1 ☎ 020 7247 2431, ⓦ laden.co.uk; ⊖ Aldgate East or Shoreditch High Street Overground; map pp.192–193. Beloved of the edgier London celebs, this East End showroom showcases loads of independent designers, and is great for exuberant dressers on a budget. Mon–Fri 11am–6.30pm, Sat 11am–7pm, Sun 10.30am–6pm.

Stumper and Fielding 107 Portobello Rd, W11 ☎ 020 7229 5577; ⊖ Notting Hill Gate; map pp.274–275. The dry English wit of the name says it all: high-style hipster-gentleman come here to get suited and booted in hand-sewn leather brogues, well-cut tweeds, retro top hats and natty bow ties. Everything is presented beautifully,

30

DEPARTMENT STORES

Although all London's **department stores** offer a huge range of high-quality goods under one roof, most specialize in fashion and food. Many are worth visiting just to admire the scale, architecture and interior design, and the majority have cafés or restaurants.

Fortnum & Mason 181 Piccadilly, W1 ☎020 7734 8040, ⓦ fortnumandmason.com; ⊖ Green Park or Piccadilly Circus; map p.78. Beautiful and eccentric three hundred-year-old store with heavenly murals, cherubs, chandeliers and fountains as a backdrop to its quintessentially English offerings. Justly famous for its fabulous, pricey food and fancy afternoon teas, it also specializes in the best and most upmarket designer clothes, furniture, luggage and stationery, with a fabulous new jewellery room at prices that *will* break the bank. Mon–Sat 10am–9pm, Sun noon–6pm.

Harrods 87–135 Brompton Rd, Knightsbridge, SW1 ☎020 7730 1234, ⓦ harrods.com; ⊖ Knightsbridge; map pp.250–251. Expensive and a little stuffy, with a number of of lah-dee-dah quirks – don't dare to enter wearing clothes that "may reveal intimate parts of the body", or a backpack on your back, or you may fall foul of the dress code – Harrods is most notable for its Art Nouveau tiled food hall, the huge toy department and its swanky designer labels. And, of course, its memorial statue of Princess Diana and Dodi, erected by previous owner Mohamed Al-Fayed. Mon–Sat 10am–8pm, Sun noon–6pm.

Harvey Nichols 109–125 Knightsbridge, SW1 ☎020 7235 5000, ⓦ harveynichols.com; ⊖ Knightsbridge; map pp.250–251. Absolutely fabulous, sweetie, "Harvey Nicks" has eight floors of designer collections and shop assistants who look like models. The gorgeous cosmetics department is frequented by A- and Z-listers alike, while the fifth-floor food hall and associated bars and restaurants offers frivolous goodies at high prices. Mon–Sat 10am–8pm, Sun noon–6pm.

John Lewis 300 Oxford St, W1 ☎020 7629 7711, ⓦ johnlewis.co.uk; ⊖ Oxford Circus; map p.78.

Famous for being "never knowingly undersold", this reliable, much loved and trusted institution can't be beaten for basics. Every kind of button, pen and rug can be found here, along with reasonably priced and well-made clothes, furniture and household goods, and an excellent, enormous beauty hall. Mon–Wed, Fri & Sat 9.30am–8pm, Thurs 9.30am–9pm, Sun noon–6pm.

★ **Liberty** 210–220 Regent St, W1 ☎020 7734 1234, ⓦ liberty.co.uk; ⊖ Oxford Circus; map p.78. A fabulous emporium of luxury with a whiff of Art Nouveau bohemia, this exquisite store, with its mock-Tudor exterior, is most famous for its fabrics, design and accessories, but also has an excellent reputation for both mainstream and high fashion. The perfume, cosmetics, gift and household departments are recommended, too, and there's a good kids' section. Mon–Sat 10am–8pm, Sun noon–6pm.

Marks & Spencer 458 Oxford St, W1 ☎020 7935 7954, ⓦ marksandspencer.com; ⊖ Marble Arch; map p.78. London's largest branch of this cosy British institution (with more than one thousand outlets worldwide) offers a huge range of own-brand clothes, food, homeware and furnishings. The underwear is essential, the ready-meals good value, and the clothes well made and reliable, if sometimes unexciting. Mon–Sat 8am–9pm, Sun noon–6pm.

★ **Selfridges** 400 Oxford St, W1 ☎0800 123 400 ⓦ selfridges.com; ⊖ Bond Street; map p.78. This huge, airy palace of clothes, food and furnishings was London's first great department store and remains its best – and certainly its most stylish. The vast mens- and womenswear departments offer designer gear and casual lines alongside hipper, younger names and labels. The food hall is superb, too. Mon–Sat 9.30am–9pm, Sun noon–6pm.

interspersed with well-worn icons including vintage typewriters and rusty old bikes. Mon–Fri & Sun 10am–6pm, Sat 9am–7pm.

Tatty Devine 236 Brick Lane, E2 ☎020 7739 9191; Shoreditch High Street Overground, map pp.192–193; 44 Monmouth St ☎020 7836 2685, map p.132, ⊖ Covent Garden; ⓦ tattydevine.com. Keeping its East End indie aesthetic even while expanding into a prime West End location, Tatty Devine remains as fresh and playful as it did a decade ago. Its colourful jewellery, much of it plastic and all handmade in Britain, has given rise to a

host of imitators, but the original is still the best. Brick Lane: Mon–Fri 10am–6.30pm, Sat 11am–6pm, Sun 10am–5pm; Monmouth St: Mon–Wed, Fri & Sat 11am–7pm, Thurs 11am–8pm, Sun noon–5pm.

Topshop 214 Oxford St, W1 ☎0844 848 7487, ⓦ topshop .co.uk; ⊖ Oxford Circus; map p.78. A long-standing hit with both celebs and mere mortals, Topshop's flagship store is still the place to check out the new season must-haves – including a limited edition section and maternity gear – at a snip of the designer prices. Mon, Tues, Fri & Sat 9am–9pm, Wed & Thurs 9am–10pm, Sun 11.30am–6pm.

30

VINTAGE, RETRO AND SECONDHAND

Absolute Vintage 15 Hanbury St, Spitalfields, E1 ☎020 7247 3883; ⊖ Liverpool Street or Aldgate East map pp.192–193; 79 Berwick St, Soho, W1, map p.100; ⓦabsolutevintage.co.uk. A Spitalfields treasure trove of 1920s to 1980s clobber, heavy on 1970s gear, with one of the biggest collections of vintage shoes and bags in the UK, all at affordable prices. There's a slightly more glamorous sister store, Blondie, just around the corner, selling preloved women's designer pieces (same hours), and another Absolute Vintage in Soho. Spitalfields: daily 11am–7pm; Soho: Mon–Sat 10am–7pm, Sun noon–6pm.

Annie's Vintage Costume & Textiles 12 Camden Passage, N1 ☎020 7359 0796, ⓦanniesvintage clothing.co.uk; ⊖ Angel; map pp.284–285. This well-stocked, pricey shop, draped in shimmering, fragile fabrics and specializing in fabulous 1920s and 1930s glamour – from sequinned party dresses and embroidered Chinese jackets to Jazz Age petticoats and pyjamas – is a firm favourite with stylists and movie production artists. Daily 11am–6pm.

★ **Beyond Retro** 110–112 Cheshire St, E2 ☎020 7613 3636; ⊖ Liverpool St or Shoreditch High Street Overground, map pp.192–193; 58 Great Marlborough St ☎020 7434 1406, map p.97; 92 Stoke Newington Rd ☎020 7923 2277, map p.291; ⓦbeyondretro.com. Cavernous warehouse of twentieth-century classics, with thousands of well-priced goodies including faded jeans, 1950s frocks, battered cowboy boots, punk gear and 1920s evening gowns. Their sister store in Great Marlborough Street, Soho, glams it up a bit, while the Dalston branch on the Stoke Newington borders provides the same excellent service – and a cool café – for local fashionistas. Cheshire St: Mon–Wed, Fri & Sat 10am–7pm, Thurs 10am–8pm, Sun 11.30am–6pm; Soho: Mon–Wed & Sat 10.30am–7.30pm, Thurs & Fri 10.30am–8.30pm, Sun 11am–6pm; Dalston: Mon–Wed, Fri & Sat 10am–7pm, Thurs 10am–8pm, Sun 11.30am–6pm.

Blitz 55–59 Hanbury St, E1 ☎020 7377 0730, ⓦblitzlondon.co.uk; Shoreditch High Street Overground; map pp.192–193. This self-styled vintage department store spreads its five big rooms – filled with not only clothes, but also vinyl and furniture – across two floors of a Victorian brick warehouse. It's difficult to leave empty-handed. Mon–Wed & Sun 11am–7pm, Thurs–Sat 11am–8pm.

The Emporium 330–332 Creek Rd, SE10 ☎020 8305 1670; Cutty Sark DLR or Greenwich train station from Charing Cross; map p.315. Swanky and stylish store specializing in 1940s to 1960s clothes, mostly for men but also for women, featuring kitsch and well-preserved bras, compacts, eyewear and cigarette-holders. Wed–Sun 10am–6pm.

Rokit 101 & 107 Brick Lane, E1 ☎020 7375 3864, ☎020 7247 3777; ⊖ Aldgate East or Shoreditch High Street Overground; map pp.192–193; 225 Camden High St, NW1 ☎020 7267 3046, map pp.284–285; 42 Shelton St, WC2 ☎020 7836 6547, map p.132; ⓦrokit.co.uk. Quintessential Brick Lane retro, nicely presented – you'll find sparkly knits, cocktail dresses, petticoats and rollerskates, plus racks of men's gear dating back to the 1940s–80s. Brick Lane branches: Mon–Fri 11am–7pm, Sat & Sun 10am–7pm; Camden: daily 10am–7pm; Covent Garden: Mon–Sat 10am–7pm, Sun 11am–6pm.

★ **The Vintage Emporium** 14 Bacon St, E1 ☎020 7739 0799, ⓦvintageemporiumcafe.com; Shoreditch High Street Overground; map pp.192–193. Gorgeous shop, just off Brick Lane, selling British and French gear from the 1890s to the 1950s, with a fine selection of shimmering flapper frocks and floaty tea dresses. The cool upstairs tearoom serves its dainty cakes and teas by the light of puttering candles. Mon–Fri noon–7pm, Sat & Sun 10am–7pm; café Mon–Fri 11am–10pm, Sat & Sun 10am–10pm.

What the Butler Wore 131 Lower Marsh, SE1 ☎020 7261 1353, ⓦwhatthebutlerwore.co.uk; ⊖ Waterloo or Lambeth North; map p.216. Colourful Sixties boutique, evoking the groovy spirit of Carnaby St with its original Mod shift dresses, shiny patent accessories and super-slim men's suits, and the occasional designer piece from the likes of Ossie Clark or Nina Ricci. Mon–Sat 11am–6pm.

SHOES

★ **Irregular Choice** 35 Carnaby St, W1 ☎020 7494 4811, ⓦirregularchoice.com; ⊖ Oxford Circus; map p.97. Footwear doesn't get much more flamboyant, or frivolous, than this: a Mad Hatter's tea party of flowers, fruit, gewgaws and knickknacks adorning patterned pumps, flats, wedges and stilettos, all with wonderful names like Lost My Marbles and Abigail's Party. Mon–Wed 10am–7pm, Thurs–Sat 10am–8pm, Sun 11am–7pm.

Natural Shoe Store 13 Neal St, WC2 ☎020 7836 5254, ⓦthenaturalshoestore.com; ⊖ Covent Garden; map p.132. Socially responsible and ecologically sound shoes – mostly stylish, always comfortable and sometimes strange, with a great selection of Birkenstocks. Good value, but not cheap. There's another branch at 325 King's Road. Mon–Wed & Sat 10am–7pm, Thurs & Fri 10am–8pm, Sun noon–6pm.

★ **Tracey Neuls** 29 Marylebone Lane, W1 ☎020 7935 0039, ⓦtraceyneuls.com; ⊖ Bond Street; map p.89. Quirkily presented and lovingly crafted, Tracey Neuls' sculptural shoes are playful, comfortable and inspired, with genius innovations (heels that look higher than they are) and witty details that make you smile. Mon–Fri 11am–6.30pm, Sat & Sun noon–5pm.

The VIVOBAREFOOT Experience 64 Neal St, WC2 ☎020 7379 5959, ⓦvivobarefoot.com; ⊖ Covent Garden; map p.132. A temple to the "barefoot shoe", with its ultra-thin, puncture resistant and allegedly health-giving soles. Lots of funky running shoes, of course, but also pretty pumps, Mary Janes and boots for women, many made with vegan materials, plus desert boots for men and cool Chelsea boots for kids. Mon–Sat 10.30am–7pm, Sun noon–6pm.

BOOKS

While the chain bookstores struggle to stay afloat, London remains blessed, for now, with a number of local, independent and specialist bookshops. Bloomsbury and Charing Cross Road are excellent hunting grounds; the latter, in particular, along with Cecil Court (ⓦcecilcourt.co.uk) – the little lane that runs between Charing Cross Road and St Martins Lane – is particularly good if you're looking for secondhand oddities and rare titles.

30

GENERAL INTEREST AND CHAINS

Blackwell's 100 Charing Cross Rd, WC2 ☎020 7292 5100, ⓦbookshop.blackwell.co.uk; ⊖ Tottenham Court Road or Leicester Square; map p.100. The London flagship of Oxford's academic bookshop is bigger than it looks and has a much wider range than you might expect. Its academic stock is, unsurprisingly, excellent, but so too is its range of travel and fiction titles. Mon–Sat 9.30am–8pm, Sun noon–6pm.

★ **Foyles** 113–119 Charing Cross Rd, WC2 ☎020 7437 5660, ⓦfoyles.co.uk; ⊖ Tottenham Court Road; map p.100. Long-established, huge and famous London bookshop with an unrivalled selection of titles on all subjects, including antiquarian books, a café and and Ray's Jazz Shop for music. In 2014 they'll be moving next door; the plan is to combine print books with digital products and all manner of events and services, to create a flagship bricks-and-mortar bookstore for the digital age. If anyone can do it, Foyles can. Mon–Sat 9.30am–9pm, Sun noon–6pm.

Hatchard's 187 Piccadilly, W1 ☎020 7439 9921, ⓦhatchards.co.uk; ⊖ Piccadilly Circus; map p.78. A little overshadowed by the colossal Waterstones down the road, and actually part of the Waterstones group, the venerable Hatchard's, founded in 1797, holds its own when it comes to quality fiction, biography, history and travel. The regal interiors are only fitting for a bookseller by appointment to HM the Queen. Mon–Sat 9.30am–7pm, Sun noon–6pm.

Waterstones 203–206 Piccadilly, W1 ☎0843 290 8549, ⓦwaterstones.com; ⊖ Piccadilly Circus; map p.78. This flagship bookstore – Europe's largest – occupies the former Simpson's department store building and boasts a café, bar, gallery and events rooms as well five floors of books. Many other branches around town. Mon–Sat 9am–10pm, Sun 11.30am–6pm.

INDEPENDENT AND SPECIALIST

Arthur Probsthain 41 Great Russell St, WC1 ☎020 7636 1096, ⓦapandtea.co.uk; ⊖ Tottenham Court Road; map p.120. With another branch in the nearby School of Oriental and African Studies, this impressive old store, opposite the British Museum, specializes in books on the arts and cultures of Africa and The Middle East, with a small art gallery and a good little tearoom downstairs. Mon–Fri 9.30am–5.30pm, Sat noon–4pm.

Bookmarks 1 Bloomsbury St, WC1 ☎020 7637 1848, ⓦbookmarks.uk.com; ⊖ Tottenham Court Road; map p.120. Leftist and radical books in the heart of Bloomsbury, with a wide range of political biography, history, theory and assorted political ephemera. Mon noon–7pm, Tues–Sat 10am–7pm.

Books for Cooks 4 Blenheim Crescent, W11 ☎020 7221 1992, ⓦwww.booksforcooks.com; ⊖ Ladbroke Grove; map pp.274–275. Anything and everything to do with food at this wonderful new and used bookshop, which also has a tiny café (get there early for lunch) and cooking demonstrations. Tues–Sat 10am–6pm.

★ **Daunt Books** 83 Marylebone High St, W1 ☎020 7224 2295, ⓦdauntbooks.co.uk; ⊖ Bond Street or Baker Street; map p.89. Wide and inspirational range of travel literature, guidebooks and more, presented by expert staff in the beautiful, galleried interior of this famous Edwardian shop. Other branches. Mon–Sat 9am–7.30pm, Sun 11am–6pm.

Gay's the Word 66 Marchmont St, WC1 ☎020 7278 7654, ⓦgaystheword.co.uk; ⊖ Russell Square; map p.120. Venerable community bookshop, famed for the weekly lesbian discussion groups, and offering an extensive collection of lesbian and gay classics, pulps, contemporary fiction and nonfiction, plus cards and calendars. Mon–Sat 10am–6.30pm, Sun 2–6pm.

Gosh! 1 Berwick St, WC1 ☎020 7636 1011, ⓦgoshlondon.com; ⊖ Tottenham Court Rd; map p.100. All manner of graphic novels, comics and art and design books for the casually curious to the serious collector, with gorgeous vintage items, small-press oddities and superhero standards. Daily 10.30am–7pm.

Idler Academy 81 Westbourne Park Rd, W2 ☎020 7221 5908, ⓦidler.co.uk; ⊖ Royal Oak or Westbourne Park; map pp.274–275. With its aim to promote "cultivated leisure", this is a delightfully quirky bookstore whose "academy" hosts one-off events and courses ranging from ukulele lessons and supper clubs to instruction in calligraphy, ancient philosophy and urban foraging. Co-owner and author Tom Hodgkinson produces the annual hardback journal *The Idler*, whose writings

30

"campaign against the modern work ethic". Fri & Sat 10am–6pm, Sun 11am–5pm.

John Sandoe 10 Blacklands Terrace, SW3 ☎ 020 7589 9473, ⓦ johnsandoe.com; ⊖ Sloane Square; map p.265. One of London's finest literary bookshops, with a personally selected range of titles crammed into three floors of an eighteenth-century building; whether you're after classic genre fiction or obscure tomes on psychology, this is the place to come. Mon–Sat 9.30am–6.30pm, Sun 11am–5pm.

London Review Bookshop 14 Bury Place, WC1 ☎ 020 7269 9030, ⓦ lrbshop.co.uk; ⊖ Tottenham Court Rd; map p.120. All the books reviewed in the august literary journal and many more in this tranquil Bloomsbury bookstore. Particularly strong on literary fiction, poetry, history, politics and current affairs, it hosts regular readings and events and has a nice little coffee shop. Mon–Sat 10am–6.30pm, Sun noon–6pm.

Lutyens & Rubinstein 21 Kensington Park Rd, W11 ☎ 020 7229 1010, ⓦ lutyensrubinstein.co.uk; ⊖ Ladbroke Grove; map pp.274–275. Classy bookstore, established by the literary agents of the same name, selling a hand-selected range of classics, works in translation and art and design books, with lots of unusual literary gifts and very friendly staff. Mon–Sat 10am–6pm, Sun 11am–6pm.

★ **Persephone Books** 59 Lamb's Conduit St, WC1 ☎ 020 7242 9292, ⓦ persephonebooks.co.uk; ⊖ Russell Square or Holborn; map p.120. Lovely bookshop offspring of a publishing house that specializes in neglected twentieth-century writing by women. The books are beautifully produced, all with endpapers in a textile design from the relevant period. Mon–Fri 10am–6pm, Sat noon–5pm.

School of Life 70 Marchmont St, WC1 ☎ 020 7833 1010, ⓦ theschooloflife.com; ⊖ Russell Square; map p.120. A bijou store, home to the School of Life, which aims to offer "good ideas for everyday living" – relationships, work, play, politics, philosophy – with its books, short courses, meals, "sermons" and workshops. The shop sells notebooks and gifts as well as books. Mon–Fri noon–6pm.

★ **Society Club** 12 Ingestre Place, W1 ☎ 020 7437 1433, ⓦ thesocietyclubsoho.wordpress.com; ⊖ Piccadilly Circus; map p.100. Very cool little Soho spot – bookshop, gallery, coffee house, cocktail bar – with friendly resident dogs and the feel of a bohemian salon. Stock includes Soho-specific titles, vintage erotica and a little section devoted to Charles Bukowski, along with new literary fiction and first editions from authors as varied as

TOP 5 ENGLISH CLASSICS

A Gold See p.431
Berry Bros & Rudd See p.432
Hatchards See p.429
Liberty See p.426
Vivienne Westwood See p.425

Will Self, Daphne du Maurier and Nancy Mitford. Regular launches, readings and events. Mon–Fri noon–11pm, Sat 12.30–8pm.

★ **Stanfords** 12–14 Long Acre, WC2 ☎ 020 7836 1321, ⓦ stanfords.co.uk; ⊖ Covent Garden; map p.132. The world's largest specialist travel and map bookshop, selling pretty much any map of anywhere, plus a huge range of books, guides, literature, travel accessories and gifts. There's a small café. Mon & Wed–Fri 9am–8pm, Tues 9.30am–8pm, Sat 10am–8pm, Sun noon–6pm.

SECONDHAND AND ANTIQUARIAN

★ **Any Amount of Books** 56 Charing Cross Rd, WC2 ☎ 020 7836 3697, ⓦ anyamountofbooks.com; ⊖ Leicester Square; map p.100. Wonderful, sprawling secondhand bookshop stocking everything from obscure 50p bargains to rare and expensive first editions. Especially strong on fiction, the arts and literary biography. Daily 10.30am–9.30pm.

Pleasures of Past Times 11 Cecil Court, WC2 ☎ 020 7836 1142; ⊖ Leicester Square; map p.97. An absolute treasure, open since the 1960s and focusing on showbiz titles. You'll also find nineteenth-century fairytale collections, curious conjuring manuals and prewar children's fiction along with intriguing music hall paraphernalia and theatrical postcards. Tues & Wed noon–6pm, Thurs–Sat 11am–6pm.

Quinto 72 Charing Cross Rd, WC2 ☎ 020 7379 7669, ⓦ quintobookshop.co.uk; ⊖ Leicester Square; map p.100. Another Charing Cross Rd treasure, this secondhand bookshop has a huge choice, from battered paperbacks to precious first editions, and regularly refreshes its stock. Mon–Sat 9am–9pm, Sun noon–8pm.

South Bank Book Market Under Waterloo Bridge on the South Bank, SE1; ⊖ Waterloo or Embankment; map p.216. A book market by the Thames, opposite the BFI Southbank, offering everything from current and pulp fiction to obscure textbooks and modern European poetry – most of it reasonably priced, although rarely a complete bargain. Daily early morning till late, rain or shine.

FOOD AND DRINK

As you'd expect of a city that has some of the best restaurants in the world, London offers great shopping for the most discerning of food buffs. In the centre of town, **Soho** and **Covent Garden**, in particular, are a gourmand's delight: the former is particularly good for Chinese supermarkets and Italian delicatessens. **Marks & Spencer** is excellent for fresh foods and quality ready-meals, as are the major department-store food halls (see box, p.426), while **specialist stores** and the many local **food markets** (see p.433) – Borough Market, Broadway Market and Maltby Street have the highest profile – offer a more atmospheric shopping experience. The specialist **beer, wine and spirits** outlets listed are the pick of central London's numerous retailers, but you'll also find ever-improving ranges in the main supermarkets.

PATISSERIE AND CONFECTIONERY

Konditor & Cook 22 Cornwall Rd, SE1 ☎020 7633 3333, ⓦkonditorandcook.com; ⊖ Waterloo; map p.216. More than a cut above your average bakery, Konditor & Cook (with six branches; this is the original, a historic old store in the back streets of Waterloo) make the most wonderful cakes, tarts, meringues, truffles and biscuits. Mon–Wed 7.30am–6.30pm, Thurs & Fri 7.30am–7pm, Sat 8.30am–5pm.

Paul A Young 143 Wardour St, W1 ☎020 7437 0011, ⓦpaulayoung.co.uk; ⊖ Oxford Circus; map p.100. Artisan chocolate that's beyond your wildest dreams, handmade daily and with seasonal flavours including Yorkshire rhubarb and stem ginger, lemon basil and almond, and the extremely rare voatsiperifery pepper. Regular chocolate tasting and making events, too. Branches in Islington and the City. Mon–Wed, Fri & Sat 10am–8pm, Thurs 10am–9pm, Sun noon–7pm.

Treacle 110 Columbia Rd, E2 ☎020 7729 0538, ⓦtreacleworld.com; ⊖ Bethnal Green; map pp.192–193. Avoiding the cutesy smugness that came with much of the cupcake craze, this bare-bones little tearoom in the heart of the flower market keeps things real, celebrating British baking with scrumptious fairy cakes, Victoria sponges and fruit loaves, with racks of postwar crockery and cake stands to boot. Sat noon–5pm, Sun 9am–4pm.

CHEESE

★ **Neal's Yard Dairy** 17 Shorts Gardens, WC2 ☎020 7240 5700; ⊖ Covent Garden, map p.132; 6 Park St, Borough Market, SE1 ☎020 7367 0799; ⊖ Borough, map pp.226–227; ⓦnealsyarddairy.co.uk. Pungent store packed to the rafters with quality cheeses from around the British Isles, with a few exceptionally good choices from further afield. You can taste before you buy. Covent Garden: Mon–Sat 10am–7pm; Borough: Mon–Sat 9am–6pm.

Paxton & Whitfield 93 Jermyn St, SW1 ☎020 7930 0259, ⓦpaxtonandwhitfield.co.uk; ⊖ Piccadilly Circus; map p.66. Quintessentially English, two hundred-year-old cheese shop offering a very traditional range of English and European varieties, plus fine wines and ports, and fabulous cheesy gifts. Regular cheese tasting and matching events. Mon–Sat 9.30am–6pm, Sun 11am–5pm.

COFFEE AND TEA

Algerian Coffee Stores 52 Old Compton St, W1 ☎020 7437 2480, ⓦalgcoffee.co.uk; ⊖ Leicester Square; map p.100. With its original dark wood fittings and glass display cases, and its rich, dark fragrance, this unassuming

old store, here since 1887, looks and feels much as it must have done 125 years ago. Choose from hundreds of coffees – from house blends to rare beans – and grab a quick espresso for just £1. Mon–Wed 9am– 7pm, Thurs & Fri 9am–9pm, Sat 9am–8pm.

The Tea House 15 Neal St, WC2 ☎020 7240 7539, ⓦteahouseltd.com; ⊖ Covent Garden; map p.132. The distinctive red-tiled and black facade conceals two fragrant floors of teas – black, green, white and caffeine-free – with a wealth of accessories including infusers, teapots and cosies. Mon–Wed 10am–7pm, Thurs–Sat 10am–8pm, Sun 11am–7pm.

WORLD FOOD

A. Gold 42 Brushfield St, E1 ☎020 7247 2487, ⓦagoldshop.com; ⊖ Liverpool Street; map pp.192–193. Next door to Jeanette Winterson's *Verde's* (see p.378), *A. Gold* is a similarly classy old establishment, a "village shop" selling peculiarly British foodstuffs: spiced ginger wine, sugar mice, lemon curd, home-made Scotch eggs, Kendal mint cake and the like. On weekday lunchtimes they make delicious overstuffed artisan sandwiches to take away, too. Mon–Fri 10am–4pm, Sat & Sun 11am–5pm.

★ **Brindisa** Floral Hall, Stoney St, Borough Market, SE1 ☎020 7407 1036, ⓦbrindisa.com; ⊖ Borough; map pp.226–227. If you're craving Ibérico ham, pimientos, *manchego* and salt cod, this upmarket contemporary Spanish deli is the place for you; they also do an amazingly good takeaway barbecue chorizo sandwich. Tues–Thurs 10am–5.30pm, Fri 10am–6pm, Sat 8.30am–5pm.

Gazzano's 167 Farringdon Rd, EC1 ☎020 7837 1586; ⊖ Farringdon; map p.150. This splendid Clerkenwell deli has been keeping the area in honest Italian food for nearly a century; fabulous fresh pastas and pestos, hams, cheeses and olives, along with coffee, biscotti, an enormous range of dried pastas and everything in between. Tues–Fri 8am–5.30pm, Sat 9am–5pm, Sun 10am–2pm.

I. Camisa & Son 61 Old Compton St, W1 ☎020 7437 7610, ⓦcamisa.co.uk; ⊖ Leicester Square; map p.100. The whole classic Italian deli range packed into one small, wonderfully old-fashioned Soho space. Excellent cheeses, salamis, pastas and dried foods, plus Italian wines and spirits. Mon–Sat 9.30am–6pm.

Loon Fung Supermarket 42–44 Gerrard St, W1 ☎020 7437 7332, ⓦloonfung.com; ⊖ Leicester Square; map p.100. This warren of a supermarket in the heart of Chinatown offers every kind of Chinese food item you can imagine, and probably some you can't. There's also a huge range of foods and groceries in the shops of neighbouring Newport St, Newport Place and Lisle St. Daily 10am–8pm.

30

Taj Stores 112 Brick Lane, E1 ☎020 7377 0061, ⓦ tajstores.co.uk; ⊖ Aldgate East; map pp.192–193. Big Bangladeshi supermarket established in 1936, offering everything from halal meats, herbs and spices to fish, fresh fruit and veg, plus ingredients from other countries including India, Thailand, Malaysia and Jamaica. Daily 9am–9pm.

BEER, WINE AND SPIRITS

Berry Bros & Rudd 3 St James's St, SW1 ☎0800 280 2440, ⓦ bbr.com; ⊖ Green Park; map p.66. This glorious three hundred-year-old wine merchant houses a huge range of fine wines – from £5 to £25,000 – in a ravishing seventeenth-century building. Mon–Fri 10am–6pm, Sat 10am–5pm.

Gerry's 74 Old Compton St, W1 ☎020 7734 4215, ⓦ gerrys.uk.com; ⊖ Leicester Square; map p.100. Characterful old Soho store, crammed with the best, most eclectic and sometimes downright weird range of spirits you'll find anywhere in London, including a fine range of absinthe; vodka is a speciality. Mon–Thurs & Sat 9am–6.30pm, Fri 9am–7.30pm, Sun noon–6pm.

The Real Ale Shop 371 Richmond Rd, TW1 ☎020 8892 3710, ⓦ realale.com; ⊖ Richmond; map p.341. Microbrews and craft beers from around the world, including ciders, perries and wines, and regularly changing cask ales from local breweries. Mon noon–7pm, Tues–Thurs 10am–9pm, Fri 10am–10pm, Sat 10am–9pm, Sun 11am–7pm.

Vintage House 42 Old Compton St, W1 ☎020 7437 2592, ⓦ vintagehouse.co.uk; ⊖ Leicester Square; map p.100. The creaking shelves of this old, family-run drinker's paradise in the heart of Soho are crammed with wines, brandies and more than 1350 malt whiskies. Mon–Fri 9am–11pm, Sat 10am–11pm, Sun noon–10pm.

MUSIC

While the **megastores** have collapsed under the might of the MP3, a number of independent and specialist **music shops** in London cater for nostalgists and musos hunting for vinyl and CDs. Berwick Street in Soho, and London's markets (see opposite), especially Camden, are good sources of vinyl.

Gramex 25 Lower Marsh, SE1 ☎020 7401 3830; ⊖ Waterloo or Lambeth North; map p.216. A splendid find for classical music and jazz lovers, this eccentric new and secondhand record store features CDs and vinyl, and comfy leather armchairs to sample or discuss your finds at leisure. Mon–Sat 11am–7pm.

Harold Moores Records 2 Great Marlborough St, W1 ☎020 7437 1576, ⓦ hmrecords.co.uk; ⊖ Oxford Circus or Tottenham Court Road; map p.97. Two welcoming floors of CDs and vinyl, mostly classical and jazz, with rare releases and lots of contemporary, avant-garde selections. Mon–Sat 10am–6.30pm.

★ **Honest Jon's** 278 Portobello Rd, W10 ☎020 8969 9822, ⓦ honestjons.com; ⊖ Ladbroke Grove or Westbourne Park; map pp.274–275. A fine selection of jazz, soul, funk, r'n'b, rare groove, reggae, world music and more in this West London stalwart, with current releases, secondhand finds and reissues. Mon–Sat 10am–6pm, Sun 11am–6pm.

Rough Trade 130 Talbot Rd, W11 ☎020 7229 8541; ⊖ Ladbroke Grove, map pp.274–275; Rough Trade East: 91 Brick Lane, E1 ☎020 7392 7788; ⊖ Aldgate East or Shoreditch High Street Overground, map pp.192–193. ⓦ roughtrade.com. The musos' favourite, this historic indie specialist has knowledgeable, friendly staff and a dizzying array from electronica to hardcore and beyond. There's a second, huge, branch, Rough Trade East, in the Old Truman Brewery. Regular in-store performances at both. Rough Trade: Mon–Sat 10am–6.30pm, Sun 11am–5pm; Rough Trade East: Mon–Thurs 8am–9pm, Fri 8am–8pm, Sat 10am–8pm, Sun 11am–7pm.

★ **Sister Ray** 34 Berwick St, W1 ☎020 7734 3297, ⓦ sisterray.co.uk; ⊖ Tottenham Court Road; map p.100. This is a record store in the old mode, a sizeable, long-established and well-informed vinyl specialist, specializing in cool music from the 1960s up to the present day, and offering anything from spacerock to psychobilly. Mon–Sat 10am–8pm, Sun noon–6pm.

Sounds that Swing 88 Parkway, NW1 ☎020 7267 4682, ⓦ nohitrecords.co.uk; ⊖ Camden Town; map pp.284–285. The bricks and mortar outlet of the groovy No Hit Records label, with a very Camden Town rockabilly vibe, this colourful vinyl and CD store offers an eclectic, personally selected range from blues/folk via rockabilly to garage punk. Daily noon–6pm.

GIFTS AND ODDITIES

Ignore the Beefeater teddy bears and tacky comedy T-shirts – London can be a splendid place for souvenirs. In addition to the city's many fabulous museum stores (the shops at the V&A, London Transport Museum, the Wellcome Collection and the Southbank Centre, by the Royal Festival Hall, yield particularly rich pickings), and its department stores (see box, p.426) – Liberty and Selfridges are the best for gifts – London has plenty of offbeat places that are perfect for out-of-the-ordinary gifts.

Duke of Uke 88 Cheshire St, E2 ☎020 3583 9728, ⓦdukeofuke.co.uk; ⊖ Whitechapel or Liverpool Street or Shoreditch High Street Overground; map pp.192–193. Lively, welcoming and much-loved little uke-nuts' hub, stuffed to the rafters with ukuleles, banjos and harmonicas, some of them vintage. Check the website for details of live jams, singalongs and beginners' classes. Tues–Fri noon–7pm, Sat & Sun 11am–6pm.

Hamleys 188–196 Regent St, W1 ☎0871 704 1977, ⓦhamleys.com; ⊖ Oxford Circus; map p.78. You may well hear this grand old toy store – a London landmark, standing on this spot for 250 years – before you see it. Just listen for the clamour of shrieking kids on the rampage – Hamleys has no less than seven floors of fun, from wooden rocking horses to Wii games, to entice them. Mon–Wed 10am–8pm, Thurs & Fri 10am–9pm, Sat 9.30am–8pm, Sun noon–6pm.

★ **International Magic** 89 Clerkenwell Rd, EC1 ☎020 7405 7324, ⓦinternationalmagic.com; ⊖ Chancery Lane or Farringdon; map p.150. Eccentric, family-owned little magic store selling more tricks and accessories, along with instruction manuals and DVDs, than it is possible to imagine (unless you're a mindreader). Mon–Fri 11.30am–6pm, Sat 11.30am–4pm.

Limelight Movie Art 313 King's Rd, SW3 ☎020 7751 5584, ⓦlimelightmovieart.com; ⊖ South Kensington; map p.265. Though the generally high prices mean it's geared mainly towards serious collectors, you can still pick up original movie posters and lobby cards – from Bowie to Buster Keaton – at this glamorous and glossy Chelsea shop. Mon–Sat 11.30am–6pm.

Little Shop of Horrors 11 Mare St, E8 ☎020 7998 3617, ⓦviktorwyndofhackney.co.uk; ⊖ Bethnal Green or Old Street; map p.190. Wonderfully macabre little Hackney gallery/store: a time-warped Cabinet of Wonders with a freakshow vibe. From two-headed teddy bears to African masks, animal skulls to Arabian swords, you'll find plenty to enchant you in this spooky spot. It's the base of the Last Tuesday Society, which hosts regular events on generally Gothic themes. Sat noon–7pm or by appointment.

Lomography Gallery Store 3 Newburgh St, W1 ☎020 7434 1466; ⊖ Oxford Circus, map p.97; 117 Commercial St ☎020 7426 0999, map pp.192–193; ⓦlomography .com. For anyone who thinks photography lost its soul when it went digital, this super-stylish store sells all the cult analogue cameras including the Lomo LC-A, the Diana and the Lomo Lubitel, with lots of cheapies too. Newburgh St: Mon–Sat 11am–7pm, Sun noon–5pm; Commercial St: daily 11am–7pm.

Pollock's Toyshop Central Ave, South Piazza, Covent Garden, WC1 ☎020 7379 7866, ⓦpollocks -coventgarden.co.uk; ⊖ Covent Garden; map p.132. If Hamleys feels a bit commercial, head for this tiny cupboard of a place on Covent Garden piazza, where the toys – Victorian curiosities, toy theatres, wooden games, vintage puzzles – appeal to adults as much as kids. Great cards, too. Mon–Sat 10.30am–6pm, Sun 11am–4pm.

30

MARKETS

London's markets are more than just a cheap alternative to high-street shopping: you haven't really got to grips with London unless you've rummaged through the junk at Brick Lane on a Sunday morning, or haggled over a leather jacket at Camden. Do keep an eye out for **pickpockets**, however.

Alfie's Antique Market 13–25 Church St, NW8 ☎020 7723 6066, ⓦalfiesantiques.com; ⊖ Marylebone; map p.89. Vast indoor market in the Parisian flea market style, offering fantastic vintage and antiques from Art Deco earrings to priceless modernist ceramics. Great café, too. Tues–Sat 10am–6pm.

Bermondsey (New Caledonian) Bermondsey Square, SE1; ⊖ London Bridge; map pp.224–225. Antiques from obscure nautical instruments to pricey furniture. The serious collectors arrive at dawn. Fri 4am–1pm.

Berwick Street Berwick and Rupert streets, W1; ⊖ Piccadilly Circus; map p.100. This famous fruit and veg market is a piece of living Soho history, with ferociously fast vendors working the crowds like showmen, though the street food and the cool indie stalls are the big pull nowadays. Mon–Sat 9am–6pm.

Borough 8 Southwark St, SE1 ☎020 7407 1002, ⓦboroughmarket.org.uk; ⊖ London Bridge; map pp.226–227. Fine-food heaven – suppliers from all over the UK converge to sell organic and artisan goodies from around the world, and there are regular cooking demos. The Victorian structure, with its slender wrought-iron columns, is lovely. Prices are high, and Sat can be a crush; go early. Thurs 11am–5pm, Fri noon–6pm, Sat 8am–5pm.

Brick Lane Brick Lane, Cygnet and Sclater streets, E1; ⊖ Aldgate East or Liverpool Street or Shoreditch High Street Overground; map pp.192–193. Huge, sprawling, cheap and frenzied, the famous East End market has become a fixture on the hipster circuit. Fruit and veg, household tat, clothes, antique furniture, scratched records, new young designers and broken spectacles – it's hard to say what you can't find here, most of it going for a song; great food stalls, too. The coolest gear is sold in and around the Old Truman Brewery, at the Backyard Market (ⓦbackyardmarket.co.uk), the Tea Rooms (ⓦbricklane-tearooms.co.uk) and the Sunday Upmarket (ⓦsundayupmarket.co.uk). Brick Lane: Sun 9am–5pm; Backyard/Tea Rooms: Sat 11am–6pm, Sun 10am–5pm; Upmarket: Sun 10am–5pm.

30

Brixton Electric Ave, Pope's, Brixton Station and Atlantic rds, SW9 ⓦbrixtonmarket.net; ⊖ Brixton; map pp.310–311. Centred on Electric Ave, and spilling out along the neighbouring streets, this huge, energetic market (see p.434) is the centre of Brixton life, offering fruit and veg, African and Caribbean foods, beauty products, records, clothes and fabrics. Cool vintage stalls, food vendors and indie shops cluster in "Brixton Village" and Market Row, the arcades off Atlantic Rd and Coldharbour Lane, while Brixton Station Rd also sees a farmers' market on Sunday (10am–2pm) and themed markets each Sat (10am–5pm). Arcades: Mon 8am–6pm, Tues–Sun 8am–11.30pm; street stalls: Mon, Tues & Thurs–Sat 8am–6pm, Wed 8am–3pm; shops: daily 8am–7pm.

★ **Broadway Market** Broadway Market, E8 ⓦbroadwaymarket.co.uk; ⊖ Bethnal Green; map p.291. Running from the Regent's Canal down to London Fields, this trendy foodie favourite offers terrific organic and artisan produce, and you can pick up vintage clothes, cool crafts and one-off accessories in the shops alongside. Sat 9am–5pm.

Camden Camden High St to Chalk Farm Rd, NW1 ⓦcamdenlock.net; ⊖ Camden Town; map pp.284–285. This legendary market – once beloved of hippies, punks and goths, and now a firm favourite with European tourists – is actually a gaggle of markets, a mass of hundreds of stalls – arts, crafts and clubwear, records, furniture, trinkets and jewellery, and, in the Stables Market area especially, excellent vintage/antique stuff – segueing into each other to create one enormous shopping district. Lively shops add hip designers, antique dealers, restaurants, bars and booksellers to the mix. Daily, roughly 9.30am–6pm, with more stalls at the weekend.

Chatsworth Road Chatsworth Rd, E5 ⓦchatsworthroade5.co.uk/market; Hackney Central Overground; map p.190. Regenerated old Clapton market with an as yet unpretentious neighbourhood feel, catering to the mixed local population with vintage clothes, fab food stalls, used books, arts and crafts and plants. Sun 11am–4pm.

★ **Columbia Road** Columbia Rd, E2 ⓦcolumbiaroad .info; Shoreditch High Street or Hoxton Overground; map pp.192–193. Fabulous, funky flower market in the heart of the East End, with bargains galore, especially late in the day. Get here early, grab breakfast in one of the many cafés or coffee stalls, and check out the area's increasingly hip shops while you're at it. Sun 8am–3pm.

Greenwich Greenwich High Rd, SE10 ⓦgreenwichmarket.net; Greenwich train station from Charing Cross or Cutty Sark DLR; map p.315. Sprawling set of covered flea markets with some 150 stalls selling everything from bric-a-brac to furniture. Tues, Wed & Fri–Sun are best for arts, crafts and food; for antiques and vintage come on Tues, Thurs and Fri. The surrounding streets, and the shops inside the covered market, offer more treasures. Stalls Tues–Sun 10am–5.30pm.

Maltby Street Maltby St, SE1; ⊖ Tower Bridge; map pp.224–225. Rapidly rivalling the nearby Borough Market, this lower-key (and cheaper) foodie destination huddles under the arches near Tower Bridge and spreads along Maltby and Druid streets down to Bermondsey Spa. Most action is on the lively Ropewalk, which has some excellent pop-up bars and streetfood stalls. Sat 9am–2pm, Sun 11am–4pm.

Petticoat Lane Middlesex St and around, E1; ⊖ Liverpool Street; map pp.192–193. Cheap, cheerful and multicultural, this famous clothes and bric-a-brac market (there's a lot of tat) is big, bustling and deliciously ungentrified. Famously, it's where Lord Alan Sugar, of *The Apprentice* fame, started out as a young stall trader. Mon–Fri 10am–4pm, Sun 9am–3pm.

Portobello Road Portobello and Golborne rds, W10 and W11 ⓦshopportobello.co.uk; ⊖ Ladbroke Grove or Notting Hill Gate; map pp.274–275. Probably the best way to approach this enormous market, or rather markets, is from the Notting Hill end, winding your way through the antiques and bric-a-brac down to the fruit and veg, and then via the hip fashion stalls under the Westway to the thriving vintage scene at Portobello Green (ⓦportobellofashionmarket.com). The Golborne Rd market is cheaper and less crowded, with antique and retro furniture on Fri and Sat (food and bric-a-brac Mon–Thurs). Antique market: Sat 8am–6pm; Portobello Road: Fri–Sun; Golborne Rd: Mon–Sat.

Ridley Road Ridley Rd, E8; Dalston Kingsland Overground; map p.291. A bustling, very cheap food and clothes market in the heart of Hackney. African and Caribbean fruit, veg and fish predominate, but there are also Turkish and Asian staples and a long line of shops offering fabrics, hair and beauty products, old gospel albums, cheap shoes and much else. Mon–Thurs 6am–6pm, Fri & Sat 6am–7pm.

Spitalfields Commercial St, between Brushfield and Lamb streets, E1 ⓦspitalfields.co.uk; ⊖ Liverpool St; map pp.192–193. The East End's historic Victorian fruit and veg hall now houses an upmarket designer/makers, crafts, arts, vintage and antique market, with rotating themed markets each Saturday. The surrounding shops and restaurants are excellent, too. Market: Mon–Fri 10am–5pm, Sat 11am–5pm, Sun 9am–5pm; shops & restaurants: daily.

WIMBLEDON

Activities and sports

Many of the crucial international fixtures of football, rugby and cricket take place in the capital, and London also hosts one of the world's top tennis tournaments, Wimbledon. London is the only city to have hosted the Olympics three times, and the 2012 Olympics supplied a number of new world-class arenas in the Olympic Park (see p.202). Domestically, football (soccer) remains the most popular sport, with London clubs Chelsea and Arsenal among Europe's top teams. The rest of the sporting calendar is chock-full of quality events, from the sedate pleasures of county cricket to the idiosyncrasies of greyhound racing. For those who'd rather compete than spectate, there's a wide range of facilities, including inexpensive access to swimming pools, gyms, tennis courts, while even golf enthusiasts can find a course within the city limits.

31

SPECTATOR SPORTS

For the top international events, it can be almost impossible to track down a ticket without paying over the odds through a ticket agency. Should you be thwarted in your attempts to gain admission, you can often fall back on **TV or radio coverage**. BBC Radio 5 live (909 & 693 Mhz) has live commentaries on almost all major sporting events, while one of the free-to-view TV channels nearly always carries live transmission of international rugby and soccer. To watch some sports (including live Premiership football), you'll need to find a TV that has the Sky stations – many pubs show Sky games (sometimes on big screens) to draw in custom.

FOOTBALL

The English **football** (soccer) season runs from mid-Aug to early May, when the **FA Cup Final** at Wembley finishes off the season. There are four professional leagues: at the top is the twenty-club Premiership, followed by the Championship and Leagues One and Two, each of which has 24 clubs. There are London clubs in every single division, with around five or six in the Premiership at any one time. Over the decades, London's most successful club by far has been **Arsenal**. However, since the arrival of Russian oil tycoon Roman Abramovich, fellow London club **Chelsea** has had a resurgence, winning the league for the first time in fifty years in 2005, and twice more since then.

Tickets Tickets for most Premiership games start at £40–50 and are virtually impossible to get hold of on a casual basis, though you may be able to see one of the Cup fixtures. It's a lot easier and cheaper to see a game in the Championship or one of the lower leagues, or to go on a stadium tour (see club websites for details).

Fixtures Most Premiership fixtures kick off at 3pm on Saturday, though there's also an early and late kick-off on Saturday, plus a couple on Sunday and the occasional midweek match; all matches, apart from the Saturday 3pm kick-offs, are broadcast live on Sky TV.

NATIONAL STADIUM

Wembley Stadium Wembley Way (90,000 capacity) ☎ 0844 800 2755, ⓦ wembleystadium.com; ⊖ Wembley Park or Wembley Central. The new stadium, designed by Norman Foster and featuring a massive steel arch, is the world's most expensive football ground, but it'll never reach the iconic status of the old stadium, constructed for the 1924 British Empire Exhibition, and the main focus of the 1948 Olympic Games. The stadium's most famous features were its "twin towers", forever associated with England's victory here in the 1966 World Cup Final. Erected as a mute reference to the old Raj, they were, in fact, only added in 1963, to celebrate the hundredth anniversary of the Football League. Guided tours are available (daily 10am–4pm; £16).

FOOTBALL CLUBS

Arsenal (Premiership) Emirates Stadium, Ashburton Grove, N7 (60,000 capacity) ☎ 020 7619 5000, ⓦ arsenal.com; ⊖ Arsenal.

Brentford (League One) Griffin Park, Braemar Rd (12,300 capacity) ☎ 0845 345 6442, ⓦ brentfordfc.co.uk; Brentford train station from Waterloo.

Charlton Athletic (Championship) The Valley, Floyd Rd, SE7 (27,000 capacity) ☎ 0871 226 1905, ⓦ cafc .co.uk; Charlton train station from Charing Cross.

Chelsea (Premiership) Stamford Bridge, Fulham Rd, SW6 (41,800 capacity) ☎ 020 7835 6000, ⓦ chelseafc .com; ⊖ Fulham Broadway.

Crystal Palace (Premiership) Selhurst Park, Whitehorse Lane, SE25 (26,000 capacity) ☎ 020 8768 6010, ⓦ cpfc.co.uk; Selhurst train station from Victoria.

Dagenham & Redbridge (League Two) Victoria Rd, Dagenham (6000 capacity) ☎ 020 8592 1549, ⓦ daggers.co.uk; ⊖ Dagenham.

Fulham (Premiership) Craven Cottage, Stevenage Rd, SW6 (25,000 capacity) ☎ 0843 208 1222, ⓦ fulhamfc .com; ⊖ Putney Bridge.

Leyton Orient (League One) Matchroom Stadium, Brisbane Rd, E10 (9200 capacity) ☎ 0871 310 1881, ⓦ leytonorient.com; ⊖ Leyton.

Millwall (Championship) The Den, Zampa Rd, SE16 (20,000 capacity) ☎ 020 7232 1222, ⓦ millwallfc.co.uk; South Bermondsey train station from London Bridge.

Queens Park Rangers (Championship) Loftus Road Stadium, South Africa Rd, W12 (18,300 capacity) ☎ 020 8743 0262, ⓦ qpr.co.uk; ⊖ White City.

Tottenham Hotspur (Premiership) White Hart Lane Stadium, Tottenham High Rd, N17 (36,000 capacity) ☎ 0844 499 5000, ⓦ tottenhamhotspur.com; White Hart Lane train station from Liverpool Street.

West Ham United (Championship) Upton Park, Green St, E13 (35,500 capacity) ☎ 020 8548 2748, ⓦ whufc .com; ⊖ Upton Park.

Wimbledon (League Two) Kingsmeadow, Kingston-upon-Thames (4850 capacity) ☎ 020 8547 3528, ⓦ afcwimbledon.co.uk; Norbiton train station from Waterloo.

CRICKET

The cricket season runs from April to September. If you're new to the sport, the best introduction is to go to an inter-county **Twenty20** knock-out match, which take place in the evening, lasts three hours and represents the game at its most frenetic. The other option is to attend a match, either in one of the **one-day competitions** or in the old-fashioned **county championship**. Games in the latter take place over the course of four days and are never sold out. Two county teams are based in London: **Middlesex**, who play at Lord's, and **Surrey**, who play at The Oval.

Two international sides visit each summer and play a series of **Test matches** against England, which last up to five days. In tandem with the full-blown five-day Tests, there's also a series of **one-day internationals**, two of which are usually held in London.

Tickets Test match tickets can be difficult unless you book months in advance, and cost £30 and upwards. However, not all matches last the full five days, so tickets for the fifth day are usually sold on the day and can cost as little as £10. Tickets for Twenty20 matches, one-day competitions and county championship matches cost in the region of £15–20.

CRICKET GROUNDS

Lord's St John's Wood, NW8 (28,000 capacity) ☎ 020 7616 8500, ⓦ lords.org; ⊖ St John's Wood.
The Oval Kennington Oval, SE11 (23,500 capacity) ☎ 020 7820 5700, ⓦ kiaoval.com; ⊖ Oval.

RUGBY

There are two types of rugby played in England. Thirteen-a-side **Rugby League** is played almost exclusively in the north of England. However, the Super League does feature one London club, **London Broncos**, who play at the Twickenham Stoop. The season runs from February to September, and games traditionally take place on Sundays at 3pm, but there are now as many matches on Friday and Saturday. The final of the knock-out Challenge Cup is traditionally held at Wembley Stadium (see opposite).

In London, however, virtually all rugby clubs play fifteen-a-side **Rugby Union**, which has upper-class associations. Two teams in the Premiership play in London: **Harlequins**, who play at the same stadium as the London Broncos, and **Saracens**, who play at the Allianz Park in Hendon. Despite their names, **London Wasps** and **London Irish** play outside the city. Matches are traditionally on Saturdays at 3pm and the season runs from September until May, finishing off with the two knock-out finals organized by the European Rugby Cup – these are known as the Heineken Cup and the Challenge Cup.

Tickets International matches are played at Twickenham Stadium, but unless you're affiliated to a rugby club, it's tough (and expensive) to get a ticket. A better bet is to go and see a Premiership game, where there's bound to be an international player or two on display – you can usually get in for £20–40.

MAJOR RUGBY STADIUMS AND CLUBS

Harlequins Twickenham Stoop Stadium, Langhorn Drive, Twickenham (14,800 capacity) ☎ 020 8410 6000, ⓦ quins.co.uk; Twickenham train station from Waterloo.

Twickenham Stadium Whitton Rd, Twickenham (82,000 capacity) ☎ 0871 222 2120, ⓦ rfu.com; Twickenham train station from Waterloo.

TENNIS

Tennis in England is synonymous with **Wimbledon**, the only Grand Slam tournament still played on grass. The Wimbledon championships last a fortnight, in the last week of June and the first week of July. An easier opportunity to see big-name players is the Men's Championship at **Queen's** Club in Hammersmith, which finishes a week before Wimbledon. Many of the male tennis stars use this tournament to acclimatize themselves to English grass-court conditions.

Tickets Getting hold of a ticket for Wimbledon is a bit of a palaver. You really need to camp overnight if you want to get one of the five hundred day tickets for the show courts (prices from around £35–90); otherwise, if you get there by 9am, you should get admission to the outside courts (where you'll catch some top players in the first week of the tournament), which costs £15–20. Avoid the middle Saturday, when thousands of people camp overnight, and don't bother queuing for show court tickets on the last five days as all seats are pre-sold. For advance tickets, you have to enter a public ballot: send a stamped, addressed envelope to the club for an application form (available from the August preceding the championship) and return it by December 31. As with Wimbledon, you have to apply for Queen's tickets in advance, although there are ground tickets (£20) and a limited number of show court returns on sale at 10am each day (£35–100). For priority booking, you need to put your name on the Mailing List and you will be sent an application form in January.

TENNIS CLUBS

All England Lawn Tennis and Croquet Club Church Rd, Wimbledon, SW19 ☎ 020 8944 1066, ⓦ wimbledon .com; ⊖ Southfields or Wimbledon Park.
Queen's Club Palliser Rd, Hammersmith, W14; ☎ 020 7386 3400, ⓦ queensclub.co.uk; ⊖ Barons Court.

GREYHOUND RACING AND MOTORSPORT

Wimbledon Plough Lane ☎ 0870 840 8905, ⓦ lovethedogs.co.uk; ⊖ Wimbledon Park or Earlsfield train station from Waterloo. The most central London venue for watching greyhound racing (Fri & Sat evenings). Trackside admission costs £6. Evening meetings usually start around 7.30pm and finish at 10.30pm, and generally include around a dozen races. The stadium also hosts stock-car and banger races, every Sunday from October to April (ⓦ spedeworth .co.uk), with tickets from £14.

31

PARTICIPATING SPORTS

The following section lists most of the **sporting activities** possible in the capital. As a rule, the most reasonably priced facilities are provided by community leisure and sports centres, where you can simply turn up and pay to use the facilities. Most boroughs also have membership schemes that allow you to use the facilities for free or give discounts to regular users.

GOLF

At most places you don't need to be a member – a pay-and-play round costs in the region of £15 – but it's advisable to book ahead at the weekend. There are also a few (often quite transitory) places closer to the centre, where you can hone your driving and putting for less. For more information visit ⓦ londongolf.info.

Central London Golf Centre Burntwood Lane, SW17 ⓣ 020 8871 2468, ⓦ clgc.co.uk; Earlsfield train station from Vauxhall. "Central" might be stretching it, but still a decent nine-hole pay-and-play course and a floodlit driving range. Daily 7am to 1hr before sunset.

Lee Valley Golf Course Meridian Way, N9 ⓣ 020 8803 3611, ⓦ visitleevalley.org.uk; Ponders End train station from Liverpool Street. Public eighteen-hole course set in the watery landscape along the River Lee. Mon–Fri 8am to dusk, Sat & Sun 7am to dusk.

Richmond Park Golf Club Roehampton Gate, Priory Lane, SW15 ⓣ 020 8876 3205, ⓦ richmondparkgolf club.org.uk; Barnes train station from Waterloo or bus #371 or #65 from ⊖ Richmond. Two long-established eighteen-hole courses and a driving range. Daily 7am to 30min before sunset.

HORSERIDING

Strange though it might seem, there are places in the metropolis where you can **saddle up**, though at a price – £25/hr is the average. It's usually possible to borrow a hard hat, but you must wear shoes or boots with a heel.

Hyde Park Stables 63 Bathurst Mews, W2 ⓣ 020 7723 2813, ⓦ hydeparkstables.com; ⊖ Lancaster Gate. The only stables in central London, situated on the north side of Hyde Park. An hour's ride or lesson in a group costs from £69, or from £95 for a private lesson. Mon–Fri 7.30am–5pm,

Sat & Sun 9am–5pm.

Lee Valley Riding Centre 71 Lee Bridge Rd, E10 ⓣ 020 8556 2629, ⓦ visitleevalley.org.uk; Clapton train station from Liverpool St. Stables over in northeast London by the River Lee. A 1hr class will cost around £25, whereas private lessons cost upwards of £35/30min. Mon–Thurs 7.15am-9pm, Fri–Sun 8am–7pm.

Wimbledon Village Stables 24 High St, SW19 ⓣ 020 8946 8579, ⓦ wvstables.com; ⊖ Wimbledon. Hack over the wilds of Wimbledon Common and Richmond Park from £55/hr. Private lessons available from British Horse Society-approved instructors from £75/hr. Tues–Sun 9.30am–4.30pm.

TENNIS

There are loads of outdoor **courts** in council-run parks, costing £7.50–10/hr; the downside is that they're rarely perfectly maintained. If you want to book in advance, you might have to join the local borough's scheme (£20–30/year); we've given phone numbers for courts in the main central London parks or visit ⓦ londontennis.co.uk. During the day it's generally possible to turn up and play within half an hour or so, except in July and August, when Wimbledon (and decent weather) spurs a mass of couch potatoes into activity.

Battersea Park SW11 (19 floodlit courts) ⓣ 020 8871 7542, ⓦ batterseapark.org; Battersea Park train station from Victoria.

Highbury Fields Baalbec Rd, N1 (11 courts, 7 of them floodlit) ⓣ 020 7226 2334; ⊖ Highbury & Islington.

Holland Park W8 (6 courts) ⓣ 020 7602 2226; ⊖ High Street Kensington.

Hyde Park Tennis and Sports Club South Carriage Drive, W2 (6 courts) ⓣ 020 7262 3474, ⓦ royalparks .gov.uk; ⊖ South Kensington or Knightsbridge.

CLIMBING WALLS

Indoor climbing centres are run by serious climbers, and you must be a registered climber to climb unsupervised. Registration is fairly straightforward, however, and you can rent helmet, harness and footwear when you get there; total novices should book themselves on a course.

The Castle Green Lanes, N4 ⓣ 020 8211 7000, ⓦ castle-climbing.co.uk; ⊖ Manor House. London's hippest climbing centre is housed in a Victorian water pumping station that looks like a Hammer Horror Gothic castle. Mon–Fri noon–10pm, Sat & Sun 10am–7pm.

Mile End Climbing Wall Haverfield Rd, E3 ⓣ 020 8980 0289, ⓦ mileendwall.org.uk; ⊖ Mile End. Smaller climbing centre housed in an old pipe-bending factory in the East End's Mile End Park. Mon–Thurs noon–9.30pm, Fri noon–9pm, Sat & Sun 10am–6pm.

Westway Climbing Centre Crowthorne Rd, W10 ⓣ 020 8969 0992, ⓦ westwaysportscentre.org.uk; ⊖ Latimer Road. Large-scale climbing centre in a leisure centre that's tucked under the Westway flyover. Mon–Wed & Fri 9.30am–10pm, Thurs 8am–10pm, Sat & Sun 8am–8pm.

OPEN-AIR SWIMS

If you fancy an alfresco dip, a swim will cost you £5 or less at the places listed below:

Brockwell Lido Brockwell Park, SE24 ☎ 020 7274 3088, ⓦ fusion-lifestyle.com; Herne Hill train station from Victoria or St Pancras. Laidback lido at the heart of Brixton's Brockwell Park. May & Sept Mon–Fri 6.30–10am & 4–8pm, Sat & Sun 8am–6pm; June–Aug Mon–Fri 6.30am–8pm, Sat & Sun 8am–6pm; reduced hours in winter.

Hampstead Ponds Hampstead Heath, NW3 ☎ 020 7485 5757, ⓦ cityoflondon.gov.uk; ⊖ Hampstead. The Heath has three natural ponds: the Women's and Men's ponds are on the Highgate side (bus #214 from ⊖ Kentish Town), while the Mixed Bathing pond is nearer Hampstead. Daily 7 or 8am to 9pm or dusk.

Hampton Pool Hampton High St, Hampton ☎ 020 8255 1116, ⓦ www.hamptonpool.co.uk; Hampton train station from Waterloo. Heated outdoor pool on the western edge of Bushy Park, about a mile's walk from Hampton Court Palace. Open all year; phone for hours.

London Fields Lido London Fields, E8 ☎ 020 7254 9038, ⓦ gll.org; London Fields train station from Liverpool Street. Refurbished interwar lido with a 164ft heated outdoor pool. Open daily all year round, but hours vary (Tues eve women only).

Oasis 32 Endell St, WC2 ☎ 020 7831 1804, ⓦ gll .org; ⊖ Covent Garden. The outdoor pool is small, but the water is a bath-like temperature and it's open all year. Other facilities include a gym, a health suite with sauna and sunbed, massage and squash courts. Mon–Fri 6.30am–10pm, Sat & Sun 9.30am–6pm.

Parliament Hill Lido Gordon House Rd, NW5 ☎ 020 7485 3873; Gospel Oak Overground. Beautiful 200ft by 90ft open-air pool with Art Deco touches and notoriously chilly water. Daily: May to mid-Sept 7am–6.30pm; mid-Sept to April 7am–noon.

Pools on the Park Old Deer Park, Richmond ☎ 020 8940 0561; ⊖ Richmond. Not in Richmond Park, but in the Old Deer Park near the Thames, adjacent to a modern leisure centre. Easter to Sept: Mon 6.30am–7.45pm, Tues–Fri 6.30am–8pm, Sat & Sun 7am–5.45pm.

Serpentine Lido Hyde Park, W2 ☎ 020 7706 3422, ⓦ serpentinelido.com; ⊖ Knightsbridge. Offers 110yd of swimming in Hyde Park's lake, plus a paddling pool; deck chairs and sun loungers for rent. May Sat & Sun 10am–6pm; June to mid-Sept daily 10am–6pm.

Tooting Bec Lido Tooting Bec Rd, SW16 ☎ 020 8871 7198; bus #249 from ⊖ Tooting Bec. At 300ft by 100ft, this is England's (and one of Europe's) largest freshwater, open-air pools. Late May daily 6am–6pm; June–Aug daily 6am–8pm; Sept daily 6am–5pm.

31

Islington Tennis Centre Market Rd, N7 (2 floodlit outdoor and 6 indoor courts) ☎ 020 7700 1370, ⓦ aquaterra.org; ⊖ Caledonian Road.

Lincoln Inn's Fields, WC2 (3 courts) ☎ 020 7437 3662; ⊖ Holborn.

Paddington Recreation Ground Randolph Ave, W9 (12 floodlit courts) ☎ 020 7641 3642; ⊖ Maida Vale.

Regent's Park South Lower Circle, NW1 (12 courts, 4 floodlit) ☎ 020 7486 4216, ⓦ royalparks.org.uk; ⊖ Baker Street.

SPAS, GYMS AND LEISURE CENTRES

Below is a selection of the best-equipped and most central multipurpose **leisure centres**: almost all have gyms, fitness classes and pools; for local addresses visit ⓦ yell.com.

Ironmonger Row Baths 1 Norman St, EC1 ☎ 020 3642 5521, ⓦ spa-london.org; ⊖ Old Street. Newly refurbished, this place has a steam room, sauna, small plunge pool, masseurs, a lounge area with a large pool – from £25 for three hours. Women: Mon 11am–6pm, Thurs 10am–5.30pm, Fri 10am–9pm; Men: Tues 10am–9pm, Thurs 6–9pm; Mixed: Mon 6–9pm, Wed 10am–9pm, Sat & Sun 9am–6pm.

Porchester Spa Porchester Rd, W2 ☎ 020 7792 3980, ⓦ better.org.uk; ⊖ Bayswater or Queensway. Built in the 1920s, the Porchester's baths are well worth a visit for the Art Deco tiling alone. Admission is around £25 for a three-hour session, and entitles you to use the saunas, steam rooms, plunge pool, jacuzzi and swimming pool. Men: Mon, Wed & Sat 10am–10pm; Women: Tues, Thurs & Fri 10am–10pm, Sat 10am–2pm; Mixed Sun 4–10pm.

The Sanctuary 12 Floral St, WC2 ☎ 0845 521 4567, ⓦ sanctuary.com; ⊖ Covent Garden. Women-only spa in the centre of London: the interior is filled with lush tropical plants. It's a major investment at over £50 for day/ eve membership, but your money gets you unlimited use of the pool, jacuzzi, sauna and steam room, plus one sunbed session. Mon, Wed & Fri 9.30am–10pm, Tues & Thurs 9.30am–6pm, Sat & Sun 9.30am–8pm.

WHITE WATER SPORTS

Lee Valley White Water Centre Station Rd, Waltham Cross ☎ 0845 677 0606, ⓦ gowhitewater.co.uk; Waltham Cross train station from Liverpool Street. Thanks to the 2012 Olympics, London has a whitewater rafting centre on the edge of the city, where you can shoot the rapids in a raft, canoe or kayak. Rafting starts at around £50; canoe/kayak paddling from £25. Wed–Sun 10am–6pm; longer hours in summer.

DIANA MEMORIAL PLAYGROUND

Kids' London

London is a great place for children and it needn't overly strain the parental pocket. Buskers and jugglers provide free entertainment at Covent Garden (see p.130) and the South Bank (see p.214), where a traffic-free riverside walk stretches from the London Eye to Tower Bridge. And if you don't fancy the walk, plenty of boats stop off at piers along the way (see p.23). The spread of children's shows is at its best during school holidays, and at Christmas there's a glut of traditional British pantomimes, stage shows based on folk stories or fairy tales, invariably featuring a showbiz star, and often with an undercurrent of innuendo for the adults. If that's too passive, there are plenty of indoor play centres where kids can burn off excess energy. And of course, London Zoo (p.286) and the Aquarium (see p.219) are sure-fire winners.

THEATRE, PUPPETRY AND CIRCUSES

Shows that appeal to children play in the West End all the time. What follows is a pretty selective rundown of theatre, puppetry and circuses that are consistently aimed at kids.

Half Moon Young People's Theatre 43 White Horse Rd, E1 ☎020 7709 8900, ⓦhalfmoon.org.uk; Limehouse DLR or ⊖ Stepney Green. Well-established theatre that hosts touring youth shows, puts on its own productions and runs a programme of workshops and theatre sessions for over-5s. Oct–April Sat 11.30am & 2pm; all tickets £6.

Little Angel Puppet Theatre 14 Dagmar Passage, off Cross St, N1 ☎020 7226 1787, ⓦlittleangeltheatre.com; ⊖ Angel. Puppet theatre, which specializes in table-top, rod and glove puppetry, with shows usually on Saturdays and Sundays at 11am and 2pm. Extra performances during holidays. Adults £12, children £10. All tickets £5 on Fridays.

Polka Theatre 240 The Broadway, SW19 ☎020 8543 4888, ⓦpolkatheatre.com; ⊖ Wimbledon or South Wimbledon. Aimed at kids aged up to 12, this is a specially designed junior arts centre, with two theatres, a playground, a café and a toyshop. Storytellers, puppeteers and mime artists make regular appearances. Tickets from £10.

Puppet Theatre Barge Little Venice, W2 ☎020 7249 6876, ☎07836 202745, ⓦpuppetbarge.com; ⊖ Warwick Avenue. Wonderfully imaginative string marionette shows on a unique fifty-seat barge moored in Little Venice from October to July, and at Richmond in August and September. Shows start around 3pm at weekends and in the holidays. Adults £10, children £8.50.

Unicorn Theatre 147 Tooley St, SE1 ☎020 7645 0560, ⓦunicorntheatre.com; ⊖ London Bridge. The oldest professional children's theatre in London lives in modern, purpose-built premises near City Hall in Southwark. Shows run the gamut from storytelling sessions and traditional plays to creative-writing workshops and mime and puppetry. Tickets from £10.

Zippo's Circus ☎0871 210 2100, ⓦzippos.co.uk. Zippo's Circus performs in and around London for much of the year. It's a totally traditional, big-top circus offering a variety of standard acts from clowning and tightrope walking to acrobatic budgies and equine tricks, compered by an old-fashioned ringmaster. Adults £7–20, children £5–16.

PARKS

Right in the centre of the city, there are plentiful green spaces, such as **St James's Park** (see p.67) and **Regent's Park** (see p.283), providing playgrounds and ample room for general mayhem, as well as a diverting array of city wildlife. If you want something more unusual than ducks and squirrels, head for one of London's several **city farms** (see p.442), which provide urbanites with a free taste of country life. Below is a list of the best parks and playgrounds.

Battersea Park Albert Bridge Rd, SW11 ☎020 8871 7539 (playground), ⓦbatterseapark.org; Battersea Park or Queenstown Road train station from Victoria. The park has an excellent free adventure playground, a boating lake and a children's zoo (see p.271). Park: daily 8am to dusk; free. Playground: phone for times; free. Zoo: summer daily 10am–5.30pm; winter closes 4.30pm; adults £8.75, children under 16 £6.50.

Camley Street Natural Park 12 Camley St, NW1 ☎020 7833 2311, ⓦwildlondon.org.uk; ⊖ King's Cross St Pancras. Canalside wildlife haven, run by the London Wildlife Trust, with pond dipping and a good info centre. See p.129. Summer daily 10am–5.30pm; winter closes 4.30pm. Free.

Coram's Fields 93 Guilford St, WC1 ☎020 7837 6138, ⓦcoramsfields.org; ⊖ Russell Square. Very useful, centrally located playground with lots of water and sand play plus mini-farm with hens, rabbits, sheep, goats and ducks.

32

MUSEUMS

Museums are an obvious diversion and many of the big museums are free of charge. The **Science Museum** (see p.257), the **Natural History Museum** (see p.260) and the **National Maritime Museum** (see p.317), in particular, have hi-tech, hands-on sections that will keep young kids busy for hours, and they might even learn something while they're at it. At the other end of the scale, the **London Dungeon** (see p.232) and **Madame Tussauds**, with its infamous Chamber of Horrors (see p.93), remain very popular with teenagers, but are among the most expensive sights in the entire city.

Smaller museums specifically designed with children in mind include the **Horniman Museum** (see p.313), which houses an aquarium, and the **Kew Bridge Steam Museum**, which runs a miniature steam train on Sundays throughout the summer (see p.333). There are also museums devoted to childhood and toys, from the atmospheric **Pollock's Toy Museum** (see p.104) to the much larger V&A outpost, the **Museum of Childhood** (see p.202).

MUSIC

There are plenty of **free music** options worth looking out for: the Barbican (see p.413) puts on excellent weekend foyer concerts; the Royal Festival Hall at the South Bank (see p.414) and the National Theatre (see p.418) run regular seasonal festivals where you can catch some world-class music. In addition, most of the established orchestras run special **children's concerts**: look out for the London Philharmonic Orchestra (ⓦlpo.co.uk), London Symphony Orchestra (ⓦlso.co.uk) and National Children's Orchestra (ⓦnco.org.uk).

Adults admitted only if accompanied by a child. Veggie café (March–Nov). See p.122. Daily 9am to dusk. Free.

Hampstead Heath NW3 ☎020 7485 4491, ⓦcityoflondon.gov.uk; ⊖ Hampstead, Gospel Oak or Hampstead Heath train station. Nine hundred acres of grassland and woodland, with superb views of the city. Excellent kite-flying potential, too, and plenty of playgrounds, sports facilities, music events and fun days throughout the summer. See p.302. Open daily 24hr.

Hyde Park/Kensington Gardens W8 ☎0300 061 2000, ⓦroyalparks.org.uk; ⊖ Hyde Park Corner, Knightsbridge, Lancaster Gate or Queensway. Hyde Park is central London's main open space and features the Diana Fountain in which the kids can dip their feet; in Kensington Gardens (daily 6am to dusk), adjoining its western side, you can find the famous Peter Pan statue and a groovy

playground also dedicated to Princess Diana. See p.238. Daily 5am–midnight.

Kew Gardens Richmond, Surrey ☎020 8332 5000, ⓦkew.org; ⊖ Kew Gardens. Come here for the edifying open spaces, though the glasshouses usually go down well too, and there's a small aquarium in the basement of the Palm House. Adults £14.50, children under 17 free. See p.336. Daily 9.30am–5.30pm or dusk.

Richmond Park Richmond, Surrey ☎0300 061 2200, ⓦroyalparks.org.uk; ⊖ Richmond or Richmond train station from Waterloo. A fabulous stretch of countryside, with opportunities for duck-feeding, deer-spotting, mushroom-hunting and cycling. Playground situated near Petersham Gate or toddlers' play area near Kingston Gate. See p.343. Daily: March–Sept 7am–dusk; Oct–Feb 7.30am–dusk.

CITY FARMS

Free fun is available at (most of) the city's various working farms, the majority of them located in London's East End. The website ⓦfarmgarden.org.uk is also worth a visit for details of other, smaller gardens and wildlife havens in London.

Brooks Farm Skelton's Lane Park, Leyton, E10 ☎020 8539 4278, ⓦbrooks-farm.org; ⊖ Leyton. Very much a community resource, this farm has cows, pigs, goats, Shetland ponies, llamas and a pygmy hedgehog, as well as its own allotments, an adventure playground and lots of activities. Tues–Sun: April–Oct 10.30am–5pm; Nov–March 9.30am–4pm. Free.

Freightliners Farm Sheringham Rd, N7 ☎020 7609 0467, ⓦfreightlinersfarm.org.uk; ⊖ Highbury & Islington or Holloway Road. Small farm with a non-slaughtering policy, with goats, hens, ducks, turkeys, guinea fowl, geese, sheep, pigeons, bees and giant rabbits. Farm shop and lovely veggie *Strawbale* café (Thurs–Sun only). Tues–Sun 10am–4pm. Free.

Hackney City Farm 1a Goldsmith's Row, E2 ☎020 7729 6381, ⓦhackneycityfarm.co.uk; Hoxton Overground. Converted brewery that's now a small city farm housing calves, sheep, pigs, hens, guinea pigs, ducks, geese, rabbits, bees and Larry the Donkey. Food forest for foraging in and the original, superb *Frizzante* café. Tues–Sun 10am–4.30pm. Free.

Kentish Town City Farm 1 Cressfield Close, off Grafton Rd, NW5 ☎020 7916 5421, ⓦktcityfarm.org.uk;

⊖ Chalk Farm or Kentish Town. Five acres of farmland with cows, pigs, goats, sheep and chickens. Daily activities for kids, including pony rides at the weekend (£2). Daily 9am–5pm. Free.

Mudchute City Farm Pier St, E14 ☎020 7515 5901, ⓦmudchute.org; Mudchute, Crossharbour or Island Gardens DLR. One of the largest city farms in Europe, with great views of Canary Wharf and over two hundred farmyard fowl and animals, llamas, alpacas, an aviary, an equestrian centre and a pets' corner with chipmunks, gerbils, ferrets and the like. Fantastic *Frizzante* café (closed Mon), too. Daily 9am–5pm. Free.

Spitalfields City Farm Buxton St, E1 ☎020 7247 8762, ⓦspitalfieldscityfarm.org; Shoreditch High Street Overground. Another tiny East End farm (with a shop and café) housing sheep, donkeys, goats, pigs, ducks, geese, rabbits and guinea pigs. Also runs a propagation scheme, an organic vegetable garden and an eco-chic café and market every Sunday. Tues–Sun: April–Sept 10am–4.30pm; Oct–March 10am–4pm. Free.

Stepney City Farm Stepney Way, E1 ☎020 7790 8204, ⓦstepneycityfarm.org; ⊖ Stepney Green. A working farm (and rural haven) in the East End, with cows, pigs, goats, sheep, donkeys, rabbits, ferrets and guinea pigs. Also has a collection of birds of prey, a café and farm shop, and a Saturday farmers' market. Tues–Sun 10am–4pm. Free.

KIDS GO FREE

Don't underestimate the value of London's **public transport** as a source of fun – and remember kids travel free (see p.22). **The Underground** is a buzz for a lot of kids, and you can get your bearings while entertaining your offspring by installing them in the front seats on the top deck of a red **double-decker bus**. The driverless **Docklands Light Railway** (see p.22) is another source of amusement, too – grab a seat at the front of the train and pretend to be the driver.

Surrey Docks Farm Rotherhithe St, SE16 ☎020 7231 1010, ⓦsurreydocksfarm.org.uk; Surrey Quays Overground. A corner of southeast London set aside for cattle, goats, sheep, donkeys, chickens, pigs, ducks, ferrets, rabbits, guinea pigs and bees in hives, with a smithy, a dairy and the really top notch *Frizzante* café (Tues–Sun). Daily 10am–5pm; closes 4pm in winter; £3.

Vauxhall City Farm 165 Tyers St, SE11; ☎020 7582 4204, ⓦvauxhallcityfarm.org; ⊖ Vauxhall. Little city farm with sheep, goats, pigs, ferrets, rabbits, guinea pigs, ducks, hens, llamas, Shetland ponies, a horse and Waffle the goose. Wool spinning every Sat, and other activities at weekends and on holidays. Wed–Sun 10.30am–4pm. Free.

INDOOR ADVENTURE PLAY CENTRES AND SWIMMING POOLS

Most local leisure centres offer "soft play" sessions for pre-school toddlers during the week. Listed below are some of the bigger operations which also cater for older children.

Bramley's Big Adventure 136 Bramley Rd, W10 ☎020 8960 1515, ⓦbramleysbig.co.uk; ⊖ Latimer Road or Ladbroke Grove. Indoor play centre with sophisticated equipment suitable for children up to 11 and magazines for bored adults. £4–6 for 2hr or more. Mon–Fri 10am–6pm, Sat & Sun 10am–6.30pm.

Discover 385–387 Stratford High St, E15 ☎020 8536 5555, ⓦdiscover.org.uk; ⊖ Stratford. A hands-on interactive creative learning centre with a great outdoor play garden, aimed at story-building for under-11s. £4.50. Tues–Fri 10am–5pm, Sat & Sun 11am–5pm.

Waterfront Leisure Centre High St, Woolwich, SE18 ☎020 8317 5000, ⓦbetter.org.uk; Woolwich Arsenal DLR. Massive adventure swimming pool with 100ft-plus slide, wave machine, waterfall and all the usual aquatic high-jinks. Under-3s free; tickets from around £4. Mon–Fri 7am–10.30pm, Sat & Sun 8am–9.30pm; adventure pool more limited hours.

32

THE GREAT FIRE OF LONDON

Contexts

History

The citizens of London are universally held up for admiration and renown for the elegance of their manners and dress, and the delights of their tables…The only plagues of London are the immoderate drinking of fools and the frequency of fires. William Fitzstephen, companion of Thomas Becket

Conflagrations and drunkenness certainly feature strongly in London's complex two-thousand-year history. What follows is a highly compressed account featuring riots and revolutions, plagues, fires, slum clearances, lashings of gin, Boris Johnson and the London people. For more detailed histories, see our book recommendations (see p.462).

Roman Londinium

Although there is evidence of scattered Celtic settlements along the Thames, no firm proof exists to show that central London was permanently settled before the arrival of the Romans. **Julius Caesar** led two small cross-Channel incursions in 55 and 54 BC, but it wasn't until nearly a century later, in **43 AD**, that a full-scale invasion force of some forty thousand Roman troops landed in Kent. Britain's rumoured mineral wealth was certainly one motive behind the Roman invasion, but the immediate spur was the need of Emperor Claudius, who owed his power to the army, for an easy military triumph. The Romans, under Aulus Plautius, defeated the main Celtic tribe of southern Britain, the Catuvellauni, on the Medway, southeast of London, crossed the Thames and then set up camp to await the triumphant arrival of Claudius, his elephants and the Praetorian Guard.

It's now thought that the site of this first Roman camp was, in fact, in Westminster – the lowest fordable point on the Thames – and not in what is now the City. However, around 50 AD, when the Romans decided to establish the permanent military camp of **Londinium** here, they chose a point further downstream, building a bridge some 50yd east of today's London Bridge. London became the hub of the Roman road system, but it was not the Romans' principal colonial settlement, which remained at **Camulodunum** (modern Colchester) to the northeast.

In 60 AD, the East Anglian people, known as the Iceni, rose up against the invaders under their queen **Boudicca** (or Boadicea) and sacked Camulodunum, slaughtering most of the legion sent from Lindum (Lincoln) and making their way to the ill-defended town of Londinium. According to archeological evidence, Londinium was burnt to the ground and, according to the Roman historian Tacitus, whose father-in-law was in Britain at the time (and later served as its governor), the inhabitants were "massacred, hanged, burned and crucified". The Iceni were eventually defeated, and Boudicca committed suicide (62 AD).

In the aftermath, Londinium emerged as the new commercial and administrative (though not military) **capital of Britannia**, and was endowed with a military fort for around a thousand troops, an imposing basilica and forum, a governor's palace,

122	200	296	312
Emperor Hadrian visits Londinium	The Romans build a defensive wall around the city	Emperor Constantius ends the civil war in Britain and northern Gaul	Christianity becomes the state religion throughout the Roman Empire

LEGENDS

Until Elizabethan times, most Londoners believed that London had been founded around 1000 BC as New Troy or *Troia Nova* (later corrupted to Trinovantum), capital of Albion (aka Britain), by the Trojan prince **Brutus**. At the time, according to medieval chronicler Geoffrey of Monmouth, Britain was "uninhabited except for a few giants", several of whom the Trojans subsequently killed. They even captured one called Goemagog (more commonly referred to as Gogmagog), who was believed to be the son of Poseidon, Greek god of the sea, and whom one of the Trojans, called Corineus, challenged to unarmed combat and defeated.

For some reason, by late medieval times, Gogmagog had become better known as two giants, **Gog and Magog**, whose statues can still be seen in the Guildhall (see p.169) and on the clock outside St Dunstan-in-the-West (see p.155). According to Geoffrey of Monmouth's elaborate genealogical tree, Brutus is related to Leir (of Shakespeare's *King Lear*), Arthur (of the Round Table) and eventually to **King Lud**. Around 70 BC, Lud is credited with fortifying New Troy and renaming it *Caer Ludd* (Lud's Town), which was later corrupted to Caerlundein and finally London.

temples, bathhouses and an amphitheatre (see p.171). Archeological evidence suggests that Londinium was at its most prosperous and populous from around 80 AD to 120 AD, during which time it is thought to have evolved into the empire's fifth largest city north of the Alps.

Between 150 AD and 400 AD, however, London appears to have sheltered less than half the former population, probably due to economic decline. Nevertheless, it remained strategically and politically important and, as an imperial outpost, actually appears to have benefited from the chaos that engulfed the rest of the empire during much of the third century. In those uncertain times, **fortifications** were built, three miles long, 20ft high and 9ft thick, whose Kentish ragstone walls can still be seen near today's Museum of London (see p.169), home to many of the city's most significant Roman finds.

In 406 AD, the Roman army in Britain mutinied for the last time and invaded Gaul under the self-proclaimed Emperor Constantine III. The empire was on its last legs, and the Romans were never in a position to return, officially abandoning the city in **410 AD** (when Rome was sacked by the Visigoths), and leaving the country and its chief city at the mercy of the marauding Saxon pirates, who had been making increasingly persistent raids on the coast since the middle of the previous century.

Saxon Lundenwic and the Danes

Roman London appears to have been more or less abandoned from the first couple of decades of the fifth century until the ninth century. Instead, the **Anglo-Saxon** invaders, who controlled most of southern England by the sixth century, appear to have settled, initially at least, to the west of the Roman city. When Augustine was sent to reconvert Britain to Christianity, the Saxon city of **Lundenwic** was considered important enough to be granted a bishopric in 604, though it was Canterbury, not London, that was chosen as the seat of the Primate of England. Nevertheless, trade flourished once more during this period, as attested by the Venerable Bede, who wrote of London in 730 as "the mart of many nations resorting to it by land and sea".

410	604	878	1066
The Romans withdraw from Britain	Mellitus, the first Bishop of London, begins the first St Paul's Cathedral	King Alfred defeats the Vikings and England is divided between Danelaw and Wessex	William the Conqueror defeats King Harold at the Battle of Hastings

In 841 and 851 London suffered Danish Viking attacks, and it may have been in response to these raids that the Saxons decided to reoccupy the walled Roman city. By 871 the **Danes** were confident enough to attack and established London as their winter base, but in 886 Alfred the Great, King of Wessex, recaptured the city, rebuilt the walls and formally re-established London as a fortified town and a trading port. After a lull, the Vikings returned once more during the reign of Ethelred the Unready (978–1016), attacking in 994, 1009 and 1013. Finally the Danes, under Swein Forkbeard, captured London, and Swein was declared King of England. He reigned for just five weeks before he died, allowing Ethelred to reclaim the city in 1014, with help from King Olaf of Norway.

In 1016, following the death of Ethelred, and his son, Edmund Ironside, the Danish leader Cnut (or Canute), son of Swein, became King of All England, and made London the **national capital** (in preference to the Wessex base of Winchester), a position it has held ever since. Danish rule lasted only 26 years, however, and with the death of Cnut's two sons, the English throne returned to the House of Wessex, and to Ethelred's exiled son, **Edward the Confessor** (1042–66). Edward moved the court and church upstream to Thorney Island (or the Isle of Brambles), where he built a splendid new palace so that he could oversee construction of his "West Minster" (later to become Westminster Abbey). Edward was too weak to attend the official consecration and died just ten days later: he is buried in the great church he founded, where his shrine became a place of pilgrimage for centuries. Of greater political and social significance, however, was his geographical separation of power, with royal government based in the **City of Westminster**, while the **City of London** remained the commercial centre.

1066 and all that

On his deathbed, in the new year of 1066, the celibate Edward made **Harold**, Earl of Wessex, his appointed successor. Having crowned himself in the new abbey – establishing a tradition that continues to this day – Harold went on to defeat his brother Tostig (who was in cahoots with the Norwegians), but was himself defeated by **William of Normandy** (aka William the Conqueror) and his invading Norman army at the Battle of Hastings. On Christmas Day of 1066, William crowned himself king in Westminster Abbey. Elsewhere in England, the Normans ruthlessly suppressed all opposition, but in London, William granted the City a charter guaranteeing to preserve the privileges it had enjoyed under Edward. However, as an insurance policy, he also built three forts in the city, of which the sole remnant is the White Tower, now the nucleus of the **Tower of London**.

Over the next few centuries, the City waged a continuous struggle with the monarchy for a degree of self-government and independence. After all, when there was a fight over the throne, the support of London's wealth and manpower could be decisive, as **King Stephen** (1135–54) discovered, when Londoners attacked his cousin and rival for the throne, Mathilda, daughter of Henry I, preventing her from being crowned at Westminster. Again, in 1191, when the future **King John** (1199–1216) was tussling with William Longchamp over the kingdom during the absence of Richard the Lionheart (1189–99), it was the Londoners who made sure Longchamp remained

1089	1189	1209	1215
Cluniac Monastery established in Bermondsey	Henry Fitz-Ailwin becomes the first Mayor of London	Old London Bridge completed	Magna Carta signed – Mayor of London is one of the signatories

cooped up in the Tower. For this particular favour, London was granted the right to elect its own sheriff, or lord mayor, an office that was officially acknowledged in the Magna Carta of 1215.

Occasionally, of course, Londoners backed the wrong side, as they did when they turned up at Old St Paul's to accept **Prince Louis of France** (the future Louis VIII) as ruler of England during the barons' rebellion against King John in 1216, and again with Simon de Montfort, when he was engaged in civil war with **Henry III** (1216–72) during the 1260s. As a result, the City found itself temporarily stripped of its privileges. In any case, London was chiefly of importance to the medieval kings as a source of wealth, and traditionally it was to the Jewish community, which arrived in 1066 with William the Conqueror, that the sovereign turned for a loan. By the second half of the thirteenth century, however, the Jews had been squeezed dry, and in 1290, after a series of increasingly bloody attacks, **London's Jews** were expelled by Edward I (1272–1307), who turned instead to the City's Italian merchants for financial assistance.

From the Black Death to the Wars of the Roses

London backed the right side in the struggle between Edward II (1307–27) and his queen, Isabella, who, along with her lover Mortimer, succeeded in deposing the king. The couple's son Edward III (1327–77) was duly crowned, and London enjoyed a period of relative peace and prosperity, thanks to the wealth generated by the wool trade. All this was cut short, however, by the arrival of the Europe-wide bubonic plague outbreak, known as the **Black Death**, in 1348. This disease, carried by black rats and transmitted to humans by flea bites, wiped out something like two-thirds of the capital's 75,000 population in the space of two years. Other epidemics followed in 1361, 1369 and 1375, creating a volatile economic situation that was worsened by the financial strains imposed on the capital by having to bankroll the country's involvement in the Hundred Years' War with France.

Matters came to a head with the introduction of the poll tax, a head tax imposed in the 1370s on all men regardless of means. During the ensuing **Peasants' Revolt** of 1381, London's citizens opened the City gates to Wat Tyler's Kentish rebels and joined in the lynching of the archbishop, plus countless rich merchants and clerics. Tyler was then lured to meet the boy-king Richard II at Smithfield, just outside the City, where he was murdered by Lord Mayor Walworth, who was subsequently knighted for his treachery. Tyler's supporters were fobbed off with promises of political changes that never came, as Richard unleashed a wave of repression and retribution.

After the Peasants' Revolt, the next serious disturbance was **Jack Cade's Revolt**, which took place in 1450. An army of 25,000 Kentish rebels – including gentry, clergy and craftsmen – defeated King Henry VI's forces at Sevenoaks, marched to Blackheath, withdrew temporarily and then eventually reached Southwark in early July. Having threatened to burn down London Bridge, the insurgents entered the City and spent three days wreaking vengeance on their enemies before being ejected. A subsequent attempt to enter the City via London Bridge was repulsed, and the army was dispersed with yet more false promises. The reprisals, which became known as the "harvest of heads", were as harsh as before – Cade himself was captured, killed and brought to the capital for dismemberment.

1290	1305	1337–1453	1380	1415
Jews expelled from London	William Wallace executed at Smithfield	Hundred Years' War	Chaucer's Canterbury Tales published	Henry V wins the Battle of Agincourt

JOHN WYCLIFFE AND THE LOLLARDS

Parallel with the social unrest of the 1370s were the demands for clerical reforms made by the scholar and heretic **John Wycliffe**, whose ideas were keenly taken up by Londoners. A fierce critic of the papacy and the monastic orders, Wycliffe produced the first translation of the Bible into English in 1380. He was tried for heresy at Lambeth Palace, and his followers, known as **Lollards**, were harshly persecuted. In 1415, the Council of Constance, which burned the Czech heretic Jan Hus at the stake, also ordered Wycliffe's body to be exhumed and burnt.

A decade later, the country was plunged into more widespread conflict during the so-called **Wars of the Roses**, the name now given to the strife between the cousins within the rival noble houses of Lancaster and York. Londoners wisely tended to sit on the fence throughout the conflict, only committing themselves in 1461, when they opened the gates to the Yorkist king Edward IV (1461–70 and 1471–83), thus helping him to depose the mad Henry VI (1422–61 and 1470–71). In 1470, Henry, who had spent five years in the Tower, was proclaimed king once more, only to be deposed again a year later, following Lancastrian defeats at the battles of Barnet and Tewkesbury.

Tudor London

The **Tudor** family, which with the coronation of **Henry VII** (1485–1509) emerged triumphant from the mayhem of the Wars of the Roses, reinforced London's pre-eminence during the sixteenth century, when the Tower of London and the royal palaces of Whitehall, St James's, Richmond, Greenwich, Hampton Court and Windsor provided the backdrop for the most momentous events of the period. At the same time, the city's population, which had remained constant at around fifty thousand since the Black Death, increased dramatically, trebling in size during the course of the century.

One of the crucial developments of the century was the English **Reformation**, the separation of the English Church from Rome, a split initially prompted not by doctrinal issues, but by the failure of Catherine of Aragon, first wife of **Henry VIII** (1509–47), to produce a male heir. In fact, prior to his desire to divorce Catherine, Henry, along with his lord chancellor, Cardinal Wolsey, had been zealously persecuting Protestants. However, when the Pope refused to annul Henry's marriage, Henry knew he could rely on a large amount of popular support, as anti-clerical feelings were running high. By contrast, Henry's new chancellor, Thomas More, wouldn't countenance divorce, and resigned in 1532. Henry then broke with Rome, appointed himself head of the English Church and demanded both citizens and clergy swear allegiance to him. Very few refused, though More was among them, becoming the country's first Catholic martyr with his execution in 1535.

Henry may have been the one who kickstarted the English Reformation, but he was a religious conservative, and in the last ten years of his reign he succeeded in executing as many Protestants as he did Catholics. Religious turmoil only intensified in the decade following Henry's death. First, Henry's sickly son, **Edward VI** (1547–53), pursued a staunchly anti-Catholic policy. By the end of his short reign, London's churches had lost their altars, their paintings, their relics and virtually all their statuary. After an abortive attempt to secure the succession of Edward's Protestant cousin, Lady Jane

1422	1455–85	1476	1483
Riot ensues after victory of City of London over the City of Westminster in a wrestling match	Wars of the Roses	William Caxton sets up the first printing press in the precincts of Westminster Abbey	Death of the Princes in the Tower, Edward V and his brother the Duke of York

---

DISSOLUTION OF THE MONASTERIES

Henry's VIII's most far-reaching act was his **Dissolution of the Monasteries**; a programme to close down the country's monasteries and appropriate their assets, commenced in 1536 in order to bump up the royal coffers. Medieval London boasted over a hundred places of worship and some twenty religious houses, with two-thirds of the land in the City belonging to the Church. The Dissolution changed the entire fabric of both the city and the country: London's property market was suddenly flooded with confiscated estates, which were quickly snapped up and redeveloped by the Tudor nobility.

Grey, the religious pendulum swung the other way for the next five years with the accession of "**Bloody Mary**" (1553–58). This time, it was Protestants who were martyred with abandon at Tyburn and Smithfield.

Despite all the religious strife, the Tudor economy remained in good health for the most part, reaching its height in the reign of **Elizabeth I** (1558–1603), when the piratical exploits of seafarers Walter Raleigh, Francis Drake, Martin Frobisher and John Hawkins helped to map out the world for English commerce. London's commercial success was epitomized by the millionaire merchant Thomas Gresham, who erected the **Royal Exchange** in 1571, establishing London as the premier world trade market.

The 45 years of Elizabeth's reign also witnessed the efflorescence of a specifically **English Renaissance**, especially in the field of literature, which reached its apogee in the brilliant careers of **Christopher Marlowe**, **Ben Jonson** and **William Shakespeare**. The presses of **Fleet Street**, established a century earlier by William Caxton's apprentice Wynkyn de Worde, ensured London's position as a centre for the printed word. Beyond the jurisdiction of the City censors, in the entertainment district of Southwark, whorehouses, animal-baiting pits and theatres flourished. The carpenter-cum-actor James Burbage designed the first purpose-built playhouse in 1576, eventually rebuilding it south of the river as the **Globe Theatre**, where Shakespeare premiered many of his works. The theatre has since been reconstructed (see p.228).

From Gunpowder Plot to Civil War

On Elizabeth's death in 1603, James VI of Scotland became **James I** (1603–25) of England, thereby uniting the two crowns and marking the beginning of the **Stuart dynasty**. His intention of exercising religious tolerance after the anti-Catholicism of Elizabeth's reign was thwarted by the public outrage that followed the **Gunpowder Plot** of 1605, when Guy Fawkes and a group of Catholic conspirators were discovered attempting to blow up the king at the state opening of Parliament. James, who clung to the medieval notion of the divine right of kings, inevitably clashed with the landed gentry who dominated Parliament, and tensions between Crown and Parliament were worsened by his persecution of the Puritans, an extreme but increasingly powerful Protestant group.

Under James's successor, **Charles I** (1625–49), the animosity between Crown and Parliament came to a head. From 1629 to 1640 Charles ruled without the services of Parliament, but was forced to recall it when he ran into problems in Scotland, where he was attempting to subdue the Presbyterians. Faced with extremely antagonistic MPs,

1512	1534	1553–58	1561	1571
Royal Dockyards established in Woolwich	Henry VIII breaks with the Roman Catholic Church	Queen Mary reinstates Catholicism	Lightning strikes Old St Paul's and the spire falls to the ground	The opening of the Royal Exchange in the City

Charles attempted unsuccessfully to arrest several of their number at Westminster. Acting on a tip-off, the MPs fled by river to the City, which sided with Parliament. Charles withdrew to Nottingham, where he raised his standard, the opening military act of the **Civil War**. London was the key to victory, and as a **Parliamentarian stronghold** it came under attack almost immediately from Royalist forces. Having defeated the Parliamentary troops to the west of London at **Brentford** in November 1642, the way was open for Charles to take the capital. Londoners turned out in numbers to defend their city, some 24,000 assembling at **Turnham Green**. A stand-off ensued, Charles hesitated and in the end withdrew to Reading, thus missing his greatest chance of victory. A complex system of fortifications was thrown up around London, but was never put to the test. In the end, the capital remained intact throughout the war, which culminated in the execution of the king outside Whitehall's Banqueting House in January 1649.

For the next eleven years England was a **Commonwealth** – at first a true republic, then, after 1653, a Protectorate under **Oliver Cromwell**, who was ultimately as impatient of Parliament and as arbitrary as Charles had been. London found itself in the grip of the Puritans' zealous laws, which closed down all theatres, enforced observance of the Sabbath and banned the celebration of Christmas, which was considered a papist superstition.

Plague and fire

Just as London proved Charles I's undoing, so the ecstatic reception given to **Charles II** (1660–85) helped ease the **Restoration** of the monarchy in 1660. The "Merry Monarch" immediately caught the mood of the public by opening up the theatres, and he encouraged the sciences by helping the establishment of the **Royal Society** for Improving Natural Knowledge, whose founder members included **Christopher Wren**, **John Evelyn** and **Isaac Newton**.

The good times that rolled in the early period of Charles's reign came to an abrupt end with the onset of the **Great Plague** of 1665. Epidemics of bubonic plague were nothing new to London – there had been major outbreaks in 1593, 1603, 1625, 1636 and 1647 – but the combination of a warm summer and the chronic overcrowding of the city proved calamitous in this instance. Those with money left the city (the court moved to Oxford), while the poorer districts outside the City were the hardest hit. The extermination of the city's dog and cat population – believed to be the source of the epidemic – only exacerbated the situation by allowing the flea-carrying rat population to explode. In September, the death toll peaked at twelve thousand a week, and in total an estimated hundred thousand lost their lives.

A cold snap in November extinguished the plague, but the following year London had to contend with yet another disaster, the **Great Fire** of 1666. As with the plague, outbreaks of fire were fairly commonplace in London, whose buildings were predominantly timber-framed, and whose streets were narrow, allowing fires to spread rapidly. However, this particular fire raged for five days and destroyed some four-fifths of the City of London (see box, p.452).

Within five years, nine thousand houses had been rebuilt with bricks and mortar (timber was banned), and fifty years later **Christopher Wren** had almost single-handedly

1588	1599	1605	1642–51	1643
Defeat of the Spanish Armada	Globe Theatre opens on Bankside	Gunpowder Plot foiled	Civil War	Cheapside Cross torn down by iconoclasts

THE GREAT FIRE

In the early hours of September 2, 1666, the **Great Fire** broke out at Farriner's, the king's bakery in Pudding Lane. The Lord Mayor refused to lose any sleep over it, dismissing it with the line "Pish! A woman might piss it out." Pepys was also roused from his bed, but saw no cause for alarm. Four days and four nights later, the Lord Mayor was found crying "like a fainting woman", and Pepys had fled, having famously buried his Parmesan cheese in the garden: the Fire had destroyed some four-fifths of the City of London, including 87 churches, 44 livery halls and 13,200 houses. The medieval city was no more.

Miraculously, there were only eight recorded fatalities, but one hundred thousand people were made homeless. "The hand of God upon us, a great wind and the season so very dry", was the verdict of the parliamentary report on the Fire, but Londoners preferred to blame Catholics and foreigners. The poor baker eventually "confessed" to being an agent of the pope and was executed, after which the following words, "but Popish frenzy, which wrought such horrors, is not yet quenched", were added to the Latin inscription on the Monument (see p.178), and only erased in 1830.

rebuilt all the City churches and completed the world's first purpose-built Protestant cathedral, **St Paul's**. Medieval London was no more, though the grandiose masterplans of Wren and other architects had to be rejected due to the legal intricacies of property rights within the City. The **Great Rebuilding**, as it was known, was one of London's most remarkable achievements – and all achieved in spite of a chronic lack of funds, a series of very severe winters and continuing wars against the Dutch.

Religious differences once again came to the fore with the accession of Charles's Catholic brother, **James II** (1685–88), who successfully put down the Monmouth Rebellion of 1685, but failed to halt the "Glorious Revolution" of 1688, which brought the Dutch king William of Orange to the throne, much to most people's relief. **William** (1689–1702) and his wife **Mary** (1689–95), daughter of James II, were made joint sovereigns, having agreed to a Bill of Rights defining the limitations of the monarch's power and the rights of his or her subjects. This, together with the Act of Settlement of 1701 – which among other things barred Catholics, or anyone married to one, from succession to the throne – made Britain the first country in the world to be governed by a **constitutional monarchy**, in which the roles of legislature and executive were separate and interdependent. A further development during the reign of **Anne** (1702–14), second daughter of James II, was the Act of Union of 1707, which united the English and Scottish parliaments.

Georgian London

When Queen Anne died childless in 1714 (despite having given birth seventeen times), the Stuart line ended, though pro-Stuart or Jacobite rebellions continued on and off until 1745. In accordance with the Act of Settlement, the succession passed to a non-English-speaking German, the Duke of Hanover, who became **George I** (1714–27) of England. As power leaked from the monarchy, the king ceased to attend cabinet meetings (which he couldn't understand anyway), his place being taken by his chief minister. Most prominent among these chief ministers or "prime ministers", as they

1645	1649	1649–60	1652
Archbishop of Canterbury, William Laud, executed on Tower Hill	King Charles I executed in Whitehall	The Commonwealth of England	Pasqua Rosée opens the first coffee house in London

THE GIN CRAZE

It's difficult to exaggerate the effects of the gin-drinking orgy which took place among the poorer sections of London's population between 1720 and 1751. At its height, **gin consumption** was averaging two pints a week for every man, woman and child, and the burial rate exceeded the baptism rate by more than 2:1. The origins of this lay in the country's enormous surplus of corn, which had to be sold in some form or another to keep the landowners happy. Deregulation of the distilling trade was Parliament's answer, thereby flooding the urban market with cheap, intoxicating liquor, which resulted in an enormous increase in crime, prostitution, **child mortality** and general misery among the poor. Papers in the Old Bailey archives relate a typical story of the period: a mother who "fetched her child from the workhouse, where it had just been 'new-clothed', for the afternoon. She strangled it and left it in a ditch in Bethnal Green in order to sell its clothes. The money was spent on gin." Eventually, in the face of huge vested interests, the government was forced to pass an Act in 1751 that restricted gin retailing and brought the epidemic to a halt.

became known, was **Robert Walpole**, the first politician to live at **10 Downing Street**, and effective ruler of the country from 1721 to 1742.

Meanwhile, London's expansion continued unabated. The shops of the newly developed **West End** stocked the most fashionable goods in the country, the volume of trade more than tripled and London's growing population – it was by now the largest city in the world, with a population rapidly approaching one million – created a huge market for food and other produce, as well as fuelling a building boom. In the City, the **Bank of England** – founded in 1694 to raise funds to conduct war against France – was providing a sound foundation for the economy. It could not, however, prevent the mania for financial speculation that resulted in the fiasco of the **South Sea Company**, which in 1720 sold shares in its monopoly of trade in the Pacific and along the east coast of South America. The "bubble" burst when the shareholders took fright at the extent of their own investments, and the value of the shares dropped to nothing, reducing many to penury and almost wrecking the government, which was saved only by the astute intervention of Walpole.

Wealthy though London was, it was also experiencing the worst mortality rates since records began in the reign of Henry VIII. Disease was rife in the overcrowded immigrant quarter of the East End and other slum districts, but the real killer during this period was **gin** (see box above).

Policing the metropolis was an increasing preoccupation for the government. It was proving a task far beyond the city's three thousand beadles, constables and nightwatchmen, who were, in any case, "old men chosen from the dregs of the people who have no other arms but a lantern and a pole", according to one French visitor. As a result, **crime** continued unabated throughout the eighteenth century, so that, in the words of Horace Walpole, one was "forced to travel even at noon as if one was going into battle". The government imposed draconian measures, introducing **capital punishment** for the most minor misdemeanours. The prison population swelled, transportations began and 1200 Londoners were hanged at Tyburn's gallows.

Despite such measures, and the passing of the Riot Act in 1715, rioting remained a popular pastime among the poorer classes in London. Anti-Irish riots had taken place

1665	1666	1694	1702	1710
The Great Plague kills 100,000 people	The Great Fire of London	Bank of England established	*The Daily Courant*, the world's first daily newspaper, published on Fleet Street	Completion of St Paul's Cathedral, designed by Christopher Wren

in 1736; in 1743 there were further riots in defence of cheap liquor; and in the 1760s there were more organized mobilizations by supporters of the great agitator **John Wilkes**, calling for political reform. The most serious insurrection of the lot, however, were the **Gordon Riots** of 1780, when up to fifty thousand Londoners went on a five-day rampage through the city. Although anti-Catholicism was the spark that lit the fire, the majority of the rioters' targets were chosen not for their religion but for their wealth. The most dramatic incidents took place at Newgate Prison, where thousands of inmates were freed, and at the Bank of England, which was saved only by the intervention of the military – and John Wilkes, of all people. The death toll was in excess of three hundred, 25 rioters were subsequently hanged, and further calls were made in Parliament for the establishment of a proper police force.

Nineteenth-century London

The **nineteenth century** witnessed the emergence of London as the capital of an empire that stretched across the globe. The world's largest enclosed **dock system** was built in the marshes to the east of the City, Tory reformer **Robert Peel** established the world's first civilian **police force** and the world's first public-transport network was created, with horse-buses, trains, trams and an underground railway.

The city's population grew dramatically from just over one million in 1801 (the first official census) to nearly seven million by 1901. **Industrialization** brought pollution and overcrowding, especially in the slums of the East End. Smallpox, measles, whooping cough and scarlet fever killed thousands of working-class families, as did the cholera outbreaks of 1832 and 1848–49. The **Poor Law** of 1834 formalized **workhouses** for the destitute, but these failed to alleviate the problem, in the end becoming little more than prison hospitals for the penniless. It is this era of slum life and huge social divides that Dickens evoked in his novels.

Architecturally, London was changing rapidly. **George IV** (1820–30), who became Prince Regent in 1811 during the declining years of his father, George III, instigated several grandiose projects that survive to this day. With the architect **John Nash**, he laid out London's first planned processional route, Regent Street, and a prototype garden city around **Regent's Park**. The Regent's Canal was driven through the northern fringe of the city, and Trafalgar Square began to take shape. The city already boasted the first secular public museum in the world, the **British Museum**, and in 1814 London's first public art gallery opened in the suburb of Dulwich, followed shortly afterwards by the National Gallery, founded in 1824. London finally got its own university, too, in 1826.

The accession of **Queen Victoria** (1837–1901) coincided with a period in which the country's international standing reached unprecedented heights, and as a result Victoria became as much a national icon as Elizabeth I had been. Though the intellectual achievements of Victoria's reign were immense – typified by the publication of Darwin's *The Origin of Species* in 1859 – the country saw itself above all as an imperial power founded on industrial and commercial prowess. Its spirit was perhaps best embodied by the great engineering feats of **Isambard Kingdom Brunel** and by the **Great Exhibition** of 1851, a display of manufacturing achievements from all over the world, which took place in the Crystal Palace, erected in Hyde Park.

1720	1750	1751	1759	1760
The South Sea Bubble causes financial ruin for many	Westminster Bridge opens	The Gin Act brings the decades of London's Gin Craze to an end	British Museum opens	City of London gates demolished

THE CHARTIST MOVEMENT IN LONDON

The **Chartist movement**, which campaigned for universal male suffrage (among other things), was much stronger in the industrialized north than in the capital, at least until the 1840s. Support for the movement reached its height in the revolutionary year of 1848. In March, some ten thousand Chartists occupied Trafalgar Square and held out against the police for two days. Then, on April 10, the Chartists organized a mass demonstration on Kennington Common. The government panicked and drafted in eighty thousand "special constables" to boost the capital's four thousand police officers, and troops were garrisoned around all public buildings. In the end, London was a long way off experiencing a revolution: the demo took place, but the planned march on Parliament was called off.

Despite being more than twice the size of Paris, London did not experience the political upheavals of the French capital – the terrorists who planned to wipe out the cabinet in the **1820 Cato Street Conspiracy** were the exception (see p.86). Mass demonstrations and the occasional minor fracas preceded the passing of the **1832 Reform Act**, which acknowledged the principle of popular representation (though few men and no women had the vote), but there was no real threat of revolution. London doubled its number of MPs in the new parliament, but its own administration remained dominated by the City oligarchy.

The birth of local government

The first tentative steps towards a cohesive form of metropolitan government were taken in 1855 with the establishment of the **Metropolitan Board of Works** (**MBW**). Its initial remit only covered sewerage, lighting and street maintenance, but it was soon extended to include gas, fire services, public parks and slum clearance. The achievements of the MBW – and in particular those of its chief engineer, **Joseph Bazalgette** – were immense, creating an underground sewer system (much of it still in use), improving transport routes and wiping out some of the city's more notorious slums. However, vested interests and resistance to reform from the City hampered the efforts of the MBW, which was also found to be involved in widespread malpractice.

In 1888 the **London County Council** (**LCC**) was established. It was the first directly elected London-wide government, though as ever the City held on jealously to its independence (and in 1899, the municipal boroughs were set up deliberately to undermine the power of the LCC). The arrival of the LCC coincided with an increase in working-class militancy within the capital. In 1884, 120,000 gathered in Hyde Park to support the ultimately unsuccessful London Government Bill, while a demonstration held in 1886 in Trafalgar Square in protest against unemployment ended in a riot through St James's. The following year the government banned any further demos, and the resultant protest brought even larger numbers to Trafalgar Square. The brutality of the police in breaking up this last demonstration led to its becoming known as "Bloody Sunday".

In 1888 the Bryant & May matchgirls won their landmark **strike action** over working conditions, a victory followed up the next year by further successful strikes by the gasworkers and dockers. Charles Booth published his seventeen-volume *Life and*

1780	1811	1812	1814	1826
Gordon Riots	London's population exceeds one million	Prime Minister Spencer Perceval becomes the first (and so far) last PM to be assassinated	The last Frost Fair takes place on the frozen River Thames	London University opens

Labour of the People of London in 1890, providing the first clear picture of the social fabric of the city and shaming the council into action. In the face of powerful vested interests – landlords, factory owners and private utility companies – the LCC's Liberal leadership attempted to tackle the enormous problems, partly by taking gas, water, electricity and transport into municipal ownership, a process that took several more decades to achieve. The LCC's ambitious housing programme was beset with problems, too. Slum clearances only exacerbated overcrowding, and the new dwellings were too expensive for those in greatest need. Rehousing the poor in the suburbs also proved unpopular, since there was a policy of excluding pubs, traditionally the social centre of working-class communities, from these developments.

While half of London struggled to make ends meet, the other half enjoyed the fruits of the richest nation in the world. Luxury establishments such as *The Ritz* and Harrods belong to this period, which was personified by the dissolute and complacent Prince of Wales, later **Edward VII** (1901–10). For the masses, too, there were new entertainments to be enjoyed: music halls boomed, public houses prospered and the circulation of populist newspapers such as the *Daily Mirror* topped one million. The first "Test" cricket match between England and Australia took place in 1880 at the Kennington Oval in front of twenty thousand spectators, and during the following 25 years nearly all of London's professional football clubs were founded.

From World War I to World War II

Public patriotism peaked at the outbreak of **World War I** (1914–18), with crowds cheering the troops off from Victoria and Waterloo stations, convinced the fighting would all be over by Christmas. In the course of the next four years London experienced its first aerial attacks, with Zeppelin raids leaving some 650 dead, but these were minor casualties in the context of a war that destroyed millions of lives and eradicated whatever remained of the majority's respect for the ruling classes.

At the war's end in 1918, the country's social fabric was changed drastically as the voting franchise was extended to all men aged 21 and over and to women of 30 or over. Equal voting rights for women – hard fought for by the radical **Suffragette** movement led by Emmeline Pankhurst and her daughters before the war – were only achieved in 1928, the year of Emmeline's death.

Between the wars, London's population increased dramatically, reaching close to nine million by 1939, and representing one-fifth of the country's population. In contrast to the nineteenth century, however, there was a marked shift in population out into the **suburbs**. Some took advantage of the new "model dwellings" of LCC estates in places such as Dagenham in the east, though far more settled in "Metroland", the sprawling new suburban districts that followed the extension of the Underground out into northwest London.

In 1924 the **British Empire Exhibition** was held, with the intention of emulating the success of the Great Exhibition. Some 27 million people visited the show, but its success couldn't hide the tensions that had been simmering since the end of the war. In 1926, a wage dispute between the miners' unions and their bosses developed into the **General Strike**. For nine days, more than half a million workers stayed away from work, until the government called in the army and thousands of volunteers to break the strike.

1836	1851	1858	1863
The first railway is built in London between London Bridge and Greenwich	Great Exhibition held in Hyde Park	The Great Stink when the smell of untreated waste in the Thames reached an unprecedented level	The first section of the Underground opens between Paddington and Farringdon

THE BLITZ

The Luftwaffe bombing of London in World War II – commonly known as the **Blitz** – began on September 7, 1940, when in one night alone some 430 Londoners lost their lives, and over 1600 were seriously injured. It continued for 57 consecutive nights, then intermittently until the final and most devastating attack on the night of May 10, 1941, when 550 planes dropped over one hundred thousand incendiaries and hundreds of explosive bombs in a matter of hours. The death toll that night was over 1400, bringing the total killed during the Blitz to between twenty thousand and thirty thousand, with some 230,000 homes wrecked. Along with the East End, the City was particularly badly hit: in a single raid on December 29 (dubbed the "Second Fire of London"), 1400 fires broke out across the Square Mile. Some say the Luftwaffe left St Paul's standing as a navigation aid, but it came close to destruction when a bomb landed near the southwest tower; luckily the bomb didn't go off, and it was successfully removed to the Hackney marshes where the 100ft-wide crater left by its detonation is still visible.

The authorities were ready to build mass graves for potential victims, but were unable to provide adequate air-raid shelters to prevent widespread carnage. The corrugated steel **Anderson shelters** issued by the government were of use to only one in four London households – those with gardens in which to bury them. Around 180,000 made use of the tube, despite initial government reluctance, by simply buying a ticket and staying below ground. The cheery photos of singing and dancing in the Underground which the censors allowed to be published tell nothing of the stale air, rats and lice that folk had to contend with. And even the tube stations couldn't withstand a direct hit, as occurred at Bank in January 1941, when over a hundred died. The vast majority of Londoners – some sixty percent – simply hid under the sheets and prayed.

The economic situation deteriorated even further after the crash of the New York Stock Exchange in 1929, with unemployment in Britain reaching over three million in 1931. The Jarrow Marchers, the most famous protesters of the **Depression** years, shocked London on their arrival in 1936. In the same year thousands of British fascists tried to march through the predominantly Jewish East End, only to be stopped in the so-called **Battle of Cable Street** (see p.194). The end of the year brought a crisis within the Royal Family, too, when Edward VIII abdicated following his decision to marry Wallis Simpson, a twice-divorced American. His brother, **George VI** (1936–52), took over.

There were few public displays of patriotism with the outbreak of **World War II** (1939–45), and even fewer preparations were made against the likelihood of aerial bombardment. The most significant step was the evacuation of six hundred thousand of London's most vulnerable citizens (mostly children), but around half that number had drifted back to the capital by the Christmas of 1939, the midpoint of the "phoney war". The Luftwaffe's bombing campaign, known as the **Blitz** (see box above), lasted from September 1940 to May 1941. Further carnage was caused towards the end of the war by the pilotless V-1 "doodlebugs" and V-2 rockets, which caused another twenty thousand casualties.

Postwar London

The end of the war in 1945 was followed by a general election, which brought a landslide victory for the Labour Party under **Clement Attlee**. The Attlee government

1908	1911	1926	1936
London hosts the Olympic Games and Britain wins the most medals	London population exceeds seven million	The General Strike lasts for nine days	Police, fascists and anti-fascist protesters clash in the Battle of Cable Street in the East End

created the **welfare state**, and initiated a radical programme of **nationalization**, which brought the gas, electricity, coal, steel and iron industries under state control, along with the inland transport services. London itself was left with a severe accommodation crisis, with some eighty percent of the housing stock damaged to some degree. In response, prefabricated houses were erected all over the city, some of which were to remain occupied for well over forty years. The LCC also began building huge housing estates on many of the city's numerous bombsites, an often misconceived strategy which ran in tandem with the equally disastrous New Towns policy of central government.

To lift the country out of its gloom, the **Festival of Britain** was staged in 1951 on derelict land on the south bank of the Thames, a site that was eventually transformed into the Southbank Arts Centre. Londoners turned up at this technological funfair in their thousands, but at the same time many were abandoning the city for good, starting a slow process of population decline that has continued ever since. The consequent labour shortage was made good by mass **immigration** from the former colonies, in particular the Indian subcontinent and the West Indies. The first large group to arrive was the 492 West Indians aboard the SS *Empire Windrush*, which docked at Tilbury in June 1948. The newcomers, a large percentage of whom settled in London, were given small welcome, and within ten years were subjected to **race riots**, which broke out in Notting Hill in 1958.

The riots are thought to have been carried out, for the most part, by "Teddy Boys", working-class lads from London's slum areas and new housing estates, who formed the city's first postwar youth cult. Subsequent cults, and their accompanying music, helped turn London into the epicentre of the so-called **Swinging Sixties**, the Teddy Boys being usurped in the early 1960s by the "Mods", whose sharp suits came from London's Carnaby Street. Fashion hit the capital in a big way, and, thanks to the likes of The Beatles, The Rolling Stones and Twiggy, London was proclaimed hippest city on the planet on the front pages of *Time* magazine.

Life for most Londoners, however, was rather less groovy. In the middle of the decade London's local government was reorganized, the LCC being supplanted by the **Greater London Council** (**GLC**), whose jurisdiction covered a much wider area, including many Tory-dominated suburbs. As a result, the Conservatives gained power in the capital for the first time since 1934, and one of their first acts was to support a huge urban motorway scheme that would have displaced as many people as did the railway boom of the Victorian period. Luckily for London, Labour won control of the GLC in 1973 and halted the plans. The Labour victory also ensured that the Covent Garden Market building was saved for posterity, but this ran against the grain. Elsewhere, whole areas of the city were pulled down and redeveloped, and many of London's worst tower blocks were built.

Thatcherite London

In 1979 **Margaret Thatcher** won the general election for the Conservatives, and the country and the capital would never be quite the same again. Thatcher went on to win three general elections, steering Britain into a period of ever greater social polarization. While taxation policies and easy credit fuelled a consumer boom for the professional

1948	1951	1952	1953
London hosts the Olympic Games	Festival of Britain held on the South Bank	London's tram system is abandoned	Coronation of Queen Elizabeth II

THE BIG BANG

In 1986, at the same time as homelessness and unemployment were on the increase, the so-called "**Big Bang**", which abolished a whole range of restrictive practices on the Stock Exchange, took place. The immediate effect of this deregulation was that foreign banks began to take over brokers and form new, competitive conglomerates. The side effect, however, was to send stocks and shares into the stratosphere, shortly after which they inevitably crashed, ushering in a recession that dragged on for the best part of the next ten years. The one great physical legacy of the Thatcherite experiment in the capital is the **Docklands** development (see p.205), a new business quarter in the derelict docks of the East End, which came about as a direct result of the Big Bang.

classes (the yuppies of the 1980s), the erosion of the manufacturing industry and weakening of the welfare state created a calamitous number of people trapped in long-term unemployment, which topped three million in the early 1980s. The Brixton riots of 1981 and 1985 and the Tottenham riot of 1985 were reminders of the price of such divisive policies, and of the long-standing resentment and feeling of social exclusion rife among the city's black youth.

Nationally, the Labour Party went into sharp decline, but in London the party won a narrow victory in the GLC elections on a radical manifesto that was implemented by its youthful new leader **Ken Livingstone**, or "Red Ken" as the tabloids dubbed him. Under Livingstone, the GLC poured money into projects among London's ethnic minorities, into the arts and, most famously, into a subsidized fares policy which saw thousands abandon their cars in favour of inexpensive public transport. Such schemes endeared Livingstone to the hearts of many Londoners, but his popular brand of socialism was too much for the Thatcher government, who, in 1986, abolished the GLC, leaving London as the only European capital without a directly elected body to represent it.

Abolition exacerbated tensions between the poorer and richer boroughs of the city. Rich Tory councils like Westminster proceeded to slash public services and sell off council houses to boost Tory support in marginal wards. Meanwhile in impoverished Labour-held Lambeth and Hackney, millions were being squandered by corrupt council employees. **Homelessness** returned to London in a big way for the first time since Victorian times, and the underside of Waterloo Bridge was transformed into a "Cardboard City", sheltering up to two thousand vagrants on any one night. Great efforts were made by nongovernmental organizations to alleviate homelessness, not least the establishment of a weekly magazine, the *Big Issue*, which continues to be sold by the homeless right across London, earning them a small wage.

Thatcher's greatest folly, however, was the introduction of the **Poll Tax**, a head tax levied regardless of means, which hit the poorest sections of the community hardest. The tax also highlighted the disparity between the city's boroughs. In wealthy, Tory-controlled Wandsworth, Poll Tax bills were zero, while those in poorer, neighbouring, Labour-run Lambeth were the highest in the country. In 1990, the Poll Tax provoked the first full-blooded riot in central London for a long time, and played a significant role in Thatcher's downfall later that year.

1956	1966	1971	1973
Clean Air Act	England win the World Cup at Wembley	Decimal currency introduced	Britain joins the EEC

LONDON IN FILM THROUGH THE DECADES

As early as 1889 Wordsworth Donisthorpe made a primitive motion picture of Trafalgar Square, and since then London has been featured in countless films. Below is a snapshot selection of films culled from each decade since the 1920s.

Blackmail (Alfred Hitchcock, 1929). The first British talkie feature film, this thriller stars the Czech actress Anny Ondra and has its dramatic finale on the dome of the British Museum.

The Adventures of Sherlock Holmes (Alfred Werker, 1939). The Baker Street detective has made countless screen appearances, but Basil Rathbone remains the most convincing incarnation. Here Holmes and Watson (Nigel Bruce) are pitted against Moriarty (George Zucco), out to steal the Crown Jewels.

Passport to Pimlico (Henry Cornelius, 1948). The quintessential Ealing Comedy, in which the inhabitants of Pimlico, discovering that they are actually part of Burgundy, abolish rationing and closing time. Full of all the usual eccentrics, among them Margaret Rutherford in particularly fine form as an excitable history don.

The Ladykillers (Alexander Mackendrick, 1955). Delightfully black comedy set somewhere at the back of King's Cross (a favourite location for filmmakers). Katie Johnson plays the nice old lady getting the better of Alec Guinness, Peter Sellers and assorted other crooks.

Blow-Up (Michelangelo Antonioni, 1966). Swinging London and some less obvious backgrounds (notably Maryon Wilson Park, Charlton) feature in this metaphysical mystery about a photographer (David Hemmings) who may unwittingly have recorded evidence of a murder.

Jubilee (Derek Jarman, 1978). Jarman's angry punk collage, in which Elizabeth I finds herself transported to the urban decay of late twentieth-century Deptford.

My Beautiful Laundrette (Stephen Frears, 1985). A surreal comedy of Thatcher's London, offering the unlikely combination of an entrepreneurial Asian (Gordon Warnecke), his ex-National Front boyfriend (Daniel Day-Lewis) and a laundrette called Powders.

Naked (Mike Leigh, 1993). David Thewlis is brilliant as the disaffected and garrulous misogynist who goes on a tour through the underside of what he calls "the big shitty" – life is anything but sweet in Leigh's darkest but most substantial film.

Dirty Pretty Things (Stephen Frears, 2002). Entertaining romantic thriller set in London's asylum-seeking, multicultural underbelly, shot through with plenty of humour and lots of pace.

The King's Speech (Tom Hooper, 2011). Moving, funny account of King George VI's battle to overcome his stammer, after finding himself catapulted onto the throne following the abdication of Edward VIII.

Twenty-first-century London

On the surface at least, **twenty-first-century London** has come a long way since the bleak Thatcher years. Funded by money from the National Lottery and the Millennium Commission, the face of the city has certainly changed for the better: the city's national museums have been transformed into state-of-the-art visitor attractions, and all of them are free; there are new pedestrian bridges over the Thames; and Tate Modern towers like a beacon of optimism over the South Bank.

The creation of the **Greater London Assembly** (**GLA**), along with an American-style Mayor of London, both elected by popular mandate, ended fourteen years without a city council. The Labour government, which came to power on a wave of enthusiasm

1986	1991	2000	2005
GLC abolished leaving London without a central government	The first buildings at Canary Wharf completed	Establishment of the Greater London Authority (GLA)	July 7 a series of terrorist bombs across the London transport network leaves 56 dead

in 1997, did everything it could to prevent the election of the former GLC leader **Ken Livingstone** as the first mayor, but, despite being forced to leave the Labour Party and run as an independent, he won a resounding victory in the 2000 mayoral elections.

Livingstone was succeeded by Boris Johnson in 2008, but his lasting legacy has been in **transport**. As well as creating more bus routes and introducing more buses, he successfully introduced a **congestion charge** for every vehicle entering central London (see p.23). As a result, traffic levels in central London have been reduced, and, although the congestion charge hasn't solved all the city's problems, at least it showed that, with a little vision and perseverance, something concrete can be achieved.

Livingstone was also instrumental in winning the **2012 Olympics** for London, by emphasizing the Games' regenerative potential for a deprived area of London's East End. For a moment, London celebrated wildly – the euphoria was all too brief. A day after hearing the news about the Olympics, on **July 7, 2005**, London was hit by four **suicide bombers** who killed themselves and over fifty innocent commuters in four separate explosions: on tube trains at Aldgate, Edgware Road and King's Cross and one on a bus in Tavistock Square. Two weeks later a similar attack was unsuccessful after the bombers' detonators failed. Despite everyone's worst fears, however, these two attacks proved to be isolated incidents and not the beginning of a concerted campaign.

The **2010 election** produced no overall winner and resulted in a hung parliament for only the second time since World War II. The Conservatives formed a coalition with the Liberal Democrats and began the harshest series of spending cuts since 1945. In August 2011, against a background of deepening economic hardship, London suffered the worst **riots** since the 1980s, not just in areas such as Tottenham (where the riots began) and Brixton, but across the capital, from Bromley to Waltham Forest.

2012 proved a great year for London, with the celebrations of the Queen's **Diamond Jubilee** (sixty years on the throne), and a very successful and distinctive **Olympic Games,** further boosting London's international status and the mood of the city. The capital's economy, too, remains buoyant, despite the government's austerity measures, but the biggest problem is **housing**. While wealthy foreigners are happy to invest in buildings like the Shard, and luxury flat developments, affordable housing is thin on the ground, and some imaginative thinking is going to be necessary if a full-blown accommodation crisis is to be avoided.

2008	2010	2011	2012
Boris Johnson becomes Mayor of London	Boris Bikes free cycle hire scheme introduced	August riots in London	London hosts the Olympic Games

Books

Given the enormous number of books on London, the list below is necessarily a selective one, with books marked ★ being particularly recommended. London still has many excellent independent bookshops (see p.429). Most of the books recommended are in paperback, but the more expensive books can often be bought secondhand online.

TRAVEL, JOURNALS AND MEMOIRS

John Betjeman *Betjeman's London*. A selection of writings and poems by the then Poet Laureate, who spearheaded the campaign to save London's architectural heritage in the 1960s.

★ **James Boswell** *London Journal*. Boswell's diary, written in 1792–93 when he was lodging in Downing Street, is remarkably candid about his frequent dealings with the city's prostitutes, and is a fascinating insight into eighteenth-century life.

John Evelyn *The Diary of John Evelyn*. In contrast to his contemporary, Pepys, Evelyn gives away very little of his personal life, but his diaries are full of inside stories of court life from Queen Anne to James II.

Ford Madox Ford *The Soul of London*. Experimental, impressionist portrait of London published in 1905.

Doris Lessing *Walking in the Shade 1949–62*. The second volume of Lessing's autobiography, set in London in the 1950s, deals with the literary and theatre scenes and party politics, including her association with the Communist Party, with which she eventually became disenchanted.

George Orwell *Down and Out in Paris and London*. Orwell's tramp's-eye view of the 1930s, written from first-hand experience. The London section is particularly harrowing.

★ **Samuel Pepys** *The Diary of Samuel Pepys*. Pepys kept a voluminous diary while he was living in London from 1660 until 1669, recording the fall of the Commonwealth, the Restoration, the Great Plague and the Great Fire, as well as describing the daily life of the nation's capital. Penguin's *The Diary of Samuel Pepys*, although abridged from eleven volumes, is still massive; but contains a selection of all the best bits.

Christopher Ross *Tunnel Visions*. Witty and perceptive musings of popular philosopher Ross as he spends a year working as a station assistant on the tube at Oxford Circus.

Iain Sinclair *Hackney, That Rose-Red Empire: a Confidential Report*; *Liquid City*; and *London Orbital*. Sinclair is one of the most original (and virtually unreadable) London writers of his generation. *Hackney* is an absorbing biography of the author's favourite borough. *Liquid City* contains beautiful photos and entertaining text about London's hidden rivers and canals; and *London Orbital* is an account of his walk round the M25, delving into obscure parts of the city's periphery.

HISTORY, SOCIETY AND POLITICS

Peter Ackroyd *Dickens*; *Blake*; *Sir Thomas More*; *Thames: Sacred River* and *London Under*. Few writers know quite as much about London as Ackroyd does, and London is central to all three of his biographical subjects – the result is scholarly, enthusiastic and eminently readable. *London: The Biography* is the massive culmination of a lifetime's love affair with a living city and its intimate history.

★ **Paul Begg** *Jack the Ripper: The Definitive History*. This book, whose author has given talks to the FBI on the subject, sets the murders in their Victorian context and aims to debunk the myths.

Piers Dudgeon *Our East End: Memoirs of Life in Disappearing Britain*. Packed with extracts from written accounts and diaries as well as literary sources, this is a patchwork of the East End with its legendary community spirit and a dash of realism.

Clive Emsley *The Newgate Calendar*. Grim and gory account of the most famous London criminals of the day – Captain Kidd, Jack Sheppard, Dick Turpin – with potted biographies of each victim, ending with an account of his execution. Starting out as a collection of papers and booklets, *The Newgate Calendar* was first published in 1828 and was second in popularity only to the Bible at the time of publication, but is now difficult to get hold of.

Juliet Gardiner *The Blitz: the British Under Attack*. A far-reaching account of the Blitz which dispels some of the myths, combining first-hand accounts with some surprising statistics.

★ **Jonathan Glancey** *London Bread and Circuses*. In this small, illustrated book, the *Guardian*'s architecture critic extols the virtues of the old LCC and visionaries like Frank Pick, who transformed London's transport in the 1930s, discusses the millennium projects (the "circuses" of the title) and bemoans the city's creaking infrastructure.

★ **Ed Glinert** *The London Compendium*. Glinert dissects every street, every park, every house and every tube station and produces juicy anecdotes every time. The same author's *East End Chronicles: 300 Years of Mystery and Mayhem* is a readable revelation of all the nefarious doings of the East End, sorting myth from fact, and hoping the spirit will somehow survive in spite of Docklands.

Rahila Gupta *From Homebreakers to Jailbreakers: Southall Black Sisters*. The story of a radical Asian women's group which, against all the odds, was founded in London in 1979 and became internationally famous for campaigning for all disempowered black women.

Sarah Hartley *Mrs P's Journey: The Remarkable Story of the Woman Who Created the A–Z Map*. The tale of Phyllis Pearsall, the indomitable woman who survived a horrific childhood and went on to found London's most famous mapmaking company – you won't feel the same about the A–Z again.

Rachel Lichtenstein and Iain Sinclair *Rodinsky's Room*. A fascinating search into the Jewish past of the East End, centred on the nebulous figure of David Rodinsky.

Peter Linebaugh *The London Hanged*. Superb, Marxist analysis of crime and punishment in the eighteenth century, drawing on the history of those hanged at Tyburn.

Jack London *The People of the Abyss*. The author went undercover in 1902 to uncover the grim reality of East End poverty.

Henry Mayhew *London Labour and the London Poor*. Mayhew's pioneering study of Victorian London, based on research carried out in the 1840s and 1850s.

Roy Porter *London: A Social History*. This immensely readable history is one of the best books on London published since the war, particularly strong on the saga of the capital's local government.

Stephen Porter *The Great Plague of London*. Drawing on various contemporary sources, Porter paints a vivid picture of what it was like to live with a horror which killed seventy thousand Londoners.

Maude Pember Reeves & Polly Toynbee *Round About a Pound a Week*. From 1909 to 1913, the Fabian Women's Group, part of the British Labour Party, recorded the daily budget of thirty families in Lambeth living in extreme poverty. This is the accompanying comment, which is both enlightening and enlightened.

John Stow *A Survey of London*. Stow, a retired tailor, set himself the unenviable task of writing the first-ever account of the city in 1598, for which he is now rightly revered, though at the time the task forced him into penury.

Judith R. Walkowitz *City of Dreadful Delight: Narratives of Sexual Danger in Late-Victorian London*. Weighty feminist tract on issues such as child prostitution and the Ripper murders, giving a powerful overview of the image of women in the fiction and media of the day.

★ **Ben Weinreb & Christopher Hibbert** *The London Encyclopaedia*. More than a thousand pages of concisely presented information on London past and present, accompanied by the odd illustration. The most fascinating book on the capital.

Jerry White *London in the Eighteenth Century; London in the Nineteenth Century; London in the Twentieth Century*. Comprehensive history of the most momentous centuries in the city's history.

Sarah Wise *The Blackest Streets: The Life and Death of a Victorian Slum*. A meticulously researched work which reveals the depths of poverty in the area north of Bethnal Green Road.

ART, ARCHITECTURE AND ARCHEOLOGY

T.M.M. Baker *London: Rebuilding the City after the Great Fire*. In 1666 the heart of the City of London was destroyed; this book covers not only Wren churches but other less well-known public and private buildings and is beautifully illustrated.

Felix Barker & Peter Jackson *The History of London in Maps*. A beautiful volume of maps, from the earliest surviving chart of 1558 to the new Docklands, with accompanying text explaining the history of the city and its cartography.

Bill Brandt *London in the Thirties*. Brandt's superb black-and-white photos bear witness to a London lost in the Blitz.

Reuel Golden *London: Portrait of a City*. A treasure trove of photographs sourced from archives worldwide as well as from such famous names as Bailey, Beaton and Cartier Bresson, this book captures London from Victorian times through the Swinging Sixties, from the Festival of Britain to the 2012 Olympics.

Elaine Harwood & Andrew Saint *London*. Part of the excellent Exploring England's Heritage series, sponsored by

English Heritage. It's highly selective, though each building is discussed at some length and is well illustrated.

Leo Hollis *The Stones of London*. An illuminating social history of London illustrated by studying twelve of the city's buildings ranging from the iconic (Westminster Abbey) to the obscure (a tower block in the East End).

Derek Kendall *The City of London Churches*. A beautifully illustrated book, comprised mostly of colour photos, covering the remarkable City churches, many of them designed by Wren after the Great Fire.

Andrew Richard Kershman *London's Monuments*. A stroll around some of the well-known and the more obscure monuments of the city.

Nikolaus Pevsner and others *The Buildings of England*. Magisterial series, started by Pevsner, to which others have added, inserting newer buildings but generally respecting the founder's personal tone. London comes in six volumes, plus a special volume on the City churches.

Arnold Schwartzman *London Art Deco: A Celebration of the Architectural Style of the Metropolis During the Twenties*

and Thirties. Generously illustrated, this book bears witness to the British version of Art Deco in the likes of the Savoy and the Hoover building.

Anthony Sutcliffe *Architectural History of London.* A weighty tome, extensively illustrated, which traces the history of building in London from the Romans to the twenty-first century.

Richard Trench & Ellis Hillman *London under London.*

Fascinating book revealing the secrets of every aspect of the capital's subterranean history, from the lost rivers of the underground to the gas and water systems.

David Whitehead & Henning Klattenhof *London – the Architectural Guide.* A chronological study from the Romans to the present day with excellent colour photographs and information about architects and styles as well as buildings.

LONDON IN FICTION

Peter Ackroyd *English Music; Hawksmoor; The House of Doctor Dee; The Great Fire of London;* and *Dan Leno and the Limehouse Golem.* Ackroyd's novels are all based on arcane aspects of London, wrapped into thriller-like narratives, and conjuring up kaleidoscopic visions of various ages of English culture. *Hawksmoor,* about the great church architect, is the most popular and enjoyable.

★ **Monica Ali** *Brick Lane.* Acute, involving, and slyly humorous, novel about a young Bengali woman who comes over with her husband to live in London's East End.

Martin Amis *London Fields; Yellow Dog.* Short sentences and cartoon characters, Amis's novels tend to provoke extreme reactions in readers. Love 'em or hate 'em, these two are set in London.

J.G. Ballard *The Drowned World; Concrete Island; The Millennium People; High Rise.* Wild stuff. *The Drowned World,* Ballard's first novel, is set in a futuristic, flooded and tropical London. In *Concrete Island,* a car crashes on the Westway, leaving its driver stranded on the central reservation, unable to flag down passing cars. In *The Millennium People* the middle classes turn urban terrorist. In *High Rise,* the residents of a high-rise block of flats in East London go slowly mad.

Samuel Beckett *Murphy.* Nihilistic, dark-humoured vision of the city, written in 1938, and told through the eyes of anti-hero Murphy.

Elizabeth Bowen *The Heat of the Day.* Bowen worked for the Ministry of Information during World War II, and witnessed the Blitz first-hand from her Marylebone flat; this novel perfectly captures the dislocation and rootlessness of wartime London.

Anthony Burgess *A Dead Man in Deptford.* Playwright Christopher Marlowe's unexplained murder in a tavern in Deptford provides the background for this historical novel, which brims over with Elizabethan life and language.

Angela Carter *The Magic Toyshop; Wise Children. The Magic Toyshop* was Carter's celebrated 1967 novel, about a provincial woman moving to London, while *Wise Children,* published a year before her untimely death, is set in a carnivalesque London.

G.K. Chesterton *The Napoleon of Notting Hill.* Written in 1904, but set eighty years in the future, in a London divided into squabbling independent boroughs – something prophetic there – and ruled by royalty selected on a rotational basis.

J.M. Coetzee *Youth.* Claustrophobic, semi-autobiographical novel by South African Booker Prize-winner, centred on a self-obsessed colonial, struggling to find the meaning of life and become a writer in London in the 1960s.

★ **Arthur Conan Doyle** *The Complete Sherlock Holmes.* Deerstalkered sleuth Sherlock Holmes and dependable sidekick Dr Watson penetrate all levels of Victorian London, from Limehouse opium dens to millionaires' pads. *A Study in Scarlet* and *The Sign of Four* are based entirely in London.

Joseph Conrad *The Secret Agent.* Conrad's wonderful spy story is based on the botched anarchist bombing of Greenwich Observatory in 1894, and exposes the hypocrisies of both the police and the anarchists.

Daniel Defoe *Journal of the Plague Year.* An account of the Great Plague seen through the eyes of an East End saddler, written some sixty years after the event.

Charles Dickens *Bleak House; A Christmas Tale; Little Dorrit; Oliver Twist.* The descriptions in Dickens' London-based novels have become the clichés of the Victorian city: the fog, the slums and the stinking river. *Little Dorrit* is set mostly in Borough and contains some of his most trenchant pieces of social analysis. Much of *Bleak House* is set around the Inns of Court that Dickens knew so well.

Maureen Duffy *Capital.* First published in 1975, the novel is like a many-layered sandwich full of startling flavours, as the focus shifts from the central character, an unbalanced squatter with an obsession with London's past and future, to vivid slices of history.

Nell Dunn *Up the Junction; Poor Cow.* Perceptive and unsentimental account of the downside of south London life in the 1950s after the hype of the Festival of Britain.

George Gissing *New Grub Street; The Nether World. New Grub Street* is a classic 1891 story of intrigue and jealousy among London's Fleet Sthacks. The *Nether World* is set among the poor workers of Clerkenwell.

Graham Greene *The Human Factor; It's a Battlefield; The Ministry of Fear; The End of the Affair.* Greene's London novels are all fairly bleak, ranging from *The Human Factor,* which probes the underworld of the city's spies, to *The Ministry of Fear,* which is set during the Blitz.

Patrick Hamilton *Hangover Square; Twenty Thousand Streets Under the Sky.* The first is a story of unrequited love and violence in Earl's Court in the 1940s, while the latter is a trilogy of stories set in seedy 1930s London.

Neil Hanson *The Dreadful Judgement*. A docu-fiction account in which modern scientific methods and historical knowledge are applied to the Fire of London so vividly you can almost feel the heat.

Aldous Huxley *Point Counter Point*. Sharp satire of London's high-society wastrels and dilettantes of the Roaring Twenties.

Henry James *The Awkward Age*. Light, ironic portrayal of London high society at the turn of the twentieth century.

Hanif Kureishi *The Buddha of Suburbia; Love in a Blue Time; My Ear at His Heart*. The Buddha of Suburbia is a raunchy account of life as an Anglo-Asian in late-1960s suburbia, and the art scene of the 1970s; *Love in a Blue Time* is a collection of short stories set in 1990s London; *My Ear at His Heart* is a biography of Kureishi's father from his privileged childhood in Mumbai to a life in Bromley.

Andrea Levy *Small Island*. A warm-hearted novel in which postwar London struggles to adapt to the influx of Jamaicans who in turn find that the land of their dreams is full of prejudice.

Colin MacInnes *Absolute Beginners; Omnibus*. Absolute Beginners, a story of life in Soho and Notting Hill in the 1950s – much influenced by Selvon (see above) – is infinitely better than the film of the same name. *Omnibus* is set in 1957, in a Victoria Station packed with hopeful black immigrants; white welfare officer meets black man from Lagos with surprising results.

Somerset Maugham *Liza of Lambeth*. Maugham considered himself a "second-rater", but this early novel, written in 1897, about Cockney lowlife, is packed with vivid local colour.

★ **Ian McEwan** *Saturday*. Set on the day of a protest march against the war in Iraq, this book captures the mood of London post-9/11, as the main character is forced to consider his attitude to this and many other issues.

Timothy Mo *Sour Sweet*. Very funny and very sad story of a newly arrived Chinese family struggling to understand the English way of life in the 1970s, written with great insight by Mo, who is himself of mixed parentage.

Michael Moorcock *Mother London*. A magnificent, rambling, kaleidoscopic portrait of London from the Blitz to Thatcher by a once-fashionable, but now very much underrated, writer.

Iris Murdoch *Under the Net; The Black Prince; An Accidental Man; Bruno's Dream*. Under the Net was Murdoch's first, funniest and arguably her best novel, published in 1954, starring a hack writer living in London. Many of her subsequent works are set in various parts of middle-class London and span several decades of the second half of the twentieth century.

George Orwell *Keep the Aspidistra Flying*. Orwell's 1930s critique of Mammon is equally critical of its chief protagonist, whose attempt to rebel against the system only condemns him to poverty, working in a London bookshop and freezing his evenings away in a miserable rented room.

Jonathan Raban *Soft City*. An early work from 1974 that's both a portrait of, and paean to, metropolitan life.

★ **Derek Raymond** *Not till the Red Fog Rises*. A book which "reeks with the pervasive stench of excrement" as Iain Sinclair (see below) put it, this is a lowlife spectacular set in the seediest sections of the capital.

Barnaby Rogerson (ed) *London: Poetry of Place*. A delightful pocket-sized book complete with potted biographies of the poets.

Edward Rutherford *London*. A big, big novel (perhaps too big) that stretches from Roman times to the present and deals with the most dramatic moments of London's history. Masses of historical detail woven in with the story of several families.

Samuel Selvon *The Lonely Londoners*. "Gives us the smell and feel of this rather horrifying life. Not for the squeamish", ran the quote from the *Evening Standard* on the original cover. This is, in fact, a wry and witty account of the African-Caribbean experience in London in the 1950s.

★ **Iain Sinclair** *White Chappell, Scarlet Tracings; Downriver; Radon Daughters*. Sinclair's idiosyncratic and richly textured novels are a strange mix of Hogarthian caricature, New Age mysticism and conspiracy-theory rant. Deeply offensive and highly recommended.

Stevie Smith *Novel on Yellow Paper*. Poet Stevie Smith's first novel takes place in the publishing world of the London of 1930s.

Zadie Smith *White Teeth; NW*. White Teeth is her highly acclaimed and funny first novel about race, gender and class in the ethnic melting pot of north London. *NW* follows the fortunes of four Londoners from a council estate through the labyrinth of urban life in northwest London.

John Sommerfield *May Day*. Set in the revolutionary fervour of the 1930s, this novel is "as if Mrs Dalloway was written by a Communist Party bus driver", in the words of one reviewer.

Muriel Spark *The Bachelors; The Ballad of Peckham Rye*. Two London-based novels written one after the other by the Scots-born author, best known for *The Prime of Miss Jean Brodie*.

Edith Templeton *Gordon*. A tale of sex and humiliation in postwar London, banned in the 1960s when it was published under a pseudonym (Louisa Walbrook).

Rose Tremain *The Road Home*. The moving story of Lev, an Eastern European economic migrant, who heads for London and finds the streets are not paved with gold in the late twentieth century.

Sarah Waters *Affinity; Fingersmith; Tipping the Velvet; and The Night Watch*. Racy modern novels set in Victorian London: *Affinity* is set in the spiritualist milieu, *Fingersmith* focuses on an orphan girl, while *Tipping the Velvet* is about lesbian love in the music hall. *The Night Watch* is a tale of London during World War II.

Evelyn Waugh *Vile Bodies*. Waugh's target, the "vile bodies" of the title, are the flippant rich kids of the Roaring Twenties, as in Huxley's *Point Counter Point* (see p.465).

Patrick White *The Living and the Dead*. Australian Nobel Prize-winner's second novel is a sombre portrait of family life in London at the time of the Spanish Civil War.

P.G. Wodehouse *Jeeves Omnibus*. Bertie Wooster and his stalwart butler, Jeeves, were based in Mayfair, and many of their exploits take place with London showgirls and in the Drones gentlemen's club.

★ **Virginia Woolf** *Mrs Dalloway*. Woolf's novel relates the thoughts of a London society hostess and a shell-shocked war veteran, with her "stream-of-consciousness" style in full flow. *The London Scene* consists of six musings on Woolf's favourite London walks, originally written for *Good Housekeeping* in 1932.

SPECIALIST GUIDES

Jill Billington *London's Parks and Gardens*. An expensive coffee-table item, but the photos are beautiful.

Judi Culbertson & Tom Randall *Permanent Londoners*. An illustrated guide to the finest of London's cemeteries, from Westminster Abbey and St Paul's to the Victorian splendours of Highgate and Kensal Green. Very good on biographical histories of the deceased, too.

Andrew Duncan *Secret London*. With boundless enthusiasm, Duncan takes you along the lost rivers, unmasks the property tycoons, exposes dead tube stations and uncovers just about every undiscovered nook and cranny in the city.

Paul Goldsack *River Thames: In the Footsteps of the Famous*. Written in conjunction with English Heritage this is a racy romp up the river, spotting connections with the famous and the infamous.

David Long *Hidden City: The Secret Alleys, Courts and Yards of London's Square Mile*. This book will send you scurrying through narrow alleyways in search of historical relics.

Roger Tagholm *Walking Literary London*. Twenty-five walks in central and outer London, visiting birthplaces, homes and tombstones. Good maps, photos and transport details.

Jean Moorcroft Wilson *Virginia Woolf's London*. A book of place, tracing Woolf's connections with Kensington, Bloomsbury and Richmond, and the footsteps of some of her characters.

Christian Wolmar *The Subterranean Railway*. A fascinating history of the tube, the world's first underground railway and product of the vision of Victorian pioneers.

Glossary of architectural terms

Aisle Clear space parallel to the nave of a church, usually with lower ceiling than the nave.

Altar Table at which the Eucharist is celebrated, at the east end of a church. (When the church is not aligned to the geographical east, the altar end is still referred to as the "east" end.)

Ambulatory Passage behind and around the chancel.

Apse The curved or polygonal east end of a church.

Arcade Row of arches on top of columns or piers, supporting a wall.

Baldachin Canopy over an altar.

Barbican Defensive structure built in front of main gate fortress.

Barrel vault Continuous rounded vault, like a semi-cylinder.

Blue plaque English Heritage plaques placed on a building associated with a prominent figure (who must have been dead for at least 25 years).

Boss A decorative carving at the meeting point of the lines of a vault.

Buttress Stone support for a wall; some buttresses are wholly attached to the wall, others, known as "flying buttresses", take the form of a tower with a connecting arch.

Capital Upper section of a column or pier, usually carved.

Chancel Section of a church where the altar is located.

Choir Area in which the church service is conducted; next to or same as chancel.

Clerestory Upper storey of nave, containing a line of windows.

Coffering Regular recessed spaces set into a ceiling.

Corbel Jutting stone support, often carved.

Crenellations Battlements with square indentations.

Fan vault Late Gothic form of vaulting, in which the area between walls and ceiling is covered with stone ribs in the shape of an open fan.

Finial Any decorated tip of an architectural feature.

Gallery A raised passageway.

Hammerbeam Type of internal roofing in which horizontal beams support vertical timbers that connect to and support the roof.

Lady Chapel Chapel dedicated to the Virgin, often found at the east end of major churches.

Lantern Structure on top of a dome or tower, often glazed to let in light.

Listed building A building which has been put on English Heritage's protected list; buildings are classed (in descending order of importance) Grade I, Grade II* and Grade II.

Misericord Carved ledge below a tip-up seat, usually in choir stalls.

Nave The main part of a church on the other (usually western) side of the crossing from the chancel.

Oriel Projecting window.

Palladian Eighteenth-century classical style adhering to the principles of Andrea Palladio.

Pediment Triangular space above a window or doorway.

Perpendicular Late Gothic style, about 1380–1550.

Piano nobile Principal floor of a large house usually located above the ground floor.

Pilaster Flat column set against a wall.

Reredos Painted or carved panel at the back of an altar.

Rood screen Wooden screen supporting a crucifix (or rood), separating the choir from the nave; few survived the Reformation.

Rose window Large, circular window, divided into vaguely petal-shaped sections.

Stalls Seating for clergy in the choir area of a church.

Tracery Pattern formed by narrow bands of stone in a window or on a wall surface.

Transept Sections of the main body of a church at right angles to the choir and nave.

Tympanum Panel over a doorway, often carved in medieval churches.

Vault Arched ceiling.

Glossary of British terms

Bill	Restaurant check	Lift	Elevator
Biscuit	Cookie or cracker	Lorry	Truck
Bonnet	Car hood	Motorway	Highway
Boot	Car trunk	NHS	National Health Service
British Rail	State railways (1945–97)	Off-licence	Liquor store
		Pants	Underwear
Caravan	Trailer	Petrol	Gasoline
Car park	Parking lot	Pudding	Dessert
Cheap	Inexpensive	Queue	Line
Chemist	Pharmacist	Quid	Pound (money)
Chips	French fries	Return ticket	Round-trip ticket
Coach	Bus	Roundabout	Rotary interchange
Crisps	Potato chips	Single ticket	One-way ticket
Dodgy	Suspect or unreliable	Stalls	Orchestra seats
Dustbin	Trash can	Stone	Fourteen pounds (weight)
First floor	Second floor	Subway	Pedestrian passageway
Fiver	Five-pound note	Sweets	Candy
Flat	Apartment	Tap	Faucet
Fortnight	Two weeks	Tenner	Ten-pound note
Ground floor	First floor	Tights	Pantyhose
High Street	Main Street	Tory	Conservative (politics)
Hire	Rent	Trainers	Sneakers
Jam	Jelly	Trousers	Pants
Jelly	Jell-O	Tube/Underground	Subway (train)
Jumper	Sweater	Whig	Liberal (politics)
Leaflet	Pamphlet		

COCKNEY RHYMING SLANG

The term **Cockney** originally meant cock's egg or misshapen egg such as a young hen might lay, in other words, a lily-livered townie as opposed to a strong countryman. From the seventeenth century, it was used as a pejorative term for any Londoner, but was later appropriated by Londoners to describe themselves (and their accent). Traditionally, to be a true Cockney, you had to be born within earshot of the **Bow Bells** (see p.164), an area estimated to be roughly a five-mile radius around the City. However, with increased traffic noise, and no maternity ward in the near vicinity, this traditional definition is of little use nowadays.

As for **Cockney rhyming slang**, it's basically a coded language, where a word is replaced by two or more words, the last one of which rhymes with the original. For example, instead of the word "stairs" you have "apples and pears"; a piano (pronounced "pianner") is a "Joanna"; and pinch becomes "half-inch". The general theory is that it evolved in the criminal underworld of the **East End** as a secret means of communication, and many folk nowadays think of Cockney rhyming slang as a bit of a joke. In actual fact, it's alive and well, you just need to know a few basic rules. For a start, Londoners often don't use the part of the phrase which rhymes with the original at all. In other words, rather than say "butcher's hook" (for "look"), they say "Have a butcher's at that"; instead of "loaf of bread" (for "head"), you hear "Use your loaf!", and when it's cold, it's "tat'ers" not "potatoes in the mould". Rhyming slang is constantly evolving, too, with public figures providing rich pickings: Brad Pitt (shit), Posh & Becks (specs) and Gordon Brown (clown). For the latest rhyming slang, and all the old favourites, visit ⓦ cockneyrhymingslang.co.uk.

Small print and index

A ROUGH GUIDE TO ROUGH GUIDES

Published in 1982, the first Rough Guide – to Greece – was a student scheme that became a publishing phenomenon. Mark Ellingham, a recent graduate in English from Bristol University, had been travelling in Greece the previous summer and couldn't find the right guidebook. With a small group of friends he wrote his own guide, combining a highly contemporary, journalistic style with a thoroughly practical approach to travellers' needs.

The immediate success of the book spawned a series that rapidly covered dozens of destinations. And, in addition to impecunious backpackers, Rough Guides soon acquired a much broader readership that relished the guides' wit and inquisitiveness as much as their enthusiastic, critical approach and value-for-money ethos.

These days, Rough Guides include recommendations from budget to luxury and cover more than 200 destinations around the globe, as well as producing an ever-growing range of eBooks and apps.

Visit **roughguides.com** to see our latest publications.

Rough Guide credits

Editors: Alice Park, Olivia Rawes
Layout: Jessica Subramanian
Cartography: Ed Wright, Katie Bennett
Picture editor: Marta Bescos
Proofreader: Anita Sach
Managing editor: Mani Ramaswamy
Assistant editor: Dipika Dasgupta
Production: Charlotte Cade
Cover design: Wilf Matos, Dan May, Jessica Subramanian

Editorial assistant: Olivia Rawes
Senior pre-press designer: Dan May
Creative operations manager: Jason Mitchell
Operations coordinator: Helen Blount
Publisher: Joanna Kirby
Publishing director (Travel): Clare Currie
Commercial manager: Gino Magnotta
Managing director: John Duhigg

Publishing information

This tenth edition published February 2014 by
Rough Guides Ltd,
80 Strand, London WC2R 0RL
11, Community Centre, Panchsheel Park,
New Delhi 110017, India
Distributed by Penguin Random House
Penguin Books Ltd,
80 Strand, London WC2R 0RL
Penguin Group (USA)
345 Hudson Street, NY 10014, USA
Penguin Group (Australia)
250 Camberwell Road, Camberwell,
Victoria 3124, Australia
Penguin Group (NZ)
67 Apollo Drive, Mairangi Bay, Auckland 1310,
New Zealand
Penguin Group (South Africa)
Block D, Rosebank Office Park, 181 Jan Smuts Avenue,
Parktown North, Gauteng, South Africa 2193
Rough Guides is represented in Canada by Tourmaline
Editions Inc. 662 King Street West, Suite 304, Toronto,
Ontario M5V 1M7
Printed in Singapore by Toppan Security Printing Pte. Ltd.
© Rob Humphreys and Samantha Cook, 2014

Maps © Rough Guides
Contains Ordnance Survey data © Crown copyright and
database rights 2014
No part of this book may be reproduced in any form
without permission from the publisher except for the
quotation of brief passages in reviews.
496pp includes index
A catalogue record for this book is available from the
British Library
ISBN: 978-1-40933-783-6
The publishers and authors have done their best to ensure
the accuracy and currency of all the information in **The
Rough Guide to London**, however, they can accept
no responsibility for any loss, injury, or inconvenience
sustained by any traveller as a result of information or
advice contained in the guide.
1 3 5 7 9 8 6 4 2

Help us update

We've gone to a lot of effort to ensure that the tenth edition of **The Rough Guide to London** is accurate and up-to-date. However, things change – places get "discovered", opening hours are notoriously fickle, restaurants and rooms raise prices or lower standards. If you feel we've got it wrong or left something out, we'd like to know, and if you can remember the address, the price, the hours, the phone number, so much the better.

Please send your comments with the subject line "**Rough Guide London Update**" to ✉ mail@uk .roughguides.com. We'll credit all contributions and send a copy of the next edition (or any other Rough Guide if you prefer) for the very best emails.

Find more travel information, connect with fellow travellers and plan your trip on ⓦ roughguides.com

ABOUT THE AUTHORS

Rob Humphreys has lived in London for over 20 years. He has travelled extensively in Scotland and central Europe writing books for Rough Guides. He recently qualified as a City of London Tour Guide and spends his spare time directing shows on the Puppet Theatre Barge.

Samantha Cook (samanthacookeditorwriter.weebly.com) was born in London and has lived in the capital all her life. A freelance writer and editor, she has written many Rough Guides, including travel guides to the USA; New Orleans; Kent, Sussex and Surrey; the Best Places to Stay in Britain on a Budget, and Vintage London. She also wrote the Rough Guide to Chick Flicks and contributed to a number of Rough Guides' film titles.

Acknowledgements

Samantha Cook Thanks to Rob, fab co-author, friend and London neighbour; to editor Alice Park, who, as ever, made the whole editorial process a pleasure – and who flew the flag for South London with gusto – and to Ed Wright, cartographer extraordinaire, for his excellent work on the maps. Above all, thanks to Greg Ward, for everything.

Readers' updates

Thanks to all the readers who have taken the time to write in with comments and suggestions (and apologies if we've inadvertently omitted or misspelt anyone's name):

Ali Bell; Ingmar Hemsen; Ed Hutchings.

Photo credits

All photos © Rough Guides except the following:
(Key: a-above; b-below/bottom; c-centre; f-far; l-left; r-right; t-top)

p.1 Getty Images/Flickr RM
p.2 Robert Harding Picture Library/Peter Barritt
p.4 Getty Images/Gary Yeowell
p.6 Getty Images/Justin Guariglia
p.7 Alamy Images/Nigel Dickinson
p.9 AWL Images/Travel Pix Collection (b); Getty Images/ AWL Images RM (t); Frank Whitney (c)
p.10 Alamy Images/John Kellerman
p.11 Alamy Images/Alex Segre (b); Alamy: Gregory Wrona (c)
p.12 Alamy Images/Roger Hutchings (t); Axiom Photographic Agency/Marc Jackson (b)
p.13 Getty Images/Fraser Hall (t); Latitudestock (c)
p.14 Alamy Images/Directphoto.org (b); Ian Shaw (t); Dreamstime.com/Guppyimages (cl)
p.15 Alamy Images/John Kellerman (t); Axiom Photographic Agency/Chris Martin (c)
p.16 Alamy/ilpo musto
p.17 Alamy/Scott Hortop Travel
p.18 Getty Images/Jeremy Walker
p.34 Getty Images/Peter Adams
p.57 Axiom Photographic Agency/James Morris (bl)
p.65 Getty Images/Peter Adams
p.69 Corbis/Atlantide Phototravel
p.76 SuperStock/Sara Janini
p.87 Alamy Images/Alex Segre
p.95 Getty Images/Ludovic Maisant
p.106 Alamy Images/Brain Harris
p.111 Alamy Images/Imagepast (br); Interfoto/Getty Images/Travel Ink (t)
p.118 Dreamstime.com/Anizza
p.130 Getty Images/Travelpix Ltd

p.142 Getty Images/Ed Pritchard
p.148 Alamy Images/M.Sobreira
p.154 Getty Images/Dominic Burke
p.161 Alamy Images/Paul Carstairs (tl)
p.177 Getty Images/Rudi Sebastian (t)
p.180 Getty Images/Travelpix Ltd
p.188 Alamy Images/Rudolf Abraham
p.195 Alamy Images/Alistair Laming (br); Gregory Wrona (tl)
p.205 Alamy Images/Brian Anthony
p.214 Getty Images/Pawel Libera
p.248 Getty Images/Eric Nathan
p.259 Alamy Images/Peter D Noyce (tr)
p.280 Alamy Images/ilpo musto
p.293 Alamy/Fotomaton (t)
p.309 Alamy/Chris Lawrence
p.354 The Zetter Townhouse/Andreas von Einsiedel
p.393 Alamy Images/Steve Vidler (bl); HugoPhotoArt (t)
p.412 Getty Images/Ian Gavan
p.417 Alamy Images/Patrick Ward
p.423 Blitz
p.427 Alamy Images/Bjanka Kadic (br)
p.435 Getty Images/Clive Brunskill
p.440 Dorling Kindersley/Max Alexander
p.444 Getty Images/Imagno

Front cover Souvenirs for sale at Portobello Road market © Getty Images/Kimberley Coole
Back cover London skyline from St Paul's © Tim Draper (t); Row of houses in Notting Hill © Alamy Images/ Anthony Shaw (bl); Columbia Road Flower Market © Axiom Photographic Agency/Mark Thomas (br)

Index

Maps are marked in grey

Q

R

Maps

Index

Listings key

■ Accommodation
● Restaurant/café
■ Bar/pub/club
● Shop

City plan

The **city plan** on the pages that follow is divided as shown:

Map symbols

🚻	Toilets	⧫	Place of interest	▲	Peak	▦	Building
✉	Post office	@	Internet café	⛴	Boat	➡	Church
ⓘ	Tourist information	⊤	Gardens/fountain	○	Train station	◯	Stadium
✚	Hospital	☉	Statue	⊖	Underground station	▨	Park
☪	Mosque	⌣	Bridge	⊖	Overground station	⊞	Christian cemetery
✡	Synagogue	⊠	Gate	⊖	DLR station	●–●	Cable car

Key bus routes in central London